National Innovation Systems

2/44

National Innovation Systems

A Comparative Analysis

Edited by
RICHARD R. NELSON

New York Oxford
OXFORD UNIVERSITY PRESS
1993

Oxford University Press

Oxford   New York   Toronto
Delhi   Bombay   Calcutta   Madras   Karachi
Kuala Lumpur   Singapore   Hong Kong   Tokyo
Nairobi   Dar es Salaam   Cape Town
Melbourne   Auckland   Madrid

and associated companies in
Berlin   Ibadan

Copyright © 1993 by Oxford University Press, Inc.

Published by Oxford University Press, Inc.,
200 Madison Avenue, New York, New York 10016

Oxford is a registered trademark of Oxford University Press

Library of Congress Cataloging-in-Publication Data
National innovation systems : a comparative analysis /
edited by Richard R. Nelson.
p.   cm.   Includes bibliographical references and index.
ISBN 0-19-507616-8 — ISBN 0-19-507617-6 (pbk.)
1. Technological innovations.   2. Technology and state.
I. Nelson, Richard R.
T173.8.N36   1993   338.9′26—dc20   92-342

1 2 3 4 5 6 7 8 9

Printed in the United States of America
on acid-free paper

Acknowledgments

We, the authors of the chapters in this book and the members of the steering committee, are indebted to many parties for making this project possible. We would like to thank the American Enterprise Institute, Columbia University's Center on Japanese Economy and Business, and the German Marshall Fund of the United States for providing the basic funding that enabled us to start the project and carry it through. Funds provided by the Sloan Foundation to the Consortium on Competition and Cooperation proved invaluable when, at the end, our expenses outran our basic funding.

Our basic strategy for writing a book together was to meet together several times so that all of us could discuss chapter drafts and help each other toward something that was coherent, as contrasted with being a collection of freestanding country essays. These meetings were hosted by Columbia University's School of International and Public Affairs, by the Maastrict Economic Research Institute on Innovation and Technology, by the Science Policy Research Unit of the University of Sussex, and by Stanford University's Center for Economic Policy Research. Many thanks to our hosts and conference organizers.

Finally we, the participants in this project, would like to thank each other. It was a fascinating and rewarding venture for us. Each of us learned much from the others. We together hope that you, the readers, will learn as much as we did about a fascinating set of issues.

Contents

Contributors, ix

1. Technical Innovation and National Systems, 3
   Richard R. Nelson and Nathan Rosenberg

Part I Large High-Income Countries, 23

2. The U.S. National Innovation System, 29
   David C. Mowery and Nathan Rosenberg

3. The Japanese System of Innovation: Past, Present, and Future, 76
   Hiroyuki Odagiri and Akira Goto

4. The National System for Technical Innovation in Germany, 115
   Otto Keck

5. National Innovation Systems: Britain, 158
   William Walker

6. The French National System of Innovation, 192
   François Chesnais

7. The National System of Innovation: Italy, 230
   Franco Malerba

Part II Smaller High-Income Countries, 261

8. Comparing the Danish and Swedish Systems of Innovation, 265
   Charles Edquist and Bengt-Åke Lundvall

9. The Canadian System of Industrial Innovation, 299
   Donald G. McFetridge

10. The Australian Innovation System, 324
    Robert G. Gregory

Part III Lower Income Countries, 353

11. National System of Industrial Innovation: Dynamics of Capability Building
    in Korea, 357
    Linsu Kim

12. National Systems Supporting Technical Advance in Industry:
The Case of Taiwan, 384
Chi-Ming Hou and San Gee

13. National Systems Supporting Technical Advance in Industry:
The Brazilian Experience, 414
Carl J. Dalhman and Claudio R. Frischtak

14. National Systems of Innovation Supporting Technical Advance in Industry:
The Case of Argentina, 451
Jorge M. Katz and Nestor A. Bercovich

15. The Innovation System of Israel: Description, Performance, and
Outstanding Issues, 476
Morris Teubal

Part IV National Innovation Systems, 503

16. A Retrospective, 505
Richard R. Nelson

Index, 525

Contributors

Nestor A. Bercovich
National Council for Scientific and
  Technological Research

François Chesnais
Directorate for Science Technology
  and Industry
OECD

Carl Dahlman
Industrial Development Division
World Bank

Professor Charles Edquist
Department of Technology and Social
  Change
Linkoping University

Claudio Frischtak
Industrial Development Division
World Bank

Professor Akira Goto
Department of Economics
Hitosubashi University

Professor Robert Gregory
Department of Economics
Australia National University

Chi-Ming Hou
Director, Institute of International
  Economy
Chung-hun Institute for Economic
  Research

Professor Jorge Katz
Economic Commission
Latin America and the Caribbean

Professor Otto Keck
Department of Political Science
Free University of Berlin

Professor Linsu Kim
College of Business Administration
Korea University

Bengt-Åke Lundvall
Institut for Produktion
Aalburg Universitet Center

Professor Franco Malerba
Universita Commerciale
L. Bocconi

Professor Donald McFetridge
Department of Economics
Carleton University

Professor David Mowery
Center for Research Management
University of California, Berkeley

Professor Richard Nelson
School of International and Public
  Affairs
Columbia University

Professor Hiroyuki Odagiri
Institute of Socio-Economic Planning
University of Tsukuba

Professor Nathan Rosenberg
Department of Economics
Stanford University

Dr. Gee San
Research Fellow and Deputy Director
Institute of International Economy
Chung-Hua Institute for Economic
    Research

Professor Morris Teubal
Department of Economics
Hebrew University

Professor William Walker
Science Policy Research Unit
University of Sussex

Steering Committee
for National Innovation Project

Claude Barfield
American Enterprise Institute

Professor Giovanni Dosi
Department of Economics
University of Rome

Professor Christopher Freeman
Science Policy Research Unit
University of Sussex

Professor Hugh Patrick
Graduate School of Business
Columbia University

Professor Keith Pavitt
Science Policy Research Unit
University of Sussex

Professor Nathan Rosenberg
Department of Economics
Stanford University

Professor Jon Sigurdson
Institute for Policy Science
Saitama University

Professor Luc Soete
Department of Economics
University of Limburg

Professor David Teece
Haas School of Business
University of California, Berkeley

National Innovation Systems

1

Technical Innovation and National Systems

RICHARD R. NELSON
NATHAN ROSENBERG

WHAT IS THIS STUDY ABOUT

This book is about national systems of technical innovation. The heart of the work consists of studies of 15 countries, including the large market-oriented industrialized ones, several smaller high-income countries, and a number of newly industrializing states. The studies have been carefully designed, developed, and written to illuminate the institutions and mechanisms supporting technical innovation in the various countries, the similarities and differences across countries and how these came to be, and to permit at least preliminary discussion of how the differences matter.

The book has been written more despite than because of the recent great interest in the topic considered. The slowdown of growth since the early 1970s in all of the advanced industrial nations, the rise of Japan as a major economic and technological power, the relative decline of the United States, and widespread concerns in Europe about being behind both have led to a rash of writing and policy concerned with supporting the technical innovative prowess of national firms. At the same time the enhanced technical sophistication of Korea, Taiwan, and other NICs has broadened the range of nations whose firms are competitive players in fields that used to be the preserve of only a few, and has led other nations who today have a weak manufacturing sector to wonder how they might emulate the performance of the successful NICs. There clearly is a new spirit of what might be called "technonationalism" in the air, combining a strong belief that the technological capabilities of a nation's firms are a key source of their competitive prowess, with a belief that these capabilities are in a sense national, and can be built by national action.

It is this climate that has given rise to the current strong interest in national innovation systems, and their similarities and differences, and in the extent and manner that these differences explain variation in national economic performance. There may now be more awareness and research on such national differences than on any other area where comparative institutional analysis would seem interesting and illuminating.

The project that led to this book was born of the current strong interest in national innovation systems,[1] and came out of a belief on the part of the participants that much of the writing and argument on this subject has been somewhat hyped and rather haphazard. In addition, many of the allegedly comparative studies concentrated on one country—in recent times Japan—with comparisons with other countries mainly implied. The actual comparative studies tended to involve only two or a very small group of countries. This fact is serious in view of the absence of a well-articulated and verified analytic framework linking institutional arrangements to technological and economic performance. In the absence of such a framework, there were (and are) only weak constraints on the inclinations of analysts to draw possibly spurious causal links between differences in institutional structures that clearly are there, and differences in performance that clearly are there also. Different authors have focused on different things, and made different arguments about why some feature was an important factor behind strong or weak performance. The broadening of the set of countries considered simultaneously seemed an important way to tighten these constraints by enlarging the number of "points" that a causal theory had to "fit."

The way we have been putting the matter clearly signals that the orientation of this project has been to carefully describe and compare, and try to understand, rather than to theorize first and then attempt to prove or calibrate the theory. However, a comparative study such as this requires, at least, some agreement on basic terms and concepts.

There is, first, the concept of a national innovation system itself. Each of the terms can be interpreted in a variety of ways, and there is the question of whether, in a world in which technology and business are increasingly transnational, the concept as a whole makes much sense. Consider the term "innovation." In this study we interpret the term rather broadly, to encompass the processes by which firms master and get into practice product designs and manufacturing processes that are new to them, if not to the universe or even to the nation. We do so for several reasons. First, the activities and investments associated with becoming the leader in the introduction of a new product or process, and those associated with staying near the head of the pack, or catching up, are much less sharply distinguishable than is commonly presumed. Moreover, the strictly Schumpeterian innovator, the first firm to bring a new product to market, is frequently not the firm that ultimately captures most of the economic rents associated with the innovation. Second, much of the interest in innovative capability is tied to concern about economic performance, and here it is certainly the broader concept rather than the narrower one (the determinants of being first) that matters. This means that our orientation is not limited to the behavior of firms at the forefront of world's technology, or to institutions doing the most advanced scientific research, although in some countries the focus is here, but is more broadly on the factors influencing national technological capabilities.

Then there is the term "system." Although to some the word connotes something that is consciously designed and built, this is far from the orientation here. Rather the concept is of a set of institutions whose interactions determine the innovative performance, in the sense above, of national firms. There is no presumption that the system was, in some sense, consciously designed, or even that the set of institutions involved works together smoothly and coherently. Rather, the "systems" concept is that of a set of institutional actors that, together, plays the major role in influencing innovative performance. The broad concept of innovation that we have adopted has forced us to consider much more than simply the actors doing research and development. Indeed, a problem with the broader definition of innovation is that it provides no sharp guide to just what should be included in the innovation system, and what can be left out. More on this later.

Finally, there is the concept of "national" system. On the one hand, the concept may be too broad. The system of institutions supporting technical innovation in one field, say pharmaceuticals, may have very little overlap with the system of institutions supporting innovations in another field, say aircraft. On the other hand, in many fields of technology, including both pharmaceuticals and aircraft, a number of the institutions are or act transnational. Indeed, for many of the participants in this study, one of the key interests was in exploring whether, and if so in what ways, the concept of a "national" system made any sense today. National governments act as if it did. However, that presumption, and the reality, may not be aligned.

The studies in this project are unified by at least broad agreement on the definitional and conceptual issues discussed above. They were also guided by certain common understandings of the way technical advance proceeds, and the key processes and institutional actors involved, that are now widely shared among scholars of technical advance. In a way these understandings do provide a common analytic framework, not wide enough to encompass all of the variables and relationships that likely are important, not sharp enough to tightly guide empirical work, but broad enough and pointed enough to provide a common structure in which one can have some confidence. This basic common structure is discussed in the following section.

Technical Advance: An Overview of the Processes and Institutions Involved

To understand national innovation systems, it is essential to understand how technical advance occurs in the modern world, and the key processes and institutions involved. This section aims to provide such an overview.

We begin by describing two essential, and to some extent conflicting, aspects of technical advance. In the modern era most technologies are associated with various fields of science that illuminate them, and lend invaluable understanding and technique to efforts to advance technology. At the same time efforts at innovation almost always involve a large element of trial and error and try again learning. Next we turn to the institutions involved in industrial innovation, starting with firms, and then considering supporting institutions such as universities and government agencies and policies. We also point to some important intersectoral and intercountry differences. Finally we consider the concept of "national systems" and flag some issues about the relevance of national borders in a world in which business and technology are increasingly transnational.

THE INTERTWINING OF SCIENCE AND TECHNOLOGY

Today, R&D facilities, staffed by university trained scientists and engineers attached to business firms, universities, or government agencies, are the principal vehicles through which technological advance proceeds, in fields such as electrical equipment and systems, chemical products and processes, and aviation. Most contemporary examinations of national capabilities in technology focus on these kinds of institutions and industries. One of the principal messages of this chapter is that this view of technical advance and its sources is somewhat too narrow. However, it certainly is a central part of the picture.

An important characteristic of technical advance in all of the above fields, and in many other areas, is that it is strongly supported by various fields of science. However, the connections between science and technology are complex and vary in certain respects from field to field in certain essential respects.

Science as Leader and Follower

It is widely believed that new science gives rise to new technology. Although we shall argue that this is at best an oversimplification, the statement is quite true in regard to the rise of the electrical equipment industries. The very existence of these industries is inseparable from the history of theoretical and experimental physics in the nineteenth century. The emergence of electricity as a new source of power, and the wide range of new products that came to be built on it—incandescent light, telephone, gramophone—were the legitimate offspring of a scientific research enterprise that began with Faraday's demonstration of electromagnetic induction in 1831. Several decades later Maxwell's research opened up vast new vistas that led to Hertz's confirmation, in 1887, of the existence of radio waves and the possibility of detecting them at a distance, and then to modern radio and television (Cohen, 1948 and Dunsheath, 1962).

Thus, the discovery of radio waves, which gave birth to radio and television, occurred *not* because scientists were searching for useful applications of their research. Rather, Hertz was pursuing a logic internal to the discipline of science itself, exploring the implications of an earlier theory by searching for empirical evidence that might confirm the theory. Hertz searched for—and found—radio waves because an earlier scientific theory had predicted their existence. Establishing their existence led to the work of Marconi and others in wireless communication.

In contrast with the electrical equipment industries, the industries producing chemical products, or using chemical reactions in the manufacture of other products, long antedated the rise of modern science. Some, such as tanning and dyeing and brewing, are almost as old as civilization itself.

However, in the last four or five decades of the nineteenth century, a systematic body of scientific knowledge about chemistry grew up that laid a new basis for chemical-based innovation. Chemistry became a laboratory discipline in which research could be carried out by trained professionals making use of well-understood methods and experimental procedures. In the 1860s Kekule managed to disentangle the molecular structure of benzene, a breakthrough of major significance for thousands of aromatics, including dyes and drugs, but ultimately, for all of organic chemistry. These new understandings were invaluable in enabling scientists in industry to search constructively for new chemical compounds and to devise better production processes (Beer, 1959).

These stories about advances in physics and chemistry as scientific disciplines appear to show scientific development as autonomous, evolving according to an internal logic of its own, with technology being illuminated as a by-product. But appearances are deceiving. Faraday followed the tradition of his mentor, Humphrey Davy, in having a strong interest in practical devices and a belief in the value of science in inventing. Modern chemistry grew out of the ancient discipline of alchemy, which was concerned with finding ways to transform base materials into valuable ones.

The advent of new technologies often leads to scientific work aimed at understanding these technologies, so as to enable them to be improved. Sometimes new technology leads to whole new scientific disciplines. Sadi Carnot's work in the early part of the nineteenth century, which led to the new field of thermodynamics, was largely motivated by theoretical interest in the workings of the steam engine (Cardwell, 1971). The science of polymer chemistry emerged in the twentieth century, in large part resulting from research, performed inside industrial laboratories, to develop materials that could better fulfill the changing requirements of industry.

In addition, the rise of the modern chemical industry led to the rise of a new discipline expressly aimed to service its needs—chemical engineering. Chemical engineering involved not simply the practical application of the science of chemistry, but the merger of chemistry and mechanical engineering. Somewhat more precisely, chemical engineering involved the application of mechanical engineering skills and methods to the specialized task of producing chemical products on a large scale.

A modern chemical process plant is not a scaled-up version of the laboratory glass tubes and reactors in which scientific discoveries were originally made. Such scaling-up is neither technically nor economically feasible. Rather, entirely different processes have to be invented. The transition from the glass equipment with which W. H. Carothers produced the first polymers in the DuPont laboratories, or the transition from the laboratory synthesis of polyethylene, or terephthalic acid, to the large-scale commercial manufacture of such products, is a transition that involved years of serious development effort and significant further inventive activity. Indeed, the complexities of the transition are so great that chemical engineers have devised a unique transitional technology for it, the pilot plant.

The rise of scientific understanding supporting aircraft design reflects a similar story. Again the technology, or a primitive version of it, came first, and the "science" or engineering discipline developed to support it. Thus the frail apparatus that the Wright brothers managed to get airborne for a few seconds in 1903 had very little well-understood "science" behind its design. However, the promise of those early flying machines gave rise to the modern disciplines of aerodynamics and aeronautical engineering.

Thus saying that new technologies have given rise to new sciences is at least as true as the other way around. And it is more on the mark to say that with the rise of modern science-based technologies, much of science and much of technology have become intertwined. This is the principal reason why, in the present era, technology is advanced largely through the work of men and women who have university training in science of engineering. This intertwining, rather than serendipity, is the principal reason why, in many fields, university research is an important contributor to technical advance, and universities as well as corporate labs are essential parts of the innovation system.

Thus, the problems, or observations, that originate in industry are explored not only by industrial scientists. They feed into, and stimulate, the entire scientific community. Edison's attempts, in 1883, to improve the incandescent lamp led him to observe the flow of electricity inside the lamp, across a gap separating a hot filament from a metal wire. Edison had observed the existence of electrons before their existence had even been postulated. Although Edison did not appreciate the significance of his observations at the time, the Edison Effect formed the basis for much twentieth-century science, including atomic physics and the numerous electronics technologies.

The Limits of Science, Learning by Trying, and Cumulative Incremental Technological Advance

It is insufficiently appreciated that successful innovation in high technology industries often is not so much a matter of invention, as a patent examiner would define invention, as it is a matter of design, in the sense of trying to devise a product or process that will achieve a desirable cluster of performance characteristics, subject to certain cost constraints. This engineering design capability is a very sophisticated and costly business. McDonnell Douglas recently estimated that the redesign of the wing for a new wide-bodied jet that would be a successor to the DC-10 would likely cost a billion dollars. Moreover, determining where "design" ends and "research" begins is a matter of some real difficulty as soon as one deals with relationships that cannot be optimized by referring to the codified data in the engineering handbooks.

Those aiming for a major design advance almost always are in a position of not knowing whether a design will work or how well it will until they test it out. In the chemical industries, a pilot plant may be thought of as an intermediate-scale technology, incorporating design principles and mechanical expertise that have no counterpart in laboratory research. Its ultimate purpose is to increase the confidence in the technical feasibility and the underlying economics of a larger-scale plant that is both newly designed and involves a very large financial commitment. Such designing activity is far from laboratory research in the sense that it cannot be deduced from the findings of that research.

In some essential respects, a new aircraft prototype performs a role that is close to that of the pilot plant in the chemical processing industries. In both cases there are significant uncertainties attached to technical designs that incorporate significant elements of novelty. Since the technical uncertainties readily translate into huge financial losses if new designs are prematurely introduced into practice, it is prudent to test on a small scale, and to resolve the expensive uncertainties at the technological frontier in a less costly rather than more costly fashion. Testing of aircraft prototypes and chemical pilot plants are specialized modalities for the reduction of technological uncertainties in innovation.

Through such vehicles as building and testing pilot plants and prototypes, and testing experimental new drugs, the activities aimed to advance technology generate new knowledge as well as new products and processes. As we have noted, in many cases new scientific understanding follows rather than leads, as when the science of aerodynamics created theoretical understanding of the factors determining lift and drag, after the first flying machines had been built and flown, or when William Shockley developed a theory of holes and electrons in semiconductors to explain how and why the transistor he and his colleagues at Bell Labs devised actually worked. The new device or process that works, sort of, or surprisingly well, stimulates both efforts to explain and understand, and efforts to refine, improve, and variegate.

The Wright Brothers' 1903 machine was scarcely more than a large, ungainly bicycle with attached wings. (The resemblance to the bicycle was no coincidence, since the Wright Brothers had previously been designers as well as manufacturers of bicycles.) Their airplane's parts were secured by baling wire and glue, and its total flight was only a few hundred yards. Not until the 1930s did aircraft shed their struts and external bracing wire, the non-load-carrying skin involving the use of doped fabrics, and assume their stressed-skin monocoque construction form. Only with the design and development of the DC-3 did the airplane finally become a reliable means of transportation on commercial routes (Miller and Sawers, 1970).

But the performance gap that separates the DC-3 of 50 years ago from today's wide-bodied aircraft, equipped with powerful jet engines, swept-back wings, sophisticated electronics, and capable of flying over most weather turbulence, is also immense. It almost has to be said of the airplane that everything of economic significance is attributable to the subsequent improvements, since 1903, that have been made within the original, crude framework of the Wright Brothers' flying machine.

The point made here with respect to performance improvement of aircraft is, in fact, a point of broad generality. Most industrial R&D expenditures are on products that have long been in existence—such as aircraft, automobiles, and cameras (which have been in existence fully 150 years). It is these existing products that serve to define the framework within which improvements can be identified and undertaken. Even the transistor, which has so drastically transformed the world in the second half of the twentieth century, has been around for more than 40 years. Its introduction in the late 1940s laid the groundwork for the continuing microelectronics revolution. Yet the original transistor was a fragile, unreliable, and expensive piece of apparatus. It was only the subsequent improvements in that original, primitive device that made the later microelectronics revolution possible.

In this as in other cases, the advance of technology went hand in hand with the advance of science. The invention of the transistor in 1948 rapidly transformed solid-state physics from a small subspecialty into the largest subdiscipline of physics. This was true within the university scientific community as well as within private industry. Similarly, the advent of the laser in the 1960s, along with the feasibility of using optical fibers for transmission purposes, led to a great expansion in the science of optics, where advances in science now offered the prospect of sharply increased economic payoffs. It is important not to confuse the highly valued autonomy of the individual scientist, in shaping his or her own research agenda, with the determination of research-funding agencies to commit resources to those areas of scientific research that appear to offer the most attractive future returns. Public and private institutions may well be expected to define future returns rather differently, but neither is likely to be indifferent to the size of these returns.

THE MAJOR INSTITUTIONAL ACTORS

Because of many misconceptions, it is well to recapitulate just what the rise of science based technology led to, and what it did not. The rise of science based technology did lead to a dramatic change in the nature of the people and institutions involved in technical advance. Through much of the nineteenth century strong formal education in a science provided an inventor with little or no advantage in problem solving, although from time to time inventors would consult with scientists. By 1900 formal training in chemistry was becoming virtually a requirement for successful inventive effort in the chemical products industries. By 1910 or so the days when unschooled geniuses such as Thomas Alva Edison could make major advances in the electrical technologies where coming to an end, and the major electrical companies were busy staffing their laboratories with university trained scientist and engineers.

Firms and Industrial Research Laboratories

By the beginning of World War I the industrial research laboratory, a facility dedicated to research and the development of new or improved products and processes, and staffed by university trained scientists and engineers, had become the principal locus of technical advance in the chemical and electrical industries, and was beginning to become important more and more widely. The industrial laboratories were teamed with universities that trained their new R&D scientists and engineers, and that undertook research in the new applied sciences and engineering disciplines as well as in the more traditional basic sciences.

As we have stressed, the rise of science based technologies, and industrial research laboratories dedicated to "invention," did not lead to routinization of innovation, as some predicted. R&D continues to be an activity in which dead ends often are reached, and a lot of trying, testing, and revising is required before a successful result is achieved.

There are several reasons why the industrial research laboratory, rather than university laboratories or government facilities, became the dominant locus of the R&D part of innovation in most (but not all) fields. First, after a technology has been around for a period of time, to orient R&D fruitfully, one needs detailed knowledge of its strengths and weaknesses and areas where improvements would yield big payoffs, and this knowledge tends to reside with those who use the technology, generally firms and their customers and suppliers. In addition, over time firms in an industry tend to develop capabilities for doing certain kinds of R&D that, although drawing on public scientific knowledge, transcends it, being largely based on practice. Second, profiting from innovation in many cases requires the integration of activity and planning of R&D, production, and marketing, which tends to proceed much more effectively within an organization that itself does all of these. For these reasons, although it is common to see a significant university or other outsider role in inventing and innovating when a technology is just coming into being (as biotechnology in the early 1980s), the process of cumulative improvement and variegation, which we have pointed out accounts for the majority of R&D and innovation, tends to be the business of incumbent firms.

It is important, however, to recognize the lack of distinctness surrounding the concept of R&D. Partly the matter is one of accounting and nomenclature. Many small firms engage in significant design and development work, yet do not have a formally designated R&D department or facility; their design and development work may or may not be accounted and reported as R&D. In many firms process engineering is located organizationally in production not in R&D; again, the work involved may or may not be counted as R&D. But the matter is not simply, or basically, one of nomenclature. The lines between R&D, and other activities, such as designing products for particular customers, problem solving on production processes, or monitoring a competitor's new products, are inherently blurry. In a number of industries even firms at the frontier invest significant resources in staying up with relevant developments elsewhere in science and technology, including prominently the work and achievements of other firms.

In developing countries, what is an innovation for an indigenous firm may largely involve learning to produce a product or employ technology that has been employed for some time by firms in the highly industrialized economies. Learning to make or use a product may require a considerable amount of study as well as the taking apart of products and processes to find out how they work, that is, "reverse engineering." Although generally not so counted, reverse engineering is very much like R&D. As cases such as the economic development of Korea show, as a company and a country catch on, such work increasingly reaches out to build something different and begins to get counted as R&D.

Moreover, even if it is defined quite broadly, R&D usually is only a small part of the resources and problem solving that go into innovation. The amounts that must be invested in new equipment and plant to produce a new product, or embody a new process, generally exceed the R&D costs many fold. New organizations may be called for, or a different division of work, or new skills on the part of the work force, and new approaches in marketing. It may take considerable time and effort to get these changes made and the new system operating smoothly. And, as we have stated earlier, in many cases innovation is a continuing business, with product and process engineers learning from experience and making modifications on that basis, customers' feeding back complaints and suggestions, management learning how to smooth out rough spots, and so on.

Thus although the chapters that follow will discuss R&D spending, R&D must be recognized as only part of the larger innovation picture. In many of the chapters discussion of R&D will be augmented by descriptions and analyses of the different kinds of firms active in innovation. Thus it has been argued that the style of management and organization common in U. S. firms, although once a source of innovative strength, is now a disadvantage, and that various aspects of Japanese firms help them to be effective innovators. An important objective of this study is to illuminate and explore propositions such as these.

Other Institutional Actors

The modern industrial laboratory and the modern research university grew up as companions. The details of this companionship have been considerably different from one country to another, as later chapters will indicate. In general, however, universities play an extremely important role in technical advance, not only as places where industrial scientists and engineers are trained, but as the source of research findings and techniques of considerable relevance to technical advance in industry.

Universities in most countries are, first, the places where much of the basic research in fundamental sciences such as physics is undertaken, although the reliance on universities as a locus of basic research, as contrasted with national laboratories, varies across countries. Research in basic sciences such as physics tends to be guided by the internal logic of the discipline rather than by expectation of particular practical application. Although occasionally research in basic science will provide understandings or techniques that directly lead to product or process advances, as has been the case recently in molecular biology, this is not usual. However, even if a nation has only narrow economic motives in funding university research, it cannot afford to completely neglect the basic sciences, since training in these is an essential part of training in the applied sciences and engineering disciplines.

Many fields of academic science are expressly applications orientated. The very names "material science," "computer science," and "pathology" signal fields of inquiry closely linked to particular practical problems. So too the engineering disciplines, which were expressly established not only to train people for work in industry, but also to develop the scientific foundations of industrial technologies.

In certain cases, university based institutions have been directly oriented toward helping a particular industry or other client advance its technologies. Thus the agricultural experimentation stations, attached to the land grant universities of the United States, are an important source of new technology for farmers, and for a wide range of agriculture product processing industries. In countries that have a significant pharmaceutical industry, university faculty in medical schools tend to have close relationships with firms in the industry. In several countries, certain engineering schools have a mandated responsibility to provide help to firms in the region. In many countries, including the United States and Germany, universities are the home of institutes designed to help particular industries.

In almost all nations universities now are funded to a substantial degree by governments. However, the organization and means of funding, and orientation of university research, differ significantly across nations. It is widely believed that the American university system provides more effective stimulus and help to technical advance than university systems in most other countries. One purpose of this project is to investigate this and kindred propositions. There is a related question. To the extent that a nation's universities support technical advance, how effectively is this support channeled to help national firms? Many observers of the American system have argued that in many cases foreign firms are benefiting as much as American. To what extent is this true, or general, and what are the implications?

Recent American complaints, moreover, could easily be duplicated elsewhere. Great Britain provided a remarkable degree of intellectual leadership in the field of molecular biology, but most of the commercial exploitation of this research, so far, has been in the United States. Earlier in this century, in fact until the Second World War, Germany was undoubtedly the world leader in the sciences of aerodynamics, in large measure due to Prandtl's great contributions at the University of Göttingen and, later, at the Kaiser Wilhelm Institute for Fluid Mechanics. Nevertheless, the American commercial aircraft designers and aeronautical engineers benefited immensely by being able to draw on German aerodynamic research (Hallion, 1977).

Government laboratories also are an important part of many national innovation systems. In the United States, government laboratories play important roles in, for example, the fields of agriculture, health, and nuclear energy. However, with only a few exceptions, agriculture being a major one, in the United States government laboratories are tied to public sector missions in contrast to being established to help civilian industry. And, again with a few exceptions, in the United States the universities, rather than government laboratories, are seen as the appropriate sites for fundamental research.

In other countries public laboratories play a significantly larger, or different, role. Thus the Federal Republic of Germany has a network of Max Planck Institutes dedicated to basic research, and Fraunhofer Laboratories dedicated to applied research. Much of the latter's work is aimed at helping industry. In France, a substantial share of government funded basic research is undertaken in public laboratories that are independent of universities. This project aims to map out some of these salient differences.

Today public monies support not only research at universities and government laboratories, but R&D in industry. For the most part government support of industrial R&D in the United States has been limited to projects of direct governmental interest, principally those involving military and space needs. But as the new Sematech venture shows, even the United States is not adverse to using public monies to help the development of industrial technologies that are principally of civilian use, if a strong "public interest" argument can be articulated. In many other countries, simply helping an important industry has been accepted as a suitable governmental mission. These differences are an important subject of this comparative study.

As we have already stressed, innovation involves much more than R&D, and the set of institutions that influences the technological capabilities of a nation and how these are advanced extends far beyond those that directly impinge on innovation. The character and effectiveness of a nation's system of schooling, training, and retraining not only determine the supply of skills from engineer to machine tender, but also influence the attitudes of workers toward technical advance. So too do the patterns of labor—management bargaining and negotiation, dispute resolution, and the degree of mutual commitment of firm and workers. Financial institutions, and the way firms are governed and controlled, profoundly influence the technical activities that are feasible and that managers choose to undertake.

More generally, it is somewhat artificial to try to describe and analyze a nation's innovation system as something separable from its economic system more broadly defined, or to depict the policies concerned with innovation as quite apart from those concerned with the economy, education, or national security. The descriptions of national innovation systems that will be presented in the following chapters, although concentrating on the institutions and mechanisms discussed above, will inevitably in some cases go well beyond these.

Interindustry Differences

Some characteristics of technical advance and the principal institutional actors are quite general, holding across a wide range of industries. However, there are important interindustry differences in the nature of technical change, the sources, and how the involved actors are connected to each other, and it is useful to sketch some of these here. Nations differ in the mix of industries and these differences alone strongly influence the shapes of national innovation systems.

A number of industries produce products that can be characterized as complex systems. Much of electrical technology is of this sort. An aircraft is a complex system. The size of the system, in terms of the number of critical components, can be very large, as in jet aircraft or telecommunication systems, or relatively small, as in a television set or an automatic loom. In either case technical advance in system–product technologies tends to proceed through a combination of improvements in components, and modifications in overall system design to take advantage of or drive these, punctuated from time to time by the introduction of a significantly new system.

Technical advance in such fields generally stems from the work of component and material producers, as well as systems designers. In general the larger the system, the greater the role of the component producers. However, the effective incorporation of better components into a system often requires significant R&D work by system assemblers. The integration of component and systems R&D generally involves some combination of independent initiatives mediated by the market, contracting, and express cooperation, with the balance differing from industry to industry and from country to country. In some cases government programs may facilitate coordination.

In some systems technologies users of the system play a major role in inducing technical advance, and they may directly support it. Thus the major airlines will often engage in extensive discussion with airframe manufacturers regarding the modifications they desire, and what they will pay for. In turn, this may lead to extended discussions between the airplane producer and the designers and producers of engines.

In the case of a drastic new aircraft design, such as the Boeing 747 or 767, the manufacturer may not even proceed to the advanced design stage until it has substantial purchase commitments from airline buyers. A firm such as Boeing, moreover, functions as a designer and assembler of new aircrafts, but is dependent on thousands of outside component suppliers. Similarly, IBM can also be described as a designer and assembler of complex, system-like products, and is dependent on a large number of outside component suppliers. In both the Boeing and IBM cases, components suppliers, like ultimate product buyers, may be in many different countries. In both cases, also, components suppliers may perform significant amounts of R&D. In the case of IBM computers, where the number of ultimate buyers is very large, such buyers are less intimately involved in shaping the details of product design than in the case of aircraft, where the number of buyers is far smaller.

Technical advance in the industries producing fine chemical products, from synthetic materials to pharmaceutical, is different in a number of respects. First, in these industries innovation largely involves the introduction of discrete new products or product classes, such as nylon or valium, that are not in general subject to the continuing incremental improvement that marks systems technologies. However, they may be subject to tailoring to fit the needs of different kinds of customers, or for new uses. Indeed a striking aspect of technical advance in these fields is the discovery of new uses by producers or users. Second, since the products do not involve complex systems, input suppliers in general do not play a big role; however, process equipment suppliers may. Indeed in some cases new products may require major process innovation. Process equipment suppliers often do the key design work here. In many cases chemical product companies and equipment suppliers may cooperate. And although product innovation may be discrete in these industries, process innovation after the initial design may be continuous and incremental as described earlier.

Still other industries produce bulk commodities, from steel to milk. Here product innovation is minimal and technical change basically involves new or improved ways to produce or process the product in question. Equipment and input suppliers and processing firms often are the major sources of innovation. Where product producers are large they may do a considerable amount of process R&D on their own or contract for it. Where the product suppliers are small, they may bond together to get work done on production processes or modes of processing products, or on standards for inputs and outputs. Governmental agencies may organize and fund such work. Under such arrangements close and durable modes of interaction may form between producer cooperatives and the input suppliers, and processing firms.

TECHNOLOGICAL COMMUNITIES, BOUNDARIES, AND NATIONAL INNOVATION SYSTEMS

Technological advance proceeds through the interaction of many actors. Above we have considered some of the key interactions involved, between component and systems producers, upstream and downstream firms, universities and industry, and government agencies and universities and industries.

The important interactions, the networks, are not the same in all industries or technologies. We have pointed to differences between systems technologies and chemical product technologies in the nature of interindustry interactions. In some technologies universities play a key role, for example, pharmaceuticals and computers. In others they play a more modest one, for example, aircraft and steel. Government funding is important in some industries, such as aircraft and agriculture, and unimportant in others. But although its shape and character differ, in virtually all fields one must understand technical advance as proceeding through the work of a community of actors.

To what extent are there "national" communities? To what degree, and through what mechanisms, do the individuals and institutions that advance technology divide up into "national systems?"

We suspect that the answer to this question varies over time and from field to field. The nineteenth-century history of the evolution of shoe making machinery in the United States involved a collection of mechanic-inventors, familiar with various aspects of the shoe making process, and with each other's inventions in the form of artifacts and products (see Thomson, 1989). The community was national because the relevant American industries used technology that was different than in Europe, because of physical proximity, and because of shared language and culture. Studies of the rise of Bessemer steel technology in the United States (Allen, 1983) and Great Britain (Morison, 1966) show two different national communities at work, with some international exchange, but with the bulk of the interaction among nationals. The dyestuffs industry grew up as a largely German industry. In this case common training in German universities, and links between the company laboratories and the universities, clearly delineated the network. In the United States and Denmark, communities concerned with farming and the processing of farm products grew up associated with government-supported research programs, and cooperatives of various sorts. Military contracting, a reserved military market, and military R&D money built and protected distinctly American technological communities in semiconductors, computers, and jet aircraft in the early days of those technologies.

The discussion above has been of particular fields of technology, where for a variety of reasons distinctly national communities of actors formed. But what of the proposition that there are national systems in a broader sense, encompassing very wide ranges of technology, although perhaps specializing and stressing a narrower range? What might define and delineate these broader national systems?

Certainly the policies and programs of national governments, the laws of a nation, and the existence of a common language and a shared culture define an inside and outside that can broadly affect how technical advance proceeds. Put another way, national differences and boundaries tend to define national innovation systems, partly intentionally, partly not. Further, general perceptions about national societies and cultures tend to reify national systems.

Thus for the quarter century after World War II both Americans and citizens of other countries recognized a distinctly American model that had a number of particular features. In the first place, as writers such as Servan Schreiber (1968) pointed out in the late 1960s, in many of the key industries American firms were larger than their European countries, spent more on R&D, and had a distinctive management style. Furthermore the U. S. government spent much more on industrial R&D than did the European governments, principally through defense contracts. The U. S. university research system was stronger. To a very large extent firms situated in America were American owned, and although overseas branches were becoming increasingly important, by far most establishments owned by Americans operated in the United States. Most of the goods produced by American firms were sold overwhelmingly to the domestic market. Although foreigners were coming to the U. S. universities in increasing numbers, most of the students being taught and the faculty of American universities were Americans, and the graduates went to work in American firms. The monies of the U. S. government were almost exclusively spent in U. S. institutions.

As we shall see, the innovation systems of the major European industrial nations differed in important aspects from the American. One can argue that the European systems were much less strictly "national" systems than was the American. For one thing, even the largest of the European nations was small compared with the United States, and as a result there was much more importing and exporting as a percentage of GNP. For another, increasingly over the period there was a sense of European community that in some ways eroded the significance of national borders and particular citizenship. Third, and foreshadowing subsequent broader developments, American firms in European countries were playing a significant role in many industries. However, as well shall see, in the early postwar era there was a strong sense that although subject to strong influences from abroad, there was a distinctive and to a large extent self-contained English, German, and French systems.

Until the 1970s there was no strong competitor to the American system as a broad model of how an innovation system should be designed. This standing as a model system was a natural reflection of the U. S. technological preeminence that marked the postwar years. Earlier, the United States had been an imitator in many respects. The American research university that arose early in the twentieth century was consciously modeled on the German university system, and the R&D organization of American chemical companies similarly was patterned on a German model. We note that this proclivity of both private and public institutions to reform themselves toward what are regarded as the leading models is a strong force toward similarities in national innovation systems.

As European productivity and income levels have caught up with American levels, and Japan has emerged as a leading economic and technological power, the attraction of the American model has waned, and Japanese institutions have waxed as targets for emulation. Many strongly held beliefs about the Japanese innovation system are, at best, only partly correct. Nonetheless, it is widely thought that the Japanese government targets certain key civilian technologies and orchestrates work on them, and that this, as well as strong interfirm cooperation, leads to a more powerful and efficient innovation system. These features currently are the models of fashion in Europe, and, to an increasing degree, in the United States.

The rise of Japan as a model has enhanced the belief that an explicit national technology policy can be effective; indeed it is now widely argued that a nation will fall progressively behind if it does not have an explicit technology policy. This has led over the past decade to a rash of national programs designed to enable national industries to stay ahead or catch up technologically. These will be discussed in later chapters.

NATIONAL SYSTEMS AND TRANSNATIONAL TECHNOLOGY

Although the notion that there are distinctly national communities of technologists fits the evidence in some cases, it does not fit so well in others. Thus the early history of radio was one of transnational activity, involving inventors and companies in Great Britain, the United States, and Western Europe, all building on each other's work. The development of synthetic fibers involved similar transnational interactions. This is not to argue that the networks of interaction were not more dense within countries or regions than across borders; however, the latter interactions were sufficiently important that the idea that there were in these fields nearly disjoined technological communities does not ring right.

There is good reason to believe that in recent years, just as the idea of national innovation systems has become widely accepted, technological communities have become transnational as never before. There has been, first, a strong trend for manufacturing business firms to become multinational. This trend was set, initially, by American based firms; somewhat later European and Japanese firms joined in. In the 1980s international joint ventures on particular product design and development projects, or on large scale research projects, began to crop up in a number of industries.

These developments partly result from and certainly reinforce other trends toward internationalization of technology. Engineers and applied scientists now are taught pretty much the same thing in schools in different countries. The dramatic lowering of national barriers to trade following the war, and the recent convergence of living standards and factor prices in the major industrial nations, means that, increasingly, firms face roughly the same market environment wherever their home base. For both of these reasons, by the mid-1980s the technologies known and employed in the major industrial nations were pretty much the same in most industries. Two decades earlier there were major differences across the industrialized countries in the technologies employed and even in what the engineers knew how to do. But no longer.

More fundamentally, the internationalization of business and technology erodes the extent to which national borders, and citizenship, define boundaries that are meaningful in analyzing technological capabilities and technical advance. And these developments have both stimulated and been reinforced by the rise of transnational public programs of R&D support, such as Eureka, and the increasing activity of organizations such as the E.C. All this raises the following question: "to what extent does it make sense any more to talk about "national innovation systems?"".

As will be shown in the following chapters, although there are many areas of similarity between the systems of countries in comparable economic settings, there still are some striking differences as well. Japanese firms in the semiconductor business tend to be different than American, German, or French firms. The university systems are different and play different roles in the national R&D systems. The development paths of Korea and Taiwan have been very different and so too are their present organization of industry and structure of R&D.

And the reasons for these differences reside, to a significant degree, in differences in national histories and cultures including the timing of a country's entry into the industrialization process. These have profoundly shaped national institutions, laws, and policies (Landes, 1969). How they have will be one of the central topics of the chapters that follow. Also, at the present time many national governments are committed to trying to define, and protect, or advance, what are regarded as specifically national technological capabilities in key areas.

On the other hand, although there certainly are durable and important differences in national characteristics that shape national innovation systems and constrain their evolution, these systems have shown striking adaptability. U. S. public support of university research across the board became policy only after World War II and, if one reflects on it, it seems incompatible with the traditional American norm of small government. And countries clearly copy each other. The American copying of German higher education was repaid when the Europeans later copied American large scale public finance of university research. Europeans and Americans recently have been attempting to copy what they see as successful cooperative research programs in Japan, although adding important national wrinkles. And although important national differences remain, it is not clear how much these matter to "national" firms who often have the opportunity to set up shop in another country when it is advantageous to do so.

There is a tension caused by the attempts of national governments to form and implement national technology policies, in a world where business and technology are increasingly transnational. We discuss some of the key issues later.

A GUIDE TO THIS VOLUME

The sequencing of the country studies that are the heart of this volume is an important part of its analytic structure. Although each study can stand alone on its own merits, the principal purpose of this project has been to map out what is similar and what is different about national systems.

Above we have laid out some of the shared understandings about technological change, and the processes and institutions involved, that have broadly guided the work. We have tried to highlight the wide range of factors, organizations, and policies influencing the capabilities of a nation's firms to innovate, in the broad sense in which we are using that term.

This fact posed a problem regarding the overall design of the study. The desire for comparability seemed to call for a relatively elaborate list of things all country chapters would cover. Yet it was apparent that the most interesting features of a country's innovation system varied significantly across countries, and we wanted our study to highlight these. Limits on resources and space foreclosed doing both.

Our compromise involved two strategic decisions. First, we agreed on a limited list of features all country studies would describe, for example, the allocation of R&D activity and the sources of its funding, the characteristics of firms and the important industries, the roles of universities, and government policies expressly aimed to spur and mold industrial innovation. Beyond these the authors were encouraged to select and highlight what they thought were the most important and interesting characteristics of their country. But second, considerable effort was put into identifying the kinds of comparisons—similarities or differences—that seemed most interesting and important to make. In general these did not involve comparisons across all countries, but rather among a small group where for various reasons comparison was apt.

Thus because they are the countries that currently are in the technological avant-garde, various comparisons between the United States and Japan have been made by others, and we felt we needed to explore these, and other interesting differences and similarities that came to light in the course of discussion of the country chapters as these developed. Since a central objective of the study was to broaden comparison, the description and analysis of Germany, and to some extent those of Britain and France, were designed, along with those of the United States and Japan, to enable comparisons to be drawn in areas that seemed relevant. On reflection, it became clear that interesting comparisons among Italy, France, and Britain could be drawn. Part I contains chapters on these five large relatively affluent countries. The introduction aims to point the reader's attention toward the similarities and differences that, in discussions among the group, seemed most salient.

Part II contains studies of several high-income countries that are small, in the sense that their population is small and hence their internal markets are limited. The innovation systems of Denmark, Sweden, Canada, and Australia all reflect that they are "small" high-income countries in the above sense. Comparisons across these countries are also interesting because all have a strong natural resources or agricultural base.

Part III contains studies of five lower income countries struggling with the industrialization problem, some with striking success and others with less. The chapters on Korea, Taiwan, Brazil, Argentina, and Israel provide a fascinating comparative picture of the evolving innovation systems of an important group of developing countries, that have structured themselves in different ways and that have had quite different experiences with industrialization.

As stated at the outset of this chapter, this study aimed to explore the usefulness and the limitations of the concept of national innovation systems, not to reify the term. In the concluding chapter we will look back, and try to provide an assessment of the extent to which it has been useful to try to carve out something called an innovation system from the complex and variegated institutional structures that make up national economies, and the extent to which this is artificial and awkward. We also shall reflect on the manner and extent to which national institutions matter in a world where business, trade, and technology are increasingly transnational, and on the future of national systems in such a world.

Although the reader must be the judge, we, the authors, come away from our shared intellectual voyage with the belief that, yes, it does make sense to think of national innovation systems, if one is careful to recognize the shadiness and, to some extent, the arbitrariness of both the institutional and national borders. We also believe we have shed significant new light on what is similar and what is different about national systems, and the reasons behind the similarities and differences.

We are far less sure about another central issue. That is the extent to which the particular features of a nation's technical innovation system matter centrally in affecting a nation's overall economic performance in such dimensions as productivity and income and their growth, export, and import performance.

There are certain matters we are sure about, because both general understanding and the comparative case study evidence point to them strongly, and we will discuss these in the concluding chapter. One is that in manufacturing at least, the efforts of governments and universities may support, but cannot be a substitute for the technological efforts of firms. Another is the importance of a nation's education and training system. A third is that a nation's fiscal monetary and trade policies must spur, even compel, national firms to compete on world markets. However, we, the authors, have been impressed by the diversity of "national systems" that seem to be compatible with relatively strong, and weak, economic performance in particular contexts. Partly this may be because there are a variety of alternative arrangements for accomplishing basically the same thing; a number of our studies, when looked at together, suggest that this is so. Partly it may be because the performance of the innovation system is a larger factor behind economic performance in some contexts than in others.

But we are getting ahead of our story.

NOTE

1. We will discuss the concept of a "national innovation system" in more detail later. Three of the participants in this project more or less independently began to use the term and the basic conception in our work which fed into Dosi et al. (1988). See the chapters there by Freeman, Lundvall, and Nelson in Part V, which was titled "National Innovation Systems."

REFERENCES

Allen, R. C. (1983). "Collective Invention." *Journal of Economic Behavior and Organization* 1(4): 1–24.

Beer, J. (1959). *The Emergence of the German Dye Industry.* Urbana, IL: University of Illinois Press.

Cardwell, D.S.L. (1971). *From Watt to Clausius.* Ithaca: Cornell University Press.

Cohen, I. B. (1948). *Science, Servant of Man.* Boston: Little, Brown.

Dosi, G., Freeman, C., Nelson, R., Silverberg, G., and Soete, L. (1988). *Technical Change and Economic Theory.* London: Pinter Publishers.

Dunsheath, P. (1962). *A History of Electrical Engineering.* London: Faber & Faber.

Freeman, C. (1988). "Japan, a New System of Inno-vation." In G. Dosi, C. Freeman, R. Nelson, G. Silverberg, and L. Soete (eds.), *Technical Change and Economic Theory.* London: Pinter Publishers.

Hallion, R. (1977). *Legacy of Flight.* Seattle: University of Washington Press.

Landes, D. (1969). *The Unbound Prometheus.* Cambridge, England: Cambridge University Press.

Lundvall, B. A. (1988). "Innovation as an Interactive Process: From User–Producer Interaction to the National System of Innovation." In G. Dosi, C. Freeman, R. Nelson, G. Silverberg, and L. Soete (eds.), *Technical Change and Economic Theory.* London: Pinter Publishers.

Miller, R., and Sawers, D. (1970). *The Technical*

Development of Modern Aviation. New York: Praeger.

Morison, E. (1966). "Almost the Greatest Invention." In E. Morison, (ed.), *Man, Machines, and Modern Times.* Cambridge, MA: MIT Press.

Nelson, R. R. (1988). "Institutions Supporting Technical Change in the United States." In G. Dosi, C. Freeman, R. Nelson, G. Silverberg, and L. Soete (eds.), *Technical Change and Economic Theory.* London: Pinter Publisher.

Servan Schreiber, J. J. (1968). *The American Challenge.* New York: Atheneum Press.

Thomson, R. (1989). *The Path to Mechanized Shoe Production in the United States.* Chapel Hill, NC: University of North Carolina Press.

PART I

LARGE HIGH-INCOME COUNTRIES

Part I is concerned with the innovation systems of six large affluent highly industrialized nations (Table I.1). We note that the statistics for Germany relate to the old Federal Republic, rather than the newly unified country. The purpose of this introduction is to provide some basic statistics about these countries.

First, the countries are populous. Each one had a population exceeding 50 million, with the United States having over 200 million people, and Japan over 100 million. This differentiates this group of countries sharply from the group of small affluent countries that are the subject of Part II.

And all are affluent. If one measures living standards by gross domestic product (GDP) per capita using exchange rates to convert the nondollar currencies into dollars, as of 1989 Japan stood at the top of the pack, with the United States and West Germany close, and with Italy and the United Kingdom bringing up the rear of this group. Measures of living standards are very sensitive to how currencies are compared. If "purchasing power parity" as contrasted with the official exchange rate is used to effect conversion, the United States moves to the top by a considerable distance, and the other five are seen as bunched at a level about 70% of that in the United States. By either measure, the population of these countries is very well off compared with those of the countries considered in Part III.

Although all of these countries are affluent now, the six differ significantly in when they began their strong economic development. Great Britain was the pioneer in the first industrial revolution, with the United States following strongly by the mid-nineteenth century; Germany's strong development begins later in the nineteenth century, with France and Italy lagging. At the turn of the century Japan had hardly begun her modernization. By the beginning of World War II the United States had a large per capita income lead. Great Britain was a clear second, then Germany, France, and Italy, with Japan by far at the bottom of the per capita league, although not necessarily last in terms of command of technology.

Of the countries in this group Japan had the highest growth of gross domestic product per capita over the period between 1965 and 1988, with the United Kingdom and the United States slowest. It is not coincidental that of these countries Japan had the highest ratio of gross domestic investment to gross domestic product.

It may surprise some readers that of these countries, after the United States, Japan had the smallest ratio of exports to GDP. There is an obvious strong negative correlation between the size of the internal market of a country and its exports as a fraction of gross national product (GNP). However, it is West Germany that is off the regression line, not Japan, although it should be noted that a large share of its exports went to neighboring European states. In all of these countries manufacturing exports accounted for the majority of total exports. In the small high-income countries treated in Part II, exports generally accounted for a significantly larger fraction of GDP than in the countries in Part I.

The literacy rate in all of these countries is very high, as is the enrollment ratio in secondary education, although here the United Kingdom and Italy lag somewhat behind the rest. The United States has a significantly larger fraction of students going on to third-level education than do the other countries. However, there may be something of a statistical artifact here in that secondary education is more intensive in some of the other countries than in the United States.

A smaller fraction of university students in the United States major in science and engineering, compared with the situation in some other countries, particularly Japan and West Germany. Reflecting this Japan, not the United States, stands at the top of the list in countries in terms of scientists and engineers as a fraction of the total population. The United States follows with West Germany a close third.

Table I.1. Comparison of the Six Large High-Income Countries

	United States	Japan	West Germany	France	United Kingdom	Italy
GDP/capita, 1989 official exchange rates	19,840	21,020	18,480	16,090	12,810	13,330
GDP/capita, 1988 purchasing power parity	19,558	14,228	14,161	13,603	13,428	12,985
Population, 1988	246,329	122,613	61,451	55,873	57,065	57,441
Average growth rate GDP/ hour average 1965–1988	1.6	4.3	2.5	2.5	1.8	3.0
Gross domestic invest/GDP average 1965–1988	16	29	19.5	23.5	21	23
Manufacturing output/GDP	22	29	44	27	27	27
Manufacturing exports/ GDP	5	9	24	13	17	14
Total exports/GDP	7.4	16.5	32.4	17.0	20.7	15.5
Literacy rate	>95	>95	>95	>95	>95	>95
Secondary level enrollment rate	98	96	94	92	83	75
Third-level enrollment rate	60	28	30	31	22	24
Scientists and engineers/ population	0.33	0.48	0.25	0.19	0.17	0.12
R&D/GNP	2.9	2.9	2.9	2.3	2.3	1.2
Private R&D/total R&D	48	78	64	42	49	42
Business R&D/total R&D	72.5	66.0	72.2	58.9	67.0	57.2
Private business R&D/total business R&D	66.4	98.0	86.5	69.0	68.2	71.7

The United States, Japan, and West Germany stand at the top of the group in R&D as a fraction of GDP. France and Britain stand lower, with Italy far behind. In all of these countries the majority of R&D is undertaken in business enterprises. However, a significantly larger fraction of that work is financed by government in the United States, the United Kingdom, and France as contrasted with Japan and Germany, largely reflecting differences in the military R&D budget.

2

The U. S. National Innovation System

DAVID C. MOWERY
NATHAN ROSENBERG

A descriptive analysis of the U. S. national innovation "system" is a gargantuan task, made all the more ambitious by our efforts to begin this discussion in the early twentieth century. We then examine the pre-World War II and postwar U. S. innovation "systems." In the introductory and the concluding sections of the paper, we summarize some of the elements that appear to distinguish this national innovation system from those of other industrial and industrializing economies. Because of the dearth of reliable quantitative data for the pre-1953 era, most of our comparative assessments cover the postwar period or are largely qualitative. Moreover, the lack of data on other dimensions of the post-1953 U. S. innovation system (e.g., comprehensive statistics on the adoption of new technologies) means that our quantitative discussion of this period relies heavily on R&D investment data, with all of their limitations.

One of the most salient distinguishing traits of the U. S. innovation system is its enormous scale—for a substantial portion of the postwar era, the national R&D investment of the United States was larger than those of all other OECD nations combined. The relative importance of three key sectors within the U. S. innovation system—industry, universities, and the federal government—as performers and as funders of R&D also contrasts somewhat with the role of these institutions in other national innovation systems. The roles of these three sectors have changed considerably during the past 70 years.

Another structural contrast between the U. S. and other national innovation systems that is particularly noteworthy for the postwar period is the importance of new firms in the commercialization of new technologies within the U. S. economy. Relatively small startup firms have played a significant role in the development and diffusion of microelectronics, computer hardware and software, biotechnology, and robotics during the past four decades. Their role appears to have been more significant within the U. S. economy than in the other economies included in this comparative analysis, with the possible exceptions of Taiwan and Denmark. This role may decline somewhat in importance in the future, an issue to which we return later.

Two public policies in particular contributed to contrasts between the structure of the U. S. national innovation system and those of other nations. The antitrust statutes of the United States have had complex effects on the structure and performance of this innovation system. Another policy-related point of contrast concerns the important role of military R&D and procurement within the U. S. innovation system. Frequently cited as an important source of commercial strength in high-technology industries during the early postwar years, this large military R&D investment may now yield a far smaller commercial payoff.

Although it has invested large sums in R&D throughout the postwar period, the U. S. federal government has not based this investment on any economic strategy. The fragmented structure of R&D programs' finance and administration in both the Executive branch and Congress has supported a high degree of pluralism and diversity in publicly funded R&D programs. Conversely, however, this structure has precluded any comprehensive oversight of the structure or economic effects of publicly financed R&D. Evaluations of the economic benefits flowing from the large public R&D investment in the postwar United States are rare.

Some indicators of the basic research capabilities of the U. S. innovation system (e.g., the share of postwar Nobel Prizes won for research performed within U. S. laboratories, or citation analyses of scientific papers) suggest that the research performance of the system is very strong. The U. S. innovation system has not succeeded, however, in maintaining pre-1973 rates of growth in real earnings; nor has it enabled U. S. productivity growth to match that of other industrial economies or prevented a significant deterioration in the U. S. current account. U. S. economic performance has been impaired by many factors during the past 2 decades, and the national R&D system is by no means the sole contributor to widening trade deficits or to slow growth in earnings and productivity. Nor are economic indices necessarily the most appropriate criteria for an evaluation of the performance of this system. Nevertheless, these perceived deficiencies are driving much of the current debate over the structure of U. S. innovation and trade policies.

The recent technological performance of U. S. firms appears to be relatively weak in several areas. U. S. firms have been slower than their counterparts in a number of other industrial economies to adopt new manufacturing technologies and, some observers suggest, do not utilize these technologies (e.g., robotics, computer-integrated manufacturing) as intensively or as effectively as foreign firms.[1] Detailed comparisons of the performance of U. S. and Japanese automobile firms suggest that U. S. firms have been hampered by much longer development cycles for new products. Still other analyses have faulted the ability of U. S. firms in a wide array of industries to commercialize new technologies rapidly and effectively. These weaknesses, especially the first (in view of the importance of capital costs in investment decisions), may be only loosely related to the structure and performance of U. S. institutions for R&D. Nevertheless, this and other evidence (some of which, such as international trade performance, is affected by other factors, such as macroeconomic policy), has provoked a wide-ranging debate over the need for new ways of organizing and funding public and private R&D within the U. S. economy. This debate is discussed briefly later.

Discussion of new approaches to the organization and finance of innovation in the United States has been parallelled by signs of change in the structure of the innovation systems of Western Europe and Japan. Institutional change in all three of these economic regions is occurring simultaneously with growing international trade in high-technology products and increasing international interdependence of "national" innovation systems. National trade and technology policies appear to be more and more tightly interconnected. Change in the international environment, combined with the weak apparatus for the formulation and oversight of technology policy in the

United States, has created serious challenges for U. S. policymakers in the coordination of trade and technology policies. We briefly discuss this issue in our concluding section.

THE U. S. SYSTEM BEFORE 1945

The Origins of U. S. Industrial Research

The expansion of the American economy during the late nineteenth and early twentieth centuries combined with innovations in transportation, communications, and production technologies yielded manufacturing operations of unprecedented scale (Chandler, 1977). These production operations built on a long-established pattern of technological innovation and adaptation that relied largely on mechanical skills, rather than on formal scientific research. As David (1975), Rosenberg (1972), and others have noted, growth in manufacturing productivity and output in the nineteenth century U. S. economy was achieved in part through the development of the "American system of manufactures" for the production of light machines and other mechanical devices.

Innovation in this sector did not rely heavily on scientific research.[2] The resource endowment of the United States, which favored the development of machinery for agricultural and transportation applications, its enormous, protected domestic market, and the ability of the United States to exploit foreign sources of knowledge (importing machinery, blueprints, and skilled tinkerers from Europe and elsewhere) all supported these developments.[3] But innovation during much of this period, which supported growth in U. S. productivity and per capita income to levels exceeding those of Great Britain by 1913 (Nelson, 1990), relied on few of the institutions associated with R&D in the late twentieth century.

The enormous mass-production operations that typified much of U. S. manufacturing during this period also were associated with a system of work organization and hierarchy that if not unique to the United States was more systematically pursued in this economy. The twentieth–century "American system of manufactures" was inspired by the theories and experiments of Frederick Taylor and by the practices of Henry Ford (among others), and spurred by the challenges of managing an ethnically diverse and heterogeneous workforce. This system emphasized the division of operations into very narrow, relatively unskilled tasks, each of which was performed repeatedly by a single worker who was closely supervised by lower-level managers. Specialized capital equipment also was utilized in the repeated performance of these tasks—high levels of capital intensity and specialization made for high costs of design changes and meant that long production runs of a single product design were central elements of this manufacturing system. Workers had little responsibility for the pace and structure of the work process or for product quality. Fluctuations in product demand were often managed through layoffs.

Each element of this system reinforced others—unstable employment and narrowly defined work classifications both supported low levels of firm investment in worker training and skills. Elaborate job classification systems received additional support in unionized establishments, since unions derived considerable power over both members and management by defending these systems. A number of observers have suggested that this "Fordist/Taylorist" system of work organization contributed to an adversarial atmosphere of labor–management relations and low levels of investment in worker skills that have impeded U. S. firms' efforts to adopt new technologies and improve product quality (Walton and McKersie, 1990; Lazonick, 1991).

The materials analysis and quality control laboratories that were established within many of these new, large factories were among the first industrial employers of scientists and research personnel. These plant-level laboratories gradually expanded and were supplemented by the foundation of central laboratories devoted to longer term research. Although the development of much of the original testing and materials analysis research was a response to changes in the structure of production, the expansion and elaboration of these activities reflected change in the organizational structure of the firm. The development of these research facilities was associated with expansion and diversification of the firm's activities and products and substitution of intrafirm control of these activities for market control.

Structural change in many large U. S. manufacturing firms, including their investment in industrial research, was influenced by U. S. antitrust policy. The increasingly stringent judicial interpretation of the Sherman Antitrust Act in the late nineteenth century made agreements among firms for the control of prices and output more frequent targets of civil prosecution. The 1895–1904 U. S. merger wave, particularly the surge in mergers after 1898, was in part a response to this new legal environment. Finding that the legality of informal or formal price-fixing and market-sharing agreements was under attack, firms resorted to horizontal mergers to control prices and markets.[4] Effective use of mergers for this purpose frequently required strong central control of the firm's subsidiaries.

The influence of antitrust policy on the growth of industrial research, however, extended beyond its effects on corporate structure. The incentives created by the Sherman Act for horizontal mergers were reduced by the *Northern Securities* decision of 1904. Nonetheless, judicial interpretations of the Sherman Act and Justice Department prosecution of a widening array of firms increased corporate reliance on industrial research and innovation to forestall or offset the effects of antitrust prosecution. Industrial research supported corporate diversification and the use of patents to attain or retain market power without running afoul of antitrust law.[5]

These early research laboratories focused in part on developing inventions created by in-house research, but also monitored the environment for technological threats and opportunities for the acquisition of new technologies, in many cases through the purchase of patents or firms. Many of Du Pont's major product and process innovations, for example, were obtained by the firm at an early point in their development, often on the advice of the central research laboratory (Mueller, 1962; Hounshell and Smith, 1988). For much of the pre-1940 period, Du Pont research focused on developing inventions acquired from external sources; nylon and neoprene were exceptions to this rule. The research facilities of AT&T, General Electric, and, to a lesser extent, Eastman Kodak, performed similar monitoring roles during this period.[6]

The Growth of Industrial Research

Although recent historiography on U. S. industrial research has focused primarily on the electrical industry (an exception is Hounshell and Smith, 1988), the limited data on the growth of industrial research activity during the early twentieth century suggest that it was dominated by the chemicals industry and related industries. The chemicals, glass, rubber, and petroleum industries accounted for nearly 40% of the number of laboratories founded during 1899–1946. The chemicals sector also dominated research employment during 1921–1946. In 1921, the chemicals, petroleum, and rubber industries accounted for slightly more than 40% of total research scientists and engineers in manufacturing. The dominance of chemicals-related industries as research employers was supplemented during the period by industries whose product and process technologies drew heavily on physics. Electrical machinery and instruments accounted for less than 10% of total research employment in 1921. By 1946, however, these two industries contained more than 20% of all scientists and engineers employed in industrial research in U. S. manufacturing, and the chemicals-based industries had increased their share to slightly more than 43% of total research employment.

Table 2.1 provides data on research laboratory employment for 1921, 1927, 1933, 1944, and 1946 in 19 two-digit manufacturing industries and in manufacturing overall (excluding miscellaneous manufacturing industries). Employment of scientists

Table 2.1. Employment of Scientists and Engineers in Industrial Research Laboratories in U.S. Manufacturing Firms, 1921–1946

	1921	1927	1933	1940	1946
Food/beverages	116	354	651	1712	2510
	(.19)	(.53)	(.973)	(2.13)	(2.26)
Paper	89	189	302	752	770
	(.49)	(.87)	(1.54)	(2.79)	(1.96)
Chemicals	1102	1812	3255	7675	14066
	(5.2)	(6.52)	(12.81)	(27.81)	(30.31)
Petroleum	159	465	994	2849	4750
	(1.83)	(4.65)	(11.04)	(26.38)	(28.79)
Rubber products	207	361	564	1000	1069
	(2.04)	(2.56)	(5.65)	(8.35)	(5.2)
Stone/clay/glass	96	410	569	1334	1508
	(.38)	(1.18)	(3.25)	(5.0)	(3.72)
Primary metals	297	538	850	2113	2460
	(.78)	(.93)	(2.0)	(3.13)	(2.39)
Fabricated metal products	103	334	500	1332	1489
	(.27)	(.63)	(1.53)	(2.95)	(1.81)
Nonelectrical machinery	127	421	629	2122	2743
	(.25)	(.65)	(1.68)	(3.96)	(2.2)
Electrical machinery	199	732	1322	3269	6993
	(1.11)	(2.86)	(8.06)	(13.18)	(11.01)
Transportation equipment	83	256	394	1765	4491
	(.204)	(.52)	(1.28)	(3.24)	(4.58)
Instruments	127	234	581	1318	2246
	(.396)	(.63)	(2.69)	(4.04)	(3.81)
Total (including R&D employment n.e.c.).	2775	6320	10927	27777	45941

Note: Figures in parentheses represent research intensity, defined as employment of scientists and engineers per 1,000 production workers.

Source: Mowery (1981).

and engineers in industrial research within manufacturing grew from roughly 3,000 in 1921 to nearly 46,000 by 1946.[7] The ordering of industries by research intensity is remarkably stable—chemicals, rubber, petroleum, and electrical machinery are among the most research-intensive industries, accounting for 48–58% of total employment of scientists and engineers in industrial research within manufacturing, throughout this period. Similar stability is revealed in the geographic concentration of industrial research employment during this period. Five states (New York, New Jersey, Pennsylvania, Ohio, and Illinois) contained more than 70% of the professionals employed in industrial research in 1921 and 1927; their share declined modestly, to slightly more than 60%, by 1940 and 1946. The major prewar research employers remained among the most research-intensive industries well into the postwar period despite the growth in federal funding for research in industry. Chemicals, rubber, petroleum, and electrical machinery accounted for more than 53% of industrial research employment in 1940 and represented 40.3% of research employment in industry in 1984 (National Science Foundation, 1985).

An exception to the pattern of stability in research intensity is transportation equipment, which increased in research intensity throughout the period, and by 1946 was among the five most research-intensive manufacturing industries. The upward movement in the relative research intensity of this industry (which includes aircraft) is attributable to federal support of research and federal procurement during 1940–1946, and to the rapid growth of the automobile industry throughout 1921–1946. Government funding of wartime research in industry also contributed to research employment growth within electrical machinery and instruments after 1940.

Schumpeter argued (1954) that in-house industrial research had supplanted the inventor–entrepreneur (a hypothesis supported by Schmookler, 1957) and would reinforce, rather than erode, the position of dominant firms. The data on research employment and firm turnover among the 200 largest firms suggest that during 1921–1946 at least, the effects of industrial research were consistent with his predictions. Industrial research significantly improved firms' prospects for remaining in the ranks of the 200 largest firms during this period (Mowery, 1983). The growth of industrial research during 1921–1946 among the 200 largest firms is associated with a decline in turnover within this group. Industrial research contributed to the stabilization of market structure in the unstable economic environment of the 1921–1946 period (Edwards, 1975; Kaplan, 1964; Collins and Preston, 1961). To the extent that federal antitrust policy contributed to industrial research investment by large firms during this period, the policy paradoxically may have aided the survival of these firms and the growth of a relatively stable, oligopolistic market structure in some U. S. manufacturing industries. Interestingly, and in contrast to the usual statement of one of the Schumpeterian "hypotheses," these results suggest that firm conduct (R&D employment) was an important influence on market structure (turnover).

Publicly Funded Research and the Universities

In spite of the permissive implications of the "general welfare" clause of the U. S. Constitution, federal support for science prior to World War II was limited by a strict interpretation of the role of the federal government. During World War I, the military operated the R&D and production facilities for the war effort; with the exception of the munitions industry, where the federal government relied on Du Pont, the necessary technical and scientific expertise simply was not available in the private sector. When one of the armed services identified a scientific need, a person with the appropriate qualifications was drafted into that branch. One legacy of wartime programs for technology development was the National Advisory Committee on Aeronautics (NACA), founded in 1915 to "investigate the scientific problems involved in flight and to give advice to the military air services and other aviation services of the government" (Ames, 1925). NACA, which was absorbed by the National Aeronautics and Space Administration in 1958, made important contributions to the development of new aeronautics technologies for both civilian and military applications throughout its existence, but was particularly important during the era before 1940.

For 1940, the last year that was not dominated by the vast expenditures associated with wartime mobilization, total federal expenditures for research, development, and R&D plant amounted to $74.1 million. Of that, Department of Agriculture expenditures amounted to $29.1 million, or 39%. In 1940, the Department of Agriculture's research budget exceeded that of the agencies that would eventually be combined in the Department of Defense, whose total research budget amounted to $26.4 million. Between them, these categories accounted for 75% of all federal R&D expenditures. The claimants on the remaining 25%, in descending order of importance, were the Department of the Interior ($7.9 million), the Department of Commerce ($3.3 million), the Public Health Service ($2.8 million), and the National Advisory Committee on Aeronautics ($2.2 million).

Federal expenditures for R&D throughout the 1930s constituted 12–20% of total U. S. R&D expenditures. Industry accounted for about two-thirds of the total. The remainder came from universities,[8] state governments, private foundations, and research institutes. One estimate suggests that state funds may have accounted for as much as 14% of university research funding during 1935–1936 (National Resources Planning Board, 1942, p. 178). Moreover, the contribution of state governments to nonagricultural university research appears from these data to have exceeded the federal contribution.

To a greater extent than was true of Germany or Great Britain, industrial and academic research developed in parallel in the United States. The pursuit of research was recognized as an important professional activity within both U. S. industry and higher education only in the late nineteenth century, and research in both venues was influenced by the example (and in the case of U. S. industry, by the competitive pressure) of German industry and academia.

Linkages between academic and industrial research were powerfully influenced by the decentralized structure and funding of the U. S. higher education system, especially public universities. Public funding meant that the size of the U. S. higher education system outstripped that of such European nations as Great Britain.[9] Of equal or greater importance, however, was the fact that public funding for many U. S. universities was provided by state governments, rather than by the federal government. The politics of state funding meant that both the curriculum and research of U. S. public universities were more closely geared to commercial opportunities than was true in many European systems of higher education.[10] Especially within emerging subfields of engineering and, to a lesser extent, within mining and metallurgy, state university systems often introduced new programs as soon as the requirements of the local economy became clear.

The use of scientific knowledge and problem-solving techniques in industry was accelerated by growth in the pool of technically trained personnel—especially engineers. This expansion was the result in part of growth in the number of engineering schools and programs in the second half of the nineteenth century. The training of these engineers was, to be sure, often elementary in character and did not prepare them for work at the scientific frontier. Indeed, before 1940 there are few if any areas of scientific research in which U. S. universities or scholars could be described as operating at the scientific frontier.

Although the situation was improving in the decade before 1940, Cohen (1976) noted that virtually all "serious" U. S. scientists completed their studies at European universities, and Thackray et al. (1985) argue that American chemistry research during this period attracted attention (in the form of citations in other scientific papers) as much because of its quantity as its quality.[11] Interestingly, recent citation analyses suggest that American physics research had begun to acquire a world-class research reputation by the 1930s, before the infusion of scientific brilliance resulting from the emigration to the United States of European scientists.[12] The rise of American physics research to scientific eminence is reflected as well in the award of Nobel Prizes to Langmuir, Millikan, Compton, and Davisson in physics during this period—two of these recipients made their pathbreaking discoveries as employees of major U. S. industrial research laboratories. Nevertheless, the current eminence of U. S. scientific research in a broad array of disciplines is largely a postwar phenomenon.

Regardless of the quality of the scientific research performed within the U. S. research system before World War II, it was the larger body of scientific knowledge, and not merely frontier science, that was relevant to the needs of an expanding industrial establishment.[13] Thus, engineers and other technically trained personnel served as valuable carriers of scientific knowledge. As a result, the number of people bringing the knowledge and methods of science to bear on industrial problems was vastly greater than the limited number of individuals that society chose to label "scientists" at any particular time. Moreover, as was noted above, the scale of the U. S. higher educational system exceeded those of other industrial nations during this period. As in the postwar Japanese research system, this broad-based system of training scientists and engineers aided the diffusion and utilization of advanced scientific and engineering knowledge. Even where it did not advance the knowledge frontier, higher education appears to have been an important instrument for scientific and engineering "catch-up" in the United States during the early twentieth century.

Agricultural Research

Although the focus of this and other papers is technical advance in industry, the U. S. agricultural sector deserves brief mention. Agricultural products have long been important U. S. exports, and U. S. industrial development for much of the last 150 years relied heavily on the exploitation of linkages between agriculture and industry, as in the development of advanced technologies for food processing and in the growth of a U. S. technological advantage in farm machinery and equipment (Patel and Pavitt,

Table 2.2. Defense R&D as a Share of Federal R&D Spending, 1960–1990

Year	Percent	Year	Percent
1960	80	1976	50
1961	77	1977	51
1962	70	1978	49
1963	62	1979	48
1964	55	1980	51
1965	50	1981	54
1966	49	1982	61
1967	52	1983	64
1968	52	1984	66
1969	54	1985	67
1970	52	1986	69
1971	52	1987	69
1972	54	1988	67
1973	54	1989 (est.)	60
1974	52	1990 (est.)	65
1975	51		

Source: Budget of the U.S. Government (Washington, D.C.: US Government Printing Office, 1989).

1986). The data cited above note the prominent role of agriculture as a recipient of federal and state research funds during the pre-1940 era.

Much of the foundation for the extensive system of publicly supported higher education in the United States was in fact laid down during the nineteenth century as a means of financing research and other services for the agricultural sector. The Morrill Act of 1862 provided the wherewithal for the founding of state universities to pursue research and education in the "agricultural and mechanical arts." Further support for agricultural research was provided in the Hatch Act of 1887 and the Adams Act of 1906, which established state experimental stations to perform agricultural research. Table 2.2 includes data on funding for the pre-1940 period and illustrates two points: (1) the important role of state funds in financing this research system, a role that was greater during the pre-1940 period than in the postwar period; and (2) the sizable portion of the budget devoted to extension activities, including testing and support for the dissemination of best-practice techniques in an "industry" in which local conditions and problems required considerable modification of seeds, techniques, and equipment.

Extension activity appears to have been especially important for the pre-1940 growth of U. S. agriculture, which was almost entirely extensive rather than intensive in character (Parker, 1972). Figure 2.1 illustrates the nearly flat trend in output per acre or per man-hour for the pre-1940 period. Much of the growth in agricultural output during this period depended on the expansion of cultivated land and the dissemination of seed strains that were suited to local growing conditions. These functions relied as much on extension as on scientific research. Beginning in 1940, however, agricultural productivity grew rapidly, as a result of the exploitation of advances in biological and chemistry research. Hybrid seed corn, for example, came into widespread use only in the late 1930s. The scientific research component of this considerable state and federal investment in agricultural research and extension thus began to reap substantial payoffs only after a number of decades.[14]

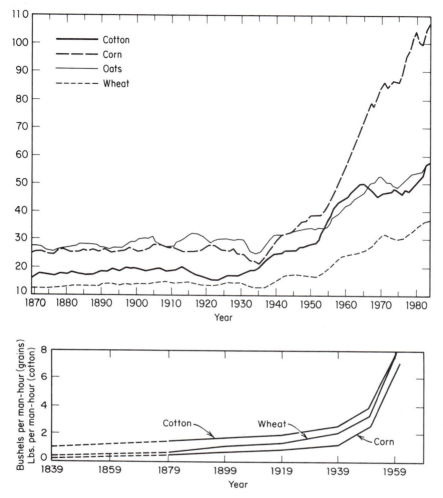

Figure 2.1. Output per acre, 1868–1984. Source: U.S.D.A., Agricultural Statistics, 1962, 1982, 1987. From W. N. Parker, "Agriculture." In L. E. David, R. A. Easterlin, and W. N. Parker (eds.), *American Economic Growth,* p. 374. New York: Harper & Row, 1972.

Conclusion

Much of the structure of the private sector components of the U. S. national innovation system took shape during the 1900–1940 period. Closely linked with the rise of the giant multiproduct corporation that began at the turn of the century, industrial research contributed to the stability and survival of these firms. Before 1940 federal support for research that was not agricultural was very limited and may well have been exceeded by state government support. Although university research budgets before 1940 were miniscule by later standards, the system was one in which the requirements of industry, agriculture, and mining were recognized and accommodated. As research within industrial establishments grew in importance, university research during this period often involved various forms of collaboration with private industry.

THE POSTWAR SYSTEM

Introduction

World War II transformed the U. S. R&D system. Federal government support for industrial and academic research expanded dramatically, although in contrast to other nations, nongovernmental institutions retained primary responsibility for the performance of much of this R&D. World War II also transformed the global technological and competitive environment within which U. S. firms operated. The United States emerged from wartime as an unchallenged leader in a much broader range of technologies than was true at any point before 1940, and federal funding built a strong scientific research capability during the postwar years. Moreover, the demands of reconstruction were to prolong U. S. technological and economic supremacy. Because a central point of contrast between the prewar and postwar research systems is the upsurge in federal government involvement in the national R&D system, this section devotes considerable attention to the contours of federal R&D support in basic, commercial, and military research.

World War II and Its Aftermath

With war preparations and the entry of the United States into World War II in December 1941, the bucolic picture of federal R&D expenditures discussed above was transformed. Funding for the primary categories of prewar R&D, which were not war related, grew only slightly during the war in dollar terms and declined substantially in real terms. Total federal R&D expenditures (in 1930 dollars) rose from $83.2 million in 1940 to a peak of $1,313.6 million in 1945. Over the same period, the research expenditures of the Department of Defense rose from $29.6 to $423.6 million (in 1930 dollars).

The success and the organizational structure of the massive federal wartime R&D program yielded several important legacies. The successful completion of the Manhattan Project, whose research budget in the peak years 1944 and 1945 substantially exceeded that of the Department of Defense, created a research and weapons production complex that eventually would usher in the age of truly "big science." Paradoxically, the Manhattan Project's success in creating weapons of unprecedented destructive power contributed to rosy postwar perceptions of the constructive possibilities of large-scale science for the advance of societal welfare.

Far smaller in financial terms, but highly significant as an institutional innovation, was the Office of Scientific Research and Development (OSRD), a civilian agency directed by Vannevar Bush. The OSRD was not under military control. Although it employed federal funds on wartime scientific research projects, OSRD entered into contracts with the private sector for the performance of that research and allowed full reimbursement of research costs. OSRD also relied heavily on universities as research performers. The largest single recipient of OSRD grants and contracts during wartime (and the inventor of that device beloved of university research administrators, institutional overhead) was M.I.T., with 75 contracts for a total of more than $116 million. The largest corporate recipient of OSRD funds, Western Electric, accounted for only $17 million (Pursell, 1977, p. 364).

The contrast between the organization of wartime R&D in World War I and World War II reflects the far more advanced state of development of university and private sector research capabilities during the second global conflict. The contractual arrangements developed by OSRD during World War II allowed the Office to tap the broad array of private sector scientific capabilities that had developed during the inter-war period.[15] Members of the scientific community were called on to recommend and to guide as well as to participate in scientific research with military payoffs. OSRD was not subordinated to the military and had direct access to the President and to the pertinent congressional appropriations committees.

The success of these wartime contractual arrangements with the private sector contributed to a feature of postwar publicly funded American R&D that distinguishes it from both the prewar period and other countries.[16] In 1940 federal R&D went to support research performed within the federal establishment itself—by government civil servants, as in the National Bureau of Standards, the Department of Agriculture, and the Public Health Service, or by state institutions financed by federal grants, as in the agricultural experiment stations. In the postwar period, by contrast, most federal R&D funds have supported the performance of research by nongovernmental organizations.

Postwar R&D Expenditures

Two salient features of postwar R&D spending are the magnitude of the overall national R&D investment and the size of the federal R&D budget. Throughout this period, federal R&D spending has been a large fraction of a very large national R&D investment. The total volume of resources devoted to R&D since the end of World War II is large not only by comparison with our earlier history, but also by comparison with other Organization for Economic Cooperation and Development (OECD) member countries. Indeed, as late as 1969, when the combined R&D expenditures of the largest foreign industrial economies (West Germany, France, the United Kingdom, and Japan) were $11.3 billion, those for the United States were $25.6 billion. Not until the late 1970s did the combined total for those four countries exceed that of the United States (Danhof, 1968, p. 192).

Of the two components of national R&D spending, private and federal spending, the latter has been more volatile, reaching a peak of about two-thirds of total R&D in the mid-1960s and declining substantially after this point. Over the same period, private R&D has tracked GNP growth more closely and therefore has grown more steadily (see Table 2.3). Total R&D spending was slightly more than 1% of GNP in the immediate postwar years. The percentage grew rapidly in the second half of the 1950s and peaked at almost 3% in the mid-1960s, after which it declined until the second half of the 1970s.

Within the postwar R&D system, federal expenditures have financed somewhere between one-half and two-thirds of total R&D, the great bulk of which is performed by private industry. In 1985 73% of all federally funded R&D was performed in private industry, and only 12% in federal intramural laboratories (although 47% of all R&D

Table 2.3. Sources of Funds for Research and Development by Sector: 1953–1989 (Dollars in Millions)

| | Current Dollars | | | | | Real (1982) Dollars[a] | | | | | | |
Year	United States	Federal Govt.	Industry	Universities and Colleges	Other Nonprofit	United States	Federal Govt.	Industry	Universities and Colleges	Other Nonprofit	Total Private[b]	Federal (%)
1953	5,124	2,753	2,245	72	54	19,744	10,590	8,671	276	208	9,155	53.6
1955	6,172	3,502	2,520	88	62	22,760	12,923	9,282	326	229	9,837	56.8
1960	13,523	8,738	4,516	149	120	43,648	28,191	14,591	479	387	15,457	64.6
1965	20,044	13,012	6,548	267	217	59,351	38,532	19,384	791	643	20,818	64.9
1970	26,134	14,892	10,444	461	337	62,405	35,636	24,851	1,111	807	26,769	57.1
1975	35,213	18,109	15,820	749	535	59,883	30,986	26,679	1,302	916	28,897	51.7
1980	62,594	29,453	30,914	1,326	901	73,237	34,548	36,067	1,565	1,057	38,689	47.2
1985	107,757	51,668	52,358	2,377	1,354	96,999	46,463	47,188	2,131	1,217	50,536	47.9
1989 (est.)	132,350	62,700	64,035	3,800	1,815	105,029	49,720	50,863	3,007	1,439	55,309	47.3

[a]Based on GNP implicit price deflator.

[b]Total for three columns including industry, universities and colleges, and other nonprofit.

Sources: National Science Foundation, SRS. National Patterns of R&D Resources (1989). NSF 89-308.

was financed by the federal government). The remaining 15% is a critical component of federal R&D spending. Approximately 3% of federal R&D supports federally funded research and development centers (FFRDCs) administered by universities and colleges, 3% is allocated to other nonprofit institutions, and 9% supports university research.[17]

Federal funds have been especially important in supporting basic research. Although that share has been declining for the past several years and now is at its lowest level in 20 years, federal funds still represent two-thirds of total basic research spending. Only 15% of federally funded basic research currently is performed within the federal research establishment. Universities have increased in importance as basic research performers during this period. In 1953, less than one-third of all basic research was performed in universities and FFRDCs at universities and colleges. In recent years, however, these institutions have performed more than one-half of all basic research.

Support for basic research is concentrated in a few agencies within the federal budget. By far the largest federal obligations are in the Department of Health and Human Services, where the basic research budget consists overwhelmingly of the expenditures of the National Institutes of Health. The next largest obligations, in descending order, are in NSF, DOD, DOE, and NASA.

Military R&D Funding

The military services have dominated the federal R&D budget for the past 30 years, falling below 50% of federal R&D obligations in only 3 years (see Table 2.4). In 1960 defense research constituted no less than 80% of federal R&D funds. It declined sharply from that level (a decline offset by the growth of the space program) and hovered around the 50% level until the early 1980s, when it rose swiftly again.

The dominant role of the defense budget within the total federal R&D budget has another important implication. The defense R&D budget is far more development intensive than the rest of the federal R&D budget. This characteristic of the dominant component of federal R&D spending imparts a strong bias to the overall federal R&D budget in favor of development. If the 1982 federal budget is broken down into defense

Table 2.4. Trends in Federal R&D Expenditures

Year	Obligations (in Billions of Dollars)				Defense (%)	All Other (%)
	Defense[a]	All Other	Total	Basic Research[b]		
1960	6.1	1.5	7.6	0.6	80	20
1965	7.3	7.3	14.6	1.4	50	50
1970	8.0	7.3	15.3	1.9	52	48
1975	9.7	9.3	19.0	2.6	51	49
1980	15.1	14.7	29.8	4.7	51	49
1985	33.4	16.1	49.5	7.8	67	33
1990 (est.)	44.0	23.3	67.3	11.2	65	35

[a]Includes military-related programs of the Departments of Defense and Energy.
[b]Included in totals for conduct of R&D.
Source: Budget of the U.S. Government, 1990. Executive Office of the President, Office of Management and Budget, "Special Analysis J" (1989, 1990).

and nondefense components, the share of basic, applied, and development expenditures within each total is as follows:

1983 Federal R&D Expenditures[18]

	Defense (%)	Nondefense (%)
Basic	3.2	33.7
Applied	11.0	35.3
Development	85.8	31.0
Total	100.0	100.0

Sources:

1958 data: National Science Foundation, *Research and Development in Industry: 1974,* Tables B-3, B-6, and B-9.

1972 data: National Science Foundation, *National Patterns of Science and Technology Resources: 1980,* Tables 37–39.

1986 data: National Science Foundation, *National Patterns of Science and Technology Resources: 1989,* Tables B-25, B-26, and B-27. Implicit GNP deflator used for conversion to 1987 dollars.

The largest items in the DOD R&D budget involve the development of advanced weapons systems, construction and testing of prototypes, and so on. Conversely, DOD devotes a smaller share of its R&D budget to basic and applied research than any other major federal R&D funding agency.[19]

As a result of the development emphasis in defense R&D and the large size of the defense R&D budget, the distribution of the federal R&D budget across industry sectors is highly concentrated. Nearly 80% of all federal R&D in 1984 went to two industry sectors—aircraft and missiles (over 50%) and electrical machinery (over 25%).[20] Nonelectrical machines was a distant third, and motor vehicles and other transportation equipment fourth (see Table 2.5).

Have military expenditures strengthened the commercial innovative capabilities of U. S. firms during the postwar period? Assessing the commercial impact of military R&D spending is complicated by the fact that the influence of military R&D spending can easily be confounded with that of military procurement. The benefits that are sometimes perceived to flow from military R&D are in fact frequently the product of military R&D plus massive military procurement. This overlap between the influence of Pentagon R&D spending and Pentagon procurement is accentuated by the practice of paying a percentage of military procurement contracts to defense suppliers as an "independent R&D" allowance that is generally not included in either the formal defense R&D budget or the reported R&D expenditures of recipient firms.

In the semiconductor industry, for example, the role of military procurement may well have outweighed the direct influence of military R&D expenditures (Utterback and Murray, 1977). The large procurement needs of the military and NASA were vital in the early years of new product development in electronics. From the mid-1950s to the late 1960s, the federal government (mainly the military and NASA) accounted for a large, although declining, share of the output of semiconductor devices. By the end of the 1960s the computer industry displaced the military as the largest end user market for integrated circuits. Profits and overhead from military procurement contracts supported company-funded R&D and thereby may have generated more civil-

Table 2.5. R&D Funds by Industry

R&D Funds by Industry	Total	1958 Federal	Company
Current dollars			
Total	8389	4759	3630
Chemicals and allied products	792	126	666
Industrial chemicals	553	110	443
Drugs and medicines and other chemicals	239	16	223
Petroleum refining and extraction	246	12	234
Rubber products	89	21	68
Primary metals	131	14	117
Ferrous metals and products	80	2	78
Nonferrous metals and products	51	12	39
Fabricated metal products	162	57	105
Nonelectrical machinery	781	343	438
Electrical machinery	1969	1337	632
Communication equipment and electronic components	868	615	253
Motor vehicles and other transportation equipment	856	296	560
Aircraft and missiles	2609	2276	333
Professional and scientific instruments	294	137	157
Scientific and mechanical measuring instruments	156	93	63
Optical, surgical, photographic, and other instruments	138	44	94
All other manufacturing industries	343	78	265
Nonmanufacturing industries	117	62	55
1989 constant dollars			
Total	35674	20238	15437
Chemicals and allied products	3368	536	2832
Industrial chemicals	2352	468	1884
Drugs and medicines and other chemicals	1016	68	948
Petroleum refining and extraction	1046	51	995
Rubber products	378	89	289
Primary metals	557	60	498
Ferrous metals and products	340	9	332
Nonferrous metals and products	217	51	166
Fabricated metal products	689	242	447
Nonelectrical machinery	3321	1459	1863
Electrical machinery	8373	5686	2688
Communication equipment and electronic components	3691	2615	1076
Motor vehicles and other transportation equipment	3640	1259	2381
Aircraft and missiles	11095	9679	1416
Professional and scientific instruments	1250	583	668
Scientific and mechanical measuring instruments	663	395	268
Optical, surgical, photographic, and other instruments	587	187	400
All other manufacturing industries	1459	332	1127
Nonmanufacturing industries	498	264	234

R&D Funds by Industry	Total	1972 Federal	Company
Current dollars			
Total	19552	8017	11535
Chemicals and allied products	1932	189	1741
Industrial chemicals	1031	171	860
Drugs and medicines and other chemicals	901	18	881
Petroleum refining and extraction	468	15	454

Table 2.5. R&D Funds by Industry (*Continued*)

R&D Funds by Industry	1972 Total	Federal	Company
Rubber products	377	123	255
Primary metals	277	12	264
Ferrous metals and products	146	3	144
Nonferrous metals and products	130	10	121
Fabricated metal products	253	12	243
Nonelectrical machinery	2158	401	1758
Electrical machinery	4680	2367	2313
Communication equipment and electronic components	2913	1542	1370
Motor vehicles and other transportation equipment	2010	326	1684
Aircraft and missiles	4950	3970	978
Professional and scientific instruments	838	161	678
Scientific and mechanical measuring instruments	163	13	151
Optical, surgical, photographic, and other instruments	675	148	527
All other manufacturing industries	902	10	890
Nonmanufacturing industries	707	431	277
1989 constant dollars			
Total	45730	18751	26979
Chemicals and allied products	4519	442	4072
Industrial chemicals	2411	400	2011
Drugs and medicines and other chemicals	2107	42	2061
Petroleum refining and extraction	1095	35	1062
Rubber products	882	288	596
Primary metals	648	28	617
Ferrous metals and products	341	7	337
Nonferrous metals and products	304	23	283
Fabricated metal products	592	28	568
Nonelectrical machinery	5047	938	4112
Electrical machinery	10946	5536	5410
Communication equipment and electronic components	6813	3607	3204
Motor vehicles and other transportation equipment	4701	762	3939
Aircraft and missiles	11577	9285	2287
Professional and scientific instruments	1960	377	1586
Scientific and mechanical measuring instruments	381	30	353
Optical, surgical, photographic, and other instruments	1579	346	1233
All other manufacturing industries	2110	23	2082
Nonmanufacturing industries	1654	1008	648

R&D Funds by Industry	1986 Total	Federal	Company
Current dollars			
Total	80629	27782	52847
Chemicals and allied products	9021	248	8773
Industrial chemicals	4059	247	3812
Drugs and medicines and other chemicals	4962	1	4961
Petroleum refining and extraction	NA	NA	1867
Rubber products	1075	300	776
Primary metals	NA	NA	809
Ferrous metals and products	NA	NA	388
Nonferrous metals and products	454	34	421
Fabricated metal products	622	78	544
Nonelectrical machinery	10696	1456	9239

Table 2.5. R&D Funds by Industry (*Continued*)

R&D Funds by Industry	Total	1986 Federal	Company
Electrical machinery	18030	7569	10460
Communication equipment and electronic components	12085	4392	7692
Motor vehicles and other transportation equipment	10131	2742	7390
Aircraft and missiles	16240	12099	4141
Professional and scientific instruments	5421	844	4576
Scientific and mechanical measuring instruments	NA	NA	1959
Optical, surgical, photographic, and other instruments	NA	NA	2617
All other manufacturing industries	NA	NA	3172
Nonmanufacturing industries	2716	1616	1099
1989 constant dollars			
Total	89485	30834	58652
Chemicals and allied products	10012	275	9737
Industrial chemicals	4505	274	4231
Drugs and medicines and other chemicals	5507	1	5506
Petroleum refining and extraction	NA	NA	2072
Rubber products	1193	333	861
Primary metals	NA	NA	898
Ferrous metals and products	NA	NA	431
Nonferrous metals and products	504	38	467
Fabricated metal products	690	87	604
Nonelectrical machinery	11871	1616	10254
Electrical machinery	20010	8400	11609
Communication equipment and electronic components	13412	4874	8537
Motor vehicles and other transportation equipment	11244	3043	8202
Aircraft and missiles	18024	13428	4596
Professional and scientific instruments	6016	937	5079
Scientific and mechanical measuring instruments	NA	NA	2174
Optical, surgical, photographic, and other instruments	NA	NA	2904
All other manufacturing industries	NA	NA	3520
Nonmanufacturing industries	3014	1794	1220

Sources:

1958 data: National Science Foundation, *Research and Development in Industry: 1974*, Tables B-3, B-6, and B-9.

1972 data: National Science Foundation, *National Patterns of Science and Technology Resources: 1980*, Tables 37–39.

1986 data: National Science Foundation, *National Patterns of Science and Technology Resources: 1989*, Tables B-25, B-26, and B-27. Implicit GNP deflator used for conversion to 1987 dollars.

ian spillovers than R&D that was directly funded by the military. In addition, direct financial support from the Pentagon was available for the construction of production facilities by winners of contracts under the provisions of the Defense Production Act. Much of this defense-related procurement demand also was covered by "Buy American" provisions, which further favored U. S. over foreign suppliers (Malerba, 1985).

Defense procurement lowered marketing-based barriers to entry. Lower entry barriers allowed small firms, such as General Radio, Texas Instruments, and Transitron, to direct their development efforts to meeting the performance and design requirements of a single large customer in the 1950s. The relatively modest barriers to entry were associated with the entry and rapid growth of numerous young, relatively small firms in the industry.

Granted that military–civilian technological spillovers have, at certain times and in certain industries, been a significant economic phenomenon, are they as large today as they were 20 or 30 years ago, and are spillovers likely to be rising or falling in the years ahead? The answers to these questions vary across different technologies. The commercial spillovers from defense research and procurement also appear to fluctuate over time within a specific technology. A number of factors influence the magnitude of such spillovers, but among the most important is the generic similarity of civilian and military requirements for a technology. Although generalizations on this issue are hazardous, increasing divergence in these requirements in a broad array of technologies appears to have reduced the economic importance of military–civil spillovers in recent years.

Frequently, commercial and military requirements for performance, cost, ruggedness, and so on more closely resemble one another early in the development of a new technology. This broad similarity in requirements appears to have been associated with significant spillovers in microelectronics in the early 1960s, when the demands of the commercial and military markets for miniaturization, low heat in operation, and ruggedness did not diverge too dramatically. During the 1950s and 1960s, the jet engine was applied in military strategic bombers, transports, and tankers, all of which had fuselage design and engine performance requirements that resembled some of those for commercial air transports. The jet engine was a prime example of a military spillover to the civilian economy. Over time, however, the size and even the direction of spillovers in these technologies appear to have changed.[21] The changing relationship between military and commercial technologies in microelectronics influenced the establishment of the Sematech (Semiconductor Manufacturing Technology) research consortium, funded jointly by private industry and the U. S. military (see below for further discussion).

University Research and Federal Funding

Another change in the structure of the postwar U. S. research system from its prewar outlines is the expansion of research in U. S. institutions of higher learning. Much of this growth in research of course reflects the expansion in federal support for university research during and after World War II—indeed, industrial funding now may account for a smaller share of university research than was true during the 1930s (the industry share of university research funding in the 1970s was well below that of the early 1950s).

By any measure, the expansion of academic research was immense. From an estimated level of nearly $420 million (1982 dollars) in 1935–1936, university research (excluding FFRDCs) grew to more than $2 billion (1982 dollars) in 1960 and $8.5 billion in 1985, nearly doubling as a share of GNP during 1960–1985 (from 0.13 to 0.25). The increase in federal support of university research has transformed major U. S. universities into centers for the performance of scientific research, an unprecedented role.

The huge increase in federal expenditures on university research has taken the form of contracts and grants for specific research projects. Most of the "demand" for scientific research has emanated from a centralized federal authority, although a number of federal departments and agencies with distinctly separate missions and goals have contributed to this demand. On the supply side has been a heterogeneous range of institutions, public and private, committed to both research and education, dependent on the federal government for financial support but otherwise determined to maintain their autonomy.

The federal government did not confine itself to expanding the demand for university research. Federal actions on the supply side enlarged the pool of scientific personnel and supported the acquisition of the physical equipment and facilities essential to the performance of high-quality research. After World War II, federal programs increased financial aid for students in higher education. The best known was the G.I. Bill, which provided substantial financial support to all veterans who enrolled in college-level educational programs; others include graduate fellowships supported by NSF and AEC funds, training fellowships from the National Institutes of Health, and the National Defense Education Act fellowships. Federal funds also made it possible for universities to purchase increasingly expensive scientific equipment and advanced instrumentation, central to the expansion of both research and teaching functions of the university scientific community.

By simultaneously providing funds for university education and for the support of research within the university community, the federal government strengthened the university commitment to research (a commitment that, before World War II, ran a very poor second to teaching) and reinforced the link between research and teaching. The combination of research and teaching in higher education has been carried much further in the United States than elsewhere. In Europe and Japan, for example, a larger fraction of research is carried out in specialized research institutes not connected directly with higher education and in government-operated laboratories.[22]

Research in Industry

As the above discussion makes clear, private industry retained its dominance as a performer of research amid shifts in the sources of the funding for this research. In 1985, although it performed 73% of total U. S. research and development, industry accounted for slightly more than 50% of total funding. Its continued primacy as a performer of R&D, however, meant continued growth in employment within industrial research—from less than 50,000 in 1946 (Table 2.1) to roughly 300,000 scientists and engineers in 1962, 376,000 in 1970, and almost 600,000 in 1985 (Birr, 1966; U. S. Bureau of the Census, 1987, p. 570).

Although the R&D facilities of established firms expanded greatly as a result of hostilities and the following Cold War, relatively young industrial firms have also played a prominent role in the postwar U. S. industrial innovation system. The successive waves of new product technologies that have swept through the postwar U. S. economy, including semiconductors, computers, and biotechnology, have been commercialized in large part through the efforts of new firms.[23] The role of small firms in commercializing new technologies in the United States during this period appears to contrast with the pattern in both Japan and Western Europe, where established firms in electronics, pharmaceuticals, and other industries have played a more significant role in new technology development.

Several factors have contributed to this prominent role of new, small firms in the postwar U. S. innovation system. The large basic research establishments in universities, government, and a number of private firms served as important "incubators" for the development of innovations that "walked out the door" with individuals who established firms to commercialize them. This pattern has been particularly significant in the biotechnology, microelectronics, and computer industries. Indeed, high levels of labor mobility within regional agglomerations of high-technology firms have served both as an important channel for technology diffusion and as a magnet for other firms in similar or related industries. At least one scholar has argued that the far lower levels of interfirm labor mobility in Japan would restrict technology transfer without the off-setting influence of cooperative research projects (Saxonhouse, 1982, 1986).

The foundation and survival of vigorous new firms also depend on a sophisticated private financial system that can support new firms during their infancy. The U. S. venture capital market played an especially important role in the establishment of many microelectronics firms during the 1950s and 1960s, and has contributed to the growth of the biotechnology and computer industries. Throughout the 1970s, $100–200 million of funds annually flowed into this industry from the venture capital community, and one informed observer has suggested that by the early 1980s, flows of venture capital for high-technology firms may have been as much as $2–4 billion annually. This abundant supply of venture capital was gradually supplemented by public equity offerings.[24]

Commercialization of microelectronics and biotechnology innovations by new firms was aided by a relatively permissive intellectual property regime in these industries that aided technology diffusion and reduced the burden on young firms of litigation over innovations that may have originated in part within established firms or other research installations. In microelectronics, liberal licensing and cross-licensing policies were one byproduct of the 1956 consent decree that settled the federal antitrust suit against AT&T. In biotechnology, continuing uncertainty over the strength and breadth of intellectual property protection may have discouraged litigation.

Postwar U. S. antitrust policy also contributed to the importance of startup firms. The 1956 settlement of the AT&T case significantly improved the environment for startup firms in microelectronics, because of the liberal patent licensing terms of the consent decree and because the decree prohibited AT&T from commercial activities outside of telecommunications. As a result, the firm with the greatest technological capabilities in microelectronics was effectively forestalled from entry into commercial production of microelectronic devices, creating substantial opportunities for entry by startup firms. A 1956 consent decree settling another antitrust suit against IBM also mandated liberal licensing by this pioneer computer firm of its punchcard and computer patents at reasonable rates (Flamm, 1988). The major antitrust suits of this period also may have indirectly affected the prospects for startup firms, since a number of established firms that were involved in antitrust litigation during the late 1940s and 1950s were deterred from continuing their prewar policies of technology acquisition through the acquisition of smaller firms.

During much of the postwar period, U. S. military procurement aided the growth of new firms. As was noted earlier, the U. S. military market in the 1950s and 1960s provided an important springboard for startup firms in microelectronics and computers, who faced relatively low marketing and distribution barriers to entry into this market.[25] The benefits of the military market were enhanced further by the substantial possibilities for technological spillovers from military to civilian applications. Some of the effects of military procurement on startup firms' success, and on the spillovers from military to commercial applications, were a result of policy. In contrast to European military procurement, the U. S. armed services were willing to award major procurement contracts to firms with little track record in serving the military (or, in many cases, any) market. In industries such as microelectronics, these contracts attracted startup firms as well as enterprises that historically had mainly served civilian markets and that remained concerned with extracting commercial applications from their military technology development efforts.[26]

The industrial research facilities of many of the pioneers of research, such as General Electric, Du Pont, RCA, and Kodak underwent considerable change during the postwar period. The wartime demonstration of the significant potential for commercial and military applications of scientific research, combined with vast increases in government funding for research in defense-related technologies, led a number of these firms to expand their central research facilities and to shift applied research to the product divisions.

Especially during the early postwar period, buoyant domestic and international markets supported robust profits and rapid expansion of R&D in both the central laboratories and the divisional laboratories. Central R&D facilities focused increasingly on fundamental research in many of these large firms, leaving the development and application of new technologies, as well as the improvement of established products and processes, to the divisional laboratories. Federal research contracts were awarded to the central research facility or to a dedicated divisional laboratory—for reasons of both policy (accounting regulations governing federal contracts) and security; research for government contracts often was carried out in separate facilities. In some cases, as in that of Du Pont, the use of the central laboratory and Development Department as "scanning devices," searching out promising technologies or firms for acquisition, was ruled out by senior management as a result of increasing antitrust restrictions on expansion through acquisition. As a result, internal discovery and development of new products became paramount.[27] The data on basic research for 1953 and 1960 are less reliable than those for later years, but suggest nonetheless that the share of total U. S. basic research financed by industry during the postwar period may well have been at its peak during the 1950s and early 1960s.

As the fundamental research activities of the central research laboratories expanded (expansion that often relied on federal funds), and as manufacturing firms diversified into new product lines through acquisition and internal development, the ties between the central research laboratory and the increasingly diverse and in some cases geographically distant product divisions of these firms were weakened.[28] Internal communications between the fundamental and applied research operations deteriorated, making it more difficult to commercialize the work of the central research facility and eroding the contributions of central research to the activities of the product divisions.[29]

Severe competitive pressures from foreign firms, increases in the real cost of capital, and a slowdown in the growth rate of the domestic economy in the 1970s may have caused the returns to R&D investment to decline during the mid-1970s,[30] and the rate of growth in real industry expenditures on R&D declined. Industry funding of basic research shrank, and many of the central research facilities of the giant corporations entered a period of budgetary austerity or cutbacks. After a resurgence in the early 1980s, the rate of growth in industry-funded R&D declined, and the National Science Foundation in early 1990 reported that real industry-financed R&D had declined during 1988–1989.[31]

Research in Agriculture

The rapid growth in postwar agricultural productivity (measured either in terms of yield per acre or output per hour) suggests that the returns to the federal and state investment in agricultural research (as opposed to extension) increased sharply during the postwar period. This research program is almost alone among federal R&D programs in having been the subject of a series of economic evaluations. These studies have consistently found high returns to the public investments in agricultural research (Evenson, 1982, reviews a number of these studies), and the U. S. agricultural research system has been cited in some reports (e.g., OTA 1990) as an exemplary program of support for technology adoption and adaptation. Public budgetary support for the agricultural research and extension network continued to expand during the postwar period, although the state government share of this budget declined somewhat. Developments in postwar agricultural research also point out the important interaction between research investment decisions and the appropriability of the returns, a variable influenced by intellectual property rights.

The Plant Patent Act of 1930 was an important early development in the establishment of private property rights for plant varieties, and its passage directly influenced the subsequent commercialization of hybrid strains of corn and other plant varieties. The provisions of the Plant Patent Act were expanded and strengthened in the Plant Variety Protection Act (PVPA) of 1970. The U. S. Supreme Court's 1980 decision in *Diamond v. Chakrabarty,* upholding the patentability of living organisms, further expanded the coverage of intellectual property rights in agricultural research. In response to these developments, privately financed agricultural R&D has grown rapidly and the balance of public and private funding has shifted: "private spending accounted for roughly one-fourth of total R&D relevant to agriculture in the 1950s but . . . this had risen to approximately 40 percent in the 1960s and 50 percent in the 1970s" (Evenson, 1982, p. 242). Evenson (1983) notes that the 1970 PVPA produced a dramatic increase in the development of new strains in soybeans and other crops.[32] Although the balance of public and private funding has shifted during the postwar period, the public and private research investments appear to be complementary, rather than duplicative, as one might expect in a research system that is sensitive to local political and economic demands.[33]

Although the agricultural research system's economic returns and blend of research and diffusion support have been widely praised, other analysts have criticized the system's weaknesses in scientific research, notably the failure to develop stronger expertise in molecular biology and related fields.[34] The resource allocation mechanism for the system also is hardly a model of scientific self-governance (i.e., peer review and evaluation of research proposals). Historically, two-thirds of the federal agricultural research funds provided to land-grant universities by the U. S. Department of Agriculture have been allocated among the states on a formula basis, rather than on the basis of scientific merit or research excellence (U. S. Congressional Office of Technology Assessment, 1986). The share of the federal agricultural research budget allocated on a competitive basis has slowly increased in recent years, but remains low. In both of these areas, the agricultural system appears to exhibit some tension between political responsiveness and research excellence.

Partly in response to criticism of the research performance of the agricultural research system, the balance of federal funding between extension activities and research also has shifted during the past 25 years. Federal funding for extension grew more rapidly than funding for research during 1966–1975, but these trends were reversed after 1975. Combined with expanding private investment in agricultural research, the Congressional Office of Technology Assessment has argued that the balance of the public/private system of agricultural research is tipping away from its historic support for technology adoption toward an expanded role in technology generation (1986, see Chapter 12). Nevertheless, the ability of this system to advance the agricultural research frontier remains uncertain.

POLICY CHALLENGES AND STRUCTURAL CHANGE IN THE 1980S

Introduction

Change in the international environment during the past 15 years appears to have reduced the contributions of the U. S. national innovation system to growth in domestic incomes and competitiveness. Through the early 1970s, the returns to publicly funded research were more easily captured by U. S. firms because of their considerable technological lead over foreign firms and because they performed much of the publicly funded research. In addition, the commercial competitiveness of U. S. firms in some industries may have received less support in recent years from defense spending than was true of the 1950s and 1960s.

A postwar process of convergence in both the economic and technological spheres has brought many foreign economies to levels of income per capita, productivity, and R&D investment that approach or exceed those of the United States (see Cyert and Mowery, 1987; Mowery, 1988; or Nelson, 1990, for more detailed discussion). Convergence at the aggregate level, however, is not matched by any uniform pattern of decline in the relative strength of U. S. performance in all industrial sectors. As Nelson (1990) points out, the United States has preserved its export and patenting "market share" in a number of high-technology sectors, although in such industries as scientific instruments, consumer electronics, or steel and automobiles, U. S. exports have declined dramatically. Since 1973, moreover, a number of indicators suggest that U. S. living standards (e.g., real earnings) have stagnated or declined in real terms, and aggregate productivity growth has remained low. These developments, which have both contributed to and have been exacerbated by inept U. S. macroeconomic policy, have affected U. S. debates on trade and technology policies. Restrictive trade policies and nationalistic (or xenophobic) responses to foreign investment in the United States have gained considerable currency in recent years, although the extensive offshore markets and investments of many U. S. multinational firms have tempered any moves to completely cut off foreign access to U. S. markets. Science and technology policies also are being affected by these economic and political trends.

Since foreign firms now are more technologically sophisticated and technology is more internationally mobile, the competitive advantages that accrued in the past from U. S. basic research and a strong knowledge base have been eroded. Faster international transfer of new technologies has undercut a major source of America's postwar superiority in high-technology markets.[35] Both the public and private sectors have responded to these changes in the environment. Private firms have pursued a number of new organizational approaches to exploit R&D and innovation outside of the firm—these include domestic and international consortia or alliances and domestic university-industry research linkages. The federal government also has undertaken new initiatives in research funding, trade policy, and intellectual property protection, in order to increase the domestic economic returns to public and private R&D investments in the United States. These policy initiatives may reduce some of the structural contrasts between the United States and other national innovation systems, if the influence of antitrust policy on U. S. firms' technology strategies becomes less significant and if the importance of new firms in technology commercialization declines.

The Growth (Rebirth?) of University–Industry Research Cooperation

During the past decade, financial support from industry has established a number of research facilities on university campuses to conduct research with potential commercial value. Important initiatives are coming from the federal government as well as private industry. The National Science Foundation has embarked on a program to establish a number of interdisciplinary research centers in engineering and other scientific disciplines on university campuses. The financial structure of these centers also is relatively novel, since it combines "seed-money" support from the federal government (as well, in many cases, as state and local governments) with major contributions from private corporations that are affiliated with the centers.

The phenomenon of university–industry research collaboration is not new, having been well-established before 1940. Indeed, the share of university research expenditures financed by industry appears to have declined through much of the postwar period. In 1953, industry financed 11% of university research, a share that declined to 5.5% in 1960 and 2.7% in 1978. By 1985–1986, estimates suggest that industrial funds accounted for no more than 5% of university research. The recent development of closer research ties between universities and industry represents a restoration of a linkage that was weakened during the 1950s and 1960s, rather than a fundamental departure.[36]

There is a vast array of forms of research collaboration between universities and industry, making generalizations virtually impossible. The relationship between university research and commercial technology varies considerably across industries. No single model or description of the constraints, advantages, and disadvantages of such collaboration is likely to be accurate for all university–industry collaborations.

A fundamental motive for closer ties between university and industrial research is the fact that U. S. universities account for a growing share of total U. S. basic research. In 1953, industry accounted for 58% of the combined basic research budget (from all sources) of the universities and industry; in 1978, universities accounted for 76% of the combined basic research budget of universities and industry (National Commission on Research, 1980, pp. 8–9). Nevertheless, private industry financial support of university research remains modest. Industry provided about 20% of the funds for all basic research in the mid-1980s, but it funds a much smaller percentage of the basic research performed at the universities—around 6% of the total.

The growing role of U. S. universities in the performance of basic research has been associated with a recognition by U. S. industry that more fields of research at the universities now hold out significant promise of generating findings that may be of great commercial significance. The connection between university research and commercial technology appears to be particularly close in biotechnology, a factor that influences the character of many university–industry research relationships in this field, and may distinguish them from university–industry research collaborations in other fields.[37] Increased pressure to reduce R&D costs, to monitor a wider range of emerging areas of scientific research, and to speed the commercialization of scientific research has driven many U. S. firms to attempt to develop relationships with an array of external institutions (see below for additional discussion), including research universities in the United States and abroad, to complement and enhance the payoff from their in-house R&D activities.[38]

By virtue of their mission as educational, as well as research, institutions, U. S. universities are critically important sources of scientific and engineering personnel. Participant firms can employ collaborative ventures as "filters" for hiring research personnel, observing the performance of potential researchers before making employment commitments. Moreover, the importance of people as vehicles for the transfer of scientific and technological knowledge means that the hiring by firms of the graduates of these programs facilitates the transfer of knowledge and technology from university to industry. The interdisciplinary character of modern technological and research challenges makes this training and hiring benefit particularly important.

The growing perceived economic significance of U. S. university research, combined with expanded funding of such research by non-U. S. firms, have sparked concerns that foreign firms are "unfairly" gaining access to high-quality research within the relatively open U. S. university system (the "unfairness" presumably stems from the belief that foreign, especially Japanese, universities offer fewer opportunities for U. S. firms to gain access to world-class scientific and engineering research) allows foreign firms to improve their competitiveness vis-à-vis U. S. firms (e.g., Business Week, 1989, pp. 73–74). Congressional and state legislative policymakers have raised questions about programs such as the Industrial Liaison Program of M.I.T., through which foreign firms receive briefings on academic research in exchange for financial contributions.

Although the empirical basis for this criticism appears to be rather weak and no action has yet been taken by either state or the federal governments, the debate underlines the complexities introduced by the increased quantity and rate of international flows of scientific and technological knowledge. When national innovation systems vary in their fundamental structure, a "level playing field" in this sphere is appealing in the abstract and very difficult to create in reality. Nevertheless, as policymakers and managers alike increasingly view national innovation systems as important strategic assets in global economic competition, demands for such "leveling" are likely to expand, as we note below.

Industrial Research in an Era of Structural Change

The structure of the U. S. industrial research system also appears to be undergoing significant change. Although the outcome of current experiments and reorganization cannot be predicted with confidence, competitive and cost pressures appear to be leading a number of large U. S. firms to reorganize their corporate research activities and, in particular, to exploit external sources of new technologies more aggressively. The growth in university–industry research cooperation is one example of this—others include international collaborative ventures and domestic research consortia. Even as the historic dominance of industrial research by the in-house research laboratory may be declining, changes in the policy and competitive environment may also reduce the role of new firms in the commercialization of new technologies within the U. S. economy. This section discusses both of these developments in what must be a speculative and tentative treatment.

Restructuring U. S. Industrial Research?

One of the most widespread forms of institutional innovation in the U. S. national innovation system reflects the effort by firms to develop external sources of research and development expertise. These efforts have resulted in considerable expansion of collaboration in R&D that involves U. S. and foreign firms, as well as U. S. universities.

U. S. firms have expanded both international and domestic collaborative research efforts, and both types of collaboration are responses to the same factors: the rising costs and risks of product development, the increased breadth of the scientific and technological knowledge base needed to compete in high-technology industries (reflected in instances of "technological convergence" such as the interpenetration of telecommunications and computer technologies, biotechnology and pharmaceuticals, etc.), more rapid product cycles in some industries, and more severe competitive pressure from foreign firms.[39] In addition to these factors common to both types of collaboration, change in the prospects for new startup firms in some high-technology industries may be increasing their predisposition to pursue technology commercialization through collaboration with larger domestic or foreign firms, rather than pursuing this goal independently (see below for further discussion). In some instances, these collaborative ventures have resulted in the acquisition of the smaller startup by the larger firm.

The consequences of these new organizational structures are still uncertain, since in most cases collaboration is less than 10 years old. Nevertheless, there appear to be important contrasts in structure and motives between the international and domestic research and development ventures into which U. S. firms have entered. One must distinguish among at least three broad categories of research collaboration: collaborative ventures between U. S. and foreign firms, research collaboration among U. S. firms, and domestic university–industry research collaboration. International collaborative ventures focus mainly on development, production, and marketing, rather than precommercial research. Thus far, domestic collaborations among U. S. firms have been concerned with research that is less applied in character and less closely linked to a specific commercial product. In general, however, these domestic collaborative ventures do not focus primarily on basic research despite the intentions and founding aspirations of several of them. Finally, university–industry research collaboration appears to incorporate scientific and engineering research of a more fundamental character. These different forms of collaboration are not substitutes but complements. Large U. S. corporations in the computer and electronics industries, for example, appear to utilize all three forms of collaboration simultaneously.

International collaborative ventures involving U. S. firms rarely focus on the "precommercial" research activities that are the intended target of the efforts of domestic research consortia among firms and university–industry collaborations. These ventures are a response by U. S. firms to the factors noted above as causes of domestic research collaboration, but in addition reflect the growing technological strengths of many foreign firms and the increasingly prominent role of nontariff trade barriers and government support for the development of advanced technologies. International collaboration has grown dramatically in a diverse array of U. S. manufacturing industries, although its long-term prospects appear brighter in some industries than in others. The consequences for U. S. competitiveness of such collaboration thus far appear to be fairly benign—in most cases, international collaboration is a response to, rather than a cause of, declining U. S. competitiveness. In other industries, collaboration has assisted U. S. firms in strengthening their technological and production skills.

International collaborative ventures create some complex policy issues in the trade and technology policy spheres. Along with numerous other factors, international collaborative ventures will accelerate international technology transfer in the global economy of the future. Nevertheless, the technology transfer operating within international collaborative ventures involving U. S. firms is likely to remain a two-way flow for the foreseeable future—there are few documented examples of U. S. firms "giving away" critical technological assets to foreign enterprises within these ventures. Reflecting the close and interdependent relationship between trade and technology policies, trade policy clearly influences the development of international collaborative ventures. Indeed, international private collaborative ventures appear to be an important complement to the growing number of "closed" (to foreign firms) cooperative technology development programs sponsored by governments in the industrial world.[40] Increasingly, however, trade policy formulation and implementation will be affected by the operation and existence of these ventures—notably, the internationalization of sources of R&D and components.

Change in the Role of the Startup Firm?

The revival of faith in the "magic of the market" within U. S. policymaking circles during the 1980s paradoxically has been combined with more frequent expressions of concern over the impact of the efficient U. S. capital market on the growth of new, high-technology firms.[41] The U. S. venture capital market and other institutions that have spawned innovative firms and new industries now are criticized by some observers for breeding "managerial myopia" (an excessive focus on short-term results) and providing insufficient support for technology development over the long run. Other critics suggest that the reliance on startup firms for the development of new technologies within the U. S. economy has resulted in excessive transfer of technological know-how to the foreign firms (often, Japanese firms) that recently have expanded their investments in these enterprises. In this view (which is by no means universally held), many of the widely remarked difficulties of the U. S. economy in commercializing new technologies stem in part from an excessive reliance on startup firms for commercialization.

A number of factors may change the future role of the startup firm in the commercialization of technologies within the U. S. economy. Although the evidence on both of these hypotheses is mixed, it is possible that the rate of formation of new high-technology firms may decline or that these new firms will less frequently develop into large commercial enterprises. Some recent accounts suggest that venture capital markets now are a less important source of support for startup firms, as a result of the increasing costs of new product development (especially in biotechnology and microelectronics), and the attraction of alternative investment opportunities.[42] Acquisition of startups by established U. S. and foreign firms also has become more common. Particularly in biotechnology, new firms rarely have developed into mature enterprises, instead being acquired.[43]

The changing public policy environment in the United States also may reduce the role of startup firms in the future. To the extent that postwar U. S. antitrust policy before the 1980s tended to discourage acquisitions by large industrial firms as a means to develop and commercialize new technologies, relaxation of this policy under the Reagan and Bush Administrations (see below) may increase the likelihood that startup firms will be acquired by larger enterprises, rather than remaining independent. Similarly, the effects of the efforts of the 1980s to strengthen domestic protection for intellectual property may reduce the viability of startup firms in at least one industry in which they have been very important. The passage of the Semiconductor Chip Protection Act of 1984 significantly strengthened protection for chip designs in microelectronics. In response, established semiconductor firms have become far more willing to sue startup and established firms over alleged infringement, and startup firms have been especially hard hit (Gupta, 1988). Intellectual property protection in biotechnology and computer software remains far more uncertain, however, and litigation over intellectual property may pose less of an obstacle to the establishment of new firms in these industries.

Change in the structure of markets for high-technology goods also has diminished the ability of new firms to grow considerably in size and scope. The U. S. military market no longer plays a strategic role in the computer and semiconductor industries comparable to its position in the 1960s, and the possibilities for military–civilian technology spillovers appear to have declined in many areas of these technologies. Biotechnology firms in particular are attempting to enter industries (e.g., food processing or pharmaceuticals) in the U. S. and foreign economies that are far more heavily regulated than was true of semiconductors. As a result, the costs of new product introduction and the marketing-related entry barriers faced by these firms have risen, even as the willingness of prospective purchasers to provide capital for production facilities has declined. For this and other reasons, including the greater interest by foreign firms in the technological assets of U. S. startup firms, collaborative ventures involving startup and established U. S. and foreign firms have grown considerably in recent years (Pisano et al., 1988). These ventures frequently focus on technology exchange (often combined with the acquisition by an established firm of a substantial portion of the equity of the new firm) and/or marketing (including navigating domestic and foreign product regulations), rather than joint development of new products.

Summarizing this speculative discussion, the strength and effects of these changes in the economic environment of the startup firm remain uncertain. If the formerly significant role of the startup firm in high-technology industries does diminish, a key contrast between the U. S. national innovation and those of many other nations will be reduced in importance.

Public Policy Initiatives

Along with the governments of other industrial and industrializing nations, the U. S. government during the past decade has recognized the important role of innovation in economic performance and has begun to take steps intended to increase the domestic economic payoff from the large public and private U. S. investment in R&D. The contrast between the position of the newly elected Reagan Administration in 1981, denying any role for the federal government in the development and commercialization of new civilian technologies,[44] and the Reagan Administration of 1987–1988, is dramatic. By 1987–1988, the Administration had organized a symposium on commercial applications of high-temperature superconductivity (HTS) that was restricted to U. S. nationals, had proposed legislation for speeding the development of commercial applications of HTS that included provisions to restrict access by foreign nationals to the results of publicly funded basic research in the U. S., and had launched two military-funded research programs in civilian technology development.

These initiatives, which had broad bipartisan support, represented a considerable shift in the focus of Federal programs aimed at civil technology development. Previous postwar federal programs to support civil technology development in such areas as energy, nuclear energy, and even housing construction, typically were aimed at technologies for which policymakers felt that market incentives were insufficient, causing the social returns to substantially exceed the private returns to the innovator. Federal programs designed to aid in the development of commercial applications of scientific discoveries such as HTS, however, are aimed at technologies for which the private and social returns to innovation both may be very high. Instead, these programs attempt to influence the distribution of the private returns between U. S. and foreign firms. Although the Bush Administration has expressed opposition to aggressive public support for commercial technology development as "industrial policy," the Administration is not unified in this opposition, and bipartisan Congressional pressure for action remains strong.

The Changing Relationship Between Military and Civilian Technologies
As was noted earlier, military technologies (and therefore military R&D and procurement budgets) may now be less fertile sources of commercial technologies than was true during the 1950s and 1960s. New technologies in some important areas now appear first in civil applications and are subsequently incorporated into weapons systems. Accordingly, several Pentagon research programs, such as Sematech, have focused on supporting the development of commercial technologies, in the belief that these technologies will yield advances in military applications.

A second important influence on recent Pentagon research and technology development initiatives is the changing market for the products of U. S. high-technology firms. As the military share of total demand for many high-technology systems and components (especially in computers and microelectronics) has declined, the economic viability of major defense suppliers increasingly depends on their ability to compete in civilian markets. Recent military-funded research programs thus are designed to address the commercial competitive strengths of U. S. firms.

The Sematech consortium is dedicated to the development of advanced manufacturing processes for commercial memory chips, not military components. Similar concerns led to the 1988 foundation of the National Center for Manufacturing Sciences (NCMS), funded in part by the military to support research in manufacturing technologies and to the $30 million Defense Advanced Research Projects Agency (DARPA) research program in high-definition television (HDTV) technologies begun in 1989.[45] Many (although not all) of the applications of HDTV will be in civilian markets. Both Sematech and the NCMS exclude foreign firms, and DARPA programs in HDTV also are open only to U. S.-owned firms (Wolf, 1989; Mowery and Rosenberg, 1989b).

These programs have considerable political support, but it is difficult to predict whether they will spawn similar initiatives in other technologies. Several observers have suggested that U. S. military research and procurement programs should be structured and managed to strengthen U. S. producers of civilian high-technology products (Gansler, 1989). Civilian and military policymakers in the Pentagon, however, may resist any diversion of funds in a flat or shrinking budget from military to "dual-purpose" R&D and procurement programs. The emphasis within these new military R&D programs on civilian technology development has some resemblance to earlier European initiatives. Indeed, a central justification for the subsidies extended by Western European governments to the Airbus Industrie consortium is the desire of these governments to maintain a military aerospace industrial base by supporting the commercial activities of their national firms. Needless to say, the presence of a similar program in the U. S. microelectronics industry will impede the efforts of U. S. trade policymakers to reduce European government subsidies to Airbus.

In addition to their unhappy implications for trade policy, the recent popularity of military research and procurement programs as instruments for improving the civilian technological and commercial capabilities of U. S. firms overlooks the poor track record of similar programs in Western Europe. Airbus is a technological and political (not financial) success, but it is exceptional in a list of costly programs supporting weapons development by "national champions," or European consortia of "champions," that yielded little by way of improved military security or enhanced commercial competitiveness.[46]

Intellectual Property and Antitrust

Other recent U. S. initiatives in technology policy have improved enforcement of intellectual property protection and reduced antitrust restrictions on collaboration in research. The 1982 legislation that established the Court of Appeals for the Federal Circuit has strengthened the protection granted to patentholders.[47] The U. S. government has also pursued stronger international protection for intellectual property rights in both bilateral and multilateral international trade negotiations.

In antitrust policy, the Reagan Administration adopted a substantially more lenient enforcement posture than its predecessors, arguing that international competition had significantly reduced the dangers of market power being acquired through domestic merger and acquisition activity. Justice Department guidelines and review procedures for mergers were relaxed somewhat, and major federal antitrust suits against high-technology firms were dropped or settled in the early 1980s. The Reagan Administration supported the 1984 National Cooperative Research Act, which reduced the antitrust penalties for collaboration among firms in precommercial research. The NCRA has been credited with easing the founding of the Microelectronics and Computer Technology Corporation, an early reesarch consortium involving U. S. computer and electronics firms.

The number of research consortia in U. S. industry has grown since the NCRA's passage, with 111 cooperative ventures registered under the terms of the Act from 1984 through June 1988. Some critics of the NCRA argue that more consortia would have been established, or existing consortia would be more effective, if the Act's protection against treble-damage antitrust penalties were extended beyond precommercial research. In this view, consortia that are restricted to research cannot move quickly to profitably apply new technologies commercially.[48] In response to this criticism, legislation has been introduced in the Congress to reduce antitrust penalties against consortia that engage in production, a proposal that has gained White House support.[49]

In both antitrust and intellectual property policy, the Reagan and Bush Administrations are strengthening the returns to innovators. The policy initiatives in antitrust have also been influenced by the example of Japanese success in cooperative research and technology development, although the recent antitrust legislative proposals extend the scope of cooperation well beyond the precompetitive research stage in which Japanese firms most often collaborate. This policy focus, however, fails to address one of the most serious weaknesses of the U. S. national innovation system, the slow pace of domestic adoption of new technologies in manufacturing. Policies designed to increase the rewards to innovators in some instances will increase the costs associated with the adoption of the technologies produced by the innovators, and thereby may hamper diffusion (David, 1986). Moreover, the "lessons" drawn from the Japanese experience by U. S. policymakers appear to overlook the emphasis within Japanese industry and technology policies on support for domestic technology adoption and on strong domestic competition in technology commercialization.

The Merger of Technology and Trade Policies
The growing political salience of national science and technology policies has blurred the boundaries between U. S. technology and trade policies and has complicated policy formulation in each area. Technology-intensive industries now are at the center of bilateral trade disputes and negotiations. The commercial aircraft, telecommunications equipment, computer, and microelectronics industries all were the subjects of special provisions in the 1988 Omnibus Trade and Competitiveness Act.[50]

At least one recent international negotiation dealt directly with the structural differences between the U. S. and foreign national innovation systems. Negotiations over renewal in 1988 of the U. S.–Japan Agreement on Scientific Cooperation, formerly of concern only within the scientific community, for the first time involved trade policymakers in both governments. The central trade-related issues in these talks concerned intellectual property rights within Japan and the assurance by the Japanese government of access by U. S. firms to publicly funded research in Japanese laboratories that was comparable to Japanese firms' access to publicly funded research in U. S. research facilities.[51]

Still another illustration of the influence on U. S. trade policy of the evolving technology policy agenda is intellectual property rights, which are a high priority for U. S. negotiators in the Uruguay Round of multilateral trade negotiations. Bringing intellectual property issues into trade policy (as has been done through Section 301 of the Trade Act and may be done in the future, if U. S. goals in the Uruguay Round are achieved, through the General Agreement on Tariffs and Trade) provides a powerful enforcement mechanism, restrictions on market access for the products of nations that provide insufficient protection, that current multilateral agreements lack. U. S. negotiators have also pursued this issue in bilateral negotiations with Thailand, Taiwan, South Korea, and other nations. Faced with the threat of restrictions on their firms' access to U. S. markets, these and other foreign governments have revised domestic policies to achieve standards of protection and breadth of coverage comparable to those in the United States. The intellectual property rights issue also illustrates the significant extension of the reach of trade policy issues beyond the borders of trading nations into domestic policy.

Concluding Remarks

At least some of the changes in the structure of the U. S. innovation system that are foreshadowed by these organizational experiments and public policy initiatives may revive several of the elements of this system that were characteristic of the pre-1940 period. The high-technology startup firm, for example, is normally associated with the postwar era; as was noted earlier, before 1940 much of the in-house research activity of large manufacturing firms focused on the acquisition of technologies from smaller entrepreneurial firms (or from individual entrepreneurs), often including the acquisition of the firm. Similarly, the expansion in university–industry collaboration and in the role of state governments in supporting these and other research activities involves the revival of another key component of the pre-1940 system. Still another element of the pre-1940 system, and a far less desirable one, that has been strengthened somewhat in recent years is the protectionist and isolationist tone of some contributions to the U. S. debate over trade and technology policies.

CONCLUSION

As was noted in the first part of this paper, the importance of each of three key components within the U. S. national innovation system has changed over the course of this century. In the early twentieth century research facilities in both universities and industry were established and informal linkages between at least some universities (often, public universities) and industrial research establishments were developed. The federal government played a modest role as a supporter of research in the nonagricultural sector, and state governments funded both public higher education and the "engineering extension" activities of many of these universities.

The research system that had developed within U. S. industry and academia by the end of the 1930s exceeded the size of its British counterpart, the only non-U. S. system for which reliable data exist during this period, and probably outstripped that of any other industrial economy, with the possible exception of Germany. Nonetheless, the quality of U. S. fundamental research in academia and industry was only sporadically on a par with the best of German or British research. The rise of the U. S. economy to a position of world leadership in manufacturing output and productivity during the first 15 years of this century did not rely on world-class domestic scientific research (Nelson, 1990).

This structure was transformed beyond recognition by World War II and the state of armed peace that developed within 5 years after the end of hostilities. Federal research funding expanded and displaced the role of state governments as actors in this innovation system and contributed to some weakening in the informal ties that linked many corporate and academic research institutions. The powerful role of the federal government within the postwar U. S. innovation system was not linked to any economic strategy, however, instead being motivated largely by national security concerns. During both the pre-1940 and postwar eras, little if any strategic planning underpinned public intervention in the U. S. innovation system, and policymakers devoted minimal attention to its domestic economic payoffs.

Whether or not the policy was based on a comprehensive strategy, the interaction between federal and private R&D expenditures significantly influenced the performance of the U. S. national innovation system during the postwar period. A large, well-financed federal defense R&D program increased the demand for a limited supply of professional engineers and scientists. Although that demand also expanded the supply of such trained persons (expansion aided by federal research and fellowship funds for higher education), it also raised their wages and salaries and increased the cost of privately financed R&D.[52]

Comparisons with other countries provide some support for concern over the commercial implications of defense R&D spending. Japan and West Germany have had very small military budgets since the end of World War II, and in both countries the ratios of civilian R&D to GNP have been substantially higher than in the United States for many years (National Science Board, 1981, pp. 214–215). The opportunity costs to the U. S. economy of high levels of defense R&D spending have been high. The relative economic performance of the United States, West Germany, Japan, and other advanced industrial economies in the past few decades does not support the presumption that large expenditures on military R&D have improved this nation's economic strength. Moreover, recent efforts by the military services to broaden their support of commercial innovation may create as many problems as they solve.

The historical perspective of this paper suggests that U. S. antitrust policy has exercised an important and (by comparison with other industrial nations) unique influence on the U. S. innovation system. Antitrust policy was partly responsible for the formation of the giant firms that were among the earliest investors in industrial research, and influenced their decisions to invest in industrial research. For most of the post-1945 period, antitrust policy remained an important influence on corporate R&D investment by large firms. In the case of Du Pont, R&D investment soared as the firm attempted to develop "new nylons" (largely ignoring the fact that with the exception of nylon and neoprene, the bulk of the firm's prewar innovations had been acquired, rather than originating in Du Pont fundamental research). AT&T pursued liberal licensing policies in microelectronics as a direct result of antitrust policy, leading to rapid entry into the semiconductor industry by new firms.

Antitrust policy may have led to higher postwar levels of industry-financed investment in R&D; this investment, however, did not necessarily improve the economic performance of the U. S. innovation system. Nevertheless, viewed in terms of its effects on the domestic diffusion of new technological knowledge and findings, postwar antitrust policy may well have aided the performance of the U. S. innovation system, in view of the support that this policy provided for the important role of small, startup firms in technology commercialization. Whether this structure is equally well-suited to a global environment in which technological knowledge travels almost as rapidly across national boundaries as it does within these boundaries remains uncertain (see Nelson, 1990, for additional discussion).

Recent and prospective changes in U. S. antitrust policy may reduce the extent of the contrast between U. S. and foreign nations' antitrust policies. Combined with other policy initiatives in intellectual property, a more lenient U. S. antitrust policy may reduce the importance of new firms as agents for the commercialization of new technologies. The effects of these policy changes on the adoption of new technologies, an area in which U. S. performance has been weak, are uncertain but may prove detrimental. More generally, however, the current U. S. debate over science and technology policy exhibits little awareness of the importance of technology adoption for international competitiveness, nor is there much acknowledgment of any role for public policy in supporting technology adoption. As the case of agricultural research makes clear, public programs designed to support technology adoption may perform less well in scientific research. In addition, of course, the contemporary U. S. debate's focus on trade and technology policies as containing the entirety of a "solution" to problems of competitiveness is almost certainly misguided.

In all three of the major industrial regions of the world economy—Japan, the United States, and Western Europe—far-reaching structural change now appears to be occurring in national innovation systems. In Western Europe, national innovation systems may be supplemented by a regional one, under the sponsorship of BRITE, EUREKA, RACE, JESSI, and other programs. Japan's transition from a position of "catch-up" within the global economy to a position of technological leadership in many areas also is likely to require new institutions for technology development and commercialization. The movement of the U. S. economy from a position of global technological and economic dominance to the position of first among equals is intensifying political debate over the trade and technology policies of this government through most of the postwar period. This debate paradoxically has been fueled by the success of the multilateral political and economic strategies, to which U. S. trade and technology policies contributed, in the demise of the Warsaw Pact.

Within the U. S. debate, the economic and other consequences of increased international technological interdependence in both the civilian and military spheres are only dimly perceived. It seems inevitable nonetheless that technology policy issues will figure ever more prominently on the trade and national security agenda. Even as the U. S. and other governments attempt to intervene strategically in their "national innovation systems" (treating the European Communities as a single such system), the growing economic and technological interpenetration of the major industrial and industrializing economies of the world appears to be making these "national" systems increasingly permeable.

Unfortunately, although the increased concern of a number of recent U. S. technology policy initiatives with commercial development of the fruits of basic research investments arguably is a positive development, the mercantilistic flavor of many of them is not. Proposals to restrict scientific and technological cooperation at the water's edge fly in the face of the growing interdependence of national R&D systems. To the extent that U. S. policymakers design technology initiatives that ignore the increasing interdependence of U. S. and foreign scientific and technological research, U. S. and foreign technological and economic development will be hampered.

At the international level, the challenge to policymakers seeking to manage international interdependence is spilling across all areas of economic policy. The development of macroeconomic policy coordination among the industrialized nations has required nearly two decades, and still leaves much to be desired. The problems of international interdependence and convergence in microeconomic policies and institutions are only now beginning to receive attention (Ostry, 1990). In the multilateral trade talks that almost certainly will begin shortly after the conclusion of the Uruguay Round, a multilateral antitrust or competition policy is likely to be a central topic, which may provide further impetus to some convergence in the structure of industrial nations' national innovation systems.

Although economic factors may be forcing some convergence in the structure of national innovation systems within the industrial world (just as these forces have forced some convergence in the financial systems of the industrial economies), the speed and effectiveness with which they will operate are uncertain, especially in view of the political sensitivity of many of the affected issues and interests. Moreover, our understanding of the management and organization of the innovation process is so imperfect that debates over "fair" and "unfair," "open" and "closed," or "efficient" and "inefficient" innovation systems will remain poorly informed for the foreseeable future.

NOTES

1. There is a growing literature on this topic, although it focuses on a small number of technologies and often does not present internationally comparable data. See, among others, Flamm (1988), Edquist and Jacobsson (1988), Kelley and Brooks (1988), and Jaikumar (1987).

2. "[T]he coupling between science and technological innovation remained very loose during this period [the nineteenth century] because, in many industrial activities, innovations did not require scientific knowledge. This was true of the broad range of metal-using industries in the second half of the nineteenth century, in which the United States took a position of distinct technological leadership. Indeed, following the American display at the Crystal Palace Exhibition in 1851, the British came to speak routinely of 'the American system of manufactures.' . . . In the second half of the nineteenth century, America provided the leadership in developing a new production technology for manufacturing such products as reapers, threshers, cultivators, repeating rifles, hardware, watches, sewing machines, typewriters, and bicycles" (Mowery and Rosenberg, 1989b, p. 27).

3. Concerning the characteristics of the trajectory of technological advance within the U. S. economy, Abramovitz (1986) notes that "The path of technological change which in those years [1870–1945] offered the greatest opportunities for advance was at once heavily scale-dependent and biased in a labor-saving but capital- and resource-using direction. In both respects America enjoyed great advantages compared with Europe or Japan. Large-scale production was favored by a large, rapidly growing, and increasingly prosperous population. It was supported also by a striking homogeneity of tastes. This reflected the country's comparative youth, its rapid settlement by migration from a common base on the Atlantic, and the weakness and fluidity of its class divisions. Further, insofar as the population grew by immigration, the new Americans and their children quickly accepted the consumption patterns of their adopted country because the prevailing ethos favored assimilation to the dominant native white culture. At the same time, American industry was encouraged to explore the rich possibilities of a labor-saving but capital- and resource-using path of advance. The country's resources of land, forest, and minerals were particularly rich and abundant, and supplies of capital grew rapidly in response to high returns" (p. 397).

4. See Stigler (1968). The Supreme Court ruled in the *Trans Missouri Association* case in 1898 and the *Addyston Pipe* case in 1899 that the Sherman Act outlawed all agreements among

firms on prices or market sharing. Data in Thorelli (1954) and Lamoreaux (1985) indicate a sharp increase in merger activity between the 1895–1898 and 1899–1902 periods.

5. The Du Pont Company's research activities focused increasingly on diversification out of the black and smokeless powder businesses even before the antitrust decision of 1913 that forced the divestiture of a portion of the firm's black powder and dynamite businesses. Discussing Du Pont's early industrial research, Hounshell and Smith (1989) argue that "Du Pont's initial diversification strategy was based on utilizing the company's plants, know-how, and R&D capabilities in smokeless powder (i.e., nitrocellulose) technology. The goal was to find uses for Du Pont's smokeless powder plants because political developments in Washington after 1907 [Congressional restrictions on procurement by the Navy of powder from "trusts" and the 1913 antitrust decision that forced divestiture of much of Du Pont's black powder and dynamite operations] signaled a significant decline, if not end, to Du Pont's government business" (p. 57). The 1911 consent decree settling the federal government's antitrust suit against General Electric left GE's patent licensing scheme untouched, enabling the firm to maintain an effective cartel within the U. S. electric lamp market for years to come without further acquisitions, which would have violated the consent decree (Bright, 1949). During the interwar period, Du Pont and General Electric both utilized patent licensing arrangements as a basis for international cartel agreements (see Taylor and Sudnik, 1984; Reid, 1989).

6. The ability of firms to utilize their industrial research laboratories to monitor their technological environments and evaluate patents or firms for possible acquisition was aided by stronger protection for intellectual property in the late nineteenth century. Stronger intellectual property protection increased the appropriability of the returns from innovation and facilitated the development of a market for the acquisition and sale of patents. Federal court decisions in the 1890s upholding the validity of patents covering goods not in production increased the utility of large patent portfolios for defensive purposes.

7. The data in Table 2.1 were drawn originally from the National Research Council surveys of industrial research employment, as tabulated in Mowery (1981). The surveys' coverage of research laboratories in 1921 is somewhat suspect, and the data for that year should be treated with caution.

8. "Universities" throughout this paper refers to all institutions of higher education, and therefore covers a broader and more diverse array of institutions than those defined as universities in other national innovation systems.

9. In the early 1920s, roughly 42,000 students were enrolled in British universities; the figure rose to 50,000–60,000 by the late 1930s. By contrast, American institutions of higher learning awarded over 48,000 *degrees* in 1913 alone, nearly 10 years earlier, and more than 216,000 degrees in 1940. With a total population 35% that of the United States, Britain had only about 6% as many students in higher education in the late 1930s (Briggs, 1981; U. S. Bureau of the Census, 1975, p. 386). The size of the higher educational system was an important "supply-side" influence on the growth of German industrial research; Beer (1959) cites the high rate of production of chemistry Ph.D.s by German higher education in the late nineteenth century as an important influence on the growth of industrial research in the German chemicals industry. As the supply of professional chemists exceeded available academic employment opportunities, emigration or industrial research were the only alternatives open to the German graduate chemist.

10. Even in the private universities, however, the applications of scientific research, rather than the intrinsic importance of science, were emphasized by academic administrators. Cohen (1976) notes that "By the mid-1840's the stress on practicality produced schools of science at both Harvard and Yale in which a dominant theme was the utility of the sciences" (p. 374).

11. "[F]rom comparative obscurity before World War I, American chemistry rose steadily in esteem to a position of international dominance. Almost half the citations in the *Annual Reports* [*Annual Reports in Chemistry*, described on the page as "a central British review jour-

nal"] in 1975 were to American publications. Similarly, almost half the citations to non-German-language literature in *Chemische Berichte* [the "central German chemical journal"] in 1975 went to American work. It is striking that this hegemony is the culmination of a fifty-year trend of increasing presence, and not merely the result of post-World War II developments. Second, it is clear that the increasing attention received in the two decades before World War II reflected the growing *volume* of American chemistry, rather than a changed assessment of its worth. Since World War II, however, in both *Chemische Berichte* and the *Annual Reports,* American chemistry has been cited proportionately more than is warranted by increasing quantity alone. The prominence of American work within the international literature has been sustained by quality" (Thackray et al., 1985, p. 157; emphasis in original).

12. "Around the 1920s, American physics came of age. From a state of distinct inferiority before World War I it improved until, by the early 1930s, it was the equal or superior of physics anywhere in the world . . . For example, an early citation study, covering all the reference citations found in papers published in a number of physics journals in 1934, turned up only 21 citations to papers published in the leading American journal, the *Physical Review,* in the interval 1895–1914, compared with 169 citations to the German *Annalen der Physik.* But in citations to papers published in 1930–33, the *Physical Review* beat the *Annalen* three to one, and as of 1933 it had become the most-cited of all physics journals" (Weart, 1979, p. 298).

13. Moreover, to a much greater extent in the United States than elsewhere, technically trained engineers moved into positions of industrial leadership. See Chandler (1962, p. 317).

14. Evenson (1982) argues that interregional disparities in agricultural productivity and incomes also were influenced by federal policies toward research investments: "the federal government through its investment decisions has been very influential in changing the research system, even though state governments have provided the majority of the funds. In the 1930s and 1940s it located much of its investment in the 'lagging' regions, chiefly the South. In this way it had a major impact on the regional nature of productivity" (pp. 251–253).

15. The differences in the arrangements during the two world wars between the federal government and the private sector for defense-related research and development had significant effects on the diffusion of technological know-how during and after each conflict. Limited involvement by private firms in military R&D during World War I meant that "spillovers" from military to commercial innovation were limited. World War II appears to have had a different effect. In the chemicals industry, for example, Hounshell and Smith (1988) argue that World War II created significant new competitive threats to the Du Pont Company, because of the large-scale involvement of private firms in the operation of complex chemical production processes: "Because the wartime emergncy served as a great leveler—exposing other companies to truly large-scale projects and manufacturing operations while forcing Du Pont to yield much of its proprietary knowledge—Du Pont's executives foresaw that firms such as Allied, Union Carbide, Monsanto, and Dow would become far more competitive after the war. This competition would be manifested not only in the marketplace but also in the laboratory" (p. 332).

16. For a careful, although now somewhat dated, treatment of these contractual issues, see Danhof (1968).

17. National Science Foundation (1985, p. 3). For a listing of FFRDCs by location and sponsoring agency, along with federal obligations for 1981, see National Science Board (1983, p. 310).

18. Congressional Budget Office (1984, p. 53). In addition to expenditures of the Department of Defense, defense includes expenditures for military programs in the Department of Energy.

19. Although no more than 3.2% of federal defense R&D in 1982 went to basic research, the absolute size of this budget is still very large, and basic research supported by military agencies has been a significant component of federally supported basic research. The Office of Naval Research has been a supporter of basic research for 40 years, and the Defense Advanced Research

Projects Agency (DARPA) has played a crucial role in the early stages of several research programs that have yielded significant civilian applications, most notably in computer technology (see Flamm, 1988).

20. Ergas (1987) argues that this concentration is a common feature of "mission-oriented" R&D programs: "the goals of mission-oriented R&D are centrally decided and clearly set out, generally in terms of complex systems meeting the needs of a particular government agency. . . . Concentration also extends to the range of technologies covered. Virtually by its nature, mission-oriented research focuses on a small number of technologies of particular strategic importance—primarily in aerospace, electronics, and nuclear energy. As a result, government R&D funding in these countries is heavily biased toward a few industries that are generally considered to be in the early stages of the technology life cycle" (p. 194).

21. Flamm and McNaugher (1989) suggest that changes in Defense Department R&D policy have contributed to declining military–civilian technology spillovers. They cite declines in the share of basic research in DOD R&D spending, as well as increased Congressional demands that these R&D programs yield near-term applications in weapons systems, as two factors that have reduced such spillovers.

22. See National Research Council (1982) and Okimoto and Saxonhouse (1987). Sharp (1989) argues that the less prominent role played in scientific research by European universities has contributed to the slower growth of small biotechnology firms: "A researcher at a CNRS laboratory in France, or at a Max Planck Institute laboratory in Germany, is the full time employee of that institution. As such his/her prime responsibility is to public, not private science. Moeover, as a full time employee, he/she will not find it easy to undertake the 'mix' of research frequently undertaken by an American professor, who combines an academic post with consultancy in the private sector. Indeed the tradition of funding U S academic posts for only nine months of the year, expecting the academic who wishes to carry out research in the summer to raise research funds to meet the remaining three months of salary, explicitly encourages the entrepreneurial academic. In stark contrast, his/her German opposite number at a Max Planck Institute will find all research costs, including staff and equipment, met as part of institutional overheads. The opportunity cost of leaving such a research environment for the insecurity of the small firm is all the greater since, once off the academic ladder in West Germany, it is more difficult to climb back on again. The same goes for the opposite number in France, and with the additional disincentive that French researchers are civil servants and dropping out of the system means *both* losing security of tenure/accumulated benefits *and* difficulty in re-entry should the need arise. In the circumstances, it is not perhaps so surprising that few spin-offs from public sector research arise, nor, for that matter, that in Europe most such spin-offs are to be found in the U K, where the organisation of academic science most closely matches that of the U S. In the U K, it is notable that—with the exception of Celltech and the Agricultural Genetics Company (AGC)—most of the spin-offs from biotechnology have come from the universities" (pp. 12–13).

23. This is not to deny the major role played by such large firms as IBM in computers and AT&T in microelectronics. In other instances, large firms have acquired smaller enterprises and applied their production or marketing expertise to expand markets for a new product technology. Nonetheless, it seems apparent that startup firms have been far more active in commercializing new technologies in the United States than in other industrial economies. Malerba's analysis of the evolution of the microelectronics industry in Western Europe and in the United States (1985) emphasizes the greater importance of startup firms in the United States.

24. See Perry (1986) and Mowery and Steinmueller (1991). Sharp (1989) argues that "the venture capital market in Europe is underdeveloped. The most active venture capital market is in the U K where some half dozen funds specialising in investment in biotechnology are active and an estimated total of over $1 billion invested since 1980 . . . The doyen of this market is the Rothschild Fund Biotechnology Investments Ltd (BIL)—now capitalised at $200 million and

the largest specialist fund in Europe. By contrast, the largest German venture capital fund, Techno Venture Management, established in 1984, had an initial capitalisation of $10 million and in 1989 is worth only $50 million. The availability of venture capital, however, is only one part of the equation. BIL, for example, whose investments span biotechnology and medical technology, have not found in Europe the quality of investment they are seeking. 75 per cent of their investments are in the U S, only 25 per cent in Europe, and these concentrated almost entirely in the U K. This pattern of investment is mirrored by nearly all the investment funds, all of which invest a large proportion of their investments in biotechnology in the small firm sector in the U S, and only a very small proportion in small firms in Europe" (pp. 9–10).

25. Discussing the early years of the semiconductor industry, Tilton (1971) noted that "The defense market has been particularly important for new firms . . . these firms often have started by introducing new products and concentrating in new semiconductor fields where the military has usually provided the major or only market. Fortunately for them, the armed forces have not hesitated to buy from new and untried firms. In early 1953, for example, before Transitron had made any significant sales, the military authorized the use of its gold-bonded diode. This approval has been called the real turning point for the new firms. During 1959, new firms accounted for 63 percent of all semiconductor sales and 69 percent of military sales" (p. 91). Describing a similar situation in the early computer industry, Flamm (1988) argues that "the many start-up computer firms entering the U. S. industry in the early and middle 1950s were chasing after a reasonably large market, dominated by military demand. For almost of these producers, the military was the first, and generally the best customer. About eighty different organizations, including numerous small start-ups that later merged with larger producers or disappeared, produced computers in the United States during the 1950s. The U. S. military, or defense contractors, paid for or purchased the first machines made by most of these groups" (pp. 78–79).

26. "European governments provided only limited funds to support the development of both electronic component and computer technology in the 1950s and were reluctant to purchase new and untried technology for use in their military and other systems. European governments also concentrated their limited support on defense-oriented engineering and electronics firms. The American practice was to support military technology projects undertaken by industrial and business equipment firms that were mainly interested in commercial markets. These firms viewed their military business as a development vehicle for technology that eventually would be adapted and sold in the open marketplace" (Flamm, 1988, p. 134).

27. "The happy experience of neoprene and nylon in the 1930s suggested a way in which Du Pont could stay ahead of the competition, continue to grow, and avoid antitrust litigation. By expanding its fundamental research effort dramatically, not only in the Chemical Department but also in the industrial departments, the Executive Committee expected to reap a harvest of new nylons" (Hounshell and Smith, 1988, p. 327).

28. See Graham (1986a), Wise (1985), Hounshell and Smith (1985), Sturchio (1985), and Rosenbloom (1985).

29. Graham (1986b) argued in her analysis of the RCA and Alcoa laboratories that "The problem both corporate laboratories encountered was that, while they could influence actual strategy formulation through informal but effective channels, they encountered heavy opposition at the execution stage. The operating tasks required to develop and commercialize major innovations were quite different from the tasks involved in other forms of corporate R&D activity, and the methods and priorities that were effective for these other activities proved dysfunctional for their radical innovations" (p. 189).

30. See Baily and Chakrabarti (1988, especially pp. 42–43), who argue that such a decline did occur, but attribute it largely to exhaustion of technological opportunities. The empirical research on the returns to R&D investment, to say nothing of fluctuations in these returns over time, yields mixed results [see Scherer (1983) and Griliches (1980, 1986)].

31. Markoff (1989) reports that recent survey data from the National Science Foundation indicate that inflation-adjusted R&D spending by industry shrank by 0.9% between 1988 and 1989, the first reduction in real industry-funded R&D spending since 1974–1975. For a less gloomy assessment of this development, see the *Economist* (1990, pp. 65–72).

32. "Prior to the 1970 act roughly a dozen or so public SAES and USDA breeder programs and a smaller number of private breeder programs were in place. After 1970 some 35 additional private programs were added. Of the 244 soybean varieties granted certificates since 1970, only 37 were granted to public research programs. The remainder were granted to approximately 35 different private firms" (Evenson, 1983, p. 971).

33. "Overall, the experiment stations have generally moved their work into areas where they have a comparative advantage vis-à-vis the private sector. In direct competition with market-oriented private firms, the public sector does poorly and generally does not invest heavily in research of that type. It tends to be pressed into a good deal of work of a testing a certifying nature, designed to help farmers make choices among suppliers of inputs. In recent years it has played a major role in facilitating adjustment to regulations both in the chemical inputs fields and in food technology" (Evenson, 1982, p. 275).

34. Evenson (1983) notes that "Given the major developments in the 'mother' biological sciences, particularly in molecular biology, it would seem reasonable to expect a significant proportion of the [agricultural research] system scientists to have backgrounds in this field. These data show that this is not the case. Less than one percent of the researchers in the system, even today after more than two decades of scientific revolution in the field, are trained in the field" (p. 973). Other critiques of the U. S. agricultural research system are in U. S. Congressional Office of Technology Assessment (1981, 1986).

35. Abramovitz's work on "catch-up" in postwar economic growth yields two insights into the process of relative U. S. decline. First, Abramovitz points out that the process of convergence in levels of productivity that has been underway in his sample of 16 nations since 1870 accelerated sharply after World War II, reflecting more rapid rates of international technology transfer, investment, and trade. Another important factor in more rapid postwar convergence, according to Abramovitz (1990), was the fact that change in the structure of foreign industry, consumer demand, and financial markets facilitated the absorption by foreign economies of the scale-dependent, capital-intensive, manufacturing technologies of U. S. firms. No longer was it the case that foreign economies' "underdeveloped financial markets and their still low levels of income restricted capital accumulation, while the combination of low incomes and small populations limited their domestic markets and therefore, also the base on which large-scale competitive exports could be built" (1990, p. 6).

36. Indeed, one might argue that the weakening of university–industry research linkages during a significant portion of the postwar period was the real departure from historical trends. Hounshell and Smith (1988) cite a 1945 memo from Elmer Bolton, director of what was to become the Du Pont Company's central research laboratory, that made a case for greater self-reliance by the firm in its basic research: "Three things were necessary: Du Pont had to strengthen its research organizations and house them in modern research facilities; the company's existing processes had to be improved and new processes and products developed; and 'fundamental research, which will serve as a background for new advances in applied chemistry, should be expanded not only in the Chemical Department but should [also] be increased in our industrial research laboratories and the Engineering Department.' Bolton stressed that it was no longer 'possible to rely to the same extent as in the past upon university research to supply this background so that in future years it will be necessary for the Company to provide this knowledge to a far greater extent through its own efforts.' To 'retain its leadership' Du Pont had 'to undertake on a much broader scale fundamental research in order to provide more knowledge to serve as a basis for applied research'" (p. 355). Swann (1988, pp. 170–181) also argues that research

links between U. S. universities and the pharmaceuticals industry weakened significantly in the immediate aftermath of World War II, in part as a result of vastly increased federal research funding for academic research in the health sciences.

37. This close relationship is due in part to the nature of biotechnology. Recombinant DNA and genetic engineering techniques in many ways represent radical scientific breakthroughs that are being transferred to industry and reduced to practice. In Gomory's terminology (1988), biotechnology is a "ladder" technology, that is, a case in which

> the new idea is dominant and the product forms itself around the new idea or new technology. Those who understand that idea or technology are often scientists, and they therefore play leading roles in its introduction. (p. 11)

Another example of a ladder technology cited by Gomory is the transistor. In contrast to biotechnology, of course, the transistor was first developed within industry. The different origin of these two major scientific discoveries may reflect the shifting role of industry and universities as basic research performers. An interesting empirical study of university–industry research collaboration that tends to support the characterization of biotechnology as a unique area of interaction is Blumenthal et al. (1986).

38. A recent study by the Organization for Economic Cooperation and Development (OECD, 1984) quotes a Xerox Corporation research executive's description of the firm's investment in the Center for Integrated Systems (CIS) at Stanford University: "Xerox's contribution to CIS is very small compared to what we are investing internally in the same kind of research. For little additional investment we enlarge our perspective by participating in a broad program of basic research. We envision opportunities for joint interaction with the university and with other companies, as well as the ability to recruit students. On a per-dollar basis it should be a good investment" (quoted in OECD, 1984, p. 47).

39. A consortium like Bellcore, established in the wake of the divestiture of the Bell operating companies by AT&T, is a response to a very different and unique set of circumstances. In most respects, Bellcore, serving the needs of the noncompeting businesses of the Bell operating companies, more closely resembles the Electric Power Research Institute or the Gas Research Institute than ventures such as the Software Productivity Consortium or the Microelectronics and Computer Technology Corporation (MCC).

40. Chesnais (1988) has noted that an interesting complementary relationship may be developing between closed domestic research programs in the EC and the United States, such as JESSI and Sematech, and international product development and technology exchange agreements in microelectronics: "one finds a combination between *domestic* alliances in *pre-competitive* R&D (with all of the provisos attached to this notion), and a wide range of technology exchange and cross-licensing agreements among oligopolist rivals at the international level" (1988, p. 95; emphasis in original).

41. See Ferguson (1983, 1988), Florida and Kenney (1988), Borrus (1988), White House Science Council (1988), and *Business Week*, 6/24/89. The comments of Jorde and Teece (1989) illustrate one important line of argument within this critique: "Companies like Sun Microsystems, Genentech, Compaq, Advanced Micro Devices, and Apple Computer are archetypical examples [of startups]. Whereas large integrated firms like IBM and Exxon have relied upon integration and administrative processes to effectuate coordination, the 'Silicon Valley' startups have in the main eschewed integration and relied excessively on outsourcing . . . Market processes have in some instances replaced administrative ones. This is particularly true where 'hollow corporations'—those without significant in-house research, manufacturing, and distribution—have come to replace economic activity that in an earlier period took place inside vertically integrated enterprises. In some cases this has left industries with inadequate strategic coordination, particularly when they are competing against firms located in industrial structures

that are less fragmented and which are supported by governments that engage in directed industrial policies" (p. 29).

42. See *Economist* (6/24/89, pp. 73–74). Other experts, however, assert that startup activity remains strong. According to T.J. Rodgers, CEO of Cypress Semiconductor of San Jose, California, "More chip companies were started in the five years between 1980 and 1985 than in the two decades between 1960 and 1980" (1990, p. 25).

43. See Gupta (1982). A recent article in *The Economist* (2/10/89) asserts that "The dream is dead. Biotechnology will never produce an entrepreneurial success to rival the out-of-nowhere rise of the electronics industry's Apple, Compaq, or Intel" (p. 67).

44. Glenn R. Schleede, executive associate director of the Office of Management and Budget, commented in 1981 that "By far the most important change [made in science and technology policies by the Reagan Administration] came from this administration's redefinition of the federal role. In the R&D spectrum stretching from the most esoteric basic research out through the actual commercialization of a technology, we have drawn the line for federal intervention and support back much farther toward the basic research end. In the civilian or domestic sector, we do not think the government should be funding demonstration, product development, and commercialization efforts" (quoted in Barfield, 1982, p. 41).

45. See Davis (1989). In still another new initiative, the Defense Advanced Research Projects Agency (DARPA) announced on April 9, 1990 that it was investing $4 million in Gazelle Microcircuits, a small firm in the Silicon Valley region engaged in developing gallium-arsenide components for civilian and military applications. The DARPA investment was made, and explicitly justified, as a means of denying the firm's technology to potential foreign purchasers: "The investment, made under an experimental two-year program approved by Congress, not only allows the Defense Advanced Research Projects Agency, or Darpa, to earn a return on its investment, but could also prevent the new company from having to sell its advanced technology to a foreign company."

"'They in fact had been contacted by the Japanese and they were strapped for cash,' said Richard L. Dunn, Darpa's general counsel. 'This agreement may have saved them from that.'" In the event that the firm considers such a sale of its technology, DARPA is empowered to arrange for a domestic buyer first; if no domestic buyer can be found, DARPA is allowed to recover its investment, raising the costs to a foreign firm of investing in the U. S. firm (see Pollack, 1990).

46. Nelson (1984) concludes that "one rather clear lesson of the post-World War II experience is that trying to blend commercial and military procurement objectives is a mistake. If a program is aimed specifically at enhancing competitive strength, it should stand separate from procurement programs" (p. 73). Lorell (1980) provides a good review of the history of trans-European weapons development consortia and programs.

47. See Perry (1986), among other accounts. According to Katz and Ordover (1990), at least 14 Congressional bills passed during the 1980s focused on strengthening domestic and international protection for intellectual property rights, and the Court of Appeals for the Federal Circuit created in 1982 has upheld patent rights in roughly 80% of the cases argued before it, a considerable increase from the pre-1982 rate of 30% for the Federal bench.

48. "Although the Act does take useful steps to assist innovation, the limited shelter it provides from antitrust covers only research activity. This is one reason why only 111 ventures had been registered under the Act from 1984 through June 1988" (Jorde and Teece, 1989, p. 32).

49. Harris and Mowery (1990) present a critical discussion of the Congressional legislation.

50. The Act calls for a series of reports on U. S. firms' access to foreign markets for telecommunications equipment, creates a new provision (Sec. 1315) for dealing with subsidized international consortia, widely viewed as a provision directed at Airbus; and creates new provisions for "fast-track" antidumping investigations in industries (such as microelectronics) with short product life cycles.

51. Reciprocal access is a concept that is more easily stated than implemented in national R&D systems that differ as sharply as do those of the United States, where publicly funded research accounts for nearly 50% of all national R&D and where relatively open institutions such as universities play a very important role in basic research, and Japan, in which corporate funding of R&D is far more significant. U. S. firms almost certainly would reject a policy that required assurances of equal access to the research facilities of U. S. and Japanese corporations.

52. Comparisons of the pre- and post-1940 pattern of research employment (Mowery, 1981) suggest that federal funding was associated with some displacement of research activity away from sectors receiving little or no federal research funds, such as chemicals and petroleum, and toward the sectors that did receive massive defense-related federal R&D support (instruments, electrical machinery, and transport equipment).

REFERENCES

Abramovitz, M. (1986). "Catching Up, Forging Ahead, and Falling Behind." *Journal of Economic History* 46: 385–406.

Abramovitz, M. (1990). "The Catch-Up Factor in Postwar Economic Growth." *Economic Inquiry* 28(1): 1–18.

Ames, J. (1925). Statement of NACA Chairman to the President's Aircraft Board. Washington, D. C.: U. S. Government Printing Office.

Baily, M. N., and Chakrabarti, A. K. (1988). *Innovation and the Productivity Crisis.* Washington, D. C.: Brookings Institution.

Barfield, C. E. (1982). *Science Policy from Ford to Reagan.* Washington, D. C.: American Enterprise Institute.

Beer, J. H. (1959). *The Emergence of the German Dye Industry.* Urbana, IL: University of Illinois Press.

Birr, K. (1966). "Science in American Industry." In D. Van Tassel and M. Hall (eds.), *Science and Society in the U. S.* Homewood, IL: Dorsey.

Blumenthal, D., Gluck, M., Louis, K. S., and Wise, D. (1986). "Industrial Support of University Research in Biotechnology." *Science* 231: 242–46.

Borrus, M. G. (1988). *Competing for Control.* Cambridge: Ballinger.

Briggs, A. (1981). "Social History 1900–1945." In R. Floud and D. W. McCloskey (eds.), *The Economic History of Britain Since 1700,* Vol. 2. Cambridge, England: Cambridge University Press.

Bright, A. A. (1949). *The Electric Lamp Industry.* New York: Macmillan.

Business Week (1989a). "Is the U. S. Selling Its High-Tech Soul to Japan?" 6/26/89, 117–18.

Business Week (1989b). "Advanced Bio Class? That's over in Hitachi Hall." 8/7/89, 73–4.

Chandler, A. D., Jr. (1962). *Strategy and Structure: Chapters in the History of Industrial Enterprise.* Cambridge, MA: MIT Press.

Chandler, A. D., Jr. (1977). *The Visible Hand.* Cambridge, MA: Harvard University Press.

Chesnais, F. (1988). "Technical Co-Operation Agreements Between Firms." *STI Review* 4: 51–119.

Cohen, I. B. (1976). "Science and the Growth of the American Republic." *Review of Politics* 38(3): 359–98.

Collins, N. R., and F.L.E. Preston (1961). "The Size Structure of the Largest Industrial Firms." *American Economic Review* 51: 986–1011.

Congressional Budget Office (1984). *Federal Support for R&D and Innovation.* Washington, D. C.: Congressional Budget Office.

Cyert, R. M., and Mowery, D. C., eds., *Technology and Employment: Innovation and Growth in the U. S. Economy.* Washington, D. C.: National Academy Press, 1987.

Danhof, C. (1968). *Government Contracting and Technological Change.* Washington, D. C.: The Brookings Institution.

David, P. A. (1975). *Technical Choice, Innovation, and Economic Growth.* New York: Cambridge University Press.

David, P. A. (1986). "Technology Diffusion, Public Policy, and Industrial Competitiveness." In R. Landau and N. Rosenberg (eds.), *The Positive Sum Strategy: Harnessing Technology for Economic Growth.* Washington, D. C.: National Academy Press.

Davis, B. (1989). "Pentagon Seeks to Spur U. S. Effort to Develop 'High-Definition' TV." *Wall Street Journal* 1/4/89, 29.

Davis, L. E., and North, D. C. (1971). *Institutional Change and American Economic Growth.* New York: Cambridge University Press.

Economist (1989a). "Venture-Capital Drought." 6/24/89, 73–4.

Economist (1989b). "Test-Tube Trauma." 2/10/89, 67.

Economist (1990). "Out of the Ivory Tower." 2/3/90, 65–72.

Edquist, C., and Jacobsson, S. (1988). *Flexible Automation: The Global Diffusion of New Technology in the Engineering Industry.* New York: Basil Blackwell.

Edwards, R. C. (1975). "Stages in Corporate Stability and Risks of Corporate Failure." *Journal of Economic History* 35: 418–57.

Ergas, H. (1987). "Does Technology Policy Matter?" In H. Brooks and B. Guile (eds.), *Technology and Global Industry*. Washington, D. C.: National Academy Press.

Evenson, R. E. (1982). "Agriculture." In R. R. Nelson (ed.), *Government and Technical Progress*. New York: Pergamon.

Evenson, R. E. (1983). "Intellectual Property Rights and Agribusiness Research and Development: Implications for the Public Agricultural Research System." *American Journal of Agricultural Economics* 65: 967–75.

Ferguson, C. H. (1983). "The Microelectronics Industry in Distress." *Technology Review* 86(6):24–37.

Ferguson, C. H. (1988). "Beyond Entrepreneurialism to U. S. Competitiveness: From the People Who Brought You Voodoo Economics." *Harvard Business Review* 66(3):55–62.

Flamm, K. (1988). *Creating the Computer*. Washington, D. C.: Brookings Institution.

Flamm, K., and McNaugher, T. (1989). "Rationalizing Technology Investments." In J. D. Steinbruner (ed.), *Restructuring American Foreign Policy*. Washington, D. C.: Brookings Institution.

Florida, R. L., and Kenney, M. (1988). "Venture Capital-Financed Innovation and Technological Change in the USA." *Research Policy* 17: 119–37.

Gansler, J. (1989). *Affording Defense*. Cambridge, MA: MIT Press.

Gomory, R. E. (1988). "Reduction to Practice: The Development and Manufacturing Cycle." In *Industrial R&D and U. S. Technological Leadership*. Washington, D. C.: National Academy Press.

Graham, M.B.W. (1986a). *RCA and the Videodisc: The Business of Research*. Cambridge, England: Cambridge University Press.

Graham, M.B.W. (1986b). "Corporate Research and Development: The Latest Transformation." *Technology in Society* 7: 179–95.

Griliches, Z. (1980). "R&D and the Productivity Slowdown." *American Economic Review* 70:343–48.

Griliches, Z. (1986). "Productivity, R&D and Basic Research at the Firm Level in the 1970s." *American Economic Review* 76:141–54.

Gupta, U. (1982). "Biotech Start-Ups are Increasingly Bred Just to Be Sold." *Wall Street Journal* 7/19/82, B2.

Gupta, U. (1988). "Start-Ups Face Big-Time Legal Artillery." *Wall Street Journal* 11/20/88, B2.

Harris, R. G., and Mowery, D. C. (1990). "New Plans for Joint Ventures: The Results May Be an Unwelcome Surprise." *The American Enterprise*. September/October, 52–55.

Hounshell, D. A., and Smith, J. K. (1985). "Du Pont: Better Things for Better Living Through Research." Presented at "The R&D Pioneers," Hagley Museum and Library, Wilmington, Delaware, October 7.

Hounshell, D. A., and Smith, J. K., Jr. (1988). *Science and Corporate Strategy: Du Pont R&D, 1902–1980 Strategy*. New York: Cambridge University Press.

Jaikumar, R., (1989). "Postindustrial Manufacturing." *Harvard Business Review* 64: 69–76.

Jorde, T. M., and Teece, D. J. (1989). "Competition and Cooperation: Striking the Right Balance." *California Management Review* 31, 25–37.

Kaplan, A.D.H. (1964). *Big Business in a Competitive System*. Washington, D. C.: Brookings Institution.

Katz, M. L., and Ordover, J. A. (1990). "R&D Competition and Cooperation." *Brookings Papers on Economic Activity: Microeconomics 1990*, 137–92.

Kelley, M. R., and Brooks, H. (1933). *The State of Computerized Automation in U. S. Manufacturing*. Cambridge, MA: Center for Business and Government, Kennedy School of Government, Harvard University.

Lamoreaux, N. *The Great Merger Movement in American Business, 1895–1904*. New York: Cambridge University Press.

Lazonick, W. (1990). *Competitive Advantage on the Shop Floor*. Cambridge, MA: Harvard University Press.

Lorell, M. A. (1980). *Multinational Development of Large Aircraft: The European Experience*. Santa Monica, CA: RAND Corporation.

Malerba, F. (1985). *The Semiconductor Business*. Madison, WI: University of Wisconsin Press.

Markoff, J. (1989). "A Corporate Lag in Research Funds is Causing Worry." *New York Times* 1/23/89, A1.

Mowery, D. C. (1981). "The Emergence and Growth of Industrial Research in American Manufacturing, 1899–1946." Ph.D. diss., Stanford University.

Mowery, D. C. (1983). "Industrial Research, Firm Size, Growth, and Survival, 1921–1946." *Journal of Economic History* 43:953–80.

Mowery, D. C. (1984). "Firm Structure, Government Policy, and the Organization of Industrial Research: Great Britain and the United States, 1900–1950." *Business History Review* 58:504–31.

Mowery, D. C., ed. (1988). *International Collaborative Ventures in U. S. Manufacturing*. Cambridge, MA: Ballinger Publishers.

Mowery, D. C. and Rosenberg, N. (1989a). *Technology and the Pursuit of Economic Growth*. New York: Cambridge University Press.

Mowery, D. C., and Rosenberg, N. (1989b). "New Developments in U. S. Technology Policy: Implications for Competitiveness and International Trade Policy." *California Management Review* 27:107–24.

Mowery, D. C., and Steinmueller, W. E. (1991). "Government Policy and Industry Evolution in the U. S. Integrated Circuit Industry: What Lessons for Newly Industrializing Economies?" CCC

Working Paper, Center for Research in Management, University of California, Berkeley.

Mueller, W. F. (1962). "The Origins of the Basic Inventions Underlying Du Pont's Major Product and Process Innovation, 1920 to 1950." In *The Rate and Direction of Inventive Activity*. Princeton: Princeton University Press.

National Commission on Research, (1980). *Industry and the Universities*. Washington, D. C. National Commission on Research.

National Research Council (1982). "Research in Europe and the United States." In *Outlook for Science and Technology: The Next Five Years*. San Francisco: Freeman.

National Resources Planning Board (1942). *Research—A National Resource*, Vol. 1. Washington, D. C.: U. S. Government Printing Office.

National Science Board (1981). *Science Indicators, 1980*. Washington, D. C.: U. S. Government Printing Office.

National Science Board (1983). *Science Indicators, 1982*. Washington, D. C.: U. S. Government Printing Office.

National Science Foundation (1985). *Science and Technology Data Book*. Washington, D. C.: National Science Foundation.

Nelson, R. R. (1984). *High-Technology Policies: A Five Nation Comparison*. Washington, D. C.: American Enterprise Institute.

Nelson, R. R. (1990). "U. S. Industrial Competitiveness: Where Did It Come From and Where Did It Go?" *Research Policy* 19:117–32.

Okimoto, D. I., and Saxonhouse, G. R. (1987). "Technology and the Future of the Economy." In K. Yamamura and Y. Yasuba (eds.), *The Political Economy of Japan*, Vol. 1. *The Domestic Transformation*. Stanford: Stanford University Press.

Organization for Economic Cooperation and Development (OECD) (1984). *Industry and University: New Forms of Co-operation and Communication*. Paris: OECD.

Ostry, S. (1990). *The Political Economy of Policy Making: Trade and Innovation Policies in the Triad*. New York: Council on Foreign Relations.

Parker, W. N. (1972). "Agriculture." In L. E. Davis et al. (eds.), *An Economist's History of the United States*. New York: Harper & Row.

Patel, P., and Pavitt, K. (1986). "Measuring Europe's Technological Performance: Results and Prospects." In H. Ergas (ed.), *A European Future in High Technology?* Brussels: Center for European Policy Studies.

Perry, N. J. (1986). "The Surprising Power of Patents." *Fortune* 6/23/86, 57–63.

Perry, W. J. (1986). "Cultivating Technological Innovation." In R. Landau and N. Rosenberg (eds.), *The Positive Sum Strategy*. Washington, D. C.: National Academy Press.

Pisano, G. P., Shan, W., and Teece, D. J. (1988). "Joint Ventures and Collaboration in the Biotechnology Industry." In D. C. Mowery (ed.), *Inter-

national Collaborative Ventures in U. S. Manufacturing*. Cambridge, MA: Ballinger.

Pollack, A. (1990). "Technology Company Gets $4 Million U. S. Investment." *New York Times* 4/10/90, C17.

Pursell, C. (1977). "Science Agencies in World War II: The OSRD and its Challengers." In N. Reingold (ed.), *The Sciences in the American Context*. Washington, D. C.: Smithsonian Institution.

Reich, R. B., and Mankin, E. (1986). "Joint Ventures with Japan Give Away Our Future." *Harvard Business Review* 64:78–86.

Reid, P. P. (1989). "Private and Public Regimes: International Cartelization of the Electrical Equipment Industry in an Era of Hegemonic Change, 1919–1939." Unpublished Ph.D. dissertation, Johns Hopkins School of Advanced International Studies.

Rodgers, T. J. (1990). "Landmark Messages from the Microcosm." *Harvard Business Review* January–February, 24–30.

Rosenberg, N. (1972). *Technology and American Economic Growth*. New York: Harper & Row.

Rosenberg, N., and Steinmueller, W. E. (1988). "Why Can't Americans Learn to be Better Imitators?" *American Economic Review* 78(2):229–34.

Rosenbloom, R. S. (1985). "The R&D Pioneers, Then and Now." Presented at "The R&D Pioneers," Hagley Museum and Library, Wilmington, Delaware, October 7.

Saxonhouse, G. R. (1982). "Japanese High Technology, Government Policy, and Evolving Comparative Advantage in Goods and Services" presented at the Japanese Political Economy Research Conference, Honolulu, Hawaii.

Saxonhouse, G. R. (1986). "Why Japan is Winning." *Issues in Science and Technology* 3:50–62.

Scherer, F. M. (1983). "R&D and Declining Productivity Growth." *American Economic Review* 73: 215–18.

Schmookler, J. (1957). "Inventors Past and Present." *Review of Economics and Statistics* 39: 321–33.

Schumpeter, J. A. (1954). *Capitalism, Socialism and Democracy*, 3d ed. New York, Harper & Row.

Sharp, M. (1989). "European Countries in Science-Based Competition: The Case of Biotechnology." DRC Discussion Paper #72, SPRU, University of Sussex.

Stigler, G. J. (1968). "Monopoly and Oligopoly by Merger." In G. J. Stigler (ed.), *The Organization of Industry*. Homewood, IL: Irwin.

Sturchio, J. L. (1985). "Experimenting with Research: Kenneth Mees, Eastman Kodak, and the Challenges of Diversification." Presented at "The R&D Pioneers," Hagley Museum and Library, Wilmington, Delaware, October 7.

Swann, J. P. (1988). *Academic Scientists and the Pharmaceutical Industry*. Baltimore, MD: Johns Hopkins University Press.

Taylor, G. D., and Sudnik, P. E. (1984). *Du Pont and

the International Chemical Industry. Boston: Twayne.

Thackray, A., Sturchio, J. L., Carroll, P. T., and Bud, R. (1985). *Chemistry in America, 1876–1976: Historical Indicators.* Dordrecht: Reidel.

Thorelli, H. B. (1954). *Federal Antitrust Policy.* Baltimore, MD: Johns Hopkins University Press.

Tilton, J. E. (1971). *The International Diffusion of Technology: The Case of Transistors.* Washington, D. C.: Brookings Institution.

U. S. Bureau of the Census (1975). *Historical Statistics of the United States: Colonial Times to 1970,* Vol. 1. Washington, D. C.: U. S. Government Printing Office.

U. S. Bureau of the Census (1987). *1987 Statistical Abstract of the United States.* Washington, D. C.: U. S. Government Printing Office.

U. S. Congressional Office of Technology Assessment (1981). *An Assessment of the United States Food and Agricultural Research System.* Washington, D. C.: U. S. Government Printing Office.

U. S. Congressional Office of Technology Assessment (1986). *Technology, Public Policy, and the Changing Structure of American Agriculture.* Washington, D. C.: U. S. Government Printing Office.

Utterback, J. M., and Murray, A. E. (1977). "The Influence of Defense Procurement and Sponsorship of Research and Development on the Development of the Civilian Electronics Industry." Center for Policy Alternatives working paper # 77-5, M.I.T.

Walton, R. E., and McKersie, R. B. (1989). "Managing New Technology and Labor Relations: An Opportunity for Mutual Influence." In D. C. Mowery and B. E. Henderson, eds., *The Challenge of New Technology to Labor-Management Relations.* Washington, D. C.: U. S. Department of Labor.

Weart, S. (1979). "The Physics Business in America, 1919–1940." In N. Reingold (ed.), *The Sciences in the American Perspective.* Washington, D. C.: Smithsonian Institution.

White House Science Council (1988). *High-Temperature Superconductivity: Perseverance and Cooperation on the Road to Commercialization.* Washington, D. C.: Office of Science and Technology Policy.

Wise, G. (1985). "R&D at General Electric, 1878–1985." Presented at "The R&D Pioneers," Hagley Museum and Library, Wilmington, Delaware, October 7.

Wolf, J. (1989). "Europeans Fear Obstacles by U. S. on Advanced TV." *Wall Street Journal* 5/31/89, A16.

3

The Japanese System of Innovation: Past, Present, and Future

HIROYUKI ODAGIRI
AKIRA GOTO

It was commonly believed that the history of the Japanese economy was that of a country desperately trying to catch up with technologically advanced nations. When Japan opened its country around the time of the Meiji Restoration of 1868 following more than two centuries of seclusionism, the leaders had to realize how much Japan was behind Western countries in many aspects of technology. Naturally, the government made efforts to import superior technology, hire engineers from abroad, educate its people, and encourage the entrepreneurs to assimilate foreign technologies and apply them in Japanese factories. In addition, the determination to catch up in terms of military capacity gave the government a strong incentive to support technological advances and make domestic procurement possible. Such a catch-up process has been observed in many late-developing countries, such as Prussia and Russia in the nineteenth century or South Korea and Taiwan in recent decades. Japan's experience was by no means unusual and neither were the policies taken by the government.

However, one cannot attribute Japan's "success" solely to the latecomer advantage or to government policies because neither of these can lead to successful economic development unless the private sector—investors, managers, engineers, workers—is willing and able to respond to the opportunities open to them. In fact, at the time of the Meiji Restoration, entrepreneurs appeared in various industries and most people had been sufficiently educated to read, write, and count. The willingness to start an unfamiliar business and ability to assimilate new technology were present, and these were the main moving forces behind Japan's development. It is also noted that even under the seclusionism during the Tokugawa (Edo) era, technological importation did take place (though not on a large scale) and indigenous technologies and skills were gradually developed. One aim of this chapter is to investigate the conditions necessary for successful catch-up by studying the development of Japanese industries and technologies by means of both a general historical description and industrial cases. Another aim is to study how Japanese businesses have been (and are) behaving and organizing, because such a micro aspect provides an important key to understanding the Japanese innovation system.

The paper is separated into four parts. The first section gives a historical overview of Japan's technological advance from past to present. The second section discusses the technological development of three industries—iron and steel, electrical and communication equipment, and automobiles. The next section discusses the present Japanese management system, since understanding the managerial aspects of Japanese firms is indispensable to understanding why the firms are motivated to innovate and how they maintain efficiency in innovation. The final section concludes the chapter by discussing future prospects.

FROM PAST TO PRESENT

The Tokugawa Era and Before: Up to 1868

Major technology importation before the Tokugawa era (1603–1868) took place twice. The first is from the seventh to ninth century when the emperor's government sent envoys to China and immigration was frequent from China and Korea. The second is the sixteenth century, particularly when guns were first introduced by the Portuguese. This was the period of civil war and the strong demand for guns caused a number of blacksmiths to start producing guns either by copying or with the help of Portuguese gunsmiths. The technological level in guns, ships, and other arms production soon caught up with the West.

The Tokugawa government, fearing that Christians would disobey their rule, secluded the country in 1639 and restricted foreign trade to the Chinese and the Dutch. Thus the only Western contact for Japanese was through a number of Dutchmen allowed to live in Nagasaki in Kyushu, an island in the southwest. The Tokugawa government monopolized trade, though evidence suggests that some of the powerful feudal lords under the Tokugawa rule did trade with the Chinese and other foreigners. With the request of the government the Dutch provided information on foreign affairs and science regularly, some of which were diffused to other lords. The Dutch in Nagasaki were also a source of information on many aspects of science and technology, such as medical science, biology, and geography. Several Dutch books were translated into Japanese, and a number of Japanese studied with Dutch doctors or other scientists living in the Dutch quarters of Nagasaki. Thus the seclusionism by no means implied a complete seclusion from foreign scientific and technological information. Actually, the accumulation of Western knowledge through the Dutch can be assumed to have contributed to a rapid absorption of the Western economic and technological system when the Tokugawa government opened the country to non-Dutch Western countries in 1854. For instance, the first Western-style iron furnace was made by a *samurai* who had studied with a Dutch book.

In terms of indigenous technology too, the Tokugawa era was hardly a static period. Because of the importance of agriculture and mining for the feudal lords' finances, increases in productivity in these areas were encouraged and many improvements were made and diffused. Because of the steep flow of rivers, climatic conditions (rainy season in June and typhoons in summer–autumn), and the importance of water in rice crops, much investment was directed toward improving rivers and making irrigation systems. Consequently, the technological level in civil engineering is believed to have been very high.

Machine engineering was another area for indigenous technology at the time. The innovators were called *karakuri* masters because karakuri, a moving mechanism, is the most essential part of any machine. These mechanisms were applied to many sorts of machines and tools, ranging from dolls and clocks to textile looms and rice-polishing machines.[1] Again, we will show later that there was a continuous development from such indigenous technology to imported Western technology after the Meiji Restoration. H. Tanaka, probably the most important karakuri master toward the end of the Tokugawa era, became a pioneer in the electrical equipment industry, and S. Toyoda (born a year before the Restoration) invented internationally copied looms.

Therefore, although the Japanese failed to invent steam engines, among other things, their technological level was not too much behind the West. This fact should be emphasized because it is in marked difference from the cases of many developing countries today. In addition, the educational level was high—probably higher in elementary education than the United States, Britain, France, and Germany, though lower in higher education because in these countries science education in universities had started by the early nineteenth century.

Basically there were two school systems. The first was the schools owned by feudal local governments, which were usually compulsory to the children of samurais (i.e., the employees of respective local governments). Many of them also admitted the children of wealthier farmers and merchants. The second was private schools, called *terakoya,* since many of them were run by Buddhist temples (*tera*). The length of education was various but, most typically, went from the age of 6 to 12, similar to the present elementary school system. They mainly taught reading, writing, and the use of *soroban* (abacus) to calculate. In addition to these schools for children, there were a number of private or public higher education systems. Some of these taught Japanese or Chinese studies, for instance, Confucianism. However, there were private schools teaching medical science using Dutch books. The best known of the latter case was "Tekijuku," a private school in Osaka taught by K. Ogata, who had learned Dutch medical science in Nagasaki. Among his students were Y. Fukuzawa, who later introduced Western democratic thoughts to Japan and established the first private university, Keio, and M. Ohmura, who later designed the Meiji military system (but was assassinated before the system was completed).

There were not many terakoyas and other schools in the early Tokugawa era but they became more and more popular, and, according to a very rough estimate, there were almost ten thousand such schools in Japan toward the end of the era. Many of them were small with 10 or fewer children, but there were schools with more than 500 in large cities such as Edo (Tokyo) and Kyoto. The ratio of school enrollment (or attendance) varies among estimates and among regions, ranging from about 25 to almost 100% for boys and a lower percentage for girls (Umihara, 1988). These estimates may be misleading because they may include those children enrolled as pupils but who seldom came. Nevertheless, the ratio of, let us say, 50% under the noncompulsory system is surprisingly high and shows the eagerness of parents to invest in child education. This fact suggests that the literacy rate in Japan in the seventeenth and eighteenth century was likely higher than in Europe and America. The introduction of the public education system in the Meiji era would not have been so smooth were it not for this wide educational background.

The Meiji Era: 1868–1911

The end of seclusionism in 1854 and the inauguration of a nonfeudal central government following the Meiji Restoration of 1868 prompted the Japanese government and the public at large to import advanced foreign technology and to catch up with the Western countries economically and militarily. The government thus started an organized effort to "modernize" the country, including the provision of infrastructures for transportation, communication, utilities, education, and finance.

Generally speaking, diffusion of science and technology from one country (or countries) to another can be made by transferring written information (e.g., books, papers, and drawings), people (e.g., hiring foreigners and sending Japanese to study abroad), goods (e.g., importing machines and plants), and capital (i.e., foreign direct investment). All these methods were used in Meiji Japan. Particularly in the case of importing social systems, hire (*yatoi*) of foreign teachers and advisors was common. For instance, when the Meiji government started to establish a national system of education including compulsory elementary education, an American, D. Murray, was hired as an advisor and gave American influences to the system, though these influences were diluted when nationalistic education was later emphasized.

It took about three decades of trial and error before the government could establish a countrywide elementary education system. In 1874 2 years after the government started the effort, there were about twenty thousand schools, less than half of what the government had planned. Some of these schools were converted from terakoyas and taught by former terakoya teachers. The enrollment ratio was 46% for boys and 17% for girls. By 1904 when the compulsory 6-year education system was finally established, the ratio had increased to 99% for boys and 96% for girls. Thus illiteracy among the youth was nearly absent by the beginning of this century. The secondary education system also became commonly available and by 1920 more than half of the children out of elementary schools proceeded to 2-year or 5-year secondary schools (Kaigo, 1971).

For the higher education system, particularly in the field of technology and engineering education, a British influence was introduced. Kobusho (the Ministry of Industries), itself started with the advice of a British railway engineer, hired a British, H. Dyer, to make plans for an engineering college. In 1873, Kogakuryo (the College of Engineering) was established with Dyer's plan and eight more British professors were hired besides Dyer himself who became the head. With the eagerness and high quality of both the instructors and the students, the college was quite successful. It hired more foreign (mostly British) professors and then started to replace them with Japanese graduates from the College. In 1886, the College merged with another college, established by the Tokugawa government to teach science and technology with the help of the Dutch, French, and German, and became the Engineering Department of Imperial University (later renamed the University of Tokyo). The College and the University produced graduates who later founded many of the major Japanese manufacturing companies as we will later show.

It is noteworthy that Dyer later exported his Japanese experience of engineering education to his hometown, Glasgow. He had been recommended to the Japanese government by a professor at the University of Glasgow, and came to Japan at the age of 25 right after receiving a master's degree there. The program he made for Kogakuryo emphasized the interaction between classroom studies and on-site training at the laboratory works he made within Kogakuryo as well as Kobusho's works. This balance between the two aspects of education was lacking in European schools at the time and Dyer's originality should be noted. He left in 1882 to go back to Glasgow and made efforts to introduce a similar engineering education program when a technical college was founded there. Apparently, the Japanese government emphasized engineering education at the time when more developed countries regarded pure science as superior to engineering. This background gave Dyer an opportunity to experiment with his ideas on engineering education and, with his Japanese experience, he persuaded his people of its importance.

During the early Meiji era, in particular the 1870s and early 1880s, the government built and owned plants and factories in industries such as mining, railroad, shipbuilding, machinery, and textile, because it was still difficult for the private sector to finance the required investment and take risks. In addition, personnel with advanced Western technological knowledge were scarce in the private sector. However, the government's investment program in industries was neither quantitatively spectacular compared, say, to that of today's developing countries nor always successful. In fact, most government-owned factories suffered losses and, with the tight government budget, were gradually privatized and sold to emerging private entrepreneurs (mostly merchants and ex-samurais).

The government retained plants in military-related industries, such as shipbuilding, aircraft, munitions, and steel, and in public utilities including telecommunication. The military-related production occupied a significant portion of Japan's economy at the time, because the Meiji government was keen to build up its military capacity to deal with the threat of Russia and other countries that were colonizing China. In 1907, the largest operation in machinery industry (including shipbuilding, vehicles, general machinery, tools, and parts) in terms of the number of blue-collar workers was the navy shipyard in Kure with about 21,500 employees, followed by another navy shipyard and two arsenals (Sawai, 1990). The largest private plant, Mitsubishi's Nagasaki Shipyard, ranked fifth with less than 10,000 employees, whose important customer was again the navy. The military-owned plants were also a center of technological development. They hired a large percentage of scarce engineers and imported advanced machinery from abroad. Their technology was subsequently transferred to the private sector as the engineers and skilled workers moved from the military plants to the private sector, especially during the disarmament period following the Russo-Japanese War of 1904–1905.

The military not only produced goods within its own shipyards and arsenals, but also procured them from the private sector. Since the military, for obvious defense reasons, preferred to procure goods domestically, procurement gave domestic producers in shipbuilding, steel, machines, electrical equipment, and so on, who were under competitive pressure from larger and technically advanced foreign firms, a chance to increase their production and accumulate knowledge through experience. It should be noted that Unequal Treaties the Tokugawa government was forced to sign in 1858 with the United States, the United Kingdom, the Netherlands, France, and Russia deprived the government of the right to set tariffs to imports. In 1902, for instance, the proportion of tariffs in government revenue was 5% in Japan versus 21% in the United Kingdom and 45% in the United States. Thus, until 1911 when the treaties were revised, the government had little means to protect domestic producers from foreign competitors except preferential procurement.

The economy started to grow after about two decades of the Restoration (see Table 3.1). GNP more than doubled in the 30-year period from 1885 to 1914, the year World War I started. In terms of industrial composition, food processing and textile were the largest industries before the turn of the century. Then metal, machinery, chemical, and other heavy industries started to grow fast. During the first four decades of the twentieth century, these heavy industries grew at an annual rate of more than 10% whereas the manufacturing industries as a whole grew at about 6%. Their growth was particularly rapid in the 1920s and the 1930s, and their share in the manufacturing sector exceeded 50% in the 1930s.

Technological progress was an important source of this growth. According to Minami (1981), nearly 70% of the growth of the private mining and manufacturing sector was accounted for by the "residual" factors that include technological progress. This technological progress came from both indigenous (traditional and domestic) technology and the technology imported from advanced countries. Indigenous technology was important not only on its own, particularly in traditional industries, but also in providing the ability to select among the technologies available in developed countries, and in adapting and assimilating them to fit domestic conditions. This fact was most notable in the textile industry, the second largest manufacturing industry at the time (next to food processing) and the largest exporting industry before World War II. The case study of iron and steel industry will provide another example.

This fact notwithstanding, the role of indigenous technology was limited in modern industries, such as metal and machinery, where imported technology played a far greater role. As discussed earlier, technology transfer from abroad was made through many channels. Many foreign engineers and specialists were hired, though they were gradually replaced by the Japanese educated domestically at the above-mentioned College of Engineering and other schools and those who had studied abroad and came back. Other channels of technology transfer were importation of advanced machinery (and reverse engineering), licensing agreements, and foreign direct investment into Japan. The latter two increased since the turn of the century because the government liberalized foreign direct investment and also joined the Paris Convention, though the patent system itself was introduced as early as 1885. The significant role these various means of technology transfer played in Japan's industrial and technological development will be discussed in more detail in the case studies.

The number of patents granted during July 1885 to February 1902 was 4817 (Patent Office, 1955). In comparison, the number was 27,136 in 1902 in the United States, 13,714 in the United Kingdom, 12,026 in France, and 10,610 in Germany. Hence the number of patents in Japan was hardly comparable with the Western countries. Among these 4817 patents, 2175 (45%) were related to machinery, 728 (15%) to chemicals, 52 (1%) to electric equipment, and 1862 (39%) to miscellaneous. Therefore, insofar as we can infer from the number of patents, R&D in the machinery industry seems to have been relatively active around the turn of the century.

Table 3.1. Gross National Expenditures and Production: 1875–1940

	Levels (at 1934–1936 prices)					Annual Growth Rates (%)				Composition (%)				
	1875	1885	1900	1915	1940	1875–1885	1885–1900	1900–1915	1915–1940	1875	1885	1900	1915	1940
Population (thousand)	35036	38176	44056	53110	71933	0.9	1	1.3	1.2	100	100	100	100	100
GNE (million yen)		3852	6238	8522	22848		3.3	2.1	4		100	100	100	100
Personal consumption expenditure		3284	5270	6806	13389		3.2	1.7	2.7		85.3	84.5	79.9	58.6
Government consumption expenditure		283	538	769	3377		4.4	2.4	6.1		7.3	8.6	9	14.8
Gross domestic fixed capital formation		346	703	1176	7070		4.8	3.5	7.4		9	11.3	13.8	30.9
Surplus on current account		−61	−279	−224	−988		10.7	−1.5	6.1		−1.6	−4.5	−2.6	−4.3
Exports and factor income from abroad		68	275	1020	3973		9.8	9.1	5.6		1.8	4.4	12	17.4
Imports and factor income paid abroad		129	554	1244	4961		10.2	5.5	5.7		3.3	8.9	14.6	21.7
GNE per Capita (yen)		101	142	160	318		2.3	0.8	2.8					
Production (million yen)														
Mining	7.1	21.3	90.3	290.6	763.7	11.6	10.1	8.1	3.9					
Coal	4	9.2	53.2	145.5	399.8	8.7	12.4	6.9	4.1					
Manufacturing	742.6	877.9	2101	4029.4	20210.2	1.7	6	4.4	6.7	100	100	100	100	100
Food	457.5	454	1018.5	1356.3	2634.7	−0.1	5.5	1.9	2.7	61.6	51.7	48.5	33.7	13
Textile	64.1	129.7	508.7	1133.6	3454.3	7.3	9.5	5.5	4.6	8.6	14.8	24.2	28.1	17.1
Chemicals	75.6	99.1	186.4	427.6	3342.3	2.7	4.3	5.7	8.6	10.2	11.3	8.9	10.6	16.5
Machines	4.9	12.2	68.9	362.2	5580.5	9.6	12.2	11.7	11.6	0.7	1.4	3.3	9	27.6
Iron and steel	2.3	3.2	5.8	89.1	2494.8	3.4	4	20	14.3	0.3	0.4	0.3	2.2	12.3
Nonferrous metals	6.1	13.8	22.7	145.4	556.2	8.5	3.4	13.2	5.5	0.8	1.6	1.1	3.6	2.8
Others	132.1	165.9	290	515.2	2147.4	2.3	3.8	3.9	5.9	17.8	18.9	13.8	12.8	10.6

Source: Estimates of Long-Term Economic Statistics of Japan since 1868. K. Ohkawa, M. Shinohara, and M. Umemura (eds.), Tokyo: Toyo Keizai Shinposha, 1988.

Between the Two World Wars: 1914–1945

It is reasonable to say that the Japanese economy took off around the time of World War I. As will be shown later, many companies in steel, machinery, chemical, and other heavy industries had been established by the mid-1910s and started growing. Also, the country's scientific and engineering base started to be formed. The education system, which had been expanded by this time to include several universities and other higher education institutions, started to supply many trained engineers. More and more skilled workers capable of handling advanced equipment became available. Some of them spun off with their acquired skills. Academic associations were formed and professional journals started. Access to foreign technological information became easier with the extended availability of foreign books and journals, and through trading companies.

To enhance the scientific and technological base further, various proposals were made by industrialists, policy-makers, the military, and scientists; for instance, the creation of basic research institutions, the increase in national industrial laboratories, and enhanced science and technology education. The industries felt a strong need to upgrade its scientific and technological capability to accommodate the growth of technology-based industries. World War I accelerated this trend, by convincing the military of the importance of high technology and the private sector's capability to contribute to national defense. In addition, the import of equipment and intermediate goods became difficult during the war, giving the private sector an incentive to produce previously imported advanced equipment and materials domestically, such as machine tools, various chemicals, aluminum, and steel. This fact further enhanced the need for advanced technology.

More universities and vocational schools were established by the public as well as the private sector. Several national research institutions were founded. Hiroshige (1973) counts 38 national research laboratories founded during 1914–1930 including those annexed to national universities and to the military. Some of them were founded by reorganizing existing laboratories or testing institutions. For instance, the Electric Research Institution was founded in 1918 by upgrading the laboratory within the Ministry of Communications, which dates back to 1873 when Kobusho started an experimental electrical factory within it.[2] In 1890 it had a staff of about 30 with 7 engineers, the rest being assistants and shop workers. It studied both technologies related to electric power and those related to communication; however, the major part of its duty was to test the equipment procured by the Ministry. Another example is the Industrial Research Institution established in 1900 with a staff of 20. By 1920 the staff had expanded to 220, including 48 researchers and engineers. It had five departments—inspection, chemistry [japan (a type of lacquer), matches, oil, and fat, etc.], ceramics, dye, and (since 1909) electrochemistry. Other research institutions present or established during this period include those studying measures, silk, geography, mining, fuel, and airplanes (within the navy) besides several institutions related to agriculture.

One of the largest and most productive research institutions established during this period was the Institute of Physical and Chemical Research (*Rikagaku Kenkyusho,* known as *Riken*). The proposal for Riken was first made by a chemist, J. Takamine, with the aim of fostering scientific progress and thereby contributing to industries. Thus the aim was not purely academic but also practical. After a long discussion involving businesses, the government, and the academics, it was established in 1917 with roughly half of the funds from the government and half from the private sector, and with a staff of 22, of whom 5 were full-time (including both researchers and supportive staff). In 4 years the staff increased to 63, with 30 full-time members. By 1945 it produced about 800 patents in Japan and 200 overseas. Some of them were developed to products, which Riken's subsidiary companies sold. These include chemical products, such as vitamins and photographic paper, and machinery, such as piston rings and measuring equipment. In terms of the contributions to the national economy, these products were hardly as major as, say, automobiles and electrical products.

To promote more basic research, the Science Council (*Gakujutsu Shinkokai*, known as *Gakushin*) was established in 1933 with funds from both the public and private sector. Its purpose was twofold: first, to increase research funds at universities and other research institutions, and second, to promote efficient research management by, for instance, encouraging interorganizational research collaboration. The research funds were granted both on an individual basis and on a project basis. In the beginning, most grants were given on an individual basis but, by 1942, more than 80% were given on a project basis, with each project pursued by members from a number of institutions. Among the grants given on a project basis in 1942, about two-thirds were given to the projects in the field of engineering, and the rest to medical science, natural science, social science, and humanities. The top three projects in terms of research grants were jet fuel, wireless communication, and atomic nucleus. The emphasis on military-related technology was apparent.[3]

Companies also started their own R&D laboratories. In 1923, there were 162 private R&D laboratories affiliated with companies, cooperatives, and other private foundations. Of these 71 were in chemistry (including pharmaceuticals, dye, paint, rubber, cement, ceramics, and paper), 27 in metals and machinery, and 24 in food. Among the large companies having their own laboratories were Shibaura Seisakusho and Tokyo Denki (later to be merged to become Toshiba), Mitsubishi Shipbuilding (later Mitsubishi Heavy Industries), Nippon Kokan (now NKK), Oji Paper, and Takeda, Tanabe, and Sankyo (all in pharmaceuticals). However, they include testing or development sections within factories and how many of them deserve to be called laboratories in the present sense is unknown. Most of them were small.[4]

After the breakout of the Chinese-Japanese War in 1937, the production of heavy industries increased rapidly as the expansion of armaments speeded up. Compared to the 1934–1936 average, the production of steel more than doubled and machinery almost quadrupled by 1944. The share in total manufacturing production of heavy industries (machinery, metal, and chemical) increased from 33.9% in 1931 to 55.8% in 1937, and then to 70.2% in 1942.[5]

The R&D activity also increased. Although the reliability of the data may be questioned, one survey in 1930 shows the number of research organizations (including departments and institutions within universities, government laboratories, Riken, and laboratories affiliated with private companies) to be 349 in 1930, which spent 30 million yen or 0.22% of the GNP.[6] In 1942, the number of private research organizations was 711, employing a staff of 33,400 and spending 590 million yen or approximately 1% of the GNP. In addition, there were 443 public research organizations (including university departments, etc.) employing a staff of 16,160 and spending 296 million yen.[7]

These increased production and R&D activities enabled some of the Japanese manufacturing industries to start building world-class production facilities and developing advanced products; for instance, large-scale furnace and open hearth for steel production, aircrafts, ships, alloys, and communication equipment. However, even these industries depended on American and European technology in many aspects, and imported technology actively until the late 1930s. The stoppage of technological flow from abroad during World War II had a serious impact, and the increase in R&D efforts at the time reflects Japan's desperate effort to fill the void created by this stoppage. Consequently, despite the increased R&D effort, the technological gap from the West widened in such key munitions industries as aircraft and shipbuilding, which had almost caught up with the world technological frontier before the war. This gap partly explains Japan's defeat in the war.[8]

The Post-World War II Era: 1945 to the early 1970s

The impact of World War II on the Japanese economy was, needless to say, devastating. The production index of the manufacturing industry in 1946 fell to 26% of the prewar peak level in 1934–1936 and the supply of food to 51%. Many of the plants and equipment had been destroyed by bombing during the war and others were destroyed or taken away by the Allied Forces. Still, more than two-thirds of the production capacity had been left intact in most of the heavy industries. The R&D resources that had been increased before and during the war, and the many workers who had worked in the munitions plants and gained production experience returned to civilian production. Of course, not all of these resources were useful. Some of the facilities had been hastily built or were hastily converted with little use after the war, and some of the R&D knowledge or production skills were obsolete. Yet, as Japan's military spending after the war was practically zero, most of these resources could be transferred for the purpose of civilian production.

Owing to various drastic economic measures and the boom during the Korean War, the manufacturing production regained the prewar peak level within 5 years. From the mid-1950s to 1973 (the year of the first oil crisis), the economy grew at an annual rate of approximately 10%. Various growth accounting studies show that this fast growth, which lasted almost two decades, was the result of a high rate of capital accumulation combined with technological progress.

As implied at the end of the previous subsection, after the end of the war Japan had to realize that it had again been left behind. The process of catching up started again. As in the Meiji era, it followed a dual track: encouraging the importation of advanced technology and promoting a domestic technology base. To make an effective technology transfer, the government allocated its scarce foreign currency selectively to those firms capable of adapting and improving imported technology.[9] This gave the government, notably the Ministry of International Trade and Industry (MITI), a strong power over the industries. In fact, most of the firms with adequate technological background were given the allocation of foreign currency. However, a few years delay often occurred and, as Peck and Tamura (1976, p. 553) said, "in a fast-growing economy it can be of importance whether government policy delays or speeds up the use of a particular technology by only three or four years."

Nevertheless, despite the effect this control undoubtedly had on individual firms, it seems unlikely to have affected the overall pattern and pace of technology importation in a major way. A more profound influence, in our view, was provided by the restriction of import and direct investment because the only way for foreign firms to exploit their technological superiority was to sell their technology, even though they might have preferred to export the product or start their own production in Japan. That is, Japan's restriction of trade and investment seems to have made it possible for Japan to import technology only. Therefore, the trade and capital liberalization in the 1960s and 1970s inevitably caused MITI to lose its control over technology and industries in general.

Another important consequence was that the Japanese manufacturing industries remained mostly in the hands of Japanese shareholders, in marked contrast with European countries where many U. S. firms started their own businesses or purchased existing European firms as their subsidiaries. There are exceptions such as IBM, NCR, and a number of petroleum refiners, which established their subsidiaries in Japan using the "grandfather rights" to resume their pre-World War II operations or using the "yen-based stock purchase system" that allowed foreign direct investment into Japan with strict conditions during 1958–1963. However, major firms in the automobile, electric equipment, and steel industries remained Japanese owned and the stakes foreign firms had in Japanese electric and communication equipment companies in fact decreased during the postwar period. Even after the capital liberalization in the 1970s, foreign direct investment into Japan remained low. Thus the management of most Japanese firms has been, and in large part still is, not exposed to the pressure of the international capital market. The consequence of this on corporate motivation will be discussed later.

It is difficult to evaluate these policies. On the one hand, it is fair to assume that they have substantially benefitted domestic firms. On the other hand, they may have lessened market competition by restricting entry of foreign producers either through import or investment. In addition, the restriction of foreign direct investment prevented the inflow of capital when the Japanese economy needed it. Even though the intense competition among domestic firms, and the high saving ratio after the 1950s mitigated these negative effects, the overall effect has to be assessed in a broader context.[10]

We also note that this government policy was feasible only because there were many firms eager to import technology in expectation of a high return. Since these technology-importing firms could start manufacturing those products that had been imported previously, import substitution took place reducing imports and eventually increasing exports, thereby enabling Japan to economize on precious foreign currency. The amount of foreign currency thus saved by far exceeded the payments to technology importation. Through the 1950s and 1960s the limited availability of foreign currency worked as a ceiling to economic growth, that is, economic booms could not be sustained because of acute shortage of foreign currency in boom years when imports increased. Technology importation had the long-run effect of pushing this ceiling upward and making fast economic growth sustainable.

In evaluating the role imported technology played in Japan's development, one should also note the following two facts. First, trade in technology became very active after the war in every country. Although Japan's payment to technology importation (64 billion yen) was the largest among major countries even as recently as 1988, its percentage to GNP, 0.17%, was about the same as in France (0.18%), Germany (0.17%), and the United Kingdom (0.16%), though larger than the United States (0.04%) (STA, 1990). That is, under the GATT-IMF regime, trade in both goods and technology increased worldwide and Japan is hardly peculiar in this regard, though, no doubt, it was one of the major beneficiaries of this trend.

Second, technology transfer would not have succeeded without the prewar technology base and a rapid postwar increase in R&D expenditures. As discussed earlier, heavy industries, such as machines and steel, had a large share in the 1930s and early 1940s, owing partly to the military build-up. When the war ended, a large number of researchers, engineers, and skilled workers were released from such production and could be utilized in civilian production. As for the contribution of domestic R&D effort to technology transfer, empirical findings indicate that those who imported technology also invested in their own R&D.[11] Domestic R&D was essential to enable firms to evaluate, adapt, and improve imported technology.

Emphasis on Own Innovation: Since the 1960s

As Japan became a serious competitor in the international market, the terms of technology importation became less favorable. In addition, as Japanese industries advanced technologically and became world-class, the backlog of technologies available for import decreased. Consequently, during the 1960s when the Japanese economy grew at a high rate and started to compete internationally, the need for increased efforts to develop its own technology became more urgent and government policies to promote domestic R&D began to be emphasized. However, the size of the incentives provided through tax breaks, subsidies, and low-interest loans were modest (see Table 3.2). In total, they amount to a little more than a hundred billion yen in 1983, or 2.6% of industrial R&D expenditures and 2.3% of industrial R&D expenditures plus payment to technology importation. Thus, financial incentives by the government to the private sector has been modest and doubtlessly smaller than in other countries where as much as a one-third of industrial R&D is financed by the government.

Table 3.2 also reveals a clear downward trend in the importance of subsidies: the proportion to industrial R&D was almost 8% in 1960, still lower than in other countries, but gradually declined to 2.6% in 1983. In parallel with the generally decreasing role of industrial policy in Japan's economic growth, government support to industrial R&D has been decreasing rather dramatically in the past two to three decades.

Private firms, under increased competition from other Japanese firms and from American and European firms in foreign and domestic markets (owing to liberated trade and direct investment), felt an urgent need to enhance their technological capability. Their R&D expenditures more than tripled in the latter half of the 1960s. Relative to these increased private efforts, the government policy measures were modest indeed and, in our opinion, most of the R&D projects the government supported would have taken place anyway.

One policy measure that has attracted considerable interest in the West is joint or cooperative research efforts based on the Act on the Mining and Manufacturing Industry Technology Research Association enforced in 1961. During 1961–1987, 87 such research associations (RAs) were formed. In 1983, there were 44 RAs of which 38 received subsidies of 33 billion yen, or about half of their total R&D expenditures

Table 3.2. Government Support to Industrial R&D in Japan[a,b] (in Billion Yen)

Year	(A) Total	(a) Subsidies and Research Contracts	(b) Preferential Tax Treatment	(c) Low Interest Rate Loan
1960	9.8	0.7	9.1	—
1965	16.4	3.1	13.3	—
1970	31.0	11.0	19.1	0.9
1975	64.7	29.8	33.0	1.9
1980	101.0	60.8	38.0	2.2
1983	117.7	58.7	57.0	2.0

Year	(B) R&D Expenditure by Industry	(A)/(B) (%)	(C) Payment for Technology Importation	(A)/(B + C) (%)
1960	124.4	7.88	34.2	6.18
1965	252.4	6.50	59.6	5.26
1970	823.3	3.77	155.1	3.17
1975	1684.8	3.84	211.3	3.41
1980	3142.3	3.21	326.2	2.91
1983	4560.1	2.58	493.8	2.33

[a]Adapted from Goto and Wakasugi (1988), Table 1.

[b]a is the amount of subsidies and research contracts. b is the amount of tax forgone through the preferential tax treatments to promote R&D. c is the interest payments savings due to the low interest rate loan to promote R&D. $A = (a) + (b) + (c)$.

Sources: (a) Somu-cho, "Kagaku gijyutsu kenkyu chosa hokoku" (Report on the Survey of Research and Development), each year.
(b) Documents submitted to Tax System Council.
(c) Estimated from Japan Development Bank documents.

(Wakasugi and Goto, 1985). Since the total government R&D subsidies were about 59 billion yen in the same year (see Table 3.2), we infer that more than one-half of them were supplied through RAs. This reflects an important aspect of RAs: for MITI, RAs have been a convenient way to distribute its subsidies to promote the technology MITI (and participating firms) believed important, most notably semiconductors and computers, and have been used to avoid favoring particular firms and to minimize the cost of supervising the use of subsidies. From this viewpoint, it is not surprising that only two of the 87 associations had joint research facilities; in all other cases, each member firm simply took its share of research funds and carried out the research in its own laboratory. Therefore, how coordinated the research really was among participating firms within each RA is doubtful except for a few cases.[12]

The effectiveness of these RAs in generating new technology is also doubtful. According to Wakasugi and Goto (1985) and Fujishiro (1988), RA's productivity as measured by the number of patents divided by its R&D expenditures was considerably lower than that of industries, though neither of these authors implies that it is the best measure of R&D efficiency.[13] Perhaps RAs were the product of the time of transition: the firms were then feeling a need to promote more long-range and large-scale, if not basic, research but were still unable, technologically and financially, to conduct it individually. Their role has been declining as more and more collaborative research activities are now carried out by research institutions funded jointly by companies or under intercompany technology agreements.

The first oil crisis of 1973 ended the high-growth era. Around the same time, Japan adopted a flexible exchange system, resulting in a major appreciation of yen. The annual growth rate fell from roughly 10% of the high-growth era to less than 5% in the 1970s and 1980s. There were two consequences of these drastic changes on technology. First, developing energy-saving production processes became one of the major targets in R&D for many businesses. Such R&D, together with the accumulation of incremental innovation at production sites, made it possible for Japanese manufacturing industries to increase energy efficiency. For instance, the steel industry developed the so-called oilless steel-making process and reduced energy consumption drastically. This shift in emphasis toward energy R&D was also apparent in government R&D: the proportion of energy R&D among total government R&D funding increased from 7.5% in 1975 to 16.3% in 1985 (National Science Foundation, 1988, p. 55). The Sunshine Project aimed at developing alternative energy-generating technology and the Moonlight Project to develop energy-conserving technology started in 1974 and 1978, respectively.

Second, the entire industrial structure shifted toward an energy-saving, technology-intensive, and high value-added one. Energy-intensive industries scaled down and high-technology industries expanded rapidly. The striking example of the former was the aluminum smelting industry. Japan was the second largest aluminum-producing country in the world in the early 1970s. After a decade and two oil crises, it had been virtually wiped out while the import had soared (Goto, 1988). By contrast, high-technology industries—semiconductors, computers, fine chemicals, and such—grew rapidly.

Through the 1970s to 1980s, therefore, Japanese firms had to cope with the drastically changing environment. Yet, after the two oil crises and two sharp appreciations of yen (65% against the U. S. dollar in 1977–1978, and 92% in 1986–1988), Japanese firms found their share to have considerably increased in the world export market. This increase was most prominent in high-technology products where the Japanese share rose from 7.2% in 1965 to 19.8% in 1986. We may attribute this success in Japan's adaptation to changing environment to two factors. The first is the high rate of investment in R&D and in plants and equipment. The R&D expenditures grew 4.4 times from 1973 to 1987 and, as a proportion to GNP, from 2.0 to 2.8%. The ratio of investment in plants and equipment to GNP fell gradually after the first oil crisis from about 19% in 1970, but remained at 14 to 15%, and then grew in the 1980s to reach 19% again in 1990. The amount of investment in plants and equipment in Japan even surpassed that of the United States, whose economy is 1.8 times larger than Japan's. These active investments in R&D and in plants and equipment reinforced each other, increasing productivity and improving product quality. In addition, as the second factor, the management system of Japanese firms contributed to their adapting to the rapidly changing environment, as we shall discuss later.

With increasing strength of the Japanese firms in the world market, the focus of the science and technology policy is gradually shifting from the promotion of industrial technological capability to emphasize such new issues as the promotion of basic research and the globalization of innovation. These issues will be discussed in the final section.

TECHNOLOGICAL DEVELOPMENT IN THREE INDUSTRIES

In this section, we will describe the development of three industries, iron and steel, electrical and communication equipment, and automobiles, since the Meiji era; this will complement the general historical description previously given.[14]

Iron and Steel

In 1901, the government constructed Yawata Steel Works (and then ran it) wholly dependent on German technology. This case, it has been argued, epitomizes the two salient characteristics of Japan's industrial and technological development—government support and technology importation. Is such an argument justified? Are these two characteristics really evident? A close examination of the history of the iron and steel industry actually gives a different picture.

The first attempt to produce iron and steel using Western technology was made almost a half century before Yawata. This was during the 1850s, still in the Tokugawa era but after the government opened the country to the United States, the United Kingdom, France, and Russia under military threat from these countries. Before this period, iron and steel had been produced from iron sand and charcoal using an indigenous small-scale production method. However, with the threat of Western countries, the Tokugawa government and some of the powerful feudal lords considered it urgent to construct strong cannons. Because this created a demand for quality steel, they constructed reverberating furnaces copying the technology described in a Dutch book (an example of technology import through the Dutch during the Tokugawa era) but entirely with Japanese hands. These furnaces produced wrought iron on a small scale out of pig iron made with indigenous technology. One of the engineers who made these furnaces, T. Ohshima, proposed building a blast furnace to produce pig iron. Ohshima was a samurai of Nambu Clan, northeast of Honshu. Nambu had an iron mine and thus a history of iron making. Adding to this background, Ohshima went to Nagasaki to study Dutch and learned the steel- and cannon-making technology with the book mentioned earlier. He thus knew both indigenous and Western technology, and, with the financial support of private investors, constructed a small blast furnace in Kamaishi, a city near an iron mine in Nambu. Although the production met with difficulties at first (in firebricks, ventilation, etc.), in about a year the production started to go smoothly and several more furnaces were built.

In 1874, the Meiji government decided to build a modern furnace in Kamaishi and hired Ohshima and a German engineer to plan it. The German engineer proposed building a large-scale modern mill (with a railway system to carry the product and iron ore) around two imported furnaces. Ohshima opposed this plan and instead proposed building five relatively small furnaces and using more modest transportation method. The government, which never questioned the superiority of Western technology, rejected Ohshima's plan and imported furnaces, railway cars, and other equipment from Britain and hired British engineers to construct a mill based on the German engineer's plan. It started the operation in 1890, immediately met with difficulties, and was closed down after 196 days of operation. The cause was obvious. At first, the mill used charcoal but, after a short while, the supply of such a large quantity of charcoal was found out to be impossible. It thus decided to switch to coke as fuel but the coke it could obtain did not have a sufficiently high quality. Needless to say, technology cannot be free from social and economic conditions. Apparently, neither the European engineers nor the Meiji government was aware of this simple principle in the belief of superior Western technology. By contrast, Ohshima, who knew the way iron had been produced by that time, was aware of the conditions surrounding iron production in Japan.

Kamaishi restarted its iron production several years after the government closed the mill. C. Tanaka, a private entrepreneur who bought the mill from the government, restarted the production not with the big furnace but with a new small furnace (built after Ohshima's technology). Again several improvements had to be made before the operation became commercially viable, but he could expand the production gradually and in 1894, with the help of K. Noro, a professor at the Imperial University (now University of Tokyo), repaired and improved the British-built big furnaces and succeeded in restarting them.

The lesson of Kamaishi appears to have been forgotten by the time the government built an integrated steel mill in Yawata, Kyushu. The government had been experimenting with steel production within the arsenals using the pig iron produced in Kamaishi or with traditional technology, and imported iron. However, from the military viewpoint it was considered necessary to produce steel using a modern integrated technology and on a large scale. Thus the government decided in 1896 to build a mill in Yawata and let M. Ohshima (T. Ohshima's son) make the plans. Ohshima had studied in Germany and decided to build the mill with German technology, commissioning a German company to make a detailed plan, buying German equipment, and hiring German engineers for the top engineering posts. Completed in 1901, it was a spectacularly modern and large plant. The excitement, however, did not last long. The operational problems mounted and the mill was forced to stop operations in about a year. The major problem was the different quality of coke between Germany and Japan. Yawata was chosen as the site basically because there was a big coal mine nearby, and the mill used the coke produced with this coal. The coke production mill was designed by Germans as well, who never understood the difference between German and Japanese coal and were also under a budget constraint by that time. Consequently, the coke mill was not only inadequate for Japanese coal but also inefficient owing to the use of cheaper obsolete equipment. The coke thus produced was inevitably poor in quality, and made steel production extremely difficult.

Again, like in Kamaishi, Noro was asked to improve the situation. Noro had earlier proposed his own plan for the Yawata mill, which, not surprisingly, suggested a more modest production scale and a gradual expansion. But the government rejected it and he had resigned from government posts for an unrelated reason. Noro made a thorough investigation of Yawata, improved the coke production process, and made several changes to the furnaces to fit them to the attributes of Japanese coke. These changes took a few years but in 1904 the mill restarted its operation successfully.

Yawata Mill was owned and run by the government, mostly because of its role as the supplier of steel to weapon production. Though it was obviously a dominant steel producer, private enterprises were not absent. In addition to Tanaka's Kamaishi mill, Sumitomo, Kawasaki, and Mitsubishi (in occupied Korea) entered into the market and so did Nippon Kokan (now NKK) with the initiative of K. Imaizumi, Noro's student, who had resigned from Yawata when his proposal to privatize Yawata was not accepted. Hence, private profit-seeking entry did take place. Because of the large initial investment, many of the entrants were zaibatsu companies or financially supported by zaibatsus (for instance, Asano, Okura, and other relatively small zaibatsus invested in Nippon Kokan). Some of them built integrated mills, but some imported pig iron and scrap iron from India, America, and other countries. In 1934, a partly government-owned company, Nippon Steel, was established to achieve a stable supply of steel (which the army considered indispensable). Yawata was absorbed into this company and the government urged private steel companies to join. Kamaishi and a few other companies complied with this request but Nippon Kokan, Sumitomo Metal, Kawasaki Steel, and other companies kept their independence.

Since the aim of this subsection is to show that Japan had a certain technological background when it decided to import Western technology and that technology importation alone cannot guarantee successful industrial development, we shall discuss the postwar development only briefly. In terms of innovation, two developments had a significant impact. The first is the importation of the basic oxygen furnace method from Austria and its improvement and adaptation to Japanese steel mills during the 1950s. Japan was ahead of other countries not only in the speed of adoption but also in the extent it improved the technology (see Lynn, 1982). For instance, Yawata invented the oxygen converter gas recovery system as an effective device to save energy use and reduce pollution, which has been used worldwide. The second is the introduction of the continuous casting method and strip mills during the 1950s and 1960s.

Two factors explain why these technologies were most effectively utilized in Japan. One is the strong propensity of Japanese firms to invest in production processes. Since both of these new technologies have to be embodied in capital equipment and require a large-scale integrated production flow, their advantage can be exploited only with new investment. Japanese iron and steel manufacturers in fact invested in a number of new and integrated large plants, and productivity has increased tremendously. For instance, between the two plants of Nippon Steel, a new one at Kimitsu had a labor productivity (steel production per worker) 2.5 times higher than an old one at Yawata in 1973, though Yawata's productivity itself had increased several times in the preceding 30 years (Iida, 1979). The other factor is the constant effort to improve efficiency within the plants. Some of them were conspicuous, for instance, the introduction of computers to control operation; however, some were made more at the shop-floor level based on learning by doing and workers' proposals. As we shall discuss later, Japanese firms have been relatively successful in attaining companywide involvement in productivity increase.

As a result, Japan's productivity has outpaced the other countries and the companies started to export technology, for instance, imparting know-hows in plant construction and operation to many countries including both developing countries such as Brazil and developed countries such as Italy and the United States. Since 1974 its royalty receipts have exceeded its payments, the first among Japanese industries.

Let us conclude this subsection. In terms of industrial policy, the role played by the government and the military in the development of the steel industry was obviously large (as in many other countries). Steel production is inseparable from the military needs, as exemplified by the fact that the first steel production under Western technology was made to make cannons. However, both the cases of Kamaishi and Yawata imply that the government is less qualified than the private sector in selecting appropriate technology. In either case, the government placed too much confidence in the Western technology as it was and disregarded local conditions, such as infrastructure and the accumulated indigenous technology. By contrast, T. Ohshima's and Tanaka's attempts at Kamaishi suggest that private enterprises were better suited for this purpose.

Electrical and Communication Equipment

The electrical and communication equipment industry gives another example of a combination of Japan's indigenous technology or its own R&D efforts with imported Western technology. Such a combination was feasible and effective because, though Japan technologically lagged behind America and Europe (as in other modern industries) in the late nineteenth century when electrical and communication equipment started to be introduced, the lag was not large. Take an example of the electric light. T. W. Swan invented an electric incandescent bulb in 1878 in the United Kingdom and T. A. Edison, in 1879 in the United States. The first incandescent light was exhibited in Japan in 1884, only 5 years after Edison's invention. Needless to say, all the equipment used in this exhibition was imported. However, in a similar exhibition in the following year, a domestically produced generator was already used. This generator was designed by I. Fujioka, a young professor at the College of Engineering (later the Engineering Department of the University of Tokyo, as explained earlier) who had studied with a British professor at the College. Fujioka then undertook to make a bulb. He left the university to join Tokyo Electric Light Company (now Tokyo Electric Power Company), was sent to America and Europe to learn the technology there, bought bulb-manufacturing equipment in the United Kingdom, and came back in 1887. He started the development effort and then, to continue this effort independently from Tokyo Electric Light Company, established a new company, Hakunetsusha, in 1890. Even with the equipment brought from the United Kingdom, the development met with continuous problems. For instance, following Swan's invention, his team first used cotton yarn for filament, but the result was unsatisfactory, and it took some time before they learned about Edison's use of Japanese bamboo and did the same. Hakunetsusha started selling the bulbs in 1890. Thus, although the United States was unquestionably earlier in innovation and was dominant in production size, the start of the industry in Japan did not lag by more than a generation.

As discussed earlier, Japan did not have a means to protect the domestic industries because of Unequal Treaties. Hakunetsusha met with fierce competition from imports. Its bulb cost about 60% more than the imports. The company, however, managed to survive with the booms after the Sino-Japanese war of 1894–1895 and the Russo-Japanese war of 1904–1905, and also because of the international price increase caused by an electric bulb cartel of European manufacturers in 1903. In the meantime, it continued its effort to improve the product and made two innovations, a dual coil bulb and a frosted bulb, that were copied worldwide.

Hakunetsusha consists of one-half of the present Toshiba. The other half came from Tanaka Seisakusho, established by H. Tanaka. Born in 1799, Tanaka was one of the most original and productive inventor–engineers (*karakuri* masters) in the Tokugawa era. At the age of 14, he already invented a loom. At 20 he made a "karakuri doll" with a hydraulic mechanism, which became very popular. The list of his inventions and developments is surprisingly comprehensive—a clock, a torch lamp, a furnace, a pump, a fire extinguisher, a tobacco cutter, an ice maker, a bicycle, an oil press, a rice-polishing machine, a ship, a dredger, guns, and many more. He even made the first steam engine in the country based on Western technology. In 1873, at the age of 74, he was invited by Kobusho (the Ministry of Industries) to come to Tokyo from his hometown in Kyushu to make telegraphs at the ministry's small factory. After this experience, he established his own company, Tanaka Seisakusho, in 1875 and made telegraphs, switches, and miscellaneous electrical and other equipment. For Tanaka, therefore, technological development was continuous, with little discontinuity between indigenous and Western technologies. Tanaka's role in Japan's industrial development was important also because among those under Tanaka's direction in the Kobusho factory were several engineers who later became pioneers themselves. These include S. Miyoshi, who later helped Fujioka in establishing Hakunetsusha, and K. Oki, the founder of the present Oki (to be discussed soon).

Although H. Tanaka died in 1881, his son took over and expanded the company with the production of torpedoes and mines at the request of the navy. In a few years it became one of the largest manufacturing companies at the time, but as the navy started to use competitive bids and then completed its own work, the demand decreased substantially and the company started to lose money. The main creditor to the company, Mitsui Bank, took over the virtually bankrupt company and renamed it Shibaura Engineering Works. The company's main products were steam engines, power generators, and other heavy electrical equipment.

Even though Shibaura had developed its own generators (after copying imported ones), it found its technology still behind the American's. Thus in 1910 it formed an affiliation with GE of America. GE acquired about a quarter of the share and allowed Shibaura the use of GE's technology. For instance, engineers were sent to GE to learn its technology and production methods.

Hakunetsusha, renamed Tokyo Electric in 1898, was also affiliated with GE, with GE acquiring a 55% share. Since it started with the production of electric bulbs, the main business was light electrical equipment and appliances, in contrast to Shibaura, which was biased toward heavy equipment. Thus the two were considered complementary and, with GE's support, the two merged in 1939 to become Tokyo Shibaura Electric (later Toshiba). GE owned 33% and Mitsui owned 15%. The relation with GE continued until the beginning of the war and, after the war, resumed in 1953 with GE's 24% share, though this percentage has decreased substantially since then.

Toshiba's main rival, Hitachi, is rather unique among the Japanese producers in that it relied on its own R&D efforts (together with reverse engineering) without forming any affiliation with foreign companies. It was established by N. Odaira, a graduate of the University of Tokyo's Engineering Department, in 1911 as a plant affiliated to Hitachi Mine, and became independent 9 years later. It started with the production of generators, blowers, transformers, and other heavy electrical equipment to be used in mining, but soon began selling to other customers and expanding the business to include industrial machines and lighter electrical equipment.

Hitachi never entered into any affiliation with foreign companies, in contrast to Toshiba, which affiliated with GE, Mitsubishi Electric, which affiliated in 1923 with Westinghouse (with 10% ownership), and Fuji Electric, which started in 1923 as a joint venture between Siemens (30% ownership) and Furukawa Mine. That Hitachi became the largest among these four main manufacturers must suggest either that Japan's technological lag was not serious or that Japanese engineers were capable of developing the products by themselves with the help of reverse engineering. It must also be noted that even companies with foreign affiliations made a significant amount of its own R&D efforts. Thus the two predecessors of Toshiba, Tokyo Electric and Shibaura Engineering, established their laboratories in 1918 and 1921, respectively, while affiliated with GE. Hitachi established its laboratory in 1934, though it started an independent R&D section much earlier in 1918.

Let us turn to communication equipment. The Meiji government started telegraphs as a government business in 1868 with a British engineer using equipment imported from Britain. Kobusho, the ministry, wished to supply them domestically and, as mentioned above, asked H. Tanaka to undertake it. Tanaka succeeded in making them in Kobusho's experimental factory and later in his own Tanaka Seisakusho. In 1877, only a year after A. G. Bell's invention, Kobusho experimented with the first telephone in Japan using American equipment. The engineers at the Kobusho factory started its domestic production by copying and in the next year came up with its first product, however unsatisfactory the quality was. One of the engineers, K. Oki, felt the business had a bright future and left Kobusho to start his own company named Meikosha (later Oki). The telephone business itself was not established until 1890, partly because of scepticism about its merit (for instance, hiring a messenger was thought to be a cheaper and more reliable way to convey information) and partly because of the controversy within the government as to whether the business should be run by the public or private sector. However, soon after the start (as a government business), the public was easily convinced of its convenience, and the demand surged. Both imported and domestic equipment (receivers, switchboards, wire, etc.) were used and, as the sole domestic producer, Meikosha prospered.

Western Electric (WE) of the United States saw a growing market in Japan and decided to enter through a joint venture. At first, it thought of teaming with Meikosha, but the prospering Oki proposed conditions too severe for WE to accept. WE finally decided to team with K. Iwadare, who had been WE's agent in Japan, and established Nippon Electric Co. (NEC) in 1898 with WE owning 54% of the share and Iwadare owning 33%. To start the business, NEC bought one of the largest manufacturing factories at the time, owned by S. Miyoshi but on the brink of bankruptcy as a consequence of its too rapid expansion and the depression at the time. As mentioned earlier, Miyoshi was another Tanaka disciple at the Kobusho factory and also a collaborator with Fujioka in establishing Hakunetsusha. Hence, one can see a historical connection from Tanaka, the master of pre-Meiji technology, not only to Oki but also to NEC, in addition to Toshiba.

Iwadare's career illustrates another (and newer) type of engineer at the time, that is, university educated. He studied electrical engineering at the College of Engineering a year after Fujioka, worked at Kobusho for 4 years, went to the United States and got a job at GE, came back to Japan after about a year to be an engineering manager of Osaka Electric Lamp Company, and, after 8 years, quit this post to start his own business as an agent for GE and WE. Thus, his career, like Fujioka's, is more "Western" than Oki's or Miyoshi's in that he studied technology in a university designed and taught by Westerners, and then was employed as an engineer in large companies at the time.

In the beginning, NEC not only produced telephone and other communication equipment with WE's technology, but also copied WE's management methods (including the accounting system and work management) and bought WE's supplies ranging from machines and materials to notepaper. However, it gradually replaced them with their own or with products procured domestically. With the expansion of the telephone system, the company expanded rapidly and competed against Oki and new entrants including Toshiba, Hitachi, and Fuji (whose communication equipment business was later separated as Fujitsu). NEC started the R&D department in 1926, which was expanded into a separate laboratory in 1939. From just assimilating WE's technology at first, it gradually increased its own R&D efforts and started producing innovations that surpassed WE's.

The technological and industrial development of Japan's electrical and communication equipment industry shows those characteristics that can be commonly found in many other industries. First, Japan was technologically behind America and Europe but the lag was in a tolerable range—a marked difference from present developing countries. Second, as a consequence, imported technologies were not entirely discontinuous from indigenous technologies. Third, therefore, some of the entrepreneurs/ engineers could utilize the skills and knowledge accumulated in the pre-Meiji era. Fourth, at the same time, those engineers educated by the colleges established by the Meiji government and taught by foreign professors greatly contributed to assimilating Western technology. Fifth, foreign technologies were actively imported through joint ventures, technology contracts, reverse engineering, and such. Japanese had an ability to absorb or adapt the imported technologies, and an ability to run the joint ventures successfully. It should also be noted that a strong desire to become independent of foreign dominance of technology—one may call it nationalism—was common among the entrepreneurs/engineers as illustrated most clearly by Hitachi's Odaira. Finally, a strong entrepreneurship and a strong will to enter into uncertain and unknown fields were present. This conclusion does not imply that the government played no role. It did play an important role in establishing science and engineering education systems, introducing new technologies such as the telegraph, telephone, and weaponry, guaranteeing demand through military procurement, and so forth. In our view, however, such policies would have never resulted in Japan's development were it not for the willingness and capability in the private sector.

This conclusion is reinforced by the postwar experience. Although the government continued to affect the industry through its nurturing policy during the 1950s and 1960s, procurement by Nippon Telephone and Telegram, and research done within MITI's Agency of Industrial Science and Technology and NTT laboratories, its significance was more limited than previously because of the minimal defense research and military procurement. As for the nurturing policy, the computer industry was the main subject. Yet subsidies given to the industry, its sizable portion being granted through research associations discussed earlier, were very small compared to the total R&D expenditures of the industry. Apparently, it was the competitive threat from domestic rivals and foreign giants such as IBM that fostered firms to R&D activities. Their R&D expenditures increased more than 40-fold during the 20-year period from 1965 to 1985.

The importation of technology and its improvement within Japanese laboratories and factories continued. After World War II, almost all the firms resumed their relation with American or European firms. Even firms such as Hitachi, which kept its independence before the war, entered into contracts to import technology from companies such as RCA, GE, Phillips, and Western Electric. Royalty payments thus greatly exceeded receipts. However, with continuous innovation by Japanese firms, the receipts have increased much faster than the payment: 13.4 times as opposed to

2.5 times from 1973 to 1988. Hence, though payment still dominates receipt, the difference has narrowed considerably: in 1988, payment was 1.65 times larger.[15]

Automobiles

The history of the development of the automobile industry also shows similar characteristics: the dominance of foreign producers in the beginning, a number of (domestic) entry attempts, the acquisition of technology first with reverse engineering, the gradual accumulation of technologies with learning by doing, the procurement by the military and the transportation authority, support by the government through financial incentives and standard setting, and the entrepreneurs' risk-taking behavior in the form of physical investment and R&D. After several decades of struggle, Japanese car manufacturers have now caught up with the European and American rivals technologically, and are now surpassing them in certain areas. It is therefore worthwhile to trace the Japanese experience in this industry in some detail.

The first car introduced into Japan was an European-made steam-driven one imported in 1897. However, it was in 1903 when two cars (one steam-driven and the other electric-driven) were used as buses in a large exposition that many Japanese people saw cars for the first time. One of the visitors to this exposition saw them and started an effort to make one domestically. This effort produced one steam-driven car, which had so much trouble (particularly in terms of the tires) in the test run that he gave up any commercial application. Four years later, the first domestic production of a motor-driven car was made with the main parts (including, it seems, engines) imported at first but gradually replaced by domestic production. This effort also collapsed after selling 10 cars, 8 of which were bought by the police to add to its stock of 41 European cars and 11 American cars. In the meantime, import of foreign cars increased and completely dominated the market: more than 200 cars had been imported by 1910 and 6800 by 1920. The Great Earthquake in Tokyo of 1923 increased this trend further because all the train services had been disrupted and cars were urgently needed to deliver food and other necessities. Thus by 1925 more than 16,000 cars had been imported, and in this year Ford established an assembly plant in Yokohama. This was followed by GM, which established a similar plant in Osaka 2 years later. Thus the market became dominated by these two American producers.

More than 10 attempts had been made during the Meiji era to produce cars domestically but all failed, and the first significant one was made by a company named Kaishinsha established in 1911 by M. Hashimoto, who had studied engineering in the United States for 3 years. He started the business by importing and repairing British cars, and then with the technology learned from these British cars and his experience with American cars, began to develop a passenger car domestically. His first car was a failure because of lack of the casting technology needed to make a sufficiently durable engine, but he finally succeeded in producing a viable product in 1913. He began selling this car with a brand name "Dat," but, in competition with Ford and GM, could not sell in sufficiently large numbers to make the production commercially viable.

The first government initiative was made by the army who, after a survey of military procurement policy in Britain, France, and Germany, concluded that it was urgent to foster domestic production of trucks and buses for military purposes. In 1918 it started a policy of subsidizing domestic production and civilian purchase of trucks and buses. Although the subsidy itself was modest, this policy gave an expectation of increased procurement and three companies started production. One was Kaishinsha, who, with the difficulty in the passenger car market, decided to enter into the production of trucks; the second was Tokyo Gas Electric (now defunct), which inherited the trial truck production in the arsenal; and the third was Tokyo Ishikawajima Zosensho (now IHI), which, with the profits from shipbuilding during the World War I boom, entered into the production of passenger cars and then trucks, first by disassembling a Fiat car to learn the technology and then by buying technology from Wolseley, a British company. Despite the army's support, domestic production was small. During 1919–1931, these three companies together produced 2575 cars and the market (including trucks and buses) was totally dominated by Ford, GM, and other imports.

The next governmental initiative occurred in 1930 when the Ministry of Railways made a detailed open test of the three domestic producers, and then in 1932 when the Ministry of Commerce and Industry (now MITI), in collaboration with the Ministry of Railways, urged the three companies to collaborate in a joint venture to develop a so-called "standard" car (truck and bus) with the brand name "Isuzu" (the ancestor of current Isuzu). The joint venture lasted for only 2 years with the production of 750 cars, but the experience was utilized in these companies' efforts to produce their own trucks and buses (both for military and civilian purposes).

Although the major part of Kaishinsha was absorbed in this joint venture and later by Isuzu, the business of small passenger cars (called "Datsun" by this time) was retained by G. Ayukawa, an energetic entrepreneur in the process of expanding its Nissan Zaibatsu (one of the so-called new zaibatsus), who had acquired Kaishinsha by that time. Ayukawa established Nissan Motors for this purpose. Another origin of Nissan Motors was a company called Jitsuyo Jidosha, which was started with the technological guidance of American engineers using the engines of American Harley-Davidson motorcycles. Hence, Nissan's technology originated both from a Japanese's effort to copy British and American cars and the technology brought by hired Americans.

The number of entry attempts around this time was surprisingly large. To trucks, Mitsubishi and Kawasaki made some efforts. To motorcycles and three-wheel cars, more than 10 companies made efforts, some of whom, like Daihatsu and Mazda, survived until later, and some of whom eventually exited. A number of efforts were also made in the passenger car market, including Mitsui Shipbuilding, but mostly by small-scale nonzaibatsu companies. Most failed but an important exception was Toyota. Two facts deserve emphasis. The first is the frequency of entry attempts, clearly indicating the presence of risk-taking spirits and the will as well as capability to challenge new technologies. In short, Schumpeterian entrepreneurship was abundant. Second, though this entrepreneurship was present among established zaibatsus, their role was limited. In fact, they gave up rather early. By contrast, independent entrepreneurs such as Ayukawa, Toyoda (Toyota), and Matsuda (Mazda), not to mention Hashimoto and others in the early period, were more persistent.

Sakichi Toyoda was a typical inventor and entrepreneur of pre-World War II Japan, much like Thomas Edison, though in a different field. Born in 1867 in a poor carpenter's family, he invented the first (wooden-made hand-driven) loom in 1890 after several years of struggle. He started selling the looms and making cloth using them, but the business did not prosper. The struggle continued until he invented automatic looms in 1897. This time the business was a success with a strong demand both for the looms and the high-quality cloth made with them. He worked further to improve the loom, and to make a wider cloth faster and more efficiently. The company started exporting the products and the quality of his loom was proved when the world's largest loom manufacturer, Pratt (U. K.), bought the technology for one hundred thousand pounds. It is worth noting that Toyoda's development effort over his lifetime was a purely private and independent enterprise. Though Mitsui Bussan (the largest trading company at the time, now Mitsui Co.) at one time gave financial support to Toyoda's enterprise, Sakichi parted the relationship fairly soon after a disagreement.

Sakichi's son, Kiichiro, plowed back the profits from loom sales and the fee from Pratt into the development of cars. He organized a development team by hiring engineers from fields such as steel, tools, and three-wheel cars from other companies. He visited several professors to learn about technology, some of whom were his former classmates when he studied at the University of Tokyo's Engineering Department. And he sent his engineer to the United States to visit the Ford plant and get ideas on how to make a factory, and purchase necessary machines. The team started by disassembling American cars. Finding that the American technology was far advanced, they decided to imitate Chevrolet's engine and use many of Chevrolet's and Ford's parts. As in the previous experience of Kaishinsha, casting was a problem. Although Toyoda had the casting technology to manufacture looms, they needed a more complex and finer technology to produce an engine. After a seemingly endless process of trial and learning in casting and other aspects of technology, the first viable product, a truck, was introduced in 1935 to sell to the army. A passenger car followed in 1936.

An important policy initiative was taken in 1936 to foster domestic car production. The government restricted the production to licensed companies who received financial and other support. In contrast, the biggest producers at the time, Ford and GM, were banned from increasing their production level in the future. The license was given to Toyota (Toyoda's brand name for cars), Nissan, and (later) Isuzu. Toyota and Nissan thus became the dominant producers and increased production. In 1938, the production level of Toyota and Nissan combined was 6568 for nonmilitary sales versus 12,441 of Ford and GM. For military sales, they were 5930 and 5999, respectively, showing the army's willingness to support domestic producers. Both Ford and GM exited the Japanese market in 1939, and the production level of Toyota and Nissan increased further, each exceeding 15,000 around 1941, with Isuzu following with about half the production level. By this time, most of the demand was for trucks for military purposes.

Without question, therefore, military procurement played an important role in supporting domestic car production. However, the quality of domestically produced cars never caught up with that of Ford and GM before the war. Complaints of breakdowns were frequent, including broken shafts, water dripping out of radiators, and early wear of moving parts.[16]

Except for the short period of the Korean war, the postwar production shifted to civilian uses. The big question at the time was whether Japan should protect and nurture domestic producers following the infant industry theory, or import cheaper and better-quality cars from abroad. The first view was taken mostly by MITI and the producers, whereas the latter was taken by the Ministry of Transport, the Bank of Japan, users such as taxi companies, and dealers of imported cars. The government settled on the first position and restricted imports quantitatively and with high tariffs. This protection guaranteed a growing market to domestic producers, giving them a chance to lower costs and improve quality through scale economies, learning by doing, and imported technology. Compared to this effect, the financial incentives provided by the government, such as the provision of low-interest loans through Japan Development Bank and accelerated depreciation allowed to selected equipment, seem less important. Government support specifically aimed at R&D was very limited.

To catch up technologically, Toyota relied on its own efforts but Nissan, Isuzu, and Hino imported technology from, respectively, Austin (U. K.), Rootes (U. K.), and Renault (France). In the latter case, at first they imported major parts including engines, but gradually replaced them with domestically produced ones. All these companies incorporated the technology they learned from the production of licensed models into the development of their own models such as Datsun, and terminated their relationship with the foreign producers by 1965.

These producers, all established before the war, were not the only car manufacturers. Entry attempts were many, counting nearly 30 companies between 1945 and 1960. These included ex-zaibatsu companies, such as Mitsubishi Heavy Industries, and reentrants, such as Mazda, but the majority were new independents including Honda and Suzuki, both of which started as motorcycle producers. However, except for these companies, few of them survived more than 5 years. These private efforts were against MITI's wish to integrate domestic car production to two groups, Toyota and Nissan, to attain scale economies large enough to compete against American giants after trade and capital liberalization. MITI's guidance bore some fruits in the form of a Nissan–Prince merger and an alliance between Toyota and Hino (and later Daihatsu). As a consequence, market concentration to the two groups increased, but the entry of several powerful independents kept the market highly competitive, which together with the increasing importance of global competition contributed to maintaining and even intensifying the innovation efforts of Japanese car makers.

This experience of the Japanese car industry throws lights on some key issues. How could Japan succeed in establishing its own car industry under the presence (in the prewar period) of technologically far advanced Ford and GM? Two factors appear most important. One is the presence of engineers and entrepreneurs, such as Toyoda and Ayukawa, who were willing to take risks and sustain efforts under adversity. The other is the general ability of engineers to absorb foreign technology and the ability of workers to absorb new production processes. Needless to say, the education system discussed earlier contributed to this effect. Also, the emphasis on engineering education in universities helped, as shown by the episode of Toyoda's visiting professors to ask technical questions.

As in any late-developing countries, reverse engineering was the first source of foreign technology. Visiting advanced factories of foreign producers, hiring foreign engineers, and purchasing foreign technology were other important means of acquiring technology.

The government's role was important in two aspects, military and other procurement, and the protection of domestic producers. These policies, by guaranteeing demand, encouraged investment in capital and R&D (mostly development rather than research, particularly in the early period). Nevertheless, one should recall that many entry attempts were made even before government policies or against MITI's guidance. It is misleading indeed to attribute Japan's success solely to government policies.

Concluding Remarks

This section gave three case studies to show how Japanese industries acquired and developed technology in its broad sense. Since the urgent economic target for Meiji Japan was to acquire more advanced Western technology and build competitive industries, our cases focused on "modern" industries and mostly the pre-World War II era. In these industries, intensive efforts were made to transfer technologies from the Western countries. The means were various. In steel, especially the case of Yawata Work, the basic strategy was to import a whole set—plan, technology, equipment, and personnel. In automobiles and electrical/communication equipment, reverse engineering and technology import through licence or joint ventures were common. The balance between these two means varied between the two industries. Apparently, joint ventures were more common in the electrical/communication equipment industry. The balance also varied across companies within each industry; thus, Toshiba, NEC, and Nissan relied more on imported technology than did Hitachi and Toyota. It is difficult to assess the relative merit of the two strategies.

We also revealed a significant role played by indigenous technology. A right choice of technology to import is easier to make with knowledge of indigenous technology, and imported technology has to be modified with the help of indigenous technology that is compatible with local conditions. The cases of Kamaishi and Yawata Steel Works clearly demonstrate this fact. Reverse engineering needs understanding of the basic mechanism behind products and the skills to imitate, which the masters of indigenous technology, such as H. Tanaka, tended to have.

In addition to these technology-specific factors, there were, first, the persistent efforts and inquisitive minds of industrial leaders and, second, educational background and skills of middle-to-top engineers and key workers. The government's hurried effort to establish a compulsory education system and engineering schools was clearly a contributing factor, though the effort would not have achieved its purpose were it not for the parents' enthusiasm for education and the background of widespread private education in the pre-Meiji era. Besides, education may be necessary but not sufficient to produce entrepreneurial will, which, as Schumpeter has so forcefully argued, is the key factor in economic development. A full inquiry into the factors supporting such will is beyond the scope of this study. Some of them may be similar to the Japanese business system today, to be discussed in the next section; however, some are not. For instance, long-term employment was not a norm before World War I as illustrated by NEC's Iwadare's career.[17]

Some observers stress the role zaibatsus played. Zaibatsus, such as Mitsui, Mitsubishi, and Sumitomo, were big, diversified, and family-owned businesses often with government or military connections, and were relatively strong in finance, mining, and shipbuilding as they acquired these businesses when the government privatized them. Among the three industries studied here, their presence was relatively large in steel because the investment required large funds. Even in this industry, however, they remained as followers to giant Nippon Steel. In the other two, their role was further limited. In fact, it was independent entrepreneurs who made risky investment and persistent efforts to catch up with the West technologically. Some of them had certain relations with zaibatsus, including Ayukawa, whose business expanded into one of the so-called new zaibatsus; Tanaka's company, which became partly owned by Mitsui because of bankruptcy; NEC, which formed a tie with Sumitomo after it intermediated between WE and Sumitomo in WE's entry into the wire business[18]; and Toyota's automatic looms, which were sold by Mitsui's trading company from time to time. In neither of these cases, however, did zaibatsu (that is, established zaibatsus) make a first move or become a dominant player. As Ayukawa's case suggests, zaibatsu is, after all, an enterprise that has successfully expanded and diversified; hence, it hardly differs from large diversified enterprises in other capitalist economies—from conglomerates in the United States and European countries to chaebols in Korea (see Chapter 11 on Korea) and other equivalents in developing countries. Thus, it is misleading to emphasize the peculiarities of Japan's experience in reference to zaibatsu.

Zaibatsus were dissolved after the war and the present Mitsui Group, Mitsubishi Group, or any other group is no more than a very loose federation of basically independent companies, unlike pre-World War II zaibatsu where there was a holding company that served as headquarters. Thus it is now frequently observed that a Mitsui company purchases from or sells to, say, a Mitsubishi company, or gets loans from Mitsubishi Bank. On this difference between prewar zaibatsu and present business groups, see Goto (1982) and Odagiri (1992, Chapter 7).

We have discussed the development of the three industries after World War II only briefly, because the discussion of the prewar experience alone was long enough, and the literature on the postwar experience is relatively plentiful. Komiya et al. (1988), in our view, gives the best discussion both on the postwar industrial policy in general and individual studies on the industries discussed in this section.[19]

We have discussed the general shift among Japanese industries from technology import to their own R&D efforts, and described the postwar R&D policies. More generally, the industrial policy (not particularly specific to R&D) may be summarized as follows.

1. Even in the early years the amount of government funding to industries, including subsidies, tax credits, and low-interest loans, was rather modest, though some industries, such as iron and steel, coal mining, shipping, and electric power, benefitted significantly.
2. There is a clear tendency that such government funding has decreased in amount and importance over time; in fact, it appears minimal and by no means larger than in other industrialized countries in recent years.[20]
3. The restriction on imports and foreign direct investment into Japan was probably the most important policy until the early 1970s. Restricting the growing Japanese market, already the second largest in the capitalist economy in the late 1960s, to Japanese firms who were competing intensively among themselves gave a strong incentive to invest in plants, equipment, and R&D. In addition, because postwar Japan's Peace Constitution meant that the military was no longer a significant customer to businesses, industries such as automobiles, which had been helped by military procurement before the war but was still in its infancy relative to American and European producers, might have been wiped out were the market made open to foreign competition. However, such restriction on trade and investment has

been drastically reduced in the 1960s and the 1970s so that the rates of tariff and the number of manufactured goods under import restriction are among the smallest in the world.

4. Procurement by government corporations such as Nippon Telephone and Telegraph (NTT, privatized in 1985) and Japan National Railways (split into six regional companies and privatized in 1987) helped the communication and electronic equipment industry, and the rolling stock industry, respectively. However, they now buy from foreign suppliers as well.

5. MITI's role in the collection and diffusion of information may have been significant, as it could obtain information on overseas markets through its Japan External Trade Organization (JETRO) and technological information through its Agency of Industry Science and Technology, which has a number of laboratories. However, this role has also declined as firms themselves accumulated international experiences and technological knowledge. In addition, Japanese firms have various other "networks" through, for instance, trading companies (*sogo shosha*), trade associations, and buyer–supplier relationships.

Thus, government policies, especially the protection of domestic markets, played a significant role in Japan's postwar industrial development at least until the early 1970s. However, as argued in the beginning of this chapter, government policies can attain their purposes only if the private sector is willing and able to take the opportunities given to them (or even to overcome the obstacles the policies create, as evidenced by Honda's experience). To understand why Japanese firms were willing and able, and to understand why they continue to be so despite the weakening role of government policies, one has to know how Japanese businesses today make decisions and carry out innovation efforts. This is why a detailed examination will be given in the next section on innovation inside Japanese firms. It will be preceded by descriptions of the current R&D efforts and performance in the aggregate.

INNOVATION IN TODAY'S JAPAN

Overview

Table 3.3 shows Japan's current R&D efforts in comparison to other major developed countries. Clearly, the role of government in funding R&D is smaller in Japan than in the other countries. One reason for this smaller share of government funds is the small defense-related expenditures in Japan. However, even when defense-related R&D expenditures are excluded, the proportion of government funds in total R&D expenditures is the smallest.

The share of government funds in industrial R&D expenditures is a mere 1.2% in Japan; that is, Japanese companies are financing almost all of their R&D out of their own funds. This is in contrast to other countries where 11 to 34% of industrial R&D expenditures are supported by government funds. Again, the gap narrows considerably if defense-related industries are excluded because, without aircraft and missile industries, the comparable percentage for the United States is reduced to 7.7 (Eads and Nelson, 1986). Yet, in comparison with Japan's 1.2%, a substantial gap remains between the two countries.

Table 3.3. R&D Expenditures and Personnel in Five Countries[a]

	Japan (Y)	United States ($)	Germany (DM)	France (F)	United Kingdom (£)
Total R&D expenditures (in billions, local currency)	10909	142.0	64.82	141.9	10334*
Total R&D expenditures (in billion yen)	10909	19596	4757	3068	2359*
Total R&D expenditures/GNP (%)	2.69	2.73	2.89	2.33	2.19*
Nondefense R&D expenditures/ GNP (%)	2.66	1.95	2.75	1.79	1.77*
Government funds/total R&D expenditures (%)	17.1	46.4	33.2	49.3	36.7*
Government funds/nondefense R&D expenditures (%)	16.4	25.1	29.9	33.9	21.6*
Industry expenditures/total R&D expenditures (%)	75.5	72.0	73.0	56.8***	66.4*
Industry funds/industry R&D expenditures (%)	98.6	65.7	86.8	73.0***	71.4*
Government funds/industry R&D expenditures (%)	1.2	34.3	11.3	22.4***	16.5*
R&D personnel (in thousands)	462	949*	166**	115*	102*
R&D personnel/10,000 population	37	39*	27**	21*	18*

[a]Year 1989 except *1988, **1987, and ***1983. R&D expenditures and personnel exclude humanities and social sciences in Japan and the United Kingdom but include them in other countries. Germany refers to the Federal Republic (West) before unification.

Source: Science and Technology Agency (1991).

Table 3.3 also shows the number of R&D personnel. The number of research personnel was about 462,000 in 1989, growing three times in the preceding two decades. Of these 64% of them were working in industry. Although the number of research personnel is about half that of the United States, per capita Japan has about the same number as the United States and more than the European countries. One notable feature of the Japanese research personnel is a relatively larger proportion of engineers (42% of the total research personnel in 1989) than scientists (16%).[21] The same tendency exists for university degrees: the number of Ph.Ds granted was 860 in science and 1404 in engineering in Japan in 1988. In contrast, these were 7438 and 3236 in the United States and 2894 and 1020 in Germany, respectively. The same can be said of the undergraduate students in Japan. In 1988, there were 368,000 students in engineering departments in contrast to 62,000 in science departments. This emphasis on engineering education started in the Meiji era as shown earlier.[22]

An active R&D activity results in patents and, more generally, technological progress. The number of patent application in Japan (by Japanese or foreigners) increased from 131,000 in 1970 to 341,000 in 1987. This is in marked contrast with European countries where the number of application decreased in the 1970s to the early 1980s, and with the United States, where the number increased only gradually to 134,000 in 1987. Although this international comparison of patent numbers may be biased owing to the Japanese system under which patents are granted separately even when inventions behind them were closely related technologically, the fact that the share of Japanese applications in the U. S. patents is also increasing rapidly—from

5.1% in 1970 to 20.3% in 1988—suggests that Japan's increased R&D efforts are indeed bearing fruits (STA, 1990).

Another popular measure of technological progress is the rate of change in total factor productivity (TFP), which is affected not only by R&D but also by other miscellaneous factors, such as demand shocks, and the "distance" from the best practice in the world. Table 3.4 shows an impressive rate of TFP increase in Japan, especially before 1973. The extremely high rate of economic growth in this period is explained mainly by this TFP increase, which, in turn, appears to be explained by the combination of successful technology importation and extensive domestic R&D, among other factors.

Innovation Inside Japanese Firms[23]

Motivations
Inherently, the choice of the level of R&D is a dynamic problem because the costs and returns take place at different and over many periods. Thus the firm's willingness to invest in R&D very much depends on how much the firm is inclined to growth (i.e., long-run objectives) as opposed to short-run objectives. It has often been argued that Japanese firms are more growth oriented than American or European firms. Several institutional factors are important.

It is first noted that the capital market constraints to the firm are presumably not as strong in Japan as in the United States or the United Kingdom. Most of the large

Table 3.4. Annual Productivity and Output and Input Growth in Business Sector (in Percentages)

	OECD Average	United States	Japan	Germany	France	United Kingdom
1960s to 1973						
Output	5.2	3.8	9.7	4.6	6.4	3.2
Factor input	2.4	2.3	3.5	1.8	2.1	1.2
TFP[a]	2.8	1.5	6.1	2.8	4.3	2.0
Labor productivity	4.1	2.2	8.6	4.9	5.9	3.3
Capital productivity	−0.4	0.3	−2.4	−1.1	0.6	−0.7
1973–1979						
Output	2.9	2.8	3.8	2.4	3.5	1.1
Factor input	2.2	2.9	2.0	0.6	1.4	0.9
TFP	0.7	−0.1	1.8	1.8	2.1	0.2
Labor productivity	1.6	0.3	3.2	3.4	3.5	1.3
Capital productivity	−1.4	−0.9	−3.0	−1.1	−1.2	−1.9
1979–1986						
Output	2.3	2.2	3.8	1.6	1.5	1.4
Factor input	1.7	2.2	2.1	0.8	0.2	0.3
TFP	0.6	0.0	1.7	0.8	1.3	1.1
Labor productivity	1.4	0.6	2.8	2.0	2.5	1.9
Capital productivity	−1.3	−1.0	−2.0	−1.3	−1.4	−0.8
Memorandum						
1985 capital share	32.2	34.3	22.6	34.8	30.8	32.5

[a]TFP, total factor productivity.

Source: Steven Englander, A., and Mittelstädt, A. (1988). "Total Factor Productivity: Macroeconomic and Structural Aspects of the Slowdown." *OECD Economic Studies,* No. 10, Spring.

shareholders are banks and other firms that are basically friendly to the firm. Often these shareholdings are reciprocal, that is, the firm also owns their shares.[24] As a consequence, it is unlikely that these shareholders interfere with the management of the firm unless it is in trouble. These shareholders are themselves controlled by the managers sympathetic to the management of this firm.[25]

Hence, Japanese managers tend to have a fair amount of discretionary power. They are typically promoted from within among the pool of those having worked with the company for, say, three decades and gradually climbed up the promotion ladder. They consider themselves, first and foremost, as representing the employees rather than the shareholders. Indeed, if they have worked with the employees all the time since their graduation from the schools, how can they stop feeling closer to the employees than to the shareholders with whom they have probably been acquainted only briefly or they have never met?

That managers tend to pursue growth more than the value of the firm has been put forth by many writers, most notably Marris (1964), for several reasons such as pecuniary and nonpecuniary gains managers receive from growth more than from shareholder wealth. Add to this the managers' strong identification with the employees and the employees' long-term attachment to the firms common in Japan. Whether this attachment should be called "lifetime" employment is doubtful, because it is not explicitly written in any labor contract, and de facto dismissal has taken place more frequently than is usually presumed. Yet it has been and is still regarded as a norm by both employers and employees, and the employer–employee relationship has been more stable in Japan than in any other country.

The result of these considerations is an even stronger motivation toward growth, for the employees are most concerned with the long-term survival and performance of the company and the prospects of promotion. Since the positions for promotion are larger the faster the corporate organization expands, the employees are more growth-oriented than the shareholders, and, with the weak capital market constraints and with the managers identifying themselves with the employees, it appears reasonable to assume that Japanese firms are more growth oriented and place a great emphasis on the acquisition of technological knowledge.

The Managers' Background

There is another difference between Japanese managers and American or British managers—their background. In Japan, the largest proportion of directors (who, unlike in the United States, are mostly full-time and insiders) came from production and technology departments, followed by marketing and export, which together accounted for 50 to 70%, far larger than those with financial and accounting origins, which are merely 5 to 19% (Kono, 1984, p. 33). More recently, according to the report in *Nihon Keizai Shimbun* (May 25, 1987), among the 126 presidents who assumed the post during the first 6 months of 1987 in the firms listed in the Tokyo Stock Exchange, 36% had a marketing origin and 28% had a production/R&D origin. Those with a financial origin again accounted for a mere 11%. This lack of importance of financial background is in contrast to the United States or the United Kingdom where financial experience has been found most helpful in attaining managerial positions.[26]

The better knowledge and experience of Japanese managers in production/R&D provide them with a better understanding of the potentials and limitations of R&D

projects, more accurate evaluation of the outcomes from R&D, and more favorable general attitudes toward R&D. Similarly, their better knowledge and experience in sales/marketing provide them with a keen understanding of what kinds of products are in demand in the markets. These familiarities of Japanese managers with technological seeds and market needs are particularly valuable in technologically rapidly changing markets.

R&D–Production–Sales Linkages
The Japanese internal labor market system is characterized not only by long-term attachment but also by a carefully organized training and rotation scheme. It is not unusual for the firm to provide several months of well-programmed training at the time of entry of the workers, not only so that they can acquire technical knowledge and skills but also to familiarize them with diverse activities of the firm, and then mid-career training every 5 years or so. In addition, rotation of workers from, say R&D to production in the case of engineers, or one shop to another in the case of production workers, is more common than in other countries. These practices help workers acquire a company-wide view and acquire flexibility to changing work environment.

Furthermore, long-term employment naturally leads the workers to develop personal linkages across departments. If you are working in R&D for many years, you will have many opportunities to meet and talk with other people in the company, and opportunities to visit other departments and other plants to discuss problems of mutual concern. Thus a close human relation is created between the R&D department and other departments within the firm. Consequently, the R&D staff will be more familiar with the technological needs arising from production and marketing, and the non-R&D departments will be more familiar with what is going on in the laboratories. Consequently, the company R&D departments tend to be more production based and market oriented. The advantage is that the research undertaken will be more commercially relevant and the introduction of a new product into the production and marketing stages will be faster. On the other hand, truly original and basic research may not be emphasized.

Two other features of Japanese firms make this R&D–production–sales link even more effective. One is the infrequent adoption in Japan of multidivisional forms with substantial discretion within each division. The weaker divisional separation not only fosters easy rotation across divisions (which probably is why a multidivisional form is unpopular) but also facilitates a companywide use of technological knowledge. The other is a close link with suppliers and subcontractors. The stable buyer–supplier relationship with a constant flow of information is usually observed in Japanese companies. As a result they tend to share the threat of market competition as well as the need for innovation. Improvements in the product or production process by the supplier or subcontractor will be noted and rewarded by the parent company and, if possible, will be utilized in other firms in the group. In many occasions, cooperative R&D will be carried out between the parent and the supplier(s). For instance, when an automobile assembler develops a new car model, it is essential that suitable components are developed at the same time. Such development will be done by the supplier(s) with close communication with the assembler's developing team and often with the latter's technical advice. See Asanuma (1985) and Clark and Fujimoto (1991) for a detailed study on the automobile industry, and Imai et al. (1985) for a general discussion.

Introduction of New Process/Product

The introduction of a new process or new product into production and marketing may be smoother in Japanese firms for several reasons. Most important is the close communication between R&D and production as previously discussed. In particular, in the course of developing a product or process, the production staff tends to participate from a rather early stage. This may not be efficient in terms of development itself but, since the views of the production department are reflected in the development of the final product/process, the transfer from development to production is quicker, with little bottleneck or disruption occurring in the process.

It is also not unusual that the engineers in the development team are transferred to the production department and actively involve themselves in applying the new product/process into production (Sakakibara and Westney, 1985). Such a transfer is common in the careers of Japanese engineers because the ability for research tends to reach a peak in the late thirties (or even earlier) and, afterward, the management as well as the engineers themselves tend to use their ability and expertise in more or less administrative and managerial positions in the production and R&D departments. The transfer, therefore, not only smooths the introduction of a particular new product/process in which the engineer has been involved, but also increases the technological knowledge in general in the production department. It also fosters an even tighter personal link between R&D and production.

Even if the production manager is familiar with the new product/process, its introduction to production cannot be smoothly done unless the workers are skilled and flexible. Here again the advantage of Japanese firms in terms of labor management has to be emphasized. In Japan, under the expectation of lifetime employment, the management has an ample incentive to provide training to both white-collar or blue-collar workers. Hence, in-company education, on-the-job training, and rotation are provided to the workers. Their skills are therefore not only high but also flexible and wide, which makes adaptation of a new product/process into shop-floors much easier and faster.

In this adaptation process, it is important for management to have a free hand in reorganizing the work organization. The prevalence of single and companywide trade unions in Japan is indispensable for this purpose. For instance, when automobile manufacturers introduced industrial robots, most of the welding jobs were eliminated and yet none of the Japanese firms discharged the welders for this reason. They were all retrained and transferred to other shops, such as metalwork and assembling; hence, no incidence of grievance or industrial action was reported. If, on the contrary, workers in separate jobs are organized into different unions, such transfers would have been impossible and the introduction of new processes would have caused disputes. The relation between innovation and labor relations can be indeed quite important, however distant they may appear. That Japanese firms starting production in the United Kingdom have all sought a single union representation has to be understood in this light.

Synthesis

In this section, we have looked into the inside of the so-called black box and came up with four major factors in Japanese management favorable in making large R&D efforts, making them efficiently, and applying the outcome swiftly and smoothly into manufacturing and marketing. They were a bias to growth maximization; familiarity of management with research, production, and marketing; close R&D–production–sales links; and the smooth transfer of new processes and products into production. Behind all these factors, we stressed the importance of the human aspects of management. The internal labor practices of Japanese management, particularly, a long-term worker–company attachment with internal training and internal promotion, have been conducive to the growth preference of the managers and employees, interdepartmental personal contacts, and easy adaptability of production processes to new processes and products. Innovation is predominantly a labor-intensive process. However powerful a computer may be, it needs a human brain to start with ideas and make a final evaluation of alternative projects. However labor-saving a new process may be, it needs experienced workers to install and operate it. Creating the human resources and organizations that are most suitable for these needs is the key to successful innovation.

These internal aspects, we note, must be accompanied by external factors. An organization, however capable of being efficient and flexible, need not be so unless external threats of competition and rapid changes in industrial structure exist. Competition among rival firms has been very intensive in many industries in Japan, even where the concentration ratio is not particularly low. Entry into growing industries has been fast and frequent. And shifts in industrial structure have been drastic in the past decades, with some of the top industries now fading into obscurity. These facts provided the firms with a strong sense of crisis and a motivation to be innovative. To maintain the smooth internal labor system, growth and diversification have to be sought internally and the firm has to acquire the necessary technology internally. Consequently, under the threat of competition and of rapidly changing technology and industrial structures, the firm's survival is threatened unless it keeps innovating. Competition in industries, itself a product of the Japanese management system (through the effort to grow internally and diversify, for instance), should never be disregarded as a key to a nation's technical progress.

THE FUTURE?

What shall we expect of the Japanese innovation system in the future? We suggested that the weight of government policies will further decline, particularly because the government is losing most of its control tools through deregulation and liberalization. The industries are less dependent on the government, and government–business personal relations are weakening.

There are a few signs suggesting that a change is inevitable in the Japanese management system. The first is the move by many firms toward increased offshore production. How much this move will make the R&D–production linkage difficult is an important question. The second is the change in financial markets, such as deregulation and an increase in mergers and acquisitions. Again, it is important to know how much impact this change will make on the way Japanese firms make decisions, and particularly on their attitudes toward R&D. The third is the changing environment surrounding labor relations. As the age composition of the Japanese working population is rapidly changing toward that of more senior workers, and as technological change accelerates, it will become more and more difficult for the firms to maintain lifetime employment, and some of the advantages of the Japanese management system may be lost. An increase in offshore production and immigrant workers may further add to this tendency.

The fourth is an increasing need for global research. As international technological race intensifies, and as globalization in production increases, the firm has to be alert to technological development in any part of the world, to technological needs from any production site worldwide, and to international market needs. The need for global research is therefore increasingly felt, and many companies have started establishing research institutions overseas or increasing technological collaborations with foreign firms. Whether the Japanese firm is suitable for this globalization is an interesting question. Sakakibara (1988), for instance, suggests that American managers are more experienced in employing people with different values, personalities, and educational backgrounds, and, therefore, have a higher flexibility and the adaptability needed in international transplantation of technology management. However, the heterogeneity of scientists in the United States and homogeneity in Japan (the difference being not absolute but only relative) may suggest that American scientists working in U. S.-based Japanese firms may adjust more easily than Japanese scientists working in American firms in Japan. To this extent, American firms may be handicapped in obtaining technological knowledge originating from Japan, and the language barrier may further aggravate this handicap. In addition, in view of the R&D–production link in Japanese firms, foreign firms may not be able to carry out research efficiently in Japan unless they have production facilities as well (Westney and Sakakibara, 1986).

Finally, more and more emphasis will be placed on basic research by both private firms and policy-makers. As Japan has caught up with the best practices in the world in many fields and become a leader in some of them, technological seeds that can be imported have become scarce. Even if Japanese firms find technologies they wish to import, it is now common that seller firms attach various restrictive conditions in their offer. Consequently, Japanese firms are now keen to create technology of their own, in particular in the field of basic research. In addition, recent development in high technology has demonstrated the importance of basic research for commercial success.

Many Japanese firms have thus set up basic research laboratories independently of existing research facilities that have been biased toward applied research and development. Although it is sometimes doubtful how basic their version of basic research truly is, the shift of emphasis toward the basic end of technological spectrum is apparent. The government is also emphasizing the need for more basic research, in the belief that, as the status of the Japanese economy in the world rises, its contribution to "international public goods" has to be increased as well. Basic research that contributes to the world stock of knowledge is viewed as such an international public good to which Japan is expected to contribute.

In terms of expenditures on basic research, the increase has been attained far more by industries than universities. During the 10-year period from 1977 to 1987, industries increased the expenditures by 15.8% annually and universities by 6.5%. As a consequence, whereas in 1977 universities undertook 64% of Japan's basic research and companies undertook 20%, the percentages in 1987 were 50 and 34, respectively (STA, 1990). Needless to say, universities have been traditionally assumed to be the prime and most appropriate performers of basic research because industries are unlikely to undertake research with externality and distant commercial applicability. One wonders, therefore, whether the increasing dependence on the private effort can lead to a healthy development of basic research. Insufficient funds in universities is also a problem. In 1987, R&D expenditure per researcher was 25 million yen in companies but only 10 million yen in universities (STA, 1990).

All the above discussions suggest that further changes are inevitable and necessary to the Japanese innovation system. Which way to change can gravely influence future technological performance, and innovation to create a leader's innovation system out of a follower's system, however successful it may have been in the past, is very much in need.

NOTES

We thank Chris Freeman, Richard Nelson, Hugh Patrick, and Nathan Rosenberg for helpful comments to earlier versions.

1. That the Japanese made rice-polishing machines while the West made mills reflects the difference in eating habits. Some authors suggest that this difference caused the Japanese to be good at the machines with reciprocating motion but behind the West at those with rotary motion.

2. We will show later how this factory relates to indigenous *karakuri* technology and to present Toshiba.

3. For national research institutions, Riken, and Gakushin discussed above, see Hiroshige (1973) and Kamatani (1988).

4. The data here are from *Kogyo Chosa Shuho,* 2(2), 1924, reprinted in *Nihon Kagaku Gijutsushi Taikei,* Vol. 3, Tokyo: Daiichi Hoki Shuppan, 1967.

5. See Miyazaki and Ito (1989) for further details of the historical development of the Japanese industry.

6. A survey conducted by Resources Bureau of the Government, quoted in Hiroshige (1973, p. 115).

7. A survey conducted by the Technology Agency of the Cabinet, quoted in the Agency of Industrial Science and Technology (1964, p. 125).

8. Take the case of Zero fighters known for their speed and maneuverability in the beginning. Karasawa (1986) shows that during the 5-year war period, their horsepower could be increased only by 20% whereas Americans and Germans more than doubled the horsepower of their fighters, thereby surpassing Zero fighters. Also, guns on the fighters were difficult to aim and suffered from short range and slowness. The weaker technology in communication and radar was also evident. In the army, too, the trucks and other cars had great trouble, as will be discussed later. Hence, the technological gap between Japan and America seems to have been very large by the end of the war, not to mention America's development of atomic bombs.

9. For Japan's technology importation and the role of government policy up to the mid-1970s, see Peck and Tamura (1976) and Peck and Goto (1981).

10. We will return to the discussion of the postwar industrial policy later.

11. Blumenthal (1976) and Odagiri (1983) found a significantly positive correlation between the amount of royalty payments for imported technology by industries or firms and their R&D expenditures.

12. Some authors, such as Saxonhouse (1985), emphasized the information-disseminating role of cooperative research. It is difficult to estimate how important this role was in RAs. It has been reported that in the much publicized case of the Very-Large-Scale Integrated Circuits

(VLSI) Research Association, it took considerable talent and effort (and drinks!) by the director to have the scientists from different companies mingle (Sakakibara, 1981). Since this RA was quite exceptional in having a common laboratory and a dedicated director from a third party (namely, a government research institution and not companies), we imagine that communication among scientists from different companies must have been infrequent in most other RAs.

13. Two arguments may be made. First, research subjects of the RAs are in principle closer to the basic end, need longer lead time, and have a smaller chance of success than the research subjects of individual firms. Second, when most of the actual and potential rivals are within an RA, there may be little need for protective patents, that is, to apply for patents only to preempt rivals.

14. The discussion in this section is based on miscellaneous Japanese sources including company histories published by respective companies. References will not be given individually.

15. Bureau of Statistics, Management and Coordination Agency, *Report on the Survey of Research and Development.*

16. This fact supports the discussion in footnote 7.

17. See Hirschmeier and Yui (1975).

18. When WE decided to enter the wire business in Japan, NEC recommended Sumitomo, one of the so-called four big zaibatsus before World War II, as the partner because Sumitomo had a big copper business. A new company, Sumitomo Electric Wire (now Sumitomo Electric Industries), was established, jointly owned by WE, Sumitomo, and NEC. In return, Sumitomo acquired a share of NEC.

19. For other views, see Johnson (1982) and Okimoto (1989).

20. This finding agrees with the declining government support on R&D shown in Table 3.2.

21. The number of researchers (or scientists and engineers) is difficult to compare internationally because the definition is different and the necessary data to adjust the Japanese figures to full-time equivalents are lacking. See National Science Foundation (1988).

22. The data on education are from Ministry of Education, *Gakko Kihon Chosa Houkokusho.*

23. For a more detailed discussion of the topic in this section, see Odagiri (1992).

24. As suggested at the end of the previous section, it is incorrect to attribute this ownership pattern to post-zaibatsu business groups. The discussion in the text applies to most firms whether they belong to such groups or not.

25. This reciprocal shareholding is one reason why hostile takeovers are infrequent in Japan. The labor practices in Japan are another reason. See Odagiri (1992, Chapter 5).

26. See Fidler (1981) and Kohn/Ferry (1981) for the United Kingdom and Browne and Motamedi (1977) for the United States.

REFERENCES

Agency of Industrial Science and Technology, the Ministry of International Trade and Industry. (1964). *Gijutsu Kakushin to Nihon no Kogyo: Kogyo Gijutsu-in 15 Nen no Ayumi.* [Innovation and Industries in Japan: The 15 Year History of the Agency of Industrial Science and Technology]. Tokyo: Nikkan Kogyo Shimbunsha.

Asanuma, B. (1985). "The Contractual Framework for Parts Supply in the Japanese Automotive Industry." *Journal of Japanese Studies* Summer, 54–78.

Blumenthal, T. (1976). "Japan's Technological Strategy." *Journal of Development Economics* 3: 245–55.

Browne, W. G., and Motamedi, K. K. (1977). "Transition at the Top." *California Management Review* 20(2): 67–73.

Clark K. B., and Fujimoto, T. (1991). *Product Development Performance: Strategy, Organization, and Management in the World Auto Industry.* Boston: Harvard Business School Press.

Eads, G. C., and Nelson, R. R. (1986). "Japanese

High Technology Policy: What Lessons for the United States?" In Hugh Patrick (ed.), *Japan's High Technology Industries,* 243–69. Seattle: University of Washington Press.

Fidler, J. (1981). *The British Business Elite: Its Attitudes to Class, Status and Power.* London: Routledge and Kegan Paul.

Fujishiro, N. (1988). "Computer Sangyo ni Okeru Kyodo-Kenkyu no Yakuwari." [The Role of Joint R&D in the Computer Industry]. Unpublished master's thesis, University of Tsukuba.

Goto, A. (1982). "Business Groups in a Market Economy." *European Economic Review* 19: 53–70.

Goto, A. (1988) "Japan: A Sunset Industry." In Merton Peck (ed.), *The World Aluminium Industry in a Changing Energy Era.* Washington, D. C.: Resources for the Future.

Goto, A., and Wakasugi, R. (1988). "Technology Policy." In R. Komiya, M. Okuno, and K. Suzumura (eds.), *Industrial Policy of Japan,* 183–204. New York: Academic Press.

Hiroshige, T. (1973). *Kagaku no Shakaishi* [The Social History of Science]. Tokyo: Chuo Koron Sha.

Hirschmeier, J., and Yui, T. (1975). *The Development of Japanese Business, 1600–1973.* London: George Allen & Unwin.

Iida, K. (1979). *Nippon Tekkou Gijutsu Shi* [The History of Iron and Steel Technology in Japan]. Tokyo: Toyo Keizai Shinposha.

Imai, K., Nonaka, I., and Takeuchi, H. (1985). "Managing the New Product Development Process: How Japanese Companies Learn and Unlearn." In K. B. Clark, R. H. Hayes, and C. Lorenz (eds.), *The Uneasy Alliance,* 337–75. Boston: Harvard Business School Press.

Johnson, C. (1982). *MITI and the Japanese Miracle.* Stanford: Stanford University Press.

Kaigo, M. (ed.) (1971). *Nihon Kindai Kyouiku Jiten* [Encyclopedia on Modern Education in Japan]. Tokyo: Heibon Sha.

Kamatani, C. (1988) *Gijutsu Taikoku 100 Nen no Kei: Nihon no Kindaika to Kokuritsu Kenkyuu Kikan* [The 100 Year Strategy to an Innovative Country: Japan's Modernization and the National Research Institutions]. Tokyo: Heibonsha.

Karasawa, E. (1986). "Koku Gijutsu no Hizumi." [Deficiencies in Aircraft Technology]. In K. Hasegawa (ed.), *Nihon Kindai to Senso,* Vol. 6, 193–224. [Modern Japan and Wars]. Kyoto: PHP.

Kohn/Ferry International in Conjunction with the London Business School (1981). *British Corporate Leaders—A Profile.* London: Kohn/Ferry International.

Komiya, R., Okuno, M., and Suzumura, K. (eds.) (1988). *Industrial Policy of Japan.* New York: Academic Press.

Kono, T. (1984). *Strategy and Structure of Japanese Enterprises.* London: Macmillan.

Lynn, L. H. (1982). *How Japan Innovates.* Boulder: Westview Press.

Marris, R. L. (1964). *An Economic Theory of 'Managerial' Capitalism.* London: Macmillan.

Minami, R. (1981). *Nippon no Keizai Hatten* [Economic Development in Japan]. Tokyo: Toyo Keizai Shinposha.

Miyazaki, M., and Ito, O. (1989). "Senji Sengo no Sangyo to Kigyo" [Industries and Firms during and after the War]. In T. Nakamura (ed.), *Nihon Keizaishi 7: Keikakuka to Minshuka,* 165–235. [The History of Japanese Economy, Vol. 7: Planning and Democratization], Tokyo: Iwanami Shoten.

National Science Foundation (1988). *The Science and Technology Resources of Japan: A Comparison with the United States.* Washington, D. C.: U. S. Government Printing Office.

Odagiri, H. (1983). "R&D Expenditures, Royalty Payments, and Sales Growth in Japanese Manufacturing Corporations." *Journal of Industrial Economics* 32(1): 61–71.

Odagiri, H. (1992). *Growth through Competition, Competition through Growth: Strategic Management and the Economy in Japan.* Oxford: Oxford University Press.

Okimoto, D. I. (1989). *Between MITI and the Market: Japanese Industrial Policy for High Technology.* Stanford: Stanford University Press.

Patent Office (1955). *Tokkyo Seido 70 Nen Shi* [The 70 Year History of the Patent System]. Tokyo: Hatsumei Kyokai.

Peck, M. J., and Goto, A. (1981). "Technology and Economic Growth: The Case of Japan." *Research Policy* 10(3): 222–43.

Peck, M. J., and Tamura, S. (1976). "Technology." In H. Patrick and H. Rosovsky (eds.), *Asia's New Giant,* 525–85. Washington, D. C.: The Brookings Institution.

Sakakibara, K. (1981). "Soshiki to Innovation: Jirei Kenkyu, Cho LSI Gijutsu Kenkyu Kumiai" [Organization and Innovation: A Case Study of VLSI Technology Association]. *The Hitotsubashi Review* 86(2): 160–75.

Sakakibara, K. (1988). "Managing Global Innovation: The Challenge of International Transplantation of Technology Management." Working Paper No. 8803, Hitotsubashi University.

Sakakibara, K., and Westney, D. E. (1985). "Comparative Study of the Training, Careers, and Organization of Engineers in the Computer Industry in the United States and Japan." *Hitotsubashi Journal of Commerce & Management* 20(1): 1–20.

Sawai, M. (1990). "Kikai Kogyo." [Machinery Industry]. In S. Nishikawa and T. Abe (eds.), *Nihon Keizaishi 4: Sangyo-ka no Jidai,* 213–53. Tokyo: Iwanami Shoten.

Saxonhouse, G. (1985). "Japanese Cooperative R&D Ventures: A Market Evaluation." Discussion Paper No. 156, Department of Economics, University of Michigan.

Science and Technology Agency (STA) (1990, 1991). *Kagaku Gijutsu Hakusho.* [White Paper on Science and Technology]. Tokyo: Printing Bureau of the Ministry of Finance.

Umihara, T. (1988). *Kinsei no Gakko to Kyouiku* [Schools and Education in the Tokugawa Japan]. Kyoto: Shibunkaku.

Wakasugi, R., and Goto, A. (1985). "Kyodo Kenkyu Kaihatsu to Gijutsu Kakushin." [Joint R&D and Technological Innovation]. In Y. Okamoto and T. Wakasugi (eds.), *Gijutsu Kakushin to Kigyo Kodo,* 193–217. Tokyo: Tokyo University Press.

Westney, D. E., and Sakakibara, K. (1986). "The Role of Japan-Based R&D in Global Technology Strategy." In M. Horwitch (ed.), *Technology in the Modern Corporation: A Strategic Perspective,* 217–32. Oxford: Pergamon Press.

4

The National System for Technical Innovation in Germany

OTTO KECK[1]

Germany is a special case, for several reasons. One is its recent political history. After World War II the country was divided into two states with opposed political–economic systems, the Federal Republic of Germany in the West (with a capitalist economy and a pluralist democracy) and the German Democratic Republic in the East (with a centrally planned economy and an authoritarian socialist political system). The contrast between a strong economy in the West and an acerbating economic crisis in the East was one of the reasons for the revolution that in 1989 and early 1990 brought down the socialist system in the East. By joining the Federal Republic in October 1990, the Eastern part with a population of 17 million adopted the political and economic institutions of the Western part, including those relating to technology and science.

A second factor that makes Germany a special case is the export performance of its economy. West Germany, with a population of 61 million, exported in the year 1988 goods of a total value of $323 billion, about the same as the United States ($320 billion), and more than Japan ($265 billion). On a per capita base, this is 4.0 times more that the United States and 2.4 more than Japan.[2]

Institutional forms that today are taken for granted in most national systems for technical innovation, such as the research-oriented university that combines its educational function with the advancement of scientific knowledge, and the science-based firm with an in-house R&D laboratory separated from production, were pioneered as social innovations in nineteenth-century Germany. Soon they were adopted by other countries. Also in technical education Germany provided an impulse for emulation in some other countries. Hence a historical description of the origins of the German system for technical innovation may not only help in understanding the present system in Germany, but also shed some light on the cross-fertilization among different national systems of technical innovation that occurred by emulating institutional forms across national boundaries while adapting them to specific national environments and sometimes improving them. This is the third reason why Germany may be regarded as a special case.

The performance of the West Germany economy is sometimes explained by reference to a supposed national character, in particular to the Germans' reputation for

115

being hard-working people. The gap in performance between the Western and the Eastern part of the country does not contradict such an explanation, since relative to other socialist states the economy in the German Democratic Republic did have a high standing. However, the explanation is refuted by data on annual working time. Industrial workers in Germany have a contractual working time of 1615 hours per year, compared to 2201 hours in Japan, 1904 hours in the United States, and 1775 hours in France.[3] The technical capability of German industry, built on the hard work of former generations, now enables industrial workers to work fewer hours per year than in other advanced countries.

This chapter therefore looks to institutional structures rather than national character to explain economic performance. Among the many institutions that contribute to economic performance it focuses on those that relate to the technological capability of industry. The first section describes the evolution of the innovation system up to the beginning of the twentieth century, the second carries the historical account to the present time, and the third analyzes the present system and discusses some of its challenges.

HISTORICAL ORIGINS IN THE NINETEENTH CENTURY

Among European states, Germany was a latecomer, in both political and economic terms. Its development had experienced a setback in the seventeenth century through the devastations of the Thirty Years' War, which reduced the population by about a third. The slow pace of development was reflected in the fragmentation of the country: as of 1789 there existed 314 independent territories and more than 1400 imperial knighthoods. Many of the territories had their own laws, currency, weights and measures, taxes, and custom tolls. The way to unification was cumbersome. The Napoleonic wars and the Congress of Vienna reduced the number of territories to 39 by the year 1815. In 1834 Prussia with some other German states formed a customs union to which most other German states acceded until 1867. Political union was eventually achieved in 1871. The German empire was a federal state, in which central government was responsible only for some state functions, mainly foreign policy and the military. The education system was under the jurisdiction of the federal states.[4]

Throughout the nineteenth century there was a conflict between the advocates of political reform and industrialization (coming mainly from the German bourgeoisie) and those striving to preserve the autocratic political order. One of the leading protagonists of industrial development was Friedrich List, from 1817 to 1820 professor of political economy at the University of Tübingen. When his views made him clash with the political authorities, he took refuge in exile in the United States. In opposition to the classical political economy of Adam Smith and David Ricardo he advocated an evolutionary perspective focusing on the development of the productive forces. He proposed a customs union comprising central Europe that by means of protective tolls would enable domestic industry to catch up through import substitution, using imported machinery.[5]

In the first third of the nineteenth century Germany turned to foreign countries, mainly to Britain, but also to Belgium, for new machinery and for skilled workers to bring advanced technology to its industries. New types of machinery in the cotton, woollen, and linen industries, the first steam engines, and the first locomotives were imported from Britain.

British and Belgian artisans were instrumental in transferring technical know-how to Germany in the machine-building and iron and steel industries. To protect the technological lead of its industries, Britain prohibited by law the emigration of skilled workers until 1824 and, for many of its advanced industries, up to 1843 the export of machinery, including models and drawings, as well as tools and utensils. Yet these laws were difficult to enforce, and in a number of cases the British government granted export licenses. German governments often provided financial support for the purchase of foreign machines, which were sometimes used as demonstration objects. Technical knowledge was also acquired through German visitors, often with encouragement and financial support by the government, and sometimes by industrial espionage.[6]

Given the backward state of the polity and the economy, the government had a key role in the country's development. The customs union, political unification, abolishment of traditional restrictions on the freedom to engage in business (Gewerbefreiheit), construction of roads and canals, encouragement of railway construction, and creation of a capable civil service were all important factors. And so was the mainly government-financed system for education and research in technology, science, and business.

The Education System

In the early nineteenth century, France was the center of science in the world.[7] Many German scientists, for example the chemist Justus Liebig, went to Paris to learn the state of the art. French institutions of higher education, in particular the Ecole Polytechnique, served as stimulus and model (though not always correctly represented). But unlike in France the university became the institutional focus of scientific research in Germany. This was not a preordained development. In the eighteenth century, academies of science had been founded in several German states, and scientific research was primarily their task. Many universities were in a poor state, and some voices favored the idea of abolishing them altogether.

However, some of the states managed to break away from this condition by reforming their universities or by establishing new ones with a reformed curriculum.[8] Prominent among these were the universities of Halle and Göttingen. The latter was founded in 1742 by the Kingdom of Hanover on the initiative of a noble civil servant, Gerlach Adolf von Münchhausen. Aiming to attract students from abroad (meaning from other German states) he designed a new curriculum and established the practice of selecting professors on the basis of their literary reputation derived from their publications. Göttingen soon became a center of scholarship.

Although the reforms introduced by Göttingen and other universities were important for the further development of the German university system, the origins of the orientation toward research were more widespread. In a study on the emerging chemical community in Germany, Hufbauer counted 11 laboratories in the year 1780, eight of which were located at medical departments and two at mining schools. Although these laboratories were small and poorly equipped by later standards, they are evidence that empirical scientific research had a hold at the universities.[9] In late

eighteenth century some apothecaries expanded their pharmacies into private institutes that trained pharmacists, manufactured such drugs and chemicals as were traditionally custom-made by the pharmacies, and also engaged in laboratory research.
Some of these institutes reached such a high level that their courses were certified by
the government to be equivalent to university courses.[10]

Up to the present time the standard rhetoric in Germany dates the origin of the
modern university to the founding of the Berlin University in 1809/1810. What made
Berlin special was the association of the new university with reform ideas coming from
German idealist philosophy. The new ideal of the university as proposed by Wilhelm
von Humboldt, Johann Gottlieb Fichte, Friedrich Schleiermacher, and others was
predicated on the assumption that the formation of an individual personality was
more important for human beings than the acquisition of useful knowledge and skills.
For idealist philosophy, becoming a personality was the highest goal in individual life,
the uppermost realization of human destiny that sets humans apart from animal life.
This ideal survived the fall of idealist philosophy and provided the personal orientation
(and often the personal ideology) for the more traditional groups of German intellec-
tuals throughout the nineteenth century.[11] According to its idealist conception the university was to be an autonomous community of teachers and students, where those by
devoting themselves to science would develop their individual personalities. Devotion
to science implied an orientation toward research, not only for the professors but also
for the students. Teaching at its best would introduce the student to doing creative
research.

However, the influence of the idealist conception of the university is generally
overestimated.[12] First, the key proponents of the idealistic ideal had only a short reign
in the government of the university. Wilhelm von Humboldt left his office as director
of religious affairs and public education in the Prussian Ministry of the Interior 4
months before the university was formally opened, and Fichte stepped down as the
first rector of the university after about a year. Institutional details were worked out by
civil servants in the upper echelons of the Prussian bureaucracy, and they moderated
idealism by utilitarian considerations of what type of education the Prussian state
deemed desirable for its future civil servants, lawyers, doctors, and high-school
teachers.

Second, the idealist concept of science focused on such elevating fields as philosophy, mathematics, and the humanities. Laboratory research was given low standing,
and empirical science had to fight for emancipation from the domination of idealistic
natural philosophy.[13]

Third, during the upheavals of the Napoleonic wars more than a dozen universities vanished, mainly small and poor ones. Governance of the universities by the
state bureaucracy improved as the territorial reordering increased the average size of
individual states and as general administrative reforms were introduced after the
Napoleonic wars.

By the middle of the nineteenth century the research orientation was firmly established at German universities. It was supported by an institutional base, comprising
institutes with laboratories for the natural sciences, and specialized libraries (called
"Seminars") for the humanities.[14] At Berlin, for example, funds for this institutional
base doubled every decade between 1830 and 1870. University research in Germany

rose to a high level, and in some fields, such as medicine, chemistry and physics ascended to world leadership.[15]

Student numbers did not grow between 1830 and 1870 (see Fig. 4.1), but thereafter they increased rapidly: from 14,000 in 1870 to nearly 60,000 in 1914. Government funds for the universities increased even faster than the number of students: from 1860 to 1910 by a factor of about five in real terms.[16] This expansion fostered specialization, and many universities then created separate departments for natural science.[17]

Contrary to much wishful rhetoric stressing their autonomy, the rise of the German universities took place under close supervision by state officials.[18] Most prominent among these was Friedrich Althoff, a senior official in the Prussian Ministry of Culture from 1882 to 1907, who pursued, with great zeal and political skill, a policy of expanding the Prussian universities and raising their standard still further. He filled professorial chairs with the best people in their fields and provided them with adequate facilities.[19] As he relied on a network of private confidants to make his selections, often cajoled departments into accepting his canditates, and sometimes appointed them against their will; his style produced controversy. Nevertheless, even those objecting to his ways acknowledged his merit.

Whereas in the area of science the German university system in the nineteenth century accomplished very much, it did nothing for engineering. In the mind of professors and administrators, engineering lacked the dignity of science, and for this reason it was not admitted to the university. More accurately, it was driven out, for in the late eighteenth and early nineteenth century, university education for civil servants was rather broad and, in addition to law, political economy, and political science, com-

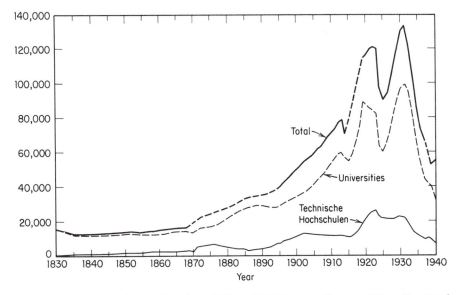

Figure 4.1. Students in higher education, 1830 to 1940. Source: Hartmut Titze, *Das Hochschulstudium in Preussen und Deutschland 1820–1944*, p. 26. Gottingen: Vandenhoek und Ruprecht, 1987.

prised the knowledge of techniques for agriculture, mining, and manufacturing. The German political economists of the eighteenth century, the so-called "cameralists," recognized the importance of these techniques for the economy and established "technology" (in German "Technologie"), in the precise meaning of this word in the sense of knowledge of techniques, as a subject for university teaching.[20]

Some engineering schools had been founded in the eighteenth century to train civil servants for government service: as administrators in the mining industry (which at that time consisted maily of state enterprises), as civil engineers and architects, or as military engineers and artillery officers. The graduates from these schools were with some exceptions reluctant to go into private industry, since this conferred a much lower social status than public service.[21]

In the early 1820s Prussia took the lead in establishing a system of schools to train technicians for private industry. It soon comprised about 20 vocational schools in the provinces providing 1-year full-time courses for craftsmen and factory shopmasters and, above the provincial schools, the Technical Institute (Gewerbeinstitut) in Berlin offering a 2-year course for technicians with the objective of enabling them to set up and manage factories.[22] Most major German states quickly followed by establishing polytechnical schools.[23]

The vocational schools expanded by offering one or more years of preparatory courses and most were gradually transformed into secondary schools for general education that differed from the traditional secondary school in Germany, the "Gymnasium," only by not teaching Latin and Greek and by stressing mathematics and natural sciences. In the 1870s their students were admitted to the university.

The polytechnical schools gradually improved their teaching and raised entrance requirements. They gained in social recognition, when their graduates were accepted for public service. To fashion themselves as equals of the universities, they stressed the use of scientific method and mathematics. The organizational politics of the polytechnical schools became part of the effort of the German engineering profession, organized since 1856 in the Union of German Engineers (Verein Deutscher Ingenieure), to obtain a social recognition equal to the university-based professions.[24]

In the 1870s the polytechnical schools were elevated to higher status. They were now called Technische Hochschulen, required similar entrance qualifications as the universities, and distinguished their graduates from lesser kinds of engineers by the special designation of *Diplom-Ingenieur*. A further step toward equal status with the universities was achieved in 1899, when after long political battles against the bitter resistance of the universities the King of Prussia decided in person to give the Technische Hochschulen in Prussia the right to grant doctoral degrees.[25] The other states soon followed.

The fact that the Technische Hochschulen made their way by emulating the universities had some negative repercussions. One was an overemphasis on theory, which led their education in a direction that may not quite have been in line with what industry needed.[26] Only in the last decade of the century, after sometimes bitter controversies, did experimental laboratories become generally established in the departments for machine construction. Here the German Technische Hochschulen in fact learned from engineering schools in the United States. The World Exposition at Chicago in 1893 demonstrated the very high standard of the American machine tool industry, and Alois Riedler, one of the leading German engineering professors, saw one of the reasons for it in the engineering education at American universities, in particular their use of laboratories.[27]

As polytechnical schools were upgraded to university level and vocational schools were transformed into secondary schools for general education, a gap opened at the middle level of technical education. There is a scattered history of specialized technical and commercial schools in the nineteenth century, but these could not fill the gap. Toward the end of the century the states created new technical schools offering courses up to 2 years. The lower technical middle schools were open to everybody who had gone through compulsory school training (normally age 6 to 14) and had 3 to 6 years of practical experience, while the higher technical middle schools normally required 4 years of elementary and 6 years of secondary school. These new schools were first established in mechanical engineering and textiles, and later also in other fields such as electrical engineering. However, the middle-level schools financed by the government were also tempted to direct their education more to careers in government than in private industry, they were slow to take up new developments in electrical technology and automobiles, and some of the smaller states could not affort them. For these reasons there existed many private technical schools, which before World War I had more students than the state schools.[28]

The basic level of technical training was provided by the traditional apprenticeship. The old craft guilds were abolished in the first half of the century, but the apprenticeship system, though beset with weaknesses and misuse, lived on with some reforms.[29] Although some of the old crafts vanished and the relative importance of the craft sector decreased in this period, the craft sector as a whole still grew and provided a pool of skilled manpower on which firms in the new industries could draw.[30] In the 1860s some firms in the machine construction industry began their own apprenticeship programs; in the 1880s firms in the electrical and optical industries did the same.

Toward the end of the nineteenth century the apprenticeship system was reorganized. Chambers of trade were charged with examination. Part-time schools were established in 1897 for further education of all those who had finished the normal school (Volksschule), supplementing the practical training in firms and craftshops. As these schools initially continued the general education of the Volksschule, some firms created their own schools, more oriented toward specialized vocational training, and had them approved by the government.[31]

Around 1900 a number of business schools were founded at the higher education level, mainly on initiatives of individuals from commerce and industry, chambers of commerce, or city governments. They later developed into university-level institutions, and some were expanded into full universities. These schools played an important role in developing business economics into a specialized subject, later taught at many universities and Technische Hochschulen.[32] Education at these schools became a routine entry into business management. Also for commercial education middle-level schools were established, the *Handelsschulen* and *Höhere Handelsschulen*. At the lowest level, the apprenticeship system trained people for commerce; so a system of several levels emerged, similar to the one for technical education.

Today it is taken for granted in most industrialized countries that the basis of all specialized training is a general education for everybody between the age of 6 and 13 or 14. Germany established general education in the eighteenth century, that is before industrialization, whereas in Britain it came only toward the end of the nineteenth century, long after industrialization. By many indicators of literacy, Germany was among the top group of European nations in the first half of the nineteenth century. In terms of primary school enrollment rate per capita, the United States and Germany were until about 1880 far above France or Britain.[33]

By the beginning of the twentieth century Germany had established a sophisticated system for education in scientific, technical, and commercial matters, reaching from elementary school to the doctoral level.[34] There were close connections between the different levels in most areas of specialization, as the teachers for the schools at a given level were normally educated at one of the higher levels. There was also a flow of knowledge between universities and Technische Hochschulen, as many areas of science such as chemistry were pursued in both, though usually with a greater emphasis on applied science in the Technische Hochschulen. And there were links between the education system and industrial firms, not only through the supply of trained personnel, but also through consultancy by professors in engineering and in areas of applied science.

The relative importance of the various schools of technical and scientific education is indicated by the data on student enrollments for Prussia given in Table 4.1. They show that the universities dominated, and that student numbers at the middle

Table 4.1. Student Enrollments in Prussia in the Years 1891 and 1911

	1891	1911
Technical schools at the middle level:		
Lower-middle		
Textiles	44	200
Machinery	574	1653
Upper-middle		
Textiles	344	800
Machinery	54	1107
Total middle-level	1016	3760
Schools in higher education		
Universities of	12826	27501
Theology		
Law		
Medicine		
Mathematics and natural science		
Economics, agriculture, forestry		
Technische Hochschulen	1910	4064
Business schools	—	1277
Mining academies	245	216
Veterinary medicine	665	635
Agriculture	544	890
Forestry	120	139
Theology	370	626
Total higher education:	16680	35348

Sources: P. Lundgreen, "Educational Expansion and Economic Growth in Nineteenth-Century German." In L. Stone (ed.), *Schooling and Society,* pp. 20–66. Baltimore: Johns Hopkins University Press, 1976 (for lower and upper middle level); Hartmut Titze, *Das Hochschulstudium in Preußen und Deutschland 1820–1944,* pp. 37–38. Göttingen: Vandenhoek and Ruprecht 1987 (for higher education).

level of technical education were of the same order of magnitude as students at Technische Hochschulen.

What set this system apart from that of other countries was not only the relatively high standard of research at universities and Technische Hochschulen, but also its large size. From 1820 to 1850 Prussia trained, relative to the size of its population, more technicians than France.[35] Measured as percentage of the 20- to 24-year-old age group, student enrollment in higher education was around the year 1880 about the same as in Sweden, but considerably larger than in France or Italy. In mathematics and natural science Germany then educated about two times more university students than did Italy and eight times more than France. In institutes of higher education other than universities, which comprise mainly technical schools, Germany trained twice as many students as Italy or France.[36] During the first decade of the twentieth century about 30,000 engineers graduated from colleges and universities in Germany compared to about 21,000 in the United States. Relative to the size of the population this means two times more in Germany than in the United States.[37] In 1913 there were about 10 times more engineering students in Germany than in England and Wales.[38]

The German universities and, by the end of the nineteenth century, also the Technische Hochschulen attracted many foreign students and served as stimulus for reform or for emulation in other countries, among them Britain, France, and the United States.[39] Sometimes they were idealized, in particular by individuals trying to promote reforms in their own countries.

Despite its strengths, the German educational system did have some weak points.[40] There were enormous tensions between universities and Technische Hochschulen and, more generally, between the neohumanistic ideals of the German bourgoisie and the worlds of industry and technology. Their intellectual orientation made university professors often averse to exploiting new ideas for commercial purposes.[41] Neither the industrialization process at large nor the system for technical and scientific education in particular was the result of a unified ideology.[42]

Specialized Research Organizations

In addition to the universities, the Technische Hochschulen, and the academies of science, central government and the federal states financed at the beginning of the twentieth century some 40 to 50 research institutes for specialized research in applied areas such as weather and atmosphere, geography and geology, health, shipbuilding, hydroengineering, biology, agriculture, fishery, and forestry.[43] Some of them had military purposes; most were oriented toward public tasks such as public health or safety regulation and some toward supporting technical innovation in the business sector.

Among the latter, a major new departure was the Imperial Institute of Physics and Technology (Physikalisch-technische Reichsanstalt, now the Physikalisch-technische Bundesanstalt), founded in 1887 mainly with finance from central government for work on standards and measures, for the development of precision instruments, and for basic research in this area. The initiative came from scientists and industrialists, among them Werner von Siemens, founder and director of the firm carrying this name, who made a donation toward the cost of the institute. Its task was defined as "physical investigations and measurements which primarily aim at solving scientific problems of great impact in theoretical or technical respect and require larger means in terms of instruments, materials and working time of observers and calculators than can be provided by private people or educational institutions."[44] By 1913 its total staff numbered 139, of which 50 were academically trained scientists and engineers.[45] The Institute served as an example for similar institutions in other countries, for example, the National Physical Laboratory in England (founded 1900), the National Bureau of Standards in the United States (1901), and the Institute of Physical and Chemical Research in Japan (1917).[46]

When the chemical industry proposed a "Chemical-Technical Imperial Institute" similar to the Physical-Technical Imperial Institute, this project became part of Friedrich Althoff's plan to set up a number of special research institutes outside the university system so as to complement the universities' research capabilities for basic and applied research.[47] American precedents such as the Rockefeller foundation had fostered in Germany the idea to tap industry as a source for research funds. About 10 million Mark were brought together until 1911, when the Kaiser-Wilhelm-Society was founded.[48] A second source of income was the membership fees of industrial firms that joined the Society. The state contributed real estate, the salaries of some of the institute directors, and in some cases further financial support. To 1914 five institutes were established: for chemistry, physical chemistry, coal research, biology, and experimental therapy. The first three, which did applied research, were nearly totally financed by industry.

Some smaller research institutes financed jointly by government and industry precede the Kaiser-Wilhelm-Society. The first may have been an experimental station founded in 1874 by the Association of Spirit Manufactureres (Verein der Spiritusfabrikanten). When in the 1880s it was associated with the Agricultural College (Landwirtschaftliche Hochschule) at Berlin, government provided the ground and the building, while the industry association paid for the equipment and operating costs.[49] At the university of Göttingen the mathematician Felix Klein persuaded industrialists to support several new institutes for applied research. One of them was an experimental station for motor aviation, which under Ludwig Prandtl's direction soon held a leading position in aerodynamics.[50] In biomedical research, private industry contributed funds to some institutes; for example, that of Emil Behring at Marburg and that of Paul Ehrlich at Frankfurt am Main.[51]

At the turn of the century dozens of foundations for scientific research were founded, some of which became the backbone of new research institutes, often affiliated with universities of Technische Hochschulen. Also some technical associations, as for example the Verein Deutscher Ingenieure, provided funds for research projects.[52]

Government Finance

In the five decades between 1860 and 1913 government funds for higher education and scientific research increased in real terms by a factor of about nine (see Table 4.2). Relative to gross national product, they more than doubled between 1860 and 1880, and thereafter they grew at about the same rate as the gross national product. As can be seen from Table 4.2, the federal states provided most of the funds for higher education and science. However, their share fell from 100% in 1860 (when there was no central government) to less than 80% in 1900.

Table 4.2. Public Expenditure for Science in Germany and the Federal Republic of Germany

Year	Total Public Expenditure for Science[a]				Contribution by	
	At Current Prices (Million Mark)	At Constant Prices (Million Mark as of 1913)	As Percent of Total Government Expenditure	As Percent of Net Social Product	Central Government (As Percent of Total)	Federal States (As Percent of Total)
German Empire						
1860	6.0	10.7	1.0	0.06	—	100.0
1870	10.5	14.7	1.1	0.08	2.2	97.8
1880	27.3	33.6	1.5	0.16	10.1	89.9
1890	32.7	37.4	1.0	0.14	18.0	82.0
1900	53.2	59.9	1.1	0.16	21.2	78.8
1910	91.2	94.8	1.1	0.20	22.9	77.1
1913	101.9	101.9	1.2	0.19	21.9	78.1
1925	282.9	206.8	2.2	0.42	39.2	60.8
1930	359.6	241.3	1.9	0.55	29.5	70.5
1938	513.4	446.6	1.6	0.52	46.8	53.2
Federal Republic						
1955	1,208	494	2.8	0.75	15.2	84.8
1960	2,352	844	4.0	0.89	26.7	73.3
1970	14,205	4,943	8.4	2.34	36.3	63.7
1980	30,249	5,038	7.1	2.31	38.2	61.8
1988	42,759	5,842	7.8	2.30	35.5	64.5

[a]In addition to research and development public expenditure for science includes expenditure for teaching and for scientific and technical services.

Sources: Data on the German empire from F. Pfetsch, *Datenhandbuch zur Wissenschaftsentwicklung.* Cologne: Zentrum für historische Sozialforschung, 1982; F. Pfetsch, "Staatliche Wissenschaftsförderung 1870–1980." In R. vom Bruch and R. A. Müller (eds.), *Formen außerstaatlicher Wissenschaftsförderung,* pp. 113–138. Stuttgart: Steiner, 1990. Data on the Federal Republic from *Bundesbericht Forschung 1984* (Bundestagsdrucksache 10/1543), 1984; Bundesminister für Forschung und Technologie, *Faktenbericht 1990 zum Bundesbericht Forschung 1988,* Bonn, 1990. Data on net social product and the price index for state consumption from W. G. Hoffmann, F. Krumbach, and H. Hesse, *Das Wachstum der deutschen Wirtschaft seit der Mitte des 19. Jahrhunderts,* pp. 598–601. Berlin: Springer, 1965; Statistisches Bundesamt, *Statistisches Jahrbuch 1989.* Stuttgart: Metzler-Poeschel, 1990.

Industry

The first major science-based industry in Germany was the *beet-sugar industry*. The close similarity of the content of the sugar beet and of cane sugar was recognized as early as 1747 by the pharmacist/chemist Andreas Sigismund Markgraf at the Berlin Academy of Sciences, who in 1753 became director of the Academy's new chemical laboratory. His successor Franz Carl Achard developed a process for extracting and refining sugar from beets. With financial support from the Prussian King he established a commercial sugar factory, which, because of high operating cost, however, became a commercial failure. When Napoleon cut off European trade with Britain, the beet-sugar industry experienced a first, though artificial boom.[53] In the late nineteenth century the beet-sugar industry became a major exporter for Germany: up to 1898 the value of sugar exports exceeded that of machinery, and in 1913 it still exceeded that of synthetic dyestuffs.[54] In addition to chemical research, this industry had a base in agricultural research. The sugar content of beets was increased from initially about 2 to 15.5%.

In 1866 the Association of the Beet Sugar Industry (Verein für die Rübenzuck-erindustrie) founded a chemical laboratory, which may have been the first institute for industrial cooperative research. In 1903 this laboratory was affiliated with the agricultural college (Landwirtschaftliche Hochschule) at Berlin and then financed jointly by government and industry.[55]

The origin of the *pharmaceutical industry* was in the private pharmaceutical institutes that existed in the early decades of the nineteenth century. Two of them later turned into chemical-pharmaceutical firms. Many of their graduates founded their own business. One of them was Heinrich Emanuel Merck, who in the 1820s began to produce pharmaceuticals on a larger scale in an apothecary shop at Darmstadt founded in 1654. By 1900 the Merck company employed 800 workers, including 50 chemists, pharmacists, engineers, and doctors; by 1913 it was the largest German firm specializing in pharmaceuticals. In 1899 the American subsidiary Merck & Co. was founded.

Also some other leaders in pharmaceuticals including Schering AG and J. D. Riedel were started by pharmacists. Still others such as von Heyden, de Han, and C. F. Boehringer started as druggists or as makers of fine chemicals. In the last third of the century technical innovation in this industry drew heavily on the advanced state of medical and biological research at the universities. By 1913 Germany was the largest exporter of pharmaceuticals with a 30.3% share of world exports, far ahead of Britain (21.3%), the United States (13%), and France (11.9%).[56]

Important lines of business in the *chemical industry* supplied inputs to the textile industry, in particular for bleaching and dyeing. Here Germany was far behind Britain and Belgium up to the middle of the nineteenth century. Around that time many German chemists worked in Britain, as the industry in Germany could not absorb all the graduates with formal university training. German firms acquired a technological and commercial lead first in synthetic dyes. The main producers were BASF, Hoechst, and Bayer, all founded in the 1860s. Later they became Germany's largest chemical companies.[57] It was in the German synthetic dyestuffs industry that scientific research first became a continuous company function separated from production.[58] This union of science and business was not always easily achieved. While BASF and Hoechst were founded as partnerships of chemists and businessmen, Bayer was started by a dye merchant and a dyer. It fell behind its competitors until, after several false starts, it hired a capable chemist, Carl Duisberg, who placed the firm's business on a new footing by synthesizing a new dye and later became the company's chief executive. By 1913 Germany produced about three-quarters to four-fifths of total world output in synthetic dyes and accounted for 90% of world exports. The main German firms had 15% of their production located abroad.[59]

Toward the end of the century new or improved processes for some bulk chemicals provided an opportunity to compete effectively with established producers. Electrolysis opened new fields of activity, and first steps were made in synthetic fibers. At the beginning of the twentieth century photochemicals and new pharmaceuticals broadened the range of business. By 1913 the German chemical industry accounted for 24 percent of world production, whereas the United States contributed 35 percent, Britain 21 percent, and France 9 percent. About 35 percent of domestic German production were exported, so Germany held a share of 27 percent of world exports, followed by Great Britain with 16 percent, France and the United States, each with a share of 10 percent.[60]

Although some parts of the industry were favored by geographic conditions (Germany had a virtual monopoly of potash at that time), the dyestuffs, synthetic fertilizers, and pharmaceutical industries are evidence that technological innovation, based on the country's educational and research systems, was the key factor that enabled the industry to establish itself as leader on the world export market. According to one estimate nearly 3000 chemists were employed in German industry by 1897.[61]

For the *mining and metal processing* industries the mining schools trained generations of administrators and managers in the eighteenth and nineteenth centuries. Professors of these schools were instrumental in the transfer of technology from abroad and their graduates pioneered some new processes, as, for example, the extraction of petrol and paraffin from lignite.[62]

In *iron and steel,* one of the central industries in the nineteenth century, application of science was a slow process. The first known instance of a chemist to be employed by an iron works dates back to 1820s, and for two decades this was the only known instance.[63] However, by the middle of the century, when railroad construction brought a boom to iron and steel production, most of the larger works employed a chemist for the analysis of ore inputs and of outputs, while smaller works commissioned their analyses to apothecaries, independent chemical institutes, or institutes at technical universities. In the 1860s the first plans for a cooperative "testing station" were discussed, but they materialized only in 1917 with the foundation of the institute for iron research within the Kaiser-Wilhelm-Society.

Although German steel output exceeded that of Britain by the end of the nineteenth century, major innovations such as the Bessemer and the Thomas processes were made in Britain, and Britain retained a technological lead. Some authors take the lower price of German steel on the world market at the beginning of the twentieth century as evidence for a technological lead by German industry and explain this lead by the existence of cartels that enabled German firms to produce more efficiently than British competitors.[64] Wengenroth has shown, however, that lower prices reflected poorer quality.[65]

The German *machine construction industry* was able to free itself by the middle of the century from dependence on British technology in some areas of machine construction, including steam locomotives.[66] In many areas British and later American firms had a technological lead until the end of the nineteenth century and beyond, although some new firms were established in Germany on the basis of new inventions, for example, printing presses.[67] Toward the end of the nineteenth century, when electric power opened new lines of machine construction and changed the design and the manufacture of many traditional machines, German firms were able to move to the technological front in additional areas.

By 1913 Germany accounted for about 27% of world production in machinery. About 26% of domestic production was exported. According to industry estimates, Germany held a 29% share of world exports, compared with 28% for Britain and 27% for the United States.[68]

The *electrotechnical industry* began with the construction of telegraph lines. The German leader was Siemens and Halske, founded in 1847 by the artillery officer Wer-

Table 4.3. Foreign Trade of Germany in the Year 1913 (in Million Marks)

Product group	Exports[a]	Imports[a]	Exports Minus Imports	RCA[b] 1913	RCA[b] 1907	Growth of Exports 1907 = 100
Agriculture, forestry, food	1,729	7,041	−5,312	−131	−139	161
Beet sugar[c]	264	0[d]	264	855	614	137
Minerals and fuels[e]	841	1,102	−261	−17	−29	168
Minerals	98	627	−529	−177	−135	103
Fuels excluding petroleum	723	290	433	101	38	183
Petroleum	21	186	−166	−212	−84	182
Wax, paraffin, soap	52	27	25	74	76	156
Chemicals and pharmaceuticals[e]	999	449	551	90	90	166
Dyes and dye products	298	21	277	275	274	126
Basic chemicals	377	281	96	39	28	192
Pharmaceuticals[f]	117	98	19	27	24	178
Explosives	101	2	99	399	316	226
Fibers and textiles[g]	1,581	873	708	69	74	108
From wool	444	241	203	71	73	101
From cotton	535	224	311	97	104	110
Leather and leather products	553	167	386	129	35	363
Rubber and rubber products	128	24	104	176	145	271
Products from wood and cork[h]	164	70	94	101	79	190
Paper, books, pictures, paintings	368	77	291	166	166	129
Products from stones and minerals[i]	34	33	1	13	−45	164
Products from clay	113	7	106	287	265	106
Glass and glass products	146	17	129	224	226	127
Products from gold and silver	74	29	45	102	222	75
Other metals and products thereof	1,903	673	1,230	113	102	164
Iron and iron products	1,336	105	1,231	264	212	169
Machinery[j]	680	80	600	223	177	176
Steam-powered vehicles[k]	75	2	73	384	333	163
Combustion engines[l]	40	2	38	317	255	255
Electrotechnical products	290	13	277	321	317	173
Vehicles[j]	161	18	142	227	106	135
Motor vehicles[m]	98	15	83	200	2	676
Rail vehicles[k]	36	2	34	295	407	164
Ships	15	29	−14	−55	−52	101
Firearms	16	2	14	233	140	275
Clocks and watches	30	30	1	11	17	114
Musical instruments	84	4	80	306	290	130
Toys	103	1	102	459	487	129
Gold and silver	101	436	−335	−135	21	41
Not adequately declared	31	2	29	(14)	(16)	(16)
Total	10,199	11,206	−1,007	0	0	144

[a]The figures include only the official category of "Spezialhandel" (i.e., imports from foreign countries into tax-free areas and exports to foreign countries from these areas are excluded).

[b]Revealed comparative advantage (RCA) for industry i is defined as $100 \times \ln [(m_i/x_i)/(\sum_j m_j/\Sigma x_j)]$, where m are imports and x are exports.

[c]Comprising categories 176b–i and 176l.

[d]Imports were 56 thousand.

[e]Coal tar and coal tar products have been moved from "Minerals and fuels" to "Chemicals."

[f]This item includes ether, alcohols, and cosmetics. It comprises product groups 4D and 4G of the German foreign trade classification, excluding for both years categories 371, 374, 375a, 377, 378, 379, and incompletely declared products, for year 1907 categories 390c, 390d, and for the year 1913 category 390b.

[g]Including textures from plant fibers and plant material, also brooms, brushes, and sieves.

ner Siemens and the mechanic J. G. Halske. The invention of the dynamoelectric principle by Werner Siemens in 1866 opened the use of electricity for power and changed this industry's relationship to science. Siemens and Halske hired the first university-trained physicists in 1872, and by 1882 the first professorial chair for electrical engineering was established at a Technische Hochschule.[69] Another major firm was AEG (Allgemeine Elektricitäts-Gesellschaft), started in 1883 on the basis of a license of the Edison patents for Germany. A third large firm founded by Johann Siegmund Schuckert (who had worked for some time with Edison in the United States) was merged in 1903 with Siemens, and from then on Siemens and AEG divided among them about half of the domestic market for electrotechnical products.

By 1913 Germany accounted for 34.9% of world production, compared with 28.9% for the United States and 16.0% for Britain.[70] About 25% of German production was exported. Germany held a 46.4% share of world exports, followed by Britain (with the strong presence of American and German subsidiaries) with 22.0% and the United States with 15.7%.

The *combustion engine and the motor vehicle* provided another new line of business in the machine construction industry. With the inventions by Otto, Diesel, Daimler, Benz, and Bosch, German firms were among the early technical leaders. However, they failed to turn this into a commercial lead. It was only after the turn of the century that motor vehicles with combustion engines were produced in larger numbers.[71] At that time the leaders were France and the United States. In 1913 France accounted for 33.4% of world exports, followed by the United States with 23.7% and Germany with 17.2%. About 40% of German production was exported.[72]

Catching up and Taking the Lead

By the beginning of the twentieth century the results of rapid industrialization became visible at home and on world markets. Although in 1870 German gross domestic product ($21 billion at 1970 U. S. relative prices) was less than that of Britain (30 billion), the United States (30 billion), and France (24 billion), by 1913 it was larger ($72 billion at 1970 U. S. relative prices) than that of Britain (68 billion) and France (47 billion), though the United States had surged ahead (176 billion). Per capita gross national product was in 1913 still about 23% lower than that of Britain, then the wealthiest country in Europe. Also Switzerland, Belgium, Denmark, the Netherlands, and Norway had a higher per capita gross national product.[73]

In all manufacturing industries, Germany had an export surplus by 1913 (see Table 4.3). The majority of exports, however, was still in the older industries, such as agriculture, fibers and textiles, or metals and metal products. The newer industries such as electrotechnical or motor vehicles contributed a small share (6.7 and 0.1%,

[h]Including carvings from plant and animal materials.

[i]Not including clay.

[j]As in the source, steam-powered vehicles are grouped with machinery rather than with rail vehicles.

[k]Comprising categories 892a–b and 893a–c for the year 1907, categories 892a–c and 893a–d for the year 1913.

[l]Comprising categories 894d–e, k, o.

[m]Road vehicles only. Comprises categories 915a–c, e.

Source: Germany, Kaiserliches Statistisches Amt, *Statistik des Deutschen Reichs,* Vols. 189 (1909) and 270 (1914).

respectively), yet they were highly dynamic, as they had a high revealed comparative advantage and rapid export growth. Highly dynamic were also machinery, coal (fuels excluding petroleum), leather and leather products, rubber and rubber products, products from wood and cork, metals and products thereof, and firearms.

Although synthetic dyes were a showpiece of a science-based industry, in 1913 dyes and dye products contributed only a third of exports in chemicals. The export to import ratio (indicated by the RCA index) in dyes and dye products is lower than in most industries, and from 1907 exports in this product group grew less than total exports.

Patenting activity in the United States can also serve as an overall indicator for the technological capability of German industry. Whereas in 1883 German firms were granted about half as many American patents as British firms, by 1913 they accounted for 34% of all foreign patents in the United States, while Britain had fallen behind with 23%.[74]

By the beginning of the twentieth century, many German firms operated on a worldwide scale.[75] Their accumulated foreign direct investment was estimated in 1914 at about 1500 million dollars. This was still significantly less than the foreign direct investment of Britain (6500 million dollars) or the United States (about 14,300 million dollars).

Within a few generations the German economy had nearly caught up with the British in terms of per capita social product, and in several industries it was now among the world's technological leaders.[76] This is not an exceptional case as other countries such as Switzerland or Denmark achieved a similar development. In the literature, the German case has often been described as an instance of the "advantages of backwardness," implying that a follower country adopting new technology from abroad can move faster than a leader country, since the latter faces some retardation as a result of old vintages of capital stock and the organizational resistance associated with old technologies.[77] Certainly Germany could not have industrialized as quickly as it did without the transfer of technology from countries such as Britain, Belgium, and later the United States. But the historical account given here suggests that it could take the lead in some industries not because of the "advantages of backwardness," but only because it established new institutional forms that enabled German firms to move quickly as new product areas or new processes were opened up by inventions and by advances in scientific knowledge.

CONTINUITY AND CHANGE IN THE TWENTIETH CENTURY

At the beginning of the twentieth century Germany was on its way to join the wealthiest countries and had a dynamic industry that was moving rapidly into world markets. But political development had not kept pace with economic development.[78] The autocratic political order blocked development toward a more democratic system and the political elite was unable to handle the foreign policy challenges that came with the country's rise to an industrial power. World War I began a series of political and economic crises that ended only toward the late 1940s.

World War I cut German industry off from its main export markets, stimulated efforts in the United States, France and Britain to substitute for German imports by domestic production, and enabled firms in neutral countries to capture market shares. The peace treaty of Versailles entailed the loss of some regions with a significant part of Germany's mineral resources, heavy reparations, and the expropriation of German patents and of direct investment in the United States, France, and Britain. A hyper-inflation in 1923 annihilated monetary assets. The short economic upswing that followed was ended by the slump of 1929. The subsequent recession was one of factors that brought the National Socialists to power in 1933.

Firms reacted to the economic crisis by increasing their effort toward different forms of nonmarket cooperation. Cartels had been a normal part of the Germany economy since the second half of the nineteenth century and could be enforced using the legal system. In the 1920s the number of domestic cartels increased, and German firms participated in many international cartels.[79] Furthermore, there was a movement towards mergers.[80] In the chemical industry the three leaders and some other firms joined in the IG Farben.[81] Technical associations such as the Association of German Engineers (Verein Deutscher Ingenieure) had for a long time provided a platform for exchange of technical information and for standardization. Economic planning during World War I led to the introduction of new standards in many industries, and these efforts were continued in the Committee for German Industry Norms DIN. For standards and norms a complex network of technical and business associations evolved.[82] The well-organized industry associations were then used by the national-socialist government to impose elements of a command economy while leaving much of formal industry structure as it was.

Their technological basis enabled German firms in some industries to return quickly to the world market after World War I. In chemicals Germany recaptured its prewar export position by 1929, and in machinery it held 35.0% of world exports by 1931, even surpassing its share as of 1913 (29.2%). The electrotechnical industry, however, recovered by 1932 a share of only 34.9%, compared with 46.4% in 1913. The motor vehicles industry, which had a prewar share of 17.2%, virtually disappeared from the world market. In the 1920s its share never exceeded 3%, and by 1928 Germany was a net importer. The case of the automobile industry reflects the difficulty German firms had in procuring the capital required for mass production. In this period, the largest German automobile manufacturer, Opel, sold out to General Motors. When in 1931 Ford completed a factory in Germany, these two companies accounted for 71% of the production capacity for passenger cars.[83]

The economic situation also affected scientific research. During the war and up to 1922 many new research institutes had been established by the state and by the Kaiser-Wilhelm-Society.[84] Some institutes of the Kaiser-Wilhelm-Society redirected their activities toward the war effort. Between 1918 and 1923 the number of institutes increased from 9 to 16, and Prandtl's institute for aerodynamics was then taken over by the Kaiser-Wilhelm-Society.

In the years after World War I a surge in student enrollment in higher education (see Fig. 4.1) resulted in unemployment for academics. Increases in government expenditure for scientific institutions did not keep pace with inflation, so the real value of salaries deteriorated and the purchase of books, equipment, and materials had to be cut.[85] As a reaction to these difficulties a new organization was founded in 1920, the *Notgemeinschaft der Deutschen Wissenschaft* (Emergency Association of German Science). It provided research money mainly to individual scientists on the basis of applications. In 1920 it received about 20 million Marks from the central government, which is 4% of all expenditure for science and higher education by states and central government together.[86] For donations to be collected from industry a special organization was created, the *Stifterverband der Notgemeinschaft der Deutschen Wissenschaft* (Donors' Union of the Emergency Association of German Science). To 1922 the Stifterverband collected a sum of about 100 million Marks, which was invested as an endowment—and a little later was virtually annihilated by inflation. The Stifterverband continued to depend on further donations, and to 1933 contributed about 1 to 3% of the income of the Notgemeinschaft. German firms provided additional funds for research through scientific societies in specific disciplines.[87]

In these years the Notgemeinschaft received some donations from abroad, for example, from the Rockefeller Foundation and the General Electric Company in the United States, However, more than 80% of its income came from the state.[88] In 1929 the Notgemeinschaft changed its name to *Deutsche Forschungsgemeinschaft*. Accordingly, the Stifterverband had to change its name and became the *Stifterverband für die Deutsche Wissenschaft*.

The Kaiser-Wilhelm-Society ran into financial problems, as its endowment, invested in government bonds, shrank as a result of inflation. From 1921 it received additional funds on a regular basis from government. From 1924 to 1933 public funds accounted for 65% of its budget; 27.8% came from domestic private sources, and 7% from foreign sources, mainly from foundations. In the wake of the slump of 1929 both government and industry reduced their funds.[89]

Nevertheless, the bleak picture of German science in the 1920s, as it is painted in the literature, appears to be overdrawn. In 1925 expenditure for higher education and science by states and central government was in real terms 2.0 times higher than in 1913 (see Table 4.2), and in 1930 it was 2.4 times higher. Obviously, the official descriptions of the state of German science in these years contain a good deal of rhetoric, which historians have barely begun to separate from reality.[90]

The scarce data that are available indicate that the industry sector in the 1920s generally increased its R&D efforts.[91] In the depression of 1929 and the following years, however, industry in Germany as in other countries laid off research personnel, reduced its spending on R&D, and concentrated on traditional rather than radically new innovations.[92]

In the period of National Socialism the number of students in higher education was drastically reduced (see Fig. 4.1). Although a large majority of academics tolerated the authoritarian rule of the National Socialists, many scientists and engineers were removed from their posts. Researchers in all fields of scholarship were forced to emigrate, including leaders in their field such as the physicist Albert Einstein and the mathematician John von Neumann. As many of the emigrees were unwilling or unable to return, the national–socialist period left a damaging effect on the quality of German science for more than one or two decades.[93]

Although some clandestine military R&D had continued during the 1920s in spite of the injunctions of the Versailles treaty, in 1935 rearmament was officially resumed and a little later a plan was implemented to make the economy independent in strategic materials. Since the planning machinery of the National Socialists was put on top of existing industrial structures, it did not radically change the innovation system.

During World War II, large parts of industrial plants were destroyed. After the war, some of what remained was taken as reparations by the allied powers. Subsidiaries of German firms abroad and all patents and trademarks were disowned. Some scientists and engineers were moved to the allied countries to be employed in military, aerospace, and nuclear technologies.[94]

After this, the two Germanys, in which the country was divided, made an astounding economic recovery. The fact that technical knowledge and skills still existed was a key factor in this. In the Eastern part of the country the Soviet Union introduced a centrally planned economy, and the existing innovation system was replaced step by step by something different.[95] In the Western part the allies abolished the planning structures of the national–socialist economy. They deconcentrated some industries effectively, in particular the chemical and steel industries; however, in other industries such as banking their deconcentration policy had only a temporary impact. Furthermore, they introduced a trade union structure that virtually avoided conflicts among specialized trade unions within firms. In all these changes the basic components of the innovation system were reconstructed: the firms and their laboratories, the schools, the universities and Technische Hochschulen, the Kaiser-Wilhelm-Society (that in 1948 became the *Max-Planck-Society*), the Deutsche Forschungsgemeinschaft (recreated in 1951), government research institutes, and business and technical associations.[96] Most organizations could take guidance in their reconstruction from their history before the national–socialist period.

THE PRESENT SYSTEM

This section focuses on the innovation system in West Germany as it existed before unification. Space does not allow us to describe the innovation system of the former German Democratic Republic and the way it is being transformed by adopting the institutional structures of West Germany. As a starting point I take the pattern of technological capabilities shown in the export performance of West German industry in the years before unification.[97]

In describing the national system for technical innovation, one has to keep in mind that in any country this is only one among several factors that account for economic performance. Other factors that deserve to be mentioned in the case of Germany but cannot be discussed in this chapter for lack of space are the system of industrial relations that has limited trade union conflict within industries, social policies and labor market policies that have eased the phasing out of noncompetitive production facilities, and the German banking system that enables banks to support the restructuring of industries.[98]

Export Performance

Table 4.4 presents the structure of West German foreign trade in the year 1988 for the all one-digit and for selected two- or three-digit commodity groups. The major German exports are machinery of various types (machines for special industries, metalworking machines, general industry machinery, and electrical machinery together had exports worth $65.8 billion U. S.), furthermore road vehicles ($54.7 billion U. S.), and

Table 4.4. West German Foreign Trade in 1988 (in Million U.S. Dollars)

SITC Classification[a]	Exports	Imports	Exports Minus Imports	RCA[b] 1988	RCA[b] 1983	Growth of Exports (1983 = 100)
0 Food and live animals	13,463	23,617	−10,154	−82	−82	182
061 Sugar and honey	355	366	−11	−29	10	91
1 Beverages and tobacco	1,847	2,498	−651	−56	−49	166
2 Crude materials excluding fuels	5,886	16,081	−10,195	−126	−131	186
233 Synthetic rubber	575	553	22	−22	10	163
26 Textile fibers and their waste	1,164	1,455	−291	−48	−39	149
28 Metalliferous ores and scrap	1,436	4,163	−2,727	−132	−151	209
3 Mineral fuels	4,210	19,173	−14,963	−177	−183	73
32 Coal, coke, and briquettes	1,467	506	961	81	80	97
33 Petroleum, petroleum products	2,002	14,710	−12,708	−225	−461	80
341 Gas, natural and manufactured	218	3,304	−3,086	−296	−154	84
4 Animal and vegetable oil and fat	872	819	53	−19	−17	129
5 Chemical and pharmaceuticals	42,810	23,752	19,058	33	47	193
53 Dyes, tanning, and colors	4,443	1,161	3,282	109	131	206
541 Medicaments and pharmaceuticals	5,074	2,956	2,118	28	48	239
55 Perfume, cosmetics, soap	2,309	1,274	1,035	34	46	217
58 Plastic materials	11,397	6,720	4,677	27	42	209
6 Basic manufactures	58,961	46,460	12,501	−2	13	188
61 Leather, leather manufactures	1,050	1,317	−267	−48	−30	170
62 Rubber manufactures	2,954	2,582	372	−12	6	207
63 Wood and cork manufactures	1,239	1,531	−292	−47	−62	222
64 Paper, paperboard, articles thereof	6,877	5,947	930	−11	−3	236
65 Textile yarn, fabrics	10,738	8,833	1,905	−6	−3	197
662 Products from clay	989	740	249	3	6	174
663 Polishing stones, abrasives etc.	1,461	781	680	37	36	219
664, 665 Glass and glassware	2,373	1,432	941	25	23	256
666 Pottery	561	312	249	33	35	193
67 Iron and steel	13,825	9,494	4,331	12	37	173
68 Nonferrous metals	6,443	7,533	−1,090	−41	−20	173
69 Other manufactures of metals	10,016	5,113	4,903	42	66	181
7 Machines and transport equipment	155,263	72,972	82,291	50	73	202
71 Power generating equipment	9,220	4,855	4,365	39	74	188
72 Machines for special industries	20,044	4,691	15,353	120	135	202
73 Metalworking machinery	5,577	1,985	3,592	78	121	203
74 General industry machinery	21,730	7,538	14,192	80	98	214
751 Office machines	1,048	1,065	−17	−27	−24	200
752 Automatic data processing equipment	4,342	6,342	−2,000	−63	−21	234
759 Parts of office and ADP machines	2,447	3,461	−1,014	−60	−22	189
761–763 Television and sound equipment	2,732	3,615	−883	−54	−46	221
764 Telecommunications equipment	3,273	3,378	−105	−29	44	173
771–775, 778 Electrical machinery	18,469	9,972	8,497	36	62	230
776 Semiconductors, valves	3,435	3,727	−292	−34	−39	300
78 Road vehicles	54,678	17,831	36,847	86	115	205
791 Railway vehicles	564	83	481	166	160	127
792 Aircraft	1,085	2,626	−1,541	−114	−39	32
793 Ships	753	339	414	54	138	72

Table 4.4. West German Foreign Trade in 1988 (in Million U.S. Dollars) (*Continued*)

SITC Classification[a]	Exports	Imports	Exports Minus Imports	RCA[b] 1988	RCA[b] 1983	Growth of Exports (1983 = 100)
8 Miscellaneous manufactured goods	35,900	37,424	−1,524	−30	−17	226
812 Sanitary, plumbing, heating fixtures	1,210	896	314	4	3	289
821 Furniture	3,989	2,797	1,192	10	19	239
84 Clothing and accessories	5,377	14,515	−9,138	−125	−108	212
87 Scientific instruments	7,952	4,004	3,948	43	56	228
881–883 Photographic goods	2,184	2,433	−249	−36	−5	205
884 Optical goods	732	670	62	−17	25	187
885 Watches and clocks	769	719	50	−19	7	192
892 Printed matter	2,926	1,123	1,803	70	95	231
893 Articles of plastics	3,976	2,097	1,879	38	48	261
894 Toys and sporting goods	1,118	1,377	−259	−46	−24	208
895 Office and stationery supplies	665	276	389	62	79	228
896 Works of art	1,344	361	983	106	−20	78
897 Jewelry	698	659	39	−20	60	157
898 Musical instruments	1,653	1,588	65	−22	−4	249
9 Goods not classified elsewhere	13,985	7,497	−3,512	−89	−2	84
951 War firearms, ammunition	684	321	363	50	104	1421
Total	323,196	250,293	72,903	0	0	191

[a]Data for one- and two-digit SITC groups in 1988 are taken from volume 1, data for three-digit groups from volume 2 of the *International Trade Statistics Yearbook*. Because of the transition from SITC 2 to SITC 3 there may be small inconsistencies between the first and the second set of data, and for some one-digit or two-digit groups the comparability to earlier years may be only approximate.

[b]Revealed comparative advantage (RCA) for industry i is defined as $100 \times \ln[(m_i/x_i)/(\sum_j m_j/\sum_j x_j)]$, where m are imports and x are exports.

chemicals and pharmaceuticals ($42.8 billion U. S.). These industries together accounted for 50.5% of exports and 27.5% of imports. Other areas with significant net exports were scientific instruments, manufactures of metals (including hand tools, fittings, and nails), power generating equipment, iron and steel manufactures, textile yarn and fabrics, plastic articles, printed matter, and furniture.

Rather than being concentrated in a few product groups, German exports are spread over many product groups. In some four-digit or five-digit industries German industry accounts for a high share of world exports: 57.7% in rotary printing presses, 53.0% in reciprocating pumps, 46.3% in textile spinning machines, 42.4% in high-pressure hydroelectric conduits of steel, 42.2% in coke of coal (one of the few areas where Germany has a natural resource advantage), and 40.0% in combined harvesters–threshers.[99] However, the contribution of this top-league to total exports is small: $4483 million U. S. or less than 2%.[100]

In some product groups, the pattern of imports reflects the country's poor endowment in natural resources, for example, in petroleum and natural gas. But there are also some high-technology sectors, in which West Germany was a net importer: ADP machines, aircraft, television and sound equipment, telecommunications, photographic goods, and semiconductors.

History goes a long way toward explaining the pattern of technological strength and weakness as it is reflected in West Germany's export performance. In most industries that today are net exporters Germany performed well on the world market in 1913 (compare Tables 4.3 and 4.4). This applies not only to those industries that now account for the bulk of German exports (machinery, electrotechnical products, motor vehicles, and chemicals), but also to manufactures of metals, in particular iron and steel, as well as textile yarns and fabrics, rubber products, paper and printed matter, products from stones and minerals, products from clay and pottery, glass and glassware, railway vehicles, jewelry, firearms, and musical instruments. Even a new product group such as plastic articles is related to industries in which Germany was strong at the beginning of the century: chemicals and machinery.

However, not all industries that were strong exporters in 1913 were still strong in the 1980s, for example, leather and leather products, products of wood and cork, and clothing. These became sensitive to the cost of unskilled or semiskilled labor, so firms had to concentrate on high-quality products or specialized inputs, be they machinery or materials.

What at first appears as historical continuity partly reflects the impact of political events on some industries that newly emerged or that took large strides in technical change. After World War II the allies prohibited R&D for military technology as well as for some areas of civilian technology, including nuclear technology, aeronautics, rocket propulsion, marine propulsion, radar, and remote and automatic control. Special permission was required for work on such things as electronic valves, ball and roller bearings, synthetic rubber, synthetic oil, and radioactivity other than for medical purposes.[101] The key injunctions remained in force until the Federal Republic became a sovereign state in 1955. They effectively wiped out the military and aeronautics industries and in some product groups kept German firms for some time away from the technological front. This is one of the reasons for the relatively poor export performance of the German aircraft, electronics, and telecommunication industries.

Historical continuity appears also at the firm level. Table 4.5 lists the 25 largest manufacturing companies in Germany. Of these 19 were founded before 1913, and three of those for which a later founding date is given (VEBA, Ruhrkohle, and Preussag) are mergers of enterprises many of which date back to the nineteenth century.

Although there have been recurrent alarms about the technical weakness of the West German industry, from the technology gap discussion in the 1960s to the eurosclerosis cries in the early 1980s, its performance has been better than these alarms made one expect.[102] Although from the mid-1970s to the mid-1980s there has been a slowly declining trend in Germany's world-market share in high-technology products however defined and also in goods with more than average research intensity, the trend was reversed in the late 1980s.[103]

Nevertheless, there are areas for concern.[104] First, West German exports are concentrated in Europe, which takes about 70%. The dynamic markets of the newly industrializing countries are less well represented than the size of their economies would suggest.

Second, to some extent the good performance in European markets is the result of trade protection against non-European imports. In the passenger car industry, for example, the countries of the European Community accounted for about 64% of exports in 1988 and were the main factor in export growth in the 1980s, whereas exports to North America declined.[105]

Table 4.5. The 25 Largest Manufacturing Companies in Germany (Year 1989)

Company	Main Activity	Founded (Year)	Sales (Billion DM)[a]	Employees (Thousand)	R&D Expenditure (Million DM)
Daimler-Benz[b]	Vehicles/electrical/ aerospace	1882	76.4	368.2	5494
Volkswagen	Vehicles	1938	65.4	250.6	2300
Siemens[c]	Electrical/electronics	1847	61.1	365.0	6875
VEBA	Energy/chemicals	1929	49.2	94.5	370
BASF	Chemicals	1865	47.6	137.0	1954
Hoechst	Chemicals	1863	45.9	169.3	2621
Bayer	Chemicals	1863	43.3	170.2	2695
RWE	Energy	1898	38.9	78.2	n.a.
Thyssen	Steel/machinery	1867	34.2	133.8	735
Bosch	Electrical	1886	30.6	174.7	1803
BMW	Vehicles	1916	26.5	66.3	ca. 3300
Ruhrkohle	Coal mining	1968	23.4	124.8	273
Mannesmann	Machinery	1890	22.3	125.8	518
Opel	Vehicles	1862	20.8	54.6	706
Metallgesellschaft	Metals/plant engineering	1881	20.1	24.5	n.a.
Ford	Vehicles	1925	19.8	48.2	n.a.
Krupp	Steel/machinery	1811	17.7	63.6	275
MAN	Machinery	1840	17.1	63.7	415
Deutsche Shell	Petroleum	1902	16.9	3.3	47
Preussag[d]	Energy/oil	1923	16.4	65.7	200
Hoesch	Steel	1871	15.9	52.0	n.a.
Degussa	Chemicals/metals	1873	14.4	33.7	422
Bertelsmann	Publishing	1835	12.5	43.7	—
IBM Deutschland	Electronics	1910	12.4	31.1	n.a.
Henkel	Chemicals	1876	11.6	38.1	359

[a]One billion = 1000 million.
[b]Not including Messerschmitt-Bölkow-Blohm (MBB), which was acquired by Daimler-Benz in 1989.
[c]Not including Nixdorf, which was acquired by Siemens in 1990.
[d]Including Salzgitter, which was acquired by Preussag in 1989.
Sources: Die Zeit, 17 August 1990, p. 24; *Handbuch der deutschen Aktiengesellschaften 1989/90.* Darmstadt: Hoppenstaedt, 1990/91; data on R&D from the firms' annual reports and personal correspondence.

Third, the dynamism of Japanese industry is about to affect a broad number of industries. Although in some smaller industries such as television and sound equipment, and photographic goods, West German firms have lost their markets to Japanese firms in recent decades, in other sectors such as machine tools they have met the Japanese challenge.[106] Patent statistics suggest, however, that Japan is improving its technological position in many industries. In the period 1975 to 1985 Japanese patents in the United States increased from 8.9 to 17.9%, while German patents grew only from 8.5 to 9.5%. Relative to population or gross domestic product, Germany has now about the same share as Japan, but the trend is a matter for concern. Japan is catching up with Germany in the chemical and mechanical industries, moving ahead in pharmaceuticals and instruments, and increasing its lead it electronics, data processing, and communications as well as in material science and transportation equipment. Moreover, Germany has relatively fewer important patents (as measured by a high frequency of citations).[107]

Research and Development in Industry

A key factor in the technological strength of any country is the innovation activities of business enterprises. R&D is only a part of these innovation activities, but in many industries it is an essential part.[108] In Germany about 63% of total national R&D is financed by the business sector, a much higher percentage than in the United States, France, Britain, or Italy, but a lower percentage than in Japan where it is 78% (see Table I.1 in the introduction to this part of the book). R&D expenditure financed by the business sector grew from 0.60% of the gross national product in 1962 to 1.87% in 1989 (see Table 4.6). This is more than in France (0.96%), in Britain (1.15%), Italy (0.50%), or the United States (1.43%), about the same as in Sweden (1.83%) and Switzerland (1.76% in 1983), but less than in Japan (1.98%).[109] At the aggregate level, government is not an important source of funds for R&D performed in the business sector. In 1987 it financed 4.9 billion DM, which is about 12% of all R&D performed by the business sector (see Table 4.7).

About 31% of domestic industrial R&D capability (as measured by R&D employees) is accounted for by the seven top spenders: Siemens, Daimler-Benz, Bayer, Hoechst, Volkswagen, and BASF.[110] Siemens alone stands for about 37% of R&D in the electrotechnical industry; Bayer, Hoechst, and BASF for about 46% in the chemical industry; and Volkswagen and Daimler-Benz for about 53% in the motor vehicle

Table 4.6. R&D Expenditure in West Germany 1962 to 1989

Year	Total National R&D (Billion DM)	Financed by Business			Performed by Business Sector			Financed by Government	Performed by Business Sector	
		Billion DM	Percent of Total	Percent of GNP	Billion DM	Percent of Total	Percent[a]	Subtotal Billion DM	Billion DM	Percent[b]
1962	4.5	2.2	47.9	0.60	2.1	47.0	98.1	2.3	0.3	13.9
1963	5.4	2.7	49.6	0.70	2.6	48.7	98.1	2.6	0.4	13.2
1965	7.9	4.1	51.3	0.89	4.0	50.2	97.8	3.7	0.6	12.3
1967	9.7	4.8	49.4	0.97	4.6	47.4	96.0	4.8	1.0	17.5
1969	12.3	6.4	52.2	1.07	6.2	50.8	97.2	5.7	1.0	14.2
1971	18.0	8.7	48.5	1.16	8.5	47.0	96.9	8.7	2.0	18.2
1973	20.5	9.6	47.0	1.05	9.4	46.2	98.2	10.4	2.3	19.5
1975	24.6	11.8	47.8	1.15	11.6	47.0	98.3	12.0	2.9	19.2
1977	27.7	14.1	50.9	1.18	13.8	49.9	98.2	12.6	2.9	16.6
1979	34.5	18.6	57.0	1.34	18.3	53.2	98.3	15.1	4.4	19.0
1981	39.4	22.1	56.1	1.43	21.4	54.4	96.9	16.7	4.8	18.2
1983	43.9	25.5	57.9	1.52	24.7	56.2	97.0	17.3	5.3	17.3
1985	52.3	31.1	59.5	1.69	30.1	57.6	96.8	20.5	6.0	16.3
1987	59.5	36.8	61.9	1.82	35.7	60.1	97.0	21.7	5.3	12.7
1989	66.7	42.4	63.5	1.87	41.1	61.6	97.0	23.0	5.4	11.3

[a]Percent of billion DM financed by business.

[b]Percent of billion DM performed by business sector.

Sources: Bundesminister für Forschung und Technologie (ed.), *Faktenbericht 1990 zum Bundesforschungsbericht 1988.* Bonn: Bundesminister für Forschung und Technologie, April 1990, Table VI/3, p. 340sq. GNP from Statistisches Bundesamt (ed.), *Statistisches Jahrbuch 1983 für die Bundesrepublik Deutschland.* Stuttgart: Kohlhammer 1983, Table 23.2, p. 528: Statistisches Bundesamt (ed.), *Statistisches Jahrbuch 1989.* Stuttgart: Metzler-Poeschel, 1989, Table 24.2, p. 542.

Table 4.7. West German R&D Expenditure in 1987 by Source or Funds and Sector of Performance (Million DM)

Sector of Performance	Source of Funds				
	Business	Government	Private Nonprofit	Abroad	Total
Business	35,739	4,899	62	629	41,329
Government	86	6,990	112	100	7,288
Higher education	525	7,814	0	0	8,339
Private nonprofit	54	157	64	9	284
Abroad	427	1,306	0	—	1,733
Total	36,831	21,166	238	738	58,973

Source: H. Echterhoff-Severitt, C. Grenzmann, R. Marquardt, E. Menner, A. Weisburger, J. Wudtke, *Forschung und Entwicklung in der Wirtschaft 1987, mit ersten Daten 1989.* Essen: SV-Gemeinnützige Gesellschaft für Wissenschaftsstatistik, 1990.

industry. Patent statistics confirm the concentration of technological capability: five German firms account for 29% of German patents in the United States.[111]

As Table 4.7 shows, 97% (35.8 billion DM) of the funds provided by the business sector are also spent in the business sector. Of this sum about 2.5 billion DM or 7% is for outside R&D performed by other business enterprises, and 338 million DM or 1% goes to institutes of cooperative industrial R&D. The latter had a total budget of 617 million DM in 1987, of which 55% was funded by the participating business enterprises, 17% by a program of the Federal Ministry for the Economy, and the rest mainly through projects in other government programs.[112] The business sector also finances some R&D performed in the higher education sector (525 million DM in 1987), in government laboratories (86 million DM), and in domestic private not-for-profit institutions (54 million DM).

According to the statistics summarized in Table 4.7 in 1987 the German business sector received 629 million DM from abroad for R&D performed for foreign sources and paid 427 million DM to foreign R&D performers. Data by the Deutsche Bundesbank put receipts at 3111 million DM and expenditure at 2549 million DM.[113] The latter figures appear to reflect more adequately the internationalization of R&D.[114] According to one estimate 40,000 R&D employees (about 14% of R&D employees in domestic industry) work in subsidiaries of foreign firms in Germany, and about the same number work abroad in subsidiaries of German firms. In 1989 Hoechst spent about 40% of its R&D funds in foreign subsidiaries, Bayer 33%, and Siemens 20%.[115]

The Education System

As Table I.1 in the introduction to Part I of this book and similar tables in other parts show, most advanced Western countries do not differ in elementary schooling (for which the literacy rate may serve as a rough indicator). However, there are significant differences in the structure and duration of second-level education. In Germany, the enrollment rate at age 17 is 98.7%, which is the highest among all OECD countries (see Table 4.8). The system of vocational training has gone through some changes as some skills disappeared, new ones emerged, and many skills changed, but it has the same basic structure as established around the turn of the century, with part of the training

Table 4.8. International Comparison of Indicators for Education

| Country | Enrollment Rate as Percent of Age Group | | | | Students Qualifying as Percent of Age Group | | | Expenditure Per Student as Percent of Per Capita GDP | |
| | Age 17 | | Age 20 | | Level 5 | Level 6 | Level 7 | Second Level | Third Level |
	Total	Part-Time	Total	Part-Time					
Australia	50.3	10.4	n.a.	n.a.	9.7	16.5	1.6	19[c]	55
Austria	n.a.	n.a.	n.a.	n.a.	3.6	6.8	0.5	37	50
Belgium	86.4	4.8	46.0	7.4	15.8	14.9	[b]	31	38
Canada	78.5	0.1	36.3	1.3	13.3	24.5	4.1	n.a.	41
Denmark	75.4	n.a.	36.4	n.a.	10.3	12.7	[b]	31	39
Finland	83.3[a]		22.4[a]		17.0	11.8	0.9	29	40
France	79.7	10.3	28.1	0.7	14.7	15.3	6.2	26	30
Germany	99.7	48.4	36.6	19.5	7.7	12.4	1.5	27	37
Greece	58.7[a]		29.0[a]		4.9	10.9	0.4	15	36
Ireland	64.7[a]		17.6[a]		1.0	10.8	5.2	25	73
Italy	n.a.	n.a.	n.a.	n.a.	0.4	7.9	1.4	n.a.	n.a.
Japan	90.5	1.6	n.a.	n.a.	11.1	21.9	1.5	23	118
Netherlands	78.3	—	31.9	0.2	16.5	6.8	[b]	22	82
New Zealand	38.8	1.4	16.1	3.0	4.1	11.2	4.5	15	56
Norway	76.2	2.0	23.4	2.8	36.3	16.1	7.3	38[d]	36
Portugal	n.a.	n.a.	n.a.	n.a.	n.a.	n.a.	n.a.	25	60
Spain	53.1[a]		n.a.	n.a.	0.1	14.7	0.5	n.a.	n.a.
Sweden	83.0[a]		9.5[a]		n.a.	n.a.	n.a.	38[d]	40
Switzerland	83.1	56.3	30.2	15.1	0.9	6.1	0.3	28[c]	52
United Kingdom	49.3	16.2	23.8	9.9	12.3	14.2	4.6	28	85
United States	89.0	0.4	35.7	3.8	12.7	24.1	9.7	29	39

[a]Full-time students only.

[b]Included in Level 6.

[c]First level and second level.

[d]Second level second stage only.

Source: Organisation for Economic Cooperation and Development, *Education in OECD Countries, 1986–87.* Paris: Organisation for Economic Cooperation and Development, 1989.

provided by business firms and other organizations that are the future employers, and part by vocational schools.[116]

The higher education sector, once a showpiece of the German education system, no longer is so. In 1985, 7.7% of the corresponding age group received a qualification of level five (as defined by the OECD), meaning completion of a course of education usually outside the university and of shorter duration and of a quality lower than a full university degree; 12.4% completed a first full university degree (level 6), and 1.5% a postgraduate education (level 7). Many other advanced industrial countries did better in all these categories: Australia, Belgium, Canada, France, Japan, Norway, the United Kingdom, and the United States (see Table 4.8).

One may argue that the quality of education varies among countries. But as far as expenditure per student is a measure, this argument does not help in the case of the German higher education sector. With 37% of per capita GDP Germany spends about the same per student as Belgium, Denmark, Greece, Norway, and the United States, but other countries spend much more, such as the Netherlands (82%) or the United Kingdom (85%). Japan is top with 118%.

Comparison with Japan shows a long-term trend in the educational level of the labor force that is unfavorable for Germany. Per 10,000 labor force, Japan had in 1965 about 8% more scientists and engineers employed in nonacademic jobs than West Germany. The difference increased by the mid-1980s to about 27%.[117]

The higher education sector has been neglected in Germany since the mid-1970s. In real terms neither expenditure nor the number of staff has grown since 1975. At the same time the number of students has increased by 65%.[118] In particular for the universities, the neglect by government has not only been financial, but also one of governance. Since the institutional reforms of the late 1960s and early 1970s ended in widespread disappointment, little has been done to install governance structures that would enable them to tackle deficiencies in teaching and to adapt with speed and flexibility to new developments in science and technology, in particular such developments that open up new connections between areas that previously were distinct and separate from each other.[119] There is a broad consensus that new structures are necessary that give the universities more responsibility and at the same time increase incentives for them to be efficient. A government report in 1988 stated bluntly that a continuation of trends may pose a risk for the whole research system.[120]

About 14% of total national R&D is performed in the higher education sector (see Table 4.7), down from about 20% in 1975. Relative to the size of their population, Japan spends about 40% and the United States about 30% more than Germany (measured in purchasing power) on R&D performed in the higher education sector. Nevertheless, in some areas German research is first rate, as indicated by the Nobel prizes won by German scientists in the 1980s. In other areas, for example, clinical research, there is a consensus that the situation is unsatisfactory.[121]

For specific research projects funds are provided through the Deutsche Forschungsgemeinschaft. In 1989 its budget was 1188 million DM, of which 61% was financed by the Federal Government and 38% by the federal states. In addition to the funding of research the Deutsche Forschungsgemeinschaft has the function of advising government in scientific matters. Except for the setting of standards for toxic substances in occupational health and safety, this function remained marginal.[122]

Closely linked to the universities are the research activities of the Max-Planck-Society (the successor to the Kaiser-Wilhelm-Society). In 1989 it comprised about 60 institutes and had a budget of 1079 million DM, of which one-half is financed by the Federal Government and the other half by the federal states. The Max-Planck-Society focuses on the natural sciences, on which it spends about 80% of its funds. Leading scientists are normally recruited from universities. The institutes usually participate in postgraduate education. Whereas its predecessor, the Kaiser-Wilhelm-Society, had major activities in applied research, and included institutes such as leather research or textile research, the Max-Planck-Society after World War II moved toward basic research, which had brought it international recognition in previous decades.[123]

The creation of better links between industry and the higher education sector was recognized in the 1980s by federal and state governments as a task for technology policy. State governments prodded universities to be more sensitive to the needs of regional industry. Most universities and, in some regions, technical and commercial colleges (Fachhochschulen) now have a special office for technology transfer.[124]

Technology Policy by Federal and State Governments

An official technology policy in the sense of a set of government policies designed to support technical change and to guide its direction has existed at the federal level only since the late 1960s, and at the state level only since the 1980s. Military R&D, which in other countries, especially in the United States, after World War II became a vehicle to support R&D far beyond the narrow boundaries of armaments, was forbidden in West Germany by allied law until 1955. Compared to countries such as the United States, Britain, or France, West Germany spends little on defense R&D: in 1989 it was 3023 million DM, or 13% of total government-financed R&D.

The Federal Ministry for Research and Technology (Bundesministerium für Forschung und Technologie), which is the main R&D spender in the Federal Government (see Table 4.9), was created in 1955 as Ministry for Atomic Questions. In the 1950s and early 1960s it had a precarious position between the Ministry for Economy on one

Table 4.9. Government Expenditure for Research and Development in 1989

	Million DM	1981 = 100
Federal government	13,900	134
By department		
Ministry for Research and Technology	7,695	130
Ministry for Defense	3,052	196
Ministry for Education and Science	1,120	127
Ministry for the Economy	992	93
By type of support		
Direct	7,094	131
Indirect	420	91
Institutional	5,414	143
National laboratories	2,354	146
Departmental laboratories	936	146
Higher education	380	139
Deutsche Forschungsgemeinschaft	610	129
Max-Planck-Society	457	129
Fraunhofer-Society	155	186
International	1,234	174
By technology (selected areas)		
Space	1,291	195
Nuclear (including fusion)	893	65
Nonnuclear energy	450	62
Information technology (including production technology)	804	214
Environment and climate	741	173
Health	542	159
Materials	549	185
Aircraft	777	163
Biotechnology	246	248
State governments	9,100	132
Higher education	8,030	
Other	1,070	
Government total	23,000	133
Tax reduction (not included in total)	674	

Source: Bundesminister für Forschung und Technologie, *Faktenbericht 1990 zum Bundesbericht Forschunt 1988.* Bonn: Bundesminister für Forschung und Technologie, 1990.

side, which as an advocate of the market order was skeptical about government involvement in industrial innovation, and the federal states on the other side, which under the West German constitution have the primary responsibility for scientific research. However, it created a secure organizational domain for itself by founding nuclear research laboratories in collaboration with federal states—at a time when the federal nuclear research laboratories in the United States were already looking for new tasks.[125]

In the public discussion of the 1960s Neo-Schumpeterians like Kenneth Galbraith and Neomarxists agreed that direct government support for industrial R&D is a necessity, and this opinion was reinforced by the public discussion on the technology gap between the United States and Europe.[126] In 1962 the responsibility of the Atom Ministry was expanded into space research and technology and its name, which previously had changed slightly several times, now became the Federal Ministry for Scientific Research. A program for electronic data processing was begun in 1966, but only in 1969, with the start of a program for new technologies, the ministry's responsibility was broadened to technology in general (and its name then became Ministry for Education and Science). Government support for civilian aircraft, begun in 1962, remained under the Ministry for the Economy, and military R&D under the Ministry of Defense.[127] In 1972 the Ministry for Scientific Research was split up in two parts: federal responsibilities for education including higher education remained in the Ministry for Education and Science, while technology and R&D outside the higher education sector became the province of the Ministry for Research and Technology.[128]

Until the 1970s the Federal Ministry for Research and Technology and its predecessors were widely regarded as successful. West German manufacturers of nuclear power plants, Siemens and AEG, managed to catch up (using American licenses) in short time, and this was claimed by the ministry and generally accepted as confirming the effectiveness of the ministry's subsidies.[129] In the mid-1970s the ministry won acceptance for the idea that government support for industrial R&D is a key in modernizing the structure of industry.[130]

However, as research by this author revealed, contrary to this image AEG and Siemens developed their nuclear reactors mainly with their own funds; most government funds were spent on reactor types that later were not used for commercial electricity generation, and the government laboratories, apart from some safety research in the 1970s and 1980s, contributed very little to the development of those reactor types that were commercially used.[131] A study by A. D. Little about the ministry's support for computers and electronic data processing cast doubt on its effectiveness as far as large computer systems were concerned.[132]

In the 1980s the failure of some large projects, for example, the fast breeder reactor and the high-temperature reactor, became obvious even to the general public. By that time the ministry had begun to learn from its experience and to strive for more effective policies.[133] As this author has argued elsewhere, the failures in government support to technology can be explained by the simple fact that if nearly all costs are financed by government, firms have an incentive to carry out a project even if they expect it to have no commercial use. This problem can be avoided by cost sharing between government.[134] The ministry has more and more adopted a strategy to finance only a fraction of project cost, usually between 30 and 70%. With some exceptions, such as space, projects financed totally by government are being phased out.

As another major policy innovation the ministry devised new programs and tailored existing ones so as to strengthen cooperation among firms or between firms and public research organizations. In selected areas such as microelectronics, robotics, computer-aided design and manufacturing, or biotechnology, criteria for subsidies are explicitly defined so as to encourage firms to participate in cooperative projects. Such projects are useful to the firms less for the funds they provide than for their informational effects: by alerting firms to technological frontiers, by pooling precompetitive technical information, and by creating links between suppliers and users of specialized inputs.[135] Since 1978 the ministry has supported research contracted by firms to other firms or to government laboratories. Annual expenditure was 28 million DM in 1989. Another program subsidizes the costs of personnel seconded by firms to research organizations. Expenditure for this program in 1989 was 22 million DM.[136]

A genuine institutional innovation was the Fraunhofer-Society, which from inauspicious beginnings in 1949 grew to a large organization carrying out applied research mainly on contract with clients in industry and government.[137] In 1989 it had a budget of about 560 million DM, of which about 155 million was provided by the federal government as institutional support that is made contingent on its success in securing contracts. Six of its institutes work for the Defense Ministry and are totally financed with public funds. The Fraunhofer-Society has close links to universities and, being dependent on contracts, a strong orientation toward serving clients. Hence it provides a link between universities and industry, and thus helped to reduce the gap that opened in the German innovation system as the Max-Planck-Society moved toward basic research.

Indirect government support included such measures as tax credits (674 million DM in 1989), subsidies, and special depreciation rates for investments in R&D up to a certain limit (449 million DM and 225 million DM, respectively, in 1989), and two programs of subsidies for R&D personnel in small and intermediate enterprises. All these programs were discontinued. Since 1983 the government experimented with support for newly created technology-oriented enterprises. Expenditure was 53.5 million DM in 1989. Although this subsidy helped to strengthen the infrastructure for risk capital, the rather small demand for it suggested that the availability of risk capital was not an important barrier to industrial innovation.[138]

Institutional support by the federal government is heavily concentrated on national laboratories (2354 million DM in 1989) and departmental laboratories (936 million DM). Both types of organizations have grown since 1981 a little faster than total government expenditure for R&D (see Table 4.9). The role of the departmental research laboratories has not been controversial, as most of them carry out R&D for noncontroversial state functions. Of the laboratories more or less directly related to industrial innovation the major ones are the *Physikalisch-Technische Bundesanstalt,* successor to the Physikalisch-technische Reichsanstalt mentioned in the first section, with an annual budget of 372 million DM, working on standards and measures; the *Bundesanstalt für Materialforschung und prüfung,* with an annual budget of 125 million DM, working on materials and on safety aspects of chemicals; and the *Bundesanstalt für Geowissenschaften und Rohstoffe,* with an annual budget of 69 million DM, working on geology and raw materials.

Since the 1970s there were attempts to diversify the work of the national laboratories into technologies outside nuclear power and to improve their links with industrial technology. Some laboratories have increasingly taken on work in environmental

R&D and climate research in recent years. Schemes were set up to help the national laboratories to spin off new firms and to improve their links with industry.

In the priority given by Federal Government to different areas of technology there have been some notable shifts in recent years (see Table 4.9). The largest share now goes to space technology. Funds for this area have been strongly increased recently as a result of a controversial political decision to participate in new ambitious Western European collaborative projects.[139] The second field of government support is nuclear technology, although the level of support for this technology was reduced by 35% since 1981. A similar reduction has been effected on nonnuclear energy technology.

Support for aircraft technology has grown by 63% since 1981 to an annual expenditure of 777 million DM. One of the largest projects is the Airbus family of passenger airplanes developed and manufactured by a European consortium of firms. Although Airbus can be regarded as a technical success, it has not yet crossed the threshold to a normal commercial business, as the participating firms were skilful to motivate their governments to spend more and more money to enlarge the Airbus family by developing more and more types of airplanes. In a controversial move the West German government has brought the German aircraft firms that so far depended on its subsidies into a system of mixed ownership with management leadership by Daimler-Benz, hoping that after the next round of subsidized projects the Airbus program will finally become a normal commercial venture.[140]

Since the 1980s, federal states and some cities supported science parks to attract new high-technology firms to their region or to facilitate the spin-off of new firms from existing research organizations. Innovation centers were established providing space and infrastructure facilities for new science-based firms. A study in 1989 found 50 innovation centers in operation and 50 more under construction or in the planning stage. Average investment was 5.5 million DM.[141] In addition some federal states have taken initiatives to create new R&D organizations. The state of North-Rhine-Westfalia, for example, created a *Wissenschaftszentrum* with several decentralized research institutes in areas such as "technology and work" and climate research.[142]

A System Fallen into Oblivion and Partly Recovered

If the German innovation system of the 1980s is put into historical perspective, one gets the impression that it reflects mainly the momentum of organizations that have existed for a long time, have survived the period of wars and crises, and since then have grown in size. In the reconstruction period after World War II each organization primarily looked after itself, and the system as such fell into oblivion. The federal states cared for their educational institutions, including higher education. The Max-Planck-Society (successor to the Kaiser-Wilhelm-Society) shed many of its activities in applied research and focused on basic research. The federal government was hesitant in assuming responsibilities for science and technology, and where it did, as in nuclear power, aerospace, and electronic data processing, its programs for supporting industrial technology were ineffective. Eager to build a secure organizational domain, the Atom Ministry and its successors build up national laboratories that contributed little to industrial technology. Many of the foundations had vanished in two inflations, and for new ones to be created (for example, the Volkswagen Foundation) it needed new stimuli such as the technology gap discussion. The old innovation system had been driven by the dynamism of the Prussian bureaucracy that because of Prussia's preponderance could force other federal states to follow suit. After World War II none of the West German federal states had the size and dynamism to take on the leadership previously provided by Prussia, and the new institutions that were built up to coordinate the technical and scientific efforts of the Federal and state governments, as, for example, the Wissenschaftsrat and the Bund-Länder-Kommission für Bildungsplanung und Forschungsförderung, were slow to assume their responsibilities and catered only to parts of the innovation system.[143]

It was only in the late 1970s and 1980s that the Federal Ministry for Research and Technology began hesitantly to assume a role as manager of a national innovation system, designed programs so as to strengthen cooperation and the flow of personnel and information between different organizations within the system, and fostered new institutions such as the Fraunhofer-Society that provided new links among different components of the system. By that time, however, the splitting up of federal responsibilities between the Federal Ministry for Research and Technology and the Federal Ministry for Education and Science had created a new barrier for policymakers to consider the system as a whole.

The fact that the system as a whole fell into oblivion is one of the reasons why German industry today shows a strong technical capability in those areas where it has a long tradition of technological strength. Where radically new areas of technology emerged in the decades after World War II, as, for example, computers and microelectronics, or where because of the post-World War II policies of the allied countries German industry had to start anew as in aircraft, industry developed less technological dynamism (with the exception of nuclear power).[144] In technologies where government organizations play a key role as customers, such as telecommunications, German industry has not regained its earlier technological dynamism.[145]

While the system was partly recovered from oblivion in the late 1970s and in the 1980s and first steps were taken by government to strengthen the links among its components, Japan has caught up with Germany or overtaken it on nearly all counts that make up for a strong national technological capability: business financed R&D as percentage of gross domestic product, patents held in the United States, scientists and engineers in nonacademic jobs per 10,000 labor force, qualifications as percent of age group in all levels of higher education, and percent of per capita gross domestic product spent per student in higher education.

Challenges

Although West German industry has performed well in export markets in the 1980s there is no reason for complacency. The fact that other countries with even less favorable endowments of natural resources such as Japan or Switzerland achieve a higher per capita gross national product shows that Germany could perform still better. The major part of exports are directed toward Western European countries. Automobile exports, which are a major factor in West Germany's export performance, have benefitted from trade protection against Japanese imports in other European countries. In the face of Japan's large scientific and technological potential German firms will face a strong competitor on the world market not only in selected industries such as photographic equipment, consumer electronics, or semiconductors, but also in those industries that so far have been traditional areas of German technological strength.

In the next few years, a good deal of the attention and energy of decision makers in industry and government as well as of the financial resources over which they decide will be devoted to reconstructing the economy in the Eastern part of the country and to establishing ties with the emerging market economies in Eastern Europe. Given the speed with which unification had to proceed because of the precarious economic situation in the former German Democratic Republic and because of the geopolitical situation, it was unavoidable that the present system of technical innovation was extended roughly as it is to the Eastern part of the country. There was no time to have a general discussion and a detailed analysis of the system's strengths and weaknesses. However, in the face of a new challenge from Japan over broad areas of technology, some reforms in the German system for technological innovation cannot wait for long if German industry is to hold its place on world markets.

One major challenge for reform is the higher education sector. Although there are areas where scientific research is first rate and some minor reforms of postgraduate education are on the way, the higher education sector is one of the weak components in the country's innovation system.

Given the close relationship between the national capability for technical innovation and the education system, there is a need for closer coordination of government policies for technology with policies for education at various levels. The separation of federal responsibilities in two ministries, one for Education and Science and one for Research and Technology, does not appear to be helpful in meeting this need.

A further challenge is the increasing internationalization of business. The trend for firms to locate different parts of their activities in different countries may have slowed down for German industry a little because of the reconstruction in the Eastern part of the country, but it will continue and may even accelerate again as German firms participate in the reconstruction of the Eastern European economies. For the Federal Government it means that its policies adopt, willingly or unwillingly, more and more the character of regional policies designed to provide the infrastructure and support systems that keep the country attractive for high-wage business activities.

Finally, there is the challenge of European unification. In the past the impact of the policies of the European Communities on the West German innovation system has been mainly in terms of project funds, which were administered in such a way as to foster links among firms and research organizations in other European countries. Although the funds were substantial for single projects, as, for example, for the JESSI project in memory chips, they make up only a few percent of the total national R&D and so far have not effected significant institutional changes within the nation's innovation system.[146] At present the combined impact of Community policies for technological innovation and of Community policies for a unified European market on the German system for technical innovation is difficult to assess, but questions concerning what form the emerging European innovation system will have, what the German innovation system may contribute to it, and how it will have to adapt to it still remain to be answered.

NOTES

1. This paper was written while the author was at the Science Center Berlin and later at the European University Institute at Florence. The author thanks Richard Nelson, Nathan Rosenberg, and Peter Walther for comments.

2. World Bank (1989, pp. 6–9); Statistisches Bundesamt (1990, p. 236).

3. *Informationsdienst des Instituts der deutschen Wirtschaft* 17, 17 (25 April 1991) p. 5.

4. Schnabel (1934) is a classic account of German history in the nineteenth century that gives due attention to science and technology. For economic history see Stolper et al. (1967), Henderson (1975), Treue (1975), Borchardt (1976), Aubin and Zorn (1973–1976, Vol. 2), Henning (1979), and Fischer (1985).

5. On List see Henderson (1984) and Schefold (1990).

6. Henderson (1954/1972; pp. 1–9, 139–166), Ritter (1961), Mieck (1965), Weber (1975), Weber (1983), Seeling (1983), and Radkau (1989).

7. Ben-David (1971, Ch. 6).

8. Turner (1974) and McClelland (1980, Chapters 2 and 3).

9. Hufbauer (1982).

10. D. Pohl (1972).

11. Turner (1980) and Ringer (1969). The university system implied a redistribution favoring the upper classes (Borchardt, 1965).

12. McClelland (1980, Chapters 4–6).

13. Schnabel (1934, Vol. 3) and Schmauderer (1976).

14. Cahan (1985) and Turner [in Jeismann and Lundgreen (1987, pp. 221–249)].

15. Ben-David (1971, pp. 186–192), and Forman et al. (1975).

16. Titze (1987, pp. 27–29) (student numbers), Pfetsch (1974, pp. 85–88, 186) (budget figures), and W. Hoffmann et al. (1965, pp. 598–601) (price index for public consumption).

17. On specialization see Lundgreen (in Jarausch, 1983, pp. 149–179) and on natural science departments Riese (1977, pp. 80–93).

18. See Ben-David (1971) and McClelland (1980).

19. See Brocke and Backhaus (both in Backhaus, in press).

20. Troitzsch (1966).

21. Lundgreen (in Sodan, 1988).

22. On the Gewerbeinstitut and the careers of some of its graduates see Henderson (1958, Chapter 6).

23. Schnabel (1925), König (1981), and Gispen (1989).

24. Ludwig and König (1981).

25. Manegold (1970).

26. Kocka (1978, p. 313) and Fischer (1978, p. 87).

27. Fischer (1978, p. 88) and König (in Sodan, 1988, pp. 186–189).

28. König (in Sodan, 1988, pp. 183–213), Harney, Lundgreen, Schmiel, Treese (all in Jeismann and Lundgreen, 1987), Grüner (1967), and Gispen (1989, Chapter 7).

29. Straatmann (in Jeismann and Lundgreen, 1987, pp. 271–281).

30. Fischer (in Aubin and Zorn, 1973–1976, Vol. 2, pp. 557–562) and Engelhardt (1984).

31. E. Hoffmann (1962) and Adelmann (1979).

32. An enthusiastic account is given by Locke (1984, Chapters 4–6).

33. Cipolla (1969) and Easterlin (1981).

34. A good contemporary description is Lexis (1904).

35. Fischer and Lundgreen (1975, p. 557).

36. Flora et al. (1983, pp. 553–663).

37. Kocka (1980, p. 96).

38. Locke (1985, p. 187).

39. Späth (in Rürup, 1979, Vol. 1, pp. 189–208) and Lundgreen (1990). For Britain see Haines (1969) and Alter (1982); for France see Paul (1972) and Fox and Weisz (1980). In the United States some of those initiating the graduate school believed to follow the German model, but, as Ben-David (1971, Chapter 8) showed, in fact built something different.

40. Ben-David (1971, pp. 129–133).

41. Some examples are given by Schmauderer (1976).

42. Landes (1969, p. 346f.) argues that ideological consensus favored German industrialization.

43. Pfetsch (1974, pp. 91–99), Lundgreen (1986), Lundgreen et al. (1986), and Lundgreen (in Vierhaus and Brocke, 1990).

44. Griewank (1927, p. 23).

45. Cahan (1989, p. 196f.).

46. Pfetsch (1970), Bortfeldt et al (1987), and Cahan (1989).

47. Johnson (1990).

48. Burchardt (1975) and Brocke and Burchardt (both in Vierhaus and Brocke, 1990).

49. Brocke (in Vierhaus and Brocke 1990, p. 90).

50. Manegold (1970).

51. Lenoir (1992).

52. Brocke (in Vierhaus and Brocke, 1990, pp. 109–119); Lundgreen (in Rürup, 1979).

53. Fischer (1978, p. 75f.) and Müller (in Lärmer, 1979, pp. 215–243).

54. W. Hoffmann et al. (1965, p. 522); exports of synthetic dyes from Beer (1959, p. 134) (exchange rate 4 Marks/dollar).

55. Brocke (in Vierhaus and Brocke, 1990, p. 90).

56. D. Pohl (1972), Vershofen (1949–58), Haber (1971, p. 133f.), and Hertner (1986, pp. 115–118).

57. Beer (1959) and Haber (1958, pp. 126–136).

58. For the laboratory of Bayer see Beer (1959).

59. Haber (1971, p. 121) and Plumpe (1990, p. 52).

60. Ausschuss (1930, p. 8; 1932, p. 85). These data differ slightly from another source cited by Haber (1971, p. 108).

61. Haber (1971, p. 14); see also Jeffrey (in Cocks and Jarausch 1990, pp. 123–142).

62. Timm (1974).

63. Troitzsch (1977, pp. 35–42).

64. Most recently Allen (1979) and Webb (1980).

65. Wengenroth (1986).

66. Fremdling (1977).

67. For printing presses see Porter (1990, pp. 180–195).

68. Ausschuss (1932, pp. 33, 85, 174).

69. Hughes (1983, Chapter 3).

70. Based on an estimate by the German electrical manufacturers association (reported by Czada, 1969, pp. 136–147). Another estimate gives figures of 31% for Germany and 35% for the United States (see Hertner 1986, p. 125).

71. W. Hoffmann et al. (1965, p. 358).

72. Ausschuss (1932, pp. 85, 238).

73. Maddison (1982).

74. Pavitt and Soete (1982).

75. Kabisch (1982), Braun (1983), Dunning (1983), Hertner (1986), and Schröter (1990).

76. Kindleberger (1975).

77. Ames and Rosenberg (1963) critically review this literature.

78. This view goes back to Veblen (1915) and Weber (1917/1980).

79. On German and international cartels see Maschke (1969), Cornish (1979), H. Pohl (1985, 1988), Wurm (1989), and Fischer (in Aubin and Zorn, 1973–1976, Vol. 2, p. 811).

80. Feldenkirchen (1988).

81. Plumpe (1990).

82. Brady (1933).

83. Ausschuss (1932, pp. 85, 174, 176, 200, 237–239) and Czada (1969, p. 144). Chandler (1990, chapters 12 and 14) provides case histories of firms in the 1920s.

84. See the list in Schreiber (1923, pp. 13–15).

85. Schreiber (1923).

86. Zierold (1968, pp. 38–39), Nipperdey/Schmugge (1970), Düwell (1971), Schroeder-Gudehus (1974), Jarausch (1985), and Feldman (1987); government expenditure for science from Pfetsch (1982, p. 65).

87. Richter (1972, 1979), Forman (1973), H. Pohl (1983), and Feldmann (in Bruch and Müller 1990).

88. Zierold (1968, p. 234), Treue (in Aubin and Zorn, 1976, Vol. 2, p. 114), and H. Pohl (1983, p. 59).

89. Witt and Düwell (both in Vierhaus and Brocke, 1990).

90. For the Kaiser-Wilhelm-Society see Witt (in Vierhaus and Brocke, 1990).

91. Haber (1971, p. 354) (for the chemical industry) and Erker (1990, p. 86) (for Siemens).

92. Plumpe (1990, pp. 471–477) (on IG Farben) and Erker (1990, p. 86) (on Siemens).

93. On science and technology under National Socialism see Beyerchen (1977), Ludwig (1974), Mertens and Richter (1979), Tröger (1986), and Jarausch (1986). On the emigration of scientists and engineers see Fleming and Bailyn (1969) and Mock (1986). On the philosophical and ideological traditions in science and technology preceding National Socialism see Ringer (1969) and Herf (1984).

94. Lasby (1971) and Gimbel (1990); for aerodynamics see Hanle (1982).

95. Bentley (1984).

96. Stamm (1981) and Osietzki (1984).

97. For formal institutional details see Geimer and Geimer (1981), Massow (1983), and Meyer-Krahmer (1992).

98. For the German trade union system good entries are Berghahn and Karsten (1989) and Markovits (1986); for labor market policies Schettkat and Wagner (1990), Matzner and Wagner (1990), and Soskice (1990); for the banking system Zysman (1984, Chapter 5).

99. All data are for 1988; see United Nations (1990).

100. According to Porter (1990) the top 50 industries (in terms of shares of total world export) in 1985 accounted in Germany for 10% of total exports, 53% in Korea, 49% in Japan, 42% in Switzerland, 34% in the United States, 30% in Sweden, 27% in Italy, and 18% in Britain.

101. Law No. 25, *Official Gazette of the Control Council for Germany* No. 6 (30 April 1946), pp. 138–143.

102. Servan-Schreiber (1968), OECD (1968, 1970), Majer (1973), and Nussbaum (1983). For a historical account of the public discussion see Krieger (1987).

103. BMFT (1989). Earlier studies on German foreign trade in high technology are surveyed by Schmietow (1988, Chapters 3 and 4). For selected areas see Grupp and Legler (1987).

104. BMFT/BMBW (1988).

105. Hild (1989).

106. Vieweg (1991).

107. Narin and Olivastro (1987).

108. According to data collected by Ifo-Institut (Penzkofer and Schmalholz, 1990), R&D accounted for 26% of total innovation expenditure in manufacturing industry in 1988.

109. All figures except for Switzerland are for the year 1987. In that year the German figure was 1.82%. See BMFT (1990, p. 378sq.)

110. Wortmann (1991, p. 39). The data on R&D expenditure in Table 4.5 also include expenditure abroad, so they cannot be directly related to national R&D capability.

111. Patel and Pavitt (1989).

112. Echterhoff et al. (1990, pp. 20, 51), BMFT (1990, pp. 50, 362).

113. Deutsche Bundesbank (1990).

114. Tulder and Junne (1988) and Wortmann (1990).

115. Wortmann (1991).

116. Sorge (1991) and Blossfeld (1992).

117. National Science Board (1987, p. 227).

118. Wissenschaftsrat (1988, pp. 121–122, 200–207, 233–259).

119. On universities see Katzenstein (1987, Chapter 7) and Oehler (1989).

120. BMFT/BMBW (1988, p. 7).

121. Wissenschaftsrat (1988, p. 64); an account of accomplishments is "Ein Wissenschafts-wunder?," *The Economist* (11 November 1989), 145–152; for bibliometric research see Daniel and Fisch (1990); for clinical research Freund (1991).

122. Stamm (1981, pp. 109–140), Zierold (1968), Nipperdey and Schmugge (1980), and Hartmann and Neidhardt (in Daniel and Fisch, 1990).

123. Vierhaus and Brocke (1990), Stamm (1981, pp. 85–108), Hohn and Schimank (1990, Chapter 4), and BMFT (1990, p. 266).

124. Schimank (1988).

125. For the Karlsruhe nuclear research center see Keck (1981, Chapter 3); for a generalization of this view see Hohn and Schimank (1990, Chapter 7); for the American discussion see Weinberg (1967).

126. Galbraith (1967/1974) and Hirsch (1974).

127. For government support to aerospace see Schulte-Hillen (1975).

128. For federal policies up to the 1970s see Bräunling and Harmsen (1975), Keck (1976), and Schmitz et al. (1976).

129. An example of the ministry's claim is BMWF (1965, p. 18); an example of its uncritical acceptance is in a report by the Commission on Monopolies (Monopolkommission, 1977, p. 367).

130. Hauff and Scharpf (1975/77).

131. Keck (1981).

132. Sommerlatte et al. (1982).

133. Lorenzen (1985).

134. Keck (1988).

135. An interesting case history is Häusler et al. (1991).

136. BMFT (1988, p. 186; 1990, p. 50).

137. Hohn and Schimank (1990, Chapter 6).

138. BMFT (1988, pp. 189; 1990, pp. 50–51), Bundesregierung (1989, pp. 99–101, 164, 166), Meyer-Krahmer et al. (1983), "Fue-Personalkostenzuschuss-Programm," *Deutsches Institut für Wirtschaftsforschung Wochenbericht* (8 March 1990), 119–122, and Kulicke and Krupp (1987).

139. Humphreys (1989, pp. 147–150) and Weyer (1990).

140. On the aircraft industry see Hornschild and Neckermann (1989).

141. Steinberg (1989).

142. Ellwein and Bruder (1982), Bruder (1983), Gibb (1985), Dose and Drexler (1987), Hilpert (1990), Hucke and Wollmann (1989), Jürgens and Krumbein (1991), Staudt (1987/88), and Sabel et al. (1989). For a survey of the activities of federal states see BMFT (1988, pp. 201–229; 1990, pp. 187–230).

143. On the early work of the Wissenschaftsrat see Berger (1974); on its later work see Block and Krull (in Daniel and Fisch, 1990).

144. For microelectronics see Friebe and Gerybadze (1984) and Malerba (1985); for nuclear power see Keck (1980 and 1981).

145. For telecommunications see Grupp (1991) and the chapter on Germany in Grupp and Schnöring (1990–1991).

146. For European community policies in science and technology see Klodt et al. (1988) and Starbatty and Vetterlein (1990).

REFERENCES

Adelmann, G. (1979). "Berufliche Ausbildung und Weiterbildung in der deutschen Wirtschaft 1871–1918." In H. Pohl (ed.), *Berufliche Aus- und Weiterbildung der deutschen Wirtschaft seit dem 19. Jahrhundert*, 9–52. Wiesbaden: Steiner.

Allen, R. C. (1979). "International Competition in Iron and Steel, 1850–1913." *Journal of Economic History* 39: 911–38.

Alter, P. (1982). *Wissenschaft, Staat, Mäzene*. Stuttgart: Klett-Cotta.

Ames, E., and Rosenberg, N. (1963). "Changing Technological Leadership and Industrial Growth." *Economic Journal* 73(3):13–31.

Aubin, H., and Zorn, W. (eds.) (1973–1976). *Handbuch der deutschen Wirtschafts- und Sozialgeschichte*, Vol. 1. Stuttgart: Union Verlag, 1973, Vol. 2. Stuttgart: Klett, 1976.

Ausschuss zur Untersuchung der Erzeugungs- und Absatzbedingungen der deutschen Wirtschaft. (1930). *Die deutsche chemische Industrie*. Berlin: Mittler.

Ausschuss zur Untersuchung der Erzeugungs- und Absatzbedingungen der deutschen Wirtschaft (1932). *Der deutsche Aussenhandel unter der Einwirkung der weltwirtschaftlichen Strukturwandlungen*. Berlin: Mittler.

Backhaus, J. G. (in press). *The Economics of Science Policy*. Berlin: Springer.

Beer, J. J. (1959). *The Emergence of the German Dye Industry*. Urbana, IL: University of Illinois Press.

Ben-David, J. (1971). *The Scientist's Role in Society*. Englewood Cliffs, NJ: Prentice-Hall.

Bentley, R. (1984). *Technological Change in the German Democratic Republic*. Boulder: Westview.

Berger, R. (1974). *Zur Stellung des Wissenschaftsrats bei der wissenschaftspolitischen Beratung von Bund und Ländern*. Baden-Baden: Nomos.

Berghahn, V. R., and Karsten, D. (1989). *Industrial Relations in West Germany*. Oxford: Berg.

Beyerchen, A. D. (1977). *Scientists under Hitler*. New Haven: Yale University Press.

Blossfeld, H. -P. (1992). "Unterschiedliche Systeme der Berufsausbildung und Anpassung an Strukturveränderungen im internationalen Vergleich." In D. Sadowski and A. Timmesfeld (eds.), *Ökonomie und Tolitik beruflicher Bildung: Europäische Entwicklungen* 45-60. Berlin: Duncker & Humblot.

BMBW/BMFT (Bundesministerium für Bildung und Wissenschaft/Bundesministerium für Forschung und Technologie) (1988). *Leistungsstand und Perspektiven von Wissenschaft, Forschung und Technologie in der Bundesrepublik Deutschland*. Bonn.

BMFT (Bundesminister für Forschung und Technologie) (1988). *Bundesbericht Forschung 1988*. Bonn.

BMFT (Bundesminister für Forschung und Technologie) (1989). *Zur technologischen Wettbewerbsfähigkeit der deutschen Industrie*. December 7.

BMFT (Bundesminister für Forschung und Technologie) (1990). *Faktenbericht 1990 zum Bundesbericht Forschung 1988*. Bonn.

BMwF (Bundesminister für wissenschaftliche Forschung) (1965). *Bundesbericht Forschung II*. (Bundestagsdrucksache V/2054).

Borchardt, K. (1965). "Zum Problem der Erziehungs- und Aus-bildungsinvestitionen im 19. Jahrhundert." In H. Aubin, E. Ennen, H. Kellenbenz, T. Mayer, F. Metz, M. Miller, J. Schmithüsen (eds.), *Beiträge zur Wirtschafts- und Stadtgeschichte*, 380–92. Wiesbaden: Steiner.

Borchardt, K. (1976). "Germany-," In C. Cipolla (ed.), *The Fontana Economic History of Europe: Vol. 4, Part 1*. Brighton: Harvester, London: Barnes & Noble.

Bortfeldt, J., Hauser, W. and Rechenberg, H. (1987). *Forschen, Messen, Prüfen*. Weinheim: Physik-Verlag.

Brady, R. A. (1933). *The Rationalization Movement in German Industry*. Berkeley, CA: University of California Press.

Braun, H.-J. (1983). "Technolgietransfer im Maschinenbau von Deutschland in die USA, 1870–1939." *Technikgeschichte* 50(3), 238–52.

Bräunling, G., and Harmsen, D. M. (1975). *Die Förderungsprinzipien und Instrumente der Forschungs- und Technologiepolitik*. Göttingen: Otto Schwartz.

Bruch, R. vom, and Müller, R. A. (eds.) (1990). *Formen ausserstaatlicher Wissenschaftsförderung*. Stuttgart: Steiner.

Bruder, W. (1983). "Innovation Behavior of Small and Medium-Scale Firms." *Research Policy* 12, 213–25.

Bundesregierung. (1989). *Bericht über die Entwicklung der Finanzhilfen des Bundes und der Steuervergünstigungen für die Jahre 1987 bis 1990*. (Bundestagsdrucksache 11/5116).

Burchardt, L. (1975). *Wissenschaftspolitik im Wilhelminischen Deutschland*. Göttingen: Vandenhoek & Ruprecht.

Cahan, D. (1985). "The Institutionalization of German Physics, 1865-1914." *Historical Studies in the Physical and Biological Sciences* 15(2): 1–65.

Cahan, D. (1989). *An Institute for an Empire*. Cambridge, England: Cambridge University Press.

Chandler, A.D., Jr. (1990). *Scale and Scope*. Cambridge, MA: Harvard University Press.

Cipolla, C. M. (1969). *Literacy and Development in the West*. Harmondsworth: Penguin.

Cornish, W. R. (1979). "Legal Control over Cartels and Monopolization, 1880–1914: A Comparison." In N. Horn and J. Kocka (eds.), *Law and the Formation of the Big Enterprises in the 19th and Early 20th Centuries*, 280–305. Göttingen: Vandenhoek & Ruprecht.

Cocks, G., and Jarausch, K. H. (eds.). (1990). *German Professions, 1800–1950*. New York: Oxford University Press.

Czada, P. (1969). *Die Berliner Elektrotechnische Industrie in der Weimarer Zeit.* Berlin: Colloquium Verlag.

Daniel, H.-D., and Fisch, R. (eds.) (1990). *Scientometrics in the Federal Republic of Germany.* (Special Issue of *Scientometrics* Vol. 19, Nos. 5–6).

Deutsche Bundesbank. (1990). "Patent und Lizenzverkehr mit dem Ausland sowie sonstiger Austausch von technischem Wissen durch Dienstleistungen in den Jahren 1988 und 1989." *Monatsberichte der Deutschen Bundesbank* 42(5): 28–43.

Dose, N., and Drexler, A. (eds.) (1987). *Technologieparks.* Opladen: Westdeutscher-Verlag.

Dunning, J. H. (1983). "Changes in the Level and Structure of International Production." In M. Casson (ed.), *The Growth of International Business,* 84–139. Winchester, MA: George Allen & Unwin.

Düwell, K. (1971). "Staat und Wissenschaft in der Weimarer Epoche." In T. Schieder (ed.), *Beiträge zur Geschichte der Weimarer Republik,* 31–74 (*Historische Zeitschrift* Beiheft 1). München: Oldenbourg.

Easterlin, R. A. (1981). "Why Isn't the Whole World Developed?" *Journal of Economic History* 41(1): 1–19.

Echterhoff-Severitt, H., Grenzmann, C., Marquardt, R., Menner, E., Weissburger, A., and Wudtke, J. (1990). *Forschung und Entwicklung in der Wirtschaft 1987.* Essen: SV-Gemeinnützige Gesellschaft für Wissenschaftsstatistik.

Ellwein, T., and Bruder, W. (1982). *Innovationsorientierte Regionalpolitik.* Opladen: Westdeutscher Verlag.

Engelhardt, U. (ed.) (1984). *Handwerker in der Industrialisierung.* Stuttgart: Klett-Cotta.

Erker, P. (1990). "Die Verwissenschaftlichung der Industrie." *Zeitschrift für Unternehmensgeschichte* 35(2): 73–94.

Feldenkirchen, W. (1988). "Concentration in German Industry 1870–1939." In H. Pohl (ed.), *The Concentration Process in the Entrepreneurial Economy Since the Late 19th Century,* 113–146. Stuttgart: Steiner.

Feldman, G. DD. (1987). "The Politics of Wissenschaftspolitik in Weimar Germany." In C. Maier (ed.), *Changing Boundaries of the Political: Essays on the Evolving Balance Between the State and Society, Public and Private in Europe.* 255–85. Cambridge, UK: Cambridge University Press.

Fischer, W. (1978). "The Role of Science and Technology in the Economic Development of Modern Germany." In W. Beranek and G. Ranis (eds.), *Science, Technology and Economic Development,* 71–113. New York: Praeger.

Fischer, W. (1985). "Deutschland 1850–1914." In W. Fischer (ed.), *Handbuch der Europäischen Wirtschafts- und Sozialgeschichte,* Vol. 5, 357–442. Stuttgart: Klett-Cotta.

Fischer, W., and Lundgreen, P. (1975). "The Recruitment and Training of Administrative and Technical Personnel." In C. Tilly (ed.), *The Formation of National States in Western Europe,* 456–561. Princeton: Princeton University Press.

Fleming, D., and Bailyn, B. (1969). *The Intellectual Migration.* Cambridge, MA: Harvard University Press.

Flora, P., Alber, J., Eichenberg, R., Kohl, J., Kraus, F., Pfenning, W., and Seebohm, K. (1983–1987). *State, Economy, and Society in Western Europe 1815–1975,* 2 Vols. Frankfurt: Campus; London: Macmillan; Chicago: St. James.

Forman, P. (1974). "Financial Support and Political Alignments of the German Physicists after First World War." *Minerva* 10(2): 39–66.

Forman, P., Heilbron, J., and Weart, S. (1975). "Physics Circa 1900." *Historical Studies of the Physical and Biological Sciences* 5: 1–185.

Fox, R., and Weisz, G. (eds.) (1980). *The Organization of Science and Technology in France 1808–1914.* Cambridge, England: Cambridge University Press.

Fremdling, R. (1977). "Railroads and German Economic Growth." *Journal of Economic History* 37(3): 583–604.

Freund, H.-J. (1991). "Problemfeld klinische Forschung." *Forschung: Mitteilungen der DFG.* 3(3): 30.

Friebe, K. P., and Gerybadze, A. (eds.) (1984). *Microelectronics in Western Europe.* Berlin: Erich Schmidt.

Galbraith, J. K. (1967/1974). *The New Industrial State.* Harmondsworth: Penguin (first edition 1967, a German translation was published in 1967).

Geimer, H., and Geimer, R. (1981). *Research Organization and Science Promotion in the Federal Republic of Germany.* München: Saur.

Gibb, J. M. (ed.) (1985). *Science Parks and Innovation Centres.* Amsterdam: Elsevier.

Gimbel, J. (1990). *Science, Technology, and Reparations.* Stanford: Stanford University Press.

Gispen, K. (1989). *New Profession, Old Order.* Cambridge, England: Cambridge University Press.

Griewank, K. (1927). *Staat und Wissenschaft im Deutschen Reich.* Freiburg: Herder.

Grüner, G. (1967). *Die Entwicklung der höheren technischen Fachschulen im deutschen Sprachbiet.* Braunschweig: Westermann.

Grupp, H. (1991). "A Quantitative Assessment of Innovation Dynamics and R&D Management in Japanese and West German Telecommunications." *R&D Management* 21(4):271–90.

Grupp, H., and Legler, H. (1987). *Spitzentechnik, Gebrauchstechnik, Innovationspotential und Preise.* Cologne: TÜV Rheinland.

Grupp, H., and Schnöring, Th. (eds.) (1990–91). *Forschung und Entwicklung für die Telekommunikation,* 2 Vols. Berlin: Springer.

Haber, L. F. (1958). *The Chemical Industry during the Nineteenth Century.* Oxford: Oxford University Press.

Haber, L. F. (1971). *The Chemical Industry, 1900–1930*. Oxford: Oxford University Press.

Haines, G. (1969). *Essays on German Influence upon English Education and Science, 1850–1919*. Hamden, CT: Archon Books.

Hanle, P. A. (1982). *Bringing Aerodynamics to America*. Cambridge, MA: Harvard University Press.

Hauff, V., and Scharpf, F. W. (1975/77). *Modernisierung der Volkswirtschaft*, 2nd ed. Cologne: Europäische Verlagsanstalt (first edition 1975).

Häusler, J., Hohn, H.-W., and Lütz, S. (1991). "The Architecture of an R&D Collaboration." Cologne: Max-Planck-Institut für Gesellschaftsforschung.

Henderson, W. O. (1954/1972). *Britain and Industrial Europe*, 3rd ed., 1972, (first edition 1954). Leicester: Leicester University Press.

Henderson, W. O. (1958). *The State and the Industrial Revolution in Prussia, 1740–1870*. Liverpool: Liverpool University Press.

Henderson, W. O. (1975). *The Rise of German Industrial Power, 1834–1914*. London: Temple Smith.

Henderson, W. O. (1984). *Friedrich List*. London: Cass.

Henning, F.-W. (1979). *Die Industrialisierung in Deutschland*, 5th ed. Paderborn.

Herf, J. (1984). *Reactionary Modernism*, Cambridge, England: Cambridge University Press.

Hertner, P. (1986). "German Multinational Enterprise Before 1914." In P. Hertner and G. Jones (eds.), *Multinationals*, 113–34. Aldershot, England: Gower.

Hild, R. (1989). "Exportboom in der Automobilindustrie." *ifo-Schnelldienst* 42(25): 19–32.

Hilpert, U. (ed.). (1990). *Regional Innovation and Decentralization*. London: Routledge.

Hirsch, J. (1974). "Scientific-Technical Progress and the Political System." *German Political Studies*, Vol. 1. 107–39. Beverly Hills: Sage.

Hoffmann, E. (1962). *Zur Geschichte der Berufserziehung in Deutschland*. Bielefeld: Bertelsmann.

Hoffmann, W. G., Grumbach, F., and Hesse, H. (1965). *Das Wachstum der deutschen Wirtschaft seit der Mitte des 19. Jahrhunderts*. Berlin: Springer.

Hohn, H.-W., and Schimank, U. (1990). *Konflikte und Gleichgewichte im Forschungssystem*. Frankfurt am Main: Campus.

Hornschild, K., and Neckermann, G. (1989). *Die deutsche Luft- und Raumfahrtindustrie*. Frankfurt am Main: Campus.

Hucke, J., and Wollmann, H. (eds.) (1989). *Dezentrale Technologiepolitik?* Basel, Switzerland: Birkhäuser.

Hufbauer, K. (1982). *The Formation of the German Chemical Community, 1720–1785*. Berkeley, CA: University of California Press.

Hughes, T. P. (1983). *Networks of Power*. Baltimore, MD: Johns Hopkins University Press.

Humphreys, P. (1989). "Policies for Technological Innovation and Industrial Change." In S. Bulmer (ed.), *The Changing Agenda of West German Public Policy*, 128–54. Aldershot, England; Dartmouth; Brokkfield, VT: Gower.

Jarausch, K. H. (ed.) (1983). *The Transformation of Higher Learning 1860–1930*. Stuttgart: Klett.

Jarausch, K. H. (1985). "The Crisis of German Professions 1918–1933." *Journal of Contemporary History* 20: 379–98.

Jarausch, K. H. (1986). "The Perils of Professionalism." *German Studies Review* 9: 107–37.

Jeismann, K.-E., and Lundgreen, P. (eds.) (1987). *Handbuch der deutschen Bildungsgeschichte*, Vol. 3. München: Beck.

Johnson, J. A. (1990). *The Kaiser's Chemists*. Chapel Hill: University of North Carolina Press.

Jürgens, U., and Krumbein, W. (eds.) (1991). *Industriepolitische Strategien*. Berlin: Edition Sigma.

Kabisch, T. R. (1982). *Deutsches Kapital in den USA*. Stuttgart: Klett-Cotta.

Katzenstein, P. J. (1987). *Policy and Politics in West Germany*. Philadelphia, PA: Temple University Press.

Keck, O. (1976). "West German Science Policy Since the Early 1960's." *Research Policy* 5: 116–57.

Keck, O. (1980). "Government Policy and Technical Choice in the West German Reactor Programme." *Research Policy* 9: 302–56.

Keck, O. (1981). *Policymaking in a Nuclear Program*. Lexington, MA: Lexington Books.

Keck, O. (1988). "A Theory of White Elephants." *Research Policy* 17:187–201.

Kindleberger, C. P. (1975). "Germany's Over-Taking of England." *Weltwirtschaftliches Archiv* 111: 253–81, 477–504.

Klodt, H., Hoffmeyer, M., Krieger-Boden, C., and Soltwedel, R. (1988). *Forschungspolitik unter EG-Kontrolle*. Tübingen: Mohr.

Kocka, J. (1978). "Entrepreneurs and Managers in German Industrialization." In T. Mathias and M. M. Tostan (eds.), *The Cambridge Economic History of Europe, Vol. 7: The Industrial Economies: Capital, Labour, and Enterprise*, Part 1, 492–589 Cambridge, Engl.: Cambridge University Press.

Kocka, J. (1980). "The Rise of Modern Industrial Enterprise in Germany." In A. D. Chandler and H. Daems (eds.), *Managerial Hierarchies*, 77–116. Cambridge, MA: Harvard University Press.

König, W. (1981). "Stand und Aufgaben der Forschung zur Geschichte der deutschen Polytechnischen Schulen und Technischen Hochschulen im 19. Jahrhundert." *Technikgeschichte* 48(1): 47–67.

Krieger, W. (1987). "Zur Geschichte von Technologiepolitik und Forschungsförderung in der Bundesrepublik Deutschland." *Vierteljahreshefte für Zeitgeschichte* 35: 247–71.

Kulicke, M., and Krupp, H. (1987). "The Formation, Relevance and Public Promotion of New Technology Based Firms." *Technovation* 6:47–56.

Landes, D. (1969). *The Unbound Prometheus.* Cambridge, England: Cambridge University Press.

Lärmer, K. (ed.) (1979). *Studien zur Geschichte der Produktivkräfte.* Berlin: Akademie Verlag.

Lasby, C. G. (1971). *Project Paperclip.* New York: Atheneum.

Lenoir, T. (1992). *Politik im Tempel der Wissenschaft.* Frankfurt am Main: Campus.

Lexis, W. (ed.) (1904). *Das Unterrichtswesen im Deutschen Reich,* 4 Vols. Berlin: Asher (also available in English).

Locke, R. R. (1984). *The End of the Practical Man.* Greenwich, CT: JAI Press.

Locke, R. R. (1985). "Relationship between Higher Educational and Managerial Cultures in Britain and West Germany." In P. Joynt and M. Warner (eds.), *Managing in Different Cultures,* 166–214. Oslo: Universitetsforlaget.

Lorenzen, H.-P. (1985). *Effektive Forschungs- und Technologiepolitik.* Frankfurt am Main: Campus.

Ludwig, K.-H. (1974). *Technik und Ingenieure im Dritten Reich.* Düsseldorf: Droste.

Ludwig, K. -H., and König, W. (eds.) (1981). *Technik, Ingenieure und Gesellschaft.* Düsseldorf: VDI-Verlag.

Lundgreen, P. (1976). "Educational Expansion and Economic Growth in Nineteenth-Century Germany." In L. Stone (ed.), *Schooling and Society,* 20–66. Baltimore, MD: Johns Hopkins University Press.

Lundgreen, P. (1986). *Standardization, Testing, Regulation.* Universität Bielefeld, Forschungsschwerpunkt Wissenschaftsforschung.

Lundgreen, P. (1990). "Engineering Education in Europe and the USA, 1750–1930." *Annals of Science* 47: 33–75.

Lundgreen, P., Horn, B., Krohn, W., Küppers, G., and Paslack, R. (1986). *Staatliche Forschung in Deutschland 1870–1980.* Frankfurt am Main: Campus.

Maddison, A. (1982). *Phases of Capitalist Development.* Oxford: Oxford University Press.

Majer, H. (1973). *Die "Technologische Lücke" zwischen der Bundesrepublik Deutschland und den Vereinigten Staaten von Amerika.* Tübingen: Mohr.

Malerba, F. (1985). *The Semiconductor Business.* London: Pinter.

Manegold, K.-H. (1970). *Universität, Technische Hochschule und Industrie.* Berlin: Duncker & Humblot.

Markovits, A. S. (1986). *The Politics of the West German Trade Unions.* Cambridge, England: Cambridge University Press.

Maschke, E. (1969). "Outline of the History of German Cartels from 1873 to 1914." In F. Crouzet, W. H. Challnor, and W. M. Stern (eds.), *Essays in European Economic History,* 226–58. London: Arnold.

Massow, V. von (1983). *Organization and Promotion of Science in the Federal Republic of Germany.* Bonn: Inter-Nationes.

Matzner, E., and Wagner, M. (1990). *The Employment Impact of New Technology.* Aldershot, England: Avebury/Gower.

McClelland, C.E. (1980). *State, Society and University in Germany 1700–1914.* Cambridge, England: Cambridge University Press.

Mehrtens, H., and Richter, S. (eds.) (1979). *Naturwissenschaft, Technik und NS-Ideologie.* Frankfurt am Main: Suhrkamp.

Meyer-Krahmer, F. (1990). *Science and Technology in the Federal Republic of Germany.* London: Longman.

Meyer-Krahmer, F., Gielow, G., and Kuntze, U. (1983). "Impacts of Government Incentives Towards Industrial Innovation." *Research Policy* 12: 153–69.

Mieck, I. (1965). *Preussische Gewerbepolitik in Berlin 1806–1844.* Berlin: de Gruyter.

Mock, W. (1986). *Technische Intelligenz im Exil.* Düsseldorf: VDI-Verlag.

Monopolkommission. (1977). *Hauptgutachten 1973/1975.* Baden-Baden: Nomos.

Narin, F., and Olivastro, D. (1987). *Identifying Areas of Strength and Excellence in F.R.G. Technology.* Report to the Bundesministerium für Forschung und Technologie.

National Science Board (United States). (1987). *Science & Engineering Indicators 1987.* Washington, D.C.: U.S. Government Printing Office.

Nipperdey, T., and Schmugge, L. (1970). *50 Jahre Forschungsförderung in Deutschland.* Bonn: Deutsche Forschungsgemeinschaft.

Nussbaum, B. (1983). *The World After Oil.* New York: Simon and Schuster (a German translation was published in 1984).

Oehler, C. (1989). *Die Hochschulentwicklung in der Bundesrepublik Deutschland seit 1945.* Frankfurt am Main: Campus.

Organisation for Economic Cooperation and Development. (1968). *Gaps in Technology: General Report.* Paris: OECD.

Organisation for Economic Cooperation and Development. (1970). *Gaps in Technology: Analytical Report.* Paris: OECD.

Osietzki, M. (1984). *Wissenschaftsorganisation und Restauration.* Cologne: Böhlau.

Patel, P., and Pavitt, K. (1989). "A Comparison of Technological Activities in West Germany and the United Kingdom." *National Westminster Bank Quarterly Review* May, 27–42.

Paul, H. W. (1972). *The Sorcerer's Apprentice.* Gainsville: University of Florida Press.

Pavitt, K., and Soete, L. (1982). "International Differences in Economic Growth and the International Location of Innovation." In H. Giersch (ed.), *Emerging Technologies,* 105–33. Tübingen: Mohr.

Penzkofer, H., and Schmalholz, H. (1990). "Zwanzig Jahre Innovationsforschung im Ifo-Institut und zehn Jahre Ifo-Innovationstest." *IFO-Schnelldienst* 43(14): 14–22.

Pfetsch, F. (1970). "Scientific Organisation and Science Policy in Imperial Germany." *Minerva* 8(4): 556–80.

Pfetsch, F. (1974). *Zur Entwicklung der Wissenschaftspolitik in Deutschland, 1750–1914.* Berlin: Duncker & Humblot.

Pfetsch, F. (1982). *Datenhandbuch zur Wissenschaftsentwicklung.* Cologne: Zentrum für historische Sozialforschung.

Plumpe, G. (1990). *Die IG-Farbenindustrie AG: Wirtschaft, Technik und Politik 1904–1945.* Berlin: Duncker & Humblot.

Pohl, D. (1972). *Zur Geschichte der pharmazeutischen Privatinstitute von 1779 bis 1873.* Doctoral Dissertation, Marburg.

Pohl, H. (1983). "Die Förderung schulischer Ausbildung und wissenschaftlicher Forschung durch die deutsche Wirtschaft von 1918 bis 1945." In H. Pohl (ed.), *Wirtschaft, Schule und Universität,* 42–77. Wiesbaden: Steiner.

Pohl, H. (ed.) (1985). *Kartelle und Kartellgesetzgebung in Praxis und Rechtsprechung vom 19. Jahrhundert bis zur Gegenwart.* Stuttgart: Steiner.

Pohl, H. (ed.) (1988). *Wettbewerbsbeschränkungen auf internationalen Märkter.* Stuttgart: Steiner.

Porter, M. E. (1990). *The Competitive Advantage of Nations.* London: Macmillan.

Radkau, J. (1989). *Technik in Deutschland.* Frankfurt am Main: Suhrkamp.

Richter, S. (1972). *Forschungsförderung in Deutschland, 1920–1936.* Düsseldorf: VDI-Verlag.

Richter, S. (1979). "Wirtschaft und Forschung." *Technikgeschichte* 46: 20–44.

Riese, R. (1977). *Die Hochschule auf dem Wege zum wissenschaftlichen Grossbetrieb.* Stuttgart: Klett.

Ringer, F. (1969). *The Decline of the German Mandarins.* Cambridge, MA: Harvard University Press.

Ritter, U. P. (1961). *Die Rolle des Staates in den Frühstadien der Industrialisierung.* Berlin: Duncker & Humblot.

Rürup, R. (ed.) (1979). *Wissenschaft und Gesellschaft,* 2 Vols. Berlin: Springer.

Sabel, C. F., Herrigel, G. B., Deeg, R., and Kazis, R. (1989). "Regional Prosperities Compared: Massachusetts and Baden-Württemberg in the 1980s." *Economy and Society* 18(4): 374–404.

Schefold, B. (ed.) (1990). *Studien zur Entwicklung der ökonomischen Theorie 10.* Berlin: Duncker & Humblot.

Schettkat, R., and Wagner, M. (eds.) (1990). *Technologischer Wandel und Beschäftigung.* Berlin: de Gruyter.

Schimank, U. (1988). "The Contribution of University Research to the Technological Innovation of the German Economy." *Research Policy* 17: 329–40.

Schmauderer, E. (1976). "Die Stellung des Wissenschaftlers zwischen chemischer Forschung und chemischer Industrie im 19. Jahrhundert." In W. TReue und K. Mauel (eds.), *Naturwissenschaft, Technik und Wirtschaft im 19. Jahrhundert,* Vol. 2, 614–53. Göttirgen: Vandenhoek & Ruprecht.

Schmietow, E. A. (1988). *Die technologische Wett-*bewerbsfähigkeit der Bundesrepublik. Bad Homburg: DIE Verlag H. Schäfer.

Schmitz, K., Riehle, R., Narr, W.-D., Koch, C., and Albrecht, U. (1976). *Der Staat und die Steuerung der Wissenschaft.* Göttingen: Otto Schwartz.

Schnabel, F. (1925). "Die Anfänge des technischen Hochschulwesens." In *Festschrift anlässlich des 100-jährigen Bestehens der Technischen Hochschule Fridericiana zu Karlsruhe,* 1–44. Karlsruhe: Müller.

Schnabel, F. (1929–1934). *Deutsche Geschichte im 19. Jahrhundert,* 3 Vols. Freiburg: Herder.

Schreiber, C. (1923). *Die Not der deutschen Wissenschaft und der geistigen Arbeiter.* Leipzig: Quelle & Meyer.

Schroeder-Gudehus, B. (1974). "The Argument for the Self-Government and Public Support of Science in Weimer Germany." *Minerva* 10: 537–70.

Schröter, H. G. (1990). "Die Auslandsinvestitionen der deutschen chemischen Industrie 1870 bis 1930." *Zeitschrift für Unternehmensgeschichte* 35(1):1–22.

Schulte-Hillen, J. (1975). *Die Luft- und Raumfahrtpolitik der Bundesrepublik Deutschland.* Göttingen: Otto Schwartz.

Seeling, H. (1983). *Wallonische Industrie-Pioniere in Deutschland.* Lüttich: Wahle.

Servan-Schreiber, J.-J. (1968). *Die amerikanische Herausforderung),* (German translation of *Le Défi Americain*), Hamburg: Hoffmann und Kampe.

Sodan, G. (ed.) (1988). *Die Technische Fachhochschule Berlin im Spektrum Berliner Bildungsgeschichte.* 1–44. Berlin: Technische Fachhochschule Berlin.

Sommerlatte, T., Beckerhoff, D., Walsh, I., Stelter, K., Klekotto, I. (1982). *Die Entwicklung der Datenverarbeitung in der Bundesrepublik Deutschland.* Report BMFT-FB-DV 82-004, Bundesministerium für Forschung und Technologie.

Sorge, A. (1991). "Strategic Fit and the Societal Effect: Interpreting Cross-National Comparisons of Technology, Organization and Human Resources." *Organization Studies* 12(2): 161–90.

Soskice, D. (1990). "Reinterpreting Corporatism and Explaining Unemployment." In R. Brunetta and C. Dell'Aringa (eds.), *Labour Relations and Economic Performance.* 170–211, London: Macmillan.

Stamm, T. (1981). *Zwischen Staat und Selbstverwaltung.* Cologne: Verlag Wissenschaft und Politik.

Starbatty, J., and Vetterlein, U. (1990). *Die Technologiepolitik der Europäischer Gemeinschaft.* Baden-Baden: Nomos.

Statistisches Bundesamt. (1990). *Statistisches Jahrbuch für das Ausland 1990.* Stuttgart: Metzler-Poeschel.

Staudt, E. (1987/88). "Technologie- und Regionalpolitik der Länder." *List-Forum* 14: 93–110.

Steinberg, R. (1989). "Innovation Centres and Their Importance for the Growth of New Technology-Based Firms." *Technovation* 9: 681–94.

Stolper, G., Häuser, K., and Borchardt, K. (1967). *The German Economy: 1870 to the Present*. London: Weidenfeld & Nicholson.

Timm, A. (1974). *Bergbau und Wissenschaft*. Dortmund: Gesellschaft für Westfälische Wirtschaftsgeschichte.

Titze, H. (1987). *Das Hochschulstudium in Preussen und Deutschland 1820–1944*. Göttingen: Vandenhoek & Ruprecht.

Treue, W. (1975). *Gesellschaft, Wirtschaft und Technik Deutschlands im 19. Jahrhundert*. München: Deutscher Taschenbuch Verlag.

Tröger, J. (ed.) (1986). *Hochschule und Wissenschaft im Dritten Reich*. Frankfurt am Main: Campus.

Troitzsch, U., (1966). *Ansätze technologischen Denkens bei den Kameralisten des 17. und 18. Jahrhunderts*. Berlin: Duncker & Humblot.

Troitzsch, U. (1977). *Innovation, Organisation und Wissenschaft beim Aufbau von Hüttenwerken im Ruhrgebiet, 1850–1870*. Dortmund: Gesellschaft für Westfälische Wirtschaftsgeschichte.

Tulder, R. van, and Junne, G. (1988). *European Multinationals in Core Technologies*. Chichester and New York: John Wiley.

Turner, S. (1974). "University Reformers and Professorial Scholarship in Germany, 1760–1806." In L. Stone (ed.), *The University in Society*, Vol. 2, 495–531. Princeton: Princeton University Press.

Turner, S. (1980). "The Prussian Universities and the Concept of Research." *Internationales Archiv für Sozialgeschichte der deutschen Literatur* 5: 68–93.

United Nations. (1990). *International Trade Statistical Yearbook*. New York: United Nations.

Veblen, T. (1915). *Imperial Germany and the Industrial Revolution*. London and New York: Macmillan.

Vershofen, W. (1949–1958). *Die Anfänge der chemisch-pharmazeutischen Industrie*, 3 Vols. Berlin: Deutscher Betriebswirte-Verlag; Aulendorf: Cantor.

Vierhaus, R., and vom Brocke, B. (eds.) (1990). *Forschung im Spannungsfeld von Politik und Gesellschaft*. Stuttgart: Deutsche Verlagsanstalt.

Vieweg, H.-G. (1991). "Der Werkzeugmaschinenbau." *IFO-Schnelldienst* 44(21): 22–9.

Webb, S. B. (1980). "Tariffs, Cartels, Technology, and Growth in the German Steel Industry, 1879–1914." *Journal of Economic History* 40(2): 309–29.

Weber, M. (1917/1980). "Parliament and Democracy in Germany." In J. Winckelmann (ed.). *Max Weber: Gesammelte politische Schriften*. 4th ed. Tübingen: Mohr.

Weber, W. (1975). "Industriespionage als technologischer Transfer in der Frühindustrialisierung Deutschlands." *Technikgeschichte* 42: 287–305.

Weber, W. (1983). "Preussische Transferpolitik, 1780–1820." *Technikgeschichte* 50: 181–96.

Weinberg, A. M. (1967). *Reflections on Big Science*. Cambridge, MA: MIT Press.

Wengenroth, U. (1986). *Unternehmensstrategien und technischer Fortschritt*. Göttingen: Vandenhoek & Ruprecht.

Weyer, J. (1990). "Strategies for the Social Construction of Technology." In H. Krupp (ed.), *Technikpolitik angesichts der Umweltkatastrophe*, 250–61. Heidelberg: Physica.

Wissenschaftsrat (1988). *Empfehlungen des Wissenschaftsrates zu den Perspektiven der Hochschulen in den 90er Jahren*. Cologne: Wissenschaftsrat.

World Bank. (1989). *The World Bank Atlas 1989*. Washington, D.C.: The World Bank.

Wortmann, M. (1990). "Multinationals and the Internationalization of R&D." *Research Policy* 19: 175–83.

Wortmann, M. (1991). *Country Study on the Federal Republic of Germany*. Commission of the European Communities, Monitor-Fast Program, Prospective Dossier No. 2: "Globalization of Economy and Technology," Vol. 17. Brussels: Commission of the European Communities.

Wurm, C. A. (ed.) (1989). *Internationale Kartelle und Aussenpolitik*. Stuttgart: Steiner.

Zierold, K. (1968). *Forschungsförderung in Drei Eochen*. Wiesbaden: Steiner.

Zysman, J. (1983). *Governments, Markets, and Growth*. Ithaca, NY: Cornell University Press.

5

National Innovation Systems: Britain

WILLIAM WALKER

There are two great puzzles in Britain's economic history. The first is why this comparatively small country on the northwest fringe of the European Continent became the hub of the eighteenth- and nineteenth-century industrial revolutions, and dominated the international economy over so long a period (the industrial supremacy of the United States in this century seems short-lived in comparison). The second is why Britain's industrial leadership begin to ebb away in the last decades of the nineteenth century, and why the decline that followed was so prolonged, continuous, and seemingly irreversible.

The period of apparent discontinuity in the late nineteenth and early twentieth centuries, when the long retreat began, has gained particular attention from historians. Explanations of the change in economic fortunes are of three main kinds. The first is that the culture and institutions that sustained industrial development in the period of expansion proved inappropriate to the new industries that emerged in the 1880s and 1890s, and which underpinned economic advance in much of the twentieth century (Landes, 1969). As Nelson and Rosenberg described in Chapter 1, the chemical and electrical industries required a greater and more systematic engagement in science and education, and the automobile industry a more scientific approach to industrial management, than had hitherto been practiced. The diffusion of new techniques was also inhibited by attachment to the old—by what historians have referred to as the "disadvantages of being first" to experience the industrial revolution.

The second explanation is that during the rise and fall of dominant nations, success initially breeds success, but within a few generations success becomes a source of failure. In the British case, resources became overextended as the Empire grew, middle class culture turned against industrial enterprise, and a rentier mentality took hold (Hobsbawm, 1987). In time, failure developed its own pathology. Industries became obsessed with defending rather than expanding their territories, the power of organized labor increased as managerial authority and competence weakened, and international opportunities were narrowed by the country's loss of nerve. During the twentieth century, Britain also escaped the traumas of invasion or defeat in war, so that its social fabric was less disturbed than in other European countries or in Japan, allowing greater institutional continuity and thus inertia.

The third explanation is that the spread of industrialization, especially in Europe and North America, was bound to undermine Britain's economic hegemony, and that conditions unusually favorable to Britain in the eighteenth and nineteenth centuries no longer applied in the twentieth century. For instance, the North Atlantic trading system lost some of its former importance, and the railways that Britain pioneered brought great improvements in transport, allowing land-locked regions of Europe and the United States to be industrialized and united politically (Mackinder, 1904). The advantages that came from being a maritime nation were thereby diminished. Moreover, by exporting its capital and technology, and by maintaining an open international trading system, Britain helped other nations to challenge its supremacy, as did the United States in the twentieth century (Stein, 1984).

For a long time, it was not generally accepted that Britain had suffered a serious loss of economic vitality. In the first half of this century, decline was to some degree masked by the military defeat of Britain's principal European rival, Germany, and by the economic misery experienced by the United States and other industrial countries during the Great Depression. Imperial markets also provided foreign income and a relatively safe haven between the Wars (Svennilson, 1954). The weakness of Britain's international position really became apparent in the 1950s and 1960s, politically through the inability to hold the Empire together, and economically through the persistent failure to match the growth rates of other industrial countries, or to stem the loss of trade shares in domestic and foreign markets.

In the postwar era, the 1960s and 1980s stand out as the decades in which the most determined and coherent efforts were made to halt the decline, with attention focused on what had come to be regarded as systemic defects in the economy and its management. However, the approaches taken could hardly have been more different. During the 1960s, the guiding assumption, whether under governments of left or right, was that the market economy could no longer be left to its own devices. The state had to intervene financially and in other ways to increase investment and improve industrial management, to ensure that economies of scale were realized and inventions turned into successful innovations, and to redress the inequities of income and opportunity that were seen as inherent to the capitalist system.

In stark contrast, the guiding assumption in the 1980s and 1990s (so far) has been that the market economy *must* be left to its own devices, and that Britain's economic deficiencies have stemmed in large part from the state's creeping protection of individuals, firms, and sectional interests, and from delusions about its managerial powers. The aim has therefore been to restore the spirit of "free enterprise" and "individual responsibility," giving the market free rein wherever possible to decide the allocation of resources. Hence the privatization of state monopolies, the attack on trade unionism, the shift away from direct taxation, and a whole range of measures and inducements that came to be known under the rubric "Thatcherism."

In the 1960s and 1980s, the ways in which Britain's "system of innovation" were conceived, and the roles ascribed to it in economic development, were thus very different. Broadly speaking, the first, implicitly Schumpeterian, of the above three explanations of economic decline held sway in the 1960s. The managed restructuring of the industrial economy, the allocation of increased resources to R&D and education, and the adoption of more systematic approaches to the management of industrial and technological activity were seen as the route to recovery.

In the 1980s, the second explanation carried greater weight. The government's deepest belief, romantic and behavioral rather than managerialist, was that the individual energies released by the emancipation from past constraints could alone drive economic modernization. Technical and other forms of advance would follow, but could not precede, the revolution in social attitudes and behavior. Restoring faith in free market capitalism, and rooting out the culture of failure, were seen as preconditions for economic and thus technological recovery.

In some respects, Britain's economic performance in the 1980s relative to other OECD countries showed an improvement over the 1960s and 1970s. Despite the macroeconomic troubles with which the decade began and ended, productivity rose strongly over much of the period, and in some areas, particularly in services, the old dynamism seemed to be returning. There were few signs, however, of a reversal of the historic decline in Britain's abilities to establish new technological capacities. Whereas other countries' spending on research and development (R&D) increased, Britain's stagnated; the share of world technological output, as measured by patents, continued to decline; and the science and education systems were beset with problems. The growth of high technology activity that did occur was substantially the result of the expansion of defense expenditure, and of U. S. and Japanese inward investment in electronics and other fields. Only in chemicals and pharmaceuticals and in a few engineering niches (aeroengines being a significant example) could it be claimed that Britain maintained its position among the leaders in the development of civil technology.

In the 1960s, industry and government were still acting in the shadow of the Empire. It was taken for granted that Britain should remain at the forefront of technology. This is not the case today. The first thing to emphasize about Britain's contemporary innovation system is therefore that its development, whether by industry or the state, has become a relatively low priority. This may be the natural economic behavior of a country that now has relatively low income levels and needs to catch up with international best practice, and whose manufacturing companies no longer match the scale or sophistication of their main foreign rivals. But it is also the consequence of the greater dynamism in Britain of services and other activities, and of a prevailing economic culture, even ideology, which has come to place quick gains before the patient, long-term development of industrial capabilities.

BRITAIN'S ECONOMIC STRUCTURE: STRENGTH OUTSIDE MANUFACTURING

Britain has a population of 57 million people. Its economic output in 1988 was £360bn ($580bn at the exchange rate then current). In both population and GDP, it is closest to France and Italy among the industrial nations. Britain's economic structure and praxis are, however, distinct from those of its European neighbors (Holland provides perhaps the nearest European equivalent). In several respects, Britain has most in common with the United States, despite the great disparity in size: the strength of resource-based industries, the scale and functioning of its capital markets, the heavy commitments to defense production, and the attachment to individualism and to liberal economic ideals.

The structural differences between the British and Continental European economies are most noticeable outside manufacturing—in agriculture, energy, and tradeable services—and in areas of manufacturing that are linked to resource trading (e.g., food processing, petrochemicals). It is in these areas that Britain's position in international commerce is strongest. As a result, the priority given to advanced manufacturing and thus to technological development has often been less evident in Britain than in other European countries.

Taking these other sectors in turn, *agriculture* forms a small, if generally efficient, part of the British economy. In 1989, it accounted for 1.5% of GDP and 1.3% of employment (see Table 5.1). Unlike Italy and France, Britain remains a net importer of agricultural produce, and with the exception of whisky, is not a significant producer of high-value items such as wine and cheese.

This nevertheless understates Britain's role in international commerce in foodstuffs. It is home to some of the world's largest food, drink, and tobacco companies whose origins can be traced back to the eighteenth and nineteenth centuries (British American Tobacco, Unilever, Rank Hovis McDougall, Tate & Lyle, Cadbury Schweppes). These firms are today highly diversified and multinational. Of the 29 British firms in the top 200 non-U. S. industrial companies in 1987, no fewer than 10 belonged in this category (Germany had none). Their combined sales were $71bn (see Table 5.2).

Where *energy* is concerned, Britain has the most extensive primary energy resources in Europe. It is still a major if declining coal producer, and during the 1970s and 1980s it became Europe's largest producer of oil, and its second largest producer of natural gas (after the Netherlands). This accounts for the substantial rise evident in Table 5.1 in the energy industries' share of national output in the late 1970s and early 1980s.

Outside the coal industry, the firms operating in this area are again highly multinational. BP and Shell are global actors and the largest firms based outside the United States, with combined sales of $144bn in 1987. Like RTZ, which is now the world's largest minerals producer and trader, they owe their positions partly to the territories, capabilities, and linkages acquired before the Empire was dismantled.

Table 5.1. Structural Change in the British Economy, 1979–1989

	GDP (%)			Employment (%)			GDP Per Employee
	1979	1983	1989	1979	1983	1989	1979–1989 (Constant Prices)
Agriculture	2.1	2.0	1.5	1.6	1.7	1.3	172
Energy, water	8.0	11.5	5.2	3.1	3.1	2.1	230
Manufacturing	28.2	23.5	22.2	31.3	26.2	23.0	245
Construction	6.1	6.0	6.9	5.3	5.0	4.7	251
Distribution, hotels	13.2	12.7	14.2	18.4	19.5	20.3	190
Transport, communications	7.6	7.0	6.9	6.4	6.4	6.0	180
Banking, finance insurance[a]	11.5	13.6	19.7	7.1	8.9	11.8	131
Other services	23.3	23.7	23.4	26.7	29.2	30.9	165
Total	100	100	100	100	100	100	206

[a]Excludes leasing.

Source: United Kingdom National Accounts, 1990 Edition. London: Central Statistical Office, 1990.

Table 5.2. Number (and Sales) of Top 500 Non-U.S. Industrial Companies, by Selected Sectors, 1987

	United Kingdom No. ($bn)	Federal Republic of Germany No. ($bn)	France No. ($bn)	Japan No. ($bn)
Principal manufacturing sectors	32(123.6)	40(314.4)	22(160.4)	92(513.1)
Chemicals, etc.	5(29.8)	9(77.9)	5(25.0)	22(69.5)
Electricals, electronics	8(33.3)	6(40.4)	6(41.9)	28(188.9)
Metals, mechanical engineering	10(25.2)	16(79.0)	4(34.1)	23(101.3)
Motor vehicles, aerospace	9(35.3)	9(117.1)	7(59.4)	19(153.4)
Selected other production sectors	32(213.3)	7(33.8)	15(65.3)	28(98.6)
Mining, petroleum[a]	10(112.5)	7(33.8)	6(43.8)	8(43.7)
Food, drink, tobacco[a]	22(100.8)	0	9(21.5)	20(54.9)
Total, selected industries	64(336.9)	47(348.2)	37(225.7)	120(611.7)

[a]Fifty percent of the sales of the Anglo-Dutch firms, Shell and Unilever, have been attributed to the United Kingdom.
Source: Derived from "The International 500." *Fortune,* August 1988.

With regard to *services,* the formation of a dynamic international capital market, based in the City of London, played an important part in Britain's rise to economic dominance in the nineteenth century. Today, Britain's position in international finance and insurance remains out of all proportion to the size of its productive economy. Following sterling's decline as an international currency in the 1950s and 1960s, the City of London retained its role as a leading financial center partly by gaining command over the burgeoning Eurodollar market, and partly by becoming a major player in the recycling of OPEC's windfall gains after the oil price rises in the 1970s. During the 1980s, the City of London has expanded at a prodigious rate, due to its financing of economic expansion in Europe and elsewhere, to its invasion by U. S. and Japanese financial companies, and to its increasing technological linkage to the New York and Tokyo capital markets. Many of the services offered by the City of London may be classed as producer services, but its clientele is international. Unlike Tokyo or Frankfurt, its recent expansion has not reflected the underlying dynamism of the domestic production base.

This is not the only area of services in which Britain has a significant international presence. In hotels (Grand Metropolitan, Trusthouses Forte), retail (Marks & Spencer, Sainsbury), air transport (British Airways), and advertising, publishing, and property, British firms have been expanding at home and abroad. They have, for instance, been among the most aggressive purchasers of assets in the United States during the 1980s, to the extent that Britain has recently surpassed Japan as the U. S.'s largest foreign investor.

Before moving on to manufacturing, three implications are worth drawing here. First, the above areas have increasingly come to form the heart of the British economy. The shift toward services is, of course, an international trend, but in Britain it has been especially pronounced. Manufacturing comprised less than one-quarter of national output in 1985, against one-third in 1960. Only the United States among the advanced countries has a lower share of output coming from manufacturing.

The increasing concentration of resources in the tradeable service sector should be seen in the British case as a sociopolitical as well as an economic phenomenon. Employment there carries greater prestige than in manufacturing, and is generally more lucrative, so that it acts as a magnet to the social elite, whose contours it increasingly defines. The leaning toward services is reflected in the composition of the government that has held power since 1979, with its domination by people whose careers have been made in services such as retail, property, finance, and law. As a consequence, there is a natural tendency among policy-makers, for instance with regard to the interest and exchange rates, to place the demands of the tradeable service sector above those of manufacturing. By the same token, the political administration often betrays limited understanding of what it takes to be a successful manufacturer in the contemporary international economy. Britain is in these respects at the opposite pole to Germany and Japan.

Second, the norms of managerial behavior in British manufacturing have become strongly influenced by practices in these other areas, and particularly by the nature and power of British capital markets. To an exceptional degree among European countries, short-run profit maximization and asset trading have become the primary objective of the business manager (Ingham, 1984; Lazonick, 1990). This may be attributed, inter alia, to the heavy reliance on stock market finance, and to the existence of a large secondary market in issued shares, which exerts pressure on companies to maximize the income of stakeholders; in the 1980s, to the use of monetary instruments, and specifically high real interest rates, as primary tools of macroeconomic policy; to the comparatively slight involvement of banks in industrial finance and decision making, and to their unwillingness to shield companies from the vagaries of financial markets; and to the ease of corporate takeover in Britain, as in the United States, which again encourages high profits and dividends to maintain stock ratings and thus the selling price of companies. The relatively open market in corporate assets has in turn fed the well-documented tendency among large firms to give growth by acquisition and merger a higher priority than organic growth, and has encouraged the "financial engineering" practiced by conglomerates such as the Hanson Trust and BTR, and even by some of Britain's largest high technology companies (GEC being a notable example).

The incentive structure thereby created helps explain why British manufacturing companies repeatedly display higher profits than their European and Japanese counterparts, while tending to invest less in fixed capital and R&D. This was well demonstrated in the recent takeover of the electronics firm, Plessey, by GEC and Siemens. International comparisons showed that GEC and Plessey had been consistently more profitable than their international rivals, and certainly more so than Siemens, but had equally consistently slipped down the league table of electronics companies measured by size and market share (Morgan et al., 1989). A recent consultant's report proudly announced that Britain's large firms were "the best in Europe," since they occupied 6 of the top 10, and 28 out of the top 50 positions when ranked according to a bundle of profitability measures (*Sunday Times,* 22 April 1990). There were only two German companies on the list.

Third, these nonmanufacturing sectors are predominantly technology users, rather than technology producers. Moreover, with the advent of information technology, they have become heavy and often highly sophisticated technology users. In 1987, the service sector accounted for one-half of British investment in plant and machinery, against one-third in 1977. In a number of contexts (e.g., bank cash dispensers, value-added networks (VANs), stock control systems, mobile telephones), Britain leads other European countries in the application of new technologies. This raises the question of whether the growth of investment in new technology in these sectors has, by pulling on the supply side, led to the establishment of new technological capabilities and to a creative interplay between users and producers in Britain.

Unfortunately, there have been few studies of this issue. Some indigenous capabilities have undoubtedly taken root (for instance, in relation to systems software and mobile telephones), leading to new competitive advantages. However, the available evidence suggests that this has been the exception rather than the rule. The main beneficiaries appear to have been foreign multinationals. In the North Sea, for instance, the more advanced technologies have been developed largely in the United States and elsewhere (Surrey and Cook, 1983). In relation to the financial and retail sectors, IBM and DEC have much the largest market shares in computing and networking, while Japanese companies dominate the market for peripherals and office equipment.

Looking on the bright side, many of these products are now being supplied from multinational facilities within the United Kingdom—the dynamism of the service sector is even leading some foreign firms to locate product development in Britain. DEC is, for instance, pioneering VAN service products in the United Kingdom because of the advanced nature of the financial service sector (Morgan and Davies, 1989). Although the amount of value that is added to their products in the United Kingdom is not known, the rapid uptake of new techniques in the British service sector seems to be one of the factors attracting multinational investment to the United Kingdom.

For all the above reasons, the relationship between the tertiary sectors and manufacturing has become an increasingly significant issue in Britain. Some argue that the growing predominance of services and the decline of the manufacturing base do not matter. According to this view, the growth of services is a sign of modernity, and reflects Britain's true comparative advantage. However, the massive trade imbalance that has developed in the 1980s suggests that macroeconomic stability may not be achievable without a stronger manufacturing base. In 1989, Britain's trade imbalance reached £22bn, or 4.5% of GDP (Table 5.3). Although this has been partly caused by misjudgments in macroeconomic policy that caused consumer demand to run ahead of supply capacities, Britain seems to be falling into a trap whereby the trade returns from an expanding service sector are being outweighed by its propensity to suck in

Table 5.3. British Trading Performance, 1978–1988 (£bn)

Year	Visible Trade						Invisibles $X - I$	Current Account $X - I$
	Exports (X)	Imports (I)	Total	Oil	Nonoil			
1978	35.0	36.6	−1.6	−2.0	+0.4		+2.5	+0.9
1980	47.1	45.8	+1.3	+0.3	+1.0		+1.7	+0.3
1982	55.3	53.1	+2.2	+4.4	−2.4		+2.5	+4.7
1984	70.3	74.8	−4.5	+6.9	−11.5		+6.7	+2.2
1986	72.7	81.4	−8.7	+4.1	−12.8		+8.9	+0.2
1988	80.2	100.7	−20.5	+2.3	−22.9		+5.6	−14.9

Source: United Kingdom Balance of Payments, 1988 Edition. London: Central Statistical Office, 1988.

imports of manufactured goods. Equally, the income growth from the expansion of tradeable services and from higher productivity is creating demand for consumer durables and other goods that the manufacturing sector cannot presently meet.

THE MANUFACTURING BASE

In 1987, manufacturing GDP in Britain amounted to £85bn, or 23% of national output. Medium- and high-technology sectors, as defined by the OECD, were responsible for 46% of manufacturing sales and 69% of exports in 1986 (Table 5.4). This placed Britain midway between Italy, which has the lowest commitment to these sectors among the major industrial countries (43% of sales and 51% of exports), and Japan, which has the highest (53% of sales and 82% of exports).

Like other industrial countries, the sectoral composition of output and trade has been moving in the direction of higher technology manufacturing, although in Britain rather gradually (from 41% of sales in 1971 to 46% in 1986). What has been most pronounced in Britain has been the decline of metal-based manufacturing, extending from iron and steel to mechanical engineering to motor vehicles, aerospace being the only exception. Contributing close to one-half of manufactured exports in 1971, the share had fallen to less than one-third in 1986. Compensating gains were made in chemicals and pharmaceuticals, electronics, and aerospace. The shares of low-technology manufacturing industries in both production and trade remained comparatively stable over the period, although the historic decline of textiles continued.

These trends suggest that a satisfactory "upward" shift in Britain's technology base occurred in the 1970s and 1980s. However, as indicators of the vitality of *British*

Table 5.4. Production and Export Shares in U.K. Manufacturing, 1971 and 1986

	Production Shares (%)		Export Shares (%)	
	1971	1986	1971	1986
Medium and high technology				
Chemicals, etc.	11.5	14.7	12.2	18.8
Electricals, electronics	9.7	11.7	12.3	19.3
Mechanical engineering	8.3	8.8	17.8	13.1
Motor vehicles	6.7	5.8	12.7	7.0
Aerospace	1.2	2.4	3.6	6.9
Other	3.6	2.8	5.0	3.6
Subtotal	41.1	46.2	63.6	68.7
Low technology				
Food, drink, and tobacco	18.0	20.6	6.4	6.8
Textiles, etc.	7.9	6.0	8.0	5.9
Metals	16.4	7.1	13.0	8.9
Paper and printing	8.8	9.3	2.4	2.7
Other	7.8	10.8	6.6	7.0
Subtotal	58.9	53.8	36.4	31.3

Source: A. Buxton, "Technology and Structural Change." NEDO, London, 1990, Tables I and II, using OECD figures and definitions.

industries, they have to be treated with caution due to the unusual weight of multinational investment in the British industrial economy. Table 5.5 shows that one-fifth of manufacturing GDP in 1987 came from foreign firms locating production in Britain, the greatest concentration of multinational investment being in the medium- and high-technology sectors (aerospace again excepted). Only Belgium has a higher proportion among European countries. By the mid-1990s, the proportion of manufacturing in foreign hands could reach one-third or even higher. Britain is now experiencing a new wave of foreign direct investment, with Japan this time in the vanguard. Many Japanese firms, particularly in the electronics and automobile sectors, have chosen Britain as their favored point of entry to the extended European market.

Hence the broad statistics of industrial production and trade provide a partial, and sometimes misleading, measure of the performance of British-based manufacturing enterprises. The structural changes in British manufacturing in recent years have been the result of both deindustrialization—the withdrawal from areas such as metalworking—and positive restructuring involving the creation of new manufacturing capacities. A substantial, even the major, part of the latter can be attributed to foreign investment. Without it, the structure of the British economy today would appear much less modern.

Further insights into the scale and sectoral distribution of *British* manufacturing can be gained by comparing Britain's large firms with those of other countries. Table 5.2 shows that Britain's share of large firms in the *Fortune* list of the top 500 non-U. S. industrial companies in 1987 was next only to that of Japan. However, one-half of them were in the areas of traditional strength in mining and petroleum, and food, drink, and tobacco. Indeed, the sales of British firms in these sectors dwarfed those from other countries ($213bn against $34bn, $65bn, and $99bn for Germany, France, and Japan, respectively). They also exceeded by a substantial margin the sales of British firms in the main manufacturing sectors ($213bn against $124bn), in contrast to the other countries where the balance was weighted heavily in the other direction.

Table 5.5. Foreign Companies' Share of U.K. Gross Value Added (1987)

	%
Motor vehicles	45
Office machinery, data processing	37
Chemicals, pharmaceuticals	32
Rubber, plastics	24
Instruments	22
Mechanical engineering	21
Electricals, electronics	17
Paper and Publishing	15
Food, drink, and tobacco	15
Metals	10
Textiles, leather, clothing	4
Timber, furniture	3
Aerospace, other transport equipment	2
Total manufacturing	19

Source: UK Census of Production (1987).

As regards the manufacturing sectors, one is struck in Table 5.2 by the relatively high incidence of British large firms. But their output is comparatively small by international standards. One reason is that Britain has very few "giant" manufacturing companies in the medium- and high-technology sectors. The average sales per firm in these areas in the *Fortune* list was $3.8bn for Britain, against $5.6bn for Japan, $7.3bn for France, and $7.9bn for Germany. In 1987, only one British manufacturing company, ICI, had sales ($18bn) that exceeded $10bn. The next largest was GEC with sales of $7.8bn. In comparison, France had five, Germany nine, and Japan twelve.

At the other end of the scale, a number of studies have shown that Britain is relatively poorly endowed with small firms (Bolton Committee, 1971; Ganguly and Bannock, 1985). Although the rate at which small firms are created may be high, so is the casualty rate. Their share of total manufacturing employment in the late 1970s, measured by establishment, was 24% in Britain compared to 30% in West Germany, 34% in the United States, 52% in Switzerland, and 54% in Japan. A recent comparison of Dutch and British productivity found that the number of persons per manufacturing enterprise in 1984 was 254 in the Netherlands and 413 in Britain (van Ark, 1990). Britain appears to lack the diversity evident in the German Handwerk sector, in Italian textile and shoe manufacturing, and in the French food and wine sectors.

There thus appears to be a lack of strength at both ends of the spectrum where manufacturing is concerned: there is no Siemens, or Fiat, or Mannesmann in Britain; but nor is there the abundance of sophisticated small firms that is found in some of these other countries. Again, one has to look outside medium- and high-technology manufacturing to find "giant" British firms (such as BP, Unilever, BAT), and to the service sector to find a profusion of relatively dynamic small firms. The growth in the number of enterprises recorded in Britain during the 1980s, including those involved in computer software, has been substantially a service sector phenomenon.

In identifying where Britain's relative strengths and weaknesses lie in manufacturing, one has to distinguish at the outset between areas where the strength is *indigenous* and where it derives from the presence of foreign multinationals. Among the former, three stand out:

1. *Chemicals and pharmaceuticals.* Here Britain possesses some of the world's leading companies (ICI, Glaxo, Beecham), although Table 5.2 has shown that British output in chemicals is dwarfed by that of Germany. Although there is significant inward investment by U. S. firms in particular, this is offset by substantial outward investment. The sector gains additional strength from the chemical and petrochemical activities of the major British oil companies.

2. *Aerospace.* As will become apparent below, strength in this sector derives largely from Britain's heavy postwar commitment to defense procurement. The leading firms are British Aerospace (airframes and guided weapons), Rolls-Royce (aeroengines), and Lucas Aerospace, Dowty and Smiths Industries (engine controls, hydraulics, and other subassemblies). For the same reason, Britain has a strong international presence in *defense electronics* (GEC—now incorporating Ferranti and Plessey—and British Aerospace Dynamics). None of these firms is strongly multinational in the sense that they locate significant R&D and production abroad. However, all are notable participants in collaborative aerospace projects within Europe and across the Atlantic.

3. *Food, drink, and tobacco.* Britain's substantial competitive advantage in this area has already been discussed. The firms have long been strongly multinational, having large production bases outside the United Kingdom.

Britain still has indigenous capabilities in telecommunications, and in electrical and mechanical engineering, but without any distinct competitive advantage outside some niches. As filières, they no longer have depth and cohesion, and thus a substantial international standing. Moreover, the privatization of the telecommunication and electric utilities appears to be causing their hitherto protected equipment suppliers to fall under foreign domination, rather than reviving their fortunes. Siemens has gained the upper hand in the telecommunications equipment industry following its acquisition of a half share in the main British supplier, GPT; and investment in the combined-cycle power plants, which are expected to provide most additional generating capacity in the 1990s, will be based on foreign technology supplied by General Electric, Asea-Brown-Boveri, and Siemens in particular.

To the areas of indigenous capability should be added those in which production in Britain relies heavily on foreign investment. Two stand out:

1. *Motor vehicles.* Ford and General Motors (Vauxhall) have had large production facilities in Britain since the 1920s (their design and R&D centers have, however, been largely moved to Germany). Ford has recently acquired Jaguar, and General Motors has acquired Lotus, the most innovative of the Britain's small car producers. The remaining British volume-car manufacturer, Rover, has become increasingly dependent on its links with Honda. The automobile industry in Britain is about to experience a period of strong expansion because of the decisions by Nissan and Toyota to locate their main European production bases in northern England.
2. *Electronics.* Companies with large manufacturing facilities in Britain include IBM, DEC, and Fujitsu following its recent takeover of ICL (computers); Hitachi, Sony, Matsushita, and Toshiba (consumer electronics); Motorola, NEC, and Intel (semiconductors); and Rank Xerox and Cannon (office electronics). Scotland now has the largest concentration of semiconductor manufacturing in Europe ("Silicon Glen"). In semiconductors there is no internationally significant capability remaining in British hands.

These judgments about Britain's indigenous strengths and weaknesses are generally supported by indicators of competitive advantage in technology and trade. Table 5.6 shows that Britain's revealed technological advantage lies in aerospace, pharmaceuticals, food products, coal and petroleum, chemicals, and mechanical engineering (in that order). A glance at Table 5.6 is sufficient to indicate that the distribution of advantage in Britain quite closely matched that of France and the United States, but that there was a strong negative correlation with that of Japan and to a lesser degree with that of Germany.

Sectoral differences in performance emerge more clearly from the trade statistics (Table 5.7). Among the medium- and high-technology industries, the trade surpluses in chemicals and aerospace increased, whereas the balance in electronics and motor vehicles changed from a slight surplus in 1978 to very large deficits in 1986 (other trade measures display similar patterns). All European countries faced deteriorating trade balances in electronics over the period in question, but the greatest decline was expe-

Table 5.6. Revealed Technological Advantage by Sector, 1978–1986[a]

	France	Germany	Japan	United States	United Kingdom
Aerospace	3.64	1.06	0.18	1.24	2.10
Pharmaceuticals	1.36	0.96	0.74	0.83	1.72
Food products	1.09	0.75	0.69	1.07	1.43
Coal and petroleum	1.75	0.71	0.81	1.35	1.13
Chemicals	0.95	1.27	0.87	0.99	1.03
Mechanical engineering	0.98	1.18	0.69	1.00	1.01
Electricals, electronics	1.24	0.79	1.21	1.03	0.95
Motor vehicles	0.60	1.06	1.54	0.69	0.68
Office equipment	0.74	0.53	1.80	0.95	0.64

[a]Revealed technical advantage (RTA) is a measure of technical specification; it is the ratio of a country's share of U.S. patenting in a given sector to its share of U.S. patenting in all product groups. An RTA in excess of 1 indicates above average specialization.

Source: Cantwell & Hodson (1990).

rienced by Britain. An important question in relation to Britain's recent industrial performance is, therefore, why the chemical and aerospace industries have done comparatively well, whereas the electronics and motor vehicle industries have fared badly.

These figures also provide a warning for Britain: multinational investment, which has been growing most strongly in these last two sectors, does not so far appear to be correcting the trade imbalance. If it is hastening the decline of indigenous capabilities and replacing them with assembly plants, as some are claiming, it may instead be worsening the trade situation. One should note, however, that the chemical sectors have also experienced strong inward investment without a deteriorating trade balance. It is

Table 5.7. U.K. Trade Balance by Sector, 1978–1986 (£m)

	Exports Minus Imports (1978)	Exports Minus Imports (1986)	Change in Balance 1978–1986
Medium and high technology			
Chemicals, drugs	+1206	+2306	+1100
Electricals, electronics	+486	−2183	−2669
Mechanical engineering	+2298	+1725	−573
Motor vehicles	+311	−4127	−4438
Aerospace	+237	+1634	+1397
Other	+376	−1332	−1708
Subtotal	+4914	−1977	−6891
Low technology			
Food, drink, tobacco	−1644	−3252	−1608
Textiles, etc.	−707	−3289	−2582
Metals	−400	−652	−252
Paper and printing	−773	−2088	−1315
Other	−1290	−3071	−1781
Subtotal	−4814	−12352	−7538
Total	+100	−14329	−14429

Source: Mayes (1987).

only where there is an underlying weakness that foreign firms can behave like cuckoos in the nest.

Come what may, the development of the British industrial economy in the 1990s will depend significantly, and to a greater extent than for other West European economies, on the behavior of foreign multinational companies: the scale of their investments, the degree of local content in their products, their willingness to locate R&D and design capabilities in Britain and to use British personnel, and their attitudes toward future investment in the United Kingdom as against other parts of Europe (now including Eastern Europe). In particular, the outcome will depend on the decisions of Japanese companies, and on how Japan generally conducts its trade relations with the enlarged European market. As always, the price of decline is a loss of economic sovereignty.

THE INNOVATION SYSTEM: PRODUCTIVITY AND R&D

So far, the picture has been one of continuing retrenchment in Britain's manufacturing industries. In one respect, however, industrial performance in Britain was more than satisfactory in the 1980s—in the growth of industrial productivity.

The Productivity Conundrum

For Britain in the 1980s, the indicators of technical progress present us with a dichotomy. As we shall see, R&D and patenting statistics suggest that Britain's technological standing continued to deteriorate. The growth of productivity was, however, the fastest among OECD countries over much of the decade. Between 1980 and 1987, output per person employed increased in real terms by 24% in the United Kingdom, against 22% in Japan, 12–14% in France, Italy, and Germany, and 7% in the United States. On the face of it, this suggests that notable advances occurred in Britain's *application* but not in its *development* of technology.

The productivity increases have become the subject of much debate among economists. There appears to be consensus on two points (Layard and Nickell, 1989; Oulton, 1990; Feinstein and Matthews, 1990). The first is that productivity growth in the 1980s was not, by and large, investment or output led. It was not until the late 1980s that manufacturing investment and output recovered sufficiently to overtake the levels reached in the late 1970s. Instead, it was particularly associated with reductions in overmanning and the scrapping of the large "tail" of inefficient plants. Freeman has referred to this as the Verdun rather than the Verdoorn effect (Freeman, 1989). The second is that there was significant improvement in the management of the remaining productive assets. This came especially from the reduced resistance to change among the labor force, and the accompanying reassertion of managerial authority within firms. Some have stressed the importance of the "shock" of 1980–1981, when the combination of domestic recession and an overvalued exchange rate threatened the survival of many firms and brought high unemployment (Metcalf, 1988). This, in turn, weakened the influence of trades unions, as did the government's refusal to intervene in wage bargaining and its legislation to curb their powers.

It remains to be seen whether the productivity improvements can be sustained in the 1990s. As recession has taken hold in the early 1990s, productivity has fallen along with industrial output. Nevertheless, it can justifiably be claimed that Britain came closer, if not close enough, to operating according to international best practice during the 1980s.

Why, then, were the gains in manufacturing productivity not accompanied by equivalent gains in Britain's innovative capabilities? One interpretation is that Britain was beginning to act as a low-wage, low-productivity economy. By the end of the 1970s, a productivity gap had opened up between Britain and other leading European economies, let alone with the United States and Japan. It was, therefore, economically rational to seek profits and strengthening competitiveness by raising productive efficiency and by improving product quality and design, rather than by pursuing monopoly rents through innovation. Except in high-technology industries where the neglect of innovation tends to be fatal, Britain could, according to this view, afford to lower the priority given to the development of new technology, for the time being at least.

Another interpretation is that changes in social relations and incentives in the 1980s strongly supported productivity improvement, but not improvement in innovative performance. The combination of a pliant labor force and strong incentives to reduce costs and maximize profits brought large gains in productive efficiency, but those same incentives discouraged investment in R&D and in new productive capacity. The growth of profits has in fact outstripped the growth of R&D and capital investment. In general, the increased surplus generated by higher productivity has tended to be absorbed by higher dividend and interest payments, and by higher taxes, or has been put aside to raise money earnings, or to engage in company purchases (Table 5.8).

A charitable view of innovation strategies in the 1980s is that, as in relation to production, priority was given to squeezing more out of less. We shall see that this applied to the approaches adopted by the government as well as producers. The government constrained spending on R&D, and made the achievement of "value-for-money" a guiding principle when defining its policies on science, R&D, education, and training, as it did in relation to every other aspect of public expenditure. Within firms, more emphasis may also have been placed on incremental innovation and improvement in design, rather than on the radical innovations that seemed appropriate when they still felt able to challenge the technology leaders.

Table 5.8. Allocation of Industrial and Commercial Surplus

	1977	1987
Gross profits (% of GDP)	15.4	18.5
Dividend and interest payments (% of gross income)	20.0	25.5
U.K. tax on income (% of gross income)	9.7	15.2
Percentage of income undistributed	62.5	51.7
Investment (% of gross income)	37.8	34.8
Industrial R&D[a] (% of gross income)	7.5	5.9
Financial surplus (% of income undistributed)	5.9	10.3

[a]Intramural R&D funded from all sources.

Source: UK National Accounts; "R&D 1988: Annual Review of Government Funded R&D," Cabinet Office, HMSO, 1989.

Although operating as a follower rather than a leader has its economic advantages, it carries the risk of growing technological backwardness. The British manufacturing economy finds itself in a paradoxical situation. Low wages and productivity levels encourage specialization in areas of relatively low technology, and lead to emphasis being placed on catching up with international best practice in both design and production. Yet Britain has, as indicated in Table 5.6, one of the most "modern" and R&D-intensive industrial structures among the OECD countries. Although the paradox may in part be resolved by operating at the low end of the high technology spectrum, British manufacturing still remains vulnerable to underinvestment in R&D, and to general inefficiency in the innovation system.

Patterns and Trends in R&D Expenditure

What, in outline, were the main trends in the scale and pattern of British R&D expenditure over the past two decades? Six aspects deserve attention.

Declining Investment in R&D Relative to Other Countries
Throughout the postwar period, Britain has been a relatively high spender on R&D. The historic trend in R&D spending has been closer to that of the United States than to that of France, Germany or Japan (see Table 5.9). From high levels in the 1960s, U. S. and U. K. expenditures on R&D as a percentage of GNP dipped in the 1970s, and then recovered somewhat in the 1980s. Second to the United States in the mid-1960s, Britain had fallen to fifth place in the mid-1980s after Sweden, Japan, Germany, and the United States. The OECD commented in 1989 that the "United Kingdom was the only country where growth in R&D expenditure [in the 1980s] was lower than growth in GDP."

Britain is also distinguished by its relatively low expenditure on basic research (Table 5.10). Per capita, it had fallen in 1987 well behind that recorded by France, Germany, and the United States (but not Japan). Moreover, the increase in the government's science budget over the previous decade was the lowest among the industrial countries.

Heavy Commitment to Defense Technology
Like the United States, Britain stands out for the unusually high proportion of funds spent on defense R&D. The proportion increased in the late-1970s and early-1980s in response to the expansion of NATO defense spending and to the launching of a number of large equipment projects. It has since declined slightly and is expected to decline more steeply as defense needs diminish. In 1986, defense accounted for 51% of gov-

Table 5.9. R&D Expenditure as a Percentage of GNP

	France	Federal Republic of Germany	Japan	United Kingdom	United States
1964	1.8	1.6	1.5	2.3	2.9
1975	1.8	2.2	2.0	2.1	2.2
1986	2.3	2.7	2.8	2.4	2.7

Source: "International Science and Technology Data Update: 1988." NSF, December 1988.

Table 5.10. Per Capita Government Expenditure on Basic Research (%)

	France	Federal Republic of Germany	Japan	United Kingdom	United States
PPP exchange rates					
1975	36.6	56.2	20.4	43.0	45.3
1987	57.7	66.0	30.6	49.1	61.1
Increase, 1975–1987 (%)	58	17	50	14	26
Official exchange rates					
1975	45.2	77.1	30.1	40.9	45.3
1987	71.8	88.1	42.2	45.3	52.9
Increase, 1975–1987 (%)	59	14	40	11	28

Source: Irvine et al. (1990).

ernment, and 20% of total R&D expenditure (this included the science budget). Removing this component of R&D expenditure thus presents Britain in a less flattering light, leaving it trailing some way behind Japan, Germany, Sweden, and Switzerland in its spending on industrial innovation.

In recent years, the manner in which Britain's defense R&D statistics are compiled has become the subject of some debate (House of Lords, 1990). Unlike its U. S. counterpart, the British Ministry of Defence spends little on basic or applied research. The great majority of funds go to development projects, and a significant proportion to activities (e.g., design and production startup) that fall outside the Frascati definition of R&D. In addition, expenditure on nuclear warhead production in the United Kingdom is counted in the government's R&D figures, so that its extent can be disguised.

However measured, the scale of resources committed to defense purposes would remain high by international standards. Moreover, those who oppose changes in definitions argue that the preproduction activities recorded as R&D still absorb a large proportion of skilled manpower, with possible opportunity costs for the wider high technology base.

The Shift from Public to Private Investment in R&D

During the 1950s and 1960s, there was a steady increase in the proportion of R&D financed by government. It peaked in the early 1970s, at around one-half of total expenditure. A significant shift has since occurred toward private financing of R&D in Britain. By 1986, the government's share of expenditure had fallen to 39%. This was due both to the higher rate of growth of industry-financed R&D and the government's own deliberate reduction of spending on civil R&D from the mid-1980s onward. The government has attempted to withdraw support from "near-market" research, and from development work generally, out of the belief that industry alone should decide which technologies to bring to market and should carry all the risks involved.

In the second half of the 1980s, a number of initiatives begun in the early 1980s were therefore terminated, including the Alvey project, which had been Britain's response to the Japanese Fifth Generation Computing Project. Only in relation to Airbus is substantial development aid still provided for civil purposes. Instead, attention has shifted to supporting precompetitive R&D, albeit less generously than in most other industrial countries. In 1987–1988, the Department of Trade and Industry (DTI) spent £92.5m on this type of R&D. The role of government R&D laboratories also declined over the period. Whereas 26% of government-funded R&D was conducted intramurally in 1975, the proportion had fallen to 16% in 1986.

Increasing International Cooperation in R&D
In virtually every area, the autonomy of the British innovation system diminished during the 1970s and 1980s. In aerospace, most technological development is now carried out in cooperation with U. S. or European partners, whether in relation to civil (Airbus) or defense (Tornado, EH101 Helicopter, European Fighter Aircraft, Harrier AV-8B) projects. In electronics, much of the R&D that is supported with public funds is now carried out under the aegis of European Community programs, with ESPRIT alone accounting for one-half of government R&D expenditure in the area of information technology. British electronics firms have also exhibited the general international leaning toward bilateral and multilateral collaboration in R&D.

Britain is therefore becoming increasingly integrated into the *European* innovation system. In defense, it is doing so enthusiastically and from a position of strength, despite its resistance to the creation of a Europe-wide defense R&D program (see below). In civilian fields, by contrast, it is very much a follower rather than a leader in Europe. Britain was not one of the main instigators of the Single European Market, and has not usually welcomed the Community's expanded role in technological development. Its desire to receive its *juste retour* has left it with no option but to participate. The lead has come instead from industries and governments in France, Germany, Italy, and (in electronics) the Netherlands, as well as from the European Commission itself (Sharp, 1989). Thus Britain has ceded its leadership in civil aerospace to France (although Rolls-Royce remains the preeminent aeroengine manufacturer); it is a reluctant participant in the European space program; and in electronics generally, it has not joined with Siemens, Thomson, Philips, Olivetti, and others in trying to mobilize resources to mount a technological challenge to U. S. and Japanese firms.

Multinational Investment in R&D
Another notable trend has been the growing proportion of R&D carried out by foreign multinational companies—increasing from 4% of total funding of industrial R&D (private and public) in 1967 to 13% in 1986 (Table 5.11). As a result, a growing part of the British innovation system has become an appendage of foreign innovation systems. This has spawned a lively, if inconclusive, debate about its effect on indigenous technological capabilities. Stoneman has argued that a potential "internal brain drain"

Table 5.11. Sources of Funds for Industrial R&D, 1967–1986 (%)

	Government	Overseas	Own Funds	Total
1967	29	4	67	100
1972	33	6	60	100
1978	29	8	63	100
1983	30	7	63	100
1986	23	13	64	100

Source: Cabinet Office (1988), Table 2.1.

is being created from domestic to foreign-owned firms, with the results of R&D conducted by the latter being used mainly to support production elsewhere in the world (Stoneman, 1989). Others have preferred to see this as a positive development, strengthening the skill-base and providing an example to local firms (Cantwell and Hodson, 1990). Wherever the truth lies, the real increase in British industrial R&D spending during the 1980s would have been smaller still without the contributions of foreign firms.

Patel and Pavitt have provided evidence of the relatively high proportion of the U. K.'s innovative output that comes from foreign firms (Patel and Pavitt, 1990). In 1981–1986, foreign multinationals accounted for a much higher proportion of U. K. patents taken out in the United States than they did for other European countries, Belgium apart (19% against a European average of 6%). They have also shown that British firms are themselves comparatively highly internationalized in their R&D activities. One-third of the patents registered in the United States by large British firms—the European average was one-fifth—came from R&D conducted outside the home country. Both statistics may be partly explained by the relatively high propensity of U. S. and British multinationals to locate R&D and production in one anothers' countries, due to the common language among other reasons.

Sectoral Shifts in R&D Spending: The Growth of Electronics

The sectoral distribution of expenditure on industrial R&D is shown in Table 5.12. The proportion spent on chemicals held roughly constant between 1975 and 1986, and was not far out of line with other advanced countries. The most striking feature of Table 5.12 is, however, the very marked growth of R&D in electronics, and the apparently higher proportion of R&D allocations to electronics in Britain than in the other cited countries. This is a puzzle, given the evidence that individual firms such as GEC and Plessey have not been high R&D spenders by international standards (Morgan et al., 1989) and that electronics has not been an area of competitive advantage for Britain. Table 5.13 shows that not only did Britain's revealed technological advantage in electronics slip over the period when R&D expenditures were increasing, but its advantage in the fastest growing areas of technologies had deteriorated sharply.

Table 5.12. Expenditure on Industrial R&D, by Sector (%)

	United Kingdom							United
					France	Germany	Japan	States
	1975	1981	1986		(1985)	(1985)	(1986)	(1985)
Chemicals	18	16	18		17	21	16	11
Mechanical engineering	7	6	5 }					
Electronics	21	33	34 }	42	33	37	39	36
Electricals	5	3	3 }					
Motor vehicles	6	5	7		10	15	14	9
Aerospace	22	20	17		19	7	2	23
Other	21	17	16		21	20	31	22
Total	100	100	100		100	100	100	100

Source: Cabinet Office (1988); NSF (1991).

Table 5.13. Britain's Revealed Technological Advantage in Fast-Growing (FG) Patenting Areas Compared with Performance Overall (All), in Chemicals, Electrical, and Mechanical Technologies

	1963–1968		1969–1976		1977–1984	
	FG	All	FG	All	FG	All
Chemical	1.02	1.07	1.14	1.04	1.44	1.16
Electrical	1.13	1.05	0.83	0.97	0.57	0.84
Mechanical	0.80	0.96	0.95	0.99	0.65	0.96

Source: Patel (1988).

It should be noted, however, that in 1985 electronics accounted for close to one-half (£237m) of multinational R&D spending in Britain, and that as much as one-third of all electronics R&D in Britain in that same year (£550m) may have been conducted for defense purposes (Walker, 1988). This being the case, only just over one-half of the electronics R&D may have been carried out by *British* firms orienting themselves toward civil markets. Moreover, this civil expenditure seems to have yielded a low return in terms of exports and economic output. The largest civil item, the telecommunications switch System X, has not been exported, and British firms have generally been unsuccessful in high-volume areas such as semiconductors and consumer electronics.

In summary, five main points emerge from this look at R&D expenditures:

1. Among the industrial countries, Britain is an average spender on R&D. Its position in the rankings has, however, been falling, and is substantially owed to the very high expenditure on defense technology.
2. In terms of industry-financed R&D, Britain now counts as a low spender among the major industrial countries.
3. Except for defense, the role of government in the support of industrial innovation diminished sharply in the 1980s.
4. R&D has become increasingly internationalized. A growing proportion of R&D carried out in Britain is funded by foreign firms, and British firms have become tied into European cooperative programs. Except for defense, they have, however, tended to be junior partners.
5. The most rapid growth of R&D expenditure has been in the field of electronics. But as little as one-half of civil electronics R&D may be carried out by British firms, and in a number of areas the return on R&D investments appears to have been low.

SOURCES OF WEAKNESS IN THE INNOVATION SYSTEM

How can the persistent weakness of the British innovation system, and the variations within it, be explained? One important factor has already been discussed. This is the relationship between the manufacturing and financial sectors, and the pattern of incentives that the latter imposes on the former. The lack of any strong desire to devise compensating mechanisms in turn reflects the diminished status of manufacturing within the contemporary British political economy.

Three other general explanatory factors deserve attention: the heavy commitment to defense technology, the shortcomings of education and training, and what may broadly be termed the problems of coordination.

Distortions Caused by Heavy Defense Spending

As noted above, the development of defense technologies occupies a large part of Britain's technological resources. Only the United States surpasses it among Western nations. More precisely, defense procurement absorbs a large proportion of high technology *engineering* resources. By comparison, chemical and other industries have been little involved in defense markets, in the postwar period at least, except as providers of materials that mostly differ little from those supplied to civil markets. Here we therefore have one possible explanation for the relatively poor performance of Britain's *engineering* industries.

Heavy spending on defense technology may be harmful to performance for three main reasons (Kaldor et al., 1986). First, it can have high opportunity costs, especially in an economy such as Britain's, which has a weak skill-base. In the British context, there also appears to have been little "spinoff" into the civil sector, partly because of the rigorous separation of civil from defense activities within the firm, as in government. Unlike the Pentagon and the Délégation Générale pour l'Armament, the Ministry of Defence has consistently refused to take any responsibility for the development of technologies that are not tied to specific defense requirements (ACOST, 1989).

Second, involvement in defense markets can influence the "style" of technological activity in large firms. The emphasis is placed on product rather than process innovation, with the result that dynamic learning effects may not be realized to the same degree as in civil areas of production. Moreover, there is a tendency toward excessive elaboration in product specifications (baroque technology), partly because there is a lack of "market discipline" when major wars are not being fought (Kaldor, 1982).

The third argument is that protected defense markets lure the large firms that act as prime contractors away from activities where risks are higher and competitive pressures more pronounced, and where sales cannot be "fixed" through negotiation with politicians and the military bureaucracy. As such, patterns of behavior are established that are not conducive to success in open civil markets.

Among economists, there is broad agreement that defense spending has sapped, rather than strengthened, Britain's industrial economy. However, there are large differences of opinion over the weight to be ascribed to this factor. It cannot provide a general explanation of Britain's long-run industrial decline, since defense procurement in peace-time only began to absorb a significant proportion of industrial output in the 1950s. Moreover, it is difficult to judge what might have happened if the defense market had not been there to prop up high technology firms.

It is also debatable whether the traditional criticisms of defense spending are as valid, in the British context, today as in the 1960s and 1970s. Under the "Levene" reforms of procurement practices, the government has forced large firms to accept a larger share of the financial risk in defense contracts, collaboration in defense projects with Germany and other countries may have brought learning and greater industrial discipline, and recently a French-style policy of export maximization has been adopted that discourages product complexity. The British defense industry had remarkable success in international markets in the 1980s—defense being the only engineering sectors where an improvement in the trade balance was recorded. Britain is now third to the United States and USSR as a defense exporter, and has overtaken France.

However one judges the historic effects of defense spending on industrial performance, the important problem now is that very substantial technological resources are locked into a market that is expected to decline, the Gulf War notwithstanding. The question is whether large parts of the aerospace and electronics industry can be transformed into capabilities able to withstand competition in crowded and highly competitive civil markets.

The Poverty of Education and Training in Britain

British industrialization did not rely on mass education. Nor did it rely on the formal training of managerial or engineering personnel. Until the late nineteenth century (perhaps even later), an education "system" did not exist in Britain, although proposals to establish one extended back to the eighteenth century. In contrast to Germany, Japan, and even the United States where organized education was the springboard for industrial advance, in Britain education was disorganized and lacked the strong association with the aims of economic development.

The deficiencies in British education have long been recognized. There have been many attempts to reform it, particularly to widen access and increase the priority given to technical education. Despite the efforts, there is broad agreement that the British education system remains one of the poorest in Europe. The following features stand out:

1. A smaller proportion of young people move into higher education, or experience any kind of further education, in Britain than in any other major industrial country. Nearly two-thirds abandon full-time study at the age of 16, one-half of which have no formal education or training thereafter (*Financial Times*, 31 October 1989).
2. Although in quantitative terms a minor part of the education system, private schools carry exceptional prestige and are much better resourced than state-supported schools. Closely connected to the Universities of Oxford and Cambridge, they still provide a high proportion of the country's economic and political elite. Education is in this respect as elitist as it is in France. However, access to private schools and then to the most prestigious universities is determined in Britain more by wealth than ability, and the graduates of this "system within a system" do not have the rigorous technical training of the French Enarques. Within the economic sphere, the British private system is oriented toward the service more than to the productive sector, and especially toward the financial sector. The French phenomenon of bright young Polytechniciens developing careers that span both government service and industrial management has no parallel in Britain.
3. Although Britain's output of scientists and engineers receiving higher education is not far out of line with that of other countries, the quality of education they receive, and their general standing within the education system, appears to be comparatively low. This applies especially to engineers, reflecting the low standing of the

engineering profession in the country at large. A number of studies have compared the pay, status, and career structures of engineers in Britain and in other European countries, and especially in Germany. They have found that the engineering profession is held in much higher regard in Germany than in Britain; that in Germany there is greater involvement of academic engineers in industry, and of engineers in industrial management; and that there is generally a stronger engineering "culture" in Germany (Fores and Bongers, 1975). The lack of the specialist institutions of technical education that are found in Germany and most other European countries (the Technische Hochschule etc.) is both symptom and cause of the shortcomings of the engineering profession in Britain.

A further claim is that the concept of "engineering" in Britain retains the nineteenth century association with strictly practical endeavor, and with learning-by-doing. It implies tacit rather than formal knowledge. There is no equivalent of the German concept of "Technik," which combines practical activity with the systematic application of technical and scientific theory.

There have been periodic attempts to reinvigorate the engineering profession in Britain, and to give it a better educational grounding. However, debates within the engineering institutes in the early 1900s, over the creation of a centralized administrative structure for technical education after 1945, and over the Finniston Inquiry's recommendation that an "engineering dimension" should be introduced at national and company levels (Finniston, 1980) all came up against two insurmountable obstacles: the conservatism of the established engineering institutes and their desire to preserve the tradition of professional self-regulation, and the lack of sufficient interest groups inside and outside government to impel reform (McCormick, 1991).

4. The most rigorous comparative studies of technical education have been conducted by Prais. He found that except at the level of the University doctorate, the output of skilled manpower is lower at all levels in Britain than in France and Germany (but less clearly below that of Japan and the United States). The greatest disparity occurred, however, at the level of the craftsman (see Table 5.14):

> Both the Germans and the French have *twice as many* qualifying each year as craftsmen as they have qualifying as technicians or with university degrees in engineering: whereas in Britain . . . the number qualifying as craftsmen is *less* than the number qualifying at higher levels. (Prais, 1988)

Table 5.14. Numbers Qualifying in Engineering and Technology, c. 1985[a]

	United Kingdom	France	Germany	Japan	United States
Doctorates	0.7	0.3	1.0	0.3	0.5
Master and "enhanced" degrees	2	6+	4+	5	4
Bachelor degrees	14	15	21	30	19
Technicians	29	35	44	18–27	17
Craftsmen	35	92	120	44	n.a.

[a]Numbers for Japan and the United States have been reduced in proportion to the U.K. population. All units in 1000s.
Source: Prais (1988).

The position appears to have worsened during the 1980s in this respect. The number of apprenticeships in British manufacturing fell by two-thirds between 1979 and 1989 (*Financial Times,* 14 March 1990).

5. Prais's findings can be generalized. The problem for Britain rests less with the education of the "top" 15% of the labor force than with the lack of skills evinced by the remaining 85%. This is the result of an inadequately funded general education system, of insufficient commitment to industrial training, and of a culture that does not set great store by intellectual achievement or technical proficiency. It is a demand- as well as a supply-side phenomenon: there is inadequate supply of skills because employers have not recognized the need for a more highly skilled labor force, and have not been prepared to pay for it (Senker, 1988); and in prestigious parts of the service sector, systematic education or training has not hitherto been a requirement (Ingham, 1984).

The poverty of engineering skills and of craftsmanship seems an important source of weakness in Britain's engineering industries. British science shows greater strength. Despite the relatively low funding levels, Britain's share of world scientific literature is comparatively high (8.2% of papers in 1986, versus 7.7% for Japan, 5.8% for West Germany, and 4.9% for France), as is its citation ratio (NSF, 1991). This may again go some way to explaining the relative strength in chemicals and pharmaceuticals, where scientific research forms a more integral part of the innovation process than in the engineering industries.

Problems of Coordination

One is here on more difficult analytical ground. How can the extent and form of economic coordination be compared across countries, and its results measured? And when does coordination become a source of rigidity rather than dynamic efficiency? In a number of respects, however, there are grounds for believing that the British system of innovation, and the industrial economy more broadly, suffer from a lack of, and often the wrong kinds of, coordination. This has frequently been observed in the following contexts.

Integration of Scientific and Technological Communities
Only in a few areas, such as the nexus of medical research, pharmaceuticals and the national health service, does the relationship between scientific research, technological development, and diffusion appear to work well in Britain, partly for reasons already discussed. The connection between the physical sciences and engineering seems especially weak. One feature of Britain is that it is comparatively poorly endowed with "bridging" institutions, such as the Fraunhofer Gesellschaft in Germany (Rothwell et al., 1988).

Organization of R&D and Product Development
Much R&D expenditure in Britain has been devoted to the development of large systems technologies in aerospace, telecommunications, power generation and other areas. Yet each has a long history of waste and disappointment: TSR-2, Concorde, Nimrod, and the air-defense system (UKADGE); System-X and its electromechanical predecessors; the advanced gas-cooled reactor (AGR); and the advanced passenger

train to mention some of the more notorious examples. Although comparisons are difficult, the record seems less impressive than in other European countries. In Britain, there appear to be special problems coping with high degrees of organizational complexity in R&D, and in settling conflicts over technology choice.

Producer–User Relations

It was noted earlier that close and mutually sustaining producer–user relations tend to be the exception rather than the rule in Britain. Where they are in evidence, as in the case of the retailer Marks & Spencer and its suppliers, they become the subject of great curiosity but not, by and large, imitation. In the retail as in other sectors, this is one reason why the British market is so easily penetrated by foreign producers. The British tradition is for the consumer to have complete freedom of choice, and to have no special responsibility toward, or common cause with, indigenous suppliers.

Managerial Coordination

From a large literature, three themes are worth drawing out. First, British management tends to be hierarchical rather than participatory, as is being demonstrated by comparisons with managerial practices in the Japanese firms setting up production facilities in Britain. The distinction between "gentlemen" and "players" that characterized nineteenth century managerial relations (Coleman and MacLeod, 1986) still has some relevance today. The German, Japanese, and Swedish traditions of industrial consensus building are notably absent from Britain. Second, Tylecote and others have argued that British industry is most successful where it is not faced with complex problems of cross-divisional coordination, such as between engineering design, production, and marketing (Tylecote, 1987). Tylecote suggests that this may be an important reason for the comparative success of British pharmaceutical companies, where decisions on production and marketing follow naturally from success in development and testing. And third, Prais has demonstrated that the larger the production facility, the less efficient are British enterprises by comparison with their foreign counterparts (Prais, 1981). Again, this appears connected with problems of handling social and technological complexity.

Banks and Industry

The close coordinating relationship between banks and industrial enterprises that has, for instance, been a feature of German and Swedish industrialization, does not exist in Britain. Banks are seldom represented on the Boards of British companies. In relation to industrial restructuring, the effective reorganization of the German aerospace industry by Deutsche Bank in the late 1980s could not have happened in Britain. Industrial restructuring in Britain occurs largely through the "market for corporate control" (i.e., through mergers and acquisitions), without the strong regulatory hand of banks, the state or other agents—except where national security or competition policies are affected.

This lack of "collective integration" in the British economy may be attributed, in some degree, to inherent features of British society: its racial and cultural heterogeneity that deny it the natural cohesion of, say, Japan or Sweden, the strong tradition of personal and institutional individualism, the long history of conflict between labor and capital, and the mistrust it has engendered, and the cultural bias against systematic thought and planning that, although sometimes a source of flexibility, can inhibit the development of organizational capabilities required for large-scale industrial development.

During the 1980s, however, the prevailing opinion in Britain was that the economy had suffered from too much, rather than too little coordination, and of the wrong sort:

> The ability of the economy to change and adapt was hampered by the combination of corporatism and powerful unions. Corporatism limited competition and the birth of new firms whilst, at the same time, encouraging protectionism and restrictions designed to help existing firms. (DTI, 1988)

Under Thatcherism, the "free market" therefore came to be regarded as the paramount form of coordination. In advocating it, the government sought to make the economy more rather than less individualistic, conforming to its vision of a market as a dynamic array of autonomous, competing entities. An enhancement of collective performance would, the government hoped, be the paradoxical outcome of increasing the strains on, and rewards to, individual economic agents.

THE STATE AND THE INNOVATION SYSTEM

Britain has an unusual political structure. It is a multinational state, a union of three "kingdoms" (Scotland, Wales, and England) and one "province" (Northern Ireland). In each kingdom there is a strong north–south divide: the Highlands and Lowlands of Scotland, the agrarian (Welsh-speaking) north and industrial (English-speaking) south of Wales, and the north and south of England, the north predominantly industrial and the south the heart of the service economy. Despite (or perhaps because of) wide economic and cultural disparities, Britain has, along with France, the most centralized political administration in Western Europe. Regional and municipal government is weak and became weaker still in the 1980s.

In modern history, the state in Britain has not acted as the catalyst of industrial and technological development as it has in France, Japan, and several other nations. Between the mid-eighteenth and last quarter of the nineteenth centuries, its economic role was confined to some regulatory functions (financial markets, property law etc.) and to the advancement and military protection of foreign trade. The next hundred years brought a gradual rising tide of state intervention in the economy. This said, it was often hesitant, usually resisted, and seldom as determined and coherent as in other countries. Moreover, it tended to be reactive—to decline, to perceived threats from other nations, to protectionism, and to the political pressures to redress past social wrongs. Unlike in France or Japan, for example, the state has not generally seen itself as a creator of new modes of production, as an entrepreneur in its own right.

The two World Wars and the Cold War were important in bringing a more active stance on technical change. They initiated and subsequently gave greater legitimacy to state sponsorship. They brought the first direct funding of R&D, the establishment and expansion of government R&D laboratories, the use of procurement as an instrument for creating new production capabilities, the creation of industries (notably nuclear and aerospace) under the wing of the state, and the use of industrial planning in energy and other areas. In general, the new technologies emerging from wartime activity gave rise to the notion that the state could, in addition to its broader economic functions, play a part in accelerating the development and diffusion of new technology.

Between the wars, the state also became an advocate of higher industrial spending on R&D. This it sought to achieve especially through the formation of industrial research associations that would allow firms to pool technical resources while sharing experience, the government providing matching funds by way of inducement. The research associations were most prominent in the 1930s, 1940s and 1950s, but have subsequently declined, although some, such as the Welding Institute, are still active (Sharp and Cook, 1988).

The 1960s, and particularly the period 1964–1970 when the Labour Party was in office, were the apogee of state intervention in the economy. Emphasis was given to import substitution, to the achievement of greater scale economies through industrial concentration, to the expansion of the education system, and to regaining technological leadership through the support of R&D and other measures. This was all intended to be achieved through increased partnership between government, the trade unions, and industrial management, which met together in the National Economic Development Council (NEDC).

The 1970s, during which there was a see-saw between Conservative and Labour administrations, can be seen with hindsight as a transitional period when the presumptions that had guided economic policy after the war began to unravel. It brought disillusion with the government's economic philosophy (and not least with Keynesianism), its managerial abilities, and its powers of omniscience. Despite efforts to revive economic fortunes, the domestic economy did not prosper, international trade shares continued their decline, and many interventionist policies came to be regarded as failures. In the industrial sector, technological resources became excessively focused on high-technology projects (Concorde, the Advanced Gas-Cooled Reactor, etc.) to the detriment of sectoral performance; and the demise of British Leyland and other large firms discredited policies that supported industrial concentration and the formation of national champions.

In part, Thatcherism was therefore a response, and naturally an opportunistic response, to perceived failure in policy. This background goes some way toward explaining the three main prongs of government policy in the 1980s: the restoration of a market economy based on competition, financial incentives and private ownership; the use of monetary instruments as the foundation of macroeconomic policy, allied to constraints on public expenditure; and the reining in of trade union power, bringing an end to the attempt to manage the economy through a partnership among labor, management, and the state.

The Market, Enterprise, and Value for Money

In contrast to the earlier period, technological performance ranked low among the government's list of concerns in the 1980s. During the first term of Mrs. Thatcher's administration, there was nevertheless considerable continuity with innovation policies laid down previously. There was even some increase in R&D support, partly in reaction to the scare over Britain's failure to keep up with U. S. and Japanese achievements in information technology, and partly because of the expansion of the defense budget as East–West relations deteriorated. The Alvey program was launched in 1981, and became one of Britain's largest efforts to strengthen national technological capabilities. It also broke new ground by encouraging cooperation between firms, and between industry and universities (i.e., better coordination was a central objective).

The Alvey program was, however, short-lived. The change of course in the mid-1980s occurred for two main reasons. The desire to reduce public expenditure led to pressure to cut government spending on innovation, as on other things. And efforts were made to bring innovation policy—and the general handling of state–industry relations—into line with the neoliberal economic principles that the government increasingly espoused. This was accompanied by an increasing centralization of control within government over budgetary allocations, with the Cabinet Office (which serves the Cabinet and Prime Minister) in particular assuming responsibility for policy coordination. Its Advisory Committee on Science and Technology (ACOST) became an important focus for discussion of the government's priorities, even if its advice was not always heeded.

We have seen that there followed, over a comparatively short period, a substantial reduction in the state's role in the innovation system. Government R&D expenditures were cut as was employment in R&D establishments, and by privatizing high-technology producers (mainly in aerospace) and users (utilities) the government lessened, by choice, its direct influence over technological decisions. This can be seen as part of a general international trend, whereby responsibility for technological development was increasingly assumed by private agents, acting alone and in concert. The British government nevertheless stands out for the zeal with which it set about abandoning its former role—testimony to the strength of its neoliberal convictions, and to the comparatively low value it had come to place on technological achievement.

The comparative disregard for technological activity was not perceived by the government to be inconsistent with its campaign to create a more dynamic economy. From the mid-1980s onward, an increasingly ideosyncratic, populist view of the sources of economic dynamism came to be propounded (Redwood, 1988). It appeared in its most unabashed form in the government's 1988 White Paper, "DTI—the department for Enterprise."

There were three central concepts. One was the "open market," which was regarded as the natural, most efficient, stable yet dynamic regulator of economic activity. Governments should stay out of the market, while taking vigorous action to ensure that it remained open and competitive. Thus "competition policy" came to form the core of the government's industrial policy. Any state activity that potentially distorted firms' relations with the market was frowned on.

The second concept was "enterprise," which gave the market its energy and creativity. It brought in new actors, challenged the old, and was the basic source of output and employment growth:

> Enterprise is fundamental to a dynamic and growing economy. Lack of enterprise played a major part in the relative decline of the British economy; its return has played a major role in the recent economic revival. The key to continued economic success lies in the further encouragement of the enterprise of our people. (DTI, 1988, p. 1)

This concept of enterprise was distinctive. It denoted a broad cultural movement: it was a romantic vision of the natural condition to which "our people" should return. At the same, it was highly individualistic. The principal actors were conceived to be individuals and individual firms (notably small firms), whose separate and competitive activities formed the market. The individual entrepreneur was also not necessarily, or even primarily, a progressive force, in the sense that he or she exploited new scientific or technical knowledge, or brought novel organizational approaches to economic activity (Edgerton and Hughes, 1989). The essential qualification was that the entrepreneur should operate a new and expanding *business,* whether it be a retail store, software house, manufacturing company, or removal firm. The "Enterprise Initiative" that was launched in the second half of the 1980s thus did not involve the implicit or explicit prioritization of innovative activity, broadly defined. It thus ran counter to the hierarchical and temporal assumptions that have lain behind innovation policies in most other advanced countries, with their stress on moving into "higher technology" areas of production.

The third guiding assumption was that the government's support for innovation should be constrained in expenditure terms. The emphasis should be placed on achieving greater "value-for-money" by raising the efficiency with which resources were used, not least by making their allocation conditional on recipients satisfying strict performance criteria. In the absence of normal market selection mechanisms, other carrots and sticks were required to act as incentives and prevent institutional sclerosis. In relation to education, to science, to R&D, and to all other areas where the state played a part in the innovation system, the requirement for demonstrable returns on investment became the lynchpin of government policy, with an effect that was often equivalent to that of high real interest rates. Long-term developments with uncertain payback were inevitably rationed.

As such, the government's approach to science and technology mirrored priorities within the economy at large. Productivity improvements and cost reductions came before expansion and the creation of new capabilities even where, as in education, there was a serious historic tendency toward underinvestment.

The Neglect of Capabilities

In practice, the government's policies remained more pragmatic than those announced in the DTI White Paper. Nevertheless, it adopted a markedly less active role in relation to technical change than its predecessors or its foreign counterparts (including the U. S. government), from which it has not departed since. The new orientation was an understandable reaction to the intrusive and ultimately wasteful policies of earlier governments. The "mission-oriented" approach that Britain shared with France and the United States, and that involved the heavy subsidy of R&D programs in aerospace, nuclear energy, and telecommunications allied to support for national champions, was unsustainable and inappropriate for a country in Britain's economic position. Instead, Britain has moved toward adopting the "diffusion-oriented" approach of more successful countries such as Germany and Sweden, even if there has as yet been insufficient commitment to creating the strong decentralized institutions that it requires (Ergas, 1984).

What has been lost on the way, however, has been recognition of the central importance of building durable technological capabilities. Although firms have primary responsibility for developing and marketing new technologies in the modern economy, the state retains an important supportive role especially if, as in Britain, firms consistently underinvest in R&D and in training. Misconceptions of what these capabilities should comprise have also become widespread. In particular, the preoccupation with individualistic enterprise has diverted attention away from the large-scale, collective, and resource-intensive nature of much contemporary technological activity. Innovation seldom comes cheap, and is always risky. Particularly in electronics (and notably semiconductors, computers, and telecommunications), the state has, like the private sector, shown little appetite for the heavy investments required to maintain strong indigenous industries.

Another aspect of the state's diminished concern for nurturing capabilities has been its growing reluctance to play a part in identifying and supporting the technologies that may have strategic value, whether in terms of supply security or their potential economic importance in the future. Two examples are symptomatic: the hesitancy in providing significant funds to support research on superconductors and the unconcern shown over the fate of Britain's remaining semiconductor and computer capacities (viz. the government's acquiescence in the sale of INMOS to SGS-Thomson, and ICL to Fujitsu). Even in the defense field, the government has greatly reduced—to nuclear warheads, cryptography, and a few others—the list of technological capabilities that it considers must survive in British hands.

Partly because so little strategic significance is attached to innovation policy, this is one of the few areas where the government has willingly ceded authority to the European Commission (while frequently criticizing its policies), and where it has allowed regional bodies to assume greater responsibilities. As a result, it has presided over the transfer of decision making to the European center at the same time as to the British periphery. In the former context it has, as we have seen, tended to fall in behind the lead provided by its European partners. An interesting example has been the attitude taken toward the Action Plan launched in 1988 to integrate the Western European armaments market. Although the British government strongly supported the liberalization of defense trade that the Action Plan sought to achieve, it resisted the creation of an accompanying European defense R&D program (EUCLID). It was mainly on French insistence that EUCLID was established (Walker and Gummett, 1989).

The dispersal of responsibility to the regions has occurred in three main ways. First, the regional development agencies (those in Scotland and Wales being the most notable examples) have tried to stimulate the development and diffusion of technology, particularly to encourage the growth of small firms and the renewal of existing sectors. By and large, their main function has been to mobilize the resources (land, skilled labor, and capital) that will attract foreign investment to their respective areas. Thus the Scottish and Welsh agencies have helped pave the way for the expansion of Japanese investment in electronics production in Scotland (mainly semiconductors) and Wales (mainly consumer goods).

Second, Local Enterprise Agencies have been established in various parts of the country, funded by combinations of local government, business, and financial institutions, to provide support facilities for small firms. By 1989, 300 had been established. And third, science parks have been created in Britain as in other countries. By 1988, 33 science parks had been constructed in Britain. The initiatives to set them up have come mainly from universities eager to find new sources of revenue when their budgets were being cut, and from regional development agencies—and not from central government (Monck et al., 1988).

Although locally important, international comparative studies of similar developments abroad have not always been flattering to Britain. In France, decentralization has been more forthright, and better coordinated and funded, whereas in Germany it has involved the extension and deepening of already strong regional infrastructures (Rothwell and Dodgson, 1989). A comparison of the development of electronics industries in Scotland (Silicon Glen) and around Grenoble shows that although substantial production capacity has been established in Scotland, it has largely involved product assembly. There is less evidence of new technologies taking root in the local soil than in the case of France (Dunford, 1989). And the technology transfer benefits claimed for science parks may have been exaggerated. Quintas (1988) found that firms located in British science parks did not have noticeably stronger ties with higher education institutes than firms located elsewhere. Although a great deal has been said in praise of these regional initiatives, their effects on British technological capabilities may therefore still be slight.

Instability in Government Policies

Looking back over the past 30 years, one is struck, when comparisons are made with other countries, by the instability—and lack of true cooperation—that have marked the state's relationship with the industrial sector in Britain. Policies have veered between the excessive managerialism of the 1960s and the equally excessive disengagement of the 1980s. In no other advanced country has the government department responsible for industrial policy so frequently changed its name, its internal organization, or its Minister (six times in the 1980s alone, against twice in the Treasury). In no other country has it set itself such ambitious tasks in one decade (the Ministry of Technology under Wedgwood Benn in the late 1960s), or willed its own disbandment in another (DTI under Ridley in the late 1980s).

In part this reflects the violent doctrinal swings that have occurred in British governance in recent decades, and the particular character of relations between the state and the production system in Britain. But it is also a symptom of economic decline, and of the evident difficulties of arresting it. Actions in one period have tended to be reactions, and often overreactions, to the perceived failure of policies during the preceding period. This is one of the vicious circles that have made it so difficult to reverse economic decline since 1945: decline has engendered policy instability, which has reduced the state's ability to orchestrate a sustained revival; and instability may itself have contributed to the downward spiral.

CONCLUSIONS

Among the countries discussed in these pages, Britain has the oldest industrial economy. For much of the eighteenth and nineteenth centuries, its innovation system had no match, generating revolutionary changes in the techniques of energy and material transformation (the coal, iron, and steam nexus), in the organization of production (the factory system), and in transportation (railways and the steam ship). Indeed, it can be argued that the modern era's systematic pursuit of technological advance originated in Britain.

The twentieth century has seen a gradual erosion in the country's industrial standing, to the extent that today it is no longer counted among the technological leaders outside a few niches. At each stage, the British economy has adapted to changing consumption patterns and production possibilities, to the extent that it now has one of the most "modern" industrial structures. However, the new industries have not, by and large, proved successful in international markets. Typically, they have been inventive in their early stages but have failed to consolidate their positions as technologies and markets have developed. How to operate as an effective follower, and to avoid becoming a laggard, has become the main industrial task.

Among the various factors that have contributed to decline in the twentieth century, four seem to stand out:

1. The nature and influence of Britain's capital markets, with their unusual dedication to short-term gain, and to trading in rather than developing productive assets;
2. The persistent underresourcing and undervaluation of education and training (except in the military field, as the Falkland and Gulf Wars have demonstrated);
3. Weakness in coordination, due inter alia to the strong tradition of individualism (at institutional as well as personal levels), and to social conflicts that have been exacerbated by decline;
4. The loss of a strong technological "culture," which is particularly evident in the low status of engineers in contemporary Britain.

Hitherto, attempts to achieve reform in Britain have been pursued in a setting of substantial national autonomy, even insularity. During the twentieth century, the main economic exemplar has been the United States because of its domination of new industries and its primacy among foreign investors in Britain, and recently because of its advocacy of neoliberal economic policies. This said, the search for new approaches has been largely internalized, choices being made with reference more to Britain's particular historical experiences and administrative traditions than to foreign practices, and often being tightly constrained by institutional inertia.

If this were to continue, there would be few grounds for believing that the above structural impediments would be any more surmountable than they have been in the past. During the 1990s, however, three notable discontinuities will occur in the context in which British economic development will have to be approached. The first is the implementation of the Single European Act and of European monetary integration, which will tie Britain more tightly into a European system of economic exchange and regulation. It will place substantial limits on the British government's abilities to implement its ideosyncratic industrial and macroeconomic policies, while exposing more cruelly any deficiencies in Britain's productive infrastructure, broadly defined.

The second change comes from the build-up of Japanese foreign investment in Britain, particularly in the electronics and automobile industries. In several areas, Britain's fortunes will depend on Japanese corporate strategies in relation to the enlarged European market, and on Japanese contentedness with Britain as a location for advanced industrial production. This will force Britain to become more open to Japanese models of industrial organization than to the U. S. models that have been influential in the past, while again exposing infrastructural inadequacies.

The third discontinuity is the ending of the East–West conflict and the need for massed armaments that accompanied it. This robs Britain of its important politico-strategic position in the defense of Northwest Europe, and in providing a bridge between the United States and Western Europe within NATO. Despite the Gulf War, this is likely to weaken Britain's economic and political ties with the United States— among external relationships, that with Japan could become as important as that with the United States—while binding Britain more tightly into the European framework. And within Britain, it will require a substantial reconfiguration of high technology engineering resources as demands for weaponry diminish.

Each of these changes poses threats to Britain's international status. From the point of view of economic development, however, they also bring significant opportunities. In particular, they will require Britain to be more open to Japanese and Continental European influences where the management of productive resources is concerned. Above all, Britain will benefit if it learns to place greater emphasis at all levels on the nurturing of *capabilities,* rather than on the extraction of quick economic returns.

One of the great ironies of Britain's current approach to Europe is that market integration is regarded as a great boon, and social integration a great threat. Yet it is the archaism and inefficiency of Britain's social institutions that seem to lie at the root of so many of its industrial weaknesses. This being the case, the most important question is whether European integration will bring modernization in Britain, not through the further extension of market mechanisms, but through the diffusion of more effective institutional practices in the educational and other fields.

REFERENCES

Advisory Council on Science and Technology (ACOST). (1989). "Defence R&D: A National Resource." London: HMSO.

Bolton Committee: Report of the Committee of Inquiry on Small Firms. (1971). London: HMSO.

Buxton, A. (1990). "Technology and Structural Change." *UK Economy Papers.* London: National Economic Development Office.

Cabinet Office. (1990). "R&D 1988: Annual Review of Government Funded Research and Development." London: HMSO.

Cantwell, J., and Hodson, C. (1990). "The Internationalisation of Technological Activity and British Competitiveness." Mimeo, University of Reading, Department of Economics.

Coleman, D., and MacLeod, C. (1986). "Attitudes to New Techniques: British Businessmen. 1800–1950." *Economic History Review* 39(4): 588–611.

Department of Trade and Industry. (1988). "DTI— the Department for Enterprise." London: HMSO.

DTI: (1988–89). Memorandum to the House of Commons Select Committee on Trade and Industry's Inquiry into Information Technology.

Dunford, M. (1989). "Technopoles, Politics and Markets: The Development of Electronics in Grenoble and Silicon Glen." In M. Sharp and P. Holmes (eds.), *Strategies for New Technologies.* New York and London: Philip Allan.

Edgerton, D., and Hughes, K. (1989). "The Poverty of Science." *Public Administration* 67(4):419–33.

Ergas, H. (1984). "Why Do Some Countries Innovate More Than Others?" CEPS Papers No. 5. Brussels: Centre for European Policy Studies.

Feinstein, C., and Matthews, R. (1990). "The Growth of Output and Productivity in the UK: The 1980s as a Phase of the Post-War Period." *National Institute Economic Review* 132, 78–90.

Finniston Report: (1979–80). "Engineering Our Future." Report of the Committee of Inquiry into the Engineering Profession, Session Cmnd 7794, January 1980.

Fores, M., and Bongers, N. (1975). "The Engineer in Western Europe." Unpublished mimeo December, (in SPRU Library).

Freeman, C. (1989). "R&D, Technical Change and Investment in the UK." In F. Green (ed.), *The Restructuring of the UK Economy.* London: Harvester Wheatsheaf.

Ganguly, P., and Bannock, G. (eds.) (1985). *UK*

Small Business Statistics and International Comparisons. London: Harper & Row.

Henderson, P.D. (1977). "Two British Errors: Their Probable Size and Some Possible Lessons." *Oxford Economics Papers* July, 159–205.

Hobsbawm, E.J. (1987). *The Age of Empire, 1875–1914.* London: Weidenfeld and Nicolson.

House of Lords. (1990). Select Committee on Science and Technology. Report on Definitions of R&D. Session 1989–90. London: HMSO.

Ingham, G. (1984). *Capitalism Divided? The City and Industry in British Social Development.* London: Macmillan.

Irvine, J., Martin, B., and Isard, D. (1990). *Investing in the Future: International Comparisons of Government Funding of Academic and Related Research.* Aldershot, England: Edward Elgar.

Kaldor, M. (1982). *The Baroque Arsenal.* London: Andre Deutsch.

Kaldor, M., Sharp, M., and Walker, W. (1986). "Industrial Competitiveness and Britain's Defence Commitments." *Lloyds Bank Review* October, 31–49.

Landes, D.S. (1969). *The Unbound Prometheus,* Cambridge, England: Cambridge University Press.

Layard, R., and Nickell, S. (1989). "The Thatcher Miracle?" Discussion Paper No. 315. London: Centre for Economic Policy Research.

Lazonick, W. (1990). "Controlling the Market for Corporate Control: The Historical Significance of Managerial Capitalism." Paper presented to the Third International Joseph A. Schumpeter meeting, June.

McCormick, K. J. (1991). "The Development of Engineering Education in Britain and Japan." In H. Gospel (ed.), *Industrial Training and Technological Innovation: A Comparative and Historical Study,* London: Routledge.

Mackinder, H. (1904). "The Geographical Pivot of History." *Geographical Journal* 23(4):421–44.

Mayes, D.G. (1987). "Does Manufacturing Matter?" *National Institute Economic Review* November, 47–58.

Metcalf, D. (1988). "Trade Unions and Economic Performance: The British Evidence." Discussion Paper 353. London: Centre for Labour Economics.

Monck, C., Porter, R., Quintas, P., Storey, D., and Wynarczyk, P. (1988). *Science Parks and the Growth of High Technology Firms.* London: Croom Helm.

Morgan, K., and Davies, A. (1989). "Seeking Advantage from Telecommunications: Regulatory Innovation and Corporate Information Networks in the UK." *Information Networks and Competitive Advantage, vol. 3 of Comparative Reviews of Telecommunications Policies and Usage in Europe,* Paris: OECD, pp. 267–317.

Morgan, K., Harbor, B., Hobday, M., von Tunzelmann, N., and Walker, W. (1989). "The GEC-Siemens Bid for Plessey: The wider European Issues." PICT Working Paper 2, SPRU, January.

Mowery, D., and Rosenberg, N. (1990). "The US National Innovation System." Draft paper prepared for the Columbia University project on national innovation systems, November.

National Science Foundation (NSF) (1991). *International Science and Technology Data Update.* NSF 91-309, Washington, D.C.

Oulton, N. (1990). "Labour Productivity in UK Manufacturing in the 1970s and in the 1980s." *National Institute Economic Review* May, 71–91.

Patel, P. (1988). "The Technical Activities of the UK: A Fresh Look." In A. Silberston (ed.), *Technology and Economic Progress.* London: Macmillan.

Patel, P., and Pavitt, K. (1990). "Large Firms in the Production of the World's Technology: An Important Case of Non-Globalisation." *Journal of International Business Studies* 22(1):1–21.

Pavitt, K. (1989–90). Evidence Given to Select Committee on Science and Technology's Report. "Definitions of R&D." House of Lords, Session.

Redwood, J. (1988). *Popular Capitalism.* London: Routledge.

Quintas, P. (1988). "Science Parks: Image and Reality." Paper prepared for the Study Group conference on Aspects of Industrial Policy, Centre for Business Strategy, London Business School, June.

Prais, S.J. (1981). *Productivity and Industrial Structure.* Cambridge, England: Cambridge University Press.

Prais, S.J. (1988). "Qualified Manpower in Engineering: Britain and Other Industrially Advanced Countries." *National Institute Economic Review* February, 76–83.

Rothwell, R., and Dodgson, M. (1989). "Regional Technology Policies: The Development of Regional Technology Transfer Infrastructures." Paper Prepared for the Third International Workshop on Innovation, Technical Change and Spatial Impacts, Cambridge, September.

Rothwell, R., Dodgson, M., and Lowe, S. (1988). "Technology Transfer Mechanisms, Part I: The United Kingdom." London: National Economic Development Office.

Senker, P. (1988). "International Competition, Technical Change and Training." SPRU/Imperial College Papers in Science, Technology and Public Policy No. 17, January.

Sharp, M. (1989). "European Technology: Does 1992 Matter?" SPRU/Imperial College Papers on Science, Technology and Public Policy No. 19, February.

Sharp, M., and Cook, P.L. (1988). "R&D Cooperation among Firms, Universities and Research Organizations in the United Kingdom." SPRU, February.

Stein, A. (1984). "The Hegemon's Dilemma: Great Britain, the United States and the International Economic Order." *International Organization* 38: 355–386.

Stoneman, P. (1989). "Overseas Financing for Industrial R&D in the UK." Paper presented to the Annual Meeting of the British Association for the Advancement of Science, Sheffield, September.

Surrey, A.J., and Cook, P.L. (1983). "The Off-Shore Petroleum Supplies Industry: British Government Policy Compared with Norwegian and French Policies." SPRU Occasional Paper No. 21, October.

Svennilson, I. (1954). *Growth and Stagnation in the European Economy.* Geneva: United Nations.

Tylecote, A. (1987). "Time Horizons of Management Decisions: Causes and Effects." *Journal of Economic Studies* 14(4):51–64.

van Ark, B. (1990). "Comparative Levels of Labour Productivity in Dutch and British Manufacturing." *National Institute Economic Review* 131:71–85.

Walker, W. (1988). "UK Defence Electronics: A Review of Government Statistics." PICT Policy Papers No. 4. London: Economic and Social Research Council.

Walker, W., and Gummett, P. (1989). "Britain and the European Armaments Market." *International Affairs* 65(3):419–42.

Wiener, M.J. (1987). "English Culture and the Decline of the Industrial Spirit." Cambridge, England: Cambridge University Press.

6

The French National System of Innovation

FRANÇOIS CHESNAIS

The French system is essentially a creation of the post-World War II period. The higher education sector, with its dual component (the Universities and the "Grandes Ecoles") dates back to the late eighteenth century and to subsequent developments at given periods of the nineteenth century. But otherwise today's institutions and mechanisms have all evolved out of those that were first built just after the Liberation from 1945 to 1949 and again from 1958 to 1966 during the first phases of the Fifth Republic. The system has several features that are quite specific to France: (1) the organization and funding of the largest part of fundamental research through a special institution, the CNRS, distinct from the higher education sector entities, which are funded by the State and governed by scientists in an uneasy relationship with public authorities; (2) a dual higher education sector producing at least one type of senior technical person little known elsewhere, namely the "Grandes Ecoles" technical experts elite of engineers cum industrial managers, cum high level political and administrative personnel; and (3) a pervasive element of State involvement in the production not just of general scientific and technical knowledge, but often of technology per se in the form of patentable and/or immediately usable products or production processes.

Special attention will be paid to this last feature. The French national system of innovation consists to a large extent of a set of vertically structured and fairly strongly compartmentalized *sectoral subsystems* often working for public markets and invariably involving an *alliance* between the State and public and/or private business enterprises belonging to the *oligopolistic* core of French industry. The most important subsystems are those that concern electrical power production (conventional and nuclear), telecommunications, space, arms production, and electronics. But the State–enterprise relationship also exists in petroleum, railroad equipment and transport systems, civil engineering, and marine technology. More generally it is present in a latent form in every field where the State has built, at some period or another, an R&D capacity and has looked, in particular, since the 1970s, for *industrial partners* to whom to transfer the technology and knowledge produced: this is now also true in the areas of medicine and agriculture. Even in the case of industrial sectors where public involvement in science and technology is low as in the chemical–pharmaceutical complex, the role of the State remains strong with respect to industrial restructuring and the provision of capital. In the last analysis, there are few "truly private" firms, enjoying little or no direct State support, among the top French firms or organizations patenting in the United States (Pavitt and Patel, 1990). L'Oréal (fine chemicals), Michelin (tires), Peugeot (cars), and Valéo (automobile parts) are among them but remain exceptions.

Large or very large firms (at France's level of course) belonging to the oligopolistic core of French business are the State's partners. In some instances, the firms concerned are classic nationalized enterprises [as EDF (Electricité de France) in conventional and nuclear electrical power]; in others, they are firms with all or a majority of their capital owned by the State, but otherwise totally normal business enterprises in their strategy and behavior (e.g., Elf-Sanofi or Thomson); in other cases again they are private corporations in the sense of being owned by private asset holders (CGE or Dassault), but they behave much in the same way as firms with public capital. For reasons of opportunity and/or political necessity (internal and external) the distribution of R&D, manufacturing, and marketing capacity between the public and private sectors and the way responsibilities are *shared* between a given State agency and its industrial partners have often *evolved* considerably over time. But the changes have *never* been of a magnitude such as to sever completely the State–capital relationship and bring the alliance to an end. The chapter examines some of the reasons for this and gives priority to two explanations: first the inherent historical weakness of French industrial capitalism along with the need it has of receiving State support and second the important, highly original role played by the élite of the "Grandes Ecoles" and the Grands Corps in creating particularly strong links between the State apparatus stricto sensu, the public or quasipublic enterprise sector, and the private industrial and financial sector. This implies that although the system was built after 1945, its configuration has nonetheless been shaped by the whole legacy of French social history.

As in the case of other countries, the French system of innovation has many component elements, is divided into different segments, and includes strata dating back to different historical phrases and forms of technological accumulation. In an old country such as France these may have roots in earlier peasant and artisan "technical cultures" going back in some instances to before the industrial revolution and the application of science and technology to production (e.g., wine making and artisan food processing) and in others to the nineteenth century (e.g., fashion and beauty products). These components of the system of innovation should not be overlooked.[1] However, despite the potential inherent opportunities they offer for competitiveness and the cohesion of the country's economic and social fabric, they have never been the object of the same attention as the large technology system-oriented parts of the innovation system. This is true of the support they receive but also of the studies they have prompted. France is a country in which there is continuous talk about the importance of SMEs and innovation, but where, barring a few exceptions, one finds only limited evidence of their role as active components of the innovation system.[2]

For an innovation system as distinct from an R&D system, the "bottom line" is the capacity to compete successfully in world markets. Consequently the chapter concludes that the French system's numerous spectacular achievements cannot hide its serious weaknesses, expressed today in the endemic vulnerability of the French trade balance as well as in the strong rigidity of the system in the face of contemporary requirements for technological change. Technology per se is not, however, the sole nor even the most important factor at work. Technological innovation stems from within given national economic, political, social, and cultural environments. The performance of a national system will be shaped by these factors. This is particularly true of France (Salomon, 1991).

THE NINETEENTH-CENTURY RECORD AND LEGACY: AN ADVANCED BUT UNBALANCED SCIENCE SYSTEM: FEW LINKAGES WITH PRODUCTION: A DUAL HIGHER EDUCATION SYSTEM

When one is examining the development of a national system of innovation, one is reading a country's economic, social, and political history through the particular prism of the conditions surrounding the use of technology in capitalist production and the choices made by the ruling class or dominant élites regarding the production and application of scientific and technological knowledge. In our case, after a brilliant start in the eighteenth century, French scientific production had to wait until the mid-twentieth century before the political and industrial conditions that would allow it to make its full contribution to military and foreign policy and of course to growth.

French Science from Colbert to Napoleon

The French Académie Royale des Sciences was founded in 1676 by Colbert with the explicit aim of fostering scientific capacities and fitting them into the machinery of government. Thus basic science was immediately synonymous with expert science seeking industrial and military applications. If the institutional establishment of scientific research in France was from the very beginning an act of State, so of course was much of manufacturing industry, in particular all the "manufactures" created under Louis XIV. Members of the Académie often provided scientific leadership for the model factories. Thus, in the second half of the eighteenth century, Berthollet and Chaptal were active in research on the chemistry of dyes connected with the manufacture of tapestries at the Gobelins, Macquer worked on porcelain at Sèvres, and Lavoisier on gunpowder at the Arsenal (Crossland, 1975; Gillipsie, 1980).

The scientific community was a strong beneficiary of the absolute Monarchy, but also from the 1740s onward under the leadership of d'Alembert, Diderot, and the group that published the Encyclopedia, a pivotal component in the political struggle against the Ancien Régime and in the *programmatic* preparation of the French Revolution. The thrust of the Encyclopedia's campaign was that for "progress" to take place and the fulfillment of science's economic and social promise to materialize, the fetter of the Ancien Régime on French nascent capitalist society had to be broken. This explains the speed at which the Revolutionary and Napoleonic governments were able to mobilize science for military and industrial purposes (Dhombres, 1988). Toward 1810 Paris housed a scientific population of a size unprecedented up to that time. This "critical mass" of talent was the start of one of the most creative periods in French science and certainly the only phase in which it exercised international scientific leadership. During the first half of the nineteenth century Paris was, in the words of von Humboldt, the "true metropolis of science to which scientists flocked from all over Europe to associate with such great scientific figures as Cuvier, Lavoisier, and Laplace"

(Gillipsie, 1980).[3] During this period the Collège de France, the Ecole Polytechnique, and the Muséum d'Histoire Naturelle were the world's leading scientific institutions.

The economic policy measures rendered necessary by the British naval blockade (the Continental system) forced the Napoleonic governments to try and root science-based innovation in industry. This led in particular to the birth of a chemical industry based on the research of Chaptal, Berthollet, and Leblanc. It included one firm that has survived until today, Saint-Gobain, and was the leading chemical industry in Europe until 1830 or so. Once the impetus of the Napoleonic State-led and State-supported policies had worn out, French private industry did nothing to pursue the necessary investment and maintain the ties with research. There were a few exceptions as in protestant Mulhouse, but they served only to prove the rule.[4] Though it was Lavoisier who founded the modern theory of chemistry, the development of the subject took place outside France, especially in Germany. As Papon has aptly put it, the relations between science and industry are those of "a very precocious divorce" (Papon, 1978, p. 20).

Inevitably French scientific leadership came to an end because of this. Though France produced later in the century leading scientific figures such as Claude Bernard and Louis Pasteur, and at the end of the century, the mathematician Poincarré and the Curies, scientific leadership passed rapidly to Germany. This process did not escape the attention of the greatest scientific figures of the time. Pasteur, who was particularly active in the defense of French science, published as early as 1868 a pamphlet with the revealing title, "Le budget de la science." After France's first humiliating military defeat by Germany in 1870, he wrote a number of articles in which he argued that one of the causes was the lack of support given to French science and technology. However, Pasteur is a fascinating example of the very peculiar relationships that grew up between science and industry in France in the second half of the nineteenth century. Pasteur worked repeatedly on problems raised by industrial activity (animal disease as in the case of silkworms, intensive production of chicken and pork, food conservation, scientifically controlled wine and beer production). Yet, he refused to move close to capitalist production and struggled to maintain the idea of fundamental, "disinterested" science (Salomon-Bayet, 1986).

Some Aspects of France's Slow Industrial Growth

A study of one of the major scientific institutions of nineteenth century France ends with the overall assessment that "the slower growth and lower productivity of French science, when viewed in comparison with German science, can be seen as a consequence of the relatively slower expansion of the French economy, especially in the chemical and metallurgical industries which grew much more rapidly across the Rhine. *In short, the French economy got the level of science it needed and could support*" (Zwerling, 1980, p. 59). The slow and uneven development of industrial capitalism in the nineteenth century has been the object of considerable study and debate.[5] I will select the features of French economic and social development in the nineteenth century that seem both the less well known and the most important.

. The first point concerns the particular strength of conservative forces vested in the agrarian structure. Because of its direct intervention in the revolutionary process in 1790, a large section of the peasantry won the right to own the land they had worked on the large estates. Agrarian reform occurred to the extent that the Church's lands were divided and sold, but many aristocratic large holdings survived the gale. In the aftermath of the Revolution and the Restauration, the agrarian base of French society, both peasant and bourgeois-aristocratic, emerged as a very strong economic and social force. Some sections of the peasantry were fairly radical at some moments (in 1847–1848 and again in the early twentieth century), but on the whole the peasantry provided one of the social foundations of political conservatism.

Rent and profit from agriculture were canalized by a strong, well-organized, and advanced *financial system,* characterized by early centralization of the monetary system under the Bank of France and a fairly concentrated banking system characterized by the presence of a small number of powerful merchant banks. Rent from the land cleverly managed, helped the growth of the financial rentiers. The high and generally stable income provided by financial investment aided French capital owners to rapidly develop strong "rentier" features with a propensity to invest in government loans, later in railway stocks, then in colonial trading companies and banks (the Bank of Algeria, of Indochina, etc.), which had the prized advantage of being private ventures vested with regalian powers (this combination has really been the "must" of the French bourgeois at all times) and finally in safe loans to foreign States. From the mid-nineteenth century onward, it became frequent for contemporaries to draw a contrast between Germany, which was strong through its industries, and France, which was strong on account of its *banks.* On the eve of the first world war, France was the *second largest exporter of capital in the world* (Britain was the first). Since it lacked Britain's industrial base, France became the first large advanced capitalist country to balance a permanent trade deficit with dividend and interest earnings from capital invested abroad.

Industrialization was handicapped by a combination of factors that made the rate of return low and the banks uninterested in investing. France's coal and iron resources were poor compared both to England and Germany. In contrast with England, French industry was not faced with any large external demand but it did nothing to create it. Later it accepted without much difficulty a very reactionary approach, socially but also economically, to the management of France's new colonial possessions. Since demographic growth was very weak and the peasantry offered only a limited market for industry, domestic demand was not inherently dynamic either. The small and rather conservative businessman studied by David Landes[6] is largely a natural outcome of this overall situation. Consequently, industrialization came about in successive bursts on the basis of exogenous *market pull* in the form of *government garanteed* and *bank consortium financed demand,* notably for railroad building (both at home and abroad), ships, and arms. The feats of French engineering were principally those of large projects, involving large or very large amounts of capital (e.g., the Suez canal) and so dependent on the banks. Many projects furthermore were already negotiated in conditions where foreign alliances and the successes of French foreign policy were of importance in securing markets for French financial–industrial consortia. The heart of concentrated French industry was almost from the outset situated in the iron and steel industry (cf. the de Wendel family group) and in products for the railways and the Army (cf. the Schneider family group). In these critical areas French industrialists, pressed for time, went abroad to England and Belgium and later to Germany to buy their technology. They even recruited their foremen and skilled operators in these countries.

Higher Education Priorities for the Training of Engineers and Experts

Although the responsibility for the divorce between science and industry, from the 1840s onward, and a weaker endogenous industrial demand for science and technology in France than in the United Kingdom, Germany, and the United States, *lies principally with French industrial capitalism,* the legacy of the Napoleonic period with regard to the organization of teaching and of research in science and technology proved in time to be a further obstacle (Gilpin, 1968; Fox and Weisz, 1980). When Napoleon undertook the reorganization of French higher education between 1806 and 1811, he largely reestablished the centralized structure fashioned in the Ancien Régime in keeping with his increasingly conservative policies in many areas. This structure gave primacy to the training of *experts* as distinct from researchers and creators. This was provided in the professional schools, which have come to be known collectively as the "Grandes Ecoles." The Ecole Polytechnique founded in 1794 provided a grounding in engineering and science, which was then built on the more advanced écoles d'application—such as the Ecole de l'Artillerie et du Génie at Metz (for artillery officers and military engineers) and the Ecole des Mines or the Ecole des Ponts et Chaussées (for civil engineers). By the same principle, the Ecole Vétérinaire at Alfort produced veterinary surgeons while the Ecole Normale Supérieure, resurrected by Napoleon in 1808, prepared the élite of the secondary teaching profession for service in the lycées; subsequent institution building took place on the same model, even when private industry took the lead. This was the case for the Ecole Centrale des Arts et Manufactures, the Ecole Municipale de Physique et de Chimie Industrielles (founded in 1882), and the Ecole Supérieure d'Electricité (1894).

In contrast to the German polytechnic schools (Technische Hochschulen), the French mode of engineering schools lacked in general the spirit of modern scientific research. Until well into the twentieth century, most of them suffered from severe parochialism. Though one had to have an extensive and broad mathematical education to be selected for one of the engineering Grandes Ecoles, the training and curriculum at each school were designed to train experts, civil servants, and managers for a particular ministry. The student at the Grandes Ecoles learned the results of science (and even here often with considerable delay since the curriculae divorced from research had difficulties in keeping up with progress), and *not the methods of science.* They became either abstract mathematicians or production engineers who applied existing knowledge, rather than research engineers who could make substantial advances in the state of the art. The gradual expansion of enrollment could not compensate for the weakness of the science base.

Not surprisingly France's nineteenth century strengths in technology, notably large-scale civil engineering, mirror the priority given to higher level technical education. Throughout most of the nineteenth century, French engineers were among the best and played an important part in the industrialization of Europe and other parts of the world. Kindleberger's remark that "the products of the Ecole des Mines performed their engineering feats in Algeria, Spain, Russia and elsewhere outside the Hexagon" (1976, p. 251) is of wider pertinence than the sole Ecole des Mines. The Suez Canal, perhaps the foremost technological feat of the nineteenth century, stands as a monument to the French engineering education of the time. However, the success of French engineers abroad did not stop the divorce of large parts of industry at home with science, nor did they guarantee the use of technology in the less progressive part of the manufacturing system.

The Weakness of the Research Base and of the Universities

Initially, the Ecole Polytechnique had been a research center; its laboratories were the best equipped in Europe and the best scientists were assembled to teach and do research. Their number included such men as Monge, Fournier, Laplace, Berthollet, and Chaptal (Dhombres, 1988). During the Revolution and the Napoleonic Empire Polytechnique was a leading center of scientific research and the first to do systematic basic research. Under the Bourbon Restauration, the Ecole Polytechnique then became a military engineering school separate from other institutions of higher education and run by the Ministry of the Army. It has kept this status to this day (see Shinn, 1981, 1984). Though it continued to be an important technological institution, it disappeared as a center of scientific research and has only started to become one again during the last 30 years.

The Ecole Normale Supérieure was initially set up to train the teachers required by the newly established system of secondary education. It passed through a precarious existence during much of the first half of the nineteenth century but was able to build up its research potential and develop its ties with the university in Paris. After Pasteur's nomination as Administrator (1857–1967) and the changes he managed to impose regarding the status of research, the Ecole finally emerged in the latter part of the century as the best training ground of French scholars and scientists (Zwerling, 1980). There the most eminent of French scientists and mathematicians were educated and taught. However, the Ecole Normale with its 30 science graduates each year represented *much too narrow a base on which to build a sound scientific edifice.* Throughout the nineteenth century and well into the 1930s the universities were stopped from providing the other indispensable component of this edifice.

The university system of the Ancien Régime had been severely condemned by the Encyclopedia and abolished by the Revolution. Once he had brought the Revolution to a halt Napoléon basically restored the old Ancien Régime University. His centrally state-controlled system incorporated faculties of sciences and letters—roughly the functional equivalent of the old faculties of arts—as well as the schools of law, medicine, pharmacy, and Protestant and Catholic theology. The faculties of science and letters, which might in principle have provided a liberal education in the traditions of the Encyclopédie, scarcely functioned at all. By the time of the Bourbon Restoration in 1815, fewer than half of the projected faculties of science had actually been opened. Insofar as the faculties of science and letters did have a role, it was above all that of providing examiners for the hierarchy of qualifications that regulated teaching and other professional careers. The duties of a faculty professor were largely those of a high-level functionary. And, unlike the "professional" faculties of law and medicine, which were well attended, the faculties of science and letters had very few students. Still less were they conceived as centers of research in the manner of the German faculties of philosophy (Fox and Weisz, 1980).

Attempts to reform and strengthen the universities took place from the 1880s onward as part of a wider policy of strengthening through education, the political and social basis of the Third Republic. Student enrollment increased significantly;

throughout France new buildings and facilities were constructed; in an attempt to create some degree of decentralization, university professors were granted a significant degree of autonomy in the handling of internal affairs—a transformation that was consecrated symbolically in 1896 by the creation of universities, composed of groups of faculties in the same town. Although they never fulfilled the hopes invested in them by the reformers, these universities reflected contemporary trends by cutting across existing institutional divisions and embracing all areas of human knowledge. For a brief period, at least, they seemed to pose a real threat to the dominance of the Grandes Écoles. However as Terry Shinn (1981, 1984) and other recent scholars have shown these had sufficiently strong social and political support to offset the challenge and maintain their domination.

Consequently, the universities played only a small part in the production of scientific and technical personnel compared with the Grandes Ecoles. In the early 1900s, for example, all the universities combined awarded only some 500 science degrees (i.e., only twice the number of admissions to the Ecole Polytechnique alone). The provincial universities often found it difficult to survive, as Paris attracted both teachers and students and the competition of the Grandes Ecoles attracted a good proportion of students away from the Universities. As a result, the universities rarely offered a base for research of any magnitude. Well into the twentieth century, the typical R&D laboratory was the small personal laboratory that came with the professor's chair. There the professor could pursue his personal inclinations with a few assistants, though the research might not be at the frontiers of scientific advance and the laboratory might be too small, ill-equipped, and isolated to be efficient (see Prestre, 1984 for the area of physics). In some cases, even a scientist of renown might not even be lucky enough to have such minimal conditions. Pierre Curie, for instance, had no research funds, no personal laboratory, not even an office of his own; his important work on magnetism was carried out primarily in a corridor, and his work with his wife Marie on radium was conducted under extremely adverse conditions. On being proposed for the Légion d'Honneur, Pierre Curie wrote to a friend: "Please be so kind as to thank the Minister, and inform him that I do not feel the slightest need of being decorated, but that I am in the greatest need of a laboratory." The Paris Radium Institute was established only in 1910, 4 years after his death. Only with the establishment of the CNRS was this situation modified.

Such is the nineteenth-century legacy regarding the organization of higher education that France has battled with throughout the twentieth century and for which no other solution has been found than expanding the number of engineering schools and thwarting repeatedly the attempt of the universities to strengthen their position along the model of other countries.

The Contradictory Balance Sheet of the 1920s and 1930s

The divorce of science from industry is expressed by the almost total absence of the kind of industrial R&D laboratory developed from the 1890s onward in the United States and Germany and so a weak French position in "science-push industries." By contrast in sectors where technological development took the form of pragmatic, step-by-step innovations as in automobiles and aeronautics, French inventors and entrepreneurs were very active. Up to World War II the French automobile industry was the second largest world producer. Panhard (today only a military firm producing tanks) and Peugeot date back to 1890 and Renault to 1899. Michelin produced the first air-tube tire in 1895. In aviation again, Frenchmen flying French planes held world records on a par with U. S. rivals up to World War II. Farman and Breguet were large world exporters of planes and Gnome and Rhone, Hispano, and Renault of airplane engines between the two wars. Technological accumulation by French firms in these areas is now secular and account of course for the rapid recovery after 1950. During the 1920s and 1930s, however, the progress and growth of these two industries went hand in hand with very slow overall economic growth and a malthusian climate largely strengthened by the negative demographic consequences of the huge human losses of the first world war.

But the 1930s were also characterized by a radical and dramatic divorce between France's well-developed automobile and aeronautics industries and the military doctrine upheld by the dominant ultraconservative French officer corps. While Breguet planes were competing with the Wrights for transatlantic records, French generals were building the Maginot line and a large fraction of the French bourgeoisie showed itself much more concerned with the dangers of bolshevism than those of nazism. The crushing defeat of 1940 followed by the close collaboration of the Vichy government with Hitler were the inevitable outcome.

PHASES IN THE BUILDING OF THE SYSTEM

Along with economic planning, an active industrial policy, and large public investments in basic infrastructures, France's vigorous institution building in science and technology and large investments in R&D must be seen as one of the central instruments of the country's fairly spectacular economic and political recovery following the end of World War II.

The Context: Recovery as a Second Tier World Power

In 1945, France, having represented a major political and military power for three centuries, had suffered a crushing defeat in May–June 1940 at the hands of one of its two major historical rivals, Germany. France owed its quite marginal presence in the camp of the 1945 victors to the decision taken in 1940 by a junior general and junior minister of the government—Charles de Gaulle—to break with authorities and proclaim the establishment of a provisional government that had initially been *devoid* of almost *any* political and social support. Although France was granted the status of an occupation power in Germany, after 1945, was granted a seat in the Security Council of the United Nations, and was allowed to retrieve most of her rights as a colonial power (a mixed blessing at the very least as the Indochina and Algerian wars of independence were to prove), she was excluded from the negotiations and agreements at Yalta and Potsdam and was not a party either to the discussions leading up to the all important Bretton Woods agreement.

In 1945, France's industrial base was small and often extremely backward technologically. The industrial base, but also the coal and iron mines and the basic economic infrastructures bore the scars of two earlier decades of chronic underinvestment, the impact of the Slump of the 1930s and the destructions of the war. But the state of industry in 1945 also reflected *secular Malthusian tendencies* on the part of a large fraction of the owners of capital and landed property.[7] The defeat in June 1940 had been the result of political and military conservatism of the French bourgeoisie, which had also taken the form of a major technological gap with Germany. France had had a number of brilliant scientists, but up to 1939 they had generally been almost completely deprived of adequate resources to carry out their research. Whatever French industry knew about industrial management was the result of a study of Taylorism and Fordism. Finally 40% of the French population was still engaged in agriculture. Although farmers carried out their activity on a fertile soil, with the backing of multisecular traditions in food and wine artisanship, the backward features of much agricultural production meant that productivity and output were very low.

Thirty years later (i.e., by the mid-1970s) France had succeeded in attaining the rank and attributes of a modern industrial power. Considered as a fraction of the total 1973 OECD GNP, France with 8% had long overtaken Great Britain (5.4%). The active population in agriculture was down to less than 10%, while yields in key products such as wheat or milk production had tripled from 1945 levels. French industry had in many sectors been restructured and had experienced quantitative but also qualitative growth. France's infrastructure in terms of railroads, electricity supply, urban transport, and telecommunications system had been overhauled and modernized and made similar infrastructure in many other countries look shabby, outdated, and underequipped. Deprived of U. S. and U. K. nuclear technology by decisions dating back to 1943–1944 and confirmed by Roosevelt in 1945–1946, France had succeeded in building her own nuclear industry including nuclear weapons, however useful or meaningful this might be. She had built one successful commercial aircraft, the Caravelle, and with the United Kingdom the supersonic plane Concorde, which was an unsuccessful commercial venture, but nonetheless a technological feat. She had taken the initiative of assembling a number of European partners to build Airbus and stay in the business of large transatlantic airliners. She had, again unwisely, moved back into large-scale level albeit second tier production (as compared with the United States) of weapons, missiles, and military aircraft. In tandem with Germany she had established a position as a driving force within the European Community and was demonstrating that the United Kingdom had made a mistake in not signing the Rome Treaty. In space she was actively rallying the Europeans within the ELDO and ESRO organizations and persuading them that they could not let the United States establish a monopoly for satellites and launchers. France would be a major founder of the European Space Agency and subsequently of Arianespace.

So, in almost every way the comparison between 1945 and 1975 shows a very different situation and a tale of considerable success. The process of growth and transformation behind this performance was closely geared to large investments in R&D and two phases of intensive S&T institution building.

Institution Building Immediately after the War

The first phase of institution building took place immediately at the end of the war.[8] In a significant and spectacular manner it began with the creation of a capacity for R&D and production in nuclear energy and subsequently for military purposes, lodged in a major agency, the Commissariat à l'Energie, CEA (October 1945). It also included the reorganization and expansion of the CNRS (November 1945) and the creation (1945) under the Ministry of Post, Telegraph and Telephone of the National Centre for the Study of Telecommunications (CNET). Among the numerous technical agencies also established at the time under the Ministry of Defence, the most important was the National Office of Aeronautical Studies and Research (ONERA), which was given a mandate both for military and civil R&D. The major public agencies in the industries which had just been nationalized in energy and basic infrastructures followed suit.

The same period saw the creation of the Office of Overseas Scientific and Technical Research (ORSTOM) (1944) responsible for doing research of interest to the French colonial empire, primarily of course in tropical agriculture; the reestablishment of the National Institute of Health (INH) by the Ministry of Public Health and Population (1945) with the task of ensuring "the direction, organisation, and co-ordination of scientific medical research," and the reestablishment of the National Institute of Agricultural Research (INRA), originally set up in 1921, suppressed in 1934, and finally reorganized in 1946 with two large centralized agricultural research complexes near Paris, in addition to several regional centers.

The most portentous step was of course the decision to move into nuclear research and production. This was subsequently to lead France into one of the largest nuclear energy production programs in the world. The responsibility for the initial move limited in principle to "civilian" industrial objectives, was shared mainly between the Gaullists and the French Communist Party (acting in this as in all cases after consultation with the Soviet Stalinist party). The alliance of these two forces provided the political but also the scientific foundation of France's entry into the military nuclear field. This was decided around 1955 after the first commissioner Joliot Curie had been ousted, before being fully implemented by de Gaulle after 1960. It was opposed by the CP for reasons related to the Cold War, but the conjunctural character of this opposition was shown later when the "force de frappe" received CP support at the end of the 1970s. The building of the CEA's central R&D laboratory and pilot plant capacities at Saclay from 1947 onward symbolized the start of a transformation of French scientific institutions. In place of the small, poorly equipped laboratories of individual professors that had characterized French science, large scientific resources were brought together in a complex of modern laboratories with teams of researchers and supporting technicians. In a country where no large firm had yet set up a major industrial R&D laboratory based on the U. S. and German model, the building of Saclay was France's first real step into twentieth-century fundamental and applied science. It is only the more regrettable that it should have been for the atom.

The CNRS

Although it was formally founded in 1939 as a belated result of the political interest for science shown by the 1936 Popular Front government led by Leon Blum, the existence of the National Centre for Scientific Research (CNRS) must really be dated from its reorganization in 1945. Its initial mandate included the responsibility to develop, orient, and coordinate all French science. Although this objective was never to be achieved, the CNRS was to have a profound impact on the organization and development of basic and long-term research, the availability of scientific and technical personnel, and the overall support of science.

Through the establishment of numerous laboratories and research facilities that it administers, the CNRS has provided France since 1945 with an infrastructure of research institutes similar to that created in Germany after 1911 by the Kaiser Wilhelm Society (today the Max Planck Society). In particular, the CNRS has been able to establish and administer laboratories in newer fields of research that could not be placed within the French university structure. Within the French system the CNRS has played the role assigned in other systems to industry and private foundations, that is, support of university research. It has supported the otherwise very weak university research by seconding researchers to university laboratories. Although these scientists remain attached to CNRS in terms of promotions and salaries, they are fully integrated into the university laboratory and its research program. The CNRS also supports university research by providing the numerous services, assistants, and equipment required by scientists, which neither the Ministry of Education nor the university budgets has supported adequately. It supports colloquia on scientific subjects and finances the attendance of French scientists at international conferences. It subvenes scientific publication and the purchase of instrumentation and provides scientists and technicians with a wide range of services including documentation, specialized training, and assistance on patentable inventions.

Institution Building in the First Phases of the Fifth Republic (1958–1966)

During the 1945–1958 period, the production and diffusion of technology were driven almost exclusively by the State and innovation capacity lodged principally in nationalized or publicly owned firms. In the second phase of institution building, which took place after the Algiers military coup, the fall of the Fourth Republic, de Gaulle's return to power, and the setting up of the Fifth Republic, innovation continued to be driven strongly by the State. But policies start to be enacted to lodge at least a part of the innovative capacity within the industry's national champions (e.g., the large public or private firms with which the State has decided to build up in order to work in close partnership with them). This is the period during which the overall framework of the State–industry relationship is established by the Commissariat au Plan, which reached its highest point of power and influence under de Gaulle in the 1960s.

Major institutional decisions in S&T first concerned space research with the creation in 1959 of a Committee for Space Research, which made proposals for a 6-year program. While all the other European countries were hesitating over embarking on a space program, political considerations, including de Gaulle's personal vision of France's and Europe's place in the world, led to the decision in 1962 to launch the proposed program and to set up a national organization for space research, the National Centre for Space Studies (CNES). The decision was also made, however, to adopt an organizational set up different from the CEA or the CNET and to involve public and private firms in the program from the outset by contracting out a large part of the R&D to the business sector.

The same pattern of State–industry relationship, based on procurement and often involving the same firms, was adopted for the arms industry, following the full scale reorganization of military R&D undertaken in the early 1960s (Kolodziej, 1987). A very strong body with quasiministerial autonomous power, the Ministerial Delegation for Armements (DMA), which later became the DGA, was set up in 1961 within the Ministry of Defence, along with a Directorate for Military Research and Testing (DRME). Military R&D was moved out of the State sector and reorganized on the basis of R&D procurement to industry. The only exception was the military atomic program, which retained a high degree of autonomy within the CEA's Directorate for Military Applications and did not use firm-based R&D procurement. Although there is considerable uncertainty about the exact cost of the nuclear military program (the "force de frappe nucléaire"), it is generally considered that between 1959 and 1966 the major atomic military, aeronautic, and space programs accounted for about 65% of public R&D expenditure. These programs were launched and were all in answer to political objectives coupled in the case of nuclear sectors with a subordinate industrial objective (Papon, 1975, 1978).

After 1965, the problems of the French computer and data-processing industries brought about a further development and yet another pattern of the State–industry alliance. Faced with the difficulties of the French computer industry and spurred once again by a hopeless U. S. embargo decision, the French government, which had let the Bull Machine Company come under U. S. control, launched a new "Major Program" in the field of data processing: the Plan Calcul. This plan took shape in 1966 with the set-up of a new private data-processing company, the International Data-Processing Company (CII), which received huge financial aid from the State. In addition, the State set up an Institute for Research into Data-Processing and Automatism (IRIA) and gave further financial assistance to the French components and peripheral equipment firms. Although IRIA is still in existence, the firms that the State has attempted to upgrade into viable competitors on world markets have suffered countless misadventures and undergone innumerable metamorphoses.

Developments in the 1970s and 1980s and the 1982 Reforms[9]

With respect to the overall structure and working of the French innovation system, the 1970s and 1980s have essentially brought about only *shifts in emphasis* in the area of overall R&D resource allocation and the location of entrepreneurial capacity, along with a clearer spelling out of features that were already contained within the system as it had been built in the two previous phases. Two developments warrant special attention.

The first has been the development, based on institutions built during the earlier periods—the DMA-DGA and the DRET within the Defense Ministry and also the CEA, the CNES, and the CNET, of a *large military–industrial complex,* which encompasses those parts of the space program that fall outside the European programs managed by the European Space Agency and the operations of the Arianespace consortium, a part of the activity in telecommunications, and the efforts made to maintain a computer and components industry. The industrial elements of the complex now represent France's most powerful and at least in appearance most successful high-technology corporations, in particular Thomson, Aerospatiale, and Matra. These firms are almost indifferently "private" firms (as in the case of Matra) or "public firms" (as with the other two).

The second novel but totally logical development concerned the steps taken first to build new links or "bridges" between the research capacity accumulated within the public sector and all firms that are ready to take the innovations to market, and later to authorize and even force public research centers *to move downstream toward the market* and to become "technological entrepreneurs" in their own right. The first category of measures included the creation of ANVAR, which is a fairly classical type of agency for technology transfer from government and university research laboratories to industry. The second category of measures, developed during the Pompidou (1971–1974) and Giscard (1974–1981) administrations, had to wait the Socialist-CP government of 1981 to be written up and pushed through. They entailed the introduction of a number of breaches in public sector characteristics of major fundamental and/or applied government research laboratories in CNRS, INRA, INSERM, and so on.

The changes are still far from a full scale privatization of public sector R&D, but they certainly represent a step in that direction. The status of the R&D laboratories was changed (in 1982 for CNRS, in 1983 for INSERM and INRA) from administrative public institutions to a new generic type of status with some attributes of private law, the "établissement public scientifique et technique." Under this new status laboratories have been empowered to establish subsidiaries, acquire shares, and seek cooperation around specific projects with scientific and industrial partners in public interest groups (GIP) and scientific groupings (GS). These possibilities give the major agencies more incentive to involve themselves in exploiting and marketing their innovations. In practice, marketing will generally be undertaken by private law subsidiaries that can more appropriately act as entrepreneurs than the research agencies themselves. An example of this was the creation, in 1983, of a firm called "Midi-Robots" to develop and market products originating directly from the work of the CNRS automation and systems analysis laboratory (LAAS) in Toulouse. The firm set up business partnerships with the government aircraft laboratory ONERA and the aerospace firms. The 1982 arrangements can also take practical form in multipartite cooperation contracts, or in the formation of an embryonic industrial undertaking and marketing activity. The GIP is particularly suitable for setting up technology transfer centers and joint CNRS/industrial teams cooperating to develop industrial prototypes. One of the first examples was the "time frequency" technology GIP, in which three leading CNRS research laboratories came together with Thomson to develop the very high-precision timepieces required for airborne navigation and telecommunications networks.

THE OVERALL STRUCTURE OF THE R&D SYSTEM

An R&D system differs on several scores from an innovation system. Reported formal R&D expenditures are only a part of the innovation-related outlays made by firms. Formal R&D data ignore the complex processes of technological accumulation whereby tacit, partly uncodified knowledge is built up and transmitted from one generation to the next within institutions, firms, and sometimes whole industries. Formal R&D captures nothing of the linkages between organizations, the feedback processes, and also the alliances and relationships of power between agencies and firms. An R&D system is at best a poor proxy to an innovation system, but since the R&D data are the only reasonably coherent and comprehensive data we possess, we have no choice but to use them before examining in the following sections some of the systemic relationships that give a better idea of the reality of the innovation system.

In the case of France the overall structure can be approached through a look at the main aggregates in terms of funding and execution shown in Figure 6.1 published by the Ministry of Research and Technology.[10] This can be considered only a first approximation, since funding arrows cannot capture *the transfer of readily applicable technology,* which occurs on a large scale between the State sector laboratories and business enterprises as a result of the policies just discussed.

The main structural characteristics are as follows:

1. The government funds approximately 50% of R&D and industry about 44%, the rest coming from foreign sources.
2. About 55% is executed in industry and 43% in the "public sector" (the lower left hand block), which includes both government research laboratories (about 27%) and higher education research (about 16%), which includes funds provided by the CNRS and general university funds as reported in OECD statistics, which are of course basically aimed at teaching and only subordinately at research.

The Allocation of Nonmilitary R&D Funds to the State Laboratories

The way in which the official budget documents and other reports are presented makes it extremely difficult to understand the precise pattern of resource allocation of funds. In 1985, a serious estimate was made by one of the Associations of engineers and is given in Figure 6.2. Several observations are required for a full understanding of the data.

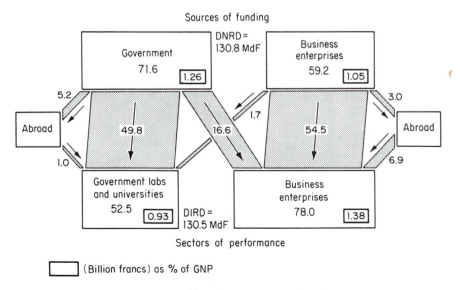

Figure 6.1. Sources of funding and sectors of performance.

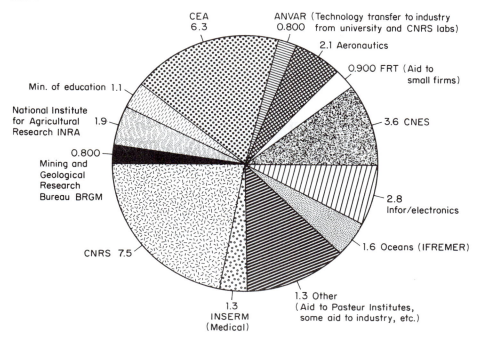

CEA
6.3

ANVAR (Technology transfer to industry
0.800 from university and CNRS labs)

2.1 Aeronautics

0.900 FRT (Aid to
small firms)

Min. of education 1.1

National Institute
for Agricultural 1.9
Research INRA

3.6 CNES

0.800
Mining and
Geological
Research
Bureau BRGM

2.8
Infor/electronics

CNRS 7.5

1.6 Oceans (IFREMER)

1.3 Other
1.3 (Aid to Pasteur Institutes,
INSERM some aid to industry, etc.)
(Medical)

Figure 6.2. The breakdown of the "budget civil de R-D" administered by the ministry of research and technology: appropriations to government laboratories and support schemes to industry. Source: Bulletin de l'Ademast, No. 10, January 1985.

1. The data cover the appropriations received through the Ministries of Industry and of Research and Technology. Following the moves made under J. P. Chevènement toward a unified system outside the military sphere, this is in fact very comprehensive and misses only the appropriations provided to the CNET in telecommunications. In 1985, they represented 3.5 billion francs (i.e., approximately the same as for CNES).

2. The appropriations made to CNRS include the expenditures it makes in its own laboratories and the funds it allocates through its own commission to university associated laboratories.

3. The CEA remains the single largest government R&D center, with a civil R&D subsidy 40% higher than that of CNES or CNET, to which a large military appropriation must be added.

4. If the appropriations made for the CEA, the CNET, the civil aeronautics program administered by the ONERA (which includes France's contribution to the R&D support given to the Airbus consortium), and the informatics/electronics sector are lumped together, then *even* independently of the *military* R&D allocation pattern that has of course exactly the same thrust, one finds an *overwhelming bias in favor of the nuclear, aeronautics, space, telecommunications, and electronics sectors* to the detriment of the chemical, biological, and life science based sectors (INRA, INSERM, IFREMER) as well as to that of the machine tool and robotics industries

and other small firm dominated sectors [which get at best a little scattered support through the FRT (Fonds de Recherche Technologique)].

Industrial R&D: The Available Data and What It Shows

We must now turn to the lower right-hand block in Figure 6.1. Industrial R&D, or R&D carried out within firms, remains significantly weak. Whereas French GERD represented 2.31% of GDP in 1987, R&D carried out in the business enterprise sector (both publicly and privately owned) represented only 1.38% (as compared with 2.11% in Japan, 2.25% in the United States, and 2.49% in Germany). As far as the R&D actually financed by firms is concerned the percentage is even lower—1.05% of GDP in 1987.

These figures are confirmed by survey data. In 1987 the Ministry of Research and Technology reported that only 1990 firms were carrying out R&D as defined by the OECD Frascati Manual. Since the Ministry includes in its survey a further 50 technical research centers that are financed collectively by firms in different industrial branches, data are provided covering 2040 firms and research centers. As a point of comparison, for the same year the industrial census reported 90,000 firms in manufacturing and services employing 10 or more people.

According to the survey the 1990 firms reporting formal R&D account for a third of industrial employment and over half of industrial output. The survey reveals, however, a dual situation in this regard: in one group of industries, which includes food processing, building materials, metallurgy, and textiles, firms doing R&D account for no more than 20% of industrial branch output; in another group, which includes energy production, electronics, data processing, aircraft, automobiles, chemicals, and pharmaceutics, such firms account for over 75% of industrial branch output. These branches account for about 87% of all R&D (Fig. 6.3).

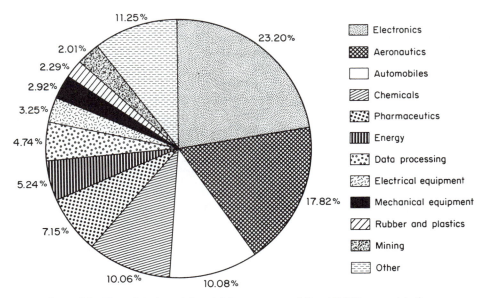

Figure 6.3. The origin by ministerial departments of direct R&D support to firms.

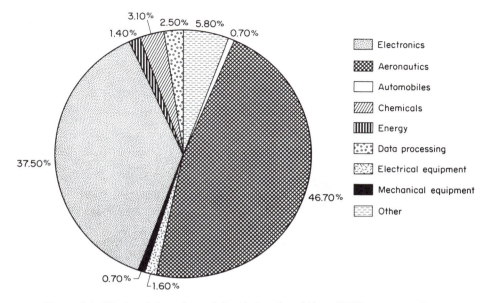

Figure 6.4. The breakdown by recipient industries of direct R&D support to firms.

Furthermore, within the group of 2040 firms and centers reporting formal R&D expenditure, effective R&D activity is concentrated within a very small group of firms. In 1987, only 7% of the organizations concerned had an R&D staff with more than 50 science and engineering research workers. *A group of no more than 150 firms accounts in fact for the bulk of French R&D.* According to the survey these firms carry out 75% of R&D and receive over 90% of direct government support for R&D. The direct support for industrial R&D is highly concentrated. Two Ministries, Defense and Post and Telecommunications, alone account for 85% of the funds channeled to firms and two sectors, aerospace and electronics, receive 83% of the total (Fig. 6.4). Here we are talking exclusively of reported R&D procurement and not of the other, possibly large, sums (which go unrecorded publicly and one quite probably very hard to really keep track of seriously), which reach industry *indirectly* through the partnerships that the large State laboratories all establish with the firms that they deem to be their opposite number in industry.

At the other end of the spectrum, among the 1990 firms reporting formal R&D, some 1450 firms employ less than 10 fully trained scientists and engineers. These firms carry out less than 8% of the recorded formal R&D and are the beneficiaries of no more than 3% of government R&D subsidies. As a result, the concentration of R&D by industrial branch is necessarily extremely high. In 1987, eight branches accounted for over 85% of total R&D expenditure: electronics, 23.2%; aircraft, 17.8%; automobiles, 10%; chemicals, 10%; pharmaceuticals, 7%; energy production, 7.2%; data processing, 5.2%; and heavy electrical material, 4.7%. By contrast industrial branches that account for a significant part of French exports (agriculture and food processing) or still represent fairly important components of French industrial GDP (metallurgy and metal working, textiles, machinery) account only for a very small fraction of industrial R&D.

Research in the Higher Education Sector

The third component of the R&D capacity is the one lodged within the higher education sector, with its dual structure of universities and separate engineering schools.

Within universities R&D is in general the privileged and closely guarded domain of *specialized laboratories that have tended again to become partly divorced from teaching.* Significant research is a feature of a handfull of universities only; the Louis Pasteur University in Strasbourg, which builds on the legacy of the German university system, Orsay (Paris IX) with its close relationships with Saclay and many CNRS laboratories, Grenoble, and Toulouse. Despite the proclamation by the 1968 and later reforms of formal university autonomy, the universities as such still have little say about research. The professors who are also heads of laboratories are jealous of their independence. They take it on themselves to ensure that teaching posts, premises, and operating budgets are allocated by University Councils along lines that represent essentially a continuation of the status quo. The more enterprising among heads of laboratories will negotiate directly with outside sources (public bodies and the CNRS in particular and now increasingly with industry) for the extra funds needed to develop high-quality research. *The swamping of the universities* by the massive surge of student enrollment under the two-fold action of demographic factors and of a call for democratization accompanied by totally insufficient resources for staff or premises has accentuated the tendency for the larger and better connected laboratories to try and isolate themselves as best they can from the situation in which the universities have been placed since the late 1970s.

The situation today is critical. Universities are part of the public sector, salaries are aligned with those in the civil service, and in a period of fiscal crisis for the State university buildings, their construction, repair, and day-to-day running costs are determined by public budgets. On other vital matters relating to the organization of teaching and research, the so-called autonomy of universities is purely formal; everything related to the administration of human and material resources falls under the strictest rules commanding public administration. The traditional conception of "public service" forbids universities to establish any kind of student entry selection; the net outcome is to negate the notion of "public service" by dramatically lowering the quality of teaching and achieving "selection through failure" after 1, 2, or 3 years.

The larger and better connected laboratories can count on the financial and material assistance of the CNRS and also increasingly on resources coming through European Community (Esprit, BRITE, RACE, etc.) programs and Eureka projects. But in many cases they are affected by an insufficient supply of young researchers stemming from the overall decline in the university system; they often consider themselves lucky when they can fill some gaps with foreign students on European or foreign country grants. Unlike the CNRS's own laboratories, the university laboratories (even those having the "associated with CNRS" status) have not been granted the EPST status discussed above so as to keep them under the Ministry of Education's strict authority and control. They remain hampered in their efforts to establish R&D contracts with industry. Discussion in the 1970s and 1980s about the need for closer university–industry relationships has not yet freed university research from the fetters of traditional state accounting procedures. The establishment of R&D contracts with firms forces laboratories to circumvent the law and to hide part of their resources from official university accountants and tax inspectors.

The other component of the education system, the engineering "Grandes Ecoles," compensate for some of the weaknesses of the university system as far as preserving the level of education is concerned, but not with respect to the needs of industry in terms of numbers of trained personnel and less still with respect to those of long-term basic research. The small size of the engineering schools and their very tough selection procedures have guaranteed the level of education, in keeping with the overall elitist requirements of the system. Lower level or "less noble" engineering schools were created during the 1960s and 1970s, but the assessment is that with a supply of about 12,500 engineers a year the system does not produce the supply required by French industry. This is thought to represent one reason for the plight of many segments of small sized industry. The laboratories of the Grandes Ecoles are much better endowed than those of the universities and the relationships with industry are naturally much stronger, but the laboratories are nearly empty. In 1982 an official report found that of 10,500 diplomas awarded, only 500 were engineering Ph.D. R&D, in particular basic or long-term research, remains weak, and in some instances is still marginal within the engineering schools. The entry selection process is still based mainly on mathematics and this discipline continues to determine the teaching curriculum in many schools. In 1987, a survey on scientific and technical personnel found 28,600 trained full-time scientists and engineers doing research within the higher education sector, but attributed only 1400 to the engineering schools. A 1985 study found 5600 people doing research within these schools (not full time), but noted that two-thirds were either from other laboratories or agencies or under contract and that only one-third were members of the normal teaching staff.

Agencies and Institutional Mechanisms for Technological Diffusion

An overview of the R&D system would be incomplete without reference to the agencies and institutional mechanisms created to disseminate scientific and technical knowledge and the technologies produced in the large public laboratories, the CNRS, and the universities.

One mechanism was discussed at the end of the previous section, namely the attribution of EPIC states (public agency with private law attributes) to certain research centers and the possibility that they could set up joint ventures with industry. But technology transfer is also the mission of several specialized agencies, both at the national and the regional level. The most important of these is ANVAR (Agence nationale pour la valorisation de la recherche), which manages a portfolio of patents (it files 1000–1200 applications at home and abroad on average a year) and finds industrial partners for CNRS and university laboratories. In 1982 a new institution was created, the CRITTs (Centres régionaux d'innovation et de transfert de technologies), which are joint venture organizations with private and public (mainly regional) financial participation and the job of enhancing regional innovation-related networks between laboratories, firms, and local governments. They can be specialized (as in Alsace in the area of new materials) or general. One finds a wide mix of financing and effective participation, which evolves over time as a firm network starts to get rooted. These institutions are obviously of great potential importance. The finance they command is, however, still absolutely marginal (see the amounts for ANVAR, the FRT (Fonds de la recherche technologique), and "other" in Fig. 6.2) in comparison with the funds channeled to the core of the system, which we will now examine.

QUALITATIVE FEATURES OF THE HIGH-TECHNOLOGY SUBSYSTEMS

The analysis of the formal R&D data yields few insights on how the innovation system really works. Given the way the system was established historically, the State occupies a pivotal position in most R&D intensive industries. Generally it relies on industrial partners to take the innovations to the market, but in some cases this task is assigned to the commercial arm of a government department. The influence of distinct and possibly rival government departments explains why the State influenced innovation system is divided vertically into strongly compartmentalized sub-systems.[11] Before discussing a number of these separately, we must examine the social foundations of the State-industry alliance.

Business and State: The Blurring of the Public–Private Distinction

An important feature of French political and social history since the end of World War II has been the progressive establishment between the State and the oligopolistic core of public and private industry of a common view of the ways of attaining economic growth, modernization, and military independence through autonomous arms production, so preserving France's "rank in the world." The events of the 1930s and 1940s brought about an understanding by the most determined group within the French ruling class (of which de Gaulle became the figurehead) that the page should be turned with respect to the classical liberal division of tasks between the State and industry. The new approach was that private capital should rally round the State, accept its help, and use it as an instrument for industrial restructuring and the channeling of financial and human resources to priority areas.[12]

The process was prepared during the Fourth Republic by setting up the Planning Commissariat, the concentration of responsibility for Finance and the Economy in one extremely powerful ministry, the nationalizations, and the setting up of the large R&D agencies. Under the Fourth Republic, the process was still hampered by two main factors: (1) the lingering of an anachronistic approach to imperial status and colonial power and the support of vested colonial interests backed by the Army, and (2) a political system based on the supremacy of the Parliament and the ploy of traditional conservative political parties and leaders (Pinay, Laniel) who were still in a position to defend the interests of the colonial lobbies and of small family business and the "shopkeepers." Between 1958 and 1961 de Gaulle put an end to this with the closing of the Algerian war, the purging of the procolonial faction within the Army and its reorientation to nuclear "force de frappe" strategical thinking, and, of course, the establishment of the Fifth Republic, which, under the label of "democracy," is today the nearest thing to "Republican Monarchy," marked by an unequaled concentration of power in the executive.

The decade that followed de Gaulle's return to power was marked by an energetic drive toward industrial restructuring and concentration. Given the highly fragmented character of most sectors of French industry, the building of much larger industrial groups and the concentration of industrial plants were, from the standpoint of French capitalism, a necessity. At the end of the 1960s, acute U. S. observers could already note that the "important force shaping corporate strategies and strategic planning is a close relationship between business and the State" (McArthur and Scott, 1989, p. 8).[13]

S. Cohen (1969, p. 51) reached much the same conclusion: "The economie concertée is a partnership of big business, the state, and, in theory though not in practice, the trade unions. The managers of big business and the managers of the state run the modern core of the nation's economy—mostly the oligopoly sectors."

Subsequent performance, in the late 1970s and 1980s, in particular in the area of industrial exports, suggests that the "national champion" policy also contributed to strengthening other important parasitic traits of French industry and finance. The task of remodeling French industry undertaken by Gaullist governments in the 1960s was completed in 1982–1983 by the additional restructuring and reorganization of corporate frontiers, which took place in 1982–1983 at the time of the so-called "nationalizations" of the first Mitterrand government. Aside from their purely ideological purpose of allowing the first socialist and CP government to seem to be "on the left," the basic purpose of 1982–1983 "nationalizations" was to give the French State and administration renewed authority and power to undertake the widespread restructuring of several major industries and, if necessary, to tread on the toes of recalcitrant capitalists while offering others (in steel and parts of petrochemicals) extremely, not to say scandalously, favorable *financial exit conditions.* In the course of the 1970s and 1980s, the oligopolistic core of French industry gained greater and greater ascendency in the State–industry partnership, as well as greater freedom of action. Price controls were suppressed in the late 1970s and early 1980s; the first Mitterrand governments planned and pushed through a full scale modernization, reorganization, and deregulation of the financial system including the Stock Exchange (the Bourse), which has proved to be particularly beneficial to the oligopolistic core of industry and banking; legislation was passed to allow public sector and nationalized firms to internationalize and to form joint ventures in France with foreign partners.

France's Unique "Power Élite": The "Grandes Écoles"

One of the most effective instruments of this near symbiosis between a State apparatus receptive to the arguments of oligopolistic industry and large firms marked by the reflex of turning to the State for support has been the system of elite production through the "*grandes écoles*" [in particular the Ecole Nationale d'Administration (ENA) and the Ecole Polytechnique] and the "grands corps." "The key fact in French planning," as noted by Granick (1964, p. 147) in the 1960s, "is that the same type of men are sitting in the management and civil service posts in this cartel: men of the grandes écoles, present and former civil servants who consider themselves technocrats." The large industrial enterprises in France, the nationalized industries, and the public sector are to a very large extent run by people who come from the same schools and are invariably members of the "grands corps," notably the Inspecteurs des Finances and the engineering corps. By "corps" is meant a highly trained expert personnel who have successfully entered Polytechnique and go on to one of the select engineering schools, in particular the Ecole des Mines, the Ecole des Ponts et Chaussées, the Ecole Nationale des Télécommunications, the Ecole Nationale Supérieure de l'Aéronautique et de l'Espace (SupAero), and the specialized schools where the Ingénieurs de l'Armement receive their last phase of training.[14]

A study of industrial managers in France made in the 1970s concluded that "the most characteristic trait in the careers of the sample studied is the frequency of the

PDG (President Director-General) coming from the public sector" (Monjardet, 1972). The study concludes that this type of career cannot be viewed any longer as simply the seduction by the private sector of an elite whose sense of public service has been weakened. Rather, it has to be seen as "an essential element in the training (acquisition of competence, or relations) of the industrial managers in France." A further recent study of the same phenomena has concluded unambiguously that this is the case: today the normal path to the top banks and industrial firms involves final schooling at Polytechnique or ENA; entry into a "grands corps" and finally a passage through the top administration or the private office of one or several Ministers (Bauer, 1987). Thus, at the heart of each of the major innovation subsystems is a group of managers, research directors, and private office Ministerial advisers belonging to the same "corps": "Mines" and "Ponts et Chaussées" in the case of electronuclear power, the Corps des ingénieurs des "télécom" in the case of telecommunications and space, the graduates from SupAero in the aerospace industries, and the Corps des ingénieurs de l'armement elsewhere in the arms industry. These people possess what Salomon (1989) calls a "lifelong passeport" to the highest and best paid jobs, within a system in which severe business failure almost unvariably goes unpunished.

SOME CHARACTERISTIC HIGH-TECHNOLOGY SUBSYSTEMS

In this section, we turn to some characteristic examples of the partnership between the State and the oligopolistic core of large public and private firms operating in the high-technology sectors other than pharmaceuticals and the new branches of the chemical sector. Figure 6.5 sets out the government agencies and their main industrial counterparts. Two sets of government agencies are indicated: those involved in technological activity either as major laboratories (CEA, ONERA), as R&D procurement agencies (DRET, CNES), or as both simultaneously (CNET), but also those politically responsible for technological strategies. The Délégation Générale à l'Armement (DGA) appears at every point in the top line, indicating the key role played by the military and the increasing influence they are now likely to exert even in telecommunications and nonmilitary space as a result of the current post-Gulf war reorientation of military–strategic priorities to space observation and telecommunications systems.

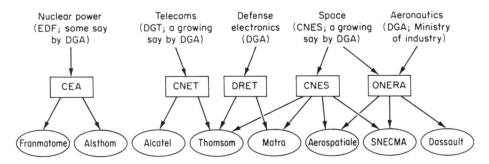

Figure 6.5. Some key relationships at the heart of the high tech innovation system. Source: Adapted from Serfati (1991).

The Military High-Technology Innovation Subsector

Although this subsector is more recent than the one in nuclear technology, its strategic position implies that we should begin with it. Expenditure on military R&D is estimated as representing *at least a third* and probably well over 35% of French public expenditure on R&D, meaning that the military subsystem of innovation is one of the largest. Military R&D is divided into three fractions: (1) the nuclear R&D undertaken at the CEA (approximately 30% of the total), (2) the R&D carried out in the State-owned traditional arsenals and arms manufactures (now less than 10%), and (3) the R&D commissioned to industrial firms through R&D contracts and procurement (over 60%), which amounts (as shown in Fig. 6.3) to about two-thirds of the total of the State's direct support to industrial R&D.

The high-technology arms industry is organized through a tightly knit relationship between private and public industry and the General Delegation for Armement (DGA). The head of this institution is a "nonpolitical" and hence a stable appointee, who is considered to be as powerful as many Ministers. The firms with which the DGA works as prime contractors are all among the largest in French industry. These firms do not compete among themselves. R&D contracts and arms procurement take place without tendering, on the basis of a functional division of tasks established by the DGA as part of its "industrial policy for arms." As a result, the French arms industry is in fact organized around a set of monopolies or duopolies: for planes and helicopters, Dassault and Aérospatiale; for aircraft engines, SNECMA; for missiles, Aérospatiale and Matra; for electronics, Thomson and Dassault-Electronique.

Given the resources at the disposal of the Ministry of Defence for R&D and arms purchases, the gradual enfeeblement of the Plan as an institutional mechanism and the persistent weakness of the Ministry of Industry, the DGA is now the strongest body in French industrial policy. As Kolodziej (1987, p. 274) has shown, the DGA is in a position through its "multiple opportunities in allocating its contracts and deploying its administrative organs to *mark French industrial planning indelibly with an arms imprint.*" Our own study of the relationships between military expenditures and competitiveness (see Chesnais and Serfati, 1990, 1992) suggests that a *large part of French high-technology industry* (perhaps really all of it outside the medical sector and pharmaceuticals) *has been shaped* by the pervasive influence of defense markets and military demand, notably the highly customized, nongeneric features of military technologies and their very low degree of transferability to civilian uses. Serfati (1991) has shown that the disastrous balance of the French electronics industry, despite the attention and financial support it has received, cannot be dissociated from the fact that the military has had priority in fixing the industry's R&D and industrial objectives. More generally in the case of a country the size of France, the effects of the arms industry and military R&D on industrial competitiveness cannot be analyzed simply in terms of alternative opportunity costs or "crowding out" processes. Because of its position at the heart of the electronics, electrical, and mechanical engineering interlocked complex of industries, arms production also affects interindustry flows of technology and shapes the *whole process of technological learning and accumulation* in these industries. In instances where new technologies emerge in the defense sector, as in laser technology, the transfer to civilian user has proved a complete failure.[15]

The power of the DGA, but also the organization of the arms related innovation subsystem and the political strength of the French military–industrial complex, cannot be dissociated from the role played by the corps of armament engineers.

> Drawn largely from the Ecole Polytechnique . . ., the army engineers form a unique and cohesive corps throughout their careers that lead almost inevitably to the highest posts within the Ministry of Defense, the DGA and, increasingly, to leadership positions throughout the nationalized and private sectors of the arms industry. . . . Sharing a common schooling and formation, they have an engineer's and technocrat's way of looking at issues. . . . *The network of corps ties goes deeper and is more extensive than the organization charts of the arms industry or of the DGA can capture.* The arms engineers who are liberally distributed throughout the weapons complex are the glue that holds the system together. Increasing numbers of the corps have no difficulty rationalizing their service to the State from the perspective of an industrialist or functionary since both activities are viewed as different aspects of a single national policy to make and sell arms. (Kolodziej, 1987, p. 278)

The overall result of these processes has been the transfer of vital decision making from the political institutions nominally in charge to this group and the organizations they work for. In economic as well as political terms (cf. the arming of Sadam Hussein), the results of "what is good for the DGA and the large arms producers is good for France" have at the best been debateable and at the worst disastrous.

The Electronuclear Subsystem: CEA, EDF, and Their Industrial Partners

Systemic relationships involving two major public organizations and large firms from the semipublic and private sectors, cemented by the Polytechnique-trained engineers belonging to the Ponts et Chaussées "Corps," also characterize this subsystem (see Fig. 6.6).

The CEA, as noted above, still has the single largest public R&D budget. Half is for military purposes; the other half (the part shown in Fig. 6.2) is for industrial objectives, where the CEA still receives nearly twice the resources as the CNET and the CNES. EDF, the large public corporation dating back from the 1945–1946 nationalizations, is the world's second largest producer of nuclear-based electrical power. It exports electricity through the European electrical grid system. Whenever (e.g., more and more rarely) tenders are called for the building of nuclear power plants a French consortium generally composed of Framatome and Alsthom/CGE will compete. France is a world leader in patents relating to nuclear production and now has the doubtful honor of being a world leader in nuclear waste disposal and/or recycling. Much of this takes place at the Hague near Cherbourg, now a major "nuclear dustbin."

The history of the nuclear subsystem falls into two main periods (Gilpin, 1968; Papon, 1975, 1977; Debeir et al., 1989). The first is that of the natural uranium–graphite–gas reactor system set up under the sway of a dual purpose military–civilian strategy with its R&D and industrial programs.[16] The second period, coinciding with de Gaulle's departure from office in 1969, was built on a clear separation between military and industrial objectives. A full-scale reorganization of the CEA was undertaken, the EDF was established with responsibility for industrial strategy, and the decision was

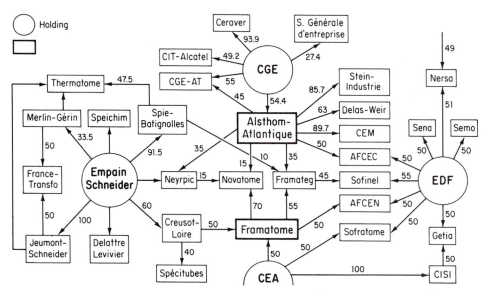

Figure 6.6. The configuration of the nuclear subsystem in the mid-1980s. Source: G. Donnadieu, *La mise en valeur des acquis de l'industrie nucleaire,* p. 34. Report to the Conseil Economique et Social, 1984.

taken to adopt the dominant U. S. enriched-uranium technology. Westinghouse's technological partnership for PWR reactors was sought and obtained on favorable conditions. The reorganization of the civil industry-oriented segment of the CEA heralded the process of semiprivatization of the government sector laboratories previously discussed. From 1970 onward a number of departments and laboratories were transformed into CEA industrial subsidiaries with private commercial law status, in particular the Compagnie générale des matières premières (COGEMA) set up in 1976, which controls, through a number of affiliated firms, the whole French nuclear fuel cycle from prospecting for and extracting natural uranium through uranium enrichment (EURODIF) to spent fuel processing via the fabrication, design, and marketing of fuels (FBFC and FRAGEMA). In 1983 all private law CEA subsidiaries were integrated in a holding company, CEA-Industries.

After an initial phase of sharp oligopolistic rivalry involving two industrial groups each allied with separate U. S. partners (Westinghouse and GE) the heavy equipment side of the innovation subsystem was organized around two poles, following one of the numerous "industrial Yaltas" (a pleasant expression for State-blessed cartel creating), which most of France's high-technology sectors have experienced at some point. The Schneider-Empain group and their lead firm in electronuclear technology, Framatome, were given the EDF contracts for nuclear reactors based on the Westinghouse PWR technology, while CGE/Alsthom, which had previously acquired the number one position in conventional heavy electric power equipment, got the orders for the complementary "standard" heavy electric equipment surrounding the nuclear plant (Debeir et al., 1989).

From the mid-1970s onward, CEA was considered to have grown well beyond the size that was required. Because of the political power of the "Grands Corps," the answer was not to slim it down but to empower it to do R&D in fields other than nuclear energy. "Innovation and industrial development" thus joined "nuclear developments" as a mission of the CEA's Technology Research and Industrial Development Institute. Nonnuclear activities include electronics and computer technology, robotics, medical instrumentation, agrofood technology, new materials, and even renewable energies. The technologies developed by the CEA are transferred to industry in a variety of ways: notably the creation of R&D partnerships with firms in the industries concerned.

CNES and the Space Industry

There is a wide interface between the military subsystem of innovation and production and the one for space R&D and related operations and space industrial production. The CNES was set up at the end of 1961. It has a legal status somewhat similar to that of the CEA, but has built up its network of technological and industrial relationships differently. The first difference is that the CNES is not a public sector laboratory since a government R&D capacity in aeronautics dates back to the 1920s and some space-related questions existed before CNES, within ONERA (civil and military aviation R&D) and ISI (Institut de Saint-Louis), which works on missiles. The second significant difference is that French space-related technological investments began once the industrial base had been rebuilt. CNES policy has always been to organize R&D procurement in industry rather than developing space technology in-house. Given the overall thrust of French industrial policy and the influence of the DGA just discussed, the firms that have been assigned prime contractor responsibilities for space programs are the same as the DGA's main partners. Matra is the lead firm in propulsion systems for the launchers and shares with Aérospatiale work on satellite platforms as well as satellite components regarding flight altitude, thermal controls, and solar generators. Thomson-CSF is the principal contractor for internal workings of the satellites, including electronic circuits and their components.

Another major difference with the CEA is that in the case of space, the scale of the resources required for R&D and operations was such that from the outset, the French projects were not conceived in purely national terms but involved international cooperation, bilaterally with the United States and even the USSR, but mainly with European States within ESRO and ELDO, and after 1975 within ESA. In contrast with nuclear energy, defense, or telecommunications, in the area of civilian space the French subsystem of innovation has *provided the overall structure and represented the backbone of Europe's involvement in space.* It is sure that without France the European commitment would not be of the scale it now is, nor Arianespace a viable competitor of the main U. S. launchers. The success has brought new problems, in particular those of France's European partners wanting to increase their industrial participation in the development and manufacture of the launchers, satellites, and space cabins. Asset holding by CNES and the four main French contractors in the Arianespace industrial consortium has progressively been brought down from over 60 to about 48%, bringing cooperation under strain, in particular since the last phases coincided with the fall in arms exports. The French government has just announced that military satellites will now represent a major priority of the DGA's investments and that closer coordination with CNES on military objectives must result. This also will put European cooperation under pressure unless it is extended to the military area, but this is not necessarily acceptable to other members of ESA and raises all the issues that have put a brake on R&D and production cooperation for military projects.

France Telecom, the CNET, and the Telecommunications Oligopoly

Prior to World War II, the equipment required by the rather underdeveloped French telephone system was supplied by the affiliates of foreign multinationals, in particular ITT and Eriksson. Since 1945, one of the permanent objectives of French policy has been to endow France with its own equipment industry and make it a leader in telecommunications. This began with the establishment of a large government laboratory, CNET, which later took over other facilities including the military radioelectricity laboratory. The Defense Ministry has always financed a fairly substantial share of the CNET's R&D budget.

Along with the building up of an R&D and innovation capacity, two other steps were taken. First a large-scale and dynamic system of public procurement managed by the DGT (Direction Générale des Télécommunications) was established. Within the P&T Ministry, the DGT plays a role somewhat similar to that of the DGA with the Ministry of Defense. As in other sectors the commercial arm of this policy is a publicly-owned private law subsidiary, French Telecomm, which has been active in equipping industry and homes with phones and now with advanced electronic equipment, in particular the Minitel videotex machine. The other step was the creation of an endogenous industrial capacity that included the acquisition of the ITT and Eriksson affiliates and their incorporation through mergers with French firms into the core nucleus of the French high-technology oligopoly. Today the manufacturing sector is highly concentrated, with CGE-Alcatel as the leading group. Alcatel now has by far the largest R&D budget in civil telecommunications. Its French R&D outlays are about twice as large as those of the following four equipment manufacturers (SAT, TRT, Matra, and Jeumont-Schneider) together.

The R&D and innovation budget for telecommunication is divided in two. About a third is allocated to the CNET, which employs a staff of 4200 people, including 1500 engineers and researchers, working in six locations. The rest goes to public or private industry in the form of R&D contracts. Again with respect to the results of CNET's R&D, the policy is to find industrial partners as early in the development process as possible. As a result, CNET holds less than 10% of all French patents in the area while the manufacturers hold almost 80%.

The telecommunication subsystem has been marked by successes as well as failures (Salomon, 1986, is highly critical). In the case of the Minitel videotex system success was built not only on correct technological decisions, but also on the large scale use of public procurement by the DGT (over 5 million terminals were bought by the DGT and offered free of charge to users), the initial subsidization of service suppliers, and the centralization of supervision and development in the hands of a single body (OECD, 1988; Cohendet and Llerena, 1991, Chapter 2). Today this system is under pressure on two scores. First, the internationalization of Alcatel (now Alcatel NV) following the acquisition by CGE/Alcatel of ITT's European industrial assets in 1987 has substantially shifted the apex of the group's economic interests to European markets.

In 1987, Alcatel NV had 75% of its turnover outside of France as against 40% in 1985. Alcatel NV has the potential to become a truly global corporation with strongly internationalized R&D activities, but it will be forced to aim its R&D strategy to the needs of all its European customers and not only those of France Telecom. Second, DGT and France Telecom are coming under increasing pressure from the European Commission to liberalize their procurement policy and reduce their direct involvement in industrial development activities.

PATENTING AND EXPORTS AS INDICATORS OF SUCCESS AND FAILURE

In the case of France, use of the term "innovation system" innovation appears legitimate. It refers to a *set of identifiable relationships* established among major political institutions, research organizations, and business enterprises, which has been *reproduced* (along with the adaptations and adjustments made necessary by changes in the economic and political context) over several decades. The mechanisms of reproduction include the role of State funding for R&D and industrial investment and the part played by an original type of political and economic *élite*.

The system also has identifiable features with respect to the type of innovation it produces. It is, to use Ergas's terminology (Ergas, 1984, 1987), one of the clearest examples of a *"mission-oriented" type of innovation system.* The model is one where *"big* is beautiful." A premium has been constantly given to *large technology intensive systems* (as in the military area, in electrical power, and in rail transport) or to products that are inherently *systemic* (e.g., aircraft or space products). As a result, markets are almost always invariably conceived by project leaders as being (or having to be) *public markets*. At home these are created through public procurement. Abroad there are invariably the outcome of political negotiations with governments, leveraged by French diplomacy, very often directed to Third World countries or erstwhile "Socialist" States and backed by a widespread use of bribery and corruption.[17]

This system of innovation does not cover the *complete* spectrum of French patenting and exports. One major sector—the chemicals, pharmaceuticals, agrochemicals complex—falls *partly* outside the pattern of relationships we have just discussed.[18] Several other activities and products for which France is successful and well known abroad (wine and brandies, luxury consumer goods, beauty products) fall *completely* outside the system. But it is quite definitely the system of innovation that the majority of Frenchmen and practically the whole educated class know and with which they generally identify themselves. It is also the one that *commands* to a considerable extent the external balance as well as industrial *growth*.

Today the system is in crisis. Its highest moment of success occurred somewhere between 1975 and 1980. This was the heyday of nuclear power plant building in France and of exports of the same large capital goods to a number of Third World countries. It was the period of spectacular growth in arms exports, leading to a situation in which military production came to represent the second most important and stable part of French engineering goods exports after automobiles and arms production became "trapped" into working over 40% for export markets, which had to win at any cost (cf. the contracts with Iraq). The space launcher Ariane-I was successfully put into orbit with a commercial mission for the first time in 1979, and the Airbus consortium finally consolidated the same year after a period of crisis with the U. K. partners. But the worm was in the fruit. One of the longstanding features of French economic performance has been the congenital weakness of industrial exports. During a transitory period, this weakness was masked by a number of successes in high-technology systemic products and the good performance of the car industry. Now that arms exports have fallen and that automobile sales have begun to collapse, the vulnerability of the system can no longer be masked.

French Technological Performance as Measured by Patenting in the United States

Today patents are considered by many scholars to represent, despite numerous caveats, a reasonable proxy for innovative activity. One drawback, which is evidenced by the French situation, is that although the granting of a patent recognizes technical novelty and may thus be one measure of technological output, *the possession of patents does not guarantee subsequent competitive commercial application, sales, and exports.* In a context where nuclear plants have practically stopped being built in the world, this is the case, for instance, for nuclear power technology. Despite this, it is interesting to look at the French data, which show the areas where France produces internationally recognized technical novelty even if this does not necessarily lead to commercially successful products.

Pavitt and Patel (1990) collected information on the national origin of U. S. patents granted over a century (1883–1987) and compared the long-term trend of French patenting with that of the United Kingdom and Germany. Outside the disruption caused by two World Wars, France has tended to improve its position compared to the United Kingdom. This trend was particularly marked from 1900 to 1910 and in the 1920s, and has occurred again since 1970: in 1987, for the first time, France was granted more U. S. patents than the United Kingdom. The comparison with Germany is also revealing. Earlier this century German patents were about four times the French level. Since the late 1950s, France has reduced this gap. German patents in the United States have stabilized to about 2.8 times the French level.

Pavitt and Patel have also calculated an index of "revealed technology advantage" (RTA), which confirms quite logically France's relative strength in sectors dominated by public procurement and State funding of technical activities. In 1981–1986, three of the first five sectors with the strongest RTA in France were in this category, as were six of the eleven with an RTA of 1.10 or more: nuclear reactors, aircraft, telecommunications, other transport (in particular, railways and railway equipment), electrical devices (in particular electrical transmission to vehicles), and normal electrical power plants.

Using the patent data in the U. S. office for 1981–1987 and for 1982–1987, the data provided on a comparable basis by patenting at the European Patent Office as well as the results of current research on patent citation, Archibugi and Pianta (1992) calculated their own index of specialization and ranked the major OECD countries according to their top five fields of technological excellence. In the case of France, Table 6.1 lists these results.

Using SIC classes instead of IPC classes and extending the data to include citations, Archibugi and Pianta present the following picture of French specialization (Table 6.2).

Table 6.1. French Technological Performance as Measured by Patenting

Patents Granted in the United States (1981–1987)				
Nuclear physics	Medical preparation	Mining	Weapons	Engineering
3.14	1.64	1.48	1.40	1.36
Patents Granted at the EPO (1982–1987)				
Nuclear physics	Building	Lighting and heating	Transport	Agriculture
2.63	1.65	1.60	1.59	1.54

Pavitt and Patel have also examined the relative performance in U. S. patenting of large firms (French and foreign controlled), State agencies, and smaller firms. Large French and foreign-based firms are particularly important in the R&D-intensive sectors (chemicals, electrical–electronics, aerospace) and in automobiles. The data confirm the strong contribution of State agencies, in particular in technologies related to energy (EDF, CEA). The overall percentage of patenting associated with smaller domestic firms is high, 37.2%, and is hardly lower than the one for the large domestic firms. This does not fit with the findings on formal R&D and points to a much greater amount of innovative activity by small firms than that reflected in the formal R&D data. It points to a largely unresearched area of the French innovation system.

Pavitt and Patel have also identified the French-owned organizations appearing in the list of the top 20 U. S. patentors for 33 sectors. Very few rank in the top U. S. 10; most of those that do are either State agencies or firms heavily dependent on State markets and State R&D funding: Creusot-Loire (now Franmatome) and CEA in the electronuclear branch; SNIAS (now Aerospatiale) and SNECMA in aerospace; and Thomson in defense-related telecommunications. Only l'Oréal (soaps, detergents, body care products) and Michelin (tires) belong completely to the private sector.

The Commercial Performance of French Innovation: Exports and Imports

In an international economic system where the social validation of production-related activities occurs mainly at the level of the market through successful commercialization, the foreign trade performance of an economy may reflect the efficiency of its innovation system better than patents.

In the case of France, foreign trade indicators reveal a serious situation (Economie et Statistiques, 1989; OECD, 1990). Despite favorable conditions regarding price competitiveness French industrial exports have experienced a long downward trend since the late 1970s, while imports have risen continuously. Recent studies stress a number of structural weaknesses; in particular, aging productive capacities, an insufficient rate of investment, a propensity (shaped by decades of selling to protected political markets) to impose higher profit margins on exports than on domestic sales, considerable difficulties on the part of executives and managers in abandoning the traditional Fordist–Taylorist model of corporate management, and significant obstacles to horizontal interindustry and intersectoral transfers of technology. These are due to the vertical organization of innovation in many sectors and to the barriers that characterize economies where arms industries occupy a central role within the high-technology complex. The system is ill-equipped to satisfy the requirements of the generic technologies. Barriers to interindustry flows of technology have been further accen-

Table 6.2. French Specialization, 1975–81 and 1982–88

Indicator	Top 5 SIC Classes With the Highest Specialization Indexes for Patents and Patent Citations				
	1	2	3	4	5
Pat.75–81	Drugs & Medicines	Agric. & Other Chem.	Guid Miss.Space Veh.	Aircr.Oth.Mech.Parts	Ship,Boat Building
Pat.82–88	Guid Miss.Space Veh.	Railroad Equipment	Soaps,Detergents	Aircr.Oth.Mech.Parts	Drugs & Medicines
Cit.75–81	Guid Miss.Space Veh.	Motorcycles & Parts	Aircr.Oth.Mech.Parts	Drugs & Medicines	Ship,Boat Building
Cit.82–88	Guid Miss.Space Veh.	Railroad Equipment	Soaps,Detergents	Ship,Boat Building	Aircr.Oth.Mech.Parts

Table 6.3. Commodity Breakdown of the Trade Balance: Customs Basis, CIF-FOB, as a Percentage of GDP

	1982	1983	1984	1985	1986	1987	1988	1989
Agrofood products	0.4	0.6	0.6	0.7	0.5	0.6	0.7	0.8
Energy	−4.9	−4.2	−4.3	−3.8	−1.8	−1.5	−1.2	−1.4
Industrial goods	0.9	1.6	2.3	1.9	0.7	−0.2	−0.7	−0.9
Consumer goods	−0.6	−0.4	−0.3	−0.3	−0.5	−0.8	−0.8	−0.7
Intermediate goods	−0.1	0.1	0.2	0.2	−0.2	−0.3	−0.4	−0.7
Producer durable goods	0.4	0.7	0.8	0.6	0.2	−0.1	−0.4	−0.3
Land transport equipment	0.6	0.6	0.8	0.7	0.6	0.4	0.4	0.3
Military hardware and other	0.6	0.6	0.9	0.8	0.7	0.5	0.5	0.5
Total	−3.6	−2.0	−1.4	−1.3	−0.6	−1.1	−1.2	−1.5

Sources: Direction générale des douanes et des droits indirects, INSEE, and OECD Secretariat estimates.

tuated by a strong element of *secrecy* stemming from the important military component of technology production: this is at least one reason for the weakness of the French electronics industry.

As shown in Table 6.3, the weaknesses in French industry are particularly pronounced in the capital and equipment goods industries. This is both a consequence of several of the factors listed above and a source per se of structural weakness. This pivot function of the capital goods industries in the diffusion of new or best practice technology is well established: when these industries begin to collapse, the performance of the entire manufacturing sector will be affected. Figure 6.7 shows that the deterioration of the French trade balance is particularly marked in the case of low-technology industries, where performance was satisfactory until the early 1980s. The deterioration has

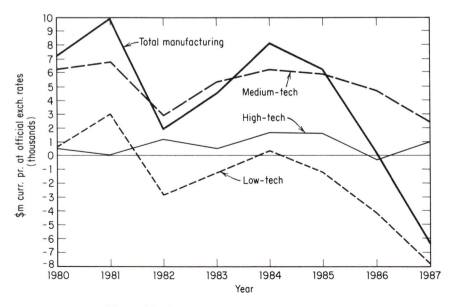

Figure 6.7. France: trade by R&D intensity groups.

also concerned the medium-technology industries, as well as the high-technology sector.

As shown in Table 6.4, the overall positive balance in the high-technology sector is really *due to only two industry groups,* drugs and medicines and aerospace (civil and military). Now that the car industry has begun to collapse in the face of German and, despite trade barriers, of Japanese competition, the structural deficiencies of French manufacturing have become evident.

The current failure of industrial exports is the inevitable outcome of what Pavitt calls the *"myopic"* traits of the industrial and technological system. It cannot be attributed to an insufficient *level* of French R&D expenditures in industry. As Barré (1988) has shown, this is comparable to that of France's major competitors, once account is made of the industrial structure by branches. But it does have a lot to do with the *structure* of industrial R&D, the *priorities* chosen, and the institutional context in which R&D is undertaken and its results taken to the market. The failure of exports is the combined result of the inherent difficulties of selling large system-like products in an economic context marked by strong monetary instability and high levels of public debt (even outside Third World countries) and of an industrial and technological structure particularly not prone to horizontal linkages between industrial branches, the exploi-

Table 6.4. France Export/Import Ratio

	1980	1981	1982	1983	1984	1985	1986	1987
Food, beverages, and tobacco	1.19	1.28	1.18	1.12	1.17	1.15	1.16	1.20
Textiles, leather, and shoes	0.86	0.85	0.77	0.79	0.81	0.81	0.72	0.68
Wood, cork, furniture	0.47	0.52	0.48	0.52	0.54	0.55	0.49	0.47
Paper and printing	0.60	0.60	0.58	0.60	0.62	0.64	0.62	0.62
Chemicals	1.03	1.11	1.00	1.16	1.19	1.19	1.13	1.12
Drugs and medicines	2.17	1.98	3.76	1.95	1.97	1.99	1.90	1.80
Petroleum refineries	0.83	0.85	0.56	0.55	0.58	0.57	0.52	0.37
Rubber, plastic	1.27	1.29	1.23	1.22	1.26	1.24	1.16	1.07
Pottery, china, glass	0.98	1.06	1.06	1.22	1.22	1.19	1.01	0.97
Ferrous metals	1.36	1.61	1.38	1.42	1.51	1.52	1.37	1.30
Nonferrous metals	0.66	0.71	0.65	0.75	0.77	0.73	0.70	0.72
Metal products	1.22	1.29	1.10	1.18	1.17	1.00	0.86	0.77
Nonelectrical machinery	1.14	1.19	1.11	1.18	1.15	1.11	0.98	0.87
Office machinery, computers	0.75	0.74	0.58	0.65	0.69	0.66	0.70	0.71
Electrical machinery	1.26	1.30	1.22	1.26	1.26	1.22	1.08	1.00
Electronic components	0.85	0.80	0.78	0.94	0.93	1.00	0.90	0.87
Other transport	1.81	2.55	2.18	2.31	2.19	2.49	1.95	1.60
Shipbuilding	2.05	3.32	1.99	3.20	3.67	2.05	2.94	2.21
Vehicles	1.74	1.58	1.32	1.35	1.49	1.41	1.33	1.21
Aerospace	1.33	1.19	1.72	1.50	2.20	2.06	1.56	1.62
Scientific instruments	0.80	0.78	0.75	0.79	0.87	0.94	0.81	0.80
Other manufacturing	0.73	0.85	0.85	0.85	0.95	0.96	0.88	0.78
NEC	2.94	3.41	4.00	4.26	4.48	4.96	3.37	2.79
Total manufacturing	1.08	1.12	1.02	1.06	1.11	1.08	1.00	0.95
Sum of above	1.08	1.12	1.02	1.06	1.11	1.08	1.00	0.95
High-technology industries	1.03	1.01	1.09	1.04	1.12	1.11	0.99	0.96
Medium-technology industries	1.16	1.21	1.09	1.18	1.21	1.19	1.11	1.05
Low-technology industries	1.01	1.08	0.94	0.96	1.01	0.97	0.91	0.86

tation of externalities, and the flexibilities required for a proper user within manufacturing of information technology. The critical assessment that several U. S. groups (cf. the MIT study of U. S. industrial competitiveness or the studies at BRIE) have recently presented regarding U. S. industrial organization (the emphasis on hierarchy, the difficulty of cooperating, the antagonistic relationships between management and workers) is pari passu applicable to French industry, with the particular rigidities of a State-led system added for good measure.

NOTES

1. For details of the way traditional production of the Bordeaux wines was established on proper scientific and technological foundations after 1945, see Ribéreau-Gayon (1972) and Peynaud (1988).
2. In the *Competitive Advantage of Nations* Michael Porter (1990) points to the software service industry, in particular for customized products not controlled by the large manufacturers, as being an industry in which France has a recognized position. For a French view, see Horaist (1986).
3. Gilpin (1968, p. 106) offers the following overall assessment:

The heroic period of French science, from 1800 to 1830, was the product of two important factors: Revolutionary and Napoleonic reforms had established institutions and an environment where French genius could flourish; and knowledge in many fields had advanced to the point where it lent itself to mastery by the peculiar strengths of the French mind. Around 1800, in chemistry, natural history, physiology, and other areas, someone was needed to bring order to the disarray of conflicting opinions and positions. Such a task required the patience, brilliance, and individuality of men like Lavoisier who founded the use of precise measurements in chemistry and systematized the subject. French genius fashioned the paradigms, or revolutionary new theories, that guided scientific research for much of the nineteenth century. As John Merz has pointed out in his History of European Thought "in France during the early part of the century the foundations of nearly all the modern sciences were laid. Many of them were brought under the rule of strict mathematical treatment."

4. Important protestant names in French industry based in the Mulhouse, Belfort, Montbeliard region include Schlumberger, Dollfus, Koechlin, and Japy with whom the Peugeot brothers later had ties by marriage (see Caron, 1987).
5. See inter alia Palmade (1961), Cameron (1961), Kindleberger (1964), and Caron (1979).
6. See Landes (1949, 1951). For counterarguments and qualifications of Landes' positions see Levy-Leboyer (1974).
7. See Stanley Hoffman's assessment of France as a "stalemate society" marked by (1) a preference for stability and protection over growth and competition, (2) a Malthusian fear of overproduction of material goods and of educated people, (3) the burden of social, religious, and political conflict, (4) the fragmented structure and conservatism of French industry, and (5) the domination of agrarian and colonial interests over domestic industrial interests (Hoffman, 1963).
8. For this section see Gilpin (1968, Chapter 6), Papon (1978, Chapter 2), OECD (1966), and Rouban (1974). A somewhat unimaginative history of the CNRS is also available; see Picard (1990).
9. For a detailed presentation of these reforms, see OECD (1986) and for a critical assessment, Salomon (1986).
10. See the lengthy annual *Rapport sur l'état de la recherche et du développement techno-*

logique, annexed each year to the *Projet de Loi de Finances* presented to tne Parliament before the discussion and vote of the French budget. This report is available each year in October.

11. The compartmentalized character of the French innovative system has recently been recognized by one of the few critical studies on technological policy produced within the French political machinery, the *"Rapport Farge":* see Commissariat Général du Plan (1989, p. 22).

12. Research by Richard Kuisel (1981) shows that this position cannot be attributed solely to left wing ideologists and the governments they inspired in 1936–1937 or 1946–1948, but was prepared in the 1930s within very conservative industrial circles to which men such as Joan Mounet belonged.

13. McArthur and Scott (1969) add that in the course of their research "it soon became evident that the *state-company relationship* and *not* the planning process *per se* was the most important determinant of corporate strategic planning in France."

14. A first class analysis in English of the "Ecoles," the "Corps," and the organization and power of the French industrial–political–financial élite can be found in Suleiman (1978).

15. The French set-up based on DGA procurement and the organization of R&D in a highly specialized subsidized firm (Compagnie Industrielle des Lasers) belonging to CGE was very successful in a purely military context but a complete failure once civil demand became important. See Cohendet and Llerena (1991, Chapter 1).

16. Although it arose from the need to avoid depending on imports of foreign-enriched uranium along with possible U. S. embargoes, the choice of a graphite-gas reactor system was really the logical outcome of the decision taken in 1956–1957 to construct plutonium-generating reactors in order to obtain plutonium for military purposes. By 1965–1966, it had become clear that the achievement of the political aim of possessing at an extremely high price nuclear weapons had led France up a blind alley with respect to the production of electricity, where cost considerations could not be waved aside as in the military field. For a detailed discussion see Papon (1975, 1979), Gilpin (1968), and Salomon (1986).

17. Through this particular way of planning for markets and winning them in arms, conventional and nuclear power production, telecommunication equipment, or urban transport systems (as well as in the large scale civil engineering operations that go along with these where some of France's most powerful industrial groups such as Bouygues are now located) corruption has crept into the pores of the French administration, political life, and society. The process has, of course, been powerfully aided by the constitutional structure of the Fifth Republic, which lays almost total and uncontrolled power into the hands of the Executive. France is not a land of Watergates or even of Colonel North type congressional and judicial investigations. The French politicians, bankers, industrialists, and generals can sleep in peace: behind a facade of formalistic legal control of legislation and administrative procedures by the Conseil Constitutionnel and the Conseil d'Etat, corruption is rampant and goes unpunished. The Parliament has no powers and the rule is that the "party of the President," be it Gaullist, Giscardian, or Socialist, must smother any difference it may have with the President and vote obediently to a man.

18. During this project there was no time to undertake the detailed work required to understand the exact configuration of the innovation system in the chemicals–pharmaceuticals–agrochemicals complex. The weight of the business enterprise component is obviously much more important than in those related to electronics and arms, but the State is present in many significant ways. The most important is the role it plays from time to time in industrial restructuring, the definition of new corporate boundaries, and the provision of finance. The last time this occurred was in 1982, with the redistribution of industrial assets between three major groups, Rhone-Poulenc, Elf-Sanofi, and CDF-Chimie, the last two of which have state capital. While R&D capacity is strongly lodged within these groups, they can also count on technology transfer from the nonprofit and public sectors. A good example concerns the results of the Institut Pasteur, which are commercialized through Diagnostics-Pasteur, a joint venture in partnership with Elf-Sanofi and Pasteur-Mérieux-Sérums et Vaccins, where the partnership is with Rhone-Poulenc.

REFERENCES

Archibugi, D., and Pianta, M. (1992). *The Techno-logical Specialization of Advanced Countries: A Report to the EEC.* Dordrecht: Kluwer Academic Publishers.

Barré, R. (1988). "La faiblesse de la recherche indus-trielle française: de quoi parle-t-on?" *Culture Technique* 18 (March): 210–19.

Bauer, M. (1987). *Les 200: comment devient-on un grand patron?* Paris: Le Seuil.

Callon, M. (1987). "La recherche française est-elle en bonne santé." *La Recherche* 186 (Avril–Mai).

Cameron, R. E. (1961). *France and the Economic Development of Europe, 1800–1914.* Princeton: Princeton University Press.

Caron, P. (1979). *An Economic History of Modern France.* New York: Columbia University Press.

Caron, P. (1987). "La capacité d'innovation tech-nique de l'industrie française." *Le Débat* 46 (Sep-tembre–Novembre).

Carter, E. C., Foster, R., and Moody, J. N. (eds.) (1976). *Enterprise and Entrepreneurs in Nine-teenth and Twentieth Century France,* Baltimore, MD: Johns Hopkins University Press.

Chesnais, F., and Serfati, C. (1990). "L'industrie d'armement: une locomotive du développement économique français?" In F. Chesnais (ed.), *Com-pétitivité internationale et dépenses militaires.* Paris: Economica.

Chesnais, F., and Serfati, C. (1992). *L'armement en France: genèse, ampleur et coûts d'une industrie.* Paris: Nathan.

Cohen, S. (1969). *Modern Capitalist Planning: The French Model.* Cambridge, MA: Harvard Univer-sity Press.

Cohendet, P., and Llerena, P. (eds.) (1991). *Modes of Use and Diffusion of New Technologies and New Knowledge: The Case of France.* BETA, Uni-versity of Strasbourg, Report for the EC MONI-TOR-FAST programme, FOP No. 228, Bruxelles.

Commissariat Général du Plan. (1989). *La Science, la Technologie, l'Innovation: une politique glob-ale, rapport de l'intergroupe Recherche et Devel-oppement Technologique.* Paris: La Documenta-tion Française, Juin.

Conseil Economique et Social. (1989). *L'économie française souffre-t-elle d'une insuffisance de recherche?* Avis et rapport, Journal officiel de la République française, vendredi 2 juin, No. 13.

Crossland, M. (1975). "The Development of a Pro-fessional Career in Science in France." *Minerva* 13(1): 38–57.

Debeir, S. C., Deléage, J. P., and Hemery, D. (1989). *Les servitudes de la puissance: une histoire de l'é-nergie en France.* Paris: Flammarion.

Dhombres, N. (1988). *Les savants en révolution, 1789–1799.* Paris: Editions de la Cité des Sciences et de l'Industrie.

Ergas, H. (1984). "Why Do Some Countries Inno-vate More than Others?" Brussels: Centre for European Policy Studies, CEPS Paper No. 5.

Ergas, H. (1987). "Does Technology Policy Matter." In B. R. Guile and H. Brooks (eds.), *Technology and Global Industry.* Washington, D.C.: National Academy Press.

Fox, R., and Weisz, G. (1980). "The Institutional Basis of French Science in the 19th Century." In R. Fox and G. Weisz (eds.), *The Organisation of Science and Technology in France, 1808–1914.* Cambridge, England: Cambridge University Press.

Gillispie, C. C. (1980). *Science and Polity in France at the End of the Old Regime.* Princeton: Prince-ton University Press.

Gilpin, R. (1968). *France in the Age of the Scientific State.* Princeton: Princeton University Press.

Granick, D. (1964). *The European Executive.* New York: Doubleday.

Hoffman, S. (1963). "Paradoxes of the French Polit-ical Community." In S. Hoffman (ed.), *In Search of France.* Cambridge MA: Harvard University Press.

Horaist, J. (1986). "Les sociétés françaises de service et d'ingénierie en informatique: historique et perspectives." *Economie et Prévisions,* 72: 33–48.

Kindleberger C. P. (1964). *Economic Growth in France and Britain.* Cambridge, MA: Harvard University Press.

Kindleberger C. P. (1976). "Technical Education and the French Entrepreneur." In E. C. Carter, R. Foster, and J. N. Moody (eds.), *Enterprise and Entrepreneurs in Nineteenth and Twentieth Cen-tury France.* Baltimore: Johns Hopkins Univer-sity Press.

Kolodziej, E. J. (1987). *Making and Marketing of Arms: The French Experience and Its Implica-tions for the International System.* Princeton: Princeton University Press.

Kuisel, R. F. (1981). *Capitalism and the State in France: Modernisation and Dirigism in the 20th Century.* Cambridge, England: Cambridge Uni-versity Press.

Landes, D. S. (1949). "French Entrepreneurship and Industrial Growth in the 19th Century." *Journal of Economic History* 9(1): 1–22.

Landes, D. S. (1959). "French Business and Busi-nessmen in Social and Cultural Analysis." In E. M. Earle (ed.), *Modern France.* Princeton: Prince-ton University Press.

McArthur, J. H., and Scott, B. R. (1969). *Industrial Planning in France.* Boston: Harvard Graduate School of Business Administration.

Monjardet, D. (1972). "Carrière des dirigeants et contrôle de l'entreprise." *Sociologie du Travail,* No. 2.

OECD (1966). *Reviews of National Science Policy: France.* Paris: OECD.

OECD (1986). *Innovation Policy: France.* Paris: OECD.

OECD (1988). *New Telecommunications Services: Videotex Development Strategies.* Paris: OECD.

OECD (1990). *Economic Surveys: France 1989–1990.* Paris: OECD.

Palmade, G. P. (1961). *Capitalisme et capitalistes français au XIXe siècle*. Paris: Armand Colin.

Papon, P. (1975). "The State and Technological Competition in France or Colbertism in the 20th Century." *Research Policy* 4: 214–45.

Papon, P. (1978). *Le pouvoir et la science en France*. Paris: Le Centurion.

Pavitt, K., and Patel, P. (1990). "L'accumulation technologique en France: ce que les statistiques de brevets tendent à montrer." *Revue d'Economie Industrielle*. 51 (Spring): 10–32. (Also available in English as a SPRU working paper.)

Peynaud, E. (1988). *Le vin et les jours*. Paris: Dunod.

Picard, S. F. (1990). *La République des Savants*. Paris: Flammarion.

Porter, M. (1990). *The Competitive Advantage of Countries*. London: Macmillan.

Prestre, D. (1984). *Physique et physiciens en France 1918–1940*. Paris: Editions des Archives Contemporaines.

République Française. (1991). *Rapport sur l'état de la recherche et du développement technologique en 1989 et 1990*, annexed to the *Projet de Loi de Finances* 1991.

Ribéreau-Gayon, J. (1972). *Problèmes de la recherche scientifique et technologique en oenologie*. Paris: Dunod.

Rouban, L. (1988). *L'Etat et la Science: La politique publique de la science et de la technologie*. Paris: Edition CNRS.

Salomon J. J. (1986). *Le Gaulois, le Cowboy et le Samourai: la politique française de la technologie*. Paris: Economica.

Salomon J. J. (1991). "La capacité d'innovation." In M. Levy-Leboyer (ed.), *Entre l'Etat et le marché: l'économie de la France au XXe siècle*. Paris: Gallimard.

Salomon-Bayet, C. (1986). *Pasteur et la révolution pasteurienne*. Paris: Payot.

Serfati, C. (1991). "Primauté des technologies militaires, faiblesse des retombées civiles et déclin de compétitivité: Le cas de l'industrie électronique française." Paper for the Conference on the Social Mastery of Technology, Maison Rhone-Alpes des Sciences de l'Homme, Lyon, September.

Shinn, T. (1981). *L'Ecole Polytechnique en France, 1794–1914*. Paris: Fondation Nationale des Sciences Politiques.

Shinn, T. (1984). "Reactionary Technologists: The Struggle over the Ecole Polytechnique 1880–1914." *Minerva* 22(3–4): 329–45.

Suleiman, E. N. (1978). *Elites in French Society: The Politics of Survival*. Princeton: Princeton University Press.

Zwerling, C. (1980). "The Emergence of the Ecole Nationale Supérieure as a Centre of Scientific Education in France." In R. Fox and G. Weisz (eds.), *The Organisation of Science and Technology in France, 1808–1914*. Cambridge, England: Cambridge University Press.

7

The National System of Innovation: Italy

FRANCO MALERBA

Italy represents one of the success stories of postwar economic growth. Over the past 40 years, GNP growth has been higher in Italy than in most other industrialized countries. Similarly, productivity and income per capita have risen rapidly and manufacturing exports have increased considerably. In a relatively short period of time Italy has been transformed from an agricultural and semi-industrialized country to an advanced industrial economy. In addition, during the 1980s Italy experienced high growth rates in R&D, although Italian international specialization remains mainly in traditional products such as textile and shoes, as well as in mechanics and industrial equipment.

What kind of national system of innovation lies at the base of the economic success story of the past 40 years? Why is it that the R&D growth of the 1980s did not translate into successful performance in high technology products?

Without considering the distinction between the developed north and center and the underdeveloped south, a full understanding of the Italian system of innovation during the 1980s and the 1990s has to start from the recognition that not one, but two innovation systems are present in Italy: a small firms network and a core R&D system. These two systems are quite different in terms of capabilities, organization, and performance. The small firms network is composed of a large population of small and medium size firms (in some cases located in industrial districts), which interact intensively at the local level. The core R&D system is composed of large firms with industrial laboratories, small high-technology firms, universities, large public research institutes, and the national government, linked through a complex organizational system at the national level.

This chapter claims that the small firms network, grown up historically on a local, regional, and vocational basis and characterized by capabilities accumulated through productive experience, has worked effectively and performed successfully during the past decades up until now. Firms in the network are engaged in rapid adoption of technology generated externally and in the adaptation and continuous improvement of this technology. The success of the system is based on the atomistic interaction of a large number of firms bound to each other by economic, local, cultural, and social factors. Firms incrementally innovate through learning by doing, by using, and by interacting with suppliers and users. They communicate in a formal as well as an informal way, share tacit knowledge, and are characterized by high labor mobility. The role of regional agencies, local public authorities, and local professional schools is effective in supporting the needs and requirements of small firms in the area.

The core R&D system, much more recent than the small firms network and developed at a much later stage than those of countries such as Germany, the United Kingdom, France, and the United States, is not characterized by advanced technological capabilities and does not perform satisfactorily in terms of innovation and international competitiveness. In Italy, in spite of relevant quantitative growth of R&D during the 1980s, some of the qualitative elements needed for an effective and successful working of such a complex system are still missing or are not fully developed. First, several industrial sectors do not have advanced research and technological capabilities. Second, public policy of R&D support still exhibits major flaws. Third, an advanced national infrastructure of services for R&D and an overall coordination of public policies are still lacking. Fourth, advanced basic research performed in universities and public research centers is very unevenly distributed across institutions. Fifth, shortages of skilled scientists and engineers are present. Finally, there is no tradition of successful industry–university cooperation in research.

It must be noted that within and across these two systems, dynamic vicious and virtuous cycles have reinforced the characteristics of each specific system. In the small firms network, horizontal and vertical linkages have generated virtuous cycles of learning and incremental innovation, which have been at the base of the successful performance of Italian small and medium firms over the past decades. In the core R&D system, the lack of advanced capabilities in several components has generated vicious cycles that have blocked the full development and the successful performance of high technology industries in Italy.

This chapter will discuss and analyze the following areas: the history and the dualism of Italian industry, the main features of the small firms network, and the core R&D system. Finally, the virtuous and vicious cycles that have taken place between and within the two systems are analyzed.

HISTORY AND BASIC FEATURES

A Recent Industrialization

Italy was a late industrializer (Graziani, 1979). Although industries such as steel, auto, electrical machinery, and chemical were in existence before World War II, Italy did not develop a modern industry until the 1950s. This meant that advanced technological and productive capabilities, managerial skills, and an infrastructure typical of other industrialized countries began to emerge only in the last 40 years (Malerba and Falzoni, 1991).

A Lack of Tradition in R&D

In Italy there is no tradition of industrial R&D that dates back to the end of last century and the first half of this century. Some centers of excellence existed in a few firms (such as Montecatini), but in general until the second half of the twentieth century Italian firms spent very little on R&D (Sapelli, 1989). As Table 7.1 shows, during the 1950s

Table 7.1. Share of R&D Expenditures on GDP[a]

	1955	1963–1964	1970s	1985–1987	1989
Italy	0.2	0.6	0.7–0.8	1.2	1.3
Germany	0.6[b]	0.3	2.3–2.4	2.7	2.9
France	0.8[c]	1.9	1.8	2.3	2.3
United Kingdom	1.6[d]	2.3	2.2	2.2	n.a.
United States	3.0[e]	3.4	2.3–2.5	2.8	2.8
Japan	n.a.	1.4	2.0	2.8	n.a.

[a]The data for the 1955 column are approximate values; [b]1954; [c]1960; [d]1956–1957; [e]1959–60.

and 1960s, Italy was a low R&D intensive country and a technological follower. During the 1950s, 1960s, and 1970s, a large part of the technical change introduced by Italian firms was through licenses obtained from foreign firms.

A High R&D Growth during the 1980s

Between 1980 and 1987, R&D expenditures grew at an annual rate of 9.9% in real terms, a value higher than most OECD countries. This was due both to an increase in R&D done by business enterprises (9.4%) and by the public sector (10.6%). The public sector became a major source of funds for R&D: between 1980 and 1987 R&D funding from the public sector grew at an annual rate of 12.6% in real terms, while funding from business enterprises grew at an annual rate of 6.5% in real terms.

A Dualistic Country in Terms of Firm Size and North–South Differences

The rapid post-World War II economic growth occurred within a dualistic economy in terms of firm size and geography. Small firms are quite numerous in traditional and specialized supplier sectors, which constitute a major part of Italian industry (see Table 7.2). In 1981 employment in plants of less than 100 employees represented 59% of total employment in industry, a share much higher than the one of the other main industrial countries with the exception of Japan. On the other hand, the core of Italian

Table 7.2. Number of Employees in Manufacturing Industry According to Pavitt's Taxonomy

	Absolute Values				Percent Values			
Sectors	1981	1971	1961	1951	1981	1971	1961	1951
Science based	329,134	237,383	180,200	97,528	5.41	4.48	4.01	2.79
Specialized suppliers	703,363	520,232	429,437	284,370	11.55	9.81	9.55	8.13
Scale intensive	1,895,526	1,764,353	1,378,429	1,048,569	31.14	33.28	30.66	29.97
Suppliers dominated	2,714,848	2,452,909	2,292,345	1,957,486	44.60	46.26	50.99	55.96
Others	444,162	326,969	215,152	110,267	7.30	6.17	4.79	3.15
Total manufacturing industry	6,087,033	5,301,846	4,495,563	3,498,220	100	100	100	100

Source: Malerba and Falzoni (1991).

industry is made up of large firms, active mainly in scale-intensive and high-technology sectors.

Most of the large Italian firms and the bulk of technologically advanced industry is located in the northern regions. The south of Italy is characterized by a limited degree of industrialization, by a low R&D intensity, and a limited diffusion of advanced technologies (Romano, 1989), as Table 7.3 shows.

The Role of Public Enterprises in R&D Growth

Another feature of the Italian industry is related to the presence of public enterprises in scale-intensive and high-technology industries such as electronics, steel, food, aerospace, and military. During the 1960s and 1970s public enterprises played a major role in maintaining an indigenous capability in sectors such as electronics and aerospace. Furthermore during the 1980s they made a major contribution to the impressive growth rate of R&D (they had a 10.8% annual real growth rate, compared to 8.6% of

Table 7.3. Italy: North–South Differences

1987	Center–North	South	Italy
Population	70	30	100
Value-added	82	18	100
Exports	90	10	100
Public sector expenditure in R&D	91	9	100
Private sector expenditure in R&D	97	3	100

Source: ISTAT

R&D/Value Added of Industrial Firms	1983
Northwest	1.4
Northeast–center	0.4
South	0.2
Italy	0.7

Source: Santarelli and Sterlacchini (1989).

	Center–North	South
Telephone density	100	59
Bank branches density	100	53
Railway electrification rates	100	43

Source: OECD (1990).

Flexible Automation	Share of Total Production Systems	Share of Total CAD Systems
Northwest	63.9	52.5
Northeast	28.4	32.9
Center	5.6	9.7
South	2.1	4.9
Italy	100.0	100.0

Source: MIP—Politecnico of Milan (1989).

private enterprises). In several circumstances their role as engine of technological change in Italy has been impaired by political obligations to save industries in crisis and to be active in the south.

The Beginning of the Internationalization Process of the 1980s

Until recently Italian industry has not shown a high degree of internationalization. Italian firms in traditional sectors such as textiles, shoes, and furniture have been major exporters, but foreign direct investments by Italian industry have been scarce (9% of total employment in 1989) and the presence of foreign multinational corporations in Italy has been limited (13% of total employment in Italy in 1989). Only recently the beginning of a move toward greater internationalization of activities and cooperative agreements has taken place in Italian industry (Onida and Viesti, 1987; Mariotti et al., 1986; Cominotti and Mariotti, 1990).

THE SMALL FIRMS NETWORK

A large part of Italian industry is composed of a large group of small and medium size firms operating in traditional industries (such as textile and clothing, shoes, furniture), in mechanics, and in equipment supplier industries. These firms are specialized in the supply of custom made products and of fashion items. Most of them assemble and integrate existing components and parts into systems for special applications or specific customers. These firms are highly profitable and quite successful internationally. Over the past decades, this group of firms has given extreme flexibility and high adaptability to Italian industry during the business cycle.

These small and medium size firms form a highly dynamic atomistic learning network. They are characterized by advanced capabilities of absorbing, adapting, improving, and tailoring new technologies (developed externally) to specific market needs.

Innovation originates not from formal R&D, but from informal learning by doing, by using, and by interacting. Engineering skills, product know-how, and understanding customers' requirements are the major sources of incremental innovations and product customization by this group of firms. These characteristics emerge clearly from Table 7.4, constructed from a major survey carried out by ISTAT in 1988 and concerning innovation in more than 8000 firms. Table 7.4 identifies the cost of innovation, the sources of innovation, and the relevance of collaboration in R&D for small firms compared to large and medium size firms.

Three types of firms can be identified in this network: firms in the industrial district, equipment producers, and traditional firms.

The Industrial District

In industrial districts, characterized by both cultural and social homogeneity and developed historically on a vocational basis, technical change occurs through horizontal linkages among a large number of small and medium size firms (Becattini, 1987, 1989). These districts are active in several industries and are located in various Italian

Table 7.4. Main Differences in the Innovation Process between Small, Medium, and Large Firms[a]

	Cost of Innovation (share of total cost)				
	R&D	Design Engineering	Productive Investments	Marketing	Percent
Small firms	8.5	16.3	70.7	4.5	100
Medium firms	12.9	17.0	65.0	5.2	100
Large firms	21.4	29.5	43.5	5.6	100
Total firms	18.0	25.2	43.5	5.4	100

	Sources of Innovation (values 1 to 6)				
	R&D	Design	Inside Proposals	Purchase of Technology	Raw Materials	Intermediate Goods
Small firms	1.7	2.8	2.0	0.3	1.2	0.8
Medium firms	2.8	3.5	2.9	0.7	1.2	0.8
Large firms	3.9	4.2	3.5	1.5	1.2	0.9
Total firms	2.1	3.1	2.3	0.5	1.2	0.8

	New Machinery	Human Skills	Professional Training	Customers Needs	Suppliers
Small firms	4.0	1.0	2.0	2.3	1.5
Medium firms	4.1	1.4	2.5	2.4	1.7
Large firms	3.9	1.7	3.1	2.7	2.1
Total firms	4.0	1.2	2.2	2.3	1.6

	Joint Ventures	Industrial Exhibitions	Public Institutions	Consultants	Imitation
Small firms	0.2	1.5	0.2	0.6	1.8
Medium firms	0.3	1.5	0.4	0.8	2.2
Large firms	0.7	1.4	0.9	1.0	2.7
Total firms	0.3	1.5	0.3	0.7	2.0

	Collaboration in R&D (share of the total number of innovative firms)				
	Total	Public Institutions	University	Customers	Suppliers
Small firms	8.8	16.8	23.6	39.4	61.2
Medium firms	20.9	24.4	37.6	37.3	55.4
Large firms	45.2	50.3	72.6	35.7	52.2
Total firms	13.9	28.2	37.9	39.4	57.4

[a]Small firms, 20–99 employees; medium firms, 100–499 employees; large firms, 500 employees and more.
Source: ISTAT (1988).

regions: textile in Prato, Como (silk), Biella, Carpi (knit); shoes in Vigevano, Barletta, and Casarano; furniture in Brianza and Udine; ceramic tile in Sassuolo; gold jewelry in Valenza Po and Arezzo; and household products in Lumezzane.

Some of these districts have been in existence for decades: such is the case of the textile districts in northern Italy. Other industrial districts grew up during the 1960s and 1970s, such as Sassuolo (Russo, 1985), Prato (Rullani and Zanfei, 1988a), and Valdarno Inferiore (Gandolfi, 1988).

In these districts the division of labor among small and medium size firms is high and the productive flexibility and adaptability to changing market demand at the final product level are substantial (Becattini, 1987; Nuti, 1988). Most firms specialize in only one stage of the production process: only a few firms eventually internalize more than one stage of the production process and eventually sell the final product. As these Italian districts are involved in a variety of technologies and industries, the organization of production varies from case to case. For example, in the shoe districts, design is developed externally, the sole and the heel are purchased from large firms, the various production stages are done by small specialized firms, and the sale and distribution by another firm (which eventually also internalizes some strategic stages of the production process such as cutting). In the textile districts, in addition to small firms specialized in a specific production stage, the fashion designer and the converter are also present. Similarly, in the ceramic tile district, vertically integrated medium size firms are present side by side with specialized small firms (CESPRI, 1990).

Local institutions and local associations play a major role in the working of the organization of the district. Regional and local governments, banks, and professional schools provide public support, financial resources, and a qualified labor force to firms. Export and distribution associations help overcome the problems faced by small firms in selling their final products on international markets. In some districts associations among firms have been created for the sharing of complex and costly production equipment.

Recently in most districts leading firms or local industrial groups have emerged. In the first case some firms, strategically located at the commercialization stage, coordinate the whole production process of the district. This is the case of the weaver at Prato, the trader in Carpi, and the converter in Como. In the second case, through acquisitions and participations, some industrial groups have been able to control (at the strategic and financial level) the production of the district without, however, interfering with the daily production of the small firms of the group.

Diffusion of process technology within the district is quite rapid. Technical change is rapidly diffused within the district through the widespread transmission of information among a large number of producers that share a common culture, have the same level of capability, and, because they are similar, are also able to transmit and assimilate tacit and noncodified knowledge. Personal contacts and the mobility of technicians among the firms play a major role in this respect (Bellandi, 1989). Interestingly enough, within the firms of the district, the diffusion of new capital equipment has been more rapid than the diffusion of electronic information systems. Firms were able to quickly adopt new machinery because they already had the technical capability to insert and adapt the new machinery in their productive organization. On the other hand, most new information systems required the drastic modification of the firms' organizations and the creation of new in-house capabilities: therefore they met resistance and delays in their diffusion within the district.

In these districts, both product and process innovations are of the incremental type. Product innovations are the result of skills in product design and ability in focusing on specific market requirements and consumer needs. Process innovations stem from learning by doing in single specific production stages.

As it will be shown later, in most cases firms in the industrial district constitute the major market for upstream equipment producers (usually located near or even within the industrial district) that introduce new innovative equipment as a result of close and continuous interaction with the downstream district firms.

Equipment Firms

The Italian industry is characterized by the presence of a large number of small and medium size equipment producers, which are highly innovative and internationally competitive. This type of firm, present in various regions in the north of Italy, also includes machine-tool and robotics producers. Table 7.5 shows that the share of pat-

Table 7.5. Italy: Size Distribution of the Firms Patenting in the United States (Percentages)

	Employees			
	0–100	100–1,000	1,000–10,000	Over 10,000
Chemicals				
1969–1974	—	8.2	26.6	65.2
1975–1979	0.3	11.2	23.6	64.9
1980–1984	2.9	11.5	16.0	69.6
Pharmaceuticals				
1969–1974	—	31.8	31.8	26.4
1975–1979	—	29.0	21.8	49.2
1980–1984	0.5	16.4	18.0	65.1
Electronics				
1969–1974	0.0	1.3	0.7	89.0
1975–1979	0.0	2.5	13.3	84.2
1980–1984	0.4	4.5	13.2	82.0
Electrical machinery				
1969–1974	0.0	9.7	6.7	83.6
1975–1979	0.0	18.3	17.5	64.2
1980–1984	1.4	15.9	10.4	72.4
Mechanical machinery				
1969–1974	9.5	18.7	13.3	58.5
1975–1979	10.1	27.2	12.7	50.0
1980–1984	16.1	26.4	10.6	46.9
Road vehicles				
1969–1974	—	5.9	8.8	85.3
1975–1979	—	2.9	5.9	91.2
1980–1984	1.4	2.8	2.8	93.0
Other transports				
1969–1974	3.4	38.0	10.3	48.3
1975–1979	6.7	26.6	6.7	60.0
1980–1984	13.8	17.2	7.0	62.0
Specialized industrial equipment				
1969–1974	4.6	22.7	22.7	50.0
1975–1979	2.9	8.7	53.6	34.8
1980–1984	7.3	15.6	43.4	33.7
Metals				
1969–1974	4.9	8.8	3.9	82.4
1975–1979	12.5	23.6	8.4	55.5
1980–1984	21.3	28.7	6.5	43.3

Source: Malerba and Orsenigo (1991).

Table 7.6. Share of Total Cost for Technological Innovation (Percentages)

Sectors	R&D 1	Design Engineering 2	Investments 3	Marketing 4	Total 5
All sectors	17.9	25.2	51.5	5.4	100.0
Pharmaceuticals	41.2	15.5	31.8	11.5	100.0
Electronics	24.3	33.4	38.4	3.9	100.0
Auto	15.3	23.5	59.4	1.8	100.0
Mechanical products	7.3	17.1	71.9	3.7	100.0
Nonelectrical equipment	16.0	33.1	46.3	4.6	100.0
Machine tools	21.0	36.9	37.4	4.7	100.0
Textile machinery	8.0	44.3	44.2	3.5	100.0
Textiles	6.4	7.3	83.3	3.0	100.0
Clothing	5.8	17.6	68.9	7.7	100.0

Source: ISTAT (1988).

ents held by small firms (with less than 100 employees) is substantial and is increasing over time.

The dynamics of entry and exit in this group of firms are high: new firms have been set up by technicians and engineers who have left other established equipment firms, or by some large users such as FIAT.

Because they are characterized by a lively entrepreneurship, a longstanding tradition of advanced technical and design skills in mechanical equipment, an effective understanding of users' needs, as well as a relevant capability of absorbing new electronics technologies in their products, equipment producers generate a continuous stream of incremental innovations in equipment. This is achieved by tailoring products to users' needs, focusing equipment to specific market segments, and improving and modifying existing equipment. Often innovations consist in system integration aimed at specific applications or at the solution of specific technical problems of the

Table 7.7. Major Sources of Innovation[a]

Sectors	R&D 1	Design 2	Inside Proposals 3	Purchase of Technology 4	Raw Materials 5	Intermediate Goods 6	New Machinery 7
All sectors	2.1	3.1	2.3	0.5	1.2	0.8	4.0
Pharmaceuticals	4.3	3.5	3.3	2.1	1.4	0.7	3.3
Electronics	3.1	4.5	2.9	0.6	1.3	1.0	3.7
Auto	4.8	4.2	3.0	0.7	1.4	1.2	4.3
Mechanical products	1.6	2.9	2.1	0.4	1.0	0.7	4.1
Nonelectrical equipment	2.7	4.2	2.5	0.5	1.1	1.0	3.4
Machine tools	2.4	3.7	2.1	0.5	1.1	1.0	3.6
Textile machinery	3.4	4.4	2.2	0.5	0.9	1.1	3.7
Textiles	1.1	1.8	1.8	0.3	1.0	0.5	4.5
Clothing	1.3	2.1	1.9	0.3	1.2	0.6	4.1

[a]Values from 1 to 6.
Source: ISTAT (1988).

users (see the nonelectrical equipment, machine tools, and textile machinery industries in Table 7.6).

Several of these firms do not have a formal R&D laboratory: their knowledge is mostly noncodified, tacit, and idiosyncratic, because it is embodied in technicians and engineers. Some firms (mainly flexible automation and robotics producers) maintain close links with engineering laboratories at the university (Camagni, 1984). Most firms use consultants for the solution of specific problems (see the nonelectrical equipment, machine tools, and textile machinery in Table 7.7).

Learning by interacting through the user–producer relationship plays a key role in the innovation process (see Table 7.8 for nonelectrical equipment, machine tools, and textile machinery). Vertical links with sophisticated users are extremely important in providing an innovative stimulus and a continuous feedback on the use of the machinery. Two main types of users may be identified: large firms (such as FIAT, Olivetti, and Zanussi) and firms in industrial districts (such as the Biella district for textile machinery and the Sassuolo district for equipment for ceramic tile production). As will be shown later, these links have generated vertical virtuous cycles in Italian industry.

Firms in Traditional Sectors

A final group of firms is composed of the large population of small and medium size firms operating in traditional industries, but not located within an industrial district. Innovative firms are not very numerous in this very heterogeneous group of firms. New product introduction is driven by marketing and production capabilities linked to fashion design, product tailoring, and market segmentation. As Table 7.7 shows for the textile and clothing industries, these firms greatly profit from the innovativeness of upstream equipment producers. Embodied technical change in terms of investments in new machinery represents the major source of change in production processes.

Human Skills 8	Professional Training 9	Customers Needs 10	Suppliers 11	Joint Ventures 12	Industrial Exhibition 13	Public Institutions 14	Consultants 15	Imitation 16
1.2	2.2	2.3	1.6	0.3	1.5	0.3	0.6	2.0
1.6	2.4	1.7	1.2	0.7	1.2	1.5	1.1	2.5
1.8	2.7	2.8	1.8	0.4	1.7	0.5	0.7	2.4
1.6	3.7	1.1	2.7	1.4	2.2	1.3	1.0	1.9
1.1	2.0	2.2	1.5	0.2	1.3	0.2	0.5	1.7
1.5	2.4	2.8	1.6	0.3	2.0	0.3	0.7	2.1
1.8	2.7	2.8	1.7	0.2	2.0	0.3	0.6	2.0
1.8	2.6	3.2	1.9	0.3	2.2	0.3	0.7	2.3
0.8	1.8	2.1	1.5	0.1	1.2	0.1	0.5	1.6
0.9	2.2	1.7	1.4	0.2	1.5	0.0	0.6	1.6

Table 7.8. Relevance of External Cooperation of Innovating Firms (Number of Firms)

Sectors	Number of Innovative Firms 1	Number of External Cooperation 2	Percent of External Cooperation 2/1	Public Institutions (%) 3/2	University (%) 4/2	Customers (%) 5/2	Suppliers National (%)	Suppliers Foreign (%) 6/2	Other Firms (%) 7/2	Industry Associations (%) 8/2	Research Consortia (%) 9/2
All sectors	8220	1140	13.9	29.1	37.9	37.9	41.4	15.9	18.1	13.5	8.5
Pharmaceuticals	154	90	58.4	27.8	108.9	14.4	6.6	6.6	30.0	18.9	21.1
Electronics	658	159	24.2	37.1	37.1	45.3	38.9	16.9		8.2	13.2
Auto	9	6	66.7	33.3	83.3	33.3	83.3	66.6			16.7
Mechanical products	1051	66	6.3	19.7	33.3	27.3	48.4	12.1	18.2	19.7	3.0
Nonelectrical equipment	1404	255	18.2	19.6	24.3	57.3	48.6	13.3	15.7	10.2	5.1
Machine tools	287	50	17.4	16.0	22.0	48.0	64.0	12.0	18.0		6.0
Textile machinery	97	32	33.0	3.1	15.6	68.8	59.3	12.5	21.9	6.3	
Textiles	714	44	6.2	22.7	9.1	27.3	59.0	11.3	9.1	22.7	11.4
Clothing	412	19	4.6	5.3		42.1	63.1	10.5	5.3	15.8	15.8

Source: ISTAT (1988).

It is interesting to note that some large Italian firms active in traditional sectors have maintained some of the attributes of the industrial district by using a very decentralized productive organization, in which a large number of small local firms are specialized in a specific stage of the production process or in the supply of a specific input.

Benetton (with more than 1330 employees and active in the wool and cotton garment industry) has been able to match a decentralized production organization (typical of Italian textile firms) with an advanced electronic sales network. It created a hierarchical system composed of independent medium size firms assembling and controlling the production of a large number of specialized independent subcontractors. Almost 80% of Benetton's production is handled by 350 external firms and artisan shops (accounting for up to 10,000 employees) specialized in labor-intensive and nontechnologically progressive operations. Benetton's distribution, on the other hand, is characterized by an advanced telematic network linking Benetton with a decentralized sales structure composed by 75 independent agent firms and 4200 selling points. This network allows Benetton to keep in close contact with customers, and to maintain control over information and market demand in different countries (Rullani and Zanfei, 1988b; Belussi and Festa, 1990).

Some large firms in traditional industries have also been able to successfully change the organization of production through the introduction of new electronics technologies. For example, Miroglio (a textile producer with 3400 employees) has been able to improve its productive efficiency through a policy of investment in new electronic equipment. Miroglio has also become competitive internationally by specializing in a production geared toward well-defined market segments (and by developing a widespread commercialization structure). Similarly, Gruppo Finanziario Tessile (GFT) (7500 employees operating in the garment industry) has chosen to specialize in the high quality segment of the market by utilizing advanced electronic-based technologies.

The Success of Policies in Favor of the Small Firm Network

Two types of policies have affected the atomistic learning network: policies aimed at fostering the adoption of capital equipment (launched by the central government) and policies aimed at developing a local technological infrastructure (launched both by the central government and by regional and local authorities).

Policies in Favor of the Adoption of New Capital Equipment
Fiscal instruments have been used in policies aimed at increasing the adoption of new capital equipment. These policies have been successful in reaching a large number of potential adopters.

The earliest provision was Law No. 1329 of 1965 (the Sabatini Law), which has proven to be a flexible instrument well suited to the needs of small and medium size firms. The Sabatini Law calls for deferred payment of the entire expenditure up to 5 years in the case of machine tool purchases, obtained through the financial institute Mediocredito Centrale. The bureaucratic procedures for obtaining these benefits are simple. In 1987, Mediocredito Centrale distributed about 444 billion lire in subsidies for more than 30,000 operations involving capital outlays of over 4000 billion lire.

To supplement the function of the Sabatini Law, another measure was passed in

1976 (Presidential Decree 902) whose purpose was to allow for the construction of new facilities or the expansion and modernization of existing ones. This provision grants low-interest loans with rates that vary according to two parameters: whether the firm is located in northern or southern Italy and what the level of economic development is in the specific area in which the firm operates. The implementation of the provision has been extremely difficult because of the highly complicated nature of the program as well as the difficulty in identifying those areas considered insufficiently developed. The result has been that the law has financed modernization projects of small and medium size firms in northern–central Italy, without achieving what the legislators intended: the articulated differentiation of the intervention over the whole country.

It should be noted that a special program for southern Italy was launched by Law 64 of 1986. This law provided low-interest loans and subsidies for research projects, purchases of real services, technological investments, and the establishment of new research centers.

A third provision giving incentives to diffusion has been Law 696 (1983), which concerns the purchase or leasing of advanced equipment such as automation equipment. It grants an additional VAT deduction of 6% off the taxable base. It should be stressed that this provision was passed as a temporary measure scheduled to lapse in 1984, but due to its success, the term was extended until 1985. Over 16,000 firms benefited. Decree law No. 318 (1987) reintroduced the same regime.

Policies for Information and Technology Diffusion
Policies for information and technology diffusion have been characterized by the blending of national policies with regional and local initiatives, which have arisen in a decentralized and bottom up manner.

Broad programs have been aimed at developing centers and structures for research, experimentation, personnel training, production upgrading, and technical consultancy. The most significant initiatives are the Tecnotex Program at Biella (in the textile industry), the Trieste Research Area (which also includes the international genetic engineering center promoted by UNIDO), and Tecnopolis in Bari (the major science park existing in Italy).

Centers of support for diffusion such as CESTEC in Lombardy, ASTER in Emilia, and DITEL in Liguria aimed at providing information and training, and organizing pilot projects and demonstrative activities to stimulate industrial awareness in the use of new technology.

Satisfactory results have been obtained by support policies focused on the creation of sectoral centers for technology transfer and general technical assistance aimed at local industry. These centers conduct experimental research, engage in design and engineering, and provide consultant services. In general, they are promoted and managed jointly by regions, regional financing companies, chambers of commerce, and, in some cases, research institutes, together with private firms and industrial associations. There are currently some 40 of these in Italy, most of them located in Emilia, Marches, and Lombardy (Lassini, 1990).

With similar objectives, the "Sprint" project in the Prato industrial district aimed at developing and installing a data transmission network. This project involved not only manufacturers but service companies, banks, government offices, and associations, so that the cost of transferring technical, financial, and commercial information for the firms in the district could be reduced. The project also included technical assistance for the introduction of process innovations in textile production.

Cooperation among firms involved in technology diffusion has also taken place. At the local level these initiatives have been quite successful. In Lombardy, for example, there are provisions designed to stimulate exchanges of technological expertise for the creation of new products, applications of new technologies, and utilization of advanced technical services such as quality and reliability testing. From 1985 to 1987, public support was granted for around 50 of these initiatives involving a total of 400 firms, whose aim was to promote the search for partners and the cooperation among firms. In general, in Italy, around 20 intercompany technical service centers have been recently established, with the direct involvement of 800 firms as partners or promoters.

In addition to these initiatives, there are around 50 formal agreements involving research institutes, public agencies, industrial associations, and major public enterprises, whose purpose is to promote the transfer of knowledge and technology. One example is Law No. 34 (1985) of the Lombardy Region. In addition to supporting innovation in small enterprises, legislation provides incentives for research contracts and consultance between universities and small firms. Another example is provided by the Autonomous Province of Trento, which has promulgated a law that supports cooperation between industry and universities (Lassini, 1990).

THE CORE R&D SYSTEM

The other side of the Italian national system of innovation is the core R&D system. This system is highly affected by technological opportunity and demand conditions. It includes a number of different segments: large oligopolistic firms, small high technology firms, universities, public research centers, central and local government.

This section argues that the Italian core R&D system grew considerably in quantitative terms during the 1980s, but at the end of the decade still had several qualitative weaknesses related to low opportunity and demand conditions. There were few large firms, few small high technology enterprises, an underdeveloped industry–university interaction, and a limited degree of internationalization. All these issues will be addressed in the following sections.

The High Quantitative Growth of the R&D System during the 1980s

During the 1980s the relative distance between Italy and the other major OECD countries (with the exception of Japan), as far as total R&D expenditures and business enterprise R&D expenditures are concerned, was reduced (see Table 7.1). The share of Italian gross domestic expenditures on R&D in OECD countries increased from 2.85% in 1981 to 3.14% in 1987, with a yearly rate of growth of 8.9% (1979–1982), 11.7% (1983–1985), and 6.6% (1986–1989) (Archibugi-Pianta, 1990).

This quantitative growth has been accompanied by major sectoral changes in the composition of business enterprise R&D, as a result of the difference in growth of production and of R&D intensity of various sectors. High-technology sectors such as electronics and aerospace significantly increased their relative importance (reaching 24 and 15%, respectively, in 1987–1988) while other sectors such as transportation (auto, ships, etc.) and chemicals reduced their share (declining to 16 and 8%, respectively, in 1987–1988).

Public support for business enterprises R&D has also significantly increased. During the 1980s the yearly compounded growth rates of government-financed R&D has been higher than that of most OECD countries. The share of government financed business enterprise R&D over total business enterprise R&D increased from 4.5% (1971) to 22.4% (1987). Government support, however, was not spread evenly across all industries. As in the other major OECD countries, this support was concentrated in aerospace, computers, and electronics.

The Limited R&D Intensity of the Italian R&D System and the Unsatisfactory International Performance in R&D Intensive Sectors

In spite of their quantitative growth during the 1980s, in 1988 Italian R&D expenditures in absolute terms and as a percentage of GDP are still much lower than those of other major OECD countries, such as the United States, Japan, Germany, France, and the United Kingdom (see Table 7.1).

Major differences between the north and the south persist. The south continues to lag far behind the north and the center (in particular the northwest Milan–Turin–Genoa triangle) in terms of R&D and technological innovation. For example, the south produces approximately 18% of the total Italian value added, and the northwest 34%. Still the south, which has a 0.2% R&D intensity, performs only 7% of all national R&D and has obtained only 0.7% of total Italian patents registered in the United States. The northwest of Italy on the contrary has 1.4, 70, and 83% respectively (Santarelli and Sterlacchini, 1989). In addition, in the south approximately 90% of R&D employees are in the public sector (mainly in universities) (Romano, 1989) and most of these employees are involved in basic research, acting independently of the local productive system.

The growth of Italian R&D expenditures did not translate into a satisfactory performance in terms of technological innovation or international competitiveness in high-technology industries. As Table 7.9 shows, the share of Italian patents registered in the United States declined from 3.4% in the early 1960s to 2.9% in the late 1980s, while the Italian share of overall OECD exports of high-technology industries declined from 4.5% in 1970 to 3.5% in 1987, mainly as a result of the high growth of Japan. Similarly, the Italian share of OECD exports in most high-technology sectors declined during the 1970s and 1980s (see Table 7.9), while there has been a deficit in the Italian balance of trade in most of these products (except for telecommunication equipment and helicopters–aircraft).

Factors Limiting the Full Development of the R&D System in Italy

What factors limit the full development of the R&D system in Italy?

Six major factors can be identified: limited endogenous generation of advanced technological opportunities, weak demand conditions, a small oligopolistic core, few small high-technology firms, an underdeveloped industry–university–research organization interface, and a still limited degree of internationalization. These six factors will now be examined in detail.

Table 7.9. Indicators of Italian Technological Performances

	Technological Balance of Payments (TBP)			
	1980–1981	1982–1983	1984–1985	1986–1987
Expenditures/R&D	0.30	0.27	0.22	0.16
Expenditures/revenues				
Total	2.80	3.80	3.50	2.90
Manufacture	3.30	4.50	3.40	3.16

Source: Falzoni (1990).

	Patents and International Competitiveness					
	Italian Share of Total Foreign Patents in the United States			Share of Total OECD Exports of High R&D Intensive Sectors[a]		
	1963–1968	1976–1981	1982–1988	1970	1980	1987
Italy	3.4	3.1	2.9	4.5	3.9	3.5

[a]Aerospace, office machines, computers, electronics and components, drugs, instruments, electrical machinery.

Italian Share of OECD Exports		
	1970–1972	1983–1985
Aerospace	2.3	4.1
Office machines	8.3	1.6
Computers	5.9	4.4
Electronic components	3.4	2.2
Telecommunications	5.0	3.8
Drugs	6.4	5.4
Instruments	2.8	2.8
Electrical machinery	5.0	4.3

Source: Malerba (1988).

Limited Endogenous Generation of Advanced Technological Opportunities

The endogenous generation of advanced scientific and technological opportunities in Italy is characterized by a fragmentation of efforts and a high variance of scientific output.

The level of research at Italian universities varies greatly across scientific fields. Areas of excellence exist in physics (particularly particle physics), space, lasers, synthetic chemistry, and optoelectronics. In several other areas, on the other hand, research has not reached advanced international standards and the presence of islands of scientific excellence is more the result of the efforts of single scientists working in isolation at the frontier than the work of teams of scientists (Dosi, 1989). This situation is aggravated by the scarce funds available for the purchase and use of advanced research equipment, the lack of advanced multidisciplinary research, and the still limited access of academicians to industry.

Recently, improvements in the organization of Italian university have occurred. In 1980, departments (around which major research areas are grouped), research doctorates, and the possibility for part-time work for university professors were introduced. In 1989, with the passage of the Italian university under the newly formed Ministry for University and Research, university research was more closely tied to teaching and training.

The introduction of the first level diploma in 1990 also aimed to change the trend of a decrease in the supply of industrial researchers, engineers, and technicians. In fact, university graduates in the science fields decreased from 11,912 in 1977 to 11,043 in 1988, while graduates in engineering decreased from 11,313 in 1977 to 10,524 in 1988 (Centro Studi IBM, 1989).

Unlike the university system, the Italian public research network does mainly mission-oriented research rather than basic research.

The Italian National Research Council (CNR) has a wide range of research activities distributed amongst quite a large number of institutes and centers (289). There is no evidence of an evaluation mechanism for internal research and there is no selection mechanism for the opening of new institutes in new scientific areas or for the closing of old ones in old scientific fields. Recently, in a wide range of research fields, the CNR has successfully launched "Finalized Projects," targeted to specific national objectives and aimed to improve cooperation in research. In addition, the CNR has focused some of its internal research activities around "Strategic Projects" concerning information technology, environment, biological systems, infrastructure, and services.

The rest of the public research network is composed of ENEA, ASI, INFN, ISS, and the experimental stations among others (see Table 7.10 for an overview). ENEA (the National Board for Nuclear and Alternative Energy Sources, under the control of the Ministry of Industry) has shown considerable dynamism by expanding its range from nuclear energy to renewable energy sources and energy conservation, to environment and health protection, to process technologies, biotechnologies for agricultural applications, advanced materials, lasers, optoelectronics, and robotics. In addition, ENEA stimulates the diffusion of new technologies among small firms. ASI

Table 7.10. The Organization of Scientific and Technological Research in Italy[a]

Source	Target
The Council of Ministers	→ CIPE
	→ CIPI
	→ Central Statistical Office—ISTAT (S 2832, R 415)
↓	
Ministers	
Budget and planning	→ ISCO
	→ ISPE
Agriculture and forestry	→ Agriculture Research Centres
	→ CNR (S 5317, R 2522)
	→ ASI
University and research	→ Universities
	→ INFN (S 1420, R 394)
Defense	→ Research Centres of Navy, Army, Air Force
	→ ENEA (S 5000)
Industry and Trade	→ Experimental stations
Labor	→ CENSIS
State enterprises	→ R&D of State enterprises
Health	→ ISS (S 1399, R 246)
Transportation and civil aviation	→ Centre for Automotive Research and Testing

[a]S, staff; R, researchers.

(Italian Space Agency) is active in space research, receives considerable public support, and collaborates with industry, universities, and CNR. The INFN (National Institute of Nuclear Physics) does research in nuclear and particle physics, has extensive international research collaboration, and has a high research reputation. The ISS (Higher Institute of Health, under the control of the Ministry of Health) conducts health research and drug testing. The Experimental Stations of the Ministry of Industry do material and product controls, testing, and certifications. These stations are small and in some cases have inadequate equipment and facilities. They are characterized by limited turnover: some of these stations have been in operation since the end of the last century, while the opening of new ones for ceramics and plastics has been rejected.

It must be noted that limited basic research is performed by the few large firms that have central corporate laboratories such as Ansaldo, FIAT, STET, ENEL, ENI, and Montedison.

Weak Demand Conditions

In Italy, demand conditions have hindered innovation in the R&D system in well defined ways.

Large firms have rarely provided innovative stimulus to domestic producers simply because in several cases they themselves have not shown a high degree of innovativeness. Until recently large firms have preferred to buy state-of-the-art components or equipment abroad when they were not available domestically, rather than stimulating a potentially innovative domestic supply.

Public procurement has rarely been used as a conscious stimulus for innovation (Pontarollo, 1986). A successful case of development of advanced capabilities concerns civil engineering firms that grew through public contracts for public works. But in general public administration normally purchases existing products from existing producers: in several cases it has, de facto, maintained unchanged historical quotas directed to domestic firms. Public procurement as a means of change has been impaired also by norms regarding public contracts, difficulties and delays in financial payments by the public sector, cumbersome bureaucratic procedures, and political or social goals.

Similarly, Italian military demand (with few relevant exceptions) has been generally less technologically progressive, smaller, and more open to imports than military demand in other European countries. In 1986, Italian expenditures on military equipment was $2500 million, versus $7100 million in the United Kingdom and $4400 million in the Federal Republic of Germany. It must be noted that 21.5% of the Italian military demand was satisfied by imports (Nones, 1988). Some cases of successful development exist, however. They are in most cases linked to participation in international programs such as Alenia in the Tornado fighter plane and Agusta in helicopters.

A Small Oligopolistic Core

One of the peculiarities of the Italian system of innovation compared to the other main advanced countries is the reduced number and the limited size of the large oligopolistic core. Italian concentration ratios in terms of R&D as well as of patents (Malerba, 1988; Malerba and Orsenigo, 1991) are higher than those of the main advanced industrialized countries (see Table 7.11). The core of industrial R&D in Italy is concentrated in a few large industrial groups: FIAT, Ferruzzi-Montedison, ENI, STET (IRI), Olivetti,

Table 7.11. R&D Concentration in Italy[a]

	Italy 1985	United States 1985	Japan 1984	United Kingdom 1978	France 1983
C5	46	16	19	41	30
C7	52	18	24	n.a.	n.a.

[a]R&D Concentration ratio: share of the major 5 and 7 R&D spenders; share of total business enterprise R&D.

Source: Malerba (1988).

and Pirelli (see Table 7.12). These six industrial groups operate in the auto, chemicals, pharmaceuticals, electronics, and tire industries.

Table 7.7 shows that the sources of innovation and the organization of the innovative process in these large companies are quite similar to the ones present in other large companies around the world. Innovation is driven mainly by internal R&D, engineering, design, and suggestions coming from other internal functional areas. External R&D contracts are mostly given to firms within the same industrial groups. R&D cooperation with public research institutions (such as CNR and ENEA) and with the university is quite common (see Table 7.8). It must be emphasized that in terms of R&D intensity at the product level, Italian firms are not at major disadvantages with respect to their international competitors. The low R&D intensity at the industry and at the country level is the result of the fact that within an industry, Italian firms are in general active in those products that have a low R&D intensity.

The new technological dynamism and R&D growth of Italian large firms during the 1980s represent the continuation of a process of technological accumulation begun by some of these firms during the 1950s and early 1960s, and interrupted during the 1970s. The period of rapid industrial reconstruction and fast growth of the 1950s and 1960s based on low labor costs and foreign licenses, and centered on mechanics, traditional sectors, and scale-intensive sectors (such as basic chemicals, auto, and steel) was characterized by indigenous technological developments in computers by Olivetti, drugs by Lepetit, nuclear energy by CNEN and INFN, lasers and electronics by CISE

Table 7.12. Italian Firms With the Largest R&D Expenditures and Patents

	(A) R&D Expenditures (Million Dollars) 1987	(B) R&D Expenditures/ Sales (Percentage)		(C) Share of Total Patents Granted to Italian Firms from the Late 1960s to the Early 1980s
		1982	1987	
FIAT	1050	2.4	3.5	5.4
STET (IRI)	422[a]	2.9	3.2[a]	4.6
Italtel	141.2	7.8	12.4	—
Montedison	290	2.6	2.7	11.9
Olivetti	330.8	4.9	5.8	5.1
ENI	149.4	0.6	1.3	5.8
Pirelli[b]	133.1	6.2	6.8	3.6

[a]SGS-Thomson is excluded.

[b]All firms of the group.

Sources: (A) and (B) Malerba (1988) and AIRI (1988); (C) Archibugi (1987).

and Politecnico of Milan, and chemicals by Donegani (Montedison). Original research and development, however, was not linked to large-scale manufacturing and to support activities such as design, engineering, and marketing, because of the lack of real commitment to a significant activity in high technologies and financial difficulties (because of increasing labor costs). Several Italian firms discontinued their research efforts and followed strategies centered on the pursuit of static efficiency (such as reduction of production costs through decentralization and rationalization of what was existing) instead of focusing on dynamic efficiency and technological innovation. Olivetti decided to remain a producer of mechanical typewriters and sold its electronics operation to General Electric in 1963; CNEN discontinued its activities in the second half of the 1960s; Lepetit was purchased by Dow Chemical; Montedison discontinued research on advanced new materials of the Donegani Institute (Malerba, 1988; Soria, 1979; Antonelli, 1984). During the period of financial crisis and labor disputes of the 1970s, although in some firms groups of researchers still continued work in advanced technological areas, the focus of the larger Italian firms moved away from innovation and R&D at the technological frontier. The extensive productive rationalization and the return to profitability in the early 1980s allowed Italian firms to invest more in R&D.

The increase in the level and intensity of R&D in the 1980s was concentrated in specific technological areas, and was linked to productive specialization (Fornengo and Silva, 1989). In the information-processing industry Olivetti followed a successful strategy in several key hardware and software areas; in microelectronics SGS (STET) closed a considerable gap in semiconductor technologies, and merged with Thomson (France); in telecommunications Italtel and Telettra developed advanced products; in robotics, firms such as DEA, Jobs, and Comau introduced a large number of innovative products; in the aerospace industry firms such as Aeritalia, Agusta and Fiat Aviazione developed specific capabilities in well-defined technologies; in the chemical and pharmaceutical industries Montedison consolidated its position in selected technological areas.

During the 1980s these firms developed vertical and horizontal cooperative agreements with other firms and institutions. Olivetti developed a network of alliances, acquisitions, and participations with hardware and software companies (Malerba, 1988); Montedison participated in or controlled several other firms; Italtel and SGS-Thomson developed a range of cooperative agreements with foreign firms. FIAT drastically changed its policy of subcontracting, reducing the number of suppliers (from 1200 in 1980 to 850 in the late-1980s) and pushing decentralization of component design and innovation through development contracts. Through these contracts, FIAT supports part of the cost of the development of a new component by its suppliers. In case of successful development, FIAT becomes the owner of the technical documentation of the component and may establish a long-term supply contract (3 to 5 years) with the same supplier. These types of development contracts increased from 28 in 1980 to 48 in 1984, while the share of FIAT purchases covered by long-term supply contracts following development contracts has increased from 3.7% in 1981 to 7% in 1984 (Enrietti and Fornengo, 1989). Despite this increase, however, the share is still quite limited as a result of the lack of advanced development capabilities by component producers, which were used for too much time to supply FIAT with products that would passively meet FIAT requirements.

Notwithstanding the high growth rates of R&D expenditures, the oligopolistic core still shows limited absolute values of R&D expenditures on an international scale and experiences difficulties in performance at the technological frontier. For a long time, large Italian firms have been accustomed to compete on a cost basis, to be active in protected domestic markets, and to maintain a technological follower strategy. In the near future, international technological competition and European integration will act as a selection mechanism that will compel big Italian industrial firms either to be innovators on a continuous basis or to assume the role of technological followers.

Few High-Technology Small Firms
Another weakness of the Italian R&D system is the limited number of new high-technology firms operating in electronics, software, biotechnology, and services. Some of these firms are closely linked to the oligopolistic core of large Italian companies, such as the small electronics firms in the Canavese region surrounding Olivetti, or the software and service companies in the Milan area. Others are linked to the few scientific parks that exist in Italy.

The organization of the innovative process in these firms is centered around design and research activities, not always formalized into an R&D laboratory. Interestingly enough, those firms that have developed internal technological capabilities are more open to external cooperation in research.

Within this restricted group, several firms innovate by integrating components, hardware, and software into systems. In most cases system integration is directed to specific final applications or to specific customers.

In Italy, demand and dynamic interdependencies have been the critical factors behind the establishment of new firms. In a sector such as software, new firms have been successful by offering a specialized, customized, or segmented product that satisfies a specific demand and by utilizing existing technology and adapting it to new applications or to potential users. These firms have grown by entering into product-related market segments, but have not reached a large size. On the other hand, cases in which new firms offer new products based on a technological innovation are rare (Raffa and Zollo, 1988). This last type of entry, however, is increasing with time, as a consequence of the growth in the number of electronics engineers and the spin-off of engineers and technicians from large corporations.

Dynamic interdependencies meant that advanced capabilities in an established industry became a major factor in the development of a new industry, as in the case of the relationship between the advanced capabilities in machinery and machine tools and the development of the robotic industry.

Weak Interfaces between University, Public Research Organizations, and Industry
Another weakness of the Italian R&D system concerns the interfaces among university, research organizations, and industry. The efficiency and effectiveness of these interfaces have been impaired by the limited number of centers of excellence in Italian universities, the limited mobility in and out of the university system, and the bureaucratic and institutional structure of universities. A survey questionnaire involving 14 universities, 25 research organizations, and 44 firms in Italy, and 49 universities, 50 research organizations, and 41 firms in the other European countries in 1988 showed that compared to European firms, Italian firms do recognize that the difficulties pre-

sented by bureaucratic constraints represent a major obstacle to cooperation with universities and other research organizations (Fornari et al., 1989).

The Still Limited (albeit Growing) Internationalization of the Italian System

As previously mentioned, the limited degree of internationalization of the Italian system has acted as a protected environment, which generated a not particularly progressive demand to Italian firms. The globalization of international technological competition and the increasing cost and complexity of R&D in several sectors have compelled Italian firms to increase their limited degree of internationalization (Cominotti and Mariotti, 1990) and to follow an articulated policy of cooperation in R&D (Vacca', 1986). Allowing for a margin of error in the sources used for the calculations (newspapers and economic magazines), it is possible to claim that the number of international cooperative agreements of Italian firms has increased during the 1980s from 96 in 1984–1985, to 181 in 1986, and to 202 in 1987, with R&D being one of the main motivations for international cooperative agreements (Malerba, 1988).

These newly established networks of international cooperative agreements in R&D broadened the knowledge base of Italian firms and provided them with complementary technological competences. Because they are still limited in number and represent a quite new phenomenon for Italian firms, however, these networks of cooperative agreements have not been able to exert major influences on the international performance of Italian firms.

The Role of Public Policy

Public policy in support of technological innovation does not have a long tradition in Italy. During the 1950s and 1960s there was no policy at all. Whereas other advanced countries began to support the electronics industry, in fact, Italian public policy focused its support on sectors with standard technologies and economies of scale, such as steel and basic chemicals, and aimed to increase the productive capacity of the country in these sectors. In most cases this policy resulted in inefficient or duplicative large plants. On the other hand, the Italian government did not intervene in high-technology sectors. In 1963, for example, only 0.8% of business enterprise R&D was funded by the state. The Government did not support Olivetti's R&D and production of computers. Nor did it intervene in the purchase of Olivetti's computer operations by General Electric in 1964. Similarly, it did not adopt any policy of support for the new semiconductor industry during those years (Malerba, 1987). Even the first attempts of policies of support of high-technology industries (Law 1089 in 1968 and Law 675 in 1977) were characterized by limited resources, and by the lack of a precise policy model.

The timing of public policy of support of high-technology sectors has been determined to a large extent by the emergence of industrial and scientific lobbies in advanced sectors, as has been the case in the decisions to support the electronics industry during the late 1970s and early 1980s and the biotechnology industry during the second half of the 1980s (Adams and Orsenigo, 1988).

In Italy, the contemporary public policy supporting innovation is implemented at three different levels. At the basic research end of the innovation process there are the Finalized Programs of the National Research Council (CNR), originally intended to guide basic research toward economic applications and to stimulate the transfer of basic results from the universities and research organizations to industry. Further downstream in the innovation process there are the National Research Plans of the Ministry of Scientific and Technological Research (MRST), designed to stimulate cooperation in R&D in high-risk projects. Finally, at the applied and development stage of the innovative process, industrial R&D is supported through the Applied Research Fund and the Technological Innovation Fund. The former aims to support applied industrial R&D, while the latter focuses on development and prototype production.

The Finalized Programs of the CNR
CNR's first Finalized Programs were launched in 1975: by 1986 they totalled 38. They included a wide range of research fields: food processing, health care, land and environment, advanced technologies, energy, and so on. Between 1976 and 1986, the financing of Finalized Programs reached 1063 billion lire: 12.3% went to the CNR institutes, 36.2% to university laboratories, and 44% to companies and other research organizations. In 1987, 10 additional Finalized Programs were approved with a projected duration of 5 years and an estimated cost of 690 billion lire for CNR, and of 300 billion lire for private partners. These Finalized Programs also include an educational component, represented by more than 1200 fellowships granted in the fields considered (Ginebri, 1987).

CNR's Finalized Programs have followed a bottom up approach. Initially, the leadership of the academic community pushed the programs toward academic research, with rather confused guidelines concerning implementation. The focus then gradually moved toward more applied research, a higher level of funding given to firms, and a greater emphasis on the coordination of the various operating units involved. It should be stressed that delays in defining objectives, selecting projects, and choosing partners created serious problems of obsolescence in the Finalized Programs.

The most significant problem that has emerged so far is the development of a cooperative approach. It is evident that cooperation between companies, universities, and other research organizations is closely related to the ability to identify unifying objectives and the capacity of industrialists or project directors to assume leadership roles. In the numerous cases where these conditions were lacking, the result was that the individual research units continued to do what they did beforehand, but with greater financial resources than before.

The National Research Programs (NRPs) of the Ministry for Scientific and Technological Research (MRST)
The NRPs were introduced in 1982. They are defined in a top-down way by the Minister of University and Research: cooperation is stimulated by defining objectives that require interdisciplinary and complementary expertise.

By the end of 1987, 9 NRPs had been approved for a total of 58 contracts and 714 billion lire in funding, of which 15% has gone to universities and government research agencies. In the case of electronics, steelmaking, and building construction (where basic research is now of limited importance) the share of these institutions has not exceeded 5%. In a field like biotechnology the share has been higher, between 5 and 10%. The share has risen even further (to almost 50%) in pharmaceutical-related projects.

The Applied Research Fund
The Applied Research Fund introduced in 1968 (Law 109) and modified in 1982 (Law 46) grants low-interest loans for research projects (up to a maximum of 40% of total expenditures in general, to 60% for projects concerning sectors included in the applied programs of the National Board for Industrial Planning-CIPI, and up to 70% for high-priority sectors) and subsidies (up to 20% of R&D expenditures). For relevant R&D projects the coverage of costs by the Applied Research Fund may reach up to 90%. The Fund is managed by the public Industrial Credit Institute IMI under the guidance of the Ministry for University and Research. The Applied Research Fund granted 4179 billion lire between 1968 and 1989. The support of the Applied Research Fund covered 5.1% of business enterprise R&D in the period 1970–1987 (7.6% between 1981 and 1987). The support has been highly concentrated in the oligopolistic core: FIAT, Olivetti, and IRI (Italtel, SGS-Thomson, Aeritalia, Selenia). Small and medium size firms have obtained a very limited share of total funds, much less than the 20% minimum share allocated by the Fund. Similarly, while a 40% share was set aside for companies located in southern Italy, a much lower share was actually granted to them.

The Technological Innovation Fund
This Fund, launched in 1982 (Law 46) and managed by the Ministry of Industry, aims to promote technological innovation and development in products and processes. It is based on low-interest loans and subsidies, and permits the funding of programs already begun. The Fund, initially designed for five industries (automotive, electronics, chemicals, steel, aeronautics), has also included support for the mechanics and agrofood industries. It has faster bureaucratic procedures and less discretion in the selection of the program than the Applied Research Fund. Until 1988, the Technological Innovation Fund granted 2314 billion lire. Also the Technological Innovation Fund has concentrated its support on the Italian oligopolistic core. The support to the activities of small and medium size firms, however, is much higher than the Applied Research Fund.

The Applied Research Fund and the Technological Innovation Fund have undoubtedly contributed to increase the technological and research capabilities of Italian industry over the past 20 years, but they still exhibit several major flaws. First, no overall coherent framework and coordination exists between the two Funds. This is in part a consequence of the political genesis of Law 46, which divided the power of managing government support for innovation among two different Ministries (Ministry of University and Research for the Applied Research Fund and Ministry of Industry for the Innovation Fund), which then aimed at total independence of action. Second, the two Funds have supported already existing activities and projects already under way, rather than stimulating totally new projects. Third, the majority of the projects are of a medium level of innovativeness rather than at the technological frontier. Fourth, no explicit policy in favor of the natality of small Schumpeterian firms in high-technology industries has been included. Fifth, the Funds use direct financial support of firms' activities (easiest to manage for the public sector), and do not rely on a broader range of policy tools (Momigliano, 1986). Sixth, the spectrum of sectors (not necessarily at the technological frontier) chosen for support is very broad, while an ex-ante selection of specific technological areas is absent. Seventh, the decision-making process and the bureaucratic procedures of the two Funds (particularly for the Applied Research Fund) are still too long.

Policies Favoring Cooperation

During the 1980s Italian public policies and major public organizations (such as CNR, ENEA, INFN and ISS, see Table 7.10) have increasingly supported cooperation in R&D. Law 240 (1981) managed by the Mediocredito Centrale (a public financial institution) provides credit in terms of low-interest loans for a period of 10 years and amounts no greater than 1 billion lire, in favor of consortia composed of small and medium size enterprises, public research agencies, and local government. The purpose of cooperation may range from scientific and technological research and technical experimentation, to the updating of managerial techniques, and to the assistance and technical consultation to cooperative member firms. The operational results of Law 240 have been meager because the procedural and bureaucratic difficulties and the organizational forms contemplated by the law (consortia of at least nine companies and multiyear duration) have proven too restrictive and complex for small and medium size enterprises. Among the major public research centers (and in addition to the previously mentioned Finalized Project launched by the CNR) since 1982 ENEA has been increasing its cooperation with industry and universities. In energy, ENEA has sought to improve the interaction with industry in terms of participation in joint research projects and of the diffusion of results to small and medium size firms. In addition, ENEA has launched "industrial promotion projects" (in microelectronics, biotechnology for agricultural applications, process technologies, advanced materials, lasers, optical technologies) concerning component testing and the creation of joint ventures with participation of universities, CNR, local governments, and firms. Also INFN has recently begun a specific program designed to commercially exploit scientific discoveries in collaboration with companies that operate in advanced technologies. Similarly, the ISS has increased interaction with industry not only in the usual phases of testing and new drugs authorization, but also in the Finalized Projects of CNR and the National Research Plans of MRST. Finally, liaison offices have been promoted with the purpose of stimulating transfer of scientific results to the industrial system. During the period 1985–1987 20 programs of this type were started, especially on the initiative of ENEA and CNR.

European Public Policy

The participation of Italian firms to European programs has helped overcome some of the weaknesses of the Italian R&D system, by opening up international networks of information exchanges and collaborations and by allowing Italian firms or research centers to cooperate with centers of excellence around Europe. It must be noted that the Italian participation in ESPRIT (12% of total ESPRIT funds) and in other programs (such as EUREKA) reflects the strengths and weaknesses of Italian industry. Large firms such as Olivetti, STET, and FIAT are present in areas such as computer-integrated manufacturing, office systems, and lasers, while small high-technology firms have a limited presence.

The specific experiences of the Italian institutions involved in European cooperation in space technologies and nuclear physics also indicate that in the long run international R&D collaboration has strongly benefited Italian firms. Italian participation in the European Space Agency and in CERN during the 1970s and the 1980s (Kluzer, 1989) shows that given advanced technological capabilities by Italian firms and institutions, the involvement in international programs has stimulated research at the frontier and has contributed to further develop skills and competences of Italian firms.

THE DYNAMICS OF THE SMALL FIRMS NETWORK AND THE CORE R&D SYSTEM: VIRTUOUS AND VICIOUS CYCLES

One of the relevant aspects of the Italian case has been the presence of interdependencies and virtuous and vicious cycles within and across the two systems of innovation.

Virtuous Cycles

Virtuous vertical innovative cycles took place between equipment producers and users. The dynamics are as follows. Technologically progressive and highly competitive users requested new advanced capital equipment to upstream producers that were therefore stimulated to satisfy users' demand with innovative equipment. With the availability of the new equipment, users were able to improve their own technological capabilities and competitiveness, and, in turn, generated new demand for additional improvements in capital equipment, and so on. A virtuous dynamic vertical cycle was then set in motion.

In Italy one of the most relevant virtuous vertical cycles of this kind existed between producers of manufacturing equipment and firms in the industrial district, as a consequence of intensive learning by doing, learning by using, and learning by interacting taking place between producers and users through formal and informal communication, share of tacit knowledge, on the spot interaction, and personnel mobility. As previously noted, in industrial districts (such as the textile one of Biella in Piedmont or the ceramic tile one of Sassuolo in Emilia), a very innovative and dynamic group of equipment producers linked to the production of the district is also present (such as textile equipment firms in Biella and producers of equipment for ceramic tile production in Sassuolo).

It must be noted that virtuous cycles have greatly affected the rate of diffusion of new technologies. Given the advanced capabilities of flexible automation producers and the proximity of several producers and users in the north of Italy, the diffusion of flexible automation has been relatively faster in Italy compared to other European countries. On the other hand, information technologies and EDP, not related to a competitive strength of Italian producers, linked to different functions within firms and acting on a different set of firms' capabilities, had a slower rate of diffusion in Italy compared to other European countries (see Table 7.13).

Virtuous cycles also took place when upstream producers with advanced technological capabilities faced a large and technologically progressive user. This is the case of the relationship between the robotics and laser industries and FIAT. In the case of robotics, FIAT had a clear perception of its needs, an advanced knowledge of its production process, and a willingness to invest a large amount of resources in new production processes; robotics producers, on the other hand, disposed of accumulated

Table 7.13. Indicators of Diffusion of Various Technologies

	Italy	Federal Republic of Germany	France	United Kingdom	United States	Japan
Number of robots[a]						
1988	8300	17700	5658	5034	32600	176000
Number of flexible manufacturing systems[b]						
1984	19	23	37	37	81	103
1988	69	117	65	82	118	190
EDP expenditures per worker[c] ($)						
1988	541	888	862	743	1103	947
1990	630	951	959	772	1262	1088
Personal computer [d] (millions)						
1988	1.2	1.7	1.7	1.9	28.0	6.1
1990	2.1	3.7	3.0	3.6	43.3	9.1
Personal computers per 100 workers[e]						
1990	9.9	13.0	13.5	13.2	36.6	14.6
Digital switching penetration[f] (share of total switching)						
1987	11.9	1.5	69.7	48.4	76.2	36.1
Digital local lines places in services[g] (millions)						
1988	1.1	.5	1.7	2.5	7.6	5.0

Sources: [a,b]CERIS, MIP—Politecnico di Milano; [c-e]ASSINFORM and NOMOS; [f,g] IEFE—Università Bocconi.

capabilities in machinery development and production and an advanced international competitiveness. Similarly, in the case of lasers FIAT promptly began a focused and interdisciplinary R&D program on the utilization of lasers in car production, which in turn benefited the production of high power lasers for industrial applications (Kluzer, 1989).

Vicious Cycles

Vicious cycles have been present when the lack of competitiveness or advanced technological capabilities in one agent hindered the introduction of innovations or the development of advanced technological capabilities by a second agent linked to the first. This in turn reinforced the noncompetitive situation or the limited capabilities of the first agent, and so on.

A clear example of vicious cycles is represented by the interactions among the various participants in the core R&D system. The uneven level of scientific research performed by the university and the public sector, the lack of technologically progressive public procurement, and the limited technological capabilities of several large firms have in fact hindered the full development of the national R&D system.

Dynamic interdependencies have also negatively affected the introduction of new technologies or the birth of new industries in Italy. The lack of a population of advanced small and medium size electronics firms highly impaired the development of small power lasers in the late 1970s (Kluzer, 1989). The limited capabilities and international competitiveness of final electronics goods producers negatively affected the development of the electronic components industry during the 1960s and 1970s (Malerba, 1987). Similarly, the limited experience and technological capabilities of the electromechanical industry during the 1950s had negative consequences on the R&D efforts of semiconductor firms during the 1960s (Malerba, 1987). Finally, the limited R&D capability in pharmaceuticals of the Italian chemical and drug companies and the fragmented R&D of the Italian food processing industry were a major cause of the late and difficult start of R&D in biotechnology during the 1980s (Galimberti et al., 1989).

CONCLUSIONS

This chapter has shown that two systems of innovation with quite different organizations may coexist within the same country. In one—the small firms network—small firms compete and interact at the local level, in most cases inserted in a homogeneous vocational, social, and cultural atmosphere. In the other—the core R&D system—large firms, new small high-technology firms, large public institutions, universities, and the national government operate in a complex web of relationships.

The very same factors that allowed for the success of the small firms network in Italy seriously impaired the effectiveness of the core R&D system, namely, vivacious individualism and entrepreneurship, strong family links, high localism, a limited oligopolistic industrial core, an inability to manage large organizations, and a rather inefficient public sector.

The case of Italy has also shown that a country can enter the club of advanced industrial economies, and even prosper and grow, without a developed formal R&D system.

These features of the Italian national system of innovation lead to wonder, however, if this situation will be sustainable in the future in the presence of a globalization of competition as well as European integration.

To survive, the small firms network will have to modify some of its basic characteristics and evolve toward a more concentrated structure, in which a limited number of leading firms or firm associations will perform a key role in both strategic and commercial terms. This is the direction that the small firms network seems to have taken in recent years.

Different predictions may be made with regard to the core R&D system. The Italian R&D system faces the choice of either remaining emarginated (as in the past) from international technological competition among advanced industrialized countries, or making the move from being a follower to a leader in some high-technology sectors.

The only way Italy can move toward a leadership position in even a limited number of fields is if the existing core is able to invest more in R&D, and if new big industrial R&D segments and new small high-technology firms enter the scene. National public policy will have to become more coherent and coordinated, universities will have to be able to supply a greater number of skilled personnel, and a more effective interface between industry and university will have to develop. In this respect globalization, while greatly increasing the competitive pressure in Italian firms, will at the same time open up new opportunities for innovation and growth by stimulating the generation, transmission, and acquisition of advanced technological knowledge and expertise.

REFERENCES

Adams, P., and Orsenigo, L. (1988). "Tecnologie emergenti e politica Industriale in Italia." *Rivista di Scienza dell'Amministrazione* 2:113–138.

Amendola, G. (1989). "La diffusione dei materiali polimerici nell'industria automobilistica." In F. Onida and R. Malaman (eds.), *Industria italiana ed alte technologie*, 310–89. Milan: F. Angeli.

Antonelli, C. (1984). "Elementi per un'analisi della politica dell'innovazione in Italia: il processo di formazione di un potenziale scientifico e tecnologico nazionale." *Economia Pubblica*. 195–522.

Antonelli, C. (ed.) (1988). *New Information Technology and Industrial Change: The Italian Case*. Dordrecht: Kluwer.

Archibugi, D. (1987). "La struttura settoriale dell'innovazione industriale in Italia." *Rivista di Politica Economica*. February 132–76.

Archibugi, D., and Pianta M. (1990). *The European Technological Specialization*. Rome: CNR.

Battaggion, M. R. (1990). "R-S e brevetti." In F. Onida and F. Malerba (eds.), *La ricerca scientifica*, 97–145. Rome: SIPI.

Becattini, G. (1987). *Mercato e forze locali: il distretto industriale*. Bologna: Il Mulino.

Becattini, G. (1989). *Modelli locali di sviluppò*. Bologna: Il Mulino.

Bellandi, M. (1989). "Capacità innovativa diffusa e sistemi locali di impresi". In G. Becattini (ed.), *Modelli locali di sviluppo*, 149–72. Bologna: Il Mulino.

Belussi, F., and Festa, M. (1990). "L'impresa rete del modello veneto". *Oltre il Ponte*, 31:3–81.

Brusco, S. (1982). "The Emilian Model: Productive Decentralization and Social Integration." *Cambridge Journal of Economics* 6:167–184.

Cainarca, G., Colombo, M., and Mariotti, S. (1989a). "An Evolutionary Pattern of Innovation Diffusion. The Case of Flexible Automation." *Research Policy* 18:59–86.

Cainarca, G, Colombo, M., and Mariotti, S. (1989b). "Sentieri di automazione ed evoluzione della struttura industriale." In G. P. Barbetta and F. Silva (eds.), *Trasformazioni strutturali delle imprese italiane*. Bologna: Il Mulino.

Camagni, R. (1984). *Il robot italiano*. Milan: Il Sole 24 Ore.

Censis - IMI (1990). *Ricerca e industria in Italia. Vent'anni di fondo IMI*. Rome: IMI-Il Sole 24 Ore.

Centro Studi Confindustria—CSC (various years). *La spesa dell'industria privata per la ricerca scientifica*. Rome.

Centro Studi IBM Italia—Assolombarda (1989). *I neolaureati in azienda*. Milan: Il Sole 24 Ore.

Cesaratto, S., Mangano, S., and Sirilli, G. (1991). "The Innovative Behaviour of Italian Firms: A Survey of Technological Innovation and R&D." *Scientometrics* 21:207–33.

Cespri (1990). "L'integrazione internazionale del sistema di industria e servizi dell'Italia: muta-menti strutturali e strategie verso il 1993." IV Rapporto CESPRI-Bocconi, Camera di Commercio, Milan

Cominotti, R., and Mariotti, S. (1990). *Italia multinazionali*. Milan: F. Angeli.

Consiglio Nazionale Ricerche (CNR) (Various years). *Annual Report*.

Contini, B., and Revelli, R. (1986). "Natalità e mortalità delle imprese italiane: risultati preliminari e nuove prospettive di ricerca." *L'Industria* 7, 2:195–232.

Dosi G. (1989). "Imprese ed istituzioni nello sviluppo di nuovi paradigmi tecnologici in Italia. In F. Onida and R. Malaman (eds.), *Industria italiana ed alte tecnologie*, 67–82. Milan: F. Angeli.

Dosi, G., and Moggi M. (1989). "Diffusione delle tecnologie elettroniche ed evoluzione della struttura industriale *contemporanea*." In G. P. Barbetta and F. Silva (eds.), *Trasformazioni strutturali delle imprese italiane*, 207–30. Bologna: Il Mulino.

Emrietti, A., and Fornengo, G. *Il Gruppo Fiat: dall'initio degli anni ottanta alle proslettive del mercato unificato*. Roma: Nuova Italia Scientifica, 1988.

Falzoni, A. (1990). "La bilancia tecnologica dei pagamenti italiana." In F. Onida and F. Malerba (eds.), *La ricera scientifica*, 147–66. Rome: SIPI.

Fornari, I., Malaman, R., and Morawetz, A. (1989). *The Relations between Public Research Organizations and Firms: The Case of Italy*. Milan. Working Paper CESPRI Universita Bocconi.

Fornengo, G., and Silva, F. (1989). *Growth Strategies of the Largest Italian Groups (1981–85)*. Manuscript: Turin.

Galimberti, I. (1989). "Le comunicazioni in fibra ottica." In F. Onida and R. Malaman (eds.), *Industria italiana ed alte tecnologie*, 197–326. Milan: F. Angeli.

Galimberti, I., and Klutzer, S. (1988). "I programmi tecnologici comuni e il loro impatto sul sistema ricerca-innovazione in Italia." In R. Malaman and P. Ranci (eds.), *Le politiche industriali della CEE*. Bologna: Il Mulino.

Galimberti, I., Gola, C., and Orsenigo, L. (1989). "Le biotecnologie." In F. Onida and R. Malaman (eds.), *Industria italiana ed alte tecnologie*, 27–112. Milan: F. Angeli.

Gandolfi, V. (1988). *Aree sistema*. Milan: F. Angeli.

Ginebri, S. (1987). "I progetti finalizzati del CNR e le loro ricadute in termini di impulsi innovativi. CESPE papers

Graziani, A. (1979). *L'economia italiana dal 1945 ad oggi*. Bologna: Il Mulino.

Gros Pietro, G. M. (1985). "L'innovazione nell'industria italiana, situazioni e problemi." *L'Industria* 6(2):217–233.

ICE (1987). *Dossier made in Italy: I beni ad alta tecnologia*. Rome.

Istat (1988). "Indagine statistica sull'innovazione tecnologica nell'industria Italiana," December.

Istat (Various years). "Indagini sulla ricerca scientifica," Rome.

Kluzer, S. (1989a). "Alcune osservazioni sull'attività di ricerca scientifica e tecnologica sui laser in Italia." In F. Onida and R. Malaman (eds.), *Industria italiana ed alta tecnologie*, 85–193. Milan: F. Angeli.

Kluzer, S. (1989b). "Il settore dei laser commerciali." In F. Onida and R. Malaman (eds.), *Industria italiana ed alta tecnolognie*. Milan: F. Angeli.

La Noce, M. (1990). *Governmental Support to Italian Industry's R-D and Technological Innovation Expenditures During the 1980s.* Manuscript: Stockholm.

Lassini, A. (1985). *Gli interventi regionali per i servizi alle imprese.* Milan: F. Angeli.

Lassini, A. (1990). "I centri di servizio all'innovazione per le piccole e medie imprese." In F. Onida and F. Malerba (eds.), *La ricerca Scienticica.* Rome: SIPI.

Malaman, R. (1989). "Lo sviluppo dei nuovi materiali ceramici." In F. Onida and R. Malaman (eds.), *Industria italiana ed alta tecnologie*, 132–226. Milan: F. Angeli.

Malerba, F. (1987). *Dalla dipendenza alla capacità tecnologica autonoma.* Milan: F. Angeli.

Malerba, F. (1988). "La dinamica di lungo periodo della R-S dell'industria italiana." *Rivista di politica economica* April. 467–96.

Malerba, F., and Falzoni, A. (1991). "Tecnologia e dinamica settoriale nello sviluppo economico italiano." In C. Filippini (ed.), *Innovazione tecnologica e servizi alle imprese.* Milan: F. Angeli.

Malerba, F., and Orsenigo, L. (1991). "L'accumulazione delle capacità tecnologiche nell'industria italiana (1969-1984)." In C. Filippini (ed.), *Innovazione tecnologica e servizi alle imprese.* Milan: F. Angeli.

Mariotti, S. (1989). "Il riordino della funzione tecnica di produzione dell'industria." In V. Balloni (ed.), *Processi di aggiustamento delle industrie negli anni 80*, 233–65. Bologna: Il Mulino.

Mariotti, S., and Colombo, M. (1987). "L'innovazione di processo nell'industria italiana." *L'Industria* 2:27–66.

Mariotti, S., and Onida, F., (1986). *L'Italia Multinazionale.* Milan: Il Sole 24 Ore.

Momigliano, F. (1985). "Determinanti, tipologia ed effetti dell'innovazione come fattore di competitività." In F. Onida (ed.), *Innovazione, competitività e vincolo energetico*, 197–286. Bologna: Il Mulino.

Momigliano, F. (1986). *Le leggi della politica industriale in Italia.* Bologna: Il Mulino.

Morandini, C. (1990). "Il ruolo delle piccole e medie imprese." In F. Onida and F. Malerba (eds.), *La ricera scientifica*, 249–91. Rome: SIPI.

Mussati, G. (1988). "Il ruolo della piccola e media impresa nella struttura industriale italiana." Centro F. Cicogna, Working Paper No. 6.

Napolitano, G., and Sirilli, G. (1990). "Technical Change in the Italian Manufacturing Industry: A User Oriented Innovation Model." ISRDS-CNR Working Paper, Rome.

Nencini, G. (1989). *La ricerca scientifica in Italia.* Rome: La Nuova Italia Scientifica.

Nones, M. (1988). *La struttura del sistema difesa-industria in Italia.* Manuscript: Genua.

Nuti, F. (1988). "Trasformazioni strutturali delle piccole e medie imprese nei distretti industriali." In the Conference "Contesto competitivo e trasformazioni strutturali delle piccole e medie imperse nei distretti industriali e nei rapporti di subfornitura." Milan, February.

OECD (1991). *Review of National Science and Technology Policy.* Italy." Paris: OECD.

Onida, F., and Malaman, R. (1989). *Industria italiana ed alte tecnologie.* Milan: F. Angeli.

Onida, F., and Malerba, F. (1990). *La ricerca scientifica.* Rome: SIPI.

Onida, F., and Viesti, G. (eds.) (1987). *Italian Multinationals.* London: Croom Helms.

Piore, M., and Sabel, C. (1984). *The Second Industrial Divide: Possibilities for Prosperity.* New York: New Basic Books.

Pontarollo, E. (1986). *Domanda pubblica e politica industriale: FS, SIP, ENEL.* Milan: Marsilio.

Raffa, M., and Zollo, G. (1987). "Innovazione e crescita delle piccole e mdie imprese del settore automazione, strumentazione e sistemi." *L'Impresa* N.2:197–226.

Raffa, M., and Zollo, G. (1988). "Dinamiche e strategie delle piccole imprese innovative." *L'Industria* 3:419–69.

Riva, A. (1983). "Sviluppo e innovazione nella piccola e media impresa." *IRER.* Milan: F. Angeli.

Romano, A. (1989). *Mezzogiorno 1992.* Milan: F. Angeli.

Rullani, E., and Zanfei, A. (1988a). "Networks between Manufacturing and Demand: Cases from Textile and Clothing Industry." In C. Antonelli (ed.), *Information Technology and Industrial Change: The Italian Case,* 57–95. Dordrecht: Kluwer.

Rullani, E., and Zanfei, A. (1988b). "Area Networks: Telematics Connections in a Traditional Textile District." In C. Antonelli (ed.), *Information Technology and Industrial Change: The Italian Case,* 97–113. Dordrecht: Kluwer.

Russo, M. (1985). "Technical Change and the Industrial District." *Research Policy* 3:329–43.

Santarelli, E., and Sterlacchini, A. (1989). "Patterns regionali di innovazione tecnologica in Italia. R-S, brevetti sull'estero, imprese innovative." *L'Industria* 1:25–56.

Sapelli, G. (1989). *Modelli di crescita e progresso tecnico. Riflessioni sull'Italia.* Manuscript: Milan.

Sirilli, G. (1987). "Patents and Inventors: an empirical study." *Research Policy.* 16:157–74.

Soria, L. (1979). *Informatica: un'occasione perduta.* Turin: Einaudi.

Vacca', S. (1986). "Internazionalizzazione delle imprese: passaggio obbligato per lo sviluppo tecnologico o veicolo di dipendenza?" *Economia e Politica Industriale* 49:3–24.

PART II

SMALLER
HIGH-INCOME
COUNTRIES

Part II is concerned with the innovation systems of four "small" high-income countries. Their levels of gross domestic product per capita are comparable to those of the countries considered in Part I, and stand high above the income levels of the countries considered in Part III. In terms of literacy rates, basic enrollment in secondary education, and in third level education, these countries look a lot like those in Part I, with Canada being very similar to the United States. However, in terms of population these countries are much smaller. Even the largest of them, Canada, has less than half the population of the large European countries, and is far smaller than the United States or Japan. The populations of the other three countries are even smaller. Thus their internal markets are much smaller than those of the countries considered in Part I.

Two of these economies, the two largest ones physically—Canada and Australia—grew up as colonies of Great Britain (with Canada also having an old French connection), which significantly shaped their economic roles and international economic connections, at least to the close of World War II. The other two are on the European continent, which also has shaped their pattern of development and trade.

Aside from its small population, Sweden in many ways now looks like the large industrialized nations in Part I. She is in their league regarding manufacuring output as a fraction of Gross Domestic Product, manufacturing exports account for most of her total exports, and her ratio of R&D to GNP is close to that of the highest of the large industrial nations. However, reflecting her small internal market, Sweden exports are a much larger fraction of her GDP than the countries considered in Part I, except for Germany.

In the other three countries manufacturing output as a fraction of Gross Domestic Product is significantly below that of the United States, the large European countries, and Japan, and manufacturing exports account for a smaller fraction of total exports. Agriculture and resource exploitation account for a larger share of economic activity than in the six large countries considered in Part I, and a larger share of exports are based on these activities. And the ratio of R&D to GNP in these countries stands significantly lower than that of the countries considered in Part I, except for Italy. This largely is associated with their smaller share of manufacturing activity in total GNP, and in particular their minor participation in some of the most R&D-intensive industries.

With the exception of Sweden, in these countries business R&D accounts for a significantly smaller fraction of total R&D. A larger fraction goes on in universities and government laboratories (Table II.1).

Table II.1. Comparison of the Four "Small" High-Income Countries

	Sweden	Denmark	Canada	Australia
GDP/capita, 1989 official exchange rates	19,300	18,450	16,960	12,340
GDP/capita, 1988 purchasing power parity	14,772	13,555	18,446	13,412
Population, 1988	8,438	5,130	25,950	16,538
Average growth rate GDP/hour average 1965–1988	1.8	1.8	2.7	1.7
Gross domestic investment GDP average 1965–1988	15	15.5	24	22
Manufacturing output/GDP	30	25	23	18
Manufacturing exports/GDP	26	19	16	5
Total exports/GDP	31	31	25	10
Literacy rate	>95	>95	>95	>95
Secondary level enrollment rate	91	107	104	98
Third level enrollment rate	31	30	58	29
Scientists and engineers/population	0.25	0.17	0.22	0.21
R&D/GNP	3.0	1.3	1.5	1.4
Private R&D/total R&D	61	47	42	61
Business R&D/total R&D	66.8	55.6	55.0	37.4
Private business R&D/total business R&D	87.0	85.9	71.8	93.3

8

Comparing the Danish and Swedish Systems of Innovation

CHARLES EDQUIST
BENGT-ÅKE LUNDVALL

SIMILARITIES AND DIFFERENCES BETWEEN DENMARK AND SWEDEN[1]

Most comparative work on national systems supporting technical change has focused on the differences between the United States and Japan. Such comparisons may be very useful as first approximations; they demonstrate, lucidly, how differences in national economic structures and institutional setups are reflected in differences in the rate and direction of technical change. In this chapter Sweden and Denmark, i.e., countries that are much more similar, are compared.

From a non-European perspective, Sweden and Denmark might seem almost identical.[2] But the closer the observer gets the more visible the differences become. In this chapter it is proposed that the Danish and the Swedish systems of innovation have quite different characteristics. It is argued that these characteristics are embedded in the economic structure and in the socioinstitutional setup and that they have strong and deep roots in the economic history of the two countries.[3]

Proximity and Common Characteristics

The distant observer is certainly right in perceiving striking similarities between Denmark and Sweden. It takes less than half an hour to cross the Sound between them, and on arrival in the neighboring state you can read its newspapers and, with a minor effort, take part in conversation with its citizens. There are few legal difficulties limiting movements across the borders. You do not have to show your passport, and you have the same right as the indigenous population to enter the labor market.

The living standard, life-style, and consumption pattern do not seem to vary much between the two societies. In both countries the public sector is in charge of systems for education and health service, which are of a comparably high quality. This is reflected in high tax rates and generally, of course, in a large public sector. Important factors behind the expansion of the public sector have been the strong Social Democratic presence in politics and the strong trade unions.

Looking back in history, we find important parallels that might partly explain the similarities of today. Both countries were industrial latecomers. In 1979 the two countries were ranked among the 10 countries having the highest GNP/capita (Sweden as number 6 and Denmark as 8). Apparently, both countries have been successful in exploiting technology to stimulate economic growth. Thus, it is easy to understand why a distant observer would tend to speak about these two small and rich countries as reflecting one single Scandinavian, or Nordic, model. One point to be made in this chapter is that such similarities in overall aggregate performance might coexist with—and even conceal—radical differences between national systems of innovation. Also, it implies that quite different institutional setups may be effective in exploiting technological opportunities. One question, however, is whether the Nordic systems of innovation, so successful historically, will remain so in the present and prospective global context.[4]

Conspicuous Differences in Indicators on Innovative Activities

Although the long-term growth records look rather similar, the most up-to-date indicators on innovative activities put Denmark and Sweden into two different leagues. We can see from Table 8.1 that Sweden is a country investing heavily in R&D whereas Denmark is characterized by an internationally very modest R&D effort. Turning to output indicators we find that Sweden is one of the countries with the highest numbers of patents per capita in the United States, whereas Denmark has a very weak record in this respect.[5]

What is the background for these dramatic differences between the two countries? We shall argue that they reflect qualitative differences in the national systems of innovation and that these differences can be understood only if we take into account specificities of the historical process of industrialization in the two countries.

We will also propose that one important, contemporary, factor behind the observed differences in registered innovative activities is the degree of economic concentration, and the related role of domestically based multinational capital in the two economies.

Table 8.1. Comparison of R&D Intensity (1985) and Number of United States Patents Per Million Inhabitants in Denmark, Sweden, United Kingdom, United States, and Japan, Annual Averages 1980–1985

Innovation Indicators	R&D Expenditures/GDP (%)	United States Patents Per Million Inhabitants 1980–1985
Denmark	1.25	27
Sweden	2.78	89
United Kingdom	2.33	41
United States	2.78	158
Japan	2.81	79

Source: R&D expenditures from OECD (1988a, p. 13). United States patents for Denmark (the average for 1980–1982) from Mjöset (1986, p. 81) and for the other countries from Patel and Pavitt (1989, p. 20).

Again, the two countries present themselves as very different as shown in Table 8.2. In Denmark the small and medium-sized enterprises dominate in manufacturing and only a few internationally small multinational firms have their home base in Denmark. In Sweden the degree of concentration in terms of ownership and control is very high, even in international terms, and the amount of capital abroad controlled by Swedish firms is large, relatively speaking.

The Structure of This Chapter as Reflecting Conceptual Matters

The rest of this chapter is divided into four main sections. The first gives a brief historical sketch of the processes of industrialization in Denmark and Sweden. The second describes the anatomy of the two systems of innovation in terms of the socioinstitutional setup, the structure of production, and the R&D system. The performance of the systems is discussed in the next section. Finally some prospective problems are addressed. This structure reflects our understanding of what constitutes a national system of innovation, as outlined below.

The national system of innovation[6] is constituted by the institutions and economic structures affecting the rate and direction of technological change in the society. Obviously, the national system of innovation is larger than the R&D system. It must, for example, include not only the system of technology diffusion and the R&D system but also institutions and factors determining how new technology affects productivity and economic growth. At the same time, the system of technological change is, of course, less comprehensive than the economy/society as a whole.[7]

We assume that technical competence is built in a cumulative process. This is the reason why we find it useful to give a brief historical sketch of the industrialization process. The cumulative character of the process of technical change reflects that interactive learning is at the center of the process of technical change. Individual agents and organizations increase their knowledge in technical matters, not in isolation from each other, but in a process of interaction, involving learning from each other as well as producing new knowledge and innovations in cooperation.[8]

We also assume learning to be a process strongly based in routine economic activities. At the firm level, it involves workers and technicians (engaged in production routines), marketing people (engaged in selling to the ordinary customers), as well as laboratory personel (engaged in routine experiments). One result from learning is that new problems are registered, and entered on the agenda of organizations. But it also

Table 8.2. Indicators of Economic Concentration and of Domestically Based Multinational Firms

	Share of Value Added in Manufacturing by the 10 Biggest Firms, 1982 (%)	Foreign Employment in Domestic Large Firms, 1984 (Absolute Number)
Denmark	14	51,000
Sweden	33	256,000

Source: Data on value added from Nordic Growth (1984, p. 185) and on foreign employment from Industriökonomisk Institut (1986, p. 61).

produces important inputs to the process of solving the problems faced by organizations engaged in searching (R&D departments, etc.).

This is the general background for the section on the anatomy of the national system of innovation. The socioinstitutional setup focuses on corporative arrangements forming a framework for interactive learning. The development blocks define areas of specialization giving such processes their content and direction. The R&D efforts, representing attempts to expand knowledge through searching rather than learning, will, as well as technology policies, be rooted partly in the production system.

Having stressed interactivity and learning, it is analytically useful to make certain distinctions with regard to the process of technical change. In the section on performance, two such distinctions are used. First, it is fruitful to distinguish between product technologies and production technologies (or process technologies) in the sphere of production. Product technologies are or are included in products (goods or services) and production technologies are used in the process of production to produce goods and services.

Second, it is also useful to make an analytical distinction between development of technologies and their diffusion.[9] The development of technology involves the production of technically feasible prototypes (inventions) and their modification and development into economically feasible technologies (innovations).[10] A breakthrough innovation is here assumed to be made only once in time and space. Everything else is diffusion, which includes absorption or assimilation of technologies developed in other countries.[11] Diffusion also includes adaptations and incremental innovations. In other words, technologies are gradually modified and changed during the whole process of technical change (i.e., also during the process of diffusion).[12]

It may sometimes be difficult empirically to make a clearcut distinction between development and diffusion. And the same artifact may sometimes be a product technology and sometimes a process technology.[13] Sometimes, but not always, a radically new product technology will also involve a need for new process technology; they may mutually condition each other. But at the same time, the distinctions prove to be very useful, as analytical tools, when it comes to analyze and characterize the performance of national systems of innovation.

The fact that a country is strong in the development of new technology, for example, does not rule out that it has great difficulty in terms of diffusion—reflecting a weak ability to absorb new technologies (products or processes) into its production system. And the fact that a country is extremely strong in terms of the diffusion of process technology does not rule out that it has great weaknesses in the diffusion of new product technologies—reflecting a weak ability to take up the production of new products, characterized by strong growth, and developed abroad. As we will see, there are examples of both these kinds.

In the section on performance, Denmark and Sweden are compared regarding their capacity to develop new technologies. We then focus on the diffusion of new process technologies and, finally, we look at the diffusion of new product technologies. The analyses demonstrate that the capability profiles of Sweden and Denmark differ in these dimensions—which confirms the usefulness of the distinctions made.

The understanding of technical change as a cumulative process based on interactive learning implies that national systems tend to be geared to follow specific trajectories. The close relation between learning and searching is crucial when it comes to moving rapidly ahead along given technological trajectories. However, the close relation might also result in locking the system of innovation into a specific trajectory in a period characterized by a change in technology paradigm. In the long run, this may cause problems in terms of stagnation, especially as it may involve a weakness in relation to the diffusion of product technologies (i.e., a weak capability to absorb new product technologies developed abroad). This problem is discussed briefly with regard to the two Nordic systems of innovation in the final section on structural and institutional problems.

There are several important elements of the national systems of innovation which we have not included in this analysis of Sweden and Denmark. Examples are the financial system and the institutional characteristics of the R&D system. It is especially true for the education and training system and the work organization.[14] We believe that the interface between technology and the development of human resources is critical for the prospective survival and growth of national systems of innovation but this perspective will have to be elaborated elsewhere.

HISTORY: THE PROCESSES OF INDUSTRIALIZATION IN SWEDEN AND DENMARK

The present profile of the two systems of innovation illustrates the cumulative character of processes of technical change and the stubborness of historically established institutional setups and economic structures. The two economies have taken part in a rapid, and far-reaching, process of internationalization. Nevertheless, it is to an important extent possible to trace their present patterns of specialization and current specific strengths and weaknesses in their systems of innovation back to how their respective economies were industrialized.

From Grain to Butter and Meat: The Establishment of the Danish Agroindustrial Complex

In the 1870s, the Danish economy was predominantly agrarian and linked to the world economy mainly through its grain exports to the United Kingdom. In this decade new competitive grain producers (Russia and the United States) entered the British market. The Danish response to the resulting dramatic fall in grain prices (40% price reduction 1880–1890), and to the ensuing crisis in Danish agriculture, was a reorientation of production from grain to pigs and cattle and, also, gradually toward more processed products.[15]

It is interesting to note that the cream separator (a continuous centrifuge), which was to play a crucial role in making the dairy industry a modern process industry, was invented almost simultaneously in Sweden and Denmark in the 1870s.[16] The rapid diffusion of this technical innovation through the Danish economy in the following decades was combined with an important social innovation—the introduction of cooperatively organized ownership of dairies. This form of organization proved to be an efficient framework for the modernization of both primary agriculture and the secondary industries refining milk and cattle into butter and meat; by 1910 90% of total exports were processed agricultural products such as bacon, butter, and cheese.[17]

In the wake of the modernization of agriculture and as farmer's income level rose, the domestic market for industrial products expanded. In the 1890s, and again in the 1930s, new home market industries developed, but it was not until the 1960s that an increasingly export-oriented manufacturing sector developed. As late as 1958, 61% of commodity exports emanated from agriculture (including agroindustrial products such as butter, cheese, and bacon) and 39% came from manufacturing. In 1968, this had been reversed: 62% came from manufacturing and 38% originated in agriculture (Andersen, 1972, p. 62ff).

As we shall see, the history of the transformation of the agroindustrial complex is reflected both in the pattern of specialization of Danish technical competence and in the organization of innovation. The cooperatively owned agroindustrial sector has been very successful in developing, producing, and marketing food products of a uniform, and high, standard. State-supported development work and quality control have interacted with the efforts of the cooperatives aiming at a high and stable quality. The success is reflected even in the present export specialization of Denmark. Butter, cheese, ham, and bacon are still dominating export products earning an important part of foreign currency. The export specialization indices presented in Table 8.3 illustrate this fact.

One strength of cooperative ownership has been its stimulation of rapid technology diffusion. A weakness has been the one-sided focus of innovative activities on process technologies.[18] The R&D efforts have generally been small in the Danish agroindustrial sector[19] and this is especially true for R&D aiming at new product technologies.

Table 8.3. Export Specialization for Main Product Groups and for Some Dominating Natural Resource-Based Export Commodities in Denmark 1973–1987[a]

Product[b] and SITC Number	1973	1979	1987
Products based on natural resources	1.3	1.5	1.6
Bacon, ham, etc. (012.1)	49.4	46.9	30.4
Prepared preserved meat (013.8)	33.6	28.7	28.8
Butter (023.0)	10.3	6.8	4.7
Oil and gas	0.7	0.8	0.8
Chemicals	0.7	0.7	0.8
Engineering	0.7	0.7	0.6
Other industry	1.2	1.1	1.4

[a]The export specialization figures in Tables 8.3, 8.4, and 8.8 are calculated as "revealed comparative advantage" indices:

$$R_{ij} = \frac{X_{ij}/X_i}{X_j/X}$$

where R_{ij} is the export specialization index of country i in commodity j, X_{ij} is exports from country i of commodity j, X_i is total exports from country i, X_j is total OECD exports of commodity j, and X are total OECD exports (Dalum et al., 1988, p. 134). If the value is 1.0 there is no specialization. The more the values deviate from 1.0, the stronger is the specialization. If the value is larger than 1.0 there is a large export of the product (group) in question. If the value is below 1.0, this is a reflexion of a small export of the relevant product.

[b]The exact content of the product groups is specified in Dalum (1989, Appendix 1).

Source: IKE database (Bent Dalum).

From Agriculture, Forestry, and Mining toward Engineering in Sweden

Sweden was, of course, also a predominantly agrarian country in the latter half of the nineteenth century. Agricultural products were also exported. From about 1830 Sweden began exporting oats to England.[20] During some years in the late 1870s, oats was the second largest export product (after wood). The export of oats decreased sharply after 1880, but was immediately replaced by a large butter export.

However, in contrast to Denmark, a large part of Swedish exports had its origin in forestry and mining rather than agriculture. And this export did not consist of plain raw materials, but of refined products. From the seventeenth century to the mid-nineteenth century iron was the main mining-based export product.[21] During the latter half of the nineteenth century new processes made possible production of cheap steel—also from the phosphor-rich iron ore abundant in Sweden. Somewhat later iron and steel began to be transformed into machinery products before export. The forestry-based export commodities were from the mid-nineteenth century "plank and boards"—processed by the sawmill industry—as opposed to timber. Later, wood was further refined and exported as pulp and paper.[22]

The fact that the export products emanating from mining and forestry were already refined products created, in the case of iron and steel, an important metallurgical capability. Hence, an important part of the nineteenth-century transformation in Sweden took place outside agriculture. In particular, the engineering industry became—and still is—a strategic sector for the modernization of the Swedish economy around the turn of the century. Employment in the engineering industry increased from 23,000 in 1890 to 63,000 in 1912, while employment in mining and iron works decreased from 35,000 to 32,000 during the same period (Gårdlund 1942, p. 279).

This expansion of the engineering industry was gradually reflected in exports. In 1880 it constituted 3% of total exports, growing to 10.5% in 1911–1913 (Senghaas, 1982, p. 131). In the interwar period the proportion of machinery and transport equipment kept growing and in 1950 its share of total export had passed 20% (Svennilson, 1954, p. 180ff). Its share of manufacturing exports was now getting close to 50% and only in the United States was this share higher among OECD countries.

The development of the Swedish engineering industries reflected a small number of specific technical innovations introduced by Swedish inventors and entrepreneurs. Among early important Swedish technical innovations we find an automatic machine for cutting matches (Lagerman invented it around 1860), the separator already mentioned above (invented in the 1870s), and new methods for processing pulp (developed by Ekman in the beginning of the 1870s). It is important to note that these three early inventions were all closely related to the export-oriented process industries.

Several important Swedish innovations in mechanical and electromechanical systems took place around the turn of the century. Several of the largest Swedish multinational firms may, actually, be regarded as originally based on single product innovations. This is certainly true for Ericsson (innovations exploiting low current technology by Lars-Magnus Ericsson), SKF (the development of ball bearing technology by Wingquist), ASEA (the development of a three-phased motor by Wenström), and Alfa Laval (the separator). The focus on single inventions and inventors might be misleading to a certain degree. All of these technological breakthroughs were, obviously, cumulative in the sense that they were built on a competence reflecting several decades of experience with metal working and with technical development in engineering.

In Sweden, an important outcome of the process of industrialization was the combination of exports based on refined and processed raw materials on the one hand and the multinational engineering firms on the other. The Swedish system of innovation still reflects this combination both in its institutional setup and in its pattern of specialization—as indicated by the export specialization indices presented in Table 8.4. In particular, it is the small number of multinational firms in the engineering industry that plays a decisive role in this system.[23]

ANATOMY: THE TWO NATIONAL SYSTEMS OF INNOVATION

Introduction

In this section we will discuss the anatomy of the Swedish and Danish systems of technological change. We begin with a discussion of the socioinstitutional setups in the two countries. The focus is on the corporative interaction between the labor unions, the welfare state, and private capital.

We then take a closer look at the patterns of specialization and the production structure in the two countries. Among other things, we point out a few strategic development blocks in each country.

Finally, we address the R&D systems and the role of the state in relation to technological change (i.e., technology policy). We end by briefly characterizing the two systems of innovation.

Social and Political Similarities and Differences

Both Denmark and Sweden are modern welfare states. The size of the public sector and, especially, of the parts engaged in social security, health care, and education put them in a class by themselves. And, since the 1930s, both countries have been char-

Table 8.4. Export Specialization for Main Product Groups and for Some Dominating Natural Resource-Based Export Commodities for Sweden 1973–1987[a]

Products[b] and SITC Number	1973	1979	1987
Product based on natural resources	1.1	1.1	1.1
Mechanical wood pulp (251.2)	20.0	31.0	20.5
Kraft paper (641.3)	18.5	24.6	24.9
Iron and steel powder (671.3)	14.8	16.9	16.7
Oil and gas	0.2	0.5	0.7
Chemicals	0.5	0.5	0.6
Engineering	1.1	1.1	1.0
Other industry	0.9	0.9	0.9

[a]For definition of export specialization index, see note *a* in Table 8.3.

[b]The exact content of the product groups is specified in Dalum (1989, Appendix 1).

Source: IKE database (Bent Dalum)

acterized by strong trade unions and by a strong political presence of Social Democratic parties.

However, there are also important differences of a social and political character between the two countries. In Sweden a stable modernist social liberal norm system dominates the political culture and institutions while political culture is less homogeneous and stable in Denmark. For example, the room for political deviations to the left and right has been greater in Denmark than in Sweden. The Social Democratic dominance of the political scene and inside the trade unions has been less continuous and hegemonic in Denmark than in Sweden.

Differences in the structure and institutions of private economic power, rooted in the history of industrialization, are also important influences on the differences in political culture in the two countries. As we have seen in Table 8.2, a small number of private firms dominate Swedish manufacturing. Also ownership and financial control are much more concentrated in Sweden than in Denmark. In Denmark the farmers' movement and the small owners have played a much more important role. The Swedish corporative interaction between big capital and labor has contributed to the stability of political development while it has been more difficult to establish long-term and corporatist social compromises in Denmark because none of the parties has been strong enough to guarantee the fulfillment of such a contract.[24]

The Labor Market
The more "modern" character of the Swedish system and its more stable context for corporatist cooperation are reflected in the institutions around the labor market. In Denmark the influence of preindustrial organizational forms is reflected in the trade union structure, as well as in the systems for training workers. The trade unions in Sweden are centralized and organized along industry lines, while the Danish unions are organized according to profession and competence. The training system in Denmark is a dual system where one of its elements may be regarded as a remnant from preindustrial artisan training.

Labor market conditions differ greatly between the two countries. In Sweden the registered unemployment rate has never in the postwar period reached 4%, while it has reached and permanently stayed above 8% in Denmark since the 1973 oil crisis. In 1990 it is about 1.5 and 10%, respectively.[25] The very low level of unemployment in Sweden means that most sectors and regions experience a severe shortage of labor. Both countries spend considerable amounts of money on labor market policy. In Sweden most of the money is used to retrain or to reemploy hit or threatened workers. In Denmark almost all of the expenditures go to cash payments to the many unemployed workers.

The Swedish Model and Its Impact on the Process of Technical Change
In Sweden a fundamental historical compromise on rationalization and technical change was established in the 1920s and 1930s. In the late 1920s and early 1930s, the leadership of the trade union movement changed its attitude to the introduction of new technology, and to rationalization of the labor process, into a much more positive one.

Originally, the trade unions had been extremely negative to Taylorism and rationalization, regarding them as threatening the workers with technological unemployment. One of the reasons for the change in attitudes was the belief—rightly or wrongly—that the Social Democratic government, established in 1933, could guarantee that new production technology would not result in widespread unemployment. Another reason was their belief that unions would be capable of appropriating what they considered their rightful share of the productivity gains. Hence, the very positive attitude toward technical change of the Swedish unions has been around for many decades now. This is one sense in which the term "Swedish model" can be used.

Johansson (1989) shows in detail how agreements between labor and capital—with regard to rationalization, technical change, and related matters—have been reached through a complex process. In the majority of conflicting issues, the unions have, in negotiations with the employers, threatened to use their privileged links with (Social Democratic) state power and to "solve" the problems through legal means. However, this threat has, normally, led to an agreement through negotiations between the labor market partners, without any formal state interference. But, indirectly, the welfare state and its commitment to full employment policies has been an important precondition for the lasting viability of this compromise. Hence, the emergence of the "Swedish model" in this sense has been characterized by an interplay between three parties: (efficient and concentrated) capital, (strong and centralized) trade unions, and the (Social Democratic) state.

The permanent shortage of workers in the postwar period means that firms compete with each other in attracting workers. One means of competition is salary. Another possibility is to make jobs more interesting and stimulating. Firms are pushed to redefine jobs in order to enlarge the scope of tasks allocated to each worker and thereby make the jobs more attractive. This means that the shortage of labor has important consequences for the quality of jobs (Edquist and Glimell, 1989, p. 43).

The shortage of labor may also influence management strategies and work organization ideas and thereby the sociotechnical and organizational design of new factories. One example, although atypical in its radicalism, is the Volvo Uddevalla factory. The shortage of labor, combined with inferior working conditions in traditional automobile assembly, has contributed to a high turnover of workers and to absenteeism—which means large costs for the employer. This has been one of the reasons why Volvo has recently designed the factory in Uddevalla according to new principles. In Uddevalla there is no moving assembly line at all. Instead a small group of workers "builds" (which is the new word for assemble) the whole car in a 2-hour cycle[26] (Edquist and Glimell, 1989, pp. 43–44).

The term "Swedish model" can also be used to denote the Swedish model for economic policy, including union-managed solidaristic wage policy, which developed after World War II. One important aspect of the Swedish model, in this sense, was acceptance of and even active support of structural change of the trade unions. If an industrial sector was ailing it was assumed to reflect low relative productivity and/or stagnating demand. General economic policies pursued by the state (through investment funds and labor market policies) and by the centralized trade unions (through solidarity wage policies, securing the largest wage increases for the lowest paid worker) combined forces in stimulating a transfer of resources from the ailing sectors to growth industries with better long-run prospects. Gösta Rehn and Rudolf Meidner were the architects behind the Swedish model of wage formation.

The Danish Model and Its Impact on the Process of Technical Change

The dominance of small scale production, and the historical importance of the cooperative movement in agriculture, has limited the influence of big capital in Denmark. One important consequence of the success of the cooperative movement in gaining control in the dominating export sectors was that it closed these strategic sectors to private capital. This is reflected in the weak position of financial capital in relation to the Danish production system.

The survival of small scale and artisan-like production has fostered a kind of corporatism, very different from the Swedish. Small, independent, entrepreneurs in Denmark will often be quite negative to central trade union power, but at the same time, often willing to cooperate, locally, with their workers and their representatives. They will often be driven by incentives less oriented toward firm growth and more toward the maintenance of an independent, and reasonably comfortable, life-style.

This small-scale corporatist model often involving a flexible use of reasonably advanced production equipment and a continuous development of incremental product innovations has its strength in flexible adaptation. But a great weakness seems to be that it does not give enough incentives to use and develop human resources inside firms. In the 1980s Danish firms have invested heavily in advanced process technologies and the disappointing outcome in terms of poor productivity performance reflects, primarily, problems with labor organization and skill development (Gjerding et al., 1990).

The workers' attitude to rationalization seems to be different in Denmark than in Sweden. Some years ago, a questionnaire sent to a representative sample of Danish citizens asked about attitudes toward "new technology." Two-thirds of the respondents expected mainly a negative impact on employment, as well as on work satisfaction. The negative expectations were strongest among the unskilled workers but, even among small owners, the negative expectations dominated (Petersen et al., 1983).

Economic policies at the national level reflect the fact that the corporative parties are weak and heterogeneous. Although incomes policies, at least until recently, was a trade union responsibility in Sweden it is the state in Denmark that has repeatedly tried to regulate incomes and wages. It has proved difficult to make incomes policies efficient without a high level of unemployment, however.

On the Structure of Production as Reflected in Development Blocks

When comparing the structure of production in Sweden and Denmark, it is useful to isolate a small number of *development blocks,* in each of the two countries. This concept was developed by the Swedish economist Erik Dahmén. Dahmén's interest is in the *transformation* of industry and trade. Therefore he focuses on changes over time within and between microentities. According to Dahmén such changes are the essence of industrial dynamics. They imply disequilibria, which should not, however, be regarded as disturbances because they are essential in transformation processes (Dahmén, 1970, 1988, p. 4).

A *development block* is a sequence of complementarities—between technological, economic, and other related factors—which by way of a series of disequilibria (or structural tensions) may result in a balanced situation.[27] Dahmén talks about development blocks and structural tensions at different levels of aggregation—from the factory floor over the interplay between enterprises to a broader socioeconomic context. We will here use the concept at a level of aggregation lower than the national economy but still not focusing on distribution of production and employment only at the level of industrial sectors.[28]

A development block will, typically, involve several domestic sectors, coupled by strong quantitative and qualitative linkages. We assume that development blocks form frameworks for interactive learning and that the specific combination of such blocks at the national level will have an important impact on the direction of processes of technological change.

Development Blocks in the Danish Economy

In the historical review we saw how an export-oriented development block had already formed around the agroindustrial activities at the beginning of this century. Still, at the end of the 1970s slightly more than 42% of total nonservice employment and nonservice exports emanated from this block (Lundvall et al., 1984, p. 23). Its present importance is also reflected in the export specialization figures for the postwar period presented in Table 8.3. The successful transformation of the Danish agriculture in the last part of the nineteenth century is still strongly reflected in the pattern of export specialization.

Actually, the block encompasses two different modes of development and two different modes of innovation. The dominating one has at its center the farmer-owned cooperative process industries. The other mode is dominated by a few large (according to a Danish standard) private food-producing firms. Some of these firms are, or have been, semipublic firms, started as licensed monopolistic producers of, for example, liquor or sugar and several of them are controlled by the old merchant and shipping firm ØK.

We have already commented on the strengths and the weaknesses of the cooperative model. The one-sided focus on standardization and rationalization of the labor process in slaughteries and dairies combined with the neglect of product innovation reflects the mode of competition and ownership in the cooperative sector. With prices given through EC regulations the competition between the different cooperative companies has been directed toward gaining access to a maximum amount of raw materials (milk, pigs, or cattle). This competition has put strong upward pressure on input prices, and the individual owners of the cooperatives have not had any strong incentives to engage in costly and uncertain long-term projects. Actually the cooperative movement has been so successful that it has eliminated most private Danish slaughter firms and dairies. Also, the process of concentration of production in the cooperative process industries has gone much further than in the privately owned sector. Now, more than two-thirds of all milk is passing through one dairy company and at present strong efforts are being made to join the last handful of cooperative slaughter firms into a single one.

Among the private companies involved in food processing, we find some of the technically most advanced Danish firms. These firms are often conglomerates, with activities in related fields of chemical production or engineering. For example, the sugar refining company developed advanced know-how in filter technology to support its main line of business. This technology was later applied by affiliated engineering firms, first to refine milk, and later to wastewater treatment, and was built into environment technology. By international standards these firms are not big, however, and they operate, typically, in specialized niches.

Until the beginning of the 1970s, two other development blocks played an important role in stimulating the growth of the economy. One was oriented toward shipping and ship-building and the other toward construction. With the international crisis in shipping, following in the wake of the oil crisis, this development block became a structural problem in Denmark as in many other countries.

The same was true for the development block oriented toward domestic construction. This block had expanded very rapidly, especially in the 1960s, and it involved not only construction as such but also the cement industry. Again we find a strong Danish technological position in cement processing machinery and production systems (F.L. Schmidt). With the oil crisis a drastic reduction in the activities inside this block took place.

Of course, not all parts of Danish production are integrated in such development blocks. In the export-oriented industrial growth, in the 1960s, a number of technically rather advanced firms in electronics expanded and became internationalized. Several of them had developed their basic, and original, competence in an interaction with domestic users—often to be found inside the public sector—but gradually they developed into enclaves.[29] These firms are engaged in medical technologies, scientific instruments, and measurement, for example.

Another, much larger group of Danish firms, in the engineering sector, produces traditional machinery or components for engineering products for larger Danish or foreign firms. The production takes place on the basis of skilled workmanship often with the help of computer-controlled machinery. It is often very flexible in terms of the products, while the connection to R&D and science is quite weak.

Development Blocks in the Swedish Economy

As in Denmark, it is possible to locate Swedish development blocks around the basic export commodities (e.g., iron and steel and wood, pulp, and paper). In these areas there has developed an infrastructure of smaller firms, service organizations, equipment producers, and research organizations, according to Stenberg (1987). In particular, the relations between specific raw material sectors and suppliers of equipment are sometimes quite important. Examples could be paper pulp producers and paper pulp machine producers or mining and mining equipment producers. This argument means, of course, clustering together specific parts of the engineering industry with its customers, implying that the relations between producers and users of various products may constitute an important relation of interactive learning.

Another development block, discussed in Stenberg (1987), is one grouped around production technology for the engineering sector. However, the engineering industry as a whole would be a very large and heterogeneous block, and it would therefore be useful to divide it into subsectors. Such an analysis might reflect the interaction between (groups of) engineering firms and their suppliers and/or customers. Such a division of the engineering industry into subblocks would be motivated also by the fact that the suppliers and customers mentioned are also, often, firms in the engineering industry.

Such an analysis would result in a number of development blocks centered around the large Swedish engineering firms or parts of them. Examples could be an electricity block (ABB Electricity, Vattenfall, etc.), an automobile block (Volvo and SAAB automobile production and their subcontractors), a telecommunication block (Ericsson, Televerket, etc.) and an aereoplane block (SAAB aeroplane production, its suppliers and the Swedish defense procurement). The Swedish development blocks might, because of the dominant role of a single or a few large firms, work differently than the Danish ones.

The relative strength of these blocks can be indicated through figures on export specialization. In Table 8.4 we have given these numbers for products based on domestic natural resources (agricultural products, wood, pulp, paper, textiles and iron and steel), oil and gas, chemicals, engineering, electronics, and transport equipment, and other industrial products. Table 8.4 illustrates the strong position still held by the sectors based on the domestic raw materials wood and iron. It also points to a relatively strong position in engineering and to a very weak position in chemicals.[30] Actually, one might argue that engineering, historically, and in a complex manner, has grown out of the raw material development block and, of course, especially the part oriented toward iron and steel. This perspective is supported by the fact that Swedish competence and R&D activity in nonferrous metals are quite weak, while it is strong both in engineering and in iron and steel (IVA, 1979a, p. 52).

The R&D System and Technology Policy

We will not try to give a detailed description of the institutions and their activities in the field of R&D and public technology policy in Sweden and Denmark in this section. For detailed presentations we refer to various national sources as well as to the OECD Reviews of National Science and Technology Policies for Sweden (OECD, 1987) and for Denmark (OECD, 1988a). Instead we will make an effort to bring forward the most characteristic aspects in a comparative perspective.

The R&D Effort

In the introduction we noted that Sweden is a big spender on R&D (2.8% of GDP) and that Denmark spends much less (1.3% of GDP).[31] Business enterprise expenditure on R&D was in 1985 1.05% of domestic product of industry in Denmark and 3.02% in Sweden—Sweden having the highest figure of all OECD countries (OECD, 1988b, Table 17). Sweden is like the large economic powers and Denmark is at a low level also compared to her fellow small countries in this respect.

Another difference is that in 1985 46.5% of all R&D was financed by public sources in Denmark but only 34.0% in Sweden. Hence more than 65% of the R&D was funded by the private sector in Sweden (OECD, 1988b Table 5). To the extent that a high proportion of private funding of R&D is an indicator of technological "maturity," Sweden is more advanced, in this respect, than Denmark. The Swedish firms have transformed themselves to R&D-based activities to a larger extent than the Danish ones.[32]

It is also important who executes R&D. Roughly a quarter of all Swedish R&D work is performed within the higher education system. The other three-quarters is performed by industry, national authorities, public, private, and cooperative research institutes, and independent consultants. However, the higher education system plays a much more prominent role in the performance of research (R) than in development (D). The basic and applied research (R) in industry is estimated at some 12% and development (D) at 88%. About half of the R&D undertaken by public authorities, institutes, etc., is research (R) and half is development (D) (OECD, 1987, p. 41). Most of the firm-based research (R) in Sweden is carried out by a handful of firms—including the pharmaceutical companies, which dominate in this respect. Most of the other corporations concentrate on more or less qualified development work (D).

The much more modest efforts in R&D in Denmark reflect several factors. To a certain degree, the low rate of investment in R&D in Denmark reflects the fact that small manufacturing firms tend to invest proportionally less in R&D than larger companies. Hence the small size of firms and the limited role of big multinational firms are important. Many of the small and medium sized Danish firms are, however, involved in development activities. For example, two-thirds of a sample of small and medium sized firms reported that they had introduced at least one new product in the market 1984–1989. However, most of these activities are not separated clearly from routine activities and do not get registered in R&D statistics.

In addition, the production structure of Danish manufacturing is a crucial determinant behind the low R&D expenditures. Several of the strategic export sectors have weak connections to a science base, and limited technological opportunities (e.g., in terms of prospects of development of radically new products such as furniture and food products). For example, in relation to value added the Danish food, drink, and tobacco industry (ISIC 31) spent 0.6% on R&D in 1987. The corresponding figure for Finland and Sweden was 1.6 and 1.7%, respectively (Nordisk FoU-statistik, 1987 og 1981–1987, 1990) Hence R&D expenditures in this sector are small in all countries. In this sense, the low overall R&D intensity in Denmark is to a large extent a consequence of the type of specialization of the economy.[33] However, the factors mentioned here cannot fully account for Denmark's limited R&D efforts. As we shall see later there seems to be a different "mode of innovation" in Denmark, based less on formalized R&D efforts.

Technology Policy
Technology policy is often identified with public R&D policy. Here, the term will be given a wider content. Technology policy includes public intervention in the process of technological change as a whole. It embraces both technological development and encouragement of the application of new technology regardless of its origin (i.e., absorption or diffusion). We will here briefly address several elements of technology policy: state support to R&D, national technology programs, support of technology diffusion, and public technology procurement.

Public support for technical R&D in Sweden is channeled through agencies such as STU (The Swedish Board for Technical Development) and is allocated, mostly, in response to initiatives from firms, institutions, and so on. Support measures consist of advisory services, grants or loans, commissions or contracts, and fellowships or prizes (for inventors). When the technology is developed, other agencies exist with the objective of providing support for later stages in the process of commercialization (OECD, 1987).[34]

During the 1980s a new element was added to the instruments of technology policy in Sweden. In late 1983 a decision was taken in Parliament to create a national

program on microelectronics components, financed by government and the participating firms jointly.[35] It has later been followed by a similar program on information
technology.[36] And in 1990 a decision was taken to launch a national program to give
state support to technology development in small and medium sized firms (mainly
subcontractors) in the engineering industry.

Danish technology policy reflects the dominance of small and medium-sized
enterprises in the economy. Public efforts to promote the application of new technology in industry strongly emphasize two objectives (OECD, 1988a, p. 59). The first is
to ensure that enterprises have access to information and advice on the application of
new technology. The second objective is to ensure that enterprises can be supplied with
solutions in areas where they have neither the personnel nor the equipment to pursue
investigations themselves. Such areas may include analyses or testing, experiments or
development, investment planning involving the procurement, commissioning, and
operation of a new production plant, organizing quality and production control systems, and other specialized activities related to technology (OECD, 1988a, p. 24).

Generally the emphasis has been on technical service organized through a net of
public or semipublic technological institutes rather than on support schemes for R&D
inside firms. The ambitions regarding industrial policy have been shifting radically
during the past decades. Until the middle of the 1980s there were few attempts to intervene besides the technical service net. In the middle of the 1980s began a short period
with a rather active policy effort.

In 1984 a technology policy initiative, with special reference to information technology, was initiated as the Technological Development Programme. This was a sizable national technology program under the Ministry of Industries, worth 1500 million Danish crowns, which was to be used over 5 years (1984–1989). The main aim of
the program was to promote the use of internationally available information technology in Danish industry as a whole, but it was also intended to stimulate independent
Danish development efforts in IT areas where there are special circumstances and
prospects (OECD, 1988a, p. 59).

This program was—officially because it had already succeeded in its goals—interrupted before 1989. Thereafter the level of ambition as regards an active technology
policy has been reduced. Except for limited programs for new materials and biotechnology, the government has moved to a policy where cost reductions, through tax
reductions and restrictive wage policy, are assumed to be sufficient to support industrial development and international competitiveness.

Obviously, Danish technology policy is biased toward diffusion rather than supporting the development of new knowledge and products. This is in sharp contrast to
the Swedish technology policy, which is very much a policy of R&D support to the
private sector. It seems as if the policy efforts in both countries tend to support the
already established mode of technological change rather than trying to correct its weak
sides. The interaction between state intervention and the market mechanism is
accordingly characterized by duplication rather than by complementarity.[37]

The technology policy initiatives mentioned above work mainly from the supply
side. There are also possibilities to intervene from the demand side.[38] One interesting
way to influence technical change from the demand side is to use public demand as a
means. Public procurement can, of course, influence the choice between existing technologies as well as which new ones are to be developed. Important consequences for

technology development might emanate from public demand when no such intentions lie behind the demand.

When analyzing the differences in procurement policies between Denmark and Sweden it is important to take into account their respective roles in international politics. While Denmark, as a member of NATO, can be quite modest in terms of independent military strength the Swedish armed neutrality is partly built on indigenous military technology. The cooperation between the state and the big private firms in ambitious projects, developing large and complex technological systems, was originally developed in areas of military importance. Typical examples were the different generations of military aircraft developed by SAAB; but there were several other large projects where the Ministry of Defense closely cooperated with the largest Swedish firms (Annerstedt, 1976). Denmark has never had any large-scale high-technology development programs in defense, space, or similar areas.

The Swedish nuclear power research program was originally oriented toward a potential Swedish atomic bomb. But when ASEA-ATOM, the development enterprise (which joined ASEA, Uddeholm, and the state) was established in 1969, the responsibility was to develop civil nuclear power. Another development enterprise, LM-Tel, joined the state (Swedish Telecom) with Ericsson in the development of telecommunication technology. In the 1950s, we find other similar cooperative enterprises focusing on, respectively, computer technology, and space technology. In the civilian sphere, public procurement in Sweden has also led to important results in the electricity field (ASEA-Vattenfall) and in railway equipment (ASEA—The State Railway Company).

Such large technology projects have not developed in Denmark. Neither the military demand, the firm structure, nor the strong noninterventionist ideology behind industrial policy has allowed such activities. The Danish state has played a role in technology areas relevant to manufacturing but through more indirect mechanisms. The most important function of the Danish state in this context has been, mostly unintentionally, to support innovation through organizing and financing professional and advanced demand for specific products. Among important examples of products, originally developed for public induced demand but later becoming hi-tech niche products with big international market shares, we find electronic hearing aids, mobile communication technology, medical instruments, and windmill technology.

This implies quite different kinds of relationships between the state and the private sector. In Sweden, a few large firms (e.g., Volvo, ASEA, SAAB, Ericsson, and Bofors) have been involved in quite intimate cooperation with state agencies. Such a close cooperation has contributed to mutual understanding between the state and the most important fraction of private capital in Sweden. In Denmark some small and medium-sized niche firms have profited from the development of an advanced public demand but most of the firms have not been involved in any formalized cooperation with the state.

An important part of technology development in Sweden takes place in a few large multinational corporations, strongly involved in big cooperative activities with professional government agencies. The working of the Danish system is quite different. The process of technical change in Denmark is organized neither by big firms nor by the state. It is quite self-organized. The only reasonably strong coordinating block in the economy has been the export-oriented, and cooperatively organized, agroindustrial sector. This sector has played a certain coordinating role as a demanding user of technologies developed by small and medium-sized firms. Even some of the strategic competencies in the small Danish high technology sector in engineering, pharmaceuticals, and chemicals can be traced back to experiences and learning made in relation to the agroindustrial complex.

The much weaker R&D effort in Denmark reflects the crucial role played by user–producer interaction in product development and the correspondingly weaker links between technical change and science. A recent study of 166 Danish product innovations in manufacturing (Christensen and Valentin, 1989) shows that almost all of the product innovations were based on knowledge already accumulated within the firms rather than on external knowledge sources. Many innovations were stimulated by users and they were also often involved during the process of development.

PERFORMANCE: THE DANISH AND SWEDISH SYSTEMS OF INNOVATION

In this section the performance of the two systems of innovation will be discussed. Performance will be expressed, first, in terms of economic growth and other macroeconomic indicators. Second, the focus is on output indicators relating more directly to the process of technical change and the national systems of innovation.

Macroeconomic Performance

Long-term economic growth rates in Denmark and Sweden were at internationally high levels during the century up to the 1960s. Since the middle of the 1960s the growth rates have become more moderate in relative terms, however. In both countries the average for the 1970s and the 1980s is clearly below the OECD average (Table 8.5). Since 1986 the Danish economy has been characterized by stagnating GNP and, presently, there are many signs pointing toward a period of zero growth also in the Swedish economy. There is also a serious productivity problem in Sweden.

These similarities in long-term trends is somewhat misleading, however. In the last decades the rythm of production and employment growth in manufacturing has been quite different in the two countries (Table 8.6). Immediately after the first oil crisis, the Danish industrial system reacted by dismissing many employees while the firms in Sweden kept their workers, absorbing the crisis in a marked slowdown in productivity growth. In the 1980s, the Danish economy had a brief period of strong growth in production and employment (1984–1987) while productivity growth was extremely slow. In this period employment in manufacturing started to fall more rap-

Table 8.5. GNP growth in Denmark, Sweden, and the OECD Average for 1960–1984

	1960–1964	1965–1969	1970–1974	1975–1979	1980–1984	1985–1986	1987–1989[a]
Denmark	5.6	4.2	2.6	2.5	1.6	3.4	−0.4
Sweden	5.2	3.6	3.4	1.5	1.5	1.8	2.2
OECD growth	5.1	5.0	3.8	3.2	2.0	2.8	2.7

[a]Preliminary figures.

Sources: 1960–1984, Mjöset (1986, p. 329) and after 1984 Dansk Ökonomi (1988).

Table 8.6. Annual Rate of Growth in GNP, Labor Productivity, and Employment in Manufacturing 1973–1985 in Denmark and Sweden

	1973–1979				1979–1985			
	y	z	n	u	y	z	n	u
Denmark	1.6	3.6	−2.0	5	2.8	1.8	1.0	9
Sweden	0.5	1.0	−0.5	2	1.6	3.1	−1.5	3

Sources: production (y), productivity (z), and employment growth (n) from Gjerding et al. (1988, p. 52); unemployment figures, averages for the periods (u) from Kongshöj Madsen (1989, p. 13).

idly in the Swedish economy. And this in spite of the two large devaluations in Sweden 1981 (10%) and 1982 (16%).

Another important difference reflected in Table 8.6 is, of course, the rates of unemployment. The Danish rate is now assumed to stabilize close to 10% while there is an extremely high demand for labor in Sweden in 1990. One result of this constellation is that some of the big Swedish firms now, actively, recruit skilled workers in Denmark. However, there are signs indicating that the Swedish rate of unemployment will increase in the near future.

The aggregate growth rates as indicators of performance imply that the prolonged relative economic success of Denmark and Sweden might now be coming to an end. The slowdown in growth to be observed since the last part of the 1960s has become more serious in the last years. In the following sections we shall look at some performance indicators more narrowly connected to technical innovation and technology diffusion. In this context it will be argued that the slowdown in economic growth, at least to a certain degree, reflects weaknesses in the national systems of technological change. Specifically, we shall look first at the capacity of the two systems to contribute to the global pool of generic technology. But, especially for small countries, the capability to absorb and diffuse new process technology and new product technology developed abroad is crucial.[39]

Development of Technologies

Technology development may involve a scale of technical advances from small incremental innovations to radical innovations and crucial contributions to generic technology. Here the focus will be on radical innovations and generic technology rather than on incremental change.[40]

Taking number of patents in the United States as an indicator of contributions to the common pool of technical knowledge we found (in Table 8.1) the Swedish contribution to be substantial (89 patents per million inhabitants) and the Danish to be very modest (27 patents per million inhabitants).

A closer study, based on Delphi methods, analyzing the specific areas in which Sweden has contributed to the global pool of technical knowledge found that the most important were electrical power, iron ore, special steel, and ship building and that the focus was almost always on developing the process technology (IVA, 1979b, p. 143ff).

In Denmark no such study has been made but it is well known that original contributions have been made in filter technology, extending the use of ultrafiltration to food processing and pharmaceuticals (artificial insulin).

But, generally, Swedish and Danish contributions have been modest and most generic technologies used in the two countries have been developed elsewhere. None of them has, for example, made any substantial contributions to the new engineering process technologies combining mechanical machines and electronics. In none of the main "mechatronic" engineering automation techniques—Computer Numerical Control-machinery (CNC), Industrial Robots, Computer Aided Design (CAD), and Flexible Manufacturing Systems (FMS)—do we find substantial Swedish or Danish innovations. Denmark is not a major producer of any of them and a partly Swedish firm (ABB) is active as a large producer only in one of the four areas—industrial robots. It is especially interesting to note that the Swedish engineering industry, which was characterized by a series of quite distinct and radical innovations almost a century ago and still presents itself as a core sector in the Swedish economy, did not contribute, more substantially, in this area (Edquist, 1989b).

The most important contributions from Denmark and Sweden to the global pool of knowledge might, however, be socioorganizational rather than technical. The cooperative form of agroorganization in Denmark and the technoeconomic system for food production based on it is an example with possible applications in many developing and eastern European countries. There is also a potential for diffusion of social and organizational forms from Sweden to other OECD countries. Some of the most visible and important experiments in this area have been developed by Volvo. Fifteen years ago, a new teamwork organization was introduced at Volvo's factory in Kalmar. And the new Volvo plant in Uddevalla represents another radical step in terms of work design (Edquist and Glimell, 1989).

Diffusion of New Process Technologies

How rapidly can a national system of technological change absorb new process technologies developed abroad? This is an important question because rapid absorption and domestic diffusion would, normally, result in a more productive and competitive national economy. Therefore, the degree of technology diffusion is a very important indicator of the performance of a national system of technological change. In this section we shall use the densities of specific automation techniques (CNC machine tools, industrial robots, CAD, and FMS) in the engineering industry as indicators for the absorption capability regarding process technology. Density is measured as the number of units per million employees in the engineering sector.

According to Table 8.7, Sweden is characterized by the most intensive use of CNC machine tools together with Japan. In industrial robots, it is number two after Japan, while it has the most intensive use of CAD systems. When it comes to the most complex and advanced technology included in the table—FMS—Sweden has a strong lead, as compared to the other countries. Sweden and Japan are well ahead of the United Kingdom, the United States, and West Germany as regards the degree of diffusion of automation technology in the engineering industry. The numbers presented in Table 8.7 refer to the end of December 1984. For industrial robots there are figures for the same set of countries also for 1987. These figures show that Sweden remains second after Japan, in terms of density, but they also indicate that the growth has been more modest in Sweden than in the other countries from 1984 to 1987 (Edquist, 1989b, Table 6).

Table 8.7. Diffusion of Flexible Automation Technologies in the Engineering Industries of Six OECD Countries (Number of Systems and Density at the End of 1984[a])

	CNC—Machine Tools	Robots	CAD	FMS
Denmark				
Stock	3,000	100	1,000	0
Density	19,230	641	6,410	0
Sweden				
Stock	6,010	1,900	1,900	15
Density	22,177	7,011	7,011	55
United States				
Stock	103,308	13,000	59,400	60
Density	11,728	1,475	6,743	7
Japan				
Stock	118,157	64,657	7,300	100
Density	22,399	12,257	1,384	19
West Germany				
Stock	46,435	6,600	11,000	25
Density	11,376	1,617	2,694	6
Great Britain				
Stock	32,566	2,623	9,000	10
Density	10,505	846	2,903	3

[a]Density reflects the total number of systems (end of 1984) divided by million of employees (1980) in the national engineering sector. For all countries except Denmark the source is Edquist and Jacobsson (1988, p. 104). The number of systems in Denmark has been estimated by methods differing from the ones used for the other countries (Kallehauge, 1989). This may imply problems of comparability. For example, the definition of CNC machine tools is wider in the Danish case—which means some overestimation of the Danish figure.

The figures demonstrate that Swedish firms are advanced users of automated engineering techniques—and this in spite of the fact than none of the flexible automation technologies was originally developed in Sweden. Comparative case studies confirm that Swedish firms have been more successful than British firms in introducing FMS systems, the success reflecting close interaction with producers, involvement of workers, and a step-by-step strategy when upgrading the technology (Haywood and Bessant, 1987).

The figures for Denmark have been gathered through many different sources and are quite uncertain, as indicated in the note to Table 8.7. They point to a high density for CNC and CAD but show extremely low values regarding industrial robots and FMS in 1984. In the years after 1984–1986, the use of CNC and CAD expanded radically. This is true also for industrial robots. But in robots the density is much lower than in Sweden and, still in 1990, there is no sophisticated FMS system in Denmark. The Danish figures point to a late, but rapid, absorption of process technology and to a specific weakness when it comes to the most advanced and complex new production systems (as FMS). Recent studies point to great difficulties in Danish firms when introducing new process technology, the difficulties reflecting a lack of technical competence but, especially, problems with qualifications and work organization. Actually, the introduction of new techniques seems, in a number of instances, to affect productivity negatively in the period 1984–1987 (Gjerding and Lundvall, 1990).

The general conclusion with regard to the technological level of process technology (in the engineering industry) is that Sweden is very advanced and that Denmark is weak in the more complex production systems.

Diffusion of New Product Technologies

An economy, or a firm, that continuously absorbs new process technology but neglects adjusting its product program to the change in the market and demand structure will sooner or later run into problems in terms of stagnation.[41] An inability to develop new products or absorb new product technologies developed abroad keeps the firm or country outside the growth sectors and products.[42]

To analyze the capacity to absorb new and advanced product technology from abroad we shall use the relative weight in exports of products with a high ratio between R&D expenditures and sales—so-called R&D-intensive products. We assume that the relative weight of such products in exports reflects the capability to absorb new product technology and to develop a production of new products and product families. One reason for focusing on R&D-intensive products is that the demand grows considerably more rapidly for these products than for other products (Table 8.10).

Table 8.8 shows that both Denmark and Sweden have a weak export specialization in R&D-intensive products. This is, however, true for almost all the small countries represented in the table. Hence, the problem is a small country problem to a certain degree. One of the two exceptions is Ireland—now a host country for multinationals producing microelectronic products but performing only the low-end activities in Ireland. It illustrates how just a few elements of the total production pro-

Table 8.8. Export Specialization Indices[a] for R&D-Intensive Products[b] in 16 OECD Countries 1961–1987

	1961–1965	1973–1979	1983–1987
Denmark	0.4	0.6	0.6
Sweden	0.7	0.9	0.8
United States	1.2	1.4	1.6
Japan	0.9	1.1	1.2
Great Britain	1.4	1.2	1.1
West Germany	1.4	1.1	1.0
Switzerland	1.6	1.8	1.4
Ireland	0.1	0.7	1.2
Netherlands	0.7	0.9	0.8
France	0.9	0.9	1.0
Belgium	0.7	0.6	0.6
Canada	0.3	0.5	0.5
Italy	0.9	0.7	0.7
Finland	0.1	0.3	0.4
Norway	0.3	0.4	0.4
Austria	0.5	0.7	0.9

[a]For definition of export specialization index, see note a in Table 8.3.

[b]The R&D-intensive products are inorganic chemicals, pharmaceuticals, plastic materials, power generating machinery, computers and peripherals, semiconductors, telecommunications equipment, machinery for production and distribution of electricity, scientific instruments, photographic supplies, watches, and clocks, and aircraft. The SITC numbers of the product groups are given in Dalum (1989, Appendix).

Source: The IKE databank and Dalum (1989).

Table 8.9. Share of Exports of Engineering Products Emanating from Industries with a High R&D Intensity[a] (%)

	1971	1975	1980	1985	1986
Sweden	23.7	23.8	25.3	29.7	28.1
United States	42.4	37.5	44.9	52.5	55.6
Japan	35.2	29.4	35.9	41.8	42.5
West Germany	24.2	24.4	27.6	30.4	29.3
France	28.7	27.2	30.0	40.1	38.4
United Kingdom	29.7	32.9	39.9	50.9	51.9
Switzerland	45.0	42.5	44.4	45.1	45.2
Netherlands	50.0	44.9	48.6	52.4	51.8
Finland	19.1	18.5	26.1	25.1	27.3
Norway	19.3	13.2	22.0	22.1	23.4
Denmark	27.5	24.4	31.2	35.6	36.3
OECD	31.2	29.5	34.1	39.3	39.1

[a]Industries with a high R&D intensity are ISIC (Rev 2): 3825 (Office machinery and Computers), 383 (Electrical Machinery), 3845 (Aerospace), and 385 (Scientific Instruments).

Source: OECD Industrial Outlook Data Base (January 1989) (COMTAP) and Edquist (1989b, Table 7).

cess may be transferred. The other more genuine exception is Switzerland, successful both in pharmaceutical products and in microelectronic based engineering products. Large countries such as the United States, Japan, the United Kingdom, West Germany and France are relatively specialized in their exports of R&D-intensive products.

Given its importance it is relevant to take a closer look at the engineering sector and its specialization in terms of R&D-intensive products. Table 8.9 demonstrates that the proportion of engineering products exported having a high R&D intensity is low in Sweden (as in West Germany, Finland, and Norway). Denmark has a stronger position in this respect, but is far behind countries such as Japan, the United States, Netherlands, and Switzerland. Accordingly, two of the small countries perform quite well on this indicator.[43]

We find that—on the whole—both Denmark and Sweden have a relatively weak position in R&D-intensive products. Taking into account that the world markets for these products grow considerably more rapidly than for other products (Table 8.10) this constitutes a long-term structural problem for both Denmark and Sweden and may, partially, explain why the growth rates in these countries are becoming low, as compared to the OECD average.

It is not too surprising that Denmark, given its weak R&D effort, has a weak position in R&D-intensive goods. But it is remarkable that Sweden, in spite of its very substantial investments in R&D, its high number of patents per million inhabitants in the United States, and its strong multinationals in engineering, has been so slow in absorbing R&D-intensive products.

PROBLEMS: STRUCTURAL AND INSTITUTIONAL STRAINS ON THE TWO SYSTEMS OF INNOVATION

In the previous section we pointed to one structural problem common to the two systems. This problem refers to the product composition of production and exports. The

Table 8.10. Differences in Annual Growth Rates (%) in the
Volume of the OECD Market, in Current Prices

Annual Growth Rates in the OECD Imports	R&D-Intensive Products[a]	Other Products
1961–1973	19.1	15.0
1973–1983	14.0	9.4

[a]For specification of R&D-intensive products, see note b in Table 8.8.
Source: Dalum (1989).

internationally most rapidly growing product groups are weakly represented in both economies. Not even Sweden, in spite of its very major efforts in R&D, has succeeded in overcoming this structural problem. But, of course, the problem takes on different forms in the two countries and we shall discuss some of these specificities separately.

The other family of problems refers to the institutional framework of the economy. Again, we find one common problem, reflecting changes in how the relationships between the national and the global economy are regulated. And again, the problem takes on quite different forms in the two economies. We shall end this chapter with a discussion of the character of this institutional problem in the Danish and the Swedish systems of innovation, respectively.[44]

Structural Problems in the Danish System

We want to point to two fundamental structural problems in the Danish economy. The first problem is that demand for the end products of the traditionally strong, development blocks around construction, shipping, and agriculture is falling or stagnating. The new hi-tech product groups in the field of electronics are still small and they have not established anything like the coherence characteristic of the old development blocks. On the contrary, after a period of innovative activities, strongly rooted in the domestic economy, they tend to establish themselves as enclaves, importing at least 90% of their components and exporting at least 90% of their final output.

The agroindustrial and food-industrial sectors are still extremely important for the health of the Danish economy and, at present (1990), a series of mergers are taking place both inside the cooperative part of the economy and in the private sector. It is an open question if this kind of regrouping will give the necessary impetus to a more offensive strategy in terms of innovative behavior. Actually, the cooperative block tends, increasingly, to play a conservative role in the Danish economy and, as long as the cooperative firms can secure acceptable prices and incomes for their owners, the incentives to develop a new strategy are quite weak. For example, we have seen that, relatively speaking, Denmark spends less on R&D in the food industry (in relation to value added) than Finland and Sweden. There might be a potential in biotechnological applications in these product areas and there is, as a matter of fact, a quite strong biotechnological competence in some Danish firms. (NOVO is the best-known example.) But this competence has been oriented mostly toward the pharmaceuticals applications and it might take some strong policy and other efforts to establish the necessary coupling and interaction between the agroindustrial complex and the biotechnology firms.

Table 8.11. The Distribution of Europe's 500 Largest Manufacturing Firms Among a Number of Small Countries

	Number of Firms	Number of Firms/Million Inhabitants
Denmark	2	0.4
Sweden	31	3.7
Norway	4	1.0
Finland	6	1.2
Austria	8	1.1
Belgium	12	1.2
Switzerland	22	3.4
Netherlands	29	2.0

Source: Forum for industriel udvikling (1988, Figure D-5).

The second structural problem is illustrated in Table 8.11. It refers to the fact that the Danish economy is extreme in its dependence on small and medium-sized firms. The two big Danish firms referred to in the table are to be found in, respectively, the dairy industry (Danish Dairy, a cooperative firm) and breweries (Carlsberg, a private firm). Outside the food industry, there are few units large enough to organize scale-intensive R&D activities. This problem is reinforced by the institutional setup of the financial sector, to be discussed in connection with the institutional problems.

It is remarkable that a small country so weak in terms of most traditional technology performance indicators (R&D intensity, process diffusion and product composition) has been able, for so long, to sustain a high level of income per capita. One interpretation might be that these indicators do not catch very well all forms of incremental innovation important to competitiveness. Another, less optimistic, interpretation is that the present stagnation signals the end of success of this model, based on modest incremental indigenous technical change.

Structural Problems in the Swedish System

Also in the case of Sweden, we shall address two structural problems, both of which point toward vulnerability and a risk for secular stagnation. The first relates to the prospective demand for its raw materials and its semimanufactured goods. The exports of wood products, pulp, paper, iron ore, steel, and so on is still very important to the dynamics of the economy. The rapid development in biotechnology and material technology might, however, in the long run result in new materials. The demand for some of the classical Swedish export products might dwindle, and the result might be stagnation and a need for a drastic transformation of the economy. We have pointed to the fact that the engineering industry focuses on the production and export of traditional, mechanical, low-R&D products with a limited growth prospect.

We have seen that the natural resource bases of Sweden and Denmark have shaped the two national systems of innovation to a very important degree.[45] However, Sweden also developed a strong mechanical engineering industry in the early parts of this century. It would, of course, be interesting to find out in detail why this happened in Sweden and not in Denmark—or Canada and Australia. At the same time the Swedish engineering industry is still mainly mechanical. It has not managed to transform itself to also produce electronics products. In this sense Sweden is locked into the mechanical trajectory in the engineering industry and still quite tied to the raw material base in other sectors of industry. Again, it would be very interesting to analyze, in detail, why Sweden did not manage to develop an IT capability (except in the case of Ericsson), while firms in other countries succeeded. In other words, why is Sweden (with a few exceptions) not producing in the new industries, which are not based on raw materials?[46]

Another kind of vulnerability emanates from the concentration in the core sector in the economy—engineering. The five largest engineering firms (Volvo, Electrolux, Ericsson, ASEA, and SKF) produced around one-fifth of the total value added in manufacturing in 1982 (Economic Growth, 1984, p. 193) and in 1976 they organized more than a fourth of total exports (IVA, 1979c, p. 82). The concentration of economic activities is even more extreme than these figures indicate. The large firms have built networks of domestic suppliers directly dependent on the performance of the large firms. And everything points toward increasing ratios of concentration since these data were produced. If these large firms do not succeed in developing efficient production in the new high-growth product areas, the problems of stagnation will become very serious for the Swedish economy. And if one or two of these large firms run into problems, it can have devastating consequences for the whole economy.[47]

A comparative advantage of the Swedish system has been its combination of advanced production methods in traditional product areas on the one hand, and corporatist institutional setups, making it easy to develop and introduce advanced process technology, on the other hand. Paradoxically, this comparative advantage might be an important factor in explaining the rigidities in the product structure. The whole institutional setup, the whole innovation system (including state policy), seems to have become geared toward movement along one trajectory. The ease with which advances have been made in this direction may have weakened the incentives to take on the more difficult task of developing the technological infrastructural basis necessary for radically new product areas.[48]

The average low-R&D character of Swedish production is a severe problem for the Swedish system of technological change. And this problem is certainly not solved spontaneously by the market. Therefore there are reasons to consider whether state intervention could mitigate the problem. A recent evaluation (Edquist, 1989b) of the activitites of The Swedish Board for Technical Change (STU) in the field of engineering technology showed that STU, in the 1980s, spent most of its resources in this field on support to process technology and a smaller—and decreasing—share on product technology. Hence, STU supports an area where Sweden performs extremely well and neglects an area that is a major problem for the Swedish system of innovation. Accordingly, a reallocation of the efforts of STU may be called for. The currently launched national program to give state support to technology in the engineering industry was partly based on the evaluation. In the new program, a more balanced allocation of the state resources between production technologies and product technologies is prescribed (Regeringens Proposition, 1990, p. 107).[49]

Institutional Problems in the Two Systems of Innovation

One fundamental characteristic of the Danish system of innovation is the absence of strong coordinating agencies. Neither the state nor concentrated capital has been powerful enough to take the lead in the process of restructuring the economy. The single strongest organized power has been the cooperative farmer's movement and, for institutional reasons, this movement has become quite myopic in relation to strategies of innovation. In the earlier period of rapid growth in demand, this absence of a coordinating force was not a serious problem. Today, with the increasingly systemic character of technology, the vulnerability of the model becomes more apparent. It is illustrated by the fact that foreign capital now, rapidly, is taking over many of the Danish niche firms characterized by advanced product technology, in, for example, electronics (Aaen, 1986).

Lately, there has been a growing awareness of this vacuum that leaves structural change to market forces and initiatives joining private firms, banks, and pension funds have resulted in a series of mergers, especially in the food industry. At the same time, the trade unions have pointed to wage earner's funds as potential candidates for organizing a more coordinated industrial restructuring. It is an open question if these different efforts will succeed in defending a reasonable degree of coherence in the Danish production and innovations systems. The prospective project of a single European market is regarded by many policy agents as the ultimate response to the structural and institutional problems of Denmark.

In Sweden there is a corresponding growing awareness of a weakening of the foundation for the Swedish model. "The Swedish model" can—as we previously saw—mean different things. If it implies the mode of wage formation developing after World War II, it is clear that it has partly disintegrated during the past 10–15 years. The difference between nominal wage increases and productivity increases has, for a considerable period, been much larger than in competing countries, which has led to a relatively high inflation in Sweden—and several devaluations around 1980. One reason for the high wage increases has been the shortage of labor.[50]

Shortage of labor and large wage increases create incentives for rationalization of production and the introduction of labor-saving process technologies (e.g., automation). And there is widespread acceptance of this in the union movement.[51] If "the Swedish model" is given the other meaning (i.e., a consensus on issues of rationalization and technical change between capital, trade unions, and the state), the model is still alive.

One fundamental problem, in this context, is the fact that the home-based multinational firms are now becoming, increasingly, footloose. ASEA's merger with Brown-Bovery from Switzerland into ABB in 1989 has now been followed up by mergers involving, for example, SAAB (with General Motors), Volvo (with Renault), and several others.[52]

In addition to the fact that the nationality of several of the largest "Swedish" firms can be questioned, the process of internationalization is also proceeding in other spheres. For example, a very important change in the 1980s was the development of a very free flow of capital across borders. This means that the possibility of pursuing an independent monetary policy in a country such as Sweden is severely restricted.[53] Further, the Swedish flow of direct investments abroad is enormous. It has increased from 5 to 55 billion Swedish crowns per year between 1980 and 1989. During the same period the foreign direct investments in Sweden remained around 5 billion per year.[54]

The trend toward internationalization has definitely weakened the structural position of the labor unions—which are still quite national—in Sweden.[55] But it has also weakened the position of the state. And capital has strengthened its position—in particular the internationalized capital. Accordingly, the power relations between the three main parties of the Swedish model have been fundamentally changed.

In other words, the process of internationalization changes, drastically, the basic workings of the Swedish model. The old model was based on the fact that the Social-Democratic state and the large firms were *mutually* dependent. If this dependency goes only one way in the future, the basis for corporatism will erode. This problem is referred to in a report to the 1989 congress of the Swedish Metal Workers Union:

> The problem today is that these multinationals do not any longer need Sweden, but the Swedish economy needs them. The "third way politics" was the last major contribution that the Swedish society could make to big business, and still expecting something in return. (Solidarisk arbetspolitik, 1989, p. 93)[56]

This brings us to an end, pointing to the possibility that the two small national systems of innovation studied here, Denmark and Sweden, are now in a critical phase.

NOTES

1. This chapter has been written within the Columbia University project on National Systems Supporting Technical Advance in Industry. We have greatly profited from discussions at the conferences organized within this project and in particular from Richard Nelson's comments. Swedish and Danish colleagues have also commented on earlier drafts. We have received valuable comments from Esben Sloth Andersen, Boel Berner, Ted Bradshaw, Martin Börjeson, Tarja Cronberg, Erik Dahmén, Bent Dalum, Mark Elam, Hans Glimell, Lars Herlitz, Mikael Hård, Björn Johnson, Maureen McKelvey, Lennart Stenberg, Elisabeth Sundin, Lars Svensson, and Hans Vallentin. The paper was written in 1990 and completed in January 1991. Accordingly it does not cover events and changes occurring thereafter (see also note 56).

2. Comparing countries with many features in common allows us to keep some variables constant. This might be effective when it comes to establishing the most crucial elements and relationships in national systems of technical change. At the same time, this chapter brings into focus some of the specific problems facing *small* national systems of innovation.

3. The comparison presented here confirms that it still is useful to assume that national borders matter when it comes to the workings of the process of technical change. If two distinct and different systems of innovation can be isolated in two countries, so close in terms of culture and space, this should be true, a forteriori, for countries more distant in these respects.

4. This issue will be discussed in the final section on structural and institutional problems.

5. Hence the conduct of Sweden looks very much like that of the large economic powers in this respect, while the conduct of Denmark is similar to other small OECD countries. The figures presented in this section also show that a country can be quite successful in terms of growth and have a high GNP/capita in spite of low R&D expenditures and a poor patenting record.

6. Alternative terms to denote the same thing are, for example, "national systems supporting technical advances" and "national systems of technological change."

7. One way—among others—to try to determine the limits of a national system of innovation would be to try to causally explain the invention, innovation, and diffusion of technologies and let the explanatory factors define the limits of the system. An attempt in this direction—but only with regard to diffusion of process technologies in the engineering industry—was made in Edquist (1989a, pp. 10–11).

8. This theoretical perspective has been developed in Andersen and Lundvall (1988), in Johnson and Lundvall (1988), and in Lundvall (1992).

9. One reason why it is useful to distinguish between development and diffusion of technologies is that the determinants differ between these stages of technological change. The analytical distinctions discussed here are dealt with in more depth in Edquist (1989b, 1991, 1992).

10. For a product technology an innovation is the first economically successful production of a product. A failed innovation is when a product has been marketed and disappeared from the market—and thereby from production. For a production technology an innovation means that new means of production are efficiently used for the first time in production—which, of course, presupposes that they have been produced earlier.

11. For process technologies diffusion means, of course, that additional producers introduce the technology in their process of production. For product technologies diffusion means that additional producers begin to produce the new product. (Hence, we do not mean diffusion to users or consumers when we talk about diffusion of product technologies.) Failed diffusion of a product technology might reflect a technological monopoly based on patents, secrecy, or other barriers to entry.

12. In small economies, the development of generic technologies and radical innovations is currently a rare phenomenon, and the most important activity in the national system of technological change is often diffusion, mainly the absorption and adaptation of technologies developed abroad.

13. For example, an industrial robot is a product technology as output and a production technology when it is used in the process of production.

14. The role of education is, for example, dealt with in Ahlström (1982) and Berner (1991).

15. There are few systematic attempts to write the history of the Danish system of innovation. In this part we have been inspired by several not very widely circulated contributions by our colleague Esben Sloth Andersen (1973, 1978a,b).

16. In Denmark the innovation was made in 1878 by Burmeister and Wain, but the separator was invented by N.J. Fjord—one of the first professors in dairying at the Danish Agricultural College, established in 1874. In Sweden the separator was invented by Gustav de Laval. Later it became one of the core products for AB Separator, a firm that later developed into the multinational firm Alfa-Laval.

17. The transformation of the Danish economy in the last quarter of the nineteenth century is an interesting illustration of the importance of social mobilization and social innovation. Actually, Grundtvig might be regarded as the most important single Danish innovator, as one who has put his marks on the modern Danish system of production and innovation. His successful ideological mobilization of the Danish peasants toward self-reliance, for example, through organizing local education in the popular "höjskoler," prepared the ground for the local organizational undertakings that gradually developed into a coordinated national movement toward farmers' cooperatives.

18. This means, for example, automation and reductions of direct labor costs in dairies and slaughterhouses.

19. Some data on this are presented in the section on the R&D effort.

20. In addition to horses used in mines many thousands were used by transport companies in London and other cities.

21. The large Swedish export of iron ore developed later.

22. Foreign demand for wood products and iron was important in the Swedish process of industrialization (Schön, 1985, p. 35).

23. This includes production of ships (until the 1980s), automobiles, mining equipment, and aeroplanes, except for the product groups already mentioned.

24. In his analysis of small country corporatism Katzenstein (1985) characterizes Denmark as having a weak partner at the capitalist side and a strong one at the labor side. We would rather

point to the fact that in Denmark none of the parties is as centralized, homogeneous, and united as their Swedish counterparts.

25. However, unemployment in Sweden is in the process of increasing in 1990.

26. If this design turns out to be unprofitable compared to automobile assembly according to traditional principles in, for example, West Germany and Japan, the conclusion may be that car assembly cannot be carried out in Sweden—for structural reasons. On the other hand, if it turns out to be profitable, the Uddevalla example may show the way for the general development of assembly work—which is one-fourth of all work in the engineering industry—in the future (Edquist and Glimell, 1989, p. 44). Another possibility is, of course, that the structural conditions change—through increased unemployment, etc.—and traditional assembly becomes viable again in Sweden. The Uddevalla factory has been addressed in more detail in Berggren (1990) and in Clarke (1989).

27. A "development block" has also been defined as a broad set of interconnected producers and users of products, developing in close interaction with each other and often supported by knowledge-producing private, or public, organizations (Stenberg, 1987, p. 46).

28. In its most complete form, a development block would include whole chains of production, final users of the products, producers of means of production, as well as independent knowledge resources. Only the United States and Japan would today contain complete development blocks in this sense within important future areas (Stenberg, 1987, pp. 46–47). Dahmén uses "development blocks" in both an ex ante and an ex post sense (Dahmén, 1988, pp. 6–7).

29. Their export and import ratios lie typically around or over 90%.

30. If sales from the Swedish-owned engineering companies abroad had been included the figure for this industry would have been much higher.

31. In relation to value added, the figures were 7.6% (Sweden) and 2.9% (Denmark). And in relation to fixed investments the percentages were 57 and 26%, respectively (Edquist, 1989b, Table 11).

32. However, the R&D expenditures (in Sweden) of Swedish firms decreased for the first time between 1987 and 1989 by 7% in real terms.

33. This particular example also indicates, however, that Denmark has a lower R&D intensity than other Nordic countries in one of her most important export sectors.

34. STU has an annual budget of about 1 billion Swedish Crowns and is the main technology policy agency in Sweden.

35. The emergence of the program has been analyzed in Glimell (1988, 1989). It has been evaluated ex post in Wennerberg (1989).

36. The first phase of the IT program has been evaluated in Arnold and Guy (1989).

37. The mechanisms behind this process are dealt with in Edquist (1989b, 1990).

38. In Edquist (1989c, 1990) supply-side as well as demand-side technology policy instruments relevant for technology development as well as for technology diffusion are discussed in more detail.

39. In this sense, the "system of technology diffusion"—including absorbtion, assimilation, and incremental change—is much more important than the R&D system for small countries. There are, therefore, strong reasons for spending as much energy on analyzing the mechanisms, institutions, and policies for acquiring foreign technology and disseminating it domestically as on the R&D system—although this is seldomly done. (To do so would be a major task, since we do not know the detailed features of the systems of technology diffusion in Denmark and Sweden.) One reason for this neglect may be that the diffusion system is less often the object of public policy intervention. Diffusion is normally left to be handled spontaneously by the market forces (although Denmark has been an exception in this respect). As we will see this may also be true when the diffusion system does not function satisfactorily—as in the case of the the diffusion of new product technology in Denmark and Sweden.

40. Incremental innovations are, in this chapter, considered to be part of the process of technology diffusion.

41. Such a combination of labor-saving technical change with lack of presence in growing markets may lead to "technological unemployment." This is the basic idea behind the Pasinetti (1981) analysis of economic growth and structural change. The argument has been adjusted and applied to small open economies in Lundvall (1987).

42. When a new product is developed in one country its diffusion to another country is often presented in the framework of product life cycle theory. However, the product life cycle model tends to understate the difficulties involved. The reason is that it may be quite complex to move complete production processes between countries. The knowledge base may involve tacit elements that are difficult to transfer or it may involve extremely complex combinations of scientific knowledge. Infrastructure and institutions in the receiving country may also not be adapted to the product family.

43. The indicators used in Tables 8.8 and 8.9 are somewhat blunt because of the rather high level of aggregation. This is because of lack of more detailed R&D data. The analysis of the diffusion of R&D-intensive product technologies in Sweden has later been developed in Edquist and McKelvey (1991).

44. In the section on problems we will address structural and institutional problems without distinguishing between those problems that can be solved through (further) political intervention in the systems of innovation and those that cannot. Such a distinction would be necessary if the policy implications of the present analysis were to be explicitly and systematically drawn out.

45. In a country such as Japan the resource base may have been less important, and civilian technology policy a more important determinant of the direction of technological change. In the United States the government-financed military R&D and procurement may have been the most important factors.

46. There are many challenging questions in this context! How do national systems of innovation use their resource base without being constrained by it (e.g., by neglecting new product areas) in later stages of development? Except for liberating the system from the domestic natural resource base (like the Japanese and Koreans), can a country also "liberate" its system of innovation from socioeconomic and cultural conditions? How do transfers between technological trajectories and paradigms actually take place?

47. As a matter of fact, both the automobile producers (SAAB and Volvo) seem to start trembling in mid-1990, having announced drastic profit reductions and considerable layoffs.

48. The large devaluations around 1980 have most probably contributed to the conservation of the product structure—by making traditional products more profitable and leaving little room for offensive ventures (in an economy of full capacity utilization).

49. In the process of implementation of this program during 1990, the resources have, to a large extent, been allocated to subcontractors within the automobile industry. This is probably related to the emerging problems for the Swedish automobile industry—and looks more like crisis management than an offensive strategy of the future.

50. However, the sum of inflation and rate of unemployment is still in 1990 relatively low—which means that the Swedish model, in this sense, has not broken down completely.

51. As we have shown earlier Sweden is good at the introduction of advanced process technology but bad at increasing productivity—which is not necessarily contradictory.

52. If only one or two of the very large and internationalized "Swedish" firms decide to move their R&D abroad the ratio between R&D expenditures and GDP would dwindle. However, this has not happened so far.

53. Previously the Swedish Central Bank could determine the domestic interest rate and adjust it to the business cycle. Now the interest rates in the surrounding world determine the Swedish one. Hence, the interest rate is no longer controlled from the political level in Sweden

but by the global market. The same seems to be becoming increasingly true for taxation—at least taxation of incomes emanating from capital.

54. And during the first half of 1990 Swedish corporations bought firms in Western Europe for a total of 72.2 billion SEK. This is to be compared to the acquisitions of U. S. firm of 32.7 billion and of Japanese of 10.5 billion. This exceptional record may, of course, have been related to the insecurity among Swedish firms concerning the future relations between Sweden and the European Community. However, during the autumn of 1990 the Swedish government declared its intention to apply for membership in the EC. A large majority in Parliament supports this.

55. This structural weakening concerns issues such as industrial democracy and codetermination. In the field of wage formation it is balanced by the shortage of labor—as long as that persists. A labor shortage may lead to problems of competitiveness (i.e., full employment contains the seeds of its own destruction). On the other hand, unions tend to accept labor-saving technical change if full employment is the case.

56. As mentioned in note 1, this chapter was written in 1990 and completed in January 1991. Hence the analysis does not address changes occurring thereafter. However, we want to mention a few events that have since occurred in Sweden. In July 1991 the Social Democratic government submitted Sweden's application for membership to the EC. In the election of September 1991 the Social Democrats were replaced by a center–right coalition government. Further, the rate of unemployment increased to about 4% in 1991. These changes are not unrelated to each other. Together they seem to strengthen the observations expressed at the end of this chapter (e.g., on the gradual disintegration of "the Swedish model," on internationalization, and on the changes in the power balance among the labor unions, the state, and private capital).

REFERENCES

Aaen, F. (1986). "Hvor dansk er dansk elektronikindustri?" Aalborg: Aalborg Universitetsforlag.

Ahlström, G. (1982). *Engineers and Industrial Growth*. London: Croom Helm.

Andersen, E. S. (1973). "Noter om industri, stat og teknisknaturvidenskabelig forskning." Köbenhavn: Danske Studerendes Fællesråd.

Andersen, E. S. (1978a). "Eksport, teknologi og forskning." Aalborg: Institut for Produktion, mimeo.

Andersen, E. S. (1978b). "Eksportudvikling, erhvervsstruktur og forskningspolitik." Aalborg: Aalborg Universitetsforlag.

Andersen, E. S., and Lundvall B. -Å. (1988). "Small National Systems of Innovation Facing Technological Revolutions—An Analytical Framework." In C. Freeman and B. -Å. Lundvall (eds.), *Small Countries Facing the Technological Revolution*. London: Pinter Publishers.

Annerstedt, J. (1976). "Några drag i den svenska statliga forskningspolitikens framväxt." In V. Andersen and R. Kalleberg (eds.), *Forskningen—staten og kapitalen*. Köbenhavn: Nordisk Sommeruniversitet.

Arnold, E., and Guy, K. (1989). "Evaluation of the IT4 Programme. Phaze I." Stockholm.

Berggren, C. (1990). *Det nya bilarbetet—Konkurrensen mellan olika produktionskoncept i svensk bilindustri 1970–1990*. Lund: Arkiv.

Berner, B. (1991). "Professional or Wage Worker? Engineers and Economic Transformation in Sweden." In C. Smith and P. Meiksins (eds.), *Engineering Class Politics*. Verso.

Christensen, J. F., and Valentin, F. (1989). "Produktinnovationer i dansk industri." Arbejdsnote 4, Institute for industrial research and social development, Copenhagen school of economics and social science.

Clarke, T. (1989). "Imaginative Flexibility in Production Engineering: The Volvo Uddevalla Plant." Paper presented at the conference "A Flexible Future," Cardiff Business School, September 19–20.

Dahmén, E. (1970). *Entrepreneurial Activity and the Development of Swedish Industry 1919–1959*. Homewood, IL: Published for the American Economic Association by R. D. Irwin.

Dahmén, E. (1988). "'Development Blocks' in Industrial Economics." *Scandinavian Economic History Review* 1:3–14. Also published in Carlsson, B. (ed.) (1987). *Industrial Dynamics*. Boston: Kluwer Academic.

Dalum, B. (1989). "Export Specialization, Competitiveness and National Systems of Innovation." Aalborg: Institut for Produktion, mimeo.

Dalum, B., Fagerberg, J., and Jörgensen, U. (1988). "Small Open Economies in the World Market for Electronics: The Case of the Nordic Countries." In C. Freeman and B-Å Lundvall (eds.), *Small Countries Facing the Technological Revolution*. London: Pinter publishers.

Dansk Økonomi. (1988). December, Köbenhavn, Det Økonomiske Råd.

Edquist, C. (1989a). "The Realm of Freedom in Modern Times? New Technology in Theory and Practice." Inaugural Lecture, *Tema T Report* 18, 1989, Department of Technology and Social Change, University of Linköping, Sweden.

Edquist, C. (1989b). "Utvärdering av statligt stöd till verkstadsindustriell teknik." Linköping, Tema Teknik och Social Förändring, mimeo (also published as *Tema T Report* 22, 1991).

Edquist, C. (1989c). "Teknisk förändring och teknikpolitik." In 'Energin, makten och framtiden— samhällsvetenskapliga perspektiv på teknisk förändring." Statens energiverk 1989:R16, Stockholm.

Edquist, C. (1990). "Technology Policy—Social, Economic and Political Aspects." *Tema T Working Paper* 75, Department of Technology and Social Change, University of Linköping, Sweden. (This report will also be published in a book entitled *Technology Policy—Towards an Integration of Social and Ecological Concerns*, Institut fur Höhere Studien, Wien, 1992.)

Edquist, C. (1992). "Technologcial and Organizational Innovations—A Conceptual Discussion and Some Notes on Consequences for Productivity and Employment." Working Paper. World Employment Programme, International Labour Organization, Geneva.

Edquist, C., and Glimell, H. (1989). "Swedish Frontiers of Change—A Guide to the Impact of New Technologies, Work Design and Management Practises." Report prepared for the Directorate for Social Affairs, Manpower and Education, OECD, mimeo (to be published by OECD).

Edquist, C., and Jacobsson, S. (1988). *Flexible Automation—The Global Diffusion of New Technology in the Engineering Industry.* Oxford: Basil Blackwell.

Edquist, C., and McKelvey, M. (1991). "Högteknologiska produkter och produktivitet i svensk industri." A study for the Swedish Productivity Delegation, in *Forskning, Teknikspridning och Produktivitet.* Expert Report number 10 of the Productivity Delegation. This report has also been published in English as a working paper at the Consortium on Competitiveness and Cooperation (CCC), the Center for Research in Management, University of California at Berkeley, 1992. The English title is "The Diffusion of New Product Technologies and Productivity Growth in Swedish Industry."

Forum for Industriel Udvikling. (1988). "Har Danmark en framtid som industrination?" Köbenhavn, mimeo.

Gårdlund, T. (1942). *Industrialismens Samhälle.* Stockholm: Tidens förlag.

Gjerding, A. N., and Lundvall, B. -Å. (1990). "Teknisk fornyelse og produktivitetsudvikling i danske industriverksamheder." PIKE-småskrift No. 8,

Institute of Production, Aalborg University Center.

Gjerding, A. N., Johnson, B., Kallehauge, L. E., Lundvall, B. -Å., and Madsen, P. T. (1988). Produktivitet og international konkurrenceevne. Aalborg: Aalborg Universitetsforlag.

Gjerding, A. N., Johnson, B., Kallehauge, L. E., Lundvall, B. -Å., and Madsen, P. T. (1990). *Den Forsvundne Produktivitet.* Köbenhavn: PJÖF:s forlag.

Glimell, H. (ed.) (1988). *Industriförnyelse i Norden. 80-talets programsatsningar på mikroelektronik.* Roskilde: Forlaget Samfundsökonomi og Planläggning.

Glimell, H. (1989). "Återerövra datapolitiken. En rapport om staten och informationsteknologi under fyra decennier." *Tema T Report* 20, 1989, Department of Technology and Social Change, University of Linköping, Sweden.

Haywood, B., and Bessant, J. (1987). "FMS in Sweden and the UK." Brighton: Innovation Research Group, Brighton Polytechnic.

Industriökonomisk Institut. (1986). "Industri i Norden: Konkurranse og samarbeid." Stavanger: Universitetsforlaget.

IVA (1979a). "Kunskap som grund för industriell utveckling." Stockholm: Ingenjörsvetenskapsakademien.

IVA (1979b). "Teknik och industristruktur." Stockholm: Ingenjörsvetenskapsakademien.

IVA (1979c). "Svensk industris långsiktiga utveckling." Stockholm: Ingenjörsvetenskapsakademien.

Johansson, A. (1989). *Tillväxt och klassamarbete— en studie av den svenska modellens Uppkomst.* Stockholm: Tiden.

Johnson, B., and Lundvall, B. -Å. (1988). "Institutional Learning and National Systems of Innovation." Paper presented at the conference on "Strategies of Flexibilization in Western Europe," Roskilde University, April, mimeo.

Kallehauge, L. E. (1989). "Spredningen af numerisk styrede værktøjsmaskiner i dansk økonomi i perioden 1980–87." PIKE-småskrift No. 3, August. Aalborg: Institut for Produktion, mimeo.

Katzenstein, P. J. (1985). *Small States in World Markets.* Ithaca: Cornell University Press.

Lundvall, B. -Å. (1987). "Technological Unemployment in a Small Open Economy." In R. Lund, et al. (eds.), *Studies in Unemployment.* Copenhagen: New Social Science Monographs.

Lundvall, B. -Å. (ed.) (1992). *National Systems of Innovation—Towards a Theory of Innovation and Interactive Learning.* London: Pinter Publishers.

Lundvall, B. -Å., Maarbjerg Olesen, N., and Aaen, I. (1984). "Det landbrugsindustrielle kompleks." Aalborg: Aalborg Universitetsforlag.

Madsen, P. K. (1989). "Orienten begynder i Malmö! Beskæftigelsespolitik i Sverige, Finland og Norge." Arbejdsnotat No. 3, Specialarbejdernes beskæftigelsesudvalg. København: Specialarbej-derforbundet, mimeo.

Mjöset, L. (ed.) (1986). *Norden dagen derpå.* Oslo: Universitetsforlaget.

Nordic Economic Growth. (1984). *Economic Growth in a Nordic Perspective.* Helsinki: Frenck-ell.

Nordisk FoU-statistik 1987 og 1981–1987 (1990).

OECD (1987). *Reviews of National Science and Technology Policy: Sweden.* Paris: OECD.

OECD (1988a). *Reviews of National Science and Technological Policy: Denmark.* Paris: OECD.

OECD (1988b). *Main Science and Technology Indicators 1982–88.* Paris: OECD.

Pasinetti, L. (1981). *Structural Change and Economic Growth.* Cambridge, England: Cambridge University Press.

Patel, P., and Pavitt, K. (1989). "Large Firms in Western Europe's Technological Competitiveness." Revised version of paper prepared for the Prince Bertil Symposium, November 1988, Stockholm.

Pavitt, K., and Patel, P. (1988). "The International Distribution and Determinants of Technological Activities." *Oxford Review of Economic Policy* 4(4).

Pedersen, J. (1986). "Afskedigelsesbeskyttelse og ansættelsestryghed for den enkelte arbejder i 7

Europæiske lande." Arbejdsnotat No. 13, Speci-alarbejdernes vækstkommission. København: Specialarbejderforbundet.

Petersen, E., et al. (1983). "Danskernes tilvärelse under krisen." *Psykologisk Skriftserie* 8(3).

Regeringens Proposition. (1990). Vissa Näringspol-itiska Frågor, Proposition No. 1989/90:88, Sver-iges Riksdag. Stockholm: Mars.

Schön, L. (1985). *Industrialismens Förutsättningar.* Malmö: Liber.

Senghaas, D. (1982). *Von Europa lernen—Entwick-lungsgeschicht-liche Betrachtungen.* Frankfurt am Main: Suhrkamp.

Solidarisk Arbetspolitik. (1989). Huvudrapport från Programkommittén om välfärden, industrins omvandling och det goda arbetet. Stockholm, Svenska Metallindustriarbetarförbundet, Kon-gress 3–9 September.

Stenberg, L. (1987). "Utvecklingsblock i förnyelse av svensk industri, Ds I 1987:3." Stockholm: Industridepartementet.

Svennilson, I. (1954). *Growth and Stagnation in the European Economy.* Geneva, United Nations, Economic Commission for Europe.

Wennerberg, S. (1989). "Nationella Mikroelektron-ikprogrammet (NMP) och Industriell Utveck-kling" (Utvärderingsrapport).

9

The Canadian System of Industrial Innovation

DONALD G. MCFETRIDGE

The purpose of this chapter is to describe the set of institutions and institutional link-ages that has evolved for the generation, diffusion, and application of knowledge in Canada. The building blocks of this innovation system are the knowledge-generating organizations including research and development performing firms, universities, other nonprofit organizations, and government laboratories. As important but less readily observed are the organizations that apply knowledge and the interactions among users and suppliers of knowledge. As Freeman (1988, p. 2) puts it:

> The national system of innovation is not just a set of laboratories but is a cumu-lative process of learning by producing, learning by using and learning by the interaction of producers and users.

The organizations comprising an innovation system can interact in a variety of ways:

1. Joint support or performance of research, development, and demonstration proj-ects.
2. Cooperation between users and suppliers to improve intermediate inputs.
3. Acquisition of knowledge and skills by employees of one organization that are transferable to other organizations or to new ventures.

Interaction can occur in a variety of dimensions or spaces. It can occur in geo-graphic space wherein individual organizations derive benefits from other organiza-tions operating in community or region or it can occur among firms making use of the same underlying technology. In this case a discovery by one organization contributes to the solution of problems in a variety of industries. Interaction also occurs between users and suppliers along the production chain in a single industry.

The importance of interaction is that it makes an innovation system more than the sum of its parts. Each organization contributes to the effectiveness of the others. Some of these contributions are priced and reflected in normal market transactions. Some are not priced and some are only vaguely perceived or defined. The existence of these cumulative external effects makes it very difficult to apply the concept of allocative efficiency to the analysis of innovation systems.

Implicit in the concept of a national system of innovation is the assumption that the interaction of domestic organizations is both more important than and to be preferred to international linkages. In the Canadian system international linkages dominate even in sectors where relatively strong domestic linkages exist. Relatively little innovation occurs in Canada without foreign participation at some stage in the process. The question in Canada has always been whether there are benefits to be derived from substituting domestic for foreign linkages. The Canadian experience shows that under certain circumstances this can be done. What is virtually impossible to resolve, even ex post, is whether this is wealth improving.

National systems of innovation are shaped by national characteristics. The Canadian system has a number of features that can be traced both to the relatively small size of its domestic market and to such unique characteristics as its natural resource endowment and vastness. Canada's small country characteristics appear to have been accentuated by its proximity to a very much larger but technologically similar country. This has contributed to the attenuation of domestic innovative linkages between, for example, the resource industries and machinery producers. On the other hand it has facilitated Canadian participation in the U. S. system, which appears to have improved technology adoption in some cases (motor vehicles) and resulted in world scale R&D mandates for affiliates in other cases. Thus the Canadian situation is unique both in the constraints on and opportunities for domestic innovation.

The next section of the chapter describes both the characteristics of the Canadian economy and how they have shaped its innovation system. The following sections describe the innovating organizations that are the building blocks of the Canadian system and the prominent linkages that exist and the resulting innovation complexes and clusters. The question of whether these systems, dominated as they are by international (largely transborder) linkages, are sufficient to generate future growth in national wealth is addressed in the concluding section.

THE CHARACTERISTICS OF THE CANADIAN ECONOMY AND THEIR IMPACT ON ITS INNOVATION SYSTEM

Canada ranks seventh among OECD members in Gross Domestic Product. A number of studies (Walsh, 1987, 1988; Soete, 1988; OECD, 1989b) have classified Canada as the smallest of the "large" OECD economies.

Industries based on natural resources have played a significant role in Canadian economic development (Canada, Royal Commission on the Economic Union, 1985, pp. 401–413). Resource industries (including agriculture) presently account for nearly 9% of Canadian GDP and 17% of Canadian exports. Resource industries account for a larger fraction of Canadian GDP than is the case in other large OECD economies (Charette et al., 1986, Table II-3).

Manufacturing accounts for a correspondingly smaller share of Canadian GDP than is the case in other large OECD economies. Canadian manufacturing activity has historically been highly protected. With some notable exceptions such as pulp and paper and nonferrous metals it has been oriented principally toward the domestic market and has been burdened by the diseconomies of small-scale production (Baldwin and Gorecki, 1986).

A major departure from this pattern occurred in 1965 with the institution of free trade in automobiles between the United States and Canada. The "Auto Pact" resulted in the rationalization of motor vehicle production on a North American basis. Canadian production of motor vehicles and parts presently accounts for 9% of Canadian manufacturing GDP and exports of these products to the United States account for 25% of Canadian merchandise exports.

The Canadian economy is closely integrated with the U. S. economy. Seventy-three percent of Canadian exports are to the United States and 69% of Canadian imports are U. S. origin. U. S. and Canadian capital markets are closely linked. Nearly 24% of the assets of nonfinancial Canadian corporations are foreign controlled with 71% of this being in U. S. hands. The figures for manufacturing are 44 and 68%, respectively. Safarian (1985, p. 9) concludes that the incidence of foreign control is higher in Canada than in any other advanced market economy with Australia, Belgium, and Ireland being the closest rivals.

Canadian and U. S. labor markets are not integrated. Immigrants to Canada have tended historically to come from the United Kingdom and more recently from Europe in general and southeast Asia. The United States accounts for roughly 8–10% of the immigrants to Canada. The United States has been the most important destination for Canadian emigrants. Migrants in general have tended to be relatively highly qualified.

Canada devotes a relatively large fraction of its resources to education. Canada ranks well ahead of the United States, Japan and the United Kingdom in terms of public expenditures on education as a proportion of GNP (Ontario Premier's Council, 1988b, p. 224). Canada ranks less highly in terms of both the rate of participation in formal education and the proportion of students completing secondary school. According to one study some 31% of Canadian students fail to complete their secondary education. This is true of only 25% of U. S., 15% of U. K., and 14% of German students (Ontario Premier's Council, 1988b, p. 221).

A more detailed study (Easton, 1988, pp. 11–13) shows that while a smaller proportion of Canadians complete secondary school than is the case in the United States, the proportion of Canadians completing university is roughly the same as in the United States and the proportion of Canadians completing some form of postsecondary education is higher.

Canadian secondary education is regarded as being somewhat weak, especially relative to far eastern countries, in science and mathematics. Canada's requirements for both scientific and entrepreneurial talent have historically been met, to a considerable degree, by immigration.

The real public rate of return on a 4-year university degree in Canada is estimated (as of 1980–1981) to lie in the 6 to 9% range depending on the region of the country (Vaillancourt and Henriques, 1986). It is 7% in Ontario and 9% in Quebec. Given that this is an average rate of return and includes returns to labor market signaling (which are private but not social benefits) it likely overstates the true marginal public rate of return. The implication is that Canada is not presently underinvesting in higher education as a whole. The chapter on Australia in this volume concludes that the same is true in that country.

Canada has a small and widely dispersed population. There are (as of 1986) only three metropolitan areas with populations in excess of one million. Urban areas in Canada tend to be widely separated frequently being in closer proximity to large U. S. cities than to each other. Some analysts (Lacroix and Martin, 1987; Britton and Gertler, 1986) concluded that the potential economies of urban agglomeration are unlikely to be fully realized outside of Toronto, Montreal, and Vancouver. They are, as a consequence, pessimistic regarding the ability of other Canadian cities to attract major R&D facilities and to generate sustained new business spinoffs.

In its historic natural resource orientation, small dispersed population, and integration with a much larger economy Canada is unique. These characteristics helped to shape an innovation system that is also unique in a number of respects.

The development of the national innovation systems of countries with small domestic markets is subject to a variety of constraints not faced by larger countries. As a result the characteristics of national systems of innovation should differ between large and small countries. Ergas (1987) has argued that large size continues to yield advantages even among the largest countries. Specifically, the United States has advantages in innovation that are not available even to Germany, France, and the United Kingdom. The Canadian innovation system has a number of small market characteristics which are accentuated by its proximity to the U. S. system.

The interaction of users and suppliers has become recognized as an important factor in the innovative process (Freeman, 1982). For small country suppliers (and users for that matter) this interaction is necessarily international. It may be burdened by the costs of communicating over long distances and of overcoming national differences in language, culture, or technological infrastructure. As a result small countries are likely to be at a disadvantage in mass market innovation.

There is some evidence that Canadian innovative activity has tended to focus on the "custom design" end of the market. De Bresson and Murray (1984) find that a disproportionate share of Canadian innovations in the machinery and equipment sector is of the custom produced or small batch variety and conclude that in this sector there is a "customized bias" in technological development. Polese and Verrault (1989) attribute the very considerable shares of international consulting engineering contracts won by Canadian firms, in part, to the nonstandardized nature of the product. The locational and technical characteristics of each job differ and this reduces the advantage accruing to firms based in large countries.

The disadvantage that small countries face in mass market innovation may result in their allocating a smaller portion of their R&D resources to applied industrial research and development and a larger portion to basic research (performed in universities or government laboratories) than large countries. Walsh (1987, pp. 107–108) observed that small countries tend to be more oriented to basic research than large countries. Canada exhibits this tendency. Canada's share of world research papers averaged 4.3% (in all fields) over the period 1973–1984. The Canadian share of external OECD patents over the period 1970–1983 was 1.4%. In contrast, Germany accounted for 6.3% of world research papers and 19.7% of external OECD patents.

Inferences regarding the tendency of small countries to perform a smaller portion of their R&D activity in their business sectors can be drawn from OECD data (OECD, 1989b, Table 7). There is a rough correspondence between GDP and the proportion of R&D performed in the business sector. Canada is an outlier in this relationship. For reasons that will be explored later, the proportion of Canadian R&D performed by the government is higher than in a number of smaller countries.

In their efforts to reduce the cost of interacting with users in other countries innovating firms based in small countries may perform more of their R&D abroad than firms based in large countries. This tendency is likely to be particularly pronounced if export sales are concentrated in a single foreign market as is the case with Canada. Pavitt and Patel (1989, Table 8) provide evidence that this tendency exists. They find that a larger proportion of the U. S. patents granted to large firms based in small countries are of foreign (i.e., outside the home country) origin than is the case with large firms based in large countries. In this respect Canada bears a fairly close resemblance to the Netherlands, Switzerland, Belgium, and Sweden. For all these countries a significant fraction of U. S. patents granted to their large firms is of either U. S. or German origin.

A second problem facing small countries is that given a minimum required scale of effort for successful innovation in most industries, they will be under greater pressure than large countries to specialize. Soete (1988) confirmed that small countries do tend to be more specialized in their innovative activity. He also finds that Canada exhibits this small country characteristic (Soete, 1988, Table 5.4).

This tendency to specialize also implies that industrial R&D spending is more concentrated (less evenly distributed among firms) in small countries than in large countries. A few world class players may account for a large fraction of a small country's industrial R&D. Van Tulder and Junne (1988, pp. 178–180) conclude from their examination of large firm R&D spending in the United States, Japan and Europe that country size and concentration of industrial R&D are negatively related. Canada conforms to this pattern. Canadian industrial R&D spending is more concentrated than that of the United States, Japan, Germany, France, the United Kingdom, or Italy but less concentrated than that of the Netherlands, Switzerland, or Sweden (see later for more detail on Canada).

It might also be conjectured that because they are less able to support specialized or "full-time" inventors, small countries might also have proportionately more part-time or individual inventors. The finding of Seguin-Dulude and Desranleau (1989) that the share of individual inventors in Canadian patents is roughly twice the share of individual inventors in U. S. patents is consistent with this reasoning.

Even with specialization, the innovative sectors of a small country are likely to be relatively thin in the sense that their fortunes ride on a few firms and, perhaps, on a few technologies. This lack of diversity is a characteristic of Canadian high-tech sectors and regions (Amesse et al., 1989). A consequence of this lack of diversity is that the failure of one firm or project can be highly disruptive. For example, it is said that the cancellation of the Avro Arrow interceptor program in 1958 resulted in the dispersal of a considerable portion of Canada's aeronautical design and engineering talent largely to the United States (Lukasiewicz, 1986). Similar concerns have been raised regarding the CANDU nuclear reactor, which has not sold well internationally. Smaller failures can be accommodated. Nichol (1985) traces the formation of many successful Ottawa information technology firms to the failure of Microsystems International, a local microchip manufacturer.

Successful imitation or adoption of new technologies developed elsewhere also requires resources. Walsh (1987, 1988) notes that industries in which there is relatively little domestic R&D spending may have difficulty assimilating technological advances made abroad and may, therefore, have difficulty remaining competitive. Small market size can handicap imitation as well as innovation. As a result small countries may be less able, hence slower, to assimilate new technologies. The rate of diffusion has been a long-standing Canadian concern (Economic Council, 1983). There has also been a recognition that one of the costs of world-scale innovative capability in a few sectors may be a reduced rate of diffusion and adoption in others.

GOVERNMENT AND UNIVERSITY R&D

Just under 20% of Canada's R&D is presently performed by the federal and provincial governments. The proportion of R&D performed in the government sector has fallen by some 47% over the past 20 years.

The decline in the share of R&D performed in government facilities is a consequence of the relatively rapid growth of business financed R&D. The Canadian experience in this regard is similar to that of the OECD as a whole (OECD, 1986, pp. 25–29).

The proportion of the national R&D effort performed within the government sector in Canada continues to be much higher than in both the large OECD economies and a number of advanced smaller economies such as the Netherlands, Sweden, Belgium, and Switzerland.

The relatively large fraction of R&D performed within the government sector may be, in part, a matter of bureaucratic choice, which can be altered over time by directions to contract-out (Senate Special Committee on Science Policy, 1972; Senate Committee on National Finance, 1984). There may, however, be other forces, most importantly the nature of the R&D activity funded by governments in Canada, at work.

The composition of government funded R&D in Canada differs from the OECD norm in a number of respects. Relatively little government R&D is devoted to defense. Relatively large amounts of R&D are devoted to agriculture, energy, and mining (OECD, 1989b, p. 44). This emphasis on the resource sectors goes back to the turn of the century (Smith, 1983). A number of provincial governments also regard the resource sectors as their top R&D priority (OECD, 1988, pp. 47–50). There may well be benefits in the form of both the accumulation of experience and project complementarity from centralizing the performance of this type of on-going process improving generic R&D. Given centralized performance there may be further benefits in terms of reduced contracting costs from the government performing the R&D itself.

Canada's most important R&D performing, supporting, and coordinating institution is the National Research Council (NRC). The NRC engages in both basic and applied research, the latter in support of both government and industry. The NRC, which opened its first laboratory in Ottawa in 1932, has also operated combined technical advisory and industrial R&D support program (Industrial Research Assistance Program, IRAP) with considerable success since 1947.

Individual provinces also maintain research councils. These organizations are of modest scale with combined R&D spending in 1987 being roughly one-quarter of the

NRC's spending. The provincial research councils are oriented toward the servicing of local industry with jointly funded R&D projects becoming more common.

Although much of the R&D performed within the government sector in Canada is intended to assist industry, doubts continue to be expressed regarding its relevance (Task Force on Federal Policies and Programs for Technology Development, 1984; Clarke and Reavely, 1988). Although there are clear exceptions, such as agricultural R&D, the basic problem appears to be a lack of communication between government laboratories and their potential clients. Numerous attempts have been made to integrate government laboratories more closely into industry innovation systems (Smith, 1983).

Universities play a number of roles in an innovation system, the education and basic research roles being the most prominent. Universities also engage in applied research. Sometimes this is on behalf of or in cooperation with industry. In other cases technologies developed in universities are licensed or are exploited in new businesses started by faculty members (academic entrepreneurs).

Canadian universities appear to have been relatively effective in fulfilling their basic research function. Canada ranks seventh in its share of world research papers (Statistics Canada, 1988, Table 41). Similarly, Canada ranked third and fourth among OECD countries in its share of publications in the fields of computers and electronics and electrical engineering respectively in 1984 (OECD, 1989a, Table 6).

Although they have been effective in their education and research functions, Canadian universities appear to have been less closely linked to the domestic industrial innovation system than are universities in other countries. The business sector funded 3.2% of Canadian university R&D in 1988 while in the United States the figure was 6.5% (National Science Foundation, 1989, Table 8-1). In Germany, Sweden, and Norway, business funds approximately 5% of university R&D (OECD, 1989b, p. 68).

While there are numerous examples of successful transfers of technology from universities to industry and of successful academic entrepreneurs (see, for example, Clifford, 1990), the impression left by very limited evidence is that Canadian universities have not served the incubator function that U. S. universities have and that technologies developed in Canadian universities are frequently exploited abroad rather than domestically (McMullan and Melnyk, 1988; Stuart-Haile, 1989; OECD, 1988; Doutriaux, 1989). Attempts have been in recent years to develop better university-industry linkages (Science Council, 1987b). Examples of linkages that have existed or have been formed in recent years are cited later.

INDUSTRIAL R&D, PATENTING, AND TECHNOLOGY ADOPTION

Major R&D Performing Firms

Canadian industrial R&D spending amounted to $4.4 billion (Cdn.) in 1988. Canada ranks tenth of the 12 largest OECD economies in its industrial R&D:GDP ratio. Canada ranks ahead of Australia and Spain but has slipped behind Italy in recent years.

Canadian industrial R&D spending is concentrated within a few firms as Table 9.1 indicates. The four largest R&D performers account for one-third of the Canadian total. The identity of the largest R&D performers is also instructive. The largest is BCE,

Table 9.1. Major Canadian Industrial R&D Performers (Self-Financed R&D Performed in Canada in Millions of Canadian $)

Company	Industry	Ownership	1989 R&D (est.)	1988 R&D	Cumulative Percentage of Canadian Total
BCE Inc.	Telecommunications equipment	Canadian	813	768	19.5
Pratt and Whitney Canada	Aeronautics	United States	247	219	25.1
IBM Canada	Information technology	United States	181	151	28.9
Atomic Energy of Canada	Nuclear	Government	166	163	33.1
Ontario Hydro	Electric power	Government	150	117	36.1
Hydro Quebec	Electric power	Government	136	129	39.4
Alcan Aluminum	Nonferrous metals	Canadian	111	105	42.0
Canadair	Aircraft	Canadian	106	91	44.3
Boeing of Canada	Aircraft	United States	91	83	46.5
CAE Industries	Aeronautics	Canadian	75	60	48.0
Imperial Oil	Petroleum products	United States	70	67	49.7
Allied Signal Canada	Electronics	United States	38	37	50.6
Inco Ltd.	Nonferrous metals	Canadian	37	33	51.5
BC Telephone	Telecommunications	United States	37	34	52.3
Digital Equipment of Canada	Information technology	United States	36	38	53.3
Shell Canada	Petroleum products	Netherlands	33	31	54.1
Mitel	Telecommunications equipment	United Kingdom	29	29	54.8
CIL	Industrial chemicals	United Kingdom	29	27	55.5
MacMillan Bloedel	Forest products	Canadian	25	24	56.1
DuPont Canada	Industrial chemicals	United States	21	18	56.6

Source: Financial Post (October 26, 1989).

which is comprised of Bell Canada, Northern Telecom and Bell-Northern Research. Pratt and Whitney is owned by United Technologies and has a world product mandate in small turbine aircraft engines. IBM Canada does software R&D in support of IBM's worldwide operations. AECL is owned by the federal government. Its principal product is the CANDU nuclear reactor and much of its research budget is spent in the support and continuing development of it.

There is a preponderance of U. S. subsidiaries, government enterprises, and utilities or utility-linked companies among the largest R&D performers in Canada. Although its spending dwarfs that of other Canadian firms, Northern Telecom R&D is quite modest in comparison with its international competitors. For example, AT&T spent over $2 billion on R&D in 1988 (Ontario Premier's Council, 1988b, p. 147).

An examination of patenting activity reveals a somewhat broader distribution of innovating activity. The largest corporate patentees of inventions of Canadian origin are listed in Table 9.2. Northern Telecom still dominates being responsible for 10% of corporate patents over the period 1982–1986.

Table 9.2. Major Corporate Recipients of Canadian Resident Patents

Firm	Industry	Ownership	Patents 1978–1982	Patents 1982–1986
Northern Telecom	Telecommunications equipment	Canadian	59	74
Canadian General Electric Company	Electrical appliances and industrial equipment	United States	25	15
DuPont Canada	Chemicals	United States	15	11
Inco	Mining	Canadian	15	8
Domtar	Paper and products	Canadian	11	9
Imperial Oil	Petroleum products	United States	10	10
Alcan	Aluminum	Canadian	11	7
Polysar	Petrochemicals	Canadian	10	8
CIL	Chemicals	United Kingdom	10	8
AECL	Nuclear	Government	8	6
Corporate total			791	774

Source: Statistics Canada (1989b, Tables 4.4 and 4.5).

Major R&D Performing Industries

The distribution of R&D spending by industry is summarized in Table 9.3. The structure of R&D in Canada differs from that of the large OECD economies in some important respects. First, Canada has a much higher proportion of its R&D in the service sector (including utilities, communications and engineering, and scientific services) than do the large OECD economies (OECD, 1986, p. 82).

Second, a much smaller proportion of Canadian industrial R&D occurs in the motor vehicles industry than is the case in both the large and the small, advanced OECD economies.

Third, a much smaller proportion of Canadian industrial R&D is in the machinery sector than is the case in both the large and many small, advanced OECD economies.

Fourth, a larger proportion of Canadian industrial R&D occurs in the basic metals and "other industries" (the largest being paper and wood products) than is the case in most other OECD economies.

The distribution of industrial R&D spending in Canada reflects both the distribution of industrial activity and the characteristics of innovative activity in Canada. Resource sectors including forest products, metals, and energy are relatively important in Canada as is R&D in support of them. Innovation in support of the resource industries has historically been oriented toward solving local process problems. Product innovations have tended to be either of the custom design or small batch variety. Large market technologies have tended to come from the United States.

As a result, domestic innovative activity in the machinery and surface transportation industries has been concentrated in fields such as logging equipment, hard-rock drilling equipment, and off-road vehicles. Canadian mass market product innovations such as the snowmobile are regarded as exceptions (De Bresson and Lampel, 1985).

Although Canada has a relatively large motor vehicle industry, it is completely integrated with that of the United States. Research, development, and engineering are

Table 9.3. Distribution of Intramural Business R&D Spending by Industry, 1988

Industry	1988 R&D Spending ($Mil Cdn)	Cumulative Share (%)	Average Annual Rate of R&D Growth 1980–1988	1986 R&D Intensity (%)
Telecommunications equipment	720	18.7	16.8	17.8
Aircraft and parts	533	30.1	13.9	13.9
Engineering and scientific services	363	36.8	20.4	22.8
Business machines	298	43.6	20.2	3.5
Other electronic equipment	293	50.3	20.7	12.8
Electric power	242	55.8	14.4	0.9
Other manufacturing industries	232	61.1	35.0	0.9
Computer services	216	66.0	32.5	15.1
Other (nonpharmaceuticals) chemical products	185	70.2	9.3	1.4
Primary metals	157	73.8	4.9	0.9
Petroleum and coal products	136	76.9	−2.1	0.5
Transportation and other utilities	134	79.9	13.1	0.4
Pulp and paper and wood products	128	82.8	8.3	0.3
Other transportation equipment	105	85.2	9.8	0.3

Source: Statistics Canada (1989c, Cat. No. 88-001, July).

centralized in the United States. The natural tendency of research, development, and engineering to locate in the larger market (and near corporate headquarters) was reinforced by the Auto Pact in 1965 under which Canada effectively traded local research development and engineering activity for more assembly jobs (Acheson, 1989).

Industrial Technology Adoption

In its 1983 report the Economic Council of Canada concluded that new technology diffuses more slowly both to Canada from abroad and within Canada than is the case in other developed countries. In their subsequent examination of the evidence McFetridge and Corvari (1986) concluded that Canada tended to be among the earliest recipients of new U. S. technologies over the period 1966–1979. They attributed this to the proximity of Canada to the United States and to the prominence of U. S. multinationals in Canada. They also noted that Canada's position in the transfer order of U. S. technologies had slipped over time. With respect to domestic diffusion the evidence was that it had been slower or less complete than in the United States in some manufacturing industries. The evidence for the service industries showed some lags by comparison with the United States but was generally inconclusive.

More systematic evidence is provided by the surveys of advanced manufacturing technology conducted by Statistics Canada (1989a) and the U. S. Department of Commerce (1989). The published results of these surveys are not comparable. They differ with respect to the sizes of establishments surveyed and the industrial groupings. Statistics Canada has prepared and will ultimately publish tabulations that match the U. S. survey more closely. These tabulations were made available to the author for statistical analysis.

Statistical analysis of the percentage of establishments in five major groups (metal fabricating, machinery, transportation equipment, electrical and electronic equipment, and instruments and related products), using each of 17 advanced manufacturing technologies, reveals that, on average, the incidence of use is greater in the United States than in Canada by some 5.6 percentage points or 44%. This difference is statistically significant. It holds across major groups and technologies.

The greater incidence of advanced manufacturing technology use in the United States is due in part to differences in both the scale of industrial establishments and the mix of industries in the two countries. Industrial establishments in the United States tend to be larger and thus more able to absorb the fixed cost of adopting new technologies than Canadian establishments. Industries that are intensive users of advanced manufacturing technologies tend to be more prominent in the United States than in Canada. An important example is the defense-related industries.

If Canadian plants were of the same scale as U. S. plants, the incidence of use of advanced manufacturing technologies in the United States would be 3.5 percentage points or 24% greater than in Canada. Correcting for the difference between the two countries in the importance of defense production would further narrow but would not eliminate the gap between them.

The remaining gap between U. S. and Canadian advanced manufacturing technology usage may be a consequence, in part, of the relative weakness of certain aspects of the Canadian innovation system. The importance of skilled personnel in facilitating the adoption of new technology has been cited in a variety of studies (see for example Julien et al., 1988). Supplier linkages may be more tenuous in Canada than in the United States, perhaps because a greater proportion of the advanced manufacturing technology used in Canada is imported. A possible remedy might be the further liberalization of restrictions on trade and migration.

LINKAGES AMONG INNOVATING ORGANIZATIONS

Horizontal Linkages

Horizontal linkages are defined here as relationships among organizations at the same stage in the innovative process. Horizontal linkages exist for two reasons. First, they are a means of internalizing externalities. That is, they are a means by which the beneficiaries of a technological improvement can contribute toward the recovery of its cost. Second, horizontal linkages are a means of realizing the benefits of specialization in research and development.

Horizontal linkages can be embedded in a wide variety of institutional arrangements. Among the more familiar are technology joint ventures and industry technology institutes. Horizontal arrangements can also embrace governments and universities. Government subsidies and tax incentives are a means of channeling support to innovators from spillover beneficiaries. Government and university laboratories may also contribute their special skills to cooperative research arrangements.

Some indication of the relative importance of various forms of formal and informal, horizontal and vertical linkages is provided by Longo (1989). His findings are reported in Table 9.4. Foreign affiliates, suppliers, and universities are the most prominent external sources of R&D. Taken together government R&D agencies and horizontal domestic linkages (with or without alliances) are also important. Customers and trade associations are relatively unimportant.

Longo also investigates the incidence and nature of technology alliances among R&D performers. He finds that over half the firms surveyed were involved in technology alliances. Foreign and domestic alliances were of roughly equal frequency.

Trade association research, development, and diffusion activities in Canada have been examined by Litvak (1985). He finds that in general there are relatively few trade associations involved in R&D or with any technical staff. The largest and oldest industry research institute is the Pulp and Paper Research Institute of Canada (Paprican), which was founded in 1925. It is supported largely by contributions from member companies. Paprican engages largely in applied process research. It has been responsible for a number of process innovations and has played an important role in solving common production problems.

There are two active research institutes in the energy industry. The Canadian Gas Research Institute conducts research on gas using appliances, gas distribution, and safety on behalf of member utilities from whom it derives 80% of its budget. It is also an associate member of the (U. S.) Gas Research Institute and benefits from research conducted by that organization. The Canadian Electrical Association conducts R&D into problems in electricity generation, transmission, and distribution on behalf of member utilities and equipment suppliers from whom it derives most of its revenue (the balance comes from the federal government).

Some research associations serve more to coordinate than to perform R&D. An example is the Canadian Steel Industry Research Association, which provides a link between the steel companies and metallurgical R&D, which is conducted largely in

Table 9.4. External Sources of R&D for Ontario R&D Performers, 1989

Source	Percentage of Respondents Ranking the Source in the Top Three
Affiliated foreign firms	24
Suppliers	23
Universities and colleges	20
Other government R&D agencies	16
National Research Council	14
Other unaffiliated firms, same industry	13
Unaffiliated firms in alliances	12
Purchasers	10
Industry research associations	10

Source: Longo (1989, p. 9).

universities and provincial research councils. Support for this R&D comes largely from federal and provincial governments and from the American Iron and Steel Institute.

A government agency that has played a prominent role in supporting, coordinating, and disseminating research in the area of heavy oil extraction is the Alberta Oil Sands Technology Research Agency (AOSTRA). AOSTRA has funded research, development, and demonstration projects jointly with petroleum companies that have evolved into commercially viable heavy oil recovery plants. AOSTRA has also funded a good deal of academic research in petroleum geology and engineering.

A more general government program that supports industrial R&D and serves as a clearinghouse for specialized technological capabilities is the National Research Council's Industrial Research Assistance Program (IRAP). The program is staffed by a network of 250 industry technology advisors operating out of 160 technology centers across Canada. It is regarded as Canada's most successful innovation support program (Supply and Services, 1990).

Other federal government programs serve largely to provide financial assistance to R&D-performing firms. Of note are the Defence Industry Productivity Program, which subsidizes R&D in the aerospace industry (Ontario Premier's Council, 1988a, Exhibit VIII.21), and the R&D tax credit provisions, which have been among the most generous in the world (United Kingdom, Inland Revenue, 1987).

Total government financial support including R&D tax credits, subsidies, and contracts amounts to approximately 20% of Canadian industrial R&D spending. It is frequently pointed out that the U. S. government directly funds some 30% of U. S. industrial R&D and that, by this standard, the level of government support in Canada is inadequate (Ontario Ministry of Industry, Trade and Technology, 1988).

The validity of this type of comparison depends on whether tax measures, subsidies, and contracts provide equivalent support to industrial R&D performers. There are reasons to believe that R&D contracts, which tend to be the means by which the government funds R&D in the United States and a number of other countries, are not equivalent, dollar for dollar, with subsidies and tax credits, so that intercountry aggregate R&D support comparisons are not meaningful.

More fundamentally, the question arises as to whether it is fruitful for governments in Canada to contract for more industrial R&D. This issue is addressed later.

To conclude, although there are numerous examples of cooperative research projects, there appear to be relatively few examples of significant institutionalized industry-wide R&D activity in Canada. There are a number of possible explanations. First, both the NRC and the provincial research councils perform and support the type of applied R&D and technology acquisition activity that might otherwise be performed by industry associations.

Second, Canada has a well-developed engineering services industry that can provide, perhaps at a lower cost, the type of specialized expertise in applying technology that an industry association might accumulate.

Third, there is the small country problem. Industrial R&D in Canada has tended to address local problems. The more broadly applicable technologies tend to come from abroad. It may be the case that in many Canadian industries, especially those outside the resource sector, the type of industry-wide yet uniquely Canadian technological problems that might be addressed by an industry association are relatively rare.

Vertical Linkages

A vertical linkage is a relationship between organizations at different stages in the innovative process. The importance of these user–supplier linkages in the innovative process has been emphasized by Rosenberg (1982), Freeman (1982), and Anderson and Lundvall (1988).

Anderson and Lundvall (1988, p. 11) have observed that it is a characteristic of small countries that the specialization pattern and technological competence of the engineering sector reflect, in part, the history of the primary sector. The Canadian experience is consistent with this observation. As will be demonstrated, much of the indigenous Canadian innovative effort has been in the service of the agriculture, mining, energy, forestry, and telecommunications industries.

The influence of user–supplier linkages on innovation in Canada has been investigated by De Bresson and Murray (1984). These authors rank Canadian industries by their number of world first innovations and adoptions over the period 1945–1978. They also rank capital goods industries according to their capacity relative to domestic demand. They find that two industries, miscellaneous ground transportation (off-road vehicles) and services to mining (air survey, exploration, and mapping) stand out as being world first innovators without being important adopters of foreign innovations. The unique requirements of Canadian geography bred a unique Canadian innovative effort in these two cases (p. 101).

Two capital goods industries are cited for their record of innovation and success at exporting and/or competing with imports. The logging equipment industry has a strong record of innovation and is highly export oriented (p. 131). The pulp and paper machinery industry has also recorded a number of world first innovations and has supplied a significant portion of domestic demand in the past (p. 133).

More generally, De Bresson and Murray find that the major innovating industries are also the major adopters of foreign technologies. The most prominent innovating industries are characterized by strong links with resource sector or government (sometimes acting on behalf of the resource sector) or public (electricity, gas, telecommunications) utility customers but not with the manufacturing sector. Prominent resource sector users of innovations or adoptions include farming (chemicals), petroleum and gas recovery, pulp and paper, smelting and refining, and hard rock mining (p. 181). The major innovating industries and their most prominent customers are listed in Table 9.5.

There are a number of Canadian examples that illustrate the essential role that users can play in defining the innovative task and in testing and refining innovations. De Bresson and Murray cite the role of the forestry company MacMillan Blodel in the design, testing, and use of a self-unloading barge for log transport. Litvak and Maule (1982) note that Imperial Oil was both the first customer and the source of the design for off-road vehicles built by Canadian Foremost.

The role of government, government utilities, and regulated utilities as users of innovation in Canada also speaks to the role of procurement in encouraging the development of domestic innovation systems and, perhaps, in strategies to "engineer comparative advantage." Polese and Verrault (1989) and the Ontario Premier's Council (1988a) argue that the prominence of Quebec-based engineering consulting firms in electricity and dam construction both in Canada and in world markets can be traced

Table 9.5. Major Innovating Industries and Their Customers, 1945–1978

Innovating Industry	Rank by Number of Innovations	Using Industries
Miscellaneous machinery and equipment	1	Wood products, mining, milling, smelting and refining
Scientific and professional equipment	2	Health and welfare services, government, mining services
Aircraft and parts	3	Aircraft and parts, government
Communications equipment	4	Communications utilities, government electrical products
Engineering and scientific services	5	Utilities, government
Industrial chemicals	6	Industrial chemicals
Electrical industrial equipment	7	Government, utilities

Source: De Bresson and Murray (1984, Tables 3 and 3.3 and List 5.3).

not only to Quebec's massive hydroelectric developments but also to Hydro-Quebec's policy of contracting out engineering requirements to local firms. Attempts by Hydro-Quebec to pursue similar policies with respect to suppliers of capital equipment (generators, transformers, cable, etc.) are described by Faucher (1989). The prospects of levering local purchases into an export industry seem less promising in this case.

Dalpé (1988) argued that Northern Telecom's status as a major exporter of telecommunications equipment (and Canada's largest R&D performer) is a result of its integration with and preferred access as a supplier of the Bell system in Canada. It is certainly the case that Northern Telecom's emergence as an innovative force began with the severance of its technological cooperation agreement with Western Electric by U. S. antitrust authorities in 1956. There is also agreement that the assurance of a domestic market was an important factor in Northern's decision to engage in the R&D projects in the 1960s and 1970s, which provided the foundation for its current success (Restrictive Trade Practices Commission, 1983, pp. 201–224). There is considerably less agreement, however, regarding the importance of full vertical integration for technological development in this industry (Globerman, 1980).

Although user–supplier linkages have contributed to innovation in Canada, it has been suggested that domestic linkages are weaker and less prevalent in Canada than elsewhere. With respect to the forestry industry in Canada, Hayter (1988) concludes:

> Although forest-product firms are the principal customers of equipment suppliers, in Canada there is no systematic co-operation between forest-product firms and equipment suppliers in the development and exploitation of technology (such co-operation exists in Scandinavia). Technological liasons between the in-house R&D groups of forest-product firms and of equipment suppliers are sporadic. R&D by equipment suppliers generally leads to the development of prototypes that are tested in the facilities of the forest-product firm (which may obtain lower prices for its willingness to be a guinea pig), by its in-house R&D group, where one exists. Similarly forest-product firms that develop a new technology normally seek a close working relationship with an equipment supplier. (p. 76)

Similarly, De Bresson and Murray (1984) find that the incidence of sustained user–supplier interaction is lower in Canada than in the United Kingdom. They conclude that there are

> few clusters of interacting industries which appears to be, in comparison to the United Kingdom, a feature peculiar to the Canadian system. An obvious factor of the lack of clusters of interacting industries in Canada is the reliance on foreign technological inputs. (p. 187)

Although sustained and successful horizontal and vertical innovative linkages can be identified in Canada, they coexist with and are often dominated by foreign linkages. This appears especially true of innovations involving capital goods. It also involves links with foreign research associations and foreign "branch plants" as both innovators and suppliers. For some (Hayter, 1988, pp. 74–75), the problem is the branch plant itself with its mandate limited to the pursuit of anything but uniquely Canadian problems. Whether this is the only form of branch plant participation in innovation in Canada and whether foreign ownership can be regarded as a causal factor in the analysis of innovation systems will be discussed further later.

Employee Mobility

Organizations that provide their employees with the knowledge and skills required to found new innovative organizations are called incubators. Employees may acquire knowledge and skills in the performance of their duties (learning by doing) or through formal in-service training. To the extent that some forms of learning necessarily occur on the job, incubator organizations are an essential complement to the formal education system. Incubators may be especially important in providing managerial skills. The role of large firms and nonmarket organizations as sources of technological entrepreneurship has been widely discussed (Miller and Cote, 1987).

The sources of technologically oriented entrepreneurship in Canada have been investigated by Litvak and Maule (1972, 1980, 1982) and Nichol (1985). These studies emphasize the international linkages in this aspect of Canada's innovation system. A significant fraction of "high-tech" entrepreneurs in Canada is either foreign born and/or foreign trained. Many entrepreneurs have also either worked abroad or been employed by foreign-owned firms.

The studies by Nichol and Litvak and Maule differ in their conclusions regarding the nature of the knowledge entrepreneurs take with them from their previous employers. Litvak and Maule (1972, pp. 4–30) find that 64% of the entrepreneurs they survey left their previous employment to exploit a specific idea or product. Nichol (1985, Table 4.20) finds that the entrepreneurs' initial product lines were competitive with those of previous employers in 30% of the cases she examines. She concludes that in the remaining 70% of the cases entrepreneurs made use of technology management skills acquired from previous employers.

Nichol provides some interesting evidence on the previous employment of high-tech entrepreneurs in the Ottawa area. Her results are summarized in Table 9.6. These results are instructive in a number of respects. First, there are two universities and a major R&D organization (the National Research Council) in Ottawa. No entrepre-

Table 9.6. Sources of High-Tech Entrepreneurship in Ottawa, 1982

Organization	Type	Percentage
Computing Devices of Canada	Foreign-owned corporation	18.9
Leigh Instruments	Canadian-owned corporation	13.2
Northern Telecom, Bell-Northern Research, Microsystems International	Canadian-owned corporation	28.3
Telesat Canada	Government corporation	3.8
Other corporate		7.5
Federal government departments and regulatory agencies		28.3
Total		100.0

Source: Nichol (1985, Table 4.18).

neurs came from these organizations. Second, Ottawa is home to the bulk of federal government employment including scientific employment. Although federal departments were the source of 28% of the technological entrepreneurs surveyed, this is a disproportionately small contribution given the federal government share of Ottawa employment.

Third, although the Bell-Northern group is an important source of technological entrepreneurship having spawned some 50 smaller companies (Ontario Premier's Council, 1988b, p. 167), much of its contribution to new high-tech entrepreneurship in Ottawa is the result of the bankruptcy of its subsidiary Microsystems International.

Fourth, Computing Devices of Canada, which is proportionately the most important incubator in the Ottawa area, has been U. S. owned since 1956. It has been a successful exporter of electronic surveillance and guidance systems to military customers for 30 years. Its employees have founded such companies as Leigh Instruments (itself an important incubator), Gandalf, and Lumonics. Thus, foreign affiliates can serve as incubators and may be superior in this regard to government scientific organizations. Whether they are superior to local firms (to the extent that the latter are an alternative) is an as yet, unanswered question.

Innovation Systems

Interaction among innovators may take place in a geographic, a technological, or an industry context. Innovative activity is frequently concentrated geographically. The benefits of geographic concentration appear to lie in the economies derived from large pools of skilled personnel and from personal communication between users and suppliers of innovation and among researchers pursuing alternative approaches to the same problem (Malecki, 1987).

The geographic distribution of innovative activity in Canada has been examined by Amesse et al. (1989). These authors report that, as of 1983, some 47% of Canadian high-tech employment was in Toronto with 22% in Montreal and 12% in Ottawa. In addition to being the largest, the Toronto high-tech sector has been established the longest and is the most diversified with significant representation in telecommunications, aerospace and information technology. Montreal is primarily aerospace, led by Pratt and Whitney, and telecommunications. Ottawa's development is the most recent. It is concentrated in the telecommunications (Bell-Northern) and information technology sectors.

In the opinion of Amesse et al. (1989) and of Lacroix and Martin (1987), Toronto, Montreal, and Ottawa qualify as Canada's only high-tech agglomerations. The OECD (1988) concludes that the "critical mass" necessary for the sustained development of new products and new technology-based firms has been reached in the western provinces in some industries. In particular critical mass has been achieved in British Columbia in telecommunications (remote terminals, signal processors, data transmission, image processors, chip design), in Alberta in electronic devices related to geophysical and seismic applications, and in Saskatchewan in electronic instrumentation and transmission devices (satellite receivers, electronic tracking systems).

Interaction among innovators also occurs in a technological and an industrial context. Technological interaction occurs when an innovation in one sector makes possible innovations in other not necessarily related sectors. The importance of this type of "innovation clustering" has been emphasized by Rosenberg (1979). Interaction can also occur among industries linked in a user–supplier relationship. De Bresson and Murray (1984) identify two complexes of frequent and sustained user–supplier linkages in metallurgy and electric power. They identify two clusters of more modest linkages in wood and chemical products.

The metallurgy complex is comprised of the nonferrous metal mining and milling (at the center) and the iron and steel and the smelting and refining industries. These industries are linked with each other and with the instruments, mining services, and industrial chemicals industries. Links with the machinery industry are relatively weak. The metallurgical complex also involves government and industry supported university research (Litvak, 1985; Hutchison et al., 1987).

The electric power complex is comprised of the power generation and distribution industry, which is a strong user of electrical industrial equipment, miscellaneous electrical products, and engineering services. This complex would also include universities such as the Ecole Polytechnique in Montreal. There is evidence of successful collaboration among universities, engineering consultants, and utilities (Hutchison et al., 1987) and between utilities and equipment suppliers (Faucher, 1989; Faucher and Fitzgibbons, 1990).

The wood cluster has pulp and paper at the center with links to logging and milling. All three are linked strongly back to the machinery industry, while some are users of innovations supplied by the miscellaneous transportation equipment and industrial chemicals industries. This cluster would also include industry research associations and the forestry institutes and laboratories of the Canadian Forestry Service as well as university forestry schools. The industry research associations have focused on localized process improvements and have been relatively successful (Hayter, 1988, Ch. 3; Miller and Blais, 1990; De Bresson and Murray, 1984). There have also been at least some cases of successful university–industry collaboration (Hutchison et al., 1987).

Although there are well-defined and relatively successful innovative linkages in the forestry industry, its critics claim that innovation in this sector has fallen well short of its potential in the areas of new forest product development and machinery (other than logging equipment) for use in the forestry industry (OECD, 1988; Science Council, 1987a). The sources of these failings are said to be inadequate R&D in the forest products companies (Hayter, 1988; Miller and Blais, 1990) and weak domestic link-ages with universities and with machinery manufacturers:

> There is little research and development carried out in British Columbia by the forestry companies. These companies do not contract out research at the universities. Forestry research at the universities is academic. Forintek . . . has an excellent laboratory facility and could contribute significantly to a turnaround in the forest sector. Some innovative products and processes have been developed at Forintek but the mechanisms for commercializing them seem inadequate. (OECD, 1988, p. 58)

A measure of the relative strength of domestic linkages in metallurgy and forestry is the proportion of patents on technologies used in these industries, which is of domestic origin. Information on the source of patents used by the pulp and paper and nonferrous metal industries is presented in Table 9.7. The process orientation of Canadian innovative activity is evident. It is also evident that although these industries generally source a larger fraction of their technology domestically than the Canadian average (approximately 7% of Canadian patents are of Canadian origin) the bulk of their technology continues to come from abroad.

The chemicals cluster is comprised of industrial chemicals, miscellaneous chemicals, and the petroleum and plastics industries. According to De Bresson and Murray (1984) these industries interact weakly with each other and strongly, as users, with engineering, machinery, and communications equipment and as suppliers with agriculture, mining, and pulp and paper. Among the types of interaction that occur in the petroleum industry are joint research, development, and demonstration projects on in situ recovery of heavy oil coordinated by the Alberta Oil Sands Technology Research Agency (AOSTRA) and joint petrochemicals research at the Institute for Chemical Science and Technology at Sarnia, Ontario. The petroleum industry has also been responsible for the development of petroleum engineering firms (Canadian firms ranked sixth in the world market in 1982) and seismic instrument firms in Alberta (Polese and Verreault, 1989; OECD, 1988).

Table 9.7. Sources of Patented Inventions for Use in Canadian Industries, 1978–1986

Industry	Type of Invention	Canadian Share (%)	U.S. Share (%)
Pulp and paper	Product	8.5	42.4
	Process	14.6	32.7
Nonferrous metal	Product	8.5	37.2
Smelting and refining	Process	15.5	38.0
Crude petroleum and natural gas	Process	13.0	72.0
Refined petroleum products	Process	8.0	64.0
Electrical power systems	Product	7.0	57.0
Communication	Product	8.0	56.0

Source: Statistics Canada, Science and Technology Indicators, 1988 (1989b, Tables 4.9, 4.10, and 4.13).

Imperial Oil (an Exxon affiliate) serves as an example of the role that a foreign owned firm can play in a national innovation system. Imperial's R&D effort includes an Exxon world research mandate in lubricating oils as well as research on domestic problems including enhanced recovery of conventional oil, recovery of heavy oil, and Arctic drilling (Clarke, 1980). Through the Exxon link foreign technology is brought to bear on Canadian problems and Canadian technology is applied internationally.

There are several other concentrations of innovative activity in Canada that are worthy of note. These are the aeronautics, telecommunications and information technology industries, and agriculture.

The aeronautics industry is a largely self-contained innovative system (De Bresson and Murray, 1984; Lambert, 1989). Among the major R&D performers are Pratt and Whitney, which has a world mandate from its U. S. parent in small turbine engines, Canadair and DeHavilland, which build airframes, and CAE Industries, which makes flight simulators. Government participation in this industry has taken the form of subsidization either directly through the Defence Industry Productivity program or indirectly through losses absorbed during the period of government ownership of DeHavilland and Canadair and through procurement.

Pratt and Whitney provides another illustration of the contribution a foreign owned firm can make to a national innovation system (De Bresson et al., 1990). In contrast, the history of Canadair and DeHavilland is one of financial difficulty and changing ownership. DeHavilland was formerly a successful builder of bush planes and is now a less successful builder of short take-off and landing passenger aircraft. It has gone from British to Canadian government to U. S. ownership. Canadair formerly built jet fighters and now builds business jets. It has gone from U. S. to Canadian government to Canadian public ownership. The history of these companies illustrates the opportunities and constraints associated with foreign ownership, the difficulties encountered by firms based in small countries in competing in world markets, and the problems posed by direct government involvement in proprietary (as opposed to generic or industry-wide) R&D decisions (Nelson, 1982).

The telecommunications industry is dominated by Bell Canada enterprises, which includes the Bell System, Northern Telecom, and Bell Northern Research. There are, in addition, a large number of other companies, both foreign and domestic, producing components, turnkey systems, and information systems (McNeil, 1986). These companies are located in western Canada as well as in the eastern high-tech agglomerations. Indeed, the largest R&D performer in western Canada is Novatel a subsidiary of Telus, formerly Alberta Government Telephones (Donville, 1991). Canada has been a major innovator in the use of satellites for telecommunications purposes (Canadian Research, 1986, p. 46). Government research is regarded as having been particularly important in this area (Dalpe, 1988).

Among the major participants in the information technology industry are the Canadian affiliates of IBM and Digital Equipment. IBM does software R&D in Canada for worldwide use. IBM is said to have been an important incubator. One of Canada's largest and most successful information technology consulting firms, DMR, was founded by former IBM employees (Pitts, 1990). There are also a large number of smaller Canadian-owned software companies that have entered the market over the past 20 years (Amesse et al., 1989; Ontario Premier's Council, 1988a, Ch. IX, X). These firms tend to make specialized products and export a large fraction of their output. Among the more important linking institutions are the institutes of computer research at the universities of Waterloo and Toronto.

At the heart of the agricultural innovation system is the network of federal government experimental farms that was begun in 1886. Its early contributions were to popularize summer-fallowing, a dryland farming technique, and to develop the "Marquis" strain of early-ripening wheat (Fowke, 1946). Both innovations increased the returns to prairie agriculture. The system has evolved to include government laboratories, agricultural colleges, and joint business–government R&D projects. The resulting crop and livestock improvements have yielded high rates of return (Nagy and Furtan, 1984; Ulrich et al., 1986; Zentner and Peterson, 1984; Widner et al., 1988; Dotto, 1987).

Innovation systems in Canada can be separated into two categories. The first category is comprised of "traditional" innovation systems in the fields of energy, metallurgy, forestry, and agriculture. These systems are oriented toward domestic process improvements. The return to innovation in these sectors comes in the form of higher rents to unique Canadian resources. Innovation in these sectors increases the profitability of selling staples on world markets.

The second category is comprised of the emergent innovation systems in aeronautics, telecommunications, and information technology. These systems have more tenuous links with Canada's natural resource endowment and more closely related to its human resource endowment. They are oriented toward product innovation. The return to innovation in these sectors comes from identifying and occupying niches in world markets for differentiated products.

The two categories of innovation systems have the common characteristics of supporting export activity and of being integrated with the innovation systems of other countries.

CONCLUSIONS

Canada's system of innovation has been shaped by its position as a thinly populated, resource-rich country adjacent to a very much larger but technologically and culturally similar country. Canada has an open innovation system with international (largely transborder) linkages dominating domestic linkages. Manifestations of the dominance of international linkages include the following:

1. A significant fraction of Canadian high-tech entrepreneurs are foreign born or trained or have foreign work experience.
2. Even in industries characterized by well-developed innovating organizations and linkages the vast bulk of the technology in use continues to come from abroad.
3. User–supplier linkages frequently involve foreign organizations as users or suppliers.
   a. Foreign firms are frequently involved in the commercialization of technologies developed in Canadian universities and research institutes.
   b. Canadian firms in the aerospace, information technology, and telecommunications equipment industries generally make a large portion of their sales abroad.

    c. The capital goods used by most Canadian industries tend to be of foreign origin or design.
4. A significant fraction of Canadian industrial R&D is performed by affiliates of foreign companies. Affiliate R&D may be limited to solving local process problems or it may support either a world product mandate (Pratt and Whitney, General Electric, Du Pont) or a world research mandate (IBM, Esso, Xerox).

Innovation in Canada has focused historically on adding value to the domestic natural resource base. It is in the resource sectors that innovation systems are the most visible. There are a number of ex post rate of return studies that conclude that this innovative effort has been highly successful. Most observers agree that the historic approach has been appropriate at least as a first step.

The Canadian system has been criticized in a number of quarters for its perceived failure to go beyond solving local process problems in the resource industries. It is argued that by comparison with the Scandinavian countries, for example, the indigenous innovative capability of the engineering (machinery) industries supplying the resource sector is quite meager. It is further argued that there has been little in the way of resource-upgrading innovation. According to this view, the innovation system has failed to reduce Canadian reliance on natural resources as has been the case in other formerly resource-oriented countries.

These failings are attributed to a lack of indigenous innovative capability in manufacturing especially in the machinery (engineering) industries. This may have reduced the productivity of other elements of the innovation system. Government and university research organizations have reported difficulties in generating local interest in their work. Similarly, threshold high-technology firms have difficulty finding domestic strategic partners.

Foreign ownership is said to be at the root of these problems. This raises the question of the extent to which foreign ownership inhibits the development of a national innovation system and, indeed, whether a national innovation system is necessarily preferred to integration into an international system.

Foreign owned firms have contributed to the development of innovation systems in Canada. They contribute toward the realization of agglomeration economies. They have served as incubators. They have served as users and suppliers at least with respect to local or small batch innovations. They have facilitated Canadian participation in the U. S. system both as users and suppliers. Large market innovative capability has, however, tended to be centralized usually in the United States. The question is whether this locational choice reflects the underlying reality of a small market next to a large market or whether it is a mere quirk of ownership.

There is reason to believe that a small country, even one in Canada's position, does have some leverage (Steed, 1989). The emergence of a strong innovative capability in the telecommunications equipment industry began with the severance of the technology cooperation agreement between Northern Electric (now Northern Telecom) and Western Electric in the United States. The wheel had to be reinvented and in this case it was. Similarly, Hydro-Quebec has successfully used purchasing policy as a means of encouraging the development of an engineering consulting industry in that province. Ontario Hydro has sourced its engineering internally and this is said to be one reason for the failure of this industry to develop in Ontario (Ontario Premier's Council, 1988a, pp. 285–300).

A large and sustained local demand can be used strategically to create domestic user–supplier innovative linkages. This type of policy is not without its costs even in the limited area in which it may be applicable. The requisite ex ante comparison of external benefits against the cost of local preference is all but impossible. The Canadian experience with two world-scale proprietary technologies that were heavily supported by government (CANDU reactor, Lermer, 1987; Challenger business jet, Borins, 1986) militates in favor of caution in pursuing this type of policy.

The alternative is to attempt to make the best of foreign linkages that will, in any event, continue to dominate the Canadian system. This would involve the following types of policies:

1. The maintenance of an open door to foreign technological and entrepreneurial talent.
2. The maintenance of market conditions and infrastructure conducive to timely domestic adoption of foreign technology.
3. The encouragement of domestic research-performing organizations to search foreign markets for compatible industrial partners where domestic partners are not available.

REFERENCES

Acheson, K. (1989). "Power-Steering the Canadian Automotive Industry." *Journal of Economic Behavior and Organization* 11: 337–51.

Amesse, F., Lamy, P., and Tahmil, B. (1989). "L'axe 40/401: Notre 'Silicon Valley' du Nord." *Gestion* 14: 15–22.

Anderson, E., and Lundvall, B. (1988). "Small National Systems of Innovation Facing Technological Revolutions: An Analytical Framework." In C. Freeman and B. Lundvall (eds.), *Small Countries Facing the Technological Revolution,* 9–36. London: Pinter Publishers.

Baldwin, J., and Gorecki, P. (1986). "Canada-U. S. Productivity Differences in the Manufacturing Sector: 1970–1979." In D. G. McFetridge (ed.), *Canadian Industry in Transition,* 211–60. Toronto: University of Toronto Press.

Borins, S. (1986). *Investments in Failure: Five Government Investments That Cost the Taxpayer Billions.* Toronto: Methuen.

Britton, J., and Gertler, M. (1986). "Locational Perspectives on Policies for Innovation." In J. Dermer (ed.), *Competitiveness through Technology: What Business Needs,* 159–75. Toronto: Lexington.

Canada, Royal Commission on the Economic Union and Development Prospects for Canada (1985). *Report Volume Two.* Ottawa: Supply and Services.

Canada, Senate Special Committee on Science Policy (1972). *Targets and Strategies for the Seventies,* Vol. 2. Ottawa: Queen's Printer.

Canada, Senate Standing Committee on National Finance (1984). *Federal Government Support for*

Technology Advancement: An Overview. Ottawa: Queen's Printer.

Canada, Supply and Services (1990). *R&D Bulletin* No. 204, March.

Canada, Task Force on Federal Policies and Programs for Technology Development (1984). *A Report to the Honourable Edward Lumley, Minister of State for Science and Technology.* Ottawa: Ministry of Supply and Services.

Charette, M., Henry, R., and Kaufman, B. (1986). "The Evolution of Canadian Industrial Structure: An International Perspective." In D. G. McFetridge (ed.), *Canadian Industry in Transition,* 61–134. Toronto: University of Toronto Press.

Clarke, P. (1980). "Research: Imperial's Long History and More of the Same." *Imperial Oil Review* 64(6): 26–29.

Clarke, T., and Reavely, J. (1988). "Problems Faced by R&D Managers in Canadian Federal Government Laboratories." *R&D Management* 18(1): 33–44.

Clifford, E. (1990). "Investors Put Faith in Quadra Logic." *Globe and Mail Report on Business* May 31, B9.

Dalpé, R. (1988). "Innovation and Technology Policy in a Small Open Economy: The Canadian Case." In C. Freeman and B. Lundvall (eds.), *Small Countries Facing the Technological Revolution,* 250–61. London: Pinter Publishers.

De Bresson, C., and Lampel, J. (1985). "Bopmbardier's Mass Production of Snowmobiles: The Canadian Exception?" *Scientia Canadiensis* 29, 133–49.

De Bresson, C., and Murray, B. (1984). "Innovation in Canada." New Westminister, Co-operative Research Unit on Science and Technology.

De Bresson, C., Niosi, J., Dalpé, R., and Winer, D. (1990). "Technological Capability, Innovation and Linkages of Domestic and Foreign Owned Firms: The Case of the Aircraft Industry." Paper presented at a Conference on Foreign Investment, Technology and Economic Growth, Ottawa, September 6–7.

Donville, C. (1991). "Novatel Pressured by Industry Boom." *Globe and Mail Report on Business* January 7, B1.

Dotto, L. (1987). "Canada-A Canadian Success Story." *University of Toronto Alumni Magazine* 15: 16–18.

Doutriaux, J. (1989). "High Technology Entrepreneurship and Academia: Are They Compatible in Canada." Ottawa: University of Ottawa, Faculty of Administration, Working Paper No. 89–9.

Easton, S. (1988). *Education in Canada.* Vancouver: The Fraser Institute.

Economic Council of Canada (1983). *The Bottom Line: Trade, Technology and Income Growth.* Ottawa: Supply and Services.

Ergas, H. (1987). "The Importance of Technology Policy." In P. Dasgupta and P. Stoneman (eds.), *Economic Policy and Technological Performance,* 51–96. Cambridge, England: Cambridge University Press.

Faucher, P. (1989). "Politique d'achat et developpement technologique: le cas d'Hydro Quebec." In *Le Marche public et le developpement technologique au Quebec: Six rapports d'etude.* Quebec: Conseil de la Science et de la Technologie.

Faucher, P., and Fitzgibbons, K. (1990). "The Political Economy of Electric Power Generation: Procurement Policy and Technological Development in Quebec, Ontario and British Columbia." Working Paper 90–03, CREDIT, University of Quebec at Montreal.

Financial Post. October 26, 1989.

Fowke, V. (1946). *Canadian Agricultural Policy: The Historical Pattern.* Toronto: University of Toronto Press.

Freeman, C. (1982). *The Economics of Industrial Innovation.* London: Pinter Publishers.

Freeman, C. (1988). "Introduction." In C. Freeman and B. Lundvall (eds.), *Small Countries Facing the Technological Revolution,* 1–8. London: Pinter Publishers.

Globerman, S. (1980). "Markets, Hierarchies and Innovation." *Journal of Economic Issues* 14, 977–98.

Hayter, R. (1988). *Technology and the Canadian Forest Products Industries.* Ottawa: Science Council of Canada Background Study No. 54.

Hutchison, W., Miller, P., Baird, N., and Bevelander, D. (1987). *R&D Links Between Firms and Universities: Six Case Studies.* Ottawa: Science Council of Canada.

Julien, P., Carriere, J., and Hebert, L. (1988). "La diffusion des nouvelles technologies dans trois secteurs industriels." Quebec: Conseil de la Science et Technologie.

Lacroix, R., and Martin, F. (1987). *Les Conse-*quences de la Decentralisation Regionale des Activites de R-D. Quebec: Conseil de la Science et de la Technologie.

Lambert, D. (1989). "Analyse de l'industrie aeronautique canadien et quebecoise: perspective de developpement." *Cahiers de Recherche,* 89–107. Montreal: Ecole des Hautes Etudes Commerciales.

Lermer, G. (1987). *AECL: An Evaluation of a Crown Corporation as a Strategist in an Entrepreneurial, Global Scale Industry.* Ottawa: Economic Council of Canada.

Litvak, I. (1985). "Canadian Trade Associations and the Promotion and Diffusion of Innovation." Ottawa: Department of Regional Industrial Expansion, Technological Innovation Studies Program, Research Report 100.

Litvak, I., and Maule, C. (1972). "A Study of Successful Technical Entrepreneurs in Canada." Ottawa: Department of Industry, Trade and Commerce, Technological Innovation Studies Program Report No. 11.

Litvak, I., and Maule, C. (1980). "Entrepreneurial Success or Failure - Ten Years Later: A Study of 47 Technologically Oriented Enterprises." Ottawa: Department of Regional Industrial Expansion, Technological Innovation Studies Program, Report No. 80.

Litvak, I., and Maule, C. (1982). "Canadian Entrepreneurship and Innovation: Six Case Studies." Ottawa: Department of Regional Industrial Expansion, Technological Innovation Studies Program, Report No. 86.

Longo, F. (1989). "Some New Findings on the Costs, Returns and Organization of R&D in Ontario." Mimeo, Toronto.

Lukasiewicz, J. (1986). "Canada's Encounter with High Speed Aeronautics." *Technology and Culture* 27: 223–61.

Malecki, E. (1987). "The R&D Location Decision of the Firm and 'Creative Regions'—A Survey." *Technovation* 5: 205–22.

McFetridge, D., and Corvari, R. (1986). "Technology Diffusion: A Survey of Canadian Evidence and Public Policy Issues." In D. G. McFetridge (ed.), *Technological Change in Canadian Industry.* Toronto: University of Toronto Press.

McMullan, W., and Melnyk, K. (1988). "University Innovation Centres and Academic Venture Formation." *R&D Management* 18(1): 5–12.

McNeil, R. (1986). "Telecommunications: A Canadian Overview." *Canadian Research* 19: 38–46.

Miller, R., and Blais, R. (1990). "Les Logiques de l'Innovation dans Six Secteurs Industriels." *Gestion* 15: 9–16.

Miller, R., and Cote, M. (1987). *Growing the Next Silicon Valley.* Lexington: Lexington Books.

Nagy, J., and Furtan, H. (1984). "Economic Cost and Returns from Crop Development Research: The Case of Rapeseed Breeding in Canada." *Canadian Journal of Agricultural Economics* 1: 1–14.

Nelson, R. (1982). *Government and Technological Progress.* New York: Pergamon.

Nichol, L. (1985). "Spin-offs and New Firm Formation: Entrepreneurship and High Technology in the Ottawa Area." Ottawa: Unpublished M. A. Thesis, University of Ottawa, Department of Geography.

Ontario, Ministry of Industry, Trade and Technology (1988). *A Commitment to Research and Development: An Action Plan.* Toronto: Queen's Printer for Ontario.

Ontario, Premier's Council (1988a). *Competing in the New Global Economy,* Vol. 2. Toronto: Queen's Printer for Ontario.

Ontario, Premier's Council (1988a). *Competing in the New Global Economy,* Vol. 1. Toronto: Queen's Printer for Ontario.

Organization for Economic Co-operation and Development (1986). *OECD Science and Technology Indicators.* Paris: OECD.

Organization for Economic Co-operation and Development (1988). *Innovation Policy: Western Provinces of Canada.* Paris: OECD.

Organization for Economic Co-operation and Development (1989a). *Major R&D Programs for Information Technology.* Paris: OECD.

Organization for Economic Co-operation and Development (1989b). *OECD Science and Technology Indicators.* Paris: OECD.

Pavitt, K., and Patel, P. (1989). "Do Large Firms Control the World's Technologies?" Mimeo, University of Sussex, Science Policy Research Unit.

Pitts, G. (1990). "DMR's Success in Past Efforts Creates Bullish View of Newly Expanding European Market." *Financial Post* (June 6), 14.

Polese, M., and Verrault, R. (1989). "Trade in Information-Intensive Services: How and Why Regions Develop Export Advantages." *Canadian Public Policy* 15(4): 376–86.

Restrictive Trade Practices Commission (1983). *Telecommunications in Canada—III, Vertical Integration.* Ottawa.

Rosenberg, N. (1979). "Technological Interdependence in the American Economy." *Technology and Culture* 20: 25–50.

Rosenberg, N. (1982). *Inside The Black Box: Technology and Economics,* Cambridge, England: Cambridge University Press.

Safarian, A. E. (1985). "Government Control of Foreign Business Investment." In J. Whalley (ed.), *Domestic Policies and the International Economic Environment,* pp. 7–56. Toronto: University of Toronto Press.

Science Council of Canada (1987a). "A Sectoral Approach to Innovation: The Case of the Forest Products Industries." Ottawa: Supply and Services.

Science Council of Canada (1987b). *University-Industry Research Centres: An Interface between University and Industry.* Ottawa: Supply and Services.

Seguin-Dulude, L., and Desranlau, C. (1989). *The*

Individual Canadian Inventor. Ottawa: Cat. No. 88–510.

Soete, L. (1988). "Technical Change and International Implications for Small Countries." In C. Freeman and B. Lundvall (eds.), *Small Countries Facing the Technological Revolution* 98–112. London: Pinter Publishers.

Smith, M. (1983). "The Role of Federal Laboratories in the Technological Development of Canadian Industry." *Journal of Canadian Studies* 17: 10–19.

Statistics Canada (1988). *The Provincial Research Organizations.* Ottawa: Cat. No. 88–201.

Statistics Canada (1989a). "Survey of Manufacturing Technologies 1989." Ottawa: Cat. No. ST-89-10.

Statistics Canada (1989b). *Science Indicators 1988.* Ottawa: Cat. No. 88–201.

Statistics Canada (1989c). *Industrial Research and Development Expenditures, 1980 to 1989.* Ottawa: Cat. No. 88–001, Vol. 13, No. 3.

Steed, G. (1989). *Not a Long Shot: Canadian Industrial Science and Technology Policy.* Ottawa: Science Council of Canada.

Stuart-Haile, M. (1989). "Technology Transfer: The Science Business." *Canadian Research* 22: 14–22.

Ulrich, A., Furtan, H., and Schmitz, A. (1986). "Public and Private Returns from Joint Venture Research: An Example from Agriculture." *The Quarterly Journal of Economics* 101: 103–30.

United Kingdom, Inland Revenue (1987). *Fiscal Incentives for R&D Spending: An International Survey.* London.

United States Department of Commerce (1989). *Manufacturing Technology 1988.* Washington, D. C.

United States National Science Foundation (1989). *National Patterns of R&D Resources.* NSF 89-308, Washington, D. C.

Vaillancourt, F., and Henriques, I. (1986). "The Returns to University Schooling in Canada." *Canadian Public Policy* 12: 449–58.

Van Tulder, R., and Junne, G. (1988). *European Multinationals in Core Technologies.* Chichester: John Wiley.

Walsh, V. (1987). "Technology, Competitiveness and the Special Problems of Small Countries" *STI Review* (Summer) 81–133.

Walsh, V. (1988). "Technology, Competitiveness and the Special Problems of Small Countries: A Review." In C. Freeman and B. Lundvall (eds.), *Small Countries Facing the Technological Revolution,* 37–66. London: Pinter Publishers.

Widner, L., Fox, G., and Brinkman, G. L. (1988). "The Rate of Return to Agricultural Research in a Small Country: The Case of Beef Cattle Research in Canada." *Canadian Journal of Farm Economics* 36: 23–36.

Zentner, R., and Peterson, W. (1984). "An Economic Evaluation of Public Wheat Research and Extension Expenditures in Canada." *Canadian Journal of Agricultural Economics* 32: 325–53.

10

The Australian Innovation System

ROBERT G. GREGORY

The distinctive characteristics of the Australian national innovation system are a low level of science and technology expenditure, a high level of government involvement in financing and undertaking research, a low level of private sector research and development, and exceptionally high dependence on foreign technology. The system has evolved in response to three dominant structural features of the economy, which can be detected very early in Australian history and have changed little.

The first structural feature is the ability of a small population to produce high living standards from the production of primary products. As an indication of these living standards, it has been estimated that a young adult convict sent to Australia during the first 40 years from the founding of the colony in 1788 could expect to live substantially longer than if he remained in the United Kingdom. The early wealth of the colony was generated by domestic production of goods and services and the export of wool, then the discovery of gold during the 1850s, and finally the export of wheat from the 1870s. Each wave of new rural production continued the pattern of combining large quantities of land, little labor, and simple technologies to further increase living standards. By the beginning of the twentieth century GDP per capita was perhaps 10–30% higher than the United States (Butlin, 1962). As a result of the efficient export of primary products there was no obvious and important direct association between economic development and the systematic application of new and *sophisticated* scientific knowledge (Schedvin, 1987).[1]

The second structural feature is that the small population and high wages led to small scale and simple manufacturing, which, as a result of high costs, found it difficult to export and compete against imports. The manufacturing sector was directed almost exclusively to the small home market, large segments were protected by tariffs, and most technologies were imported. As a result, there was a low level of private sector R&D.

The third feature is the high degree of government provision of business and social services. Economic historians talk of "colonial socialism,"[2] the evidence of which can be found in many facets of Australian life (Butlin et al., 1982).[3] Given the dominance of small scale rural production, and the tradition of "colonial socialism" a high degree of government involvement in research financing and performance was to be expected.

These structural features of the economy have been remarkably stable over Australia's 200 year history. At the end of the 1980s, about 80% of exports are still primary products, approximately half from the rural and half from the mineral sector. GDP per capita is still relatively high, although now about 10 to 15% less than the United States. The manufacturing sector continues to be small scale, accounts for 16% of GDP, and less than 10% of output is exported—mainly processed mineral and primary products. Manufacturing is protected by an average effective tariff rate of 19% and continues to import most technology. The government remains important and dominates tertiary education, R&D expenditure, and telecommunications and is a large provider of transport and banking services.

The innovation system has worked reasonably well in that Australians still enjoy high living standards. Nevertheless, attitudes and policy have been changing slowly over the last decade. There is now a strong demand for adjustments, driven by a desire to change the structure of the Australian economy, which is increasingly seen as one too dependent on a small range of primary products, prone to balance of payment problems, and not generating sufficiently fast growth rates of per capita income. The demand for adjustment is focused on increasing private sector R&D, targeting government sector research more toward national priorities, increasing competition in the research community, and expanding the education system.

The broad outline of the national innovations system is first discussed, with special attention given to the role of government and the effects of industry structure on R&D expenditure. Then the recent history of the manufacturing sector is used to explain the strong desire to change the system, particular aspects of new policies and directions are discussed and assessed, and we comment on the current fashion of linking the national innovations system to the balance of payments. Concluding comments are then presented.

THE NATIONAL INNOVATION SYSTEM AND THE GOVERNMENT–PRIVATE SECTOR BALANCE

Most of our focus is on R&D expenditure. Although, as discussed in the introductory chapter, this is only a small part of the innovation system that has been attracting significant policy interest and the economic and political forces leading to a reassessment of R&D policy are being felt in other parts of the national innovation system. Indeed, a thorough discussion of R&D policy issues should encompass most of the important conceptual issues that relate to other parts of the national innovation system.

Australia spends a relatively small fraction of GDP on R&D. Among the subgroup of OECD nations listed in Table 10.1 Australia is ranked twelfth, just ahead of New Zealand (column 1). If the same set of countries is ranked by government sector R&D expenditure (Civil) Australia is fifth (column 2). The prime reason for Australia's low R&D is private sector expenditure, which, as a fraction of GDP, is just over 20% of large spenders (column 3). When classified by sector of performance the importance of government is again evident with Australia being ranked third (column 4).

These international comparisons suggest a range of questions. Do the same influences explain each of the key facts; high government R&D, low private sector R&D, and low R&D expenditure in aggregate? Does government crowd-out the private sector? Are Table 10.1 ratios appropriate for the structure of the Australian economy?

Table 10.1. R&D Expenditure as a Ratio of GDP: Selected OECD Countries (Latest Available Data)

R&D Expenditure Total % of GDP (1)		Source of R&D Funds Government (Civil) % of GDP (2)		Source of R&D Funds Business % of GDP (3)		R&D Performance Government % of GDP (4)	
1. Switzerland	2.88	1. Netherlands	1.05	1. Switzerland	2.27	1. France	0.57
2. Japan	2.87	2. Germany	0.83	2. Japan	1.96	2. New Zealand	0.57
3. Sweden	2.82	3. Norway	0.74	3. Germany	1.81	3. Australia	0.40
4. Germany	2.78	4. France	0.73	4. Sweden	1.77	4. Netherlands	0.38
5. United States	2.66	5. Australia	0.71	5. United States	1.26	5. United Kingdom	0.37
6. Netherlands	2.40	6. Sweden	0.65	6. Netherlands	1.21	6. Germany	0.36
7. United Kingdom	2.36	7. New Zealand	0.58	7. United Kingdom	1.17	7. United States	0.31
8. France	2.29	8. Japan	0.57	8. France	0.93	8. Ireland	0.30
9. Norway	1.83	9. Canada	0.55	9. Norway	0.93	9. Japan	0.28
10. Finland	1.64	10. Ireland	0.55	10. Canada	0.58	10. Norway	0.27
11. Canada	1.35	11. Switzerland	0.54	11. Australia	0.45	11. Canada	0.26
12. Australia	1.20	12. United States	0.51	12. Ireland	0.43	12. Switzerland	0.18
13. New Zealand	0.97	13. United Kingdom	0.36	13. New Zealand	0.39	13. Sweden	0.13

Source: "Science and Technology Budget Statement, 1989–90," Australian Government Publishing Service, Canberra, 1989.

Why Is Government R&D Expenditure and Performance So High?

It has become commonplace to assert that government expenditure is too high and private sector expenditure too low, as if government has crowded-out private sector R&D. It is probably a mistake to link the two sectors in this way. First, even if crowding-out exists it is too small to explain low business sector R&D. A significant reallocation of government expenditure to the private sector, say 30% (Table 10.1), is sufficient to move the Australian government ranking from fifth to twelfth but would change the private sector ranking by only one place. Second, the Australian economy has a unique structure that might be expected to generate R&D that is above average for government and below average for business. Indeed, a case can be made that R&D expenditure and performance in both sectors are about right if OECD averages are used as benchmarks.

Table 10.2 lists government R&D expenditure by socioeconomic objectives for Australia and other OECD nations. The large differences are low Australian expenditure on energy research (Australia is energy abundant and, with the exception of electricity generation, energy is produced by the private sector) and high expenditure on agricultural research, which is about three times greater than the OECD average, excluding Australia and New Zealand. If government R&D expenditure on agriculture matched the OECD average then Australian government expenditure in total would be ranked about sixth in Table 10.1 (column 4) rather than third. Australia's position would not be exceptional.

Rural R&D expenditure by government is about half as large as all R&D undertaken in the private sector. The sector produces 4–6% of GDP but accounts for 26% of government R&D. At the state level, the sector accounts for 73 cents in every $1 spent (see Table 10.3).

Government dominance of rural R&D is quite exceptional; it accounts for 97% of all expenditure. This dominance is to be expected if the community wishes to achieve an optimal allocation of resources. Small scale rural production units make it difficult for individual producers to finance R&D and to capture its benefits to the exclusion of others. If the free market were left to determine rural R&D levels the extent of market failure would be relatively great. Other important influences that encourage government expenditure are the world dominance of Australian wool, which enables the nation to capture most of the benefits of wool R&D,[4] and the unusual physical environment, which limits the scope for rural technology imports but enables research benefits to be captured by Australian producers.

The major institution undertaking rural research is the Commonwealth Scientific

Table 10.2. Government Research Budgets by Socioeconomic Objective (1982 or Nearest Year) (cents per $100 of GDP)

	Agriculture	Industry	Energy	Environment	Health	Social	Advancement of Knowledge	Other
Australia	15.5	8.4	3.3	1.8	3.0	2.3	29.2	3.7
OECD (excluding Australia and New Zealand)	4.2	9.7	8.9	1.4	4.5	4.4	31.7	5.8

Source: OECD, *Science Resources Newsletter,* No. 7, Summer 1983.

Table 10.3. Government R&D Expenditure by Socioeconomic Objective, 1986–1987

Socioeconomic Objective	Total Percent	Commonwealth Percent	State Percent	Universities Percent
National security	9	22		
Economic development	45	55	80	24
Rural	26	24	73	10
Manufacturing	7	15	0	3
Community Welfare	22	9	17	30
Health	14	8	12	
Advancement of knowledge	24	13	3	45
Total	100	100	100	100

Source: Australian Bureau of Statistics, "Research and Experimental Development," All Sector Summary, Australia 1986–87, Cat. No. 8112.0, Table 9.

and Industrial Research Organization (CSIRO), which was created as an independent statutory authority in 1949 and succeeded the former Council of Scientific and Industrial Research (CSIR), established in 1926 to serve the research needs of the rural sector.[5] The CSIRO budget accounts for 16% of Commonwealth government expenditure on civil R&D, around 70% of rural research, 70% of mining research, and 10% of all research in Australia. Research expenditure within CSIRO is about half of that of Australian universities. Most funding is by block grant and CSIRO chooses research priorities.[6]

Rather than finance virtually all rural research from general revenue, government could provide an institutional framework to facilitate collection of private sector R&D monies to prevent free rider problems. Recently government has begun to do this. For wool, meat, wheat, and many other rural industries government now collects compulsory industry levies, and in most instances, matches them $1 for $1 to an amount equivalent to 0.5% of gross value of production. Although government is placing increased importance on moving research closer to the market place, and encouraging the private sector to finance and control more of their research needs, the sums of money collected from the rural sector are still relatively small, $37 million in 1988–1989.

The arguments for government financing R&D are different from arguments as to where R&D should be performed. Why should government undertake research rather than finance research in the private sector? There was little choice at the time decisions were made to set up government research agencies. When CSIR was established in 1926 there were few private researchers outside universities (the first Ph.D. awarded by an Australian university occurred in 1946). Immediately after World War II, when the Australian government began to plan for economic development, it could have acted to foster private research centers but the tradition of "colonial socialism," the satisfactory experience of war-time planning, and the lack of a technologically sophisticated private sector naturally led to the belief that government should take the lead. Hence the creation of CSIRO, the Institute of Advanced Studies at the Australian National University, and a number of government research organizations. Once created, these institutions showed no tendency to use government contracts to foster private R&D companies.

Australia therefore spends proportionately more government funds on R&D than the OECD average because rural production and rural exports are more important (Table 10.4). But should government expenditure be increased or reduced? The structure of the economy is quite different from the typical OECD country, but over the last 30 years rural sector dominance has declined. The rural export share has fallen from around 85% during the early 1950s to around 35% at the end of the 1980s and the GDP share from 15 to 4%. Assuming expenditure ratios were appropriate 20 or 30 years ago, these trends might be expected to lead to less rural R&D as a share of the total and less government sector R&D.[7] Neither has occurred.

Why Is Private Sector R&D Expenditure so Low?

If private R&D is classified by enterprise of product field then over 90% of expenditure is in the manufacturing sector and the reasons for low private sector R&D are to be found there. Among the more important reasons are the following.

First, the manufacturing sector is small. The sector peaked at 27% of GDP in 1968–1969 but since 1974–1975 has been contracting and is currently producing slightly more than 16% of GDP. Australia is among those OECD countries with the smallest manufacturing sector as a proportion of GDP.

Second, the typical manufacturing establishment is small scale and orientated toward serving the domestic market. Manufacturing exports, mainly low level processing of primary products, are less than 20% of manufacturing value added and most technology needs are easily imported.

Third, the manufacturing structure is biased away from high technology. Most OECD countries export more high technology products than they import (Table 10.5). Australia, however, imports seven times more high technology products than it exports.

Fourth, most large manufacturing companies are foreign multinationals that have not undertaken large quantities of R&D within Australia. In 1982–1983, 32% of manufacturing value added was under foreign control.

The influence of these factors can be grouped into the effects either of industry structure or of R&D intensity within each industry. The Bureau of Industry Economics (1990) has compared Australian private sector R&D in 1981–1982 as a proportion of manufacturing value added (0.8%) with the average of six OECD countries (4.5%).

Table 10.4. Export and Manufacturing Shares Selected Countries[a]

Country	Export Share of GDP (%)	Manufacturing (%)	Share of Exports Food/Raw Materials (%)	Energy (%)	Manufacturing Share of GDP (%)	Change 1968–1987 (%)
Australia	16	34	46	20	17	−32
United Kingdom	24	84	9	8	21	−21
Germany	29	93	6	1	32	−14
France	31	78	19	2	22	−22
Italy	20	89	9	2	23	−16
United States	9	82	15	3	19	−30
Japan	11	98	1	0	29	−8

[a]Export shares, 1988; manufacturing shares, 1987.

Sources: National Accounts, Main Aggregates, Vol. 1, 1960–1988, OECD 1990 (export share of GDP) and OECD Data Bases (share of exports).

Table 10.5. Trade in Selected Technology Based Products, OECD Ratios, 1983

Country	Ratio of Exports to Imports	Per Capita Exports US $
1. Japan	4.62	571
2. West Germany	1.95	1133
3. Switzerland	1.83	2426
4. United States	1.25	340
5. Netherlands	1.24	1313
6. Ireland	1.21	986
7. Italy	1.18	363
8. United Kingdom	1.06	568
9. France	1.06	551
10. Sweden	1.02	1060
11. Belgium	1.00	1159
12. New Zealand	0.18	110
13. Australia	0.15	73

Source: "Science and Technology Statement" 1985–86, Department of Science, Australian Government Publishing Service, Canberra, 1986, Table 14.

It concludes that if Australia possessed the same manufacturing industry structure as each of the six OECD countries R&D would increase to 1.2% on average (row 2), accounting for 11% of the Australian–OECD gap (Table 10.6). R&D intensity within industries is far more important, accounting for 60% of the gap, the remaining 29% being due to interaction effects. Australian R&D intensity has increased since 1981–1982 but the Australian–OECD gap is much the same.

There are differences of "within industry R&D intensity" between Australia and the OECD. For medium- and low-technology industries Australian R&D intensity, at current expenditure levels, is only slightly less than other OECD countries. The largest gaps occur for high technology industries, dominated by foreign multinationals, where, in almost every instance, Australian R&D is very much lower (DITAC-OECD, 1989).

Given the small manufacturing sector and industry structure, the low private sector expenditure on R&D may not be inappropriate, unless it is firmly believed that

Table 10.6. R&D Intensities and Industry Structure[a]

	A	B	C	D	E	F
Australia	0.8	0.8	0.8	1.5	1.5	1.5
Six OECD countries[b]	4.5	1.2	3.0	5.3	2.0	3.0
Gap	3.7	0.4	2.2	3.8	0.5	1.5

[a]A, The ratio of actual R&D to value added 1981. B, Australian intensity, other countries industry structure 1981. C, Australian industry structure, other countries research intensity 1981. D, Actual R&D to value added 1986–1987 (1986–1987 Australia, 1985 OECD countries). E, Australian intensity, other countries industry structure 1986–1987. F, Australian industry structure, other countries research intensity 1986–1987.

[b]Japan, United States, West Germany, United Kingdom, Sweden, and Canada.

Source: "Manufacturing Investment," Bureau of Industry Economics Research Report No. 33, Australian Government Publishing Service, Canberra, 1990, Table 6.10.

R&D expenditure determines industry structure or that it is more important for multinationals to produce research in the host country rather than import technologies.

Changing Trends

Over the past two decades there have been a number of noticeable changes in Australian attitudes and the pattern of R&D expenditure. First, there has been a dip in R&D spending from the mid-1970s until the early 1980s, most of which was concentrated in the business sector where R&D expenditure, as a proportion of GDP, approximately halved (Table 10.7). The government sector also reduced expenditure marginally, but localized to defense R&D.

Second, business sector expenditures increased from the mid-1980s and the government share began to fall. In 1978–1979 government contributed 77 cents in every research dollar. By 1987–1988 the contribution had fallen to 60 cents.[8]

Third, irrespective of the source of finance, there is a feeling that R&D should be more applied and nearer the product market. Block funding has been reduced and directed grants increased. Research agencies have been encouraged to raise private sector money. The change has been particularly marked for CSIRO, which during the early 1970s accounted for more than a quarter of the government research budget and has now been reduced to 16.0%. The share of the CSIRO budget from nondirect appropriations has increased to 30% and to change incentives CSIRO is allowed to keep royalties, which were previously paid to government general revenue. The same strategy has been applied to other government research institutions.

THE RECENT HISTORY OF MANUFACTURING

Over 90% of private sector R&D expenditure classified by industry of product field occurs in the manufacturing sector and so much current discussion and motivation

Table 10.7. Trends in Research and Development as a Ratio of GDP

Year	GERD/GDP	Business	Government Total	Civil	Defense	Government Agencies	Unis	CSIRO% of Commonwealth R&D Support
1968–1969	1.33	0.47	0.81	0.66	0.15	0.53	0.31	
1973–1974	1.21	0.39	0.79	0.67	0.12	0.50	0.32	
1976–1977	1.02	0.22	0.77	0.67	0.10	0.48	0.29	
1978–1979	1.00	0.20	0.77	0.69	0.08	0.44	0.32	27
1981–1982	1.00	0.23	0.75	0.68	0.07	0.46	0.31	29
1984–1985	1.14	0.31	0.78	0.71	0.07	0.45	0.34	23
1986–1987	1.25	0.45	0.77	0.71	0.06	0.44	0.36	20
1987–1988	1.20	0.45	0.72	0.66	0.06	0.40	0.35	—
1989–1990								16

Sources: Australian Science and Technology Data Brief Update, Department of Industry and Commerce, Australian Government Publishing Service, Canberra, June 1989. Science and Technology Budget Statement 1989–90, Australian Government Publishing Service, Canberra, 1989.

for policies to increase private sector R&D stems from dissatisfaction with the performance of manufacturing. To understand the dissatisfaction it is useful to begin at World War II when the Japanese occupied land within a hundred miles of the Australian coast. The fact that the United Kingdom was unable to direct significant resources to the defense of the Pacific, and fear of a possible future invasion, led to the decision to pursue economic development with more vigor. The development program was to be based on augmenting Australian endowments with immigrants to provide labor and foreign companies to provide capital and technology. The major policy instruments were a liberalized immigration program, including paid passages, and import protection for companies that began Australian production.

The impact of the development strategy changed Australian society. Since 1945 more than half the population increase has been immigrants and by 1981 one-fifth of the population were born overseas and 40% were either born overseas or a child of at least one overseas born parent. A large proportion of immigrant labor, especially the low skilled, was employed in the manufacturing sector behind high levels of tariff assistance. Foreign investment responded to fast population growth and automatic tariff protection. By 1968–1969 the average nominal tariff protecting manufacturing was 24% and the average effective tariff rate 35%.

A profile of manufacturing fostered by this strategy is presented in Table 10.8 where industries are grouped into quartiles according to the effective rate of assistance. Industries in the highly protected quartile were producing output behind an average effective tariff rate of 85%, which implied a net subsidy equivalent of the tariff that exceeded the wage bill; 42% of the workforce was female, 42% born overseas, and average wage, labor productivity, and capital intensity was low. The second most highly protected quartile produced behind an effective tariff rate of 48%. The postwar development policy had fostered and developed a manufacturing sector that was uneconomic, fragmented, and a drain on national resources. By the late 1960s criticism of protection policy had become widespread and there were demands for a new direction.

There was another factor lending support for a change in policy direction. It had been believed, at least since the 1930s depression, that in the face of falling relative prices rural exports would not grow at a pace sufficient to avoid balance of payments crises. It was hoped that manufacturing would develop an export capability and fill the balance of payments gap that would otherwise develop with rising living standards. The development policy, however, failed to generate large increases in manufactured exports, which were less than 7% of manufacturing turnover for 1968–1969, and largely confined to processing of foodstuffs and basic minerals. Concern for the balance of payments, however, began to dissipate with the rapid development of mineral exports, which increased their share of total exports from 11 to 34% over the period 1967–1968 to 1982–1983 (Table 10.9). It was widely believed that this new source of exports would avoid future balance of payments deficits (Gregory, 1976).

Australia therefore embarked on a new industry policy of lower tariffs. Since 1973 the average tariff has been reduced by 50% but manufacturing has not prospered. Its share of GDP has declined by 40% and since 1970 imports have increased from 17 to 25% of market supplies of manufactured goods. In addition, the share of manufactured goods in total exports has not changed substantially and Australia has not shared the experience, common among OECD countries, for import *and* export shares of each manufacturing industry to increase. Furthermore, the balance of payments has

Table 10.8. Characteristics of Manufacturing Industries: Australia 1968–1969

Quartile Ranking	Effective Rate of Assistance (%)	Capital Intensity ($)	Labor Productivity ($)	Averge Wage Per Person Employed ($)	Wage and Salary Share of Value Added (%)	Females as a Proportion of Total Number Employed (%)	Persons Employed Born Overseas as a Proportion of Total Number Employed (%)	Exports as a Proportion of Total Exports by Manufacturing Sector (%)	Imports Indirectly Allocated as a Proportion of Total Imports of Manufactured Products (%)
1	1	8581	6691	3030	45	21	31	24	11
2	28	7916	6997	3348	48	17	38	38	32
3	48	4155	5973	3088	52	24	35	15	43
4	85	3622	4963	2717	55	42	42	22	14
Manufacturing sector average	35	5774	6049	3023	50	27	37		

Source: Industries Assistance Commission, "Annual Report 1973–74," Australian Government Publishing Service, Canberra, 1974.

Table 10.9. Composition of Exports by Sector: 1967–1968 to 1987–1988

	Agricultural (%)	Mineral (%)	Manufactures (%)	Services (%)
1967–1968	54	11	18	17
1972–1973	49	18	20	13
1977–1978	39	30	17	14
1982–1983	33	34	18	15
1987–1988	34	27	21	18

Source: "Australian Exports, Performance, Obstacles and Issues of Assistance," Australian Government Publishing Service, July 1989.

not moved into surplus, apart from a few years during the early 1970s, but seems to be moving towards higher deficits (Figure 10.1).

In 1984–1985, the Australian terms of trade fell 20%, the nominal exchange rate fell 40% and foreign debt continued to increase from 4 to 30% of GDP. Government began to talk more seriously about the need for structural changes, manufacturing development, and new manufacturing exports. It was generally believed that the real exchange rate depreciation would be maintained and lead to a restructuring of the Australian economy toward increased production for import replacement and exports. As might be expected, given the lags in the system, the current account continued to deteriorate but the real exchange rate depreciation dissipated without a substantial increase in manufactured exports. Recently the current account has deteriorated further and on August 25, 1989, Moody's Investment Service downgraded its country ceiling on the ratings of Australian long term debt from Aa1 to Aa2. In October 1989, Standard and Poors also downgraded Australian debt. Among industrialized nations Australia's debt/GDP ratio is exceeded only by NZ, and no OECD country is accumulating foreign debt as fast.

Against this depressed manufacturing environment and rapid accumulation of

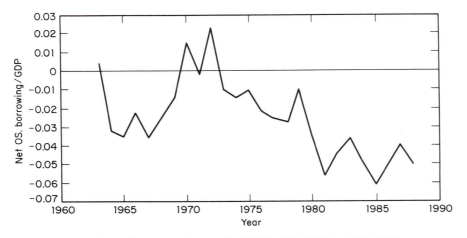

Figure 10.1. Net overseas borrowing/GNP; 1962–1963 to 1988–1989.

debt more is being asked of the National Innovation System. We now turn to a discussion of some recent initiatives.

THE NATIONAL INNOVATION SYSTEM AND IMPORTANT ISSUES OF THE DAY

With the exception of tariff protection Australian governments have been reluctant to intervene directly into industries. The dominance of tariff assistance is evident in Table 10.10 where it accounts for 92% of assistance for outputs and inputs of the manufacturing sector. There has, however, been a limited number of recent direct grants to specific industries. One major grant has been a 20% computer bounty for Australian computer production, research, design, and development, which is currently running at $47 million per annum and has grown quickly from $13.2 million in 1985–1986. Another grant is $150 million for R&D over 5 years to foreign owned motor vehicle producers. In addition, in 1989, before the election, there was $64 million grant to Kodak—a leading exporter from the manufacturing sector—not to close its Australian plant.

There is also some generalized export assistance to Australian companies. In 1988–1989, the budget of Austrade for export information, promotion, and assistance to small firms was $243 million. For motor vehicles, there is a specific program that for each export dollar earned a dollar of motor vehicles or parts can be imported duty free. This export subsidy can be substantial and the export of motor vehicle parts have increased significantly.

As in most countries there has been some concern as to the shortage of venture capital and the Australian response was to establish the Management Investment

Table 10.10. Assistance to Manufacturing, by Form: 1984–1985, 1988–1989[a]

	1984–1985	1988–1989[b]
Assistance to outputs		
Tariffs	8,994	10,880
Quantitative import restrictions	1,945	524
Bounties[c]	214	174
Export incentives[c]	133	176
Assistance to materials		
Tariffs	3,760	4,470
Quantitative import restrictions	663	263
Excise taxes	43	110

[a]Figures are in current prices. The figures for assistance to outputs and materials are, respectively, the sum of the gross subsidy equivalents and the tax on materials for individual industries, classified according to form of assistance. The summation of these amounts across industries will exceed the total for the sector due to the outputs of many industries being used by other industries as intermediate inputs.

[b]Preliminary estimates.

[c]The estimates presented in this table do not represent the actual bounty and export incentive payments in each year. The estimates measure the assistance afforded by the current rates of bounty and export incentives in each year using fixed 1983–1984 production patterns.

Source: "Industries Assistance Commission, Annual Report 1988–89," Australian Government Publishing Service, Canberra, 1989, Table A7.5.

Company Program in 1984. There are 11 Management Investment Companies (MICs) that can raise a limited amount of capital, fully tax deductible in the year of investment. The MICs raised $190 million in the early years of operation, but since then the program has not expanded. Most of the MIC investment portfolio went to activities in electronic equipment, robotics, computer software, scientific and technical services, and biomedical products.

There are three recent changes to the system that warrant special attention: the 150% R&D tax concession, the Partnerships for Development, and the expansion and reorientation of the education system.

The 150% Research and Development Allowance

In May 1985 the government announced a 150% taxation concession for R&D expenditure. The concession is to operate until June 1993, after which it will be phased down to 125%. At the present company tax rate of 39% the concession provides for an additional 19.5 cents of R&D expenditure to be recouped from normal tax liability.[9] Current cost is estimated to be $200 million, about one-seventh as large as all private sector R&D expenditure. For companies that cannot fully avail themselves of the concession there is a Grants for Industrial Research and Development Scheme (GIRD) that can grant up to 50% direct funding for R&D. Budget expenditure in 1989–1990 is estimated at $35 million.

Before discussing the 150% tax concession in depth there is a need to provide a little more background as to the structure of the manufacturing sector. Within manufacturing 54.8% of R&D expenditure takes place within three industries that produce 3.1% of GDP: appliances and electrical equipment (ASIC 3351/3352), chemical, petroleum, and coal products (ASIC 27), and motor vehicle and parts (ASIC 323). Appliances and electrical equipment, which produces 0.3% of GDP, accounts for just over one-quarter of all private sector R&D (Table 10.11). This concentration of R&D illustrates the significance of industry structure. If appliance and electrical equipment produced 1.0% of GDP rather than 0.3%, and R&D expenditure increased proportionately, then the aggregate R&D/GDP ratio would increase 50% and Australia would no longer rank so low on OECD league tables.

These three industries illustrate other important features of the economy. First, a significant fraction of R&D is under foreign control. In motor vehicles foreign ownership is 70.4%, chemicals, petroleum, and coal is 64.2% and appliances and electrical equipment is 23.4%. Consequently, effectiveness and desirability of R&D subsidies and policies need to be assessed against the behavior of multinationals.

Second, these industries do not possess any clear comparative advantage. The import share of market supplies in 1981–1982, for example, varied between 19.7% for motor vehicles (although subject to import quotas) and 65.4% for appliances and electrical equipment. Since then import shares have increased. The demand for products of these three industries account for about one-third of all Australian imports. Another indication of lack of comparative advantage is the small proportion of turnover exported, ranging between 4 and 11%, well below average for the manufacturing sector. The largest export market is New Zealand, illustrating their difficulty in exporting further afield.

Third, with the exception of chemicals, petroleum, and coal products each indus-

Table 10.11. Research and Development Expenditure and Industry Characteristics of Three Major Industries

ASIC Code	Definition	Share of Private Sector R&D (%) (86/87)	Share of GDP (%) (86/87)	Effective Tariff Rate (%) (86/87)	Import Share of Market Supplies (%)		Export Share of Turnover (%)		Major Export Market (% Export Share) (%) (81/82)	Foreign Control of R&D (%) (86/87)
					(68/69)	(81/82)	(68/69)	(81/82)		
3352/3351	Appliances and electrical equipment	30.6	0.3	30	37.9	65.4	3.0	6.0	NZ(22)	23
27	Chemical, petroleum, and coal products	13.6	1.7	12	25.3	32.3	3.0	11.0	NZ(27)	64
323	Motor vehicles and parts	10.6	1.1	86	21.6	19.7	3.0	4.0	NZ(41)	70
	Total manufacturing	90.0	19.0	19	17.0	25.4	8.0	12.0	JAP(14)	33

Sources: "Australian Trade Classified by Industry: 1968–69 to 1981–82," Industries Assistance Commission, Working Paper No. 85, Canberra (import share of market supplies, export share of turnover, and major export market). "Annual Report 1986/87," Industries Assistance Commission, Australian Government Publishing Service, Canberra (effective tariff rate). "Foreign Control in Research and Experimental Development Business Enterprises, Australia 1986–87," Australian Bureau of Statistics, Cat. No. 5330.0, Canberra (share of private sector R&D and foreign control R&D).

try is highly protected against imports. For motor vehicles, the current effective tariff rate is 86%, a reduction from a peak of 250% when the industry was protected by import quotas over the 1975–1988 period. For appliances and electrical equipment the effective tariff rate is around 30%.

Each of these features suggest a number of conjectures as to the role of R&D as a policy instrument.

How Does the Magnitude of the R&D Subsidy Compare with Other Subsidies for Industry Development?

Governments provide subsidies for other economic activities primarily in the form of import tariffs and quotas and it may be of interest to place the R&D subsidy against those of other activities. We can see from Table 10.12 that the community subsidizes transport equipment and textiles $0.48 and $0.68, respectively, for each $1 of the wage and salary bill. Those who produce clothing and footwear receive a subsidy of $0.89. At $0.19 it is clear that the government does not assist private sector R&D activity to the same extent as some manufacturing activities. Indeed, if the data are disaggregated further the tariff assistance to some activities such as cardigan and pullover production is 15 times the subsidy rate of R&D.

Do Any Special Considerations Arise from the Fact the Most of the R&D Subsidy Is Acquired by Industries with High Levels of Industry Assistance?

For an export industry without government assistance or externalities, facing fixed world prices and undertaking R&D that reduces production costs, industry and community gains from R&D are identical. The cost reduction from R&D increases invest-

Table 10.12. Government Assistance to Various Activities

ASIC Code	Definition	Assistance Per Dollar of Wage and Salaries $ 1987–1988	Net Subsidy Equivalent $ Million 1986–1987
21	Food, beverages, and tobacco	0.13	448
23	Textiles	0.68	458
24	Clothing and footwear	0.89	1005
25	Wood, wood products, and furniture	0.34	435
26	Paper, paper products, and printing	0.24	573
27	Chemical, petroleum, and coal products	0.32	462
28	Nonmetallic mineral products	0.09	85
29	Basic metal products	0.18	372
31	Fabricated metal products	0.30	595
32	Transport equipment	0.48	1188
33	Other machinery and equipment	0.33	884
34	Miscellaneous manufacturing	0.41	493
Total manufacturing		0.32	6997
150% Research and allowance concession[a]		0.19	170

[a]The estimate of the value of 150% taxation concession was calculated by assuming that all companies paid 39 cents in the dollar as company tax and fully claimed the concession (0.19).

Sources: "Annual Report 1987–1988 Industries Assistance Commision," Table A9.5, A9.7. Australian Government Publishing Service, Canberra, 1988. "Science and Technology Budget Statement 1989–1990." Australian Government Publishing Service, Canberra, 1989.

ment profitability and national income. What is good for this industry is good for the economy. This need not be so for an industry protected by import tariffs. This industry is larger because of tariffs, and given no externalities, community resources are being utilized inefficiently. In these circumstances a paradox arises.[10] Although R&D expenditure may be worthwhile for the industry, because it reduces costs and increases profits, the R&D will make the community worse off and depress national income. In response to cost reductions, imports will reduce, the industry will expand and utilize *more* resources uneconomically than before, the increased inefficient resource utilization from the output expansion exceeding the resource cost reduction from the supply curve moving downward. The industry cost reductions, from the community viewpoint, are a transfer of import revenue previously collected, some of which will be used for inefficient resource utilization by the industry and some for greater economic rents.

This argument seems to establish a strong prima facie case against R&D subsidies for industries heavily protected against imports. Can anything be said therefore, in favor of the subsidy going to highly protected industries? One possibility is that an R&D subsidy, which increases the industry's ability to cope with lower assistance levels, may be part of the political requirements of a tariff reduction strategy. However, where subsidy effects are linked to matching tariff reductions there is no industry gain from undertaking R&D and it is quickly evident that analysis of the interaction between industry R&D and government tariff strategy can become very complicated.

Where an industry is protected by a substantial tariff, the case for an R&D subsidy must rest on a much larger externality than for industries without a tariff. It may be difficult to satisfy such a requirement in Australia since most highly protected industries are dominated by oligopolies that should internalize most R&D benefits and thereby reduce the size of the externality. The case for R&D concessions seems much stronger where industry assistance is low and industry structure is atomistic, as in the rural export sector.

Do Any Special Considerations Arise from the Fact That Most of the R&D Subsidy Is Acquired by Multinationals Rather Than Australian-Owned Companies?
Much of R&D expenditure is undertaken by foreign owned companies. This may pose special problems. Suppose the concession fails to increase R&D expenditure. For an Australian company the concession becomes an income transfer from the taxpayer, in the form of company tax foregone, to the Australian shareholder who receives extra profit equal to the concession. For a foreign company the income transfer is a gift from Australian taxpayers to foreign citizens. This undesirable feature remains even when the subsidy increases R&D expenditure. Furthermore, suppose laboratories are moved to Australia to undertake work that would have been undertaken in the home country. Does Australia gain anything from this? It is difficult to see what the externality could be. There is not a well-developed private sector research capability in Australia to enable research workers to carry ideas from one laboratory to another or even from the laboratory to the factory floor.[11]

Has the Subsidy Affected the Level of R&D Expenditure?
As indicated earlier the last two decades have been difficult for manufacturing. The history of manufacturing profitability is evident in Figure 10.2, which presents indices of gross operating surplus to wages, salaries, and supplements. Profitability declined

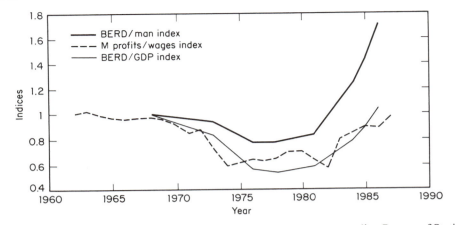

Figure 10.2. Profitability and business R&D expenditure. Source: Australian Bureau of Statistics, Australian National Accounts Cat. No. 5204-0 (various issues).

gently during the 1960s then, in 1974–1975, suddenly falls to 60% of the 1968–1969 level and remains there for 9 years. Since 1982–1983 profitability has increased, almost doubling in 8 years. We have also included an index of private sector R&D/ GDP. The two lines are remarkably close, which suggests that R&D expenditure is associated with profitability.[12] There are not many data points, but the association between R&D expenditure and profitability was not disturbed to a significant degree when the concession was introduced in 1985 (the last two data points). When R&D is deflated by manufacturing value added the impression created changes considerably and research intensity has increased toward the end of the period but the increase began before the subsidy was introduced.

On the basis of a survey of concession respondents the Bureau of Industry Economics estimates that 2 years after the beginning of the program, and for each $1 spent on the subsidy, business increased R&D in real terms by 28 cents.[13] This calculation suggests that if the subsidy is judged worthwhile and the government is allocating its budget correctly at the margin, then an extra research $1 spent in universities or CSIRO is worth only 28 cents of the $1 spent in the private sector. If we assume that the BIE estimate is correct (they suggest that it is an overestimate) and, on average, manufacturing industries that receive the subsidy are protected by tariffs, then on the basis of earlier analysis the gap between the sectors may be even wider. Since much of R&D is undertaken by multinationals the gap will widen further and the return for the concession may fall to around 15 cents, which suggests that to be a good use of public money, additional private sector R&D has to be at least five or six times more valuable than public sector research. This suggests either an inordinate premium to private sector R&D or government research is overexpanded.

Government Procurement and Partnerships for Development

In 1985–1986, federal and state governments purchased high-technology products at a cost of $3.6 billion, mainly imported from multinationals. For some time government has used this purchasing power, within an offsets program, as an industry development instrument "to gain access to internal markets and marketing facilities of large world corporations which dominate these products and leading edge technologies which otherwise would be closed to Australian companies" (Australian Civil Offsets Program, Annual Report, 1988–1989, p. 1). Under the Offsets Program major overseas suppliers trading with the Australian government must direct activities of technological significance to Australian industry, including manufacturing, export marketing, and R&D.[14]

Aerospace, telecommunication, and computer industries account for around 90% of offsets. In response to dramatic increases in the import of information technology and some general dissatisfaction with the offset program, the government introduced in 1986–1987 voluntary Partnerships for Development for the information industry. A Partner for Development would be exempt from offset requirements in return for an undertaking to increase R&D to 5% of total sales in Australia, to achieve a 50% export–import ratio within 7 years, and to achieve an average Australian value added content of 70% for exports. Partners would have access to generally available assistance programs to help them engage in product development and export activities.

The aim of the scheme is to link Australian activities into the Partner's global operations. Some idea of the potential effects of Partnerships is given in Table 10.13, which lists prepartnership exports and R&D expenditure and an estimate of the annual commitment 7 years hence.[15] It appears as though the first 15 partners have committed themselves to a 7-fold increase in exports and a 6-fold increase in R&D expenditure.

The change in performance implied by these data is extraordinary. If commitments eventuate, and a significant fraction of the increase in R&D would not have occurred without the scheme, then this program will have a much greater impact on R&D than the 150% concession. For example, the BIE estimated the 150% concession increased R&D by $54 million in 1986–1987 (Bureau of Industry Economics, 1990). The Partners are pledged to increase R&D by $220 million per annum. Another way to illustrate the importance of this scheme is to place the data against those of Table 10.14, which indicates that 12 enterprises in Australia spend at least $10 million on R&D.[16] If Partners meet their targets then, within 7 years, perhaps as many as another 10 companies will be added to the group, doubling the number of large R&D spenders and adding 20% to current R&D expenditure.

These data raise a number of interesting questions. First, we know that each year the 150% concession costs approximately $200 million and according to the BIE gen-

Table 10.13. Partners for Development

	Exports $Million	R&D $Million
Prepartnership performance	178	46
target levels 7 years hence	1202	266
Increase (%)	675	578

Source: "Australian Civil Offsets Program, Annual Report 1988–1989" Australian Government Publishing Service, Canberra.

Table 10.14. R&D Expenditure by Size of 1986–1987 Business Enterprise

Size of Expenditure ($000)	Number of Enterprises (All Industries)	Percent of Enterprises	Share of Total BERD Expenditure (All Industries) (%)
Less than 100	1692	57.7	5.5
100 to 499	899	30.7	16.5
500 to 999	183	6.2	10.6
1000 to 1999	109	3.7	12.6
2000 to 4999	67	2.2	17.4
5000 to 9999	20	0.7	12.2
10,000 or more	12	0.4	25.3
Total	2932	100.0	100.0

Source: "Research and Experimental Development, Business Enterprises, Australia," Australian Bureau of Statistics, Cat. No. 8104.0.

erates an extra $54 million of R&D. Each extra $1 of R&D carried out in the private sector, in response to the program, costs the government at least $4. What is the economic cost of the partnership program? It has minimum budgetary cost. Is this large increase in R&D free?

There seems to be two responses to this question. First, as proponents of the scheme have argued, it may be that Partners R&D can be located in most countries at much the same cost and consequently the company may be willing to respond to a mild amount of political pressure and relocate some of its R&D activities. Under these circumstances, the additional resource cost to Australia is minimal, apart from the education cost of research scientists and the subsidy. Indeed Australia has avoided imposing on itself the offsets cost. Second, it may cost the company quite a lot to meet these R&D commitments but less than the cost imposed by the Offsets program. Under these circumstances political pressure alone is not sufficient for location of R&D and the true motivating factor is the avoidance of the extra burden of the offset costs.

Expanding and Reorientating the Education System

Since its election in 1983 the Labor Government has sought to change the education system so that it is attuned better to serve the needs of the economy. There are a number of forces for change but the more important are a concern for increasing teenage unemployment and a belief that the economic and education system was not sufficiently encouraging skill formation.[17] The government has actively pursued a policy of increasing school participation and introduced an income support scheme for school children in their final 2 years of high school, subject to a parents income and asset test. About 35% of school enrollments over the age of 16 receive a payment which can be as large as $58 to $102 per week, depending on whether the student lives at home. The rise in school participation since 1983 has been dramatic; retention rates to final year of high school have increased from 35 to 63% and teenage labor seeking full-time employment has fallen from 10.9 to 5.1% of the cohort.

Policy has also been directed toward increasing enrollments in tertiary institutions. Available places have been increased as have student subsidies. Currently 42%

of tertiary students are assisted by income support (Austudy), which at the full rate varies between $69 and $243 per week. Income support for postgraduate students has been increased to $12,000–$16,000 nontaxable per annum, which is about 60–80% of average weekly earnings after tax.

There has been little analysis as to whether, on the basis of economic criteria, the tertiary education system should be expanded. However, there must be some doubt as to whether it is a good thing to expand production of a commodity that is priced so far below cost.[18] Is there any evidence that expansion of the system is a good idea? First, we look at rates of returns to graduates taken from the Income Distribution Surveys (Table 10.15). The real rate of return has been falling over the last two decades, although it remains quite high. If additional students could earn these real rates of return then expansion would seem to be warranted.

There are two qualifications. First, these rates of return have been calculated before the expanded number of students have entered the labor force and refer to *average* rather than *marginal* returns. Second, a more appropriate calculation is the rate of return at the margin, that is, what would be the average rate of return for additional entrants to the system? To address this question we use 1986 Census Data.[19] We divided university graduates and high school leavers into quintiles according to their income in 1986 and calculated a range of education returns for each quintile, on the assumption that their actual 1986 relative income level would stay the same through their working life, adjusted for cohort income growth. The alternative income stream for additional university graduates is drawn from the average of each income quintile of high school graduates who did not obtain tertiary qualifications. Thus, for each person there are five rates of return (Table 10.16). For example, we have calculated a rate of return for a person in the top income quintile of high school leavers, H1, on the basis that if he or she had acquired a degree he or she would have been in the top quintile of income earners among graduates, D1, then the calculation is repeated on the assumption that he or she would be in the second quintile, D2, and so on. If instead of dropping out after high school and being in the top quintile of high school graduates this person had completed a degree and received income in the top quintile of university graduates the rate of return would be 6.99%.[20] If the alternative income stream was in the second highest quintile of university graduates the rate of return would be negative. The overwhelming impression created from these calculations is that for a uni-

Table 10.15. Real Pretax Rate of Return to a Degree[a]

Year	Males (%)
1968/1969	24.0
1973/1974	22.4
1978/1979	19.4
1981/1982	18.3
1985/1986	16.8

[a]Assumptions: pretax total income of full-time full-year males, takes 3.3 years to complete degree, and only cost of higher education included is the opportunity cost.

Source: Chia (1990), Income Distribution Surveys (various issues), Australian Bureau of Statistics.

Table 10.16. Rate of Return to Higher Education Implied by Matching Different Parts of the High-School and Degree-Holders' Income Distribution (Posttax Income)

High School	D1 (%)	D2 (%)	D3 (%)	D4 (%)	D5 (%)
H1	6.99	Negative	Negative	Negative	Negative
H2	17.48	8.15	3.92	Negative	Negative
H3	23.12	13.50	9.38	4.42	Negative
H4	29.04	18.94	14.63	9.78	Negative
H5	50.83	38.85	33.67	28.02	12.51

Source: Chia (1990).

versity degree to provide a positive rate of return someone drawn from the income distribution of high school leavers must do as least as well, relative to degree holders, as he or she does relative to high school leavers. Given that most students who do not attend university are not qualified to enter it seems unlikely that those who gain additional places as a result of expansion will do as well as the average of all those who enter. On economic grounds, therefore, the expansion of the system must be a doubtful proposition. These calculations are obviously very crude but they do serve to highlight the important principle that it is marginal rates of return that are important rather than average returns.

Science undergraduates have maintained their share within the larger system but there has been a large reduction in demand for science places and university entry requirements have fallen considerably and are now among the lowest. At the postgraduate level the number of science Ph.D.s and Masters degrees has fallen considerably, primarily in response to poor job prospects. The proportion of Australian students within the group has also fallen. In 1973 science accounted for 50% of Ph.D. and higher degree graduations. By 1985 the proportion had fallen to 36% of the total. Engineering Ph.D.s have also declined. The growth areas have been arts and education.

Some idea of the poor job prospects for Ph.D.s in science, and the importance of the government sector as an employer, can be found from an examination of the destinations of Ph.D. graduates (Table 10.17). For those physical scientists who graduated

Table 10.17. Distribution of Higher Degree Graduates by Field of Study, 1982

	Employed in Australia			Employed Overseas (%)
	Government		Private (%)	
	Teaching (%)	Other (%)		
Physical sciences	24.5	15.3	10.2	43.9
Biomedical sciences	30.6	22.6	8.1	29.8
Engineers	14.8	8.2	32.8	39.3
Humanities, education, and economics	48.6	12.8	2.8	16.5

Source: Department of Industry, Technology and Commerce, "Measures of Science and Innovation," Australian Government Publishing Service, Canberra, 1987.

in 1982, 43.9% left for employment overseas. In biomedical sciences the proportion was 29.8%. In both disciplines the government sector, including teaching, accounted for 4 to 6 times more jobs than the private sector.

Despite clear market evidence of oversupply of scientists the view prevails among science policy advisors and the government that the country needs more scientists.[21] As this is obviously not true in *current* circumstances—in the sense that employment prospects are poor—the only legitimate arguments must focus on future requirements. There are two strands to the arguments. The first is that scientists will be needed for forthcoming structural changes in manufacturing. The second is that the average age of science researchers in universities and research institutions is increasing and, at the time that Australia will need to replace scientists, there will be a worldwide shortage.

Will there be a shortage of scientists in the future? It all depends on government policy as government employs 70% of scientists and thus effectively controls demand.[22] It also controls supply, as it determines the number of tertiary education places. In response to low job opportunities and the turning away from science by prospective graduate students the government has responded by introducing policies to increase the supply of scientists and to provide them with employment. The Australian Research Council has created new graduate scholarships and the government has recently announced The Cooperative Research Centre Scheme, which is to create 50 new research centers with an average budget of $4 million each; $2 million to be supplied by the government and $2 million by the participating institutions.[23] With respect to the private sector it is unlikely that the manufacturing sector will change sufficiently to create shortages.

Finally, we look briefly at on-the-job training. Australian wage and salary earners do not seem to have a very steep age earning's profile. For example, in 1981 in the United States a 45-year-old male earned approximately 42% more than a 25-year-old male. For Australia the gap was 13%. Earnings peak very early in Australia. After adjusting for the education level of each cohort the gap between the two countries narrows but is still substantial (Daly, 1991). The flat earning's profile has been interpreted to suggest that on-the-job training is low in Australia and the government and union movement have begun to address the issue. As from June 30, 1990 each corporation with a payroll exceeding $200,000 will be required to spend 1% of payroll on approved training courses for personnel. The unions have also sought award wage restructuring to pay greater rewards for skill.

THE NATIONAL INNOVATION SYSTEM AND THE BALANCE OF PAYMENTS

The speed at which foreign debt has recently increased in Australia, and some skepticism as to the efficacy of macro-policy instruments, has led to a debate on the interrelationships between manufacturing, science and technology policy, and the balance of payments. The debate focuses on whether governments should intervene more into the economy to foster high technology and export orientated industries. A good example of current discussions is the following, which is taken from a joint discussion paper by the Department of Industry, Technology and Commerce (DITAC) and the Organization for Economic Cooperation and Development (1989).

6.1 Australia needs to restructure and revitalize its manufacturing and service industries if it is to maintain its standard of living. The long term decline in prices for agriculture and mineral commodities together with rising domestic demand for imports of manufactures has led to a large and persistent trade deficit. This has been particularly pronounced in high technology goods. Improved export performance in high technology goods since 1981/82 has been overwhelmed by stronger growth in imports. Australian foreign debt has grown rapidly over the last seven years, rising to 30 percent of GDP in 1986–87, a level which threatens future economic growth.

6.2 Stabilizing Australia's foreign debt will require substantial structural change in manufacturing industry. The existing structural profile is skewed towards low technology and low growth industries compared to other OECD countries. At least until 1984 (the last year for which detailed data are available) Australia was generally contracting in the high technology sector, where other countries and world markets were expanding rapidly.

6.3 For the high technology industries in Australia to grow ... will require increased expenditure on R & D and technologically sophisticated machinery, as well as innovations in organizational structure, marketing and distribution. (DITAC/OECD, 1989, p. 43)

Another example is taken from the 1990–1991 Science and Technology Budget Statement (p. 1), which states,

The governments approach to realising the benefits of science and technology has been to develop a positive strategic framework which recognizes that science and technology are essential elements in addressing two of the major problems facing Australia today, namely:
- the need to develop a more internationally competitive economy based on innovation in order to solve our balance of payments problems;
- the need to integrate economic development with environmental considerations to ensure that development is ecologically sustainable.

Should the recommendation for increased expenditure on R&D and the need to foster development of high technology industries to improve export performance be accepted? Consider the following well known identity:

$$(G - T) + (I - S) = (M - X) \tag{1}$$

where G is government expenditure, T government tax revenue, I private sector investment, S private sector savings, M imports, and X exports. The DITAC/OECD paper focuses on the $(M - X)$ gap as being determined by a poor industry structure leading to a slow growth of exports (agricultural and mineral commodities) and a fast growth of imports (particularly high technology manufactured goods). To change $(M - X)$ it advocates fostering technological development in export and import competing industries to improve competitiveness. Since Eq. (1) is an identity, it follows, if this argument is correct and describes the only factors to be considered, that the right-hand side of Eq. (1) determines the left-hand side, that is, government and private sector savings and investment balances are determined by the economic performance of export and import competing industries.

The Treasury has also been concerned about the growing $(M - X)$ gap and the mounting foreign debt/GDP ratios and attributed them not to poor industry structure and inadequate technology and research and development, which might directly affect the right-hand side of Eq. (1), but to factors that determine the left-hand side, the balance between domestic savings and investment. The Treasury argues that excessive government deficits, $(G - T)$, have been largely financed from overseas borrowings. Hence, the current account deterioration during the early 1970s, and its failure to improve, is not attributed to poor industry structure leading to increased imports and a slow growth of exports but to government deficits creating economic conditions that encourage imports and discourage exports. The change in industry structure is a necessary part of financing the government deficit. Similarly, private net savings $(I - S)$ have fallen over the last decade and also contributed to the current account outcome $(M - X)$ and deterioration of the performance of the manufacturing sector. From this viewpoint, the change in international competitiveness and what appears to be an inefficient industry structure is not a cause of our economic difficulties but a symptom. The cause lies in savings and investment imbalances and, given governments desire for economic growth, must be solved by increased savings [for a discussion of these issues see Pitchford (1989), Forsyth (1990), and Gregory (1991)]. Forsyth (1990, p. 1) puts the argument most forcefully:

> Attempts to achieve a solution to the current account balance of payments problem by enhancing the competitiveness of Australian industry, increasing productivity, fostering an export culture in manufacturing and other industries, and industry restructuring are doomed to fail. This is because the outcome of the current account of payments is not determined by how competitive Australian industries are. Rather, the reverse causation is true—in the main, the current outcome determines the competitiveness of the country's industries.

> Only reforms directed toward eliminating the savings and investment distortions will reduce the deficit.

There is obviously a conflict between the pure structuralist view that $(M - X)$ is determined by industry structure and the pure macro view that $(M - X)$ outcomes are best analyzed in terms of savings and investment decisions. Since Eq. (1) is an identity either side may drive the other; the exogenous factors may lie elsewhere, or, at different times, different parts of the identity may predominate.

This conflict lies at the heart of current attitudes toward government policy and the national system of innovation. If there is a desire to improve the current account deficit then those who emphasize factors that directly affect the left-hand side of Eq. (1) are likely to recommend policies to increase the private savings ratio, reduce government deficits, and so on. This is the policy stance of the Treasury, Reserve Bank, and main stream economic advice. Those who emphasize the right-hand side of the identity are likely to recommend policies that directly encourage exports and discourage imports and tend not to see the industry structure as evolving from saving and investment decisions within a general equilibrium model. These advisors often tend not to be economists and are grouped around industry and science centers in the bureaucracy.

As might be expected government policy has adopted strands of both ideas and although there are a number of innovations in the national innovations system the prevailing ethos has remained one of nonintervention into the activities of particular industries and greater emphasis on increasing savings, especially those of the government.

CONCLUDING REMARKS

There is currently an exceptional amount of questioning of the national innovation system. The effects are evident in the changing finance of R&D between government and private sectors, reforms of the tertiary education system, the encouragement of scientific research, and a greater degree of direct government intervention into the private sector through training requirements and the creation of Partnerships for Development. The announced object of these changes is to improve the performance and structure of the economy.[24] When these changes are put against the evolution in the economy, however, it is difficult to believe that they will have a noticeable effect at the macro level, at least in the foreseeable future. Three examples will illustrate this point.

First, over the 6 years 1983–1989 Australia experienced the fastest job growth of all OECD countries. A preliminary analysis of that job growth is given in Table 10.18. The economy is evolving toward part-time and service sector workers. Those parts of manufacturing involved in substantial R&D expenditure are shrinking as a share of total employment. To date the private sector is not moving toward high technology industries or generating exceptional demands for scientists, except in information technology.

Second, it does seem strange that a country that has never had a comparative advantage in high-technology manufacturing, and enjoys high standards of living, is discussing solutions to balance of payments difficulties in terms of R&D expenditure to stimulate high-technology manufacturing. Most export growth still appears to be occurring around traditional exports and new industries of tourism and service exports rather than high-technology manufactures. If manufacturing is to make a better contribution to the balance of payments it is difficult to escape the conclusion that most

Table 10.18. Employment Population Changes 1983–1990

| | Growth Rate Aggregate E/P p.a | Share of Employment Population Change | | | | | | | |
| | | Full Time | Part Time | Male | Female | Full Time | | Part Time | |
						Male	Female	Male	Female
1983/1985	1.59	60	40	30	70	28	34	3	38
1985/1988	1.18	25	75	4	96	−9	35	12	62
1988/1990	1.31	31	69	19	81	−11	39	29	46

Sources: Australian Bureau of Statistics, Labour Force Historical Summary 1966 to 1984. Cat. No. 6204.0, Canberra 1987. Australian Bureau of Statistics, The Labour Force Australia, Cat No. 6203.0, various annual issues August 1985, August 1988, August 1990.

of that contribution will be made on the import replacement side rather than in terms of large increases in manufacturing exports.[25] It may be best to think of the national innovation system in terms of micro reforms, that is doing things better rather than thinking of the system as an instrument of macro policy that will significantly change the structure of the Australian economy.

Third, the concentration of R&D within a few firms and industries suggests that R&D policy will not have sufficient leverage on the economy as a whole.

To conclude, the current shaking up of the national innovation system, as it relates to the government sector, seems to be a good thing, although such judgments are exceptionally difficult to make. The expectations that are held as to the level of benefits to flow from the changes, however, do seem to be misplaced. There has been a significant overselling of the economic benefits of a government-led science and technology push.

NOTES

Helpful comments have been received from E. Klug, M. Teubel, K. Pavitt, Bengt Åke Lundvall, and S. Pearce.

1. It is often said that science and technology are somewhat alien to the Australian way of life. For example, an OECD Science and Technology review team stated, "we were struck by what seems to be a widespread Australian view of technology as in some sense external to national life" (OECD, 1986, p. 13). This view can be explained to a large extent by Australian history of economic development. However, it is interesting to note, by way of contrast, that establishment of the first European settlement was a direct result of support given to a scientific project proposed by the British Royal Society. Captain Cook was sent to the Pacific to observe the transit of Venus and search for the southern continent. In response to a report from the botanist on board, the British government settled New South Wales with convicts 18 years later.

The new environment did lead to some adaptations and inventions and the impact of new technologies on rural products should not be underrated. For example, many European commercial plants did not flourish in Australia. British wheat varieties were late maturing so that in many areas summer-droughts set in before the crop was ready for harvesting. William Farrer solved this problem by crossing Indian and English wheat varieties in 1901. He also began research that led to rust resistant wheat varieties. Native grasses were also not the best for grazing and imported grasses did not prosper. Eventually scientists discovered the value of subterranean clover and superphosphate.

Other well known innovations are John Ridley's grain stripper in 1842—of which it is said that four men could now do in one day the work of two men in a complete harvesting season—and R. B. Smith's stump jump plough that reduced the cost of clearing as small stumps could be left in the ground to decompose. In 1884, H. V. McKay invented the combine harvester, which could strip, thresh, and clean grain in one continuous operation. A successful company was set up to manufacture and to become Australia's largest farm machine producer before being taken over by the Canadian firm of Massey-Harris (Science and Technology in Australia 1977–78, 1978).

2. In their introductory chapter Butlin et al. (1982, p. 4) say, "we have attempted to bring the interaction of public and private decision making to the forefront. In doing so, we have had to recognize that much Western historical experience (and its related theory) has only limited value to Australia because of the prominence of governments throughout virtually the whole of Australian history in all decision making processes."

3. The first Labor government in the world was elected in the 1890s in the state of Queensland and at the Federal level in 1910. Old age and invalid pensions were introduced in 1908 and 1910, respectively, at the federal level, and even earlier in some states.

4. Of course some benefits are lost through terms of trade effects that deliver some of the cost reduction to the foreign buyer by way of lower prices.

5. Before CSIR government research was primarily financed by state government departments of agriculture but they neglected pastoral research. Research was hampered by lack of equipment, small projects, and demands of administration. In response to these factors the Commonwealth entered the research field. Rural policy, resource management, and some industry research are supported in part by a number of research bureaus within the government sector. These include the Australian Bureau of Agricultural and Resource Economics, the Bureau of Industry Economics, and the Bureau of Transport and Communications Economics.

6. In 1983 the CSIRO budget was three quarters that of the German Max Planck Gesellschaft, which accounted for 1.8% of German R&D expenditure and twice as large as the German Fraunhofergesellschaft, established specifically for the support of industry.

7. Of course, the correct calculation is to look at the rate of return to rural research. Whenever this is done the return seems quite high.

8. There is a difficulty with these figures in that the 150% R&D allowance may have changed accounting practices in the private sector to increase the proportion of expenditure eligible for the concession and thus inflate private sector R&D expenditure relative to the past.

9. There are a number of difficult conceptual problems involved in calculating this figure. Australia has now moved toward an imputation system and as the tax rates are not the same for companies and individuals the calculation can become very tricky depending on whether the company decisions are thought of as fully reflecting the tax liabilities of their shareholders.

10. This analysis applies to an industry that could not survive without protection against imports. If part of the industry could exist without the tariff then the community could gain from R&D-induced reductions in the supply curve, but the gain will be less than that measured from the cost reduction from the industry viewpoint and less than that from equivalent profitable R&D for an unassisted industry.

11. Many of the above issues are clearly illustrated by the Motor Vehicles and Components Development Grants Scheme established in 1985. The scheme provided for up to $150 million to be allocated over 5 years to assist the highly protected and foreign owned companies—Ford, General Motors Australia, Toyota, Mitsubishi, and Nissan—to develop new or substantially improved vehicles and automotive components of local design. The scheme has subsequently become less generous when the 150% allowance was introduced but to date $63 million has been paid from government revenue. Similarly $2.4 million of the Computer bounty, in addition to the 150% R&D allowance, was paid to IBM in 1989–1990.

12. This result is supported by interviews of Australian businessmen who usually indicate that R&D expenditure is first to be reduced if profitability falls.

13. Doube and Deaton (1989, p. 86) examined the rate of growth of newspaper advertisements for scientists before and after the introduction of the allowance and found no significant break in trend. They conclude that "there is no clear evidence that the scheme has increased the number of R&D jobs in Australia." This is perhaps a better test than looking at expenditure trends that are subject to reclassification in response to the tax concession.

14. To incur an offset obligation the threshold contract with the government must be above $2.5 million with an import content of more than 30%. The value of the offset obligation is 30% of the imported content of the government contract.

15. The data provide only an estimate because commitments are conditional on actual sales and in some instances the data are given as cumulative totals over the 7 years.

16. Although we do not know the current expenditure of individual partners it is clear that the maximum number of partners that could be currently spending more than $10 million is two.

17. Throughout the 1950s and 1960s Australia had one of the lowest unemployment rates among OECD nations, averaging about 1.5% of the labor force and 5% for teenagers. The average interrupted unemployment spell was about 5 weeks. During the 1970s, but particularly from 1974–1975 onward, unemployment began to increase and in 1983 peaked at 10% of the labor force. Teenage unemployment exceeded 20% and the average interrupted unemployment spell for all males increased to 43 weeks. Since 1983, strong employment growth has managed to reduce unemployment only to 6% but the interrupted unemployment spell for adult males has continued to increase and is currently 57 weeks. Over 1990–1991 unemployment will increase again.

18. Between 1973 and 1988 university places were free but rationed. To help finance the expansion a charge of about 20% of the course cost has been introduced for all students. It can be paid concurrent with the course or a tax liability accepted, indexed for inflation, which must be paid back at the rate of 2% of taxable income after the student's taxable income reaches average weekly full-time earnings. There are higher rates of repayment as income increases about this level. This system appears to have had a minimal impact on the demand for places, which are still rationed in most disciplines.

19. These data give a posttax rate of return of 9%.

20. For these data the average rate of return calculated after tax is around 9%.

21. There have been a large number of highly publicized changes in the science bureaucracy that seem designed to highlight the importance of the area. They are listed in various Science and Technology statements by the Prime Minister, and the Minister for Science, Customs and Small Business. The major changes include incorporating the Science and Technology Ministry in the economic portfolio of Industry Technology and Commerce, the creation of a Science Council, chaired by the Prime Minister, and the appointment of a Chief Scientist who reports directly to the Prime Minister. Each year there is a special Science and Technology Statement listing the government new expenditure proposals on science.

22. Among Ph.D. graduates only about 10% take their first job in the private sector (Table 10.17).

23. It is hoped that these centers will bring researchers together and create scale economies in discovery.

24. "Since the early 1980s the Governments Science and Technology policies have placed an increasing emphasis on improving research agencies' responsiveness to national economic objectives, particularly the need to promote a more open and internationally competitive economy and to facilitate structural adjustment" (P3.315 Budget Statements 1990–1991 Budget Paper No. 1).

25. This judgment may need to be qualified. The government has been paying significant subsidies for the export of motor vehicles and components as part of the Motor Vehicle Plan and the industry has been responding. Aluminium exports have also been growing.

REFERENCES

Australian Export Performance; Obstacles and Issues of Assistance. (1989). *Report of the Committee for Review of Export Market Development Assistance.* Canberra: Australian Government Publishing Service.

Bureau of Industry Economics. (1990). *Manufacturing Investment.* Research Report No. 33. Canberra: Australian Government Publishing Service.

Butlin, N. G. (1962). *Australian Domestic Product Investment and Foreign Borrowing 1861–1938/39.* Cambridge, England. Cambridge University Press.

Butlin, N. G., Barnard, A., and Pincus, J. J. (1982). *Government and Capitalism.* Sydney: Allen and Unwin.

Chia, T. T. (1990). "Returns to Higher Education in Australia." Ph.D. Thesis, Australian National University.

Daly, A. (1991). "The Labour Market in Three Countries: An International Comparison of Relative Earnings in Australia, Great Britain and the United States of America," Ph.D. Thesis Australian National University.

Department of Industry, Technology and Commerce and the OECD (1989). *Industrial R & D Investment and Structural Change in Australian Manufacturing.* Canberra: Australian Government Publishing Service.

Department of Industry, Technology and Commerce (1990). *Australian Civil Offsets Program, Annual Report 1988–89.* Canberra: Australian Government Publishing Service.

Doube, B. M., and Deaton, C. B. (1989). "Has the 150 per cent Tax Incentive Scheme Created New Jobs in R & D?" *Search* 20(3).

Forsyth, P. J. (1990). "Competitiveness, Microeconomic Reform and the Current Account Deficit." Centre for Economic Policy Research, Discussion Paper No. 228, March.

Gregory, R. G. (1976). "Some Implications of the Growth of the Mineral Sector." *Australian Journal of Agricultural Economics* 20:71–91.

Gregory, R. G. (1991). "The Current Account and Economic Policy." In *The Pacific Economy: Growth and External Stability.* Sydney: Allen and Unwin.

OECD (1986). *Review of National Science and Technology Policy: Australia.* Paris: OECD.

Pitchford, J. D. (1989). "Does Australia Really have a Current Account Problem?" *Policy* Winter 2.

Schedvin, C. B. (1987). *Shaping Science and Industry.* Sydney: Allen and Unwin.

PART III

LOWER INCOME COUNTRIES

Part III is concerned with five countries, all with levels of gross domestic product per capita significantly lower than those considered in Parts I and II, but otherwise very diverse. There is considerable intragroup variation even in current productivity and income levels, with Taiwan and Israel having (as of 1989) levels of GDP per capita roughly half of the mean of the high income countries considered earlier, but with Korea, Argentina, and Brazil having levels of GDP per capita less than half of those in Israel and Taiwan. With the exception of Israel, the countries considered in Part III all are "large" in terms of population, with Brazil being very large. However, because their income levels are low, the countries of this group, with the possible exception of Brazil, have relatively small internal markets for manufactured goods, thus putting them in the same position as the countries considered in Part II.

The countries in this group have experienced very different rates and patterns of economic growth in the period since 1960. Prior to World War II the level of per capita income in Argentina was roughly comparable to the levels of income in continental Europe. Korea, Taiwan, and Brazil had much lower levels of productivity and income. Israel (which was born only after World War II) obviously is a special case. Argentina has been marked by virtual economic stagnation over much of the post-World War II period, and today her productivity and income do not stand much higher than they did in 1960. Brazil and Israel have seen periods of very rapid growth, but have grown quite slowly in recent years. Korea and Taiwan have experienced extraordinarily rapid and sustained growth since the 1960s.

In terms of gross investment as a fraction of GDP, Taiwan stands even above Japan. Argentina has the lowest investment rate of all the countries considered in this study. The other countries are roughly in the middle.

The countries stand surprisingly close to each other in terms of manufacturing output as a fraction of GDP, and, interestingly, that fraction is roughly comparable to most of the countries of group I. However, the countries differ significantly in terms of the nature of national ownership of manufacturing companies, and in their success in generating and sustaining manufacturing exports. There is very little direct foreign ownership of firms in Korea and Taiwan. Foreign ownership is significantly higher in Brazil, and higher still in Argentina. Korea and Taiwan have been very successful in generating manufacturing exports, and in both countries manufacturing exports account for a very large share of their total exports. This also is the case for Israel: however because Israel is such a small country one would expect that exports would account for a large fraction of GDP. The exports of Brazil and Argentina account for a significantly smaller fraction of GDP, and manufacturing exports account for half or less of total exports.

The countries differ significantly in human resource development. The literacy rate in Argentina and Israel was, as of 1988, in the league with that in the high income countries. Taiwan and Korea were rapidly closing the gap. Brazil lagged behind. Regarding enrollment at the secondary school level Korea, Taiwan, and Israel are at the levels of the high-income countries or rapidly approaching them. Argentina is somewhat behind, and Brazil far behind. A similar statement holds for enrollment in postsecondary education.

The stock of scientists and engineers as a fraction of the work force in Israel may be the highest in the world. In Korea and Taiwan that ratio is significantly lower than in the industrialized high-income countries, but is rapidly growing. In Brazil and Argentina the ratio is much lower. The ratio of R&D to GNP in these countries roughly follows the pattern of the figures for the stock of scientists and engineers as a fraction of the total population.

In Korea the fraction of total R&D that is privately funded is similar to that in Japan. The figure for Taiwan is roughly comparable to that for France and Italy, with government support of R&D significantly higher than in Korea. In the other three countries by far the majority of total R&D is publicly funded, but for different reasons. In Israel the reason is that a very large share of total R&D is directed to military concerns. In Argentina and Brazil the reason is that very little R&D goes on in the manufacturing sector, with most of it at universities and laboratories that are largely funded by government (Table III.1).

Table III.1. Comparison of the Five Lower Income Countries

	Korea	Taiwan	Brazil	Argentina	Israel
GDP/capita, 1989 official exchange rates	3600	8000	2160	2520	8650
Population (World Development Report, except Taiwan)	42.4	16.2	147.3	31.9	4.5
Average growth rate, GDP/ hour average 1965–1988	6.8	6.5	3.6	0.0	2.7
Gross domestic investment/ GDP average 1965–1988	22.5	32	21.5	16.5	23
Manufacturing output/ GDP	32	—	29	31	—
Manufacturing exports/ GDP	33	—	5	3	18
Total exports/GDP	42	55.7	10	10	32
Literacy rate	88	92	78	95	95
Secondary level enrollment ratio	88	—	39	74	83
Third level enrollment ratio	36	—	11	39	34
Engineers as percent of population	0.11	—	0.04	0.06	0.47
R&D/GNP	1.0	1.16	0.4	0.5	3.7
Private R&D/total R&D	81/29	40/60	20/80	8/92	22/78
Direct foreign investment/ GDP	1.9	2.0	11.1	23.9	—

11

National System of Industrial Innovation: Dynamics of Capability Building in Korea

LINSU KIM

South Korea (hereafter Korea) has emerged as one of the fastest growing economy and has been transformed from a subsistent agricultural country into a newly industrial one during the past quarter century. As late as 1961, Korea suffered from almost all difficulties facing most poor countries today. But beginning in 1962, the Korean economy grew at an average annual growth rate of almost 9%, raising GNP per capita in current prices from $87 in 1962 to $4936 in 1989. Exports increased from a mere $40 million in 1953 to $62 billion in 1989. The share of manufactured goods in exports increased from 14.3 to 95.0% during the same period. In the mid-1960s, Korea began exporting textile, apparel, plywood, and other labor-intensive products. Ten years later, ships, steel, and construction services from Korea challenged established suppliers from the advanced countries. By the mid-1980s, computers, semiconductor memory chips, video cassette recorders, and automobiles were added to the list of Korea's major export items. By the end of the 1980s, Korea's R&D investment as a fraction of GNP and the number of scientists and engineers as a fraction of the work force were approaching the levels of some of the highly industrialized countries of Europe. What made it possible for Korea to achieve such a phenomenal growth in industrialization? Will Korea be able to sustain the growth in the future?

As a way to answer these questions, this chapter presents Korea's national system related to industrial innovation, which influences to a great extent the direction and pace of technological capability development that in turn lead to industrialization. The main focus of this chapter will be concerned with describing the industrial innovation system as of this new era in Korea's industrial history. It is, however, also important to examine how the national system in the past has worked for Korea to acquire technological capabilities that brought the country where it is today.

HOW KOREA GOT WHERE IT IS TODAY

Thirty-six years of Japanese colonialization left some industrial base, mostly in the northern part. But political and economic vacuums and chaos caused by the fall of Japanese colonial rule, arbitrary division of the nation into North and South, and ensuing civil war, which all took place between 1945 and 1953, flattened Korea as a nation with little left of its past and facing a bleak future.

Particularly, the Korean War destroyed the majority of industrial and infrastructure facilities Korea inherited from Japanese colonialization. When the Armistice was signed in 1953, the net commodity product decreased by 26% compared to the figure 10 years before, decreasing net commodity product per capita by 44% (Kim and Roemer, 1979). Ironically, the Korean War also served positively to a certain extent for the subsequent economic development, having completely transformed a traditional rigid society into a highly mobile one by forcing geographical mobility and contributed to the rapid formation of basic skills among the male labor force, most of who served compulsory military service.

Given virtually no domestic savings, about 70% of all reconstruction projects had to be financed by foreign aid. American economic assistance averaged about 10% of Korean GNP between 1953 and 1960, enabling the country to recover back to the prewar period by the time the aid was completely phased out and Korea launched its economic development program in the early 1960s.

Korea's rapid economic progress may be attributed to many economic, social, and technical factors. The most important of all may be technological capabilities, which is a combined outcome of various economic, social, and technical inputs. It is the ability to make effective use of technical knowledge in production, investment, and innovation. Technological capability enables one to assimilate, use, adapt, change, or create technology and to develop new products and processes in response to a changing economic environment. The process of acquiring technological capability is so diverse and complex that it defies a simple analysis. But this section attempts to identify both macro/general and micro factors that influenced the acquisition of technological capability in Korea.

Macro/General Factors

Macro/general factors—the process of human resource formation, the inflow of foreign technologies, the government's industrial, trade, and science/technology policies that shaped industrial structure and the direction of growth, and so on—set the stage for the rapid acquisition of technological capability.

First, human resource development may be a most basic and crucial determinant, as technological capability is embodied in people. Korea's greatest resource is its human resources. Modern education was first introduced to Korea by American missionaries and later expanded by the Japanese colonial government. But at the end of the Japanese colonial rule, only 2% of the Korean population over 14 years of age had completed secondary school, and the illiteracy rate stood at 78%.

The importance of education in the Korean government's modernization strategy can be seen in the growth of government investment in education: the share of education in the total government budget, for instance, rose from 2.5% in 1951 to over 22% in the 1980s. Government expenditures, however, accounted for only one-third of the total expenditures in education, the remainder being borne by the private sector and parents, reflecting the high commitment for education held by the Korean society. This commitment was the strongest in Korea among eight industrialized (Denmark, Germany, Italy, Japan, Sweden, Switzerland, the United Kingdom, and the United

States) and two semiindustrialized (Singapore and Korea) countries Porter (1990) studied.

As a result, enrollment in the various levels of the formal education system has increased rapidly since 1953. In the case of elementary school, enrollment has increased by over five times. Even faster growth is seen in the secondary and tertiary education levels. Secondary school enrollment increased by more than 28.5 times between 1945 and 1980, while enrollment in colleges and universities increased by almost 150 times during the same period. Table 11.1 shows that school enrollment as a percentage of the corresponding age group rose to over 100% in 1970 for the elementary school level, to over 95% in the early 1980s for the middle school level, to over 70% for the high school level, and over 25% for the tertiary level by 1980.

Several other developing countries also attained as rapid growth in elementary education as did Korea. But what was unique in Korea was the well-balanced expansion in all levels of education early enough to support its economic development. Harbison and Myers (1964) show that given GNP per capita from a regression line of 73 developing countries, Korea's level of educational achievement was furthest of that predicted by its level of economic development. That is, with a per capita income of $90, Korea's educational achievement stood fairly close to the normal pattern of human resource development for a country with a mean per capita GNP of $200. Korea's level of human resource development, when its per capita GNP reached $107, was equivalent to that of countries with a GNP per capita of $380.

Overseas training and observation were also characteristic of human resource development in Korea. Overseas training traces back to the foreign aid period in the 1950s, when a high proportion of senior personnel in government, business, and academia were exposed to foreign training, mainly in the U. S., under economic assistance

Table 11.1. Indicators of Human Resource Development in Korea

	1953	1960	1970	1980	1987
Literacy rate (%)	22.0	72.1	89.4	[a]	[a]
Enrollment as percentage of corresponding age group					
Elementary school (ages 6–11)	59.6	86.2	102.8	101.0	100.2
Middle School (ages 12–14)	21.1	33.3	53.3	94.6	98.8
High School (ages 15–17)	12.4	19.9	29.3	68.5	82.8
College/university	3.1	6.4	9.3	14.9	25.5
Graduates of vocational training centers (1000)	NA	NA	31.6	104.5	50.9
Number of graduates from tertiary schools (per 10,000 population)	NA	10[b]	11	27	54
Number of scientists and engineers[c]	4,157	16,436	65,687	174,832	361,330

[a]Illiteracy rate after the mid-1970s was so insignificant that the government ceased to collect data on it.
[b]For 1965.
[c]Cumulative number of science and engineering graduates since 1945.
Source: Ministry of Education and McGinn et al. (1980).

programs (Mason et al., 1980). The tradition of overseas training continues to this day. The ratio of third-level students training abroad to all third-level students has been twice as great in Korea as in Argentina, Brazil, and India and higher than in Mexico (Westphal et al., 1985). As a result, Korea surpassed the aforementioned newly industrializing countries by almost all indices of educational attainment. The rapid expansion of education resulted in serious unemployment problems for the educated in the 1950s and 1960s, but the formation of educated human resources, despite low per capita income, laid an important foundation for the subsequent adaptation of imported technology and development of indigenous technology. The rapid expansion of the Korean economy soon absorbed the surplus of educated workers.

Second, Korean's hard working habits in long hours may be another factor accounting for the fast acquisition of technological capability. Korea's land area is scarcely larger than New Jersey or Hungary, crossed by mountains with a relatively small portion of the land arable for more than 40 million people. In terms of population density, Korea trails only Bangladesh and Taiwan. The cramped conditions and severely cold winters appear to have forced Koreans to work hard and long whenever possible in order to survive in an unfavorable environment. The average working hours per week in manufacturing in 1985 was 53.8 hours in Korea compared to 33.1 to 42.9 in OECD countries including Japan, 44 to 48.0 hours in other Asian NICs, and 46.0 hours in Mexico (Kim, 1988). Besides, the older generation is motivated by the memory of deprivation and hard times under Japanese occupation and during the Korean War. A sense of *Geug-il* or "beat Japan" to settle old scores and national economic competition with North Korea are also major forces motivating Koreans (Porter, 1990).

Third, lacking technological capability at the outset of its economic development, Korea had to rely on foreign technology imports. However, Korea's policies concerning direct foreign investment (DFI) and foreign licensing (FL) were quite restrictive in the early years of industrialization, when technology was not a critical element and the mature technologies needed could be easily acquired through mechanisms other than DFI or FL (e.g., reverse engineering). Table 11.2 presents data on technology transfer through DFI and FL to Korea.

Consequently, the size of DFI and its proportion to total external borrowing were significantly lower in Korea than in other NICs. For example, Korea's stock of DFI in 1983 was only 7% of the size of that in Brazil, 23% of that in Singapore, and less than a half the size of that in Taiwan and Hong Kong. The proportion of DFI to total external borrowing was only 6.1% in Korea compared with 91.9% in Singapore, 45% in Taiwan, and 21.8% in Brazil (KEB, 1987). The comparative figure reflects Korea's explicit policy of promoting its "independence" from multinationals in management control.

In contrast, Korea promoted technology transfer through the procurement of turnkey plants in the early years. For example, the chemical, cement, steel, and paper industries, established in the 1960s and early 1970s, all resorted to the turnkey mode for their initial setup. But Korean firms assimilated imported technologies so rapidly that they managed to undertake subsequent expansions and upgrading with little assistance from foreigners. The rapid growth of the Korean economy has called for commensurate growth in investment for production facilities. Government policy had, however, been biased in favor of the importation of foreign capital goods and against

Table 11.2. Foreign Technology Transfer to Korea (US$ Million)

Source	62–66	67–71	72–76	77–81	82–86	Total
1. Direct foreign investment (DFI)						
Japan	8.3	89.7	627.1	300.9	875.2	1,901.2
United States	25.0	95.3	135.0	235.7	581.6	1,072.6
All others	12.1	33.6	117.3	184.0	309.7	658.7
Total	45.4	218.6	879.4	720.6	1,766.5	3,632.5
2. Foreign licensing (FL)						
Japan	—	5.0	58.7	139.8	323.7	527.2
United States	0.6	7.8	21.3	159.2	602.7	791.6
All others	0.2	3.5	16.6	152.4	258.5	431.1
Total	0.8	16.3	96.5	451.4	1,184.9	1,749.9
3. Technical consultancy						
Japan	—	12.1	7.7	20.8	89.2	129.8
United States	—	3.1	6.0	16.7	159.1	184.9
All others	—	1.6	4.8	17.2	84.0	107.6
Total	—	16.8	18.5	54.7	332.3	422.3
4. Capital goods imports						
Japan	148	1,292	4,423	14,269	20,986	41,118
United States	75	472	1,973	6,219	12,394	21,133
All others	93	777	2,445	7,490	53,338	64,143
Total	316	2,541	8,841	27,978	86,718	126,394

Source: Ministry of Finance on DFI and FL; Ministry of Science and Technology for technical consultancy data; and Korean Society for Advancement of Machinery Industry for capital goods data.

the development of a rudimentary local capital goods industry as a way to strengthen international competitiveness of the capital goods user industries. Such a policy led to massive imports of foreign capital goods, which became a major source of learning through reverse engineering by Korean firms (Kim and Kim, 1985). Of the four categories of technology transfer listed in Table 11.2, capital goods imports far surpass other means of technology transfer in terms of value. Capital goods imports were worth 34 times the value of DFI and 72 times the value of FL. The total value of capital goods imports is 21 times that of the other two categories combined, suggesting that Korea may have acquired more technology from advanced countries through the importation of capital goods than through any other means. Among NICs, the proportion of capital goods imports to total technology transfer was highest in Korea (Westphal et al., 1985).

In short, Korea restricted DFI but promoted instead technology transfer through other means such as capital goods imports. Capital was acquired in the form of foreign loans. Such a policy, designed to maintain Korea's independence from foreign multinationals, has been relatively effective in acquiring technological capability in the mature industries, as Korea's well-trained human resources and their entrepreneurship enabled the country to learn quickly from foreign capital goods.

Fourth, continued relations with the United States in the national defense has served an important role in enabling Korean firms to accumulate experience and capability. The U. S. military procurement program afforded many producers in a number of sectors with occasions for assisted learning by doing to meet exacting product specifications. Construction contractors, plywood producers, and tire makers, among others, built up their initial capability through the U. S. military contracts and later became major exporters (Westphal et al., 1985). For example, through U. S. military contracts, local construction firms learned, under the direction of the U. S. Engineering Corps, specific details of stringent U. S. specifications, the preparation of bidding documents, and management of construction projects, enabling local firms to incrementally accumulate increasingly more sophisticated construction capabilities. By the early 1970s, Korean construction firms became important contractors for the U. S. military bases in Guam and Vietnam. Capabilities accumulated in these foreign countries led Koreans to launch an aggressive expansion to the Middle East in the wake of oil crises. The U. S. military presence also reduced the defense expenditure burden of the Korean economy, enabling the country to divert more resources for industrial development.

Fifth, despite a strong backup of the U. S. military presence in Korea, Korea still had to maintain one of the largest military forces in the Free World by allocating over 36% of its annual budget to national defense. Such a national security concern, particularly during and after the Carter Administration, which expressed a possibility of the U. S. military pullout from Korea, had some impact on the development of particular industries and their technological capabilities. For example, one of the major factors the Korean government has considered in pushing hard heavy machinery industries in the late 1970s appears to be its concern to acquire capability for defense production. Although such an ambitious investment in heavy machinery industries in the absence of adequate local capability has resulted at the outset in extremely low capacity utilization and resource allocation problems, the investment over local market and local capability has put enormous pressure on both the government and private entrepreneurs to upgrade technological capability for survival. As a result, Korea became an important contender in exporting large scale plants in the Third World. The major impact of national security concern in technological capability building may be the significant improvement in precision in the machinery industry. The procurement demand of the Korean military after the Korean War also helped local consumer electronics producers to diversify into industrial electronics.

Sixth, to overcome a disadvantage of a small-sized domestic market and to take advantage of the stable nature of mature technologies on which industrialization strategy was based, the Korean government designated so-called "strategic" industries for import substitution and export promotion. Plywood, textiles, consumer electronics, and automobiles in the 1960s and steel, shipbuilding, construction services, and machinery in the 1970s are examples. These industries, which were created in violation of its static comparative advantage, had to suffer from high costs in addition to "infant industry" growing pains. To enable the industries to overcome the problems, the government used various policy mechanisms; assistance to mitigate risk and to secure stability, market protection from foreign competition, export promotion, and tax incentives and preferential financing for products and producers designated by the government. The average effective rate of protection was atypically high for the "strategic" industries. In some industries, protection quickly became redundant with firms experiencing a rapid *rite de passage* from an infant to an exporter, but in others, where technology was complex and marketing was more elaborate, protection had been relatively long lasting in order to provide a longer period of incubation (Kim, 1987).

Seventh, in contrast to Taiwan, which restricted the emergence of large enterprises, the Korean government intentionally created large firms, *chaebols,* as an instrument to bring about the economy of scale in mature technologies and in turn to develop these "strategic industries" and to lead exports and economy. The government helped the capital formation as well as the subsequent diversification of these *chaebols*. Unlike Taiwan, which did not privatize Japanese enterprises confiscated after World War II (Hou and Gee, 1990), the Korean government sold Japanese colonial properties and state-owned enterprises to selected local entrepreneurs with a favorable long-term installment payment during the inflationary period, giving local entrepreneurs a windfall capital gain. Owning all commercial banks, the government helped more significantly the formation of *chaebols* by allocating scarce foreign exchange and preferential financing at the official rates both of which were only one-half the real market rate (Jung, 1989). The state also gave them large import-substitution projects, for which these entrepreneurs imported production technology on turnkey basis with foreign loans, which was guaranteed by the government. Then, foreign debt burdens due to currency devaluations were compensated with increased low interest loans, reducing market risks for these businesses.

Where Korea differs from other developing countries in promoting big businesses was in the discipline its state exercised over these *chaebols* by penalizing poor performers and rewarding only good ones. Good performers were rewarded with new licenses in other industries, leading to further diversification. For those entering risky industries, the government rewarded entrants with licenses in more lucrative sectors, providing a cushion to nurture risky infant industries. In contrast, the government refused to bail out relatively large scale, badly managed, bankrupt firms in otherwise healthy industries, instead selected better managed *chaebols* to take over them (Amsden, 1989). The government as the controller of commercial banks was in a powerful position to punish poorly managed firms by freezing bank credits. As a result, only three of the largest 10 *chaebols* in 1965—Samsung, Lucky-Goldstar, and Ssangyong—remained on the same list 10 years later. Similarly, seven of the largest 10 in 1975 remained on the same list in 1985.

Chaebols' rapid growth and diversification have enormously affected industrial structure and market concentration in Korea. By 1977, 93% of all commodities, or 62% of all shipments, were produced under monopoly, duopoly, or oligopoly conditions, under which the top three producers accounted for more than 60% market share. The 10 largest *chaebols* accounted for 48.1% of GNP in 1980, indicating that Korean industry was even more highly concentrated than that of Taiwan or Japan. However, Chenery et al. (1986) concluded that total factor productivity as well as output grew faster in Korea's highly concentrated economy than in that of almost any other country they studied.

Eighth, the Korean government also set forth exports as something of a life or death struggle to achieve economic growth goals with the small domestic market. Thus, the government had pushed and pulled firms with threats and promises. Firms were granted unrestricted and tariff-free access to imported intermediate inputs. Firms were also granted automatic access to bank loans for working capital for all export activities, even when the domestic money supply was being tightened. These firms also had unrestricted access to foreign capital goods, as mentioned earlier, and were encouraged to integrate vertically in order to sustain international competitiveness. These incentives operated automatically constituted the crux of the Korean system of export promotion. Furthermore, the rationing of longer term bank loans was used as a carrot to draw down to new paths of exporting, encouraging diversification, and to export more than otherwise. These incentives were applied to all exporting firms, but particularly helped large firms with greater organizational, financial, and political leverage to grow even larger.

That the Korean economy was primarily export oriented appears to have affected the fast acquisition of technological capability at least in three ways. First, lump-sum investments for capacity beyond local market size to bring about the economy of scale forced local businesses to acquire technological capability fast in order to maximize capacity utilization through improving international competitiveness. Second, as producers entered the international market, the keen international competition forced them to invest significantly in technological efforts, mainly in learning by doing and reverse engineering, in order to be competitive in both quality and price. Third, informal technical assistance offered by foreign OEM (original equipment manufacture) buyers to ensure Korea-made products meeting their technical specifications provided invaluable help to Korean firms in acquiring necessary capability.

Ninth, while industrial and trade policies affected significantly the emergence and growth of local industries, particularly *chaebols,* science and technology infrastructure played little role in promoting the development of industries with mature technologies. In light of the absence of R&D capability in universities, the government established in 1966 Korea Institute of Science and Technology (KIST) as an integrated technical center and subsequently its spin-offs to meet industry's technical needs. However, the institutes suffered from poor linkages with industry at least through the mid-1970s. In these institutes, most of the overseas trained Korean researchers came from either academic fields or from R&D organizations of highly industrialized countries that undertook advanced research. Expertise was particularly lacking in manufacturing know-how and the development of prototypes, which were in great demand in the early years. Furthermore, Korean researchers could not compete with foreign licensors in supplying detailed blueprints and other manufacturing know-how, as well as being unable to assist industry in solving the problems in the crucial initial stages (Kim, 1989).

Under the aforementioned economic environment, Korean firms developed strategies at the microeconomic level to sustain growth by acquiring technological capability fast, which is the subject to be discussed below.

Microeconomic Behavior of Korean Firms

The microeconomic behavior of Korean firms in acquiring technological capability varies significantly by industry. First, industries using small batch and unit production (hereinafter small batch) such as shipbuilding and machinery focus more on developing capability to design and manufacture products than on setting up production processes, as they usually produce highly differentiated products. As a result, large firms in these industries relied heavily on the formal transfer of foreign technology primarily in the form of foreign licensings and consultancies for the initial erection of production systems and for the design of their products. These industries accounted for a disproportionately large share of Korea's total foreign licensings through the 1970s. These firms have, however, exerted increasingly their own technological efforts to strengthen their own capability and in turn to reduce their reliance on foreign licensors, as they accumulated experience in production and product design. In contrast, small firms in these industries (plus small-sized firms in the electronics and automobile industries, whose large firms deploy large batch operations) resorted primarily to their own imitative efforts to evolve organically over a long period of time, establishing their initial production facilities with primitive technologies developed by themselves and then gradually upgraded their production system and product quality through the imitative reverse engineering of foreign products and processes (Kim and Lee, 1987). Technology diffusion within these industries took rapidly through the mobility of experienced engineers from existing firms to new entrants. Particularly, engineers experienced at state-owned enterprises in the early 1950s have spun-off and played a pivotal role in emerging private firms.

Second, industries using large batch and mass production systems (hereinafter large batch) such as electronics and automobiles produce less differentiated products. Large firms in these industries were also dependent on foreign licensings but to a lesser extent than those with small batch operations. In the advent of an import substitution policy, local firms entered technical assistance agreements with leading foreign firms to import "packaged" technology (including assembly processes, product specifications, production know-how, training local technical personnel, and component parts) so as to establish the initial production system. The immediate technological task was the implementation of transferred foreign technology for the assembly of imported components and parts, whose final products had been tested and proven elsewhere, requiring only engineering (E) efforts. Most late entrants poached experienced personnel from existing firms to set up and begin their operations, resulting in a rapid diffusion of imported technologies. Then, competition stemming from new entrants, together with increasing export promotion, called for indigenous efforts to assimilate foreign technology, thus placing emphasis not only on engineering but also on limited development (D&E). Capabilities acquired through assimilation of foreign imported technology also enabled local firms to develop, through imitative engineering, related products without foreign assistance (Kim, 1980).

Third, industries using continuous processes such as chemicals, cement, paper, and steel produce the least differentiated products in highly capital-intensive processes. Since the final product and the equipment are relatively well known, but the proprietary know-how that lies in the details of the production process can make a significant difference in the productivity of these industries, the initial production system of large chemical, cement and steel plants were established on turnkey basis by Western firms. Initial production capability to operate and maintain such process-oriented plants stemmed largely from extensive training by foreign suppliers before, during, and after the erection of the initial production processes. The local firms, however, used deliberate strategies with considerable efforts to acquire capability, leading to a series of minor improvements with significant productivity increase, and to an increased taking-charge of engineering tasks in the subsequent expansions. A steel mill, for instance, relied completely on the Japanese in the first phase in 1971 for annual capacity of one million tons. But by 1981 capacity had been increased to 8.5 million tons in three expansions that were increasingly under the direction of Korean engineers. The progressive substitution of foreign engineering by local engineering is well indicated by the fall in the cost of foreign project engineering per ton from $6.13 to $0.13 during the same period (Kim, 1987). Unlike other process-oriented industries, local pharmaceutical firms in Korea started as small importers/dealers of packaged finished drugs and later entered the drug manufacturing business by packaging imported bulk drugs. Then, they gradually extended into more intricate operations, first from formulating imported raw materials and later to backward integration into chemical components production. Through this process, they grew in size and technological capability (Kim et al., 1989).

In short, given the large size investment and lack of experience and capability, large firms across industries have resorted heavily to foreign sources in order to ensure quick erection and smooth start-up. In contrast, small firms underwent a long process of imitative reverse engineering, as they lacked financial resources and organizational capability to identify and negotiate with foreign technology suppliers. Nevertheless, both large and small firms deployed deliberate, aggressive technological strategies to acquire their own technological capabilities through exerted efforts to assimilate foreign technologies from the very outset. Korean firms have acquired technological capabilities in piecemeal fashion, as successively more sophisticated capabilities have been acquired and put into practice. The process of acquisition has clearly been one of purposive efforts involving a succession of incremental steps, with production capabilities being developed somewhat in advance of engineering and innovation capabilities. The selectivity of import substitution for the elements of technology has meant continued reliance on imports for at least some elements in almost all industries, but the pattern of imports has continually shifted as local capabilities have replaced foreign ones (Westphal et al., 1985). R&D in the formal sense of the term was not important for Korea during this stage of imitating mature technologies. Industries in fact reversed the sequence of R,D&E: it started with engineering (E) for products and processes imported from abroad, and then progressively evolved into the position of undertaking substantial development (D). But research (R) was not relevant to Korea's industrialization through the 1970s. Several studies conducted in other countries also provide a similar evidence. Studies on Japanese industrial history show that its industries went through a similar pattern (Shishido, 1972; Yakushiji, 1977; Ozawa, 1974). The United States also reversed the sequence of research, development, and engineering, that is, it started with practical technologies imported from Britain, and then slowly evolved into the present position of being afforded substantial research (NAS, 1973). Brazilian and Argentinian firms began manufacturing with assembly and packing operations and eventually extended into more intricate operations. Engineering was the initiating portion of the R,D&E spectrum leading gradually to more advanced development and research efforts (Baranson, 1973; Dahlman and Frischtak, 1990; Katz and Bercovich, 1990).

The rapid acquisition of capability through such a process may be attributed to many factors. The continuous inflow of foreign technology (through formal and informal mechanisms) to learn from, the formation of highly trained human resources who were willing to learn, entrepreneur's "can do" spirit exercised freely under restricted equity participation of multinationals, and the government's orchestral role in directing *chaebols* and selectively allocating resources to them to achieve ambitious growth objectives under the pressure of the competitive international market have worked together for Korea to grow rapidly through the 1970s.

Chaebols particularly played an important role in this process, as they were in the most advantageous position in drawing best quality human resources, in identifying, negotiating, and financing foreign technology transfer, in obtaining business licenses and preferential financing from the government, in applying experience gained in one field of business to another, and in risk-taking in new businesses with existing businesses providing cushion therefor. As a result, by the end of 1970s, Korea had the largest textile plant, the largest plywood plant, the largest shipyard, the largest cement plant, and the largest heavy machinery plant in the world.

CONTEMPORARY NATIONAL SYSTEM FOR INDUSTRIAL INNOVATION

The economic environment for Korea has changed significantly in the 1980s for several reasons. First, the world economy has generally slowed down in the 1980s, affecting particularly outward-looking economies such as Korea. Second, in the wake of rising trade imbalance, North America and Europe have moved toward protectionistic policies, making it increasingly difficult for Korea to sustain export growth in industries that have led Korea's export-oriented strategy in the past. Third, Korea has lost its competitiveness in low wage based labor-intensive industries, as its real wage has risen at the average annual growth rate of 5.8% in the 1960s and 7.5% in the 1970s. Concomitantly, other developing countries with much lower wage rates are rapidly catching up with Korea in these industries. Fourth, advanced countries, particularly Japan, are increasingly reluctant to transfer technology to Korea as Korea attempts to enter industries that have been dominated by these countries. Fifth, Korea was forced to change its copyright and patent laws, preempting the imitative reverse engineering of foreign products. Such an unfavorable environment makes it imperative for Korea to enhance its own technological capabilities in order to innovate independently and to strengthen its bargaining power against foreign technology suppliers. This section focuses on Korea's national system in the 1980s that are designed to cope with these problems.

The Shift of Public Policies

In the face of such an unfavorable environment, the Korean government set out on an economic liberalization program, making a series of policy shifts in an attempt to introduce market mechanisms by reducing government intervention and to undertake a structural change towards the development of relatively more technology-based industries. First, in the face of *chaebols'* increasing economic power and its resultant monopolistic abuses such as creating scarcities, price gouging, and ruining smaller competitors, the government adopted a policy of "economic democratization" to mitigate monopolistic abuses by *chaebols.* The recently introduced Fair Trade Act along the lines of American antitrust legislation includes, among other things, the prohibition of unfair cartel practices and mutual investment among *chaebol's* affiliate companies, sets a ceiling of credit flow going to predesignated *chaebols,* and regulates their vertical and horizontal integration. Nevertheless, *chaebols* grew even bigger and economic concentration increased further: the combined sales of the five largest *chaebols* as percent of GNP increased from 12.8 in 1975 to 35.0 in 1980 and to 52.4 in 1984. Lee et al. (1986) report that the number of *chaebols* designated by the government as dominating their respective markets increased from 105 in 1981 to 216 in 1985, but only 10 were accused of having abused their economic power. Of 1172 applications for vertical or horizontal integrations, only two were rejected by the government.

Second, as part of a financial liberalization program, the government reduced regulation of nonbank financial intermediaries and denationalized commercial banks. The deregulation of nonbank financial intermediaries, many of which had long been controlled by *chaebols,* resulted in their share of total deposit liabilities from 27% in 1980 to 42% in 1984. The denationalization of commercial banks resulted in the fall of their ownership from government hands into those of *chaebols.* With increased financial resources, *chaebols* went further to buy state enterprises that were being privatized and to buy financially troubled firms. In short, the financial liberalization program enhanced the growth of *chaebols'* economic concentration. Thus, Amsden (1989, p. 137) concludes, "in the presence of large concentrations of market power, reliance on the market mechanism for reform appear to produce some perverse results, not only in Latin America but also in the Far East."

Third, since 1983, the government commenced a program to liberalize imports, raising import liberalization ratio (defined as the ratio of the number of unrestricted items to the total) from 51% in 1973 to 85% in 1984 and to 95.2% by 1988. The government also brought down the average tariff rate from 26% in 1984 to 16% in 1988. As a result, imports increased by 20.1% in 1989 compared to 2.8% in export increase, making the domestic market significantly more competitive than before.

Fourth, Korea gradually liberalized its technology transfer policies in the 1980s: Korea needs progressively more sophisticated foreign technologies than in the earlier years in order to sustain its international competitiveness in export-led industrialization. The liberalization raised the share of Korea's 999 industrial subsectors open to foreign investment from 44% in the 1970s to 66% in 1984 and to almost 90% in 1988. Foreign licensings has been completely open for all industries and for all terms and conditions. Table 11.2 presents data on technology transfer through DFI and FL to Korea. Over 48% of total DFI and 67% of royalty payments in FL since 1962 has taken place in the last 5 years (1986–1991), reflecting the liberalized public policy environment as well as the private sector's aggressiveness in acquiring more sophisticated foreign technologies. In the 1960s and 1970s, foreign companies invested in Korea to reap Korea's cheap labor costs. Now foreign companies invest to collaborate with Korean companies in relatively more technology-intensive areas.

Fifth, the government began promoting small and medium-sized industries (SMI), particularly technology-based small firms, to remedy the imbalance between the large and small business sectors. The government established "sanctuaries" for SMIs, designating 205 business territories where neither the large corporations nor their affiliates can intrude. A program called The Compulsory Lending Ratio provides that commercial (nationwide) banks should allow more than 35% of total loans to the SMIs. In addition, local or regional banks have to provide more than 80% of their total loans to these SMIs. The government also took initiatives in establishing the venture capital industry as a way to promote the emergence of technology-based small firms, when the private sector had no interest. Specifically, the government enacted a special law to establish the first venture capital firm, jointly funded by the state and a group of private firms. The government took a further step with the enactment of the Small and Medium Enterprise Formation Act in 1986, leading to the emergence of 12 venture business firms, all jointly invested by the state and private sector.

Sixth, the focus of industrial policy has shifted from the promotion of "strategic" sectors to that of innovation-related activities. That is, in the 1960s and 1970s, special incentives—tax exemptions, custom rebates, access to foreign exchange, and other forms of protection or enhancements—were granted to "strategic" industries in order to make them competitive at a world level. In contrast in the 1980s, the government abolished all industry-specific promotion acts, which had been introduced in the 1970s, and instead legislated a new industrial promotion act that ties all incentives with specific industrial activities such as the promotion of R&D and the development of human resources. However, in the late 1980s, the government designated several high-technology industries for promotion.

Finally, the government, as a way to democratize economy and society, liberalized labor movements that had been tightly controlled in the 1960s and 1970s. Given the opportunity, unionists' demands suddenly exploded disorderly, violently, and in many cases unlawfully, resulting in work stoppages, missed export delivery deadlines, lowered product quality, and wage hike beyond productivity increase. The average company suffered from 19.2 days of labor strikes in 1989, up from 5.3 days in 1987. In 1989 alone, labor disputes cost a total of about $6.2 billion in production as well as $1.36 billion in reduced exports. Korea's real wages have increased a cumulative 62.5% since 1987. When adjusted in U. S. dollar terms, the increase amounts to 91.1%, which is 2.8 times that of productivity (*Business Korea,* 1990). In short, labor disputes are a new variable that affects significantly the nation's efforts to innovate in the 1980s and 1990s.

Under these policy environments, both the government and private sector intensified their technological efforts to sustain international competitiveness. The following sections present various aspects of these technological activities.

Structural Change in R&D Activities

Since many skills and activities required in reverse engineering are also the same in R&D, activities that had been called reverse engineering have easily been transformed into activities called R&D, as Korea approached the technological frontier. Reverse engineering involved activities that sensed the potential needs in market, activities that located knowledge or products that would meet the market needs, and activities that would infuse these two elements into a new project. Reverse engineering also involved purposive search of relevant information, effective interactions among technical members within a project group and with marketing and production departments within the firm, effective interactions with other organizations such as suppliers, customers, local research institutes, and universities, and trial and error in developing a satisfactory result. Skills and activities required in these processes are in fact the same in innovation process in R&D.

Korea's R&D efforts may well be reflected in aggregate R&D investment trends. Table 11.3 shows that the total R&D investment increased from W. 10.6 billion (U S$ 28.6 million) in 1971 to W. 1878 billion (U S$ 2.37 billion) in 1987. Though the Korean economy recorded one of the world's fastest growth rates, R&D expenditure rose faster than GNP, increasing its share of GNP (R&D/GNP) from 0.32 to 1.93% during the same period. A drastic increase was seen in the late 1970s and 1980s, reflecting the shifts of government policy from the promotion of the light/mature industries to that of heavy/technology-based industries and from the assimilation of production technology to a strong drive for technological innovation. However, Korea's total

Table 11.3. Major R&D Indicators in Korea (Billion Won)

	1971	1976	1981	1987
R&D expenditures	10.67	60.90	293.13	1,878.0
Funds from government	7.29	39.18	121.73	383.0
Funds from private sources	3.38	21.72	171.40	1,495.0
Government vs. private	68:32	64:36	42:58	20:80
Manufacturing	NA	16.70	111.77	1,114.7
R&D/sales	NA	0.36	0.67	1.83
Gross national products	3,376	13,881	45,126	97,532
R&D/GNP	0.32	0.44	0.65	1.93
Number of researchers (total)[a]	5,320	11,661	20,718	52,783
Government/public institutions	2,477	3,592	5,065	9,184
Universities	1,918	4,811	8,488	17,495
Private sector	925	3,258	7,165	26,104
R&D exp/researcher (W. 1000)	4,306	5,223	14,149	35,580
Researcher/1000 population	0.08	0.33	0.54	1.27
Number of corporate R&D laboratories	1	12	65	455

[a]The figures do not include research assistants, technicians, and other supporting personnel.

Source: MOST, Science and Technology Annals, various years.

R&D expenditure amounts only to about 54% of that of the General Motors Corporation.

Government statistics indicate that basic research accounted for 16.6%, applied research for 19.6%, and development for the remaining 63.8% of the nation's total R&D expenditures in 1987. The statistics also show that the private sector accounted for 40% of the nation's basic and applied research, while universities accounted for only 28% and public R&D institutes for 32% in the same year (KIRI, 1989). These figures for basic and applied research, particularly the share of the private sector therein, appear to have been much exaggerated, as leading *chaebols* have just started a limited investment in applied research in the field of semiconductors and informatics, let alone basic research.

There has been structural change in R&D investment. The private sector has gradually assumed a larger role in the country's R&D efforts in response partly to increasing international competition and partly to policy environment conducive to private R&D activities. For example, the public sector accounted for 68% of the nation's total R&D expenditure in 1971 but for only 20% in 1987. In short, the government took initiatives in local R&D efforts when the private sector had neither the capability nor market incentives to undertake such activities. But as industrialization progressed and Korea lost its comparative advantage in labor-intensive industries, the private sector gradually took the leading role in local R&D in order to sustain its international competitiveness.

The Korean government has also promoted corporate R&D activities by offering various programs to induce the private sector to set up formal R&D laboratories. The programs include tax incentives and preferential financing to set up new laboratories and exemption from military service obligation for key R&D personnel. Spurred by these programs, the number of corporate R&D laboratories increased from one in

1970 to 122 by 1983 and to 604 in 1987, reflecting the seriousness with which Korean firms are pursuing high-technology development. Although small and medium-sized firms account for over 50% of total number of corporate R&D centers, *chaebols* dominate R&D activities (to be discussed in detail below). Table 11.3 also shows that R&D spending in the manufacturing sector has increased from W.16.7 billion (U S$ 22.25 million) in 1976 to W.1, 114.74 billion (U S$ 1.41 billion) in 1987. Even in constant prices, R&D spending has more than quadrupled during the period. This is faster than the growth of sales: R&D spending as a ratio of total sales increased from 0.39% in 1976 to 1.83% in 1987. The machinery and electronics industry spent over 4% of sales for R&D activities in 1987. However, manufacturer's R&D spending as a proportion of total sales is less than half of that of manufacturers in the United States and Japan.

One of the major mistakes made by the Korean government in developing a national system for industrial innovation has been its underinvestment in higher educational institutions. The number of universities has increased significantly from 69 in 1966 to 100 in 1985. The number of university students has increased from 131,354 to 931,884, with the proportion of high school graduates going on to universities growing from 28.2 to 38.3% during the same period. The environment for quality education and research has, however, deteriorated over this period. For example, the student–professor ratio has retrogressed from 22.6 in 1966 to 35.8 in 1985, making all universities primarily undergraduate teaching-oriented rather than research-oriented. Thus, the "publish or perish" principle is not applied.[1]

As a result, Korea has failed to develop a stock of highly trained scientists and engineers who will be necessary in the 1990s for Korea to sustain its international competitiveness. Compared to education at other levels, graduate education in science and engineering has been much neglected in terms of quantity and quality. The government's recent move to correct this discrepancy has resulted in across-the-board expansion of graduate programs in all universities in an attempt to meet future needs at least in quantity. It will take a great deal of time and effort, however, before such a move can produce quality output.

Realizing the difficulty of reforming old undergraduate teaching-oriented traditions in education, the government adopted a dual system: since all universities, public or private, under the Ministry of Education (MOE) are basically teaching-oriented, the Ministry of Science and Technology (MOST) founded a research-oriented S&T school and plans to have another one soon, establishing a new research tradition in university education.

Consequently, research activities in universities have been relatively underdeveloped. For example, though university R&D expenditures increased significantly from W.572 million ($1.5 million) in 1971 to W.198 billion ($250 million) in 1987, they account for only 5.4% of the nation's total R&D expenditures in 1971 and 10.5% in 1987, while universities account for 33.1% of the nation's R&D manpower and 78.4% of its Ph.D. level R&D manpower in 1987.

The Korean government, however, is on the move in strengthening Korea's basic research capability. For example, the government established a joint semiconductor research institute in a state university, which will be used jointly by other universities and corporate R&D centers. The government recently designated five university R&D centers in 1989 that will receive increased financial assistance in order to strengthen their R&D capabilities. The government is also in the process of enacting a "Basic

Research Promotion Law" as a way to promote the strengthening of basic research capability as one of the nation's top technological goals.

In view of the absence of R&D capability in universities, public R&D institutes have been a backbone of advanced R&D in Korea. They have also been major instruments for national R&D projects, as they are recipients of over 90% of research grants awarded by the government in "new" technology areas.

The Funding Source of Industrial R&D

Table 11.3 shows that the private sector has increasingly assumed a bigger role in the nation's R&D, accounting for 80% in 1987. The Korean government has played a significant role in helping the corporate sector secure funds for R&D activities mainly through three mechanisms: direct R&D subsidy, preferential financing, and tax incentives.

Direct R&D Subsidy
The government had no direct R&D subsidy programs through the 1970s, when Korea relied primarily on light industries for economic development. It was in the 1980s when the government introduced two schemes for direct funding of private R&D: one is "National R&D Projects" (NRP) administered by MOST in "new" technology areas focusing primarily on future problems and the other is "Industrial Base Technology Development Projects" (IBTDP) administered by the Ministry of Trade and Industry (MTI) in "existing" technology areas focusing primarily on current problems. Both schemes designate target technologies and offer direct R&D subsidy to R&D organizations.

Criteria for NRP designation include projects involving "new" (to Korea) technologies with a high risk of failure or with high economic externalities, thus warranting public support. MOST identified several target areas: localization of machinery parts and components, new materials development, semiconductor design, super-mini-computer development, energy conservation technology, localization of nuclear energy fuel, new chemical development, biotechnology development, and basic research in universities. In contrast, MTI undertakes a survey each year to identify urgent R&D projects in industrial firms and provides R&D subsidy (IBTDPs) to research organizations (public, private, and university) to undertake the projects. In 1989, 174 technologies were identified, 146 of which were designated as projects to be funded.

The government's total investment in NRPs, as shown in Table 11.4, increased significantly from W.13.3 billion (U S$ 17.7 million) in 1982 to W.55.0 billion (U S$ 69.4 million) in 1987. The government's R&D subsidy to the private sector through NRPs also increased from W.5.0 billion (U S$ 6.7 million) to W.18.1 billion (U S$ 22.8 million). However, even in the case of 1987, this amounts only to approximately U S$ 61,700 per project (equivalent to about two R&D man years) and U S$ 91,000 per participating firm. For IBTDPs, the government earmarked W.11.5 billion (U S$ 17.2 million) in 1989, about U S$ 117,936 per project. The amounts are not substantial enough to solve critical problems.

Preferential Financing for Corporate R&D
The most important mechanism for funding corporate R&D is preferential financing offered by state-controlled banks and public funds. Through the 1970s, the interest

Table 11.4. National R&D Project Investment (Billion Won)

	1982	1983	1984	1985	1986	1987
Public and industrial projects						
Projects with public leadership	8.2	13.9	16.1	17.3	27.1	28.2
Public R&D institute-industry joint projects	4.6	6.7	4.5	8.1	15.1	18.1
(matched by private sector)	5.0	12.6	9.0	13.2	46.1	49.5
Number of projects	66	106	106	186	296	370
Number of corporates involved	86	131	134	212	240	250
International joint projects	—	—	—	1.6	2.3	2.9
Basic research	—	1.0	0.9	1.5	5.0	5.0
Technical assistance to small/ medium firms	0.4	0.4	0.5	1.0	1.5	—
R&D evaluation projects	—	—	—	0.5	0.6	0.8
Total NRPs[a]	13.3	22.0	22.0	30.0	51.7	55.0

[a]National R&D Project.
Source: Science and Technology Annals (1988).

rate for R&D loans was one of the highest, reflecting the low priority of R&D in government policies. Table 11.5 shows that preferential financing amounted to W.671.6 billion (U S$ 848.0 million) in 1987, accounting for 94.3% of total corporate R&D financing (W.712.4 billion equivalent to U S$ 899.5 million) by the state that year. In contrast, direct R&D subsidy through NRPs and IBTDPs accounts for only 4% and direct investment through venture capital firms for 1.7% of the total. The total amount of public financing (W.712.4 billion) mostly in the form of preferential loans, in fact, accounted for 64% of total R&D expenditure in manufacturing in 1987. In short, the government plays a major role in funding corporate R&D through the allocation of preferential financing.

Table 11.5. Public Source of Funding for Corporate R&D (W. 100 Million)

	1982	1983	1984	1985	1986	1987
Direct R&D subsidy						
NRPs[a]	51	71	51	81	151	185
IBTDPs[a]	—	—	—	—	—	100
Inventor's prototype development	0.5	0.7	1.0	1.0	1.1	1.2
Subtotal	51.5	71.7	52.0	82.0	152.1	286.2
Direct investment through venture capital firms	2	23	31	44	60	122
Preferential financing						
Venture capital firms	221	499	601	827	905	1,000
State-controlled banks	521	879	920	880	1,352	1,730
National investment funds	—	9	33	4	193	525
Industrial development funds	95	64	91	139	195	307
Industrial technology improvement funds	—	—	—	—	316	2,654
Subtotal	837	1,451	1,717	1,942	3,252	6,716
Total	890	1,545	1,800	2,068	3,464	7,124

[a]NRPs, National R&D Projects administered by MOST in "new" technology areas; IBTDPs, Industrial Base Technology Development Projects administered by MTI in "existing" technology areas.
Source: Science and Technology Annals (1988).

Tax Incentives
Tax incentives are a major indirect mechanism in making funds available for corporate R&D. In Korea, tax incentives may be classified into five categories according to objectives associated with such incentives. Most important is tax incentives that are aimed at promoting corporate R&D investment: reduced tariffs on import of R&D equipment and supplies, the deduction of annual noncapital R&D expenditures and human resource development costs from taxable income, accelerated depreciation on industrial R&D facilities, and the exemption of real estate tax on R&D-related properties. The incentives also include a tax reduction scheme, called the Technology Development Reserve Fund, whereby an enterprise can set aside up to 20% (30% for high-technology industries) of profits before tax in any one year to be used for its R&D work in the following 4 years. The private sector did not take advantage of this scheme in early years in the absence of needs for technological activities. Other tax incentives are aimed at reducing the cost of acquiring foreign technology, promoting technology-based small firms, reducing the cost of commercializing locally generated technologies, reducing the cost of introducing new products, and promoting the venture capital industry and venture investment.

Interorganizational Cooperation

Public R&D Institutes–Industry Cooperation
In the 1980s, the government used various means to bring about effective linkages between the public R&D institutes and industry. For example, NRPs and IBTDPs, albeit insignificant in their total monetary value, were used as major means to facilitate public R&D institute–industry cooperation to develop the aforementioned target technologies. The schemes were also aimed at facilitating university involvement in the projects, but have produced only limited results. In some cases, large firms, however, tend to shy away from receiving public support in recent years in order to keep their R&D activities confidential; thus the programs now largely support small and medium-sized firms. Nevertheless, both mechanisms have led to significant joint R&D results. For example, a public R&D institute and four private firms have successfully developed and commercialized a low-density electronics switching system (TDX-1) and are now in the process of designing a high-density system (TDX-10). The same public R&D institute and three semiconductor producers completed jointly designing a 4-mega dynamic RAM (to be elaborated further below).

University–Industry Cooperation
Given the teaching orientation of almost all universities, there is fundamental lack of interplay between the universities and the private sector. This is one of the greatest weaknesses of Korea's national system for industrial innovation. Unlike universities in advanced countries that play a major role in basic as well as applied research that have important bearings on industrial R&D, almost all Korean universities suffer from insufficient facilities and their faculty members have neither the time nor the incentives to undertake serious research. Consequently, universities have lost the confidence of the private sectors, drawing almost no research funds from business circles. The government, as a way to promote university–industry cooperation, opened its NRPs to universities but universities participated in only 6 of 255 projects in 1984, involving

W.194 million, or less than 1% of total NRP expenditure (KAIST, 1986). In short, university–industry R&D cooperation in the formal sense of the term has been insignificant. But informal collaborations in the form of consultancy by individual faculty members are quite prevalent. This may be symptomatic of Korea's position as a catchup country, where technological tasks are not yet at the frontier.

Intercorporate Cooperation

A major form of intercorporate R&D cooperation is industrial research cooperatives. The technology Development Promotion Act of 1977 promotes the formation of such cooperatives, but it was not until 1982 that the first such cooperative emerged in response to direct R&D subsidies offered by NRPs. Eleven cooperatives emerged in the first year. By mid-1989, 46 industrial research cooperatives were founded involving 986 firms, 759 of which are small and medium-sized firms. The government offers various tax incentives to promote R&D cooperatives. Most existing cooperatives, however, are in name only with little substance. NRPs and IBTDPs are used as instruments to bring about effective intercorporate R&D cooperation by inviting R&D cooperatives to undertake joint research with public R&D institutes, but they neither have adequate R&D facilities nor full-time researchers to take advantage of subsidies to R&D cooperatives.

Technological Strategy of the Private Sector

As *chaebols* have been a driving force in expanding production and exports in the 1960s and 1970s, they also play a pivotal role in developing high-technology industries in Korea in the 1980s. In doing so, *chaebols* have aggressively diversified their sourcing of technologies. First, several major *chaebols* have set up outposts in Silicon Valley in California to "leapfrog" into state-of-the-art technologies by monitoring technological changes and to acquire advanced semiconductor and computer technologies. California also gave another advantage to *chaebols* by solving the most obvious obstacle to Korea's high-technology adventures—lack of experienced scientists and engineers for high-technology industries. California is populated by thousands of top-notch scientists and engineers who are Korean-Americans. Leading *chaebols* have lured away some of the best. Many of them left Korea more than a decade ago, earned Ph.D.s in America's best universities, and rose through the ranks of such leading U. S. concerns as IBM, Fairchild, Intel, and National Semiconductor. The well-financed Korean *chaebols* gave them challenging jobs and attractive compensation packages without their having to leave their American life-styles and with considerable independence. For example, Hyundai's first step on entering industrial electronics was establishing a subsidiary—Modern Electrosystems in Sunnyvale, California—manned mostly by Korean-American holders of Ph.D.s and research veterans of top U. S. semiconductor makers. Samsung also established two subsidiaries in Silicon Valley to undertake R&D activities in microelectronics and biotechnology fields, led by several Ph.D.-holding Korean-Americans, with the rest being native American engineers. Another Korean-owned start-up, ID Focus of Santa Clara, undertook market research and industrial design for Daewoo Electronics and Daewoo Telecom with a staff composed entirely of Americans. Lucky-Goldstar also established two subsidiaries for semiconductor/computer and biotechnology R&D. These subsidiaries are engaged mainly in

R&D activities for mass production in Korea. These outposts in California also serve as an "antenna" for information on research activities in advanced countries and as training posts for scientists and engineers from R&D centers and manufacturing plants in Korea (Kim, 1987).

Second, it is also *chaebols* that have successfully developed ties with multinationals, which provide important inputs in developing Korea's high technologies. Multinationals from advanced countries are looking at Korea to form consortiums for technology cooperation, as Korea is very weak in basic design and basic science but has an international competitive edge in manufacturing and process technologies. Multinationals in high-technology areas such as IBM, Hewlett-Packard, Honeywell, ATT, Monsanto, Hitachi, and Toshiba, have recently established joint ventures with Korean *chaebols* in high-technology industries. *Chaebols* have also entered extensive licensing ties with foreign high technology firms.

Third, *chaebols* developed closer ties with local public R&D institutes in the 1980s than the previous decades. Capabilities available in the public R&D institutes became relevant to *chaebols'* efforts to develop high-technology industries.

Fourth, *chaebols* have also invested aggressively in developing in-house R&D activities in order not only to absorb, assimilate, and adapt imported technologies from their outposts in Silicon Valley and from multinational partners but also to strengthen their own innovative activities. For example, Samsung set up 12 new R&D centers in the country during the 1980s, including Samsung Advanced Institute of Technology and Samsung Integrated R&D center. In 1989 alone, Samsung spent $900 million, Hyundai and Lucky-Goldstar spent $600 million each, and Daewoo spent about $300 million in R&D. Approximately 80% of the investment went for electric and electronics, about 18% for chemicals, and the remaining 2% for other fields. These four largest *chaebols* accounted for most of the nation's total industrial R&D. Leading *chaebols* have relative advantage over small or medium-sized firms in recruiting scarce, high-caliber human resources by offering attractive compensation and the best opportunities for career development among Korean firms. It is these *chaebols* that lure foreign-educated Korean scientists and engineers to their R&D centers in Korea and that recruit the top graduates from Korea's best universities. Leading scientists and engineers in *chaebols'* R&D centers and technology planning posts at headquarters are almost all foreign-educated Ph.D.s often with extensive experience at major multinational firms in advanced countries. *Chaebols* also invest most ambitiously in training to upgrade their human resources.

With the technological network, high-caliber scientific and engineering manpower, and ambitious R&D investment, *chaebols* took a leading role in moving toward the technological frontier. Illustrations in some of high-technology industries such as semiconductors, telecommunications, robotics, computers, and aircraft might shed light on how *chaebols* have managed to acquire technological capabilities to start and grow in these industries in the 1980s.

First, Korea has long participated in the semiconductor industry, involving merely simple packaging processes—bonded assembly processing by wholly owned foreign subsidiaries or joint ventures, with all parts and components imported from the parent companies and reexported back to the consignors. Then, it made a technical leap to the production of VLSI (very large-scale integrated circuit) in 1983. Large *chaebols* started the heavy betting to build a semiconductor industry and the odds were

CAPABILITY BUILDING IN KOREA

stacked in their favor: a ready access to funds syphoned from cash-cow industries, a motivated and highly skilled work force recruited from abroad, and a low labor–cost advantage. But most important of all, there were a number of distressed small semiconductor companies in the United States that were ready to sell what Korea's *chaebols* needed most—chip designs and processes—in attempts to fuel cash for survival. Samsung Semiconductor's 64K DRAM (dynamic random access memory) technology was licensed from Boisie, Idaho-based Micron Technologies, enabling Samsung to hit the market with 64K DRAM some 18 months after the first Japanese ones became commercially available. Design for Samsung's high-speed CMOS process was picked up for $2.1 million from Zytrex of California. Samsung then turned to Mostek for its 256K DRAM design. Goldstar Semiconductor signed a licensing agreement with Advanced Micron Devices in Silicon Valley for chip designs. ATT, the joint venture partner, was a source of design technology for 1M DRAM. Hyundai turned to Vitelic of San Jose for designs of 1M and 256K DRAM as well as for a variety of SRAM (static) designs. Daewoo, the fourth member of the *chaebol* chip club, got its window on the business in 1985 by injecting some $18 million into the ailing Zymos Corp, acquiring 51% equity. Silicon wafers, the most important input for chipmaking, are produced by two local firms: Korsil, a joint venture with Monsanto, and Lucky Advanced Materials, which licensed wafer processing technology from Siltec of California (now owned by Mitsubishi Metals). In short, *chaebols* relied mainly on foreign firms for design and process technologies.

Another important factor that made Korea possible to take root in the semiconductor industry was export restraints imposed on Japan after trade friction with the United States and the subsequent move upmarket by Japanese firms, opening up opportunities for Korean firms to penetrate the U. S. market. This was also true of consumer electronics and subcompact cars (Porter, 1990).

The chipmaking firms made enormous investment in both production facilities and R&D. By the end of 1988, four semiconductor producers invested over $1.3 billion in new facility investment. Total R&D expenditures increased dramatically, from $13 million in 1983 to $95 million in 1987, accounting for 10 and 22% of the total investment, respectively. Industry's aggressive R&D spending cut down Japan's lead. For example, Korea was just 6 months behind Japan in introducing the 1M DRAM.

But the road ahead was getting bumpier and is even more so today. Texas Instruments filed a suit against Samsung and eight Japanese chipmakers for infringing on its patents for DRAM designs in 1986, while Intel Corp filed a similar suit against Hyundai and its American design suppliers. Both Samsung and Hyundai ended up paying royalties on past and future sales of their memory products. Furthermore, work on the next generation of chips—the 4M DRAM—meant exploring the frontiers of semiconductor technology but also competing neck-in-neck with Japanese and U. S. companies. As the stakes have risen in the chip game, the field of players has grown smaller worldwide, meaning that few, if any, of those left in the game can be counted on to sell state-of-the-art chip design technology to Korean *chaebols*. So, Koreans had to tackle the 4M DRAM design alone. To avoid duplicate research and investment, the government stepped in and designated the R&D of the 4M DRAM as a national project. A public R&D institute played the coordinating role with three *chaebols'* participation. Samsung was the first among three *chaebols* that announced its completion of designing 4M DRAM in 1989 and 16M DRAM in 1990, only a few months after Japan.

Second, electronic switching system (ESS) and optical fiber/cable may be high-technology products in telecommunications. The Korean government (the sole buyer) decided in 1981 to shift public telephone switching from an electrical direct dialing (EDD) system to ESS in 1981. Lacking the technological capability to enter ESS production, three *chaebols* and one medium-sized firm entered foreign collaborations—two in the form of joint venture and the other two by licensing—to locally assemble foreign-designed ESS equipment. While the local producers had progressively increased the local content ratio for ESS, raising as much as 76% for some of the models by 1986, a public R&D institute organized a consortium with the four firms to develop Korea's own rural (low-density) ESS system (Time Division Exchange or TDX-1). Production experience of foreign systems plus high-caliber Korean engineering manpower recruited from abroad blended together. On completion, the design technology was transferred to the participating firms for production. TDX-1 has replaced a Swedish model since 1987. The consortium produced an improved version (TDX-1B) and exported it to the Philippines. At the same time, the consortium is undertaking a project to develop a high-density system (TDX-10) for urban use.

When Corning Glass refused to transfer optical fiber production technology to Korea in 1977, two *chaebol* copper cable producers entered a joint R&D project with a public R&D institute. After 7 years of R&D, the locally developed optical cable was tested successfully on a 35-km route in 1983. Although this local effort eventually grounded to a halt due mainly to slow progress in R&D, it nonetheless helped local firms gain bargaining power in acquiring foreign technology on favorable terms. Four *chaebols* entered licensing agreements with multinationals in 1984: Samsung with IT&T, Goldstar with AT&T, Daewoo with Canada's Northern Telecom, and Taihan with Japan's Sumitomo.

Third, Korea took an independent, reverse engineering route in developing robotics in early years. Again four leading *chaebols*—Hyundai, Samsung, Goldstar, and Daewoo—have dominated the industry. The first batch of welding robotics for *chaebol's* automobile assemblers, shipbuilders, and aerospace firms were all imported. The first batch of automatic part inserting robotics for largest electronics firms were all imported. But the users of these imported robotics were active assimilators of imported technology. Based on operating experience of foreign models and capability gained from in-house R&D efforts, they developed imitative models first to meet the subsequent needs within the plant and then to meet increasing demand within their *chaebol* groups. In contrast, some smaller *chaebols* recently entered the industry as a local dealer of foreign models as a way to gain experience. Nevertheless, these *chaebols* stepped up their R&D efforts (over $28 million in 1987 alone) in the robotics industry with the aim of cashing in on fast-growing demand both at home and abroad, giving rapid rise to technological capability and leading to the introduction of their own models. For example, Daewoo's five-axes multiple process NOVA-10 introduced in 1984 had both quality and price competitiveness to export to the United States. As in other *chaebols,* U. S.-trained Ph.D.s played a central role in initiating and expanding the robotics business at Daewoo. The government is also mapping out a comprehensive program to boost automation-related industries such as robotics production. However, robotics technology in Korea is still confined mainly to the production of robotics for simply repetitive welding works, making it difficult to turn out highly integrated products. In response to the need for more sophisticated robotics, *chaebols* such as Hyundai and Daewoo are now pursuing technology tieups with multinationals, while public R&D institutes are undertaking advanced research in areas such as artificial intelligence, vision-sensor, six-axes robotics, and a voice-recognition system.

Fourth, the computer industry has also undergone a similar route in Korea. *Chaebols* with experience in consumer electronics entered the industry through imitative reverse engineering, leading to the introduction of IBM PC (personal computer) clones. These *chaebols* rapidly expanded their businesses as OEM (original equipment manufacture) producers. Smaller *chaebols* without consumer electronics background entered first as a local dealer/service agent as a way to accumulate experience in computer technology and gradually backward integrated to the design and production of their own models (Kim et al., 1987). With a good grip on the chip business and microcomputers, Korea now tackles another national project: the design and manufacture of Korea's own super-minicomputers. Again, a team of software and hardware engineers from a public R&D institute and a number of *chaebols* have been formed to work on the project. The basic idea of the super-mini project is to buy and transplant foreign technology, in this case a super-mini design from one of the U. S. venture firms, and to progressively localize design capability.

Fifth, *chaebols* also dominate the aircraft industry. Korea's rudimentary experience in aircraft technology stemmed largely from international subcontracting and maintenance. Boeing and other U. S. aircraft makers that used Japan as a manufacturing base for bodies, parts, and components have shifted their sourcing to Korea in the facing of rising Yen. Three *chaebols* entered into close relations with U. S. manufacturers. For instance, Daewoo has supplied outer fuselages, side cockpit panels, and central fins to General Dynamics. Daewoo has also supplied upper decks for Boeing 747s and inspar wing ribs, and wing part components for Boeing-737s and wing and tail parts for a new U. S. fighter to Lockheed. Korean Air, which has accumulated aircraft technology from maintenance service of such U. S. military fighters as the F-15, F-16, and F-5 Phantom, has supplied wing tip extensions for Boeing and sheet metal assemblies for McDonnel-Douglas. In addition, Daewoo entered a joint venture with Sikorsky and Samsung exchanged a memorandum of understanding with Bell to produce helicopters in Korea for Korean military and for exports under OEM basis. These *chaebols* will participate in manufacturing the next mainstay fighters for the Korean Air Force. The U. S. government proposed that Korea buys 12 fighters as finished airplanes, produces 36 through kit assembly, and manufactures the remainder under license. Through this process, Korea hopes to acquire enough technological capability to develop its own aircraft. *Chaebols* have intensified their R&D efforts in order to assimilate foreign technologies. The Korean government also takes an active role in promoting the industry: the government legislated in 1987 Aerospace Industry Development Law and established Aerospace Technology Institute as a way to support R&D activities of the private sector.

In short, *chaebols* have deliberately taken a path—from reverse engineering to international tieups and to own research and development—to expedite and cost-minimize in acquiring technological capability in high-technology industries. When technological tasks were relatively simple, they opted to reverse-engineer foreign products. The robotics and computer industries in early years may be good examples. When technological tasks were beyond their capacity, they quickly turned to multinationals, which were willing to share technologies with Korea for various reasons. The semi-conductor, electronic switching, aircraft industries in the beginning, and the robotics, computer, and optical fiber industries in the later stage may fit this case. When Korea approached the technological frontier, where few multinationals were willing to share their technologies, Korea consolidated its efforts to develop its own products. The recent development of the 4M DRAM may be a case in point. During this process, public R&D institutes have played a pivotal role in giving rise to the bargaining power of *chaebols* in acquiring foreign technologies and in coordinating joint research efforts with *chaebols*.

Although a complaint is mounting that *chaebols* dominate high-technology industries like they did in many other sectors in the past, this dominance is considered inevitable at the initial stage owing to the great deal of risk and investment and to the absence of research-oriented universities that may incubate technical entrepreneurs who might start small technology-based venture firms. There are, however, some indications that a few venture businesses have recently appeared in high-technology fields. Expanding investment in basic research at universities, increased availability of venture capital, increasingly conducive economic environment created by the government, and the fact that *chaebols* cannot dominate a wide range of application technologies will hopefully lead to a strong appearance of small-sized venture businesses in Korea in the near future.

Other Issues

There are two other issues worth covering here: the effects of military R&D on industrial innovation and the formation of hi-tech "valleys." First, given the threat of hostilities with North Korea, national security has been one of the major concerns in Korea, making the home market unusually sophisticated and demanding. As a way to mitigate the effects of constraints imposed by foreign weapon suppliers on national security and to ensure military independence, the Korean government in the 1970s launched an ambitious program to build up local capability to develop weaponry. Its budget size was, however, $114 million in 1988, only 0.2% of that in the United States and 4% of that in France. The percent of military R&D budget to total military expenditures was only 1.5% in Korea compared to over 10% in France and the United States. The nature of projects, however, has been kept strictly confidential. And R&D has been undertaken almost strictly within the military: only 1.48% of military R&D budget was allotted to universities in 1988 (NDC, 1990). Such isolated military R&D activities appear to have suffered from lack of interaction with the rest of Korea's S&T infrastructure and also from competitive disadvantages vis-à-vis public and corporate R&D institutes in recruiting highly qualified scientists and engineers. As a result, the ambitious program has been drastically scaled down in the 1980s. The private sector is involved in manufacturing some traditional weaponry, but the spillover effects of such operations on industrial innovation appear to have been quite negligible.

Second, the government created two high-technology centers: Seoul Science Park and Daeduck Science Town, 200 km south of Seoul. Seoul Science Park started with three R&D institutes and three economic research institutes but has failed to attract private R&D centers in the vicinity. Furthermore, one of the three R&D institutes has relocated, while the second one will be relocated within a few years.

In contrast, the government has actively promoted the development of Daeduck Science Town, where it has located nine public R&D institutes and three tertiary educational institutions and attracted four private R&D laboratories. About 20 major firms plan to locate their central R&D laboratories in the Town within a few years, making the Town the first high-technology "valley" in the country.

In addition, there are signs in different parts of the country that corporate R&D laboratories in some fields tend to cluster together in the same vicinity. For example, semiconductor R&D centers and biotechnology R&D centers cluster near Seoul, telecommunications R&D laboratories near Kumi, which is known as an electronics industrial zone, and new materials R&D centers near Pohang, where POSCO has its first steel plant and its own research-oriented private university. It may be premature to regard them as high-technology "valleys" at this point but they appear to be in the incubation stage.

CONCLUDING REMARKS

Korea has been transformed from a subsistent agricultural economy into a newly industrializing one in a very short span of time. During the transformation process, Korea's economic environment has changed drastically. Protectionist moves in North America and Europe are making it increasingly difficult for Korea to sustain export growth in the industries that have led Korea's outward-looking economic strategy in the past. These countries have also put pressure on Korea to liberalize its domestic economy, forcing Korea to compete against multinationals not only in international markets but also in its domestic market. At the same time, Korea's competitiveness in labor-intensive industries had been rapidly eroded by rising real wages. Other developing countries with much lower wage rates are rapidly catching up with Korea in labor-intensive industries. Furthermore, industrialized countries, particularly Japan, are increasingly reluctant to transfer technology to Korea (Kim, 1988).

The rapid changes in economic environment have not given Korea enough time to make and consolidate a major shift in designing an appropriate national system for industrial innovation. The government has introduced in the 1980s various new policy instruments in an attempt to develop a new national system, which is yet at the formative stage. Furthermore, a consensus on the method of redesigning the institutional system and on drastic increases in resource allocation for R&D expenditure is difficult to be made. At the same time, the traditionally teaching-oriented universities could not easily be transformed into research-oriented institutions, giving gloomy implications for generating high-caliber scientists and engineers, let alone university–industry cooperation. If the formation of skilled workers in the 1950s were an important leading indicator for the subsequent development in the 1960s and 1970s, then the poor health of universities and the resultant lack of high-caliber human resources in the 1980s may be a critical warning signal for the 1990s and on.

The government took the initiatives in the 1960s and 1970s in directing and driving the private sector to achieve growth by fostering the formation of large *chaebols* through the allocation of projects and resources. This scheme appears to have helped in bringing about an economy of scale in the stable, mature industries and achieving outward-looking objectives in the past. At the same time, however, the same scheme gave rise to highly concentrated economic power within a limited number of *chaebols* and stifled the growth of small and medium-sized industries. These *chaebols* may be in an advantageous position in the 1980s in developing such industries as semiconductors and aircraft, which require a large investment. The highly concentrated market structure has, however, curtailed the market dynamism. Furthermore, highly bureaucratized large *chaebols,* which effectively functioned in the stable industries in the past, now find themselves rigid and slow in adapting to rapid changes in technology and market. Some *chaebols* have, nonetheless, managed to build up their capability to cope with the changing economic environment. They began investing heavily in R&D to give rise to existing capability in order to design and manufacture "next stage" products. But most others are highly dependent on foreign sources for new technologies.

Another problem in Korean economy is the vital missing link in the presence of related and especially supporting industries. *Chaebols* have largely focused their efforts in end products with heavy dependence on imported parts and machinery. The problem, as Porter (1990) notes, is not the cost of inputs but the effects on the innovation process. Without fluid supports from capable domestic suppliers, Korean firms will remain behind in product and process innovations.

Korea is, indeed, at the crossroad. While the government and private sector exert their efforts to redesign the national system for industrial innovation and in turn to sustain the nation's economic growth by strengthening Korea's technological capabilities, there are several critical signs, as mentioned above, that have led Korea to a serious economic crisis since 1989 and that may impede its future development.

NOTE

1. Exceptions are Korea Advanced Institute of Science and Technology (KAIST), a graduate school of applied science, and Korea Institute of Technology (KIT), an undergraduate school within the KAIST system, both of which are under the jurisdiction of MOST. All other universities and colleges are under the jurisdiction of the Ministry of Education (MOE). Another exception is POSTEC, a new research-oriented school of science and technology established by Pohang Iron and Steel Corporation (POSCO), one of the most cost-competitive steel companies in the world.

REFERENCES

Amsden, A. H. (1989). *Asia's Next Giant: South Korea and Late Industrialization.* New York: Oxford University Press.

Baranson, J. (1973). "The Drive Toward Technological Self-Sufficiency in Developing Countries." Paper presented at the Conference on Latin America-United States Economic Interactions: Conflict, Accommodation, and Policies for the Future, at the University of Texas at Austin, March 19.

Business Korea (1990). "Balancing Workers' Interests against the Nations." February, p. 31.

Chenery, H. Robinson, S., and Syrquin, M. (1986).

Industrialization and Growth: A Comparative Study. New York: Oxford University Press.

Dahlman, C. J., and Frischtak, C. R. (1990). "National Systems Supporting Technical Advanced in Industry: The Brazilian Experience." Paper presented at National Technical System Conference at Stanford University, October 18–19.

Harbison, Frederick, H., and Myers, C. S. (1964). *Education, Manpower, and Economic Growth.* New York: McGraw-Hill.

Hou, C. M., and Gee, S. (1990). "National Systems Supporting Technical Advance in Industry—The Case of Taiwan." Paper presented at National Technical System Conference at Stanford University on October 18–19.

Jung, K. H. (1989). "Business-Government Relations in Korea." In K. H. Chung and H. C. Lee (eds.), *Korean Managerial Dynamics,* 11–26. New York: Praeger.

KAIST (Korea Advanced Institute of Science and Technology) (1986). *Urinara Kwahak Gisul Gebal Systemeo Jeonge Gwajungkwa Jeonmang.* (A Study on Science and Technology Development System in Korea and Its Future Direction). Seoul: Ministry of Science and Technology.

Katz, J., and Bercovich, N. A. (1990). "Science, Technology and Socioeconomic Re-structuring: The Case of Argentina." Paper presented at National Technical System Conference at Stanford University, October 18–19.

KEB (Korea Exchange Bank) (1987). "Direct Foreign Investment in Korea." *Monthly Review* October, 3–13.

Kim, K. S., and Roemer, M. (1979). *Growth and Structural Transformation.* Cambridge, MA: Council on East Asian Studies, Harvard University Press.

Kim, L. (1980). "Stages of Development of Industrial Technology in a LDC: A Model." *Research Policy* 9:254–77.

Kim, L. (1987). *Technological Transformation in Korea: Progress Achieved and Problems Ahead.* Helsinki: World Institute for Development Economic Research, mimeo.

Kim, L. (1988). "Korea's Acquisition of Technological Capability for Internationalization: Macro and Micro Factors." *Business Review* 22(1): 183–97.

Kim, L. (1989). "Science and Technology Policies for Industrialization in Korea." In J. Suh (ed.), *Strategies for Industrial Development,* 255–272. Kuala Lumpur: Asia and Pacific Development Council.

Kim , L., and Kim, Y. (1985). "Innovation in a Newly Industrializing Country: A Multiple Discriminant Analysis." *Management Science* 31(3): 312–22.

Kim, L., and Lee, H. (1987). "Patterns of Technological Change in a Rapidly Developing Country: A Synthesis." *Technovation* 6:261–76.

Kim, L., Lee, J. and Lee, J. (1987) "Korea's Entry into the Computer Industry and Its Acquisition of Technological Capability." *Technovation* 6(4):277–93.

Kim, Y., Kim, L., and Lee, J. (1989). "Innovation Strategy of Local Pharmaceutical Firms in Korea: A Multivariate Analysis." *Technology Analysis & Strategic Management* 1(1):29–44.

KIRI (Korea Industrial Research Institutes) (1989). *Major Indicators of Industrial Technology.* Seoul: KIRI.

Lee, K. U., Urata, S. and Choi, I. (1986). "Recent Development in Industrial Organizational Issues in Korea." Mimeo, Korea Development Institute and the World Bank, Washington, D.C.

Mason, E. S., Perkins, D. H. Kim, K. S. Cole, D. C. and Kim, M. J. (1980). *The Economic and Social Modernization of the Republic of Korea.* Cambridge, MA: Council on East Asian Studies, Harvard University Press.

McGinn, N. F., Snodgrass, D. R., Kim, Y. B., Kim, S. B. and Kim, Q.-Y. (1980). *Education and Development in Korea.* Cambridge, MA: Council on East Asian Studies, Harvard University Press.

MOST (Ministry of Science and Technology) (various years). *Science and Technology Annals.* Seoul: MOST

NAS (National Academy of Sciences) (1973). *U. S. International Firms and R,D&E in Developing Countries.* Washington, D. C.: National Academy of Sciences.

NDC (National Defence College) (1990). *Gukbang yungu gebalkwa mingan yungu gebaleo gyunge ganghwa bangane kwanhan yungu.* (A proposal to strengthen the link between military and industrial R&D). Seoul: KIST Center for Science and Technology Policy.

Ozawa, T. (1974). *Japan's Technological Challenge to the West, 1950–1974: Motivation and Accomplishment.* Cambridge, MA: MIT Press.

Porter, M. E. (1990). *The Competitive Advantage of Nations.* New York: The Free Press.

Shishido, T. (1972). *Japanese Policies for Science and Technology.* Tokyo: Nikko Research Center, mimeo.

Westphal, L. E., Kim, L. and Dahlman, C. (1985). "Reflections on the Republic of Korea's Acquisition of Technological Capability." In N. Rosenberg and C. Frischtak (eds.), *International Technology Transfer: Concepts, Measures, and Comparisons* 167–221. New York: Praeger.

Yakushiji, T. (1977). *Dynamics of Policy Interventions: Government and Automobile Industry in Japan, 1900–1960.* Ph.D. dissertation, MIT, Cambridge, MA.

12

National Systems Supporting Technical Advance in Industry: The Case of Taiwan

CHI-MING HOU
SAN GEE

The Taiwan model of economic development has attracted worldwide attention. Taiwan's record of economic growth has been phenomenal and the fruits of economic growth have been widely shared by all income groups on the island. Furthermore, the improvement of the material well-being of the people was accomplished in a climate of high consumer sovereignty without undue government control, high economic stability without serious inflation or unemployment, and financial solvency without foreign debt. Also, a high degree of structural transformation took place and caused a shift from primary to secondary industries. Some countries have done as well as Taiwan in some of these areas but few, if any, have done as well as Taiwan in all of them.

It is not our intention to propagandize Taiwan's performance, but we wish to explore the role of technology in assisting Taiwan's economic achievement as we described above. As a newly industrializing country in Asia, Taiwan has been promoting technology development, which is considered one of the most important strategies for her overall economic development. However, unlike the developed countries, in Taiwan, an immediate difficulty blocking the promotion of technology development has been, and still is, the lack of skilled technicians and qualified researchers.

Furthermore, it is well known that Taiwan's economy mainly consists of small and medium enterprises (SMEs). Under such circumstances, the immediate questions that the government has to face are: Will the SMEs be able to survive given the rapid technological development in the rest of the world? Will these SMEs be capable of conducting enough research and development (R&D) to sustain their long-term competitiveness? What are the SME's major sources of technology in Taiwan? What are the possible policy options that the government has in promoting technological development among SMEs?

Because of the rapid development in science and technology, which in turn improves telecommunications and transportation, the world's economies have been quickly integrated into one unit. As such, the development of science and technology is critical to the international competitiveness both of firms and of the country. In this chapter we look at some of the technological-development experiences of Taiwan, which we hope could be useful to other developing countries as well as to further research in this field.

SOURCES OF ECONOMIC GROWTH

What has contributed to the fast growth in Taiwan? Undoubtedly a great deal of research remains to be done before an answer can be advanced, if indeed such an answer can be found at all. Work ethics, the high propensity to save, the emphasis on education, the early adoption of an outward-looking development strategy, land reform, the crucial role of foreign aid in the early stages of development, and the favorable international economic environment have all been emphasized, in various degrees, as among the most important factors contributing to Taiwan's economic success.[1] In our view, however, technological improvement, especially by the SMEs, has played the most crucial role.

We recognize it is extremely difficult to substantiate any hypothesis on the sources of economic growth, but if the Solow-type method is used, it may be computed that nearly 54% of the growth in gross domestic product from 1952 to 1979 was due to technological improvements (or the "residual"), and only 29% has been due to labor growth and 18% to capital growth.[2]

Another way of looking at this matter is through an analysis of labor productivity. For manufacturing, average labor productivity in Taiwan grew at 7.38% a year in 1953–1961, 9.15% in 1962–1971, and 3.84% in 1972–1981. For the entire period from 1953 to 1981, it grew at an average rate of 6.77% a year.[3]

Undoubtedly, the increase in the capital–labor ratio contributed to a part of the increase in labor productivity. For during the period 1953–1980, it increased at 2.8% a year.[4] Admittedly, data on capital and employment are weak, but the increase in labor productivity cannot be totally accounted for by the rising capital–labor ratio.

The improvement in the quality of the labor force must also have contributed to the increase in labor productivity. Education has played a crucial role in the improvement of the quality of the labor force. The cognitive and affective skills produced by education have contributed to efficiency in the production process, increased the labor force participation rate of women, and facilitated labor mobility, all contributing to improvement in labor productivity.[5] Available evidence suggests that the earnings of employees and workers are positively correlated with educational attainment and that earnings are basically determined by labor productivity as labor market is, or at least has been, highly competitive.[6]

The increase in the educational level of the labor force in Taiwan has been remarkable. In 1952, 42.1% of the population aged six or older were illiterate. The proportion dropped to 14.7% in 1970 and 7.4% in 1988. The proportion of the population 6 years of age or older with a secondary education was 8.8% in 1952, 26.5% in 1970, and 44.2% in 1988. The proportion of the population 6 years of age or older with a higher education was 1.4% in 1952, 3.7% in 1970, and 10.1% in 1988.[7]

Technology alone can never make a contribution to production, however crucial it may be. It has to be embodied in the labor force or capital before it can become effective. It is the sharp improvement in the quality of the labor force and the fast accumulation of capital that has enabled technology to play such a key role in the economic growth of Taiwan.[8]

But what has brought about the improvement in technology? And who has introduced this new technology to Taiwan?

THE INITIAL BASE

It is sometimes suggested that a principal reason Taiwan has been able to achieve what it has economically was the solid economic foundation that Japan had laid down before withdrawing from Taiwan in 1945. This view is, however, unfounded.

During the period of Japanese occupation from 1895 to 1945, Taiwan was always regarded as a colony that supplied raw materials and agricultural products to Japan and as a market for Japanese manufactured goods. There was never any intention on the part of Japan to industrialize Taiwan. Culturally, Japan aimed at replacing local and Chinese values, institutions, and traditions with Japanese ones.

Thus, the Chinese people as well as the native aborigines had to learn the Japanese language, and very few of them were allowed to receive schooling beyond the high school level. Those who were lucky enough to go to a college or a university were allowed to study only agriculture or commerce; they were not allowed to study engineering or the natural sciences. It is obvious that the Japanese rulers did not want the Chinese or the aborigines to acquire advanced industrial knowledge or technology.

Consequently, for the few industries that there were, they were completely under Japanese management and control. When Japan was defeated in 1945, virtually all the Japanese soldiers and citizens left Taiwan for Japan, and took with them their industrial technologies.

This is not to say that Japan did not make any contributions to Taiwan during the period of their colonial rule. Japan did set up transportation, electrical, and public health facilities and improved agricultural technology. Furthermore, under Japanese rule, primary education was widespread.

The fact that the Chinese people were forced to learn the Japanese language has also had a positive effect on Taiwan's economic development since 1945. Many industrial leaders in Taiwan grew up during the Japanese occupation. Their ability to speak and read the Japanese language and their knowledge of Japanese culture have greatly helped to facilitate Japanese investment in Taiwan and Taiwan–Japan trade, and to acquire Japanese technology in the course of Taiwan's economic development over the past 40 years or so.

It should be noted that Taiwan got a great deal of help from those Chinese who left the Chinese mainland for the island, especially after 1949. More than 2 million Chinese mainlanders came to Taiwan with the Chinese National Government. Many of them were soldiers, but a number of them were teachers, professors, businessmen, industrialists, and government officials. They were the cream of the crop of their respective groups and had been trained and had acquired experience in industrial management and technology, education, administration, and the like while in the mainland. There is little doubt that these people made a great contribution to the increases in industrial technology and development in Taiwan.

But still, the industrial base in Taiwan in the 1950s was extremely weak. All that

Taiwan was capable of exporting was principally sugar, rice, and bananas. Per capita GNP was only U S$145 in 1951, much less than that of many contemporary developing countries in Asia and Latin America. In 1988, per capita GNP was U S$6333, and, in 1989, it was estimated to be U S$7571, much higher than that of many countries that were ahead of Taiwan in 1951.

THE ECONOMIC ENVIRONMENT AND THE CHARACTERISTICS OF THE FIRMS IN TAIWAN

After the nationalist government retreated from mainland China to Taiwan, the government took over those enterprises established by the Japanese. Taiwan's economy was thus dominated by publicly owned enterprises, encompassing the power generation, petroleum, shipbuilding, sugar and agriculture products sectors, and so on. Furthermore, the statistics show that publicly owned enterprises accounted for 56.2% of total industrial value-added in 1952. There is no doubt that in those days, the publicly owned enterprises in Taiwan had capital, manpower, and technology.

By the late 1950s to the early 1960s, the situation began to change. The import substitution policies adopted in the 1950s had proven that they could not sustain rapid economic growth in a limited local market, like that of Taiwan. The efficiency problem of the publicly owned enterprises together with low factory utilization rates also called for readjustment. To react to this, the government adopted an export-promotion policy. Under this policy, the sluggish economy was not only revitalized but the policy also changed the industrial structure in Taiwan's economy.

The transformation of the industrial structure in Taiwan can be understood from the following statistics: the share of agriculture in net domestic product declined from 38.3% in 1953 to 18.0% in 1970, 9.2% in 1980 and 6.1% in 1988. The corresponding share accounted for by industry (manufacturing, construction, electricity, gas, and water) increased from 17.7% in 1953 to 34.5% in 1970, 44.7% in 1980, and 46.2% in 1988. In terms of employment, the share of agriculture was 55.6% in 1953, 36.7% in 1970, 19.5% in 1980, and 13.7% in 1988. The corresponding share of industry increased from 17.6% in 1953 to 28.0% in 1970, 42.4% in 1980, and 42.6% in 1988.

From an international trade point of view, it was in Taiwan's comparative advantage to develop labor-intensive industries, as they can be operated on a smaller scale with less capital investment. Therefore, under the export promotion policy, the small-scale private enterprises concentrating on labor-intensive industries began to flourish and quickly became the backbone of Taiwan's economy. The importance of the private sector in Taiwan can be seen in the following statistics: the share of private-enterprise value-added was 56.2% in the manufacturing sector in 1960; the comparable ratios were 84.7% for 1971 and 89.8% for 1987. In 1987, the publicly owned enterprises accounted for only 10.2% of the total value-added in the manufacturing sector, in dramatic contrast to what it was in the 1950s.

But the role of the publicly owned enterprises was also critical during the above development process. Generally speaking, publicly owned enterprises have played a supportive role in the development of private enterprises. These enterprises have often served as upstream suppliers providing stable, reliable, and low-cost raw materials to the downstream private manufacturers. Therefore, the upstream publicly owned

enterprises are actually integrated with the predominantly private downstream manufactures whereby supporting their development.

The strength of the SMEs in Taiwan can be understood from the following statistics: in 1985 there were 119,073 enterprises in the manufacturing sector in Taiwan,
however, 98.8% of them were considered to be SMEs for their paid in capital was less
than 1 million U. S. dollars; furthermore, these SMEs accounted for 28.9% of total
domestic sales and 71.1% of total earnings from export sales. Clearly, SMEs in Taiwan
are highly export oriented.

The implications of SMEs on technology development are as follows: first,
because most of the SMEs in Taiwan were developed initially based on some simple
labor-intensive processing technologies, their technology levels are generally rather
low. But as the unemployment rate dropped to less than 3% in 1971 and the economy
reached the full-employment level, the rapid increase in wages has gradually weakened
the comparative advantage of the SMEs in the labor-intensive industries. In fact, the
situation is getting worse as the shortage in unskilled labor became obvious in the
1980s. Therefore, the shortage of unskilled labor accompanied by soaring wages has
exerted tremendous pressure on the SMEs either to upgrade their technological level
or to produce higher value-added products, or both. Clearly, the SMEs in Taiwan are
now facing greater technological challenges than ever before.

Second, most of the SMEs in Taiwan have devoted relatively little resources to
research and development (R&D) due to their limited amount of capital and manpower resources. The question then is how can these SMEs compete with the other
major players in the world? Furthermore, given their limited technological capability
and limited endowment of resources, they have very little to offer to major foreign
players in the forming of strategic alliances in order to gain access to advance technology.

There is no doubt that both the entrepreneurs and the government in Taiwan
must react positively to these problems given the rapid technological development
throughout the world. In the next several sections, we wish to discuss various policies
adopted by both enterprises and the government to react to these challenges.

SOURCES OF TECHNOLOGY AND THE ROLE OF FDI ENTERPRISES

As we mentioned above, due to the various difficulties that SMEs might encounter
during the process of technological development, one of the easiest ways for them to
develop technology is to become affiliated with a major (foreign) manufacturer thus
becoming their OEM (original equipment manufacturing) supplier. Many of the
SMEs in Taiwan are satisfied with such an arrangement because they not only make
an acceptable level of profit but also avoid the risk involved in developing the technology by themselves.

The SMEs who are engaging in OEM or "technological cooperation" with foreign
firms in Taiwan frequently form alliances with Japanese firms. Taiwan's historical
background, as we discussed before, is one good reason for such a phenomenon. In
terms of foreign direct investment (FDI) in Taiwan, beginning in the early 1980s,
Japan topped the United States and became the largest FDI country investing in Taiwan.

By looking at FDI statistics, it can be seen that during the period 1952 to 1987, electronics, metal products, chemical products, and machinery and instruments were the top four industries that attracted the majority of FDI in Taiwan. In terms of the average amount of investment, the European firms invested the most, followed by U. S. and Japanese firms.

FDI enterprises in Taiwan can diffuse their technologies to domestic firms through various direct and indirect channels. One of the most typical channels for technology diffusion, from the FDI to the domestic firms, is labor mobility. One study showed, among the 161 surveyed firms in Taiwan in 1987, that hired former FDI-firm workers working as managers or technicians believed that the worker's former experience in FDI firms made a real contribution to strengthening management technology, product design, and marketing. More specifically, among these surveyed firms, 96.3% considered that those workers can make a contribution to improving their managerial technology, 85.1% of them considered that FDI workers make a contribution that improves product design, and 75.8% of them considered that FDI workers can make a contribution by improving marketing technology.[9]

Besides FDI and technical cooperation with foreign firms, there are many other sources whereby domestic firms can acquire technology. A large-scale survey was conducted by the Directorate-General of Budget Accounting and Statistics (DGBAS) of the Executive Yuan (the government) in Taiwan to study the major sources of technology of 4226 firms in manufacturing in 1985. As we can see from Table 12.1, there are 9 possible sources of technology that were listed in the survey. Of the 4226 firms 62.96% of them considered that the firm's own R&D was their major source of technology, whereas 30.64% of them considered that their technology came mainly from abroad by way of purchasing formulas and authorization or physical plants, foreign technological cooperation, foreign consultants, improving products of other countries, etc.

In Table 12.1 we organized the firms by industry and by the degree of foreign/domestic ownership. Domestic firms are denoted by DOM, firms with foreign ownership of less than 50% by FL50, and firms with foreign ownership of over 50% by FG50. As it is shown in this table, only 25.61% of DOMs consider foreign technology sources as their major channel through which to acquire technology; instead, they are more dependent on their own R&D.

Table 12.1. Percentage Distribution of Major Sources of Technology of the Firms by Industry and by Foreign Ownership[a]

	N	Total (%)	Domestic Technology			Foreign Technology						
			A	B	C	Subtotal	D	E	F	G	H	I
Total	4226	100	62.96	1.17	5.22	30.64	2.59	1.15	11.13	7.30	8.47	—
DOM	3699	100	67.35	1.28	5.73	25.61	2.32	0.96	8.05	5.39	8.89	—
FL50	207	100	38.08	0.87	3.78	57.26	3.20	0.58	31.10	14.82	7.56	—
FG50	320	100	35.95	0.22	0.89	62.90	4.94	3.59	28.09	21.57	4.71	—

[a]A, firm's own research and development; B, purchasing domestic patents; C, joint research with local research institutes; D, purchasing formula and authorization; E, purchasing the entire plant; F, foreign technology participation; G, consultancy by foreign organization; H, improving products of other countries; I, others.

Source: San (1988).

However, it is important to note that among the various sources of foreign technology, item H, namely improving products of other countries, was the most important source of foreign technology for these domestic firms. As it was vaguely defined
in the survey, we suspect that activities such as imitating, copying, or limited improvements on the existing foreign product (i.e., various reverse engineering tactics), were
their major sources of acquiring foreign technologies. Furthermore, it is reasonable to
suspect that many of the surveyed firms consider their reverse engineering efforts as
genuine R&D efforts, which undoubtedly overly exaggerates their own R&D efforts.
In contrast, firms with foreign capital participation such as FL50 or FG50 were more
heavily dependent on foreign technology through the means of foreign technology
cooperation and foreign consulting organizations and less on reverse engineering. It is
particularly significant for those FG50 firms, as their share of reverse engineering techniques under item H was very low.

The In terms of industries, for those more labor-intensive and less technology-intensive industries, such as food processing, garment, bamboo and wood products, and
paper and printing, the DOMs had lower foreign technology participation. In contrast,
for industries with higher technology intensity or more capital intensity, generally the
DOMs had higher foreign technology participation. For instance, over 30% of the
DOMs in industries such as chemical products, machinery, electronic machinery,
transportation equipment, and precision instruments reported that their major technological sources came from abroad.

The above survey results can also be examined by looking at the size of the firm.
If we consider the firms with total employees less than 100 as small firms, denoted as
Small, firms with total employees between 100 and 500 as medium-size firms, denoted
as Medium, and firms with total employees over 500 as large firms, denoted as Large,
the statistics in Table 12.2 show that the larger the firms, the more capable that they
were in attracting foreign technology, as the ratios of firms who considered foreign
technology as their major technology sources are 13.39, 27.34, and 34.45 for Small,
Medium, and Large, respectively. It should be noted that Small firms acquired technology from abroad least frequently for all of the manufacturing industries except for
the chemical products, metal, machinery, electronic machinery, transportation equipment, and precision instruments industries. Small firms in these industries had higher
foreign technology source ratios, but these industries are also more technology-intensive or capital-intensive.

Table 12.2. Percentage Distribution of Major Sources of Technology of the Firms by Size of
the Firm.[a]

	N	Total (%)	Domestic Technology			Foreign Technology						
			A	B	C	Subtotal	D	E	F	G	H	I
Total	4226	100	60.82	1.13	5.04	33.00	2.50	1.11	10.75	7.05	8.18	3.04
Small	2277	100	32.42	0.68	2.23	13.39	1.12	0.40	3.34	1.86	4.38	2.30
Medium	1597	100	42.76	0.63	3.89	27.34	2.13	1.06	10.16	6.45	5.98	1.56
Large	352	100	34.05	0.65	4.98	34.45	1.57	1.05	14.14	12.70	3.54	1.44

Source: this study.
[a]For definitions of A–I, see note *a* to Table 12.1.

By examining Small firms in the metal, machinery, electronic machinery, transportation equipment, and precision instruments industries, it is clear that item H (i.e., improving products of other countries in terms of various reverse engineering techniques) is the major source of foreign technology. Clearly, for those Small firms in the more technology-intensive industries in Taiwan, reverse engineering is still the key to acquiring technology. These firms are still far away from becoming an inventor of technology.

The larger firms have better capability in finding foreign technology cooperation partners and in inviting foreign experts as technology consultants, therefore they rely more on these two channels to acquire foreign technology. As it was found in the survey, Medium and Large firms in the manufacturing industry in Taiwan were the most common entities that either engaged in technology cooperation with foreign partners (item F) or hired foreign consultants as their major source of foreign technology.

Among the three major domestic sources of technology, namely, the firms' own research and development (A), purchasing domestic patents (B), and joint research with local research institutes (C), it is clear that the firms' own R&D in reverse engineering efforts was their most important source of technology. However, it is also clear that due to limited resources and/or diffusion channels, Small firms relied more on their own R&D efforts whereas Medium or Large firms more on conducting joint research projects with local research institutions to acqurie needed technology.

It is thus clear from data in Tables 12.1 and 12.2 that domestic firms in the manufacturing sector in Taiwan rely more on their own efforts in acquiring technology, whereas FDI firms in Taiwan rely more on foreign technology sources. In terms of the size of the firm, small firms rely more on their own R&D as their major domestic technology source, or, alternatively, on reverse engineering techniques such as imitation, copying, or improvement of existing foreign products. The larger firms by virtue of better contact with domestic research institutions and in forming alliances with foreign corporations depend on their own R&D efforts, conducting joint research projects with domestic research institutions, engaging in technology cooperation with foreign partners, and/or the hiring of foreign consultants or experts as their major acquisition channels for domestic and foreign technology.

From the above discussion, it can be seen that the firms' own R&D efforts, assistance offered by local research institutions, technology cooperation with foreign partners, foreign consultants, and reverse engineering techniques such as imitation or improvement of existing foreign products are the five major sources of technology for manufacturing firms in Taiwan. Under such circumstances, the role that the government plays in technical advance is critical, for government policies are closely involved with R&D activities, government-sponsored research institutions, regulation of technology cooperation with foreign partners, and the protection of intellectual property rights. We shall now turn to the role of the government in supporting industrial technology advancement.

THE ROLE OF THE GOVERNMENT

The government has played a very active role in the upgrading of industrial technology in Taiwan. In 1959, a "Plan of National Long-Term Development of Science" was adopted as the basic guideline of development regarding science and technology. To carry out the plan, the Council on National Long-Term Development of Science was founded with the President of Academia Sinica as its Chairman and the Minister of Education as its Vice-Chairman. The chief function of the Council is to design and carry out long-term research in the sciences. In 1967, this Council was expanded and reorganized as the National Science Council, which has become, and still is, a principal government organization that designs strategy and promotes scientific research.

But the National Science Council is only one of the government agencies that does research and promotes science and technology. There are many other research organizations as shown below. Many of the research organizations are directly under the Ministry of Economic Affairs, the Ministry of Communications, and the Ministry of Defense (development of agricultural technology is not discussed in this chapter).

Broadly speaking, the objectives of the various government plans and organizations to upgrade science and technology are 3-fold: (1) to improve the quality of life of the people especially in the area of health and to strengthen environmental protection; (2) to transform Taiwan's economic structure from being labor intensive to capital intensive and technology intensive; and (3) to develop industries necessary for a national defense system independent of foreign control.

As for the areas of scientific research, the following eight fields have been chosen as keys: (1) energy, (2) materials, (3) information, (4) automation, (5) biotechnology, (6) electron-optics, (7) hepatitis control, and (8) food technology.

At the policy level, the government has adopted (1) a strong education policy; (2) fiscal and financial policies to encourage and indeed to require business enterprises to do R&D; (3) a policy to establish government-controlled research organizations and institutes, and to support the development of high-tech industries; (4) a policy to engage in technological alliance with foreign partners to develop needed technology; and (5) technology policies to allow Taiwan to better react to the globalization of the world's economy.

EDUCATIONAL POLICY

There is little question that there has been very rapid educational growth in Taiwan; that is a reflection of not only government policy but also a strong desire for education on the part of the people that is a deep-rooted traditional value. The annual rate of increase of total student enrollment for all age groups was 4.87% for the 30 years from 1950 to 1979, the crucial years in Taiwan's development. This was substantially higher than the rate of increase in the school-age population. As a result, the enrollment rate (number of students as a percentage of the school-age population) went up from 36% in 1951–1955 to 57% in 1976–1979.[10]

It should also be noted that the growth rate became higher as the level of education became higher. That is, the growth rate of higher education (in terms of total enrollment) was higher than that of secondary education, and the growth rate of secondary education was higher than that of elementary education. This holds true both before and after the adoption of the 9-year free-education system in 1968.

Total cost per student (as measured by total expenditures per student) increased substantially in real terms for all levels of education (except private colleges and universities), indicative of the improvement in educational quality. Higher education's per student cost went up by the greatest amount—expenditure per student at public colleges and universities in 1980 was nearly 3 times as much as in 1952.

The percentage of total government expenditure for education went up from about 10% in the early 1950s to about 15% in the late 1970s. The percentage of public education expenditure in GNP went up from less than 2% in the early 1950s to more than 4% in the late 1970s.

It also should be noted that secondary education in Taiwan may be divided into three types of schools—general high schools, normal schools, and vocational schools. Promoted actively by the government, the role of vocational schools grew quickly in importance. In the 1983–1984 school year, 202 vocational schools were imparting technical skills to 404,549 students. The percentage of vocational school students was also growing as well. In 1970, the ratio of general high school students to vocational school students was 1:1, but in 1980 it was 1:2.

Over the years, the demand for higher education in Taiwan has been extraordinarily strong. It remains so today. No one reason exists to explain adequately this strong demand for higher education, or more accurately, a university or college diploma. The perceived financial returns, gains in social status, and upward mobility associated with a diploma are reinforced by an important set of social and cultural factors. A diploma is seen as the first link on the path to power, glory, and wealth or, in other words, to joining the elite of society.

The heightened expectations associated with college diplomas create difficulties in the government's efforts to promote vocational schools and in helping plug the growing requirements of economic growth. To induce more junior high school students to enter into vocational schools, rather than the regular high school, a technical college that offers a BA degree was established in 1974. Thus students in this college, who come from the vocational track, can also obtain the coveted BA degree.[11]

A strong education policy, of course, represents investment in human resources or human capital. It means that the number of people who are capable of doing useful research on industrial technology increases and the number of people who can apply research results in industrial production increases. This is of course what successful economic development requires.

While the government is actively engaging in promoting the quality of its human resources, Taiwan is also encountering a "brain-drain" problem, that is, a number of those who received education, especially higher education, have gone abroad for advanced studies and never returned. This is particularly true for students in the fields related to industrial technology such as engineering. For instance, in 1979, the total number of students in the field of engineering who returned to Taiwan after studying abroad was less than that of students who majored in the same field and went abroad for advance study by a margin of 1285 persons. This number accounts for 20.6% of the total number of students who graduated in the field of engineering in 1979 in Taiwan. If we take the above ratio to gauge the brain-drain problem (hereafter we shall call it the brain-drain ratio), then the brain-drain ratios for students in the fields of education, natural science, engineering, medicine, and agriculture were 10.0, 15.5, 3.8, 27.9, 20.6, 19.2, and 31.9%, respectively, in 1979.

In response to the brain-drain problem, the government in Taiwan has adopted various policies to attract those who study abroad to return home to work and live in

Taiwan. These policies include providing for visiting professorships at universities, and providing more flexible employment channels for Ph.D. degree holders, which allow for the circumvention of the rigid public-servant regulations required in order to join the government in Taiwan. However, the preferential treatment has not proved to be very effective.

As Taiwan rapidly transformed herself into a newly industrialized economy, the brain-drain problem seems to have improved significantly. The brain-drain ratios for the fields of law, social science, education, natural science, engineering, medicine, and agriculture were -0.5, 9.4, -1.6, 16.2, 16.8, 8.2, and 19.2%, respectively, in 1984. The most fundamental factor behind the rapid improvement in the brain-drain problem was not the government policies we described above, since the public sector and the universities can provide only a limited number of positions, but the strong demand for high-level manpower in the private sector. In the 1980s, as Taiwan was rapidly losing her comparative advantage in low-wage labor-intensive industries, the country gradually moved into technology-intensive or higher value-added industries. Under such circumstances, the demand for better technologies became fierce, which led to a stronger derived demand for a higher level of engineers who were educated and trained abroad. Furthermore, many overseas Chinese, after having accumulated many years of work experience and technological capability, began to set up their own enterprises in Taiwan because it is their homeland. Therefore, beginning in the mid-1980s, we observed a reverse in the brain-drain situation in Taiwan.

FISCAL AND FINANCIAL POLICY TO PROMOTE TECHNOLOGY DEVELOPMENT

High expenditure requirements together with the high risk of development often has become the major obstacle of firms in conducting R&D in many technology-intensive industries. This problem is particularly significant as Taiwan's various R&D indicators are significantly lower than those of many developing and developed countries. For instance, the total civilian R&D expenditure to GNP was about 0.53% during the period of 1978 to 1982, which was significantly lower than the comparable ratios of other countries such as 2.22% for Japan, 2.42% for the United States, 2.45% for West Germany, 1.90% for the Netherlands, and 0.68% for South Korea. Furthermore, from the statistics on R&D expenditure sources, it can be seen that in 1979 the government share accounted for 52% of total ROC expenditures; in 1984 it was 51.5%. Obviously, compared to many developed and developing countries, the government has shouldered too much of the burden for conducting R&D. Therefore, how to promote R&D in the private sector has become an important policy issue.

The government has adopted a number of measures to encourage business firms to intensify their R&D efforts. On the taxation side, the Statute for Encouragement of Investment (SEI) stipulates that the R&D expenses of a firm shall be deducted from the taxable income of the current year, and for equipment bought for the purpose of conducting R&D with a service life exceeding 2 years, accelerated depreciation is allowed. Furthermore, if the amount of R&D expenses of a firm in a tax year exceeds the highest amount of R&D expenditure in the five preceding years then 20% of the amount in excess thereof may be deducted from the firm's income tax payable for that year; however, the deductible amount shall not exceed 50% of the firm's income tax payable for that year.

On the financial side, the government introduced the Assistance Program for Strategic Industries (APSI) in 1982. The government initially selected 151 products as strategic products for development. By December 1987, the number of products had increased to 214. Almost half of the selected items were electronic or information products. To implement this program, the government put aside NT$ 20 billion, which is given to firms in the form of loans. These loans have been used for the installation of machinery necessary for the production of the items selected. Any qualifying firm can receive a 10-year loan with a maximum loanable amount of 80% of the total capital needed or 65% of the total expenditure required for the investment. Furthermore, a preferential interest rate, 1.75% below the prime rate of the Bank of Communications, is also charged.

Besides the APSI and SEI, there are many other assistance programs that have been introduced in the 1980s, such as the "600 million U S dollar Low-Interest Loan to Promote Export Programs," the "Assistance Program to Small and Medium-Sized Enterprises under the Sino-American Fund," and the "Assistance Program of Low-Interest Loans for Production Industries to Set Up Satellite Plants." Furthermore, there are other nonfinancial assistance programs that aim at providing consultancy services for the upgrading of managerial technology. These programs have been introduced by various government sponsored institutions (e.g., the China Productivity Center).

In addition to the "carrot" intended to attract firms to conduct more R&D, as described above, the SEI also specifically laid down minimum R&D levels for both domestic and FDI enterprises that enjoy substantial preferential tax treatment under the statute. Under the minimum R&D stipulations, if an enterprise's R&D expenditure to annual total sales ratio is lower than the prescribed standard then the enterprise is required to contribute the difference to a government controlled research and development fund for financing collective research and development projects. Basically, the required ratios vary according to the characteristics of the business and by the annual sales value of the enterprises. The range of the required ratios is from 0.5 to 1.5%. Enterprises in traditional sectors, such as the food and garment industries, have lower ratios than those of the more technology-intensive industries.

Currently, the government is actively engaged in introducing a new Industrial Upgrading Statute (IUS) to replace the SEI. The major difference between IUS and SEI is that under IUS, firms will qualify to enjoy preferential treatment only if they have shown that they meet the subscribed standards in certain areas. This includes conducting R&D, compliance with environmental protection standards, engaging in manpower training, and setting up of international marketing channels, whereas, under the SEI, a capital investment of either a newly established or an expanding firm is all that was necessary to enjoy tax-exempted preferential treatment. Clearly under the IUS, the accumulation of capital is no longer considered the only factor in promoting industrial upgrading in Taiwan.

How effective are these government policies in enhancing R&D activities in the private sector? A study was made of 1406 firms in the shoe, leather, machinery, and electronic machinery industries in Taiwan in 1987. The firm's opinions about the most effective way in which the government should respond to promote a satisfactory level of technology was studied.[12] In this study, 9 possible policy options were listed, namely (1) transferring technology through government sponsored research institutions, (2) coordination among firms to do joint research, (3) introduction of new technology from abroad, (4) educating more R&D people, (5) helping firms to establish their own brand names, (6) offering low-interest loans for R&D activities, (7) standardization of parts and components, (8) giving tax credits for R&D expenditures, and (9) others. It was found that only 7.6% of the 1406 surveyed firms regarded the offering of low-interest loans for R&D activities as the most effective way in which the government should respond to promote a satisfactory level of technology in the economy. Similarly, only 7.8% of the surveyed firms regarded giving tax credits for R&D expenditures as the most effective measure. Clearly, the survey results have shown that the majority of the surveyed firms in the sample do not consider that the tax or financial incentives, which are provided by the government, are effective in promoting technological advancement.

What, then, are the most effective ways by which the government can promote technology? The study found that 18.8% of the surveyed firms (which is the highest percentage) considered educating more R&D people to be the most effective method to upgrade technology, followed by coordination among firms to do joint research (18.6%), the introduction of new technology from abroad (17.2%), transferring technology through government-sponsored research institutions (15.6%), and helping the firms establish their own brand names (8.8%).

Clearly, the study shows that government policies geared toward educating more R&D people, coordinating joint research efforts, and introducing and transferring technologies are all critical to technology development in Taiwan, whereas financial or tax incentive policies, as discussed above, do not prove to be particularly helpful. In the next two sections, we shall take the information industry as an example to show how the government has succeeded in promoting technology development.

GOVERNMENT-SUPPORTED RESEARCH INSTITUTIONS AND THE STRATEGY TO DEVELOP THE HIGH-TECH INFORMATION INDUSTRY

Structurally, Taiwan's economy was built on a large number of SMEs, as mentioned previously. Due to their limited amount of resources for conducting R&D, SMEs rely heavily on the efforts of the government to develop technology and/or on government-sponsored research institutions to transfer technology to them. Therefore, government-sponsored research institutions are critical to technology development and diffusion in Taiwan.

To help SMEs in the information industry to overcome the various problems associated with conducting R&D, training, and marketing, the government has set up two institutions to assist firms in the industry: the Industrial Technology Research Institute (ITRI) and the Institute for the Information Industry (III). III was established in 1979; its major mission includes introducing and developing software technology, assisting government agencies and public enterprises in their computerization projects, training and educating information professionals, supplying market and technology information related to the information industry, and promoting the development and usage of computer-related technologies. In sum, the major function of III is to support activities that are undersupplied, much like the case for government-supplied public goods having positive external effects, to the member firms in the industry. More importantly, these activities, such as manpower training and the dissemination of market information, can make up for disadvantages resulting from the economies of scale that prohibit SMEs from conducting such activities.

The III programs complement ITRI's hardware development program for the electronic/information industry in Taiwan. ITRI was set up in 1973 under the direction of the Ministry of Economic Affairs. There are five major divisions in ITRI that support the development of various industrial technologies. As for the electronics industry, the Electronic Research and Service Organization (ERSO) is critical to its technology development. Basically ERSO has two major tasks: to develop needed technology for the industry and to diffuse the developed technology among the industry's firms. There are various mechanisms that can be used to diffuse the new technology, including issuing technical documents and organizing conferences for electronic firms in Taiwan; furthermore, the new technology can be transferred to individual firms through licensing agreements where royalty charges are levied on the recipient firm(s), once they employ the technology. If, however, the developed technology has marketing potential and there is the desire to set up a new joint venture to disseminate the technology then a new spin-off venture company would be established by ERSO. It is important to note that although the spin-off company is supported by ERSO's engineers and its funding is provided by the government, venture company is cautiously organized as a privately owned company. Both the technology endowment received from ERSO and the capital endowment supplied by the government aim at attracting investment from the private sector. It is hoped that the private sector can account for at least 60 to 70% of the total shares of the newly established venture company. There are at least five advantages to this kind of setup. First from an engineers point of view, the newly established venture company can provide immediate pecuniary rewards and/or professional positions, which allow them to further develop such technologies; therefore, the incentive to develop new technologies is very strong. Second, since the established venture company's new technology will be supported by the same group of engineers who developed it, the company does not have to start from scratch and can be in full operation within a very short period of time. Third, the company remains basically a privately owned company; therefore, it can be flexible and can be responsive to rapid changes in the external environment. Fourth, one of the main purposes for developing new technology is to help the private sector in Taiwan to upgrade its technological position. The government has no intention of monopolizing the technology. As a result, privately owned venture companies can serve as a conduit to diffuse new technology. Fifth, and most importantly, many entrepreneurs in the traditional sectors of the economy would like to diversify their investments to include the electronic/information industry for various reasons such as risk sharing and industrial upgrading. A venture company investment project would certainly be an ideal investment and the easiest one to invest in. The mechanisms that allow ERSO to diffuse its technology can thus be summarized in Figure 12.1.

As a result of the successful spin-off model developed by ERSO, described above, since the early 1980s, six IC chip companies began operation in Taiwan, namely UMC (1982), Advanced (1982), TSMC (1987), Coin Tek (1988), Winbord (1988), and Ten

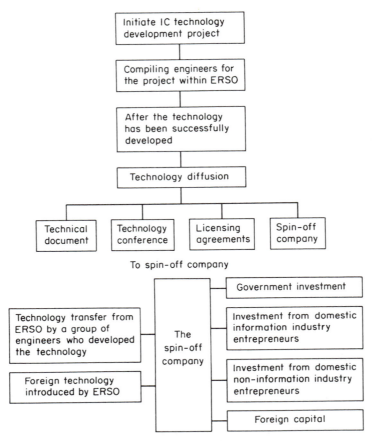

Figure 12.1. Mechanism for ERSO to diffuse its technology.

Tech (1989). They were set up in succession. Taiwan's major IC chip manufacturers in 1989 and their capacity can be summarized in Table 12.3.

It is important to note that prior to the DRAM shortage in 1988, most key industrial policy makers and entrepreneurs were in agreement on the fact that Taiwan should fully capitalize on their advantage of having a large number of SMEs in the information industry. The development of ASICs would be an ideal strategy that would fit in Taiwan's industrial structure. The relevant factors that favor development of ASICs are the fact that the design of the integrate circuits can be handled efficiently by SMEs and many talented and independent engineers would excel in the SME type of IC design firms. However, IC design firms must be incorporated into the IC fabrication network in order to complete the industrial network demanded in the production of custom chips. To facilitate this TSMC, a joint venture between ITRI and Phillips was established in 1987. TSMC is not personally involved in IC design but fabricates custom IC chips for various IC design companies. As the result of TSMC operations, the IC design firms in Taiwan have increased from just a few in 1987 to more than 50 in 1989. Clearly, prior to 1988 Taiwan's strategy to cope with the rapid

Table 12.3. Major IC Producers in Taiwan in 1989

Company	Production Began in	Sources of Capital	Sources of Technology	Manufacturing Technology	Monthly Capacity	Note
UMC	January 1982	Domestic	ERSO	1.2–5 μm CMOS	4″, 50,000 6″, 15,000	The third factory is under planning
TSMC	July 1987	Taiwan and Netherlands	ERSO	1.25 μm CMOS	6″, 12,000	The third factory is under planning
Coin Tek	July 1988	Domestic	ERSO	1.2–5 μm CMOS	5″, 30,000	The second has begun to build in 1989
Winbord	October 1988	Domestic	ERSO	1.2–5 μm CMOS	5″, 20,000	The second factory is scheduled to build in early 1990
Advanced	January 1986	Domestic	ERSO	4–5 μm CMOS	4″, 8,000	
Ten Tech	October 1988	Domestic	ERSO	2–5 μm CMOS	4″, 8,000	

Source: ERSO.

change in the IC industry was to adopt an economy of scope strategy, and not an economy of scale strategy. The country concentrated her efforts on the production of ASICs rather than standard memory chips such as DRAM. However, the worldwide DRAM shortage problem of 1988 changed this strategy.

As the shortage of DRAMs became more and more severe in mid-1988, discussions (or debates) on whether or not Taiwan should build up her own DRAM industry were intensified. A whole series of debates and discussions dragged on for several months in Taiwan. The potential risk or inherent difficulty in setting up a DRAM fabrication plant has not discouraged DRAM production proponents and some fruitful results have been produced by the discussions. First, the government has agreed to put DRAM on the list of important high-tech products. As a result of this policy, manufacturers of DRAMs can enjoy favorable tax treatment. Furthermore, non-DRAM producers can now hold more than 40% of the total shares of a company that produces DRAMs without any legal restrictions. Second, the president of TSMC has agreed to devote part of its second plant, which is scheduled to be in operation in 1990, to the production of DRAM, provided that the downstream firms can make a commitment to purchase DRAMs from TSMC—which they have. Third, two private information corporations, Vitelic and Acer, have decided to invest heavily in the production of DRAMs, because they feel that there is a potential market for DRAMs. As a non-DRAM producer, Acer's strategy to get into the production of DRAMs is to make a foreign alliance with TI. The Acer–TI DRAM fabrication plant joint venture is scheduled to be in operation by 1991. The forthcoming players in the IC industry in Taiwan can be summarized in Table 12.4.

Table 12.4. The Forthcoming IC Manufacturers After 1989 in Taiwan

Company	Monthly Capacity	Major Product	Major Technology
Mosel	6″, 6,000	BiCOMS Product, ASIC, SRAM	BiCMOS CMOS 1.0 μm
Holtek	5″, 10,000	Custom IC	CMOS 2.0 μm
Vitelic	6″, 10,000	DRAM	CMOS 1.0 μm
Silicon Integrated System	6″, 30,000	Mask DRAM	—
Acer–TI	6″, 30,000	DRAM	—
Macronix	6″, 8,000	Communication ICs	—
Utic	4″, 8,000	Linear IC	Bipolar
FORMOSA	6″, —	EPROH	—

Source: ERSO.

Furthermore, to actively respond to rapid technological development in the information industry, joint efforts similar to the SEMATECH project on submicro technology in the United States have also been launched under the coordination of the Ministry of Economic Affairs in Taiwan. In August 1989, ITRI, UMC, TSMC, Winbord, Ten Tech, and Vitelic, Taiwan's major IC chips manufacturers, and other companies in Taiwan decided to form a "technology development alliance" to develop 16M DRAM and 4M SRAM chip technology over the next 5 years. To be better prepared to handle the project, a micro electronic laboratory that meets class 10 cleanliness standards for 0.2 μm, and that has the capability of developing the technology needed to produce 0.8-μm chips, was completed. The 5-year development plan calls for an investment of 5 to 6 billion NT dollars and requires more than 200 engineers and technicians to be devoted to the project.

It is thus clear from the above discussion that Taiwan's information development strategies in the 1990s will be a more balanced combination of economy of scale (such as the development of DRAMs) and that of scope (such as the development of ASICs). It is hoped that through this combination, Taiwan's information industry will become one of the major world players in the industry.

TECHNOLOGICAL ALLIANCE WITH FOREIGN PARTNERS TO PROMOTE COMPUTER SOFTWARE DEVELOPMENT: AN EXAMPLE

One of the most fundamental strategies to promote the country's software industry is to build up its technological capabilities and develop experience in production. To do this, technological alliances with the computer giants will be necessary. Under these alliances, Taiwan can provide low-cost, quality, but relatively inexperienced, engineers to foreign partners. In turn, the foreign partners can provide their vast experience in software research and development. Clearly, both parties will mutually benefit from the alliance. The establishment of the Neotech Development Corp. (NDC) is a typical example of such a strategy.

NDC was established in 1983 with the support of III and IBM. III and IBM agreed that NDC would provide exclusive software development and design services to IBM.

On assigned projects, IBM pays both the NDC staff's salaries and the bills for all R&D equipment. During the project-development period, the NDC research staff frequently are sent to IBM plants around the world to acquire needed expertise. At the same time, IBM's engineers also are sent to NDC to guide research operations. It has been reported[13] that over the period of 1983 to 1988 that IBM paid 17 million U. S. dollars to NDC to complete various projects for IBM, primarily in the categories of information design and the development of application software (e.g., control boards for the IBM 5216 daisy wheel printer, peripherals for banking computers, peripherals for retail-house computers, and banking software). As for NDC engineers, they not only have obtained hardware facilities support from IBM but also have obtained knowledge on R&D procedures and testing techniques that could not have been easily mastered through the engineers' own efforts, but that are vital to the success of product development projects.

The success of NDC's relationship with IBM has led to another cooperation program—the establishment of International Integrated System Inc. (IIS) in 1988. Under an agreement with IBM, III put up 3.5 million U. S. dollars in capital and dispatched 70 software designers to work at IIS. IBM provided the necessary technical support for the designing of IBM software. The major difference between the IIS and NDC agreements is that IIS does not have to provide contract services to IBM exclusively, as NDC does. IIS can also provide services, such as VAN, database, and artificial intelligence services, to other independent businesses. However, the design project for the business must solely utilize IBM systems.

Clearly, a strategic alliance between IBM and III is mutually beneficial to both parties, since IBM can enhance its global competitiveness through the alliance, while its Chinese counterpart can significantly upgrade its technological capability of its software/design engineers. Also technology can be diffused to other private firms by the inevitable turnover of engineers. The latest development of NDC and IIS is that IBM's Taiwan branch has formally proposed to the board of III to merge NDC and IIS into one single company called Integrated Systems Development Corp. (ISDC). IBM has agreed to purchase 35% of ISDC shares. III will hold 45% of the shares and the remaining 20% will be held by the firm's employees. The proposal has been approved by the board of III.

Basically ISDC will engage in the kind of business that NDC and IIS have been engaging in all along. However, by combining both companies' software/design engineers, it is hoped that ISDC will have both economy of scale and the technical expertise to become a significant software/design player in the international market.[14]

THE INTERACTIONS AMONG VARIOUS GOVERNMENT-SPONSORED INSTITUTIONS AND UNIVERSITIES

Besides ITRI and III, which are directly related to industrial technology development in Taiwan, there are in the administrative structure of the government a number of institutes, councils, and the like that are charged with the responsibility of advancing science and technology in general and industrial technology in particular. They are briefly listed and described below.

I. Those that report directly to the President's office:
   1. Guidance Committee on the Development of Science
      This is an advisory body to the President.
   2. Academia Sinica
      The highest academic institution in the country, which does research in various fields.
II. Those under the Executive Yuan:
   1. Committee of Advisors on Science and Technology
      The members are now primarily scientists from other countries.
   2. Committee on Research and Development of Applied Technology
   3. National Science Council
      Under the direction of this Council, there is a data center for science and technology, a development center for precision instruments, and a bureau in charge of industrial parks.
   4. Council of Atomic Energy
      Under this council, there is a research center for atomic energy.
   5. Council of Agricultural Development
   6. Ministry of Economic Affairs
      Under this Ministry, there are 36 institutes that do research in various fields of industrial technology.
   7. Ministry of Communications
      Under this council, there are four research institutes doing research related to transportation and communications, including weather research.
   8. Ministry of Education
      The Ministry is in charge of all colleges and universities, many of which have research institutes.
   9. Administration of Public Health
      Under the administration, there are two research institutes.
   10. Ministry of Defense
      Under this ministry, there is the important Chung-Shan Science College that does research on technologies related to national defense.
   11. Taiwan Provincial Government
      Under provincial government control there are 18 research institutes doing research largely on agriculture, public health, and transportation.

Of all the above research institutions, the National Science Council plays the key role in the development of science and technology. It is charged with designing research strategy and plans, promoting basic research, pioneering applied research, improving the environment for research, cultivating and attracting research personnel, and coordinating research work undertaken by the various government agencies. It is also the principal grantor of funds to researchers at Academia Sinica and in Taiwan's colleges and universities.

The division of labor structure in technology development in Taiwan is shown in Table 12.5. In this table, it is shown that basic research is conducted mainly by Academia Sinica and the universities, while applied research, technology development, and commercialization of the technology are mainly the responsibility of various industrial technology research institutions as well as the enterprises themselves. Under

Table 12.5. The Division of Labor to Promote Technology Development in Taiwan

Type of Research	Policy Making	The Implementation of the Policies		
		Schools and Research Institutions	Government-Support Research Institution	Enterprises
Basic	Academia Sinica	Academia Sinica		
Applied research	Ministry of Education National Science Council	Universities		
Technology development Commercialized and applied	Various ministries under the ROC government	Various direct research institutions under the different levels of government	ITRI III Other government-sponsored research institutions that are not directly under the government	Private enterprises Public-owned enterprises

Source: National Science Council, Taiwan, ROC.

the above division of labor structure, one will find both advantages and disadvantages. The major advantage of the system is that limited R&D resources are pooled and the research effort can then be aimed at developing generic types of technology that can be beneficial to all the firms in the industry. In contrast, the major disadvantage of the system is that firms are more likely to rely heavily on the government as their major source of new technology.

To overcome such a deficiency, as we discussed before, policies, which rigidly require firms to meet the minimum R&D input levels if they wish to qualify for the tax exemption provision as stipulated in the SEI, have been introduced. It is thus hoped that given the SME economy in Taiwan, a more balanced R&D mixture between the government and private enterprises can be achieved.

THE INTERACTIONS BETWEEN FIRMS AND THE GOVERNMENT ON TECHNOLOGY DEVELOPMENT TO COPE WITH THE GLOBALIZATION OF THE WORLD'S ECONOMY

Due to the rapid increase in the volume of trade and investment in the world and owing to the tremendous development in science and technology during this century, the world's economy is rapidly becoming more and more integrated into a single-economy structure. However, as the globalization of the world's economy increases in momentum, both the competitive and complementary relationships, regarding technology, among firms and countries will be intensified. Therefore, how to properly react to this inevitable trend becomes critical. From the entrepreneur's point of view, one of the important strategies of firms in Taiwan, to cope with the globalization trend in the world economy, is overseas mergers. This strategy is becoming more important and is a common practice for many firms in Taiwan. There are several important economic factors that contribute to the adoption of this strategy. Financially speaking, huge foreign exchange reserves make overseas mergers feasible. Furthermore, with the appreciation of the NT dollar over the period of 1986–1988, overseas mergers have been made more affordable and attractive than exporting.

Besides the financial factors, acquiring needed technology is another major motivation for overseas mergers. The overseas mergers taken by the Acer group with Counterpoint Computers, a minicomputer manufacturing company, and PPL, a computer-control printing system company, both of which are located in the United States, is a typical example of a merger of this type. These mergers have helped Acer acquire minicomputer technology and expand her personal computer functions. The Acer group's overseas mergers are certainly not the only example of mergers being conducted by firms in Taiwan; another example is Taiwan Microtex's overseas merger with the U. S.'s Mouse System Company to enhance its technological capability.

It is frequently argued that one of the major disadvantages of SMEs in Taiwan is that most of these firms are too small to have their own marketing channels let alone have their own brand names. Therefore, the future competitive capability of the SMEs is somewhat doubtful. Many entrepreneurs in Taiwan find that overseas mergers are one of the most feasible ways to make up for this shortcoming. As a matter of fact, some entrepreneurs have even considered that it is more effective and more convenient to buy or to control a foreign marketing company that already has a marketing network set up than to start a marketing network from scratch and try to build one by themselves. Acer group's merger with DYNA, the third largest computer dealer in the United States, is a typical example of this type of marketing consideration.

Besides building a marketing channel, many of the SMEs in Taiwan find that overseas mergers with an existing company can also help them "purchase" a brand name that they can use for their products. A good example of this kind of merger is where one of the largest U. S. furniture companies, Stoneville, and her long-time OEM supplier in Taiwan merged so that the Taiwan-manufacturer could take control of both Stoneville's marketing channels and name. Clearly, Taiwan's SMEs have actually engaged in building brand names for their products as well as marketing channels through overseas mergers.

In sum, overseas mergers are appearing not only as a result of huge foreign exchange reserves and the vast appreciation of the NT dollar but are also due to the fact that it can help the domestic enterprises to vertically integrate themselves and take over a foreign firm's marketing channels, brand names, and technology. This is, obviously, a complementary and feasible strategy for domestic firms in coping with the globalization of the world's economy.

The government's policy toward overseas mergers is undoubtedly supportive, in fact, actions to promote these activities have already been taken. One of the major policy tools of the government is the providing of low-interest loans or part of the investment capital needed so that private companies can engage in overseas mergers. A typical example of this strategy is the case of WYSE Technology, a major terminal manufacturer in the United States, founded by an overseas Chinese company, and which dominates around 50% of the world's terminal market. Due to the company's diversification but unsuccessful strategies in producing personal computers, WYSE ran into serious financial trouble and looked for a strategic alliance with another firm to help the company both in the production of personal computers and also to help out with the company's finance. Mitac, one of the major personal computer manufacturers in Taiwan, was approached by WYSE and responded positively. To facilitate the merger, a venture company was quickly set up. Private capital from Mitac, China Trust, and Kuo Chiau was gathered and put in the venture company. The funds to finalize the merger, which came from these companies, were roughly 80% of the total needed to complete the merger and the remaining 20% of the funds came from the government's Central Development Fund. The merger of WYSE was thus completed. The successful experience of the WYSE case has certainly served as an important example and has set a precedent for future government involvement in supporting overseas mergers.

One must admit, however, that Taiwan overseas mergers are still in the preliminary stages of development. Since the investment banks in Taiwan are not developed to support overseas mergers very well, there is a lack of experienced international legal and accounting services and overseas mergers face many obstacles. Regardless, overseas mergers have become an important strategy of domestic firms in Taiwan. Also, overseas Chinese, in some cases but not all, will continue to play an important role in facilitating such activities.

In view of the significant role that the overseas Chinese had in promoting technology development and in response to the brain-drain problem that we have discussed earlier, the government in Taiwan set up the Hsinchu Science-based Industrial Park in 1980. Unlike the tax and duty-free export-processing zones in Kaohsiung, Nantze, and Taichung, which were designed to attract foreign investment for export expansion and to transfer technology, the park was designed primarily to attract investment in high-tech industries especially by returning students or overseas Chinese.

In this park, plants, utilities, residential housing, schools, and the like are all built with high standards. All an investor needs to do is move in and start a business. By December 1988, there were already 96 high-tech firms established in the park. Total sales of these firms went up from NT$3.3 billion in 1983 to NT$48.3 billion in 1988. Total employees in 1988 (December) numbered 16,500 with 95 of them having a Ph.D. and 696 a M. A. (M. S.) degree. Of all workers, 41% had a college education.[15]

It is increasingly apparent that the establishment of the park has attracted many experienced and well-established Chinese engineers and technicians to come back home and develop their professional careers. As a result of this "reverse" trend, a lot of advanced technology has been brought into domestic firms. Also, domestic firms in Taiwan now have more windows with which to internationalize their operations and spread the efforts of their R&D, which can further enhance their competitiveness in the world.

By recognizing the significant role of FDI in introducing technology, Taiwan has changed her policy toward FDI. In the past, the policy toward FDI could be described as "encouragement with caution." It has been stipulated in law that overseas Chinese and foreigners can invest in only certain sectors of the economy in Taiwan such as manufacturing, certain service enterprises, and scientific and technical research and development. However, the law also states that all foreign direct investment must be approved by the government. Therefore, the "apply for approval" type of administration or "positive list" scope of investment strategy was adopted by the government. To further encourage investors and firms to invest in Taiwan, the government made a bold move by changing the "positive list" in the scope of investment into a "negative list" in 1988. The major difference between the "positive list method" and the "negative list method" is clear; so long as overseas Chinese and foreigners do not make investments in the prohibited sectors listed by the government (i.e., on the negative list), their investment in Taiwan will be approved automatically by the authority-in-charge. This certainly enhances the open-door policy that is geared toward meeting the challenge of the globalization of the world's economy.

As Taiwan rapidly rushes to become an advanced industrialized country, the government has become aware of the fact that the protection of intellectual property rights must be strengthened in order to meet international standards. Furthermore, drives to encourage domestic firms to establish their own brand names for their products in international markets as well as drives to develop the software industry all have called for stricter regulations on the protection of trademarks and intellectual property. Therefore, trademark law, copyright law, and other relevant regulations are all under revision in Taiwan. For instance, in 1985 the trademark law was revised, so that penalties such as fines (with a maximum of NT$90,000), and/or imprisonment (usually not more than one year), and/or damage compensation (based on an amount equivalent to 500 to 1500 times the unit price of one community) have been introduced. Furthermore, public education on what constitutes intellectual property as well as the prosecution of violators have all been strengthened. The sincerity and determination of the government in protecting intellectual property rights are without question; after all the implementation of this policy will be beneficial to the industrial upgrading of the local economy and also will be in accordance with the drive to internationalize Taiwan's economy under the globalization of the world economy.

NATIONAL DEFENSE AND TECHNOLOGY DEVELOPMENT

It is generally believed that Taiwan has a fairly strong national defense, but little is known about the relationship between national defense and technology development. It is reasonable to assume that certain technology development is necessary for the development of a weapons system, but whether such technology is transferable or is transferred to civilian industries is quite a different matter.

Taiwan's development of military weapons has been largely determined by its relationship with the United States. Prior to January 1, 1979 when the United States and the Republic of China broke off diplomatic relations, Taiwan's national defense and the island's military-hardware needs were primarily supplied by the United States. National defense industries were hardly developed in Taiwan at that time. It is true that a 6-year development plan for 1976–1981 was adopted by the government to develop capital- and technology-intensive heavy and petrochemical industries, but no significant progress was made.

A real push for the development of national defense related industries was not made until after the severance of diplomatic relations in 1979 when the United States decided to scale down the supply of military weapons to Taiwan. The Chung-Shan Science Colleague has been the key research institute developing the technologies needed to build strong weapons systems, especially for the Air Force and the Navy. ITRI has also done research related to national defense. However, further research is needed to study how national defense has affected the technological aspect of industrial development.

R&D EXPENDITURES

The National Science Council started in 1980 to collect data and compile indicators measuring the progress made on the development of science and technology (R&D) in Taiwan. One of the indicators is expenditures on R&D. It is estimated that in 1979, total R&D expenditures for science and technology were NT$9.9 billion, constituting 0.84% of GNP or 0.91% of national income. The amount increased to NT$19.2 billion in 1983, or 0.94% of GNP or 1.02% of national income. In 1986, it increased to NT$28.7 billion, or 1.04% of GNP or 1.13% of national income.[16] But data from 1984 are not strictly comparable with data before 1984. From 1984 on, expenditures on research and development also include those in the humanities and social sciences. Such inclusion should not change the general conclusion, however, for expenditures on research for humanities and social sciences are relatively small.

In real terms, expenditures on R&D in 1986 were twice as much as in 1979. The annual growth rate averaged 9% from 1979 to 1983, and 11% from 1984 to 1986.

The amount of R&D expenditures per researcher in the science and technology fields has been quite stable. In 1986, it amounted to NT$1,034,400 a year (or US$28,730, at US$1 = NT$36).

In 1986, the government's share of total R&D expenditures was 60% whereas the share of the private sector was 40%. The government's share includes the share of public enterprises, which was 14.5% of total R&D expenditures.

The private sector includes private business enterprises, nonprofit research institutions, and foreign institutions in Taiwan. In 1986, their shares were 38.7, 0.7, and 0.5%, respectively.

In terms of trends, the government's share in total R&D expenditures has remained the same, about 60% from 1980 to 1986. But within the government, the share of public enterprises declined from an average of 20% in 1979–1981 to 15% in 1984–1986.

As for the private sector, the share of private business enterprises increased from 34% in 1979–1981 to 37% in 1984–1986. The share of nonprofit institutions declined from 5.2% in 1979–1981 to 1.3% in 1984–1986. The share of foreign institutions remained negligible.

As for the purposes of R&D expenditures, in 1986, 11% of the total was for "basic research," 38% for "applied research," and 51% for technology development.

As for private business enterprises in 1986, 3.7% of the total R&D expenditure was for basic research, 22.5% for applied research, and 73.8% for technology development. For public enterprises, 3.0% of total R&D expenditure was for basic research, 26.5% for applied research, and 70.5% for technology development. It is clear, then, for both public and private enterprises, R&D expenditures are primarily for technology development, as one would expect.

In terms of industrial distribution for both private and public enterprises, the amount of R&D expenditure per NT$1000 of sales in 1986 was only NT$4.27 for manufacturing, NT$1.06 for construction, NT$2.71 for transportation and communications, NT$6.45 for water, gas, and electricity, and NT$1.02 for mining. For all fields, total R&D expenditure amounted to only NT$4.14 per NT$1000 of sales, or 0.41% of sales. The percentage was about the same for both public and private enterprises (0.399% for private enterprises).

In 1986, for the following industries in manufacturing, R&D expenditure per NT$1000 of sales was higher than NT$5:

Chemical materials	NT$9.87
Chemical products	7.42
Rubber products	6.58
Machinery	7.94
Electrical machinery and appliances	5.98
Miscellaneous industries	6.79

For these industries, R&D expenditure was overwhelmingly for the improvement of production techniques.

Furthermore, by utilizing the survey data, which contain 246 domestic and 72 FDI electronic enterprises in Taiwan in 1986, comparisons between SMEs and large enterprises, and domestic and FDI enterprises in terms of their R&D expenditure, are made.[17] The study found that no matter which of the different R&D indicators one uses, annual R&D expenditure, annual R&D expenditure per employee (RDE), or the annual R&D expenditure to total sales ratio (RDS), FDI enterprises devote more resources to R&D than do domestic firms. However, in terms of the nationality of the FDI enterprises, it is shown that European FDI enterprises in Taiwan have placed significantly more effort on R&D than the rest of the FDI firms in Taiwan. American FDI enterprise have devoted slightly more resources on R&D than domestic firms, while Japanese FDI enterprises in Taiwan have consistently shown the least interest in R&D.

It is also found in the study that the effort of smaller firms' R&D in terms of RDE or RDS is comparable to that of the larger firms. Therefore, the R&D effort made by the firm may not be positively related to the size of the firm. Finally, it was also found that one of the most important factors in determining a firm's R&D effort is its level of technology intensity embodied in the firm (which is measured by the ratio of the total number of engineers and technicians to total number of employees in a firm), and the significance of this factor in determining a firm's R&D effort is greater than its size, government preferential treatment on R&D expenditure, or any other factor.

INDICATORS OF DEVELOPMENT IN SCIENCE AND TECHNOLOGY

It would be difficult for any country to come up with a set of indicators measuring the progress made in science and development. Surely data of this sort in Taiwan are extremely scarce. But available data suggest that a great deal of progress has been made in the development of science and technology in Taiwan.

As regards human resources, the number of persons engaged in research on the development of science and technology increased from 8345 in 1979 to 27,747 in 1986, that is, the number of researchers in science and technology in 1986 was 3.3 times as many as in 1979. In 1979, there were 12.8 researchers in science and technology per 10,000 persons in the population. In 1986, the number increased to 34.9 per 10,000 population.[18]

In terms of the educational background of the researchers engaged in research science and technology, in 1986, there were 3146 persons with doctors' degrees (11.3%

of total researchers), 6514 persons with masters' degrees (23.5% of the total), 12,485 persons with bachelors' degrees (or 45% of the total), and 6786 persons with an education in professional or vocational schools at the level of a junior college (19.7% of the total).

Of the 27,747 researchers, 47.8% were in private business enterprises, 26.8% in research institutes and organizations, and 25.4% in colleges and universities.

In terms of fields of research, 61.6% of these 27,747 researchers were in engineering, 12.6% in natural sciences, 11.0% in agriculture, 9.2% in medicine, 3.9% in social sciences, and only 1.7% in the humanities.

It may be interesting to note that those who do research in natural sciences, engineering, medicine, and agriculture were primarily B.A.s and M.A.s. On the other hand, those who do research in the humanities and social sciences are primarily Ph.D.s and M.A.s.

In absolute terms, the number of researchers in science and technology seems to be quite small, but in terms of growth rates, the number of Ph.D.s increased at 11% a year from 1979 to 1986. For M.A.s, the annual growth rate was about 12% a year. For researchers with education in professional and vocational schools the growth rate was 23% from 1979 to 1986.

A tangible result of the research has been the number of published papers. In 1986, a total of 7395 papers were published in professional or academic journals, 74% of them in Taiwan and the remainder in foreign countries. In addition, there were 4730 papers that were read but not published in journals in 1986.[19]

Another tangible result of research on science and technology has been the number of patents granted. In 1986, there were 29,511 applications for patents, of which some 12,355 were approved. Of the patents approved, 53% were by Chinese nationals and 47% by foreign nationals. This represents a substantial increase in the number filed by Chinese Nationals. In 1979, there were 10,411 applications, of which 3,686 were approved. Of the patents approved, 41% were by Chinese nationals and 59% by foreign nationals. It is evident that the number of patents approved has increased substantially, and the share accounted for by Chinese nationals has steadily increased, whereas the share given to foreign nationals has declined.

Still another indicator of the result of research on science and technology is the nature or the technology content of exports. In the 1950s, the main items of export were sugar, rice, and bananas. These products were basically land-intensive. As time went on, labor-intensive products such as textiles and shoes began to become the main items of exports. In more recent years, more technologically advanced or capital-intensive products, such as machinery in general and electrical machinery in particular as well as other types of apparatuses, have assumed a greater and greater share in total exports. By one estimate, the share of "technology-intensive" products constituted 21.9% of total merchandise exports in 1983. This proportion gradually rose to 24.3 in 1987.[20]

A NATIONAL PLAN

The government is well aware of the fact that Taiwan has to accelerate its efforts in the development of science and technology in order to upgrade its economic structure,

Table 12.6. The Key Targets of Taiwan's 10-Year Science and Technology Plan

	1986	1995	Annual Growth Rate
Total number of researchers	27,747	43,000	6.1%
Ph.D.s (percentage in total)	3,146 (11.3%)	6,600 (15%)	8.6%
M.A.s (percentage in total)	6,514 (23.5%)	15,400 (35%)	10%
R&D expenditures (NT$billion)	28.7	90.0	
Annual growth rate			13.5%
As a percentage of GNP	1.04%	2.0%	
Basic research as a percentage of total R&D	11.1%	12.0%	
Government's share in R&D	60%	40%	
Private share in R&D	40%	60%	

improve the quality of life of the people, and strengthen national defense. Conferences at all levels have been held frequently to find ways to improve technology, especially industrial technology. A 10-year plan for science and technology was adopted for the period 1986–1995. The key targets of this 10-year plan are shown in Table 12.6.

It remains to be seen, however, whether the targets in Table 12.6 will be reached. It may be noted that in Korea, the proportion of R&D expenditures constituted 1.82% of her GNP in 1986. In the same year per capita GDP for Korea was US$2365, whereas in Taiwan it was US$3688. Taiwan should achieve the 2% of GDP target by 1995.

AN APPRAISAL AND SOME CONCLUDING REMARKS

Throughout this chapter we have tried to suggest that Taiwan's economic performance has been successful in many respects, and technology has been an important contributing factor to this. We have also tried to describe the efforts of the government and the private sector to advance science and technology, especially industrial technology. These efforts, however, are far from adequate.

It must be admitted that a great deal of research remains to be done before one can understand exactly how industrial technology has been advanced in Taiwan, how technology in industry may be defined or classified for the purpose of empirical research, who introduced or applied the new or improved technologies and what they consisted of, and, finally, who failed, who succeeded, and why.

Another set of questions that remains to be answered regard government policy. Surely the government has done a great deal in advancing science and technology on Taiwan. It will be a gigantic task to evaluate what the government has done in this area, and this is something we would not attempt to do here. What follows is simply some questions about certain government policies that have an important bearing on the future development of technology.

First, we look at Taiwan's education policy. The government, in the past, has emphasized vocational or employment-specific education. This, in our view, should be modified if not totally changed. In an economy that has been, and still is, undergoing structural change, what the labor force needs is the ability to adapt to changing conditions, changing technologies, and changing production processes. In our view, it is the "general" or the "liberal arts" type of education that best prepares the labor force with such flexibility. We are not downgrading the importance of specialized or employment-specific knowledge; what we contend is simply that it is important to have a proper dose of liberal arts education in the curriculum.

Now "compulsory" or, more properly, free education will be extended from 9 to 12 years in Taiwan. It is the government's policy to emphasize vocational or professional education for the last 3 years of this period at least in terms of the number of vocational vs. general senior high schools. We suggest that serious consideration be given to the question of whether there is enough "general education" in the curriculum of vocational schools.

Second, we need to review the "pick the winners" policy. In the past the government often chose certain industries or products as strategic and favored them with preferential treatment, as described above. In our view, the industries or products that are developed should be determined by market forces; any deliberate government policy to alter the comparative advantage that an economy enjoys will distort the allocation of resources except in cases where there is market failure or externalities. To be more specific, the technology that is appropriate for an economy to adopt should be a matter that business firms decide, not the government.

It is true that the concepts of economic liberalization and internationalization have now been adopted by the government as its guiding principles in the formulation of economic policy, and government interference in the choice of technology is to be minimized. But given that the government desires to upgrade technology and the economic structure, we hope that it will resist pressure to grant special favors to any specific industries or technologies that are claimed by vested interest groups to be "strategic."

Third, a word on small and medium enterprises. Small and medium enterprises have been, and still are, a vital force for Taiwan's economy, especially the export sector. They are being confronted, and indeed have been for some time, with some special difficulties arising from the appreciation of the NT dollar and increasing competition by other developing countries where unit labor costs are much lower. As a result, some of them are being forced to move out of the country and invest abroad.

But this is not desirable for the economy as a whole, for Taiwan is still a developing economy and needs a lot of capital investment at home. Hence, it is not in a position to invest abroad on a large scale. A more desirable policy is to upgrade technology so as to increase the competitiveness of small and medium enterprises.

One reason that small enterprises shy away from spending a great deal of money to upgrade technology is that the kind of technology they need can often be imitated, and cannot be effectively protected by patents. As a result, everyone is reluctant to be an innovator, at least in regards to some types of technologies.

In our judgment, some of the government-supported research institutions such as the Industrial Technology Research Institute should double and redouble their efforts to work on the kind of technology that is appropriate for small and medium enterprises, instead of devoting their efforts primarily to "high-tech."

Finally, government-owned enterprises in Taiwan are still significant, accounting for 10.2% of total value-added in the manufacturing sector. They are often criticized as being inefficient, but this is not to say that their managers and workers are less able.

The real difficulty is that their operation is under many restrictions, there is no effective incentive systems, and, worst of all, their managers and employees have the status of a civil servant. Being a civil servant, they have a number of restrictions imposed on them, and hence they cannot be as innovative as their counterparts in private business. In our view, the best way to make them innovative, especially in upgrading or choosing appropriate technology, is to privatize those public enterprises that are not natural monopolies or related to national defense.

NOTES

The authors wish to express their thanks to Ms. Yih-shiow Chen for her assistance.

1. See, for example, Chi-ming Hou. (1988). "Relevance of the Taiwan Model of Development." In *Conference on Successful Economic Development Strategies of the Pacific Rim Nations.* Taipei: Chung-Hua Institution for Economic Research. Reprinted in *Industry of Free China,* February 1989, 9–32.

2. See Chi-ming Hou and Ching-hsi Chang. (1981). "Education and Economic Growth in Taiwan: The Mechanism of Adjustment." In *Conference on Experiences and Lessons of Economic Development in Taiwan,* 492. Taipei: The Institute of Economics, Academia Sinica.

3. Chi-ming Hou and Hui-lin Wu. (1983). "Wage and Labor Productivity in the ROC." In *Raising Productivity: Experience of the Republic of China.* Tokyo: Asian Productivity Organization. Reprinted in *Industry of Free China,* May 1985.

4. Calculated from data in Duller, H. J. (1983). *Technique in Taiwan: The Role of Technology in Taiwan's Past and Present Development.* Taipei: Sun Yat-San Institute of Social Science and Philosophy, Academia Sinica. Duller's data were provided by the Central Bank of China.

5. Hou and Chang (1981, p. 486).

6. Hou and Wu (1983, p. 65).

7. *Taiwan Statistical Data Book, 1989,* p. 7.

8. The data, as cited in note 4, imply the following rates of growth of capital in the non-agricultural sector: 2.8% in 1953–1961, 8.1% in 1962–1971, and 12.6% in 1972–1980. For the period from 1953 to 1980, the average rate of growth was 7.8% a year.

9. See San Gee. (1989). "Direct Foreign Investment and Technology Transfer in the ROC."*Proceedings of Conference on the Industrial Policies of the ROK and the ROC,* Conference Series 89-01, KDI, Seoul.

10. Hou and Chang (1981, pp. 474–481).

11. San Gee and Chao-nan Chen. (1988). *In-Service Training in Taiwan, ROC.* CIER Economic Monograph Series No. 20, CIER, Taipei, Taiwan.

12. San Gee. (1989). "Direct Foreign Investment and Technology Transfer in the ROC." *Proceedings of Conference on the Industrial Policies of the ROK and the ROC,* Conference Series 89-01, KDI, Seoul.

13. See report by Liu, P. (1989). "Big Glue Benefits from Funding R&D in Taiwan." ASIA/Pacific Business, May 15.

14. For a more detailed discussion on the information industry in Taiwan, see San Gee. (1990). "The Status and Evaluation of the Electronic Industry in Taiwan." *OECD Development Centre Technical Papers Series No. 29,* OECD June.

15. *Science and Technology Yearbook, Republic of China, 1988,* p. 416. National Science Council, Executive Yuan, in Chinese.

16. *Science and Technology Yearbook, Republic of China 1987.*

17. See San Gee. (1989). "A Comparison on R&D Expenditure among Domestic and FDI

Firms and a Study on Factors Which Determine This Expenditure—A Study on the Electronic Firms in Taiwan." *Academia Economic Papers,* the Institute of Economics, Academia Sinica, 17(1), March (in Chinese).

18. *Science and Technology Yearbook, Republic of China 1987.*
19. *Science and Technology, Republic of China 1987.*
20. *Science and Technology, Republic of China 1987.*

13

National Systems Supporting Technical Advance in Industry: The Brazilian Experience

CARL J. DAHLMAN
CLAUDIO R. FRISCHTAK

Brazil has the ninth largest GDP in the world, the sixth largest population, and the fifth largest area. Its per capita income in 1987 was US$2241, slightly above Mexico but below Argentina, South Korea, and Taiwan. The country is well endowed with natural resources, has a productive agriculture sector, and a mature and diversified industrial base. Manufacturing value-added in 1987 was US$79 billion, the ninth largest in the world, about 15% larger than that of Canada, two times that of Mexico or Korea, and almost three times that of Australia.

During the late 1960s and most of the 1970s Brazil was one of the fastest growing economies in the world. Yet in the past decade, output growth of Brazilian manufacturing industry has slowed significantly (Table 13.1). In contrast with the East Asian and several other newly industrializing countries, Brazil's average GDP and manufacturing growth were low, 2.9 and 2.2% p.a., respectively. In addition, Brazil's share of manufactured exports in manufactured output, 11.8% in 1987, is small, even though manufactured export growth has outstripped manufactured output growth since 1965.

This paper focuses on technological factors behind Brazil's faltering competitive position and the role of Brazil's innovation system. The *innovation system* is here defined as the network of agents and set of policies and institutions that affect the introduction of technology that is new to the economy. Since in the vast majority of developing countries technology is imported, the innovation system is defined very broadly to include policies toward arms-length technology transfer, intellectual property rights, importation of capital goods, and direct foreign investment. The innovation system also comprises the network of public and private institutions and agents supporting or undertaking scientific and technological activities, including research and development, diffusion, and creation of technical human capital.

The first section presents the historical and political context that gave birth to the innovation system in Brazil. It suggests that it was not until the late 1800s, with labor shortages in agriculture and depletion of mines, that there were strong enough incen-

Table 13.1. Selected Economic Indicators

	GDP Per Capita 1988 (US$)	GDP		Growth of Manufactured Output		Growth of Manufactured Exports		Share of Manufactured Exports in Output 1987 (%)
		1965–1980 (%)	1980–1988 (%)	1965–1980 (%)	1980–1988 (%)	1965–1980 (%)	1980–1988 (%)	
Brazil	2,241.07	8.8	2.9	9.8	2.2	22.1	6.2	11.8
Indonesia	476.09	8.0	5.1	12.0	13.1	13.3	35.4	44.8
Japan	23,195.02	6.5	3.9	8.2	6.7	11.9	5.3	32.4
Korea	4,078.81	9.6	9.9	18.7	13.5	31.2	14.7	103.1
Mexico	2,111.11	6.5	0.5	7.4	0.2	9.4	21.1	27.1
Thailand	1,063.30	7.2	6.0	11.2	6.8	21.3	19.3	53.3
Turkey	1,196.28	6.3	5.3	7.5	7.9	26.4	23.3	42.6

Sources: World Development Report (1990); World Tables (1989–90 edition). International Financial Statistics (December 1989).

tives for innovation and technological development. Those needs were expanded greatly with twentieth-century industrialization. Yet it is only after World War II that the government's focus on science and technology is explicit, and centered in the build-up of an institutional infrastructure and in the development of human resources. This process was formalized during the military period, particularly after 1970, when scientific and technological development became a specific policy objective.

Although the enlargement of the S&T base helped improve the competitive position of Brazilian firms in the 1970s, its impact was limited in view of the still modest importance that domestic firms attributed to technological development. The second section briefly discusses Brazil's competitive status in world markets and suggests that its faltering position is related to the limited domestic technological efforts of industrial producers. The third section shows that the modest nature of these efforts has not been offset by substantial technology imports (which have been restricted by regulatory constraints on arms-length technology transfer), direct foreign investment, and capital goods imports. Although some of these restrictions, in combination with government financial support, induced firms to engage in technological activities, relatively few producers were able to approach the international best-practice "frontier" in the 1980s.

In view of the modest technological activities undertaken by local private producers and the limited inflows of foreign technology, development efforts fall on the shoulders of the public sector. The fourth section notes that 80–90% of R&D expenditures have been undertaken by the government. Unfortunately, dispersion of these public sector R&D efforts, and weak linkages between public R&D institutes and the productive sector, have meant that the flow of useful technological services has not been commensurate with the volume of public sector resources allocated to technological activities. Finally, in human resource formation—an area in which the public sector role is critical—weak investment decisions have undermined the creation of technological capabilities for the future. The final section presents the chapter's conclusions.

HISTORICAL AND POLITICAL CONTEXT

A complex interaction between economic forces and political regimes has shaped the development of science and technology (S&T) in Brazil. This section highlights some of the salient dimensions of such interaction in order to provide a historical context for understanding many of the current features of Brazil's innovation system.

1500–1900: From Colonization to the Twentieth Century

During this phase, which spanned four centuries, Brazil was a source of agricultural and mining products for the world. Brazilian economic history during this period can be characterized as a period of boom and bust cycles of primary commodity exports. These have included sugar, gold, cotton, cocoa, rubber, and finally coffee, whose importance continued into the twentieth century and provided the economic foundation for industrialization.[1]

The main innovations during the colonial period, which lasted until 1822 when Brazil gained its independence from Portugal, were the result of agricultural technologies being transplanted to Brazil. They included new seeds (cotton), crop techniques (for tobacco, sugarcane), and the use of manure for fertilizer. Since land and slave labor were abundant during this period, there were few incentives to use land more efficiently or to mechanize production. In mining, primitive technologies were transferred as minerals were readily accessible near the surface. During this early period the country also experienced moderate development of cartography and military engineering oriented to the construction of forts, canals, bridges, and the production of weapons and munitions.[2]

The migration of the Royal Portuguese Family to Brazil in 1808, fleeing Napoleon's armies, led to the establishment of a number of scientific and technological institutions in the Brazilian colony. These included the Medical School of Bahia, the Medical School of Rio de Janeiro, the National Library, the Royal Farm, the National Museum, a gunpowder factory, an iron foundry, the School of Mines of Ouro Preto (1875), and the Agricultural Research Station of Campinas (1887).

It was not until the late 1800s, however, that there were strong economic incentives for greater attention to research and development. In mining, labor shortages, exacerbated by the abolition of slavery in 1889, combined with the depletion of the surface deposits, called for improved mining technology, a greater degree of mechanization, and a better understanding of chemistry and mineralogy. Similarly, low yields and labor shortages created a need to increase productivity in agriculture and led to the establishment of several agricultural colleges and research institutes. The Agricultural Research Station of Campinas and the Luis de Queiroz Agricultural College (both in the state of São Paulo), in particular, contributed in a major way to improve agricultural productivity, especially of export crops such as coffee, sugarcane, and cotton.[3]

1900–1946: Laying the Basis for Industry-Led Growth

The first three decades of the twentieth century saw the beginning of industrialization in Brazil. In spite of some early efforts at import substitution in the 1890s, on the eve of World War I Brazil's industrial structure was very primitive and only 3% of the labor force was employed in manufacturing.[4] The difficulty of importing industrial goods during the war strengthened the need for import substitution. However, most import substitutes were relatively simple products and did not demand much research capability or engineering manpower. Most of the technology was obtained by copying from abroad and through firm-to-firm diffusion.

An important development during the early part of this period was the spread of the railroad, which brought with it the need for increased capabilities in civil engineering and greater technological sophistication in production and use of steel (including foundry, forging, and machining operations) and steam power. The Ouro Preto School of Mines was the first civilian institution to become involved in training programs for the establishment and expansion of the railroad network. Another was the São Paulo Polytechnic, which set up a Laboratory of Material Resistance in 1926 to test materials and equipment for railroads and power plants.

The Brazilian economy, like many other Latin American primary products exporters, went into depression with the economic crash of 1929. Exports collapsed, and the lack of foreign exchange stimulated domestic production of cement, chemicals, paper, metals, and textiles. The import-substitution drive also received strong impetus from World War II, which made it difficult to obtain key inputs such as steel and capital goods. By the end of the war, the country's manufacturing sector had become quite diversified though not very competitive by world standards. Still, the technological complexity of many of the new industries increased the demand for engineers and technical support services.[5]

1947–1964: Heavy Industrialization and a Preliminary Focus on Science and Technology

This period was characterized by a strong drive toward industrialization from the second Vargas (1951–1954) and the Kubitschek governments (1956–1960). The industrial sector grew 262% in contrast to only 87% for the agricultural sector. Kubitschek's "Plano de Metas" (1956–1961) was the first organized effort focused on heavy industry and supportive infrastructure. It was built around ambitious projects in energy, transportation, steel and petroleum refining, chemicals and petrochemicals, capital goods, automobiles, and pharmaceuticals.

One of the key elements of the industrial development strategy was to induce foreign firms to set up manufacturing facilities in Brazil. This consisted not only of protecting the local market but also of offering significant subsidies and special treatment for foreign investors. By 1960, foreign subsidiaries accounted for more than 50% of the capital goods producers, 70% of chemicals (except petrochemicals), 90% of pharmaceuticals, and 100% of the nascent automobile industry.[6]

At the same time, however, significant steps were taken in the science and technology area. The National Research Council (CNPq) was established in 1951 to promote research in all areas. However, one of its main purposes, as clearly articulated by Admiral Alvaro Alberto da Mota Silva, CNPq's president from 1951 to 1955, was to prepare Brazil to use its mineral resources for the production of atomic energy.[7]

The creation of CNPq has to be seen in the context of postwar polarization, competition, and conflict. Harnessing atomic energy was perceived as the key to military power and a crucial step for accelerating the process of economic development.[8] The emphasis on science and technology during this period was also a matter of national prestige. There was an important demonstration effect from the scientific and technological activities of the advanced economies that drove countries such as Brazil to try to keep up in order to gain international stature. Much of the effort was driven by the military. Many of its personnel received training in the United States and came to appreciate the importance of a strong technological base for military power. A number of important institutions were set up by the armed forces during this period. Possibly the most successful was the Aerospace Research Center (CTA) established in 1947, which played a major role in the development of the Brazilian aviation industry as well as in the gasohol program.

In the early 1960s the Brazilian economy lost steam as ambitious projects of the Kubitschek era (which included the building of the new capital of Brasilia) and subsequent poor economic management led to growing macroeconomic imbalances. The deterioration in economic and political stability eventually led to a military coup in 1964 and to 21 years of military rule.

1964–1985: The Military Period and the Formalization of the Science and Technology Infrastructure

Economic Development Plans
The period of military rule saw many changes in the structure of the Brazilian economy and in policy-making. Greater efforts were directed toward planning for development and formalizing key programs, and increased resources were allocated to science and technology. The first military government (1964–1967) focused essentially on reestablishing macroeconomic stability and introducing important economic reforms in the tax and financial systems, whereas the one that followed gave emphasis to economic recovery and the resumption of growth. The third military government produced the "First National Development Plan" (1972–1974). The objective of that plan was to achieve sustained industrial and economic growth based on an expansion of exports and the domestic market. As part of a strategy of increasing national power, new areas (such as nuclear energy, electronics, and space research) were expected to have rapid development. The plan also expressed concern over the growing presence of multinational firms in Brazil.

The Second National Development Plan (1975–1979) set out to adjust Brazil's economy to the oil shortage by deepening the process of import substitution and moving the country toward energy self-sufficiency. Yet changes in the real exchange rate were avoided, and so was tighter fiscal and monetary control. At the same time there was growing reliance on domestic and external borrowing to finance investment and growth. Brazil entered a period of "debt-led growth."[9] By the end of 1978 Brazil's external debt had risen to $40 billion compared to only $3.5 billion in 1968 (for a more detailed discussion, see the next section). Brazil's economic situation was worsened further by the 1979 oil shock, which led to another spree of external borrowing, such that by the end of 1985 it had the largest foreign debt in the world at $100 billion. At the same time, inflation accelerated from average annual rates of 20.7% in 1970/1974 to 45.9% in 1975/1979 and 141.7% in 1980/1984. Thus, although the country maintained relatively high rates of economic growth in the 1970s, it did so at the cost of growing macroeconomic imbalances.

Science and Technology Policies and Institution-Building Efforts

Three important financing institutions relating to S&T were created during the first 3 years of the military period: FUNTEC, FINAME, and FINEP.[10] Yet only in 1968, scientific and technological development became a specific policy objective. The 1968–1969 development plan (Programa Estrategico do Desenvolvimiento—PED) defined for the first time an explicit policy for S&T at the federal level. The PED proposed the creation of a National System of Scientific and Technological Development (SNDCT), of S&T Basic Plans that would spell out the actions foreseen in the National Development plans, and of a National Fund for Scientific and Technological Development (FNDCT) to finance the SNDCT.

Since the creation of the SNDCT, three Basic Plans have been issued, covering the periods 1973–1985. The First Basic Plan of Science and Technology Development (I PBDCT—1973–1974) programmed an increase in the volume of resources for S&T by strengthening the FNDCT and other financial mechanisms. The Second Plan (II PBDCT—1975–1979) set priorities that included the development of new technologies, with research on nonconventional sources of energy, space activities, and oceanography.[11] In the area of basic research, emphasis was placed on human resource development through the National Graduate Education Plan. The Second PBDCT also identified the growing presence of multinationals and the weakness of national firms as obstacles to the development of local technology.

The Third Basic Plan of Science and Technology (III PBDCT—1980–1985) aimed at expanding the supply of S&T resources while reinforcing the technological capabilities of national firms. The Third Plan differed from the previous two in that rather than specifying government actions in the form of programs, projects, and priority activities, it established a set of policy directions that was supposed to orient the actions of the public and private sector. Furthermore, it did not present any figures on planned expenditures.

In the industrial area, the most important development was the creation of the Secretaria de Tecnologia Industrial (STI) of the Ministry of Industry and Commerce (MIC) in 1972. It was the first sectoral science and technology unit to be established within a ministry. The STI took over various S&T institutions already existing in MIC, and its activities included (1) carrying out R&D programs through its own institutes, (2) funding for technological development in public and private enterprises, and for the development of specific technologies,[12] (3) supplying technological information to firms, (4) administering a system of intellectual property rights (basically patent and trademarks) and regulating technology transfer through INPI (National Institute of Industrial Property Rights), and (5) acting as the executive secretariat of the National Council for Metrology, Normalization and Quality Control (CONMETRO).

Overall, the military period can be characterized as a time when a planning system was established for S&T and strong emphasis placed on institutional development. Science and technology were perceived as important elements for enhancing national power. The first military government represented the more liberal faction of the armed forces. The three subsequent military governments represented more nationalistic tendencies, with greater preoccupation with issues of national sovereignty and autonomy. These tendencies found expression in a strong emphasis on strengthening national technological capability in military and strategic areas such as informatics, telecommunications, the defense industry, aviation, and nuclear energy. These tendencies also led to a restrictive attitude toward international technology transfer and heavy emphasis on local technology development. The military period also exhibited a strong statist tendency, which was expressed in the drive for state participation in strategic sectors such as steel, petrochemicals and chemicals, heavy capital goods, and many important intermediate goods industries. Although it was often necessary to work with multinationals as equity partners as a way of getting access to foreign technology, the government generally sought to control the enterprises by inviting minority private national participation in order to have majority local control.

The Brazilian "miracle" was short-lived. Debt and inflation-led growth proved to be unsustainable in the longer term. As argued in the next section, a combination of macroeconomic instability, lower rates of investment, and growing inefficiencies in the use and allocation of resources led in the 1980s to a reversal of the competitive gains achieved in the Brazilian economy in the previous decade. Yet the investments made in the build-up of human resource and institutional capacity in science and technology during the military period may still prove to have far reaching consequences for the competitive position of Brazilian industry when investment levels recover. Although the technological efforts of Brazilian firms are still limited, there is growing awareness that in a more open and competitive environment the ability to innovate and produce low-cost, high-quality products will be the key to their survival. It will call for a more effective use of existing S&T infrastructure, including a more balanced development of the human resource base.

BRAZIL'S COMPETITIVE POSITION AND THE TECHNOLOGICAL EFFORTS OF BRAZILIAN FIRMS

Brazil's competitive position in the 1970s improved significantly. Between 1970 and 1980 Brazil expanded its world market share in 83 of 93 industrial segments (three-digit SITC categories) with positive manufactured exports (Table 13.2).[13] Moreover, Brazil had an impressive record of market diversification and product differentiation in the 1970s. Between 1971 and 1980, in most machinery and transport equipment segments—and in shoes, textiles, and fibers—the number of countries importing from Brazil increased, and the number of products exported in each goods category expanded. In many categories—such as office machinery, boats and ships, aircraft, and textiles—the export composition shifted to higher value-added products.[14]

Brazil's Lagging International Competitiveness in the 1980s

Since 1980, the competitive dynamics of the Brazilian economy have changed substantially, with constant or declining market shares in 46 of the 93 relevant SITC segments, including technologically sophisticated areas such as electric machinery and instruments (Table 13.2). The only significant exceptions were aircraft, telecommunications equipment, and electric distribution equipment. Moreover, in contrast with the 1970s, when 20 of 26 segments in which Brazil had achieved a "revealed" comparative advantage (i.e., normalized market shares greater than one) increased their shares, only nine segments did so in the period 1980–1987.[15] Virtually all nontraditional and nonnatural resource-based manufactured products had their gains reversed.[16] Surprisingly, this reversal even occurred in nontraditional products such as textiles, garments, travel goods, and handbags, in which Brazil could have expected to maintain its competitive position.

Brazil is now saddled with many internationally uncompetitive segments, their number having grown significantly since the early 1980s. A study of 67 manufacturing subsectors reveals that in the period 1983/1985, 45% were internationally competitive (that is, the ratio of domestic to international prices was less than one) and 7% were marginally competitive (domestic to international price ratios between 1 and 1.1). A similar comparison shows that in 1988 only 15% of the subsectors were clearly competitive, while in 12% of the cases competitiveness was marginal. These studies suggest that the proportion of fully or marginally competitive segments fell by nearly half (from 52 to 27%) between 1983/1985 and 1988.[17]

Additional evidence of a deteriorating competitive position comes from a 1989 survey of the views of 550 major industrial producers. Although most industrialists judged the Brazil's industrial sector to be more efficient than at the beginning of the decade, nearly 65% of those interviewed also perceived the extent of modernization as "insufficient" to keep up with the international price performance frontier, whereas only 3.8% thought that it was "quite adequate."[18]

Several factors explain the country's inability to sustain its competitive position. After the first oil shock in 1983, Brazil faced a further 38% decline in its terms of trade in 1977–1981. Yet, macroeconomic adjustment was postponed, and as a result Brazil's growth became increasingly debt dependent. By the late 1970s international interest rates rose rapidly, and economies driven by debt-led growth strategies became unacceptably risky for lenders once countries began to default on sovereign debt. In the case of Brazil, the flow of capital was reversed, from plus to minus 4–5% between the mid-1970s to the mid-1980s. These shocks led to severe macroeconomic instability, two major recessions, and a strong loss of confidence in the longer term prospects of the economy. Ultimately, they brought about a significant contraction in the rate of investment. The ratio of investment to GDP—after reaching nearly 25% in 1975—fell to 15–16% in 1988.

Brazil's falling performance relative to other industrializing countries has been due not only to a contraction in the rate of investment but also to inefficient resource allocation and use. Brazil has a large and diversified industrial base, the result of a relatively long process of natural and policy-induced import substitution. Beginning in the 1950s, producers were attracted to invest in new industrial segments by a combination of trade barriers, entry regulations, and fiscal, credit, and other incentives. During this period, Brazilian industry went through substantial structural change (Table 13.3). The share in value-added of traditional consumer goods sectors such as textiles, food products, beverages, and tobacco decreased significantly, whereas the shares of machinery, electrical equipment, transport equipment, and chemicals/petrochemicals increased.

In the 1970s, and within the framework of the Second National Development Plan (1974–1979), the intermediates and capital goods industries were targeted and capacity was created at very fast rates. Producers were attracted to invest in these sectors by a combination of trade barriers, entry regulations, and fiscal, credit, and other incentives. The goal was to shift resources to domestic firms so as to stimulate and enable them to invest in targeted sectors. As part of an import substitution strategy,

Table 13.2. Shifts in Market Shares for Brazil's Manufacturing Exports, 1970–1987

		Market Shares			Ratios	
SITC	Commodities	1970	1980	1987	80/70	87/80
512	Organic chemicals	0.003	0.009	0.012	3.0	1.3
513	Inorg elemnts, oxides, etc.	0.000	0.004	0.008	9.3	1.8
514	Other inorganic chemicals	0.001	0.002	0.004	1.6	1.6
515	Radioactive etc. material	0.000	0.000	0.000	0.0	37.1
521	Coal, petroleum etc. chems	0.000	0.000	0.004	5.1	68.1
531	Synt dye, nat indgo, lakes	0.000	0.001	0.001	4.2	0.7
532	Dyes nes, tanning prods	0.040	0.041	0.052	1.0	1.3
533	Pigments, paints, etc.	0.000	0.002	0.002	11.1	0.9
541	Medicinal etc. products	0.002	0.003	0.003	1.6	1.1
551	Essentl oil, perfume, etc.	0.023	0.018	0.014	0.8	0.8
553	Perfume, cosmetics, etc.	0.001	0.005	0.003	4.8	0.6
554	Soaps, cleaning etc. preps	0.000	0.006	0.002	16.1	0.4
561	Fertilizers manufactured	0.000	0.000	0.001	31.9	4.2
571	Explosives, pyrotech prod	0.002	0.041	0.168	23.8	4.1
581	Plastic materials etc.	0.000	0.003	0.007	20.4	2.4
599	Chemicals nes	0.002	0.008	0.008	3.4	1.1
611	Leather	0.021	0.029	0.032	1.4	1.1
612	Leather etc. manufactures	0.005	0.025	0.044	5.1	1.8
613	Fur skins tanned, dressed	0.000	0.001	0.002	55.4	2.4
621	Materials of rubber	0.000	0.003	0.003	16.9	0.9
629	Rubber articles nes	0.003	0.011	0.016	4.1	1.4
631	Veneers, plywood, etc.	0.025	0.023	0.022	0.9	1.0
632	Wood manufactures nes	0.003	0.012	0.010	4.7	0.8
633	Cork manufactures	0.000	0.001	0.001	18.4	0.7
641	Paper and paperboard	0.000	0.006	0.009	78.5	1.5
642	Articles of paper etc.	0.000	0.004	0.006	16.1	1.4
651	Textile yarn and thread	0.004	0.020	0.018	5.1	0.9
652	Cotton fabrics, woven	0.006	0.016	0.015	2.6	1.0
653	Woven textiles noncotton	0.001	0.004	0.002	5.3	0.6
654	Lace, ribbons, tulle, etc.	0.004	0.003	0.003	0.7	0.9
655	Special textile etc. prod	0.003	0.020	0.008	6.0	0.4
656	Textile etc. products nes	0.003	0.028	0.034	8.1	1.2
657	Floor covr, tapestry etc.	0.000	0.001	0.001	5.2	1.2
661	Cement etc. building prod	0.000	0.006	0.004	17.3	0.7
662	Clay, refractory bldg prd	0.002	0.012	0.014	6.8	1.2
663	Oth nonmetal mineral mfs	0.001	0.007	0.005	7.5	0.7
664	Glass	0.010	0.005	0.006	0.5	1.0
665	Glassware	0.000	0.004	0.006	14.6	1.6
666	Pottery	0.001	0.007	0.009	7.0	1.2
667	Pearl, prec-, semi-p stone	0.004	0.002	0.005	0.6	2.1
671	Pig iron etc.	0.026	0.073	0.145	2.8	2.0
672	Iron, stl primary forms	0.015	0.009	0.064	0.6	7.5
673	Iron and steel shapes	0.009	0.007	0.023	0.7	3.4
674	Irn, stl univ, plate, sheet	0.004	0.011	0.022	2.9	1.9
675	Iron, steel hoop, strip	0.000	0.004	0.004	34.8	1.0
676	Railwy rails etc. irn, stl	0.000	0.005	0.000	25.0	0.0
677	Irn, stl wire excl w rod	0.002	0.005	0.007	2.8	1.5

		Market Shares			Ratios	
SITC	Commodities	1970	1980	1987	80/70	87/80
678	Iron, stl tubes, pipes, etc.	0.001	0.010	0.007	8.3	0.7
679	Irn, stl castings unworkd	—	0.002	0.005	—	2.8
691	Structures and parts nes	0.000	0.002	0.004	14.9	1.5
692	Metal tanks, boxes, etc.	0.001	0.009	0.007	10.0	0.8
693	Wire products non electr	0.000	0.009	0.012	19.4	1.3
694	Stl, coppr nails, nuts, etc.	0.000	0.003	0.003	10.9	1.1
695	Tools	0.004	0.007	0.005	1.6	0.7
696	Cutlery	0.006	0.020	0.018	3.6	0.9
697	Base mtl household equip	0.001	0.012	0.007	15.2	0.6
698	Metal manufactures nes	0.000	0.003	0.003	7.8	1.2
711	Power machinery non-elec	0.000	0.013	0.014	34.5	1.1
712	Agricultural machinery	0.001	0.016	0.016	23.2	1.0
714	Office machines	0.007	0.011	0.002	1.6	0.2
715	Metalworking machinery	0.002	0.006	0.003	3.1	0.5
717	Textile, leather machnry	0.002	0.005	0.005	3.2	1.0
718	Machs for spcl industries	0.002	0.007	0.005	2.7	0.8
719	Machines nes nonelectric	0.001	0.005	0.005	5.7	0.9
722	Elec pwr mach, switchgear	0.001	0.005	0.003	5.1	0.7
723	Electr distributing mach	0.001	0.002	0.006	2.2	2.3
724	Telecommunications equip	0.001	0.005	0.010	4.7	2.0
725	Domestic electric equip	0.001	0.004	0.005	2.7	1.5
726	Electro-medcl, xray equip	0.001	0.001	0.000	1.7	0.3
729	Electrical machinery nes	0.001	0.005	0.003	3.7	0.5
731	Railway vehicles	0.000	0.016	0.004	47.4	0.3
732	Road motor vehicles	0.000	0.008	0.009	18.3	1.1
733	Road vehicles non-motor	0.000	0.007	0.001	48.0	0.2
734	Aircraft	0.000	0.003	0.011	40.5	3.3
735	Ships and boats	0.001	0.007	0.010	6.2	1.4
812	Plumbg, heating, lghtng equ	0.000	0.004	0.003	9.0	0.7
821	Furniture	0.001	0.003	0.002	1.9	0.9
831	Travel goods, handbags	0.000	0.013	0.012	41.9	1.0
841	Clothing not of fur	0.001	0.003	0.003	6.0	1.0
842	Fur etc. clothes, prod	0.000	0.017	0.004	299.8	0.2
851	Footwear	0.005	0.033	0.057	6.7	1.7
861	Instruments, apparatus	0.000	0.002	0.002	11.5	0.8
862	Photo, cinema supplies	0.001	0.007	0.010	6.7	1.4
863	Developed cinema film	0.000	0.001	0.000	2.3	0.1
864	Watches and clocks	0.000	0.001	0.001	15.1	1.5
891	Sound recorders, producrs	0.001	0.001	0.000	1.8	0.1
892	Printed matter	0.001	0.003	0.002	2.1	0.6
893	Articles of plastic nes	0.000	0.004	0.002	22.4	0.4
894	Toys, sporting goods etc.	0.001	0.006	0.003	5.7	0.5
895	Office supplies nes	0.000	0.002	0.005	13.0	2.1
896	Works of art etc.	0.000	0.000	0.000	0.7	0.1
897	Gold, silver ware, jewelry	0.004	0.002	0.003	0.6	1.3
899	Other manufactured goods	0.001	0.006	0.005	7.9	0.8
		0.002	0.007	0.008	3.5	1.1

Table 13.3. Changes in Brazil's Industrial Structure 1949–1985 Gross Value-Added (Percentage Distribution)

	1949	1963	1975	1980	1985
Nonmetallic mineral	7.4	5.2	6.2	5.7	4.3
Metal products	9.4	12.0	12.6	12.0	12.2
Machinery	2.2	3.2	10.3	10.1	9.2
Electrical equipment	1.7	6.1	5.8	7.0	7.6
Transport equipment	2.3	10.5	6.3	7.5	6.4
Wood products.	6.1	4.0	2.9	2.6	1.6
Furniture	—	—	2.0	1.8	1.4
Paper products	2.1	2.9	2.5	2.8	2.9
Rubber products	2.0	1.9	1.7	1.3	1.8
Leather products	1.3	0.7	0.5	0.5	0.6
Chemicals[a]	9.4	15.5	12.0	14.5	17.3
Pharmaceuticals	—	—	2.5	1.6	1.7
Perfumes, soap, candles	—	—	1.2	0.9	0.9
Plastic products	—	—	2.2	2.3	2.2
Textiles	20.1	11.6	6.1	6.2	6.0
Clothing and shoes	4.3	3.6	3.8	4.7	5.2
Food products	19.7	14.1	11.3	11.6	12.0
Beverages	4.3	3.2	1.8	1.3	1.2
Tobacco	1.6	1.6	1.0	0.8	0.8
Printing and publishing	4.2	2.5	3.6	2.5	1.9
Miscellaneous	1.9	1.4	3.7	2.7	2.7
Total	100.0	100.0	100.0	100.0	100.0

[a]Includes chemicals, pharmaceuticals, perfumes, and plastic products for 1949 and 1963.
Source: Baer et al. (1987, Table 3, p. 278) and IBGE.

these policies were successful. In key industrial segments, import–output ratios fell quite dramatically (Table 13.4).

However, efforts to deepen the industrial base, as well as to adjust the economy to the adverse macroeconomic shocks, were based on restricting imports. In 1986, the ratio of imports to GDP in Brazil was 5.8%, lower than Japan's (an economy nine times as large as Brazil) and one-sixth of Korea's (Table 13.5). Correspondingly, Brazil's industrial base became highly diversified. The extent of import-substitution driven diversification and absence of intraindustry specialization is suggested by extremely low ratios of manufactured imports over manufactured value-added (Table 13.5).

As noted above, Brazil is now saddled with an increasing number of internationally noncompetitive areas. They are a product, inter alia, of structural rigidities introduced by the instruments used to spur industrial development. Entry and exit barriers, overdiversified production structures, and high mandated domestic content levels slowed down mobility, tied-up resources, brought about low degrees of inter- and intraindustry specialization, and led ultimately to high cost structures.

Such policies also shielded producers from domestic and international competition. As the industrial sector matured, these protective barriers solidified, and firms became increasingly secure in their market positions. Protection from competition made firms less resilient and management less responsive to the rapid shifts in the international economy: an accelerated rate of innovation and intense technological

Table 13.4. Import–Output Ratios in Selected Industrial Segments

Industrial Segments[a]	1967	1973	1980
Mechanical equipment (66)	45.6	38.0	18.5
Electrical and telecommunications equipment (72)	13.2	22.5	15.2
Paper and paper products (25, 64)	7.5	9.2	4.8
Chemicals (231.2, 266, 42, 43, 5)	15.3	17.4	10.6

[a]Numbers in parentheses are the corresponding SITC code(s).

Source: Fasano Filho (n.d., Table 2).

and commercial rivalry were accompanied by increased protectionism in developed countries.

The Scope and Intensity of R&D Activities among Industrial Firms

The inability of Brazilian firms to keep up with the international frontier is a reflection of a highly heterogeneous industrial structure, relatively few competitive producers,[19] and limited technological efforts. Brazil's large and diversified industrial base—the result of a long process of import substitution—is insufficiently "deep." Relatively few firms are in a position to consolidate and expand international market share on the basis of substantial gains in productivity, continuous improvements in product quality and reliability, or development of new designs. Most producers have based their market position more on extensive exploitation of natural resources and reliance on low-wage labor than on the quality and productivity of labor itself and the introduction of new or better products.

Evidence strongly suggests that R&D, as a formal activity, is undertaken by relatively few firms. The number of firms declaring expenditures on R&D in their income tax returns fell from 1050 in 1976 and 1977 to 780 at the end of the 1981–1983 recession, but recovered to 1090 by 1985.[20] R&D expenditures by these firms were 0.2% of their net revenues in 1983, but doubled to 0.4% by 1985.[21] These R&D expenditures are highly concentrated. Data from 1983 show that state enterprises accounted for 62.6% of budgeted R&D outlays, with eight producers responsible for over half of the total expenditures.[22] Only about 25 private industrial groups were responsible for an additional 17.4% of expenditures (Table 13.6).

The smallness of industry-related R&D in Brazil also is reflected in the distribution of researchers (Table 13.7). In 1986 there were 52,863 researchers out of 3.5 million college graduates, a relatively low proportion; the ratio of researchers to population was 4 to 10,000, whereas in developed countries the number is about 40 to 10,000

Table 13.5. Share of Manufactured Imports in Manufacturing, Value-Added Share of Merchandise Imports in GDP Selected Countries, 1986 (%)

Indicator	Brazil	Indonesia	Japan	Korea	Mexico	Thailand	Turkey
Merchandise imports/GDP	5.8	17.8	6.5	32.2	9.4	22.0	21.0
Manufactured imports/ manufacturing value-added	10.8	102.4	31.0	74.0	32.3	83.0	51.4

Source: World Development Report (1988) and IENIN data base.

Table 13.6. R&D Outlays in Brazilian Industry, 1983[a]

Nature of Firm	Proportion of Total Outlays (%)
Public sector enterprises	62.6
Private groups	17.4
Private firms focused on individual markets	20.0

[a]Included were 1118 firms, of which 43 were public enterprises and 1075 private producers. Firms in the electric machinery and made-to-order capital goods subsectors were not included in this study. As a result, the percentage for public enterprises is biased upward.
Source: Paulinyi (1984).

inhabitants. It is striking that 91.6% of researchers worked in government, the majority in public universities (62.0%), followed by specialized S&T institutions (20%), state enterprises (3.4%), and other agencies (6.1%).

Only 8.4% of researchers were in nongovernmental jobs. Most of them worked in private universities (6.5%); relatively few worked in private research institutions (0.5%) or other agencies (0.8%). Particularly noteworthy is the minute share of researchers in private firms (0.6%). Even including state enterprises, the percentage of R&D personnel employed by the productive sector is modest, accounting for less than 4% of the total.[23]

Information compiled in the mid-1980s indicates that R&D continues to be undertaken by a narrow set of firms; a core of 366 firms can be regarded as "R&D active" (Table 13.8).[24] As expected from international experience, "technology-intensive" segments such as electronics, vehicles, and the chemical/petrochemical/pharmaceutical cluster contain the largest share of firms active in R&D. Conversely, segments such as food and beverages, textiles, garments and footwear, and leather and wood products have relatively few R&D-engaged firms, with capital goods and metal fabrication somewhere in between.

Among R&D active firms, 88 are major exporters, most concentrated in steel, vehicles, petrochemicals, chemicals, and autoparts. Some of these are world class producers in sophisticated segments (such as aircraft, missiles, high-performance pistons,

Table 13.7. Distribution of Researchers According to Place of Activity, 1986

Institution	Total		Doctorates	
	No.	%	No.	%
Universities	36,112	68.3	9,952	86.6
(public universities)	32,775	62.0	n.a.	n.a.
Specialized S&T institutions	10,856	20.5	1,358	11.8
Government agencies	3,203	6.1	82	0.7
State enterprises	1,811	3.4	38	0.3
Private institutions	727	1.4	60	0.5
Private firms	295	0.6	15	0.1
Other	111	0.2	—	—
Total	52,863	100.0	11,492	100.0

Source: Martins and Queiroz (1987).

Table 13.8. Sectoral Distribution of Export-Oriented and R&D Engaged Brazilian Firms, 1985–1988

	Industrial Sector	R&D Active	R&D Active Exporters[a]	R&D Active With No Exports	Total[b] Firms	R&D Active as % of Total Firms
I	Steel and other metals	24	17	7	517	4.6
II	Metal fabrication	9	3	6		
III	Capital goods	49	7	42	419[c]	13.8[c]
IV	Vehicles	17	12	5	70	24.3
V	Auto parts	12	8	4	139	8.6
VI	Rubber products	3	3	0	na	na
VII	Electronics	90	4	86	258	34.9
VIII	Petrochemicals	34	12	22		
IX	Chemicals	47	8	39		
X	Fertilizer	8	0	8		
XI	Pharmaceuticals/fine chemicals	13	0	13	635[d]	16.6[d]
XII	Pulp and paper	9	4	5	131	6.9
XIII	Nonmetallic minerals	12	0	12	231	5.2
XIV	Textiles, garments, footwear	8	4	4		
XV	Leather goods, wood products	4	2	2	757[e]	1.6[e]
XVI	Food and beverages	24	5	19	712	3.4
XVII	Others	3	0	3		—
C1	Metal-mechanics I–V	111	47	64	1145	9.7
C2	Electronics VII	90	4	86	258	34.9
C3	Chemicals/petrochemicals VIII–XI	102	20	82	635	16.1
C4	Traditional XIV–XVI	36	11	25	1469	2.5
Total		366	88	278	3869	9.5

[a]Drawn from the Cacex data of firms exporting over $6 million in 1985.

[b]The universe of medium to large manufacturing firms with published balance sheets, and drawn from Gazeta Mercantil, *Balanco Annual,* 1987.

[c]Includes II and III.

[d]Includes VIII–XI.

[e]Includes XIV–XV.

Source: Own compilation of R&D engaged firms based on information from ANPEI (National Association of Industrial R&D Centers), the Institute of Industrial Economics of the Federal University of Rio de Janeiro, and newsmagazines/newspaper accounts of R&D activity by individual firms.

and special alloys). Substantial production, design, and marketing experience, combined with purposeful R&D efforts, result in their competitive strength. A number of R&D active producers are multinational firms, mostly in the metal-mechanics industries (particularly vehicles), with some in rubber products and petrochemicals. Their R&D efforts were not necessarily undertaken in response to export requirements (although many were drawn to export markets in response to strong government inducements—such as the BEFIEX export program), but to local market demands (e.g., for ethanol-based engines or large hydroelectric turbines). However, the majority of R&D-engaged exporters are those that combine Brazil's traditional sources of comparative advantage (abundant natural resources and inexpensive labor) with a measure of product development and process improvements to stay competitive in world markets. They are producers of steel, autoparts, pulp and paper, chemicals, textiles, and food and beverages.

Most firms that carry out R&D but do not export are in electronics and capital goods. There are segments with traditionally high R&D intensity, as suggested by international experience, and that since the mid-1970s have expanded rapidly, behind high protectionist barriers. Although government policies and institutional support mechanisms have induced these producers to undertake substantial R&D, such activity has been insufficient to close in the technological frontier. Moreover, some efforts probably have been misdirected and wasteful. Continuously high levels of protection have allowed producers to fall behind best practice without being penalized by competition. Across-the-board import substitution also led to excessive product fragmentation, with the dispersion of technological resources. As a result, low levels of intraindustry and intrafirm specialization precluded these producers from reaping economies of scale in production and development of new products.

R&D is just one dimension of firms' technological activities, however, and possibly not the most important. Production planning and organization, troubleshooting, rescaling, raw materials adaptation, and quality control are other technological tasks that have a direct bearing on firms' competitiveness. But the fact that so few firms were engaged in R&D is significant, as firms tend to formalize R&D activities once competitive pressures require new designs and major improvements in production processes.

Moreover, despite the fact that many industrial firms are engaged in minor technological activities—ranging from the design of tools to improvements in plant layout and production processes—most of those activities have had only limited impact in bringing firms closer to best practice.[25] A detailed study of these firms' technological behavior has shown that raw material inventory was monitored by over 92% of sampled producers, but more than 81% did so manually. Similarly, nearly 93% of firms were engaged in quality control, while just 28.8% employed modern methods (such as statistical process control).[26] At the same time, only 23.5% were committed to developing new products in a systematic way. Imitation—through reverse engineering or hiring away competitors—was perceived to be the general rule in industry.[27] These findings suggest that most technology generated in Brazilian industry consists of minor innovations and adaptations—sufficient to cater to a relatively protected domestic market but inadequate to sustain its competitive position in world markets.

In sum, the evidence assembled in this section points to very limited commitment by Brazilian industrial firms to R&D and to technological development in general. As shown in the next section, such limited efforts are not offset by a regime to facilitate technology imports. The effectiveness of imported technology is hampered, in any case, by the weak absorptive capacity of Brazilian industry.

TECHNOLOGY POLICIES

Explicit policies for industrial technology development in Brazil have followed the broader industrial policies of the Government. The acquisition of foreign technology through arms-length technology transfer, capital goods imports, and direct foreign investment has been strongly influenced by the government objective of minimizing the outflow of foreign exchange and promoting import substitution. Similarly, financial incentives to foster R&D and boost the engineering consulting capabilities of

national enterprises were focused on import-substituting activities or national producers that were competing in areas dominated by multinational producers.

Arms Length Technology Transfer

Brazil's current technology transfer regime is designed to improve the bargaining position of national firms and minimize foreign exchange outflow.[28] Since 1958, the Central Bank has controlled royalty payments and has established that the maximum royalty should be 5% of net sales. The Government's main concern was that foreign firms
were using technology transfer payments as a way of remitting profits. Subsequently,
in 1962 the law governing foreign investments in Brazil[29] established strict controls on
technology transfer, which are still in effect. The law required that foreign payments
for technology transfer be registered with the Central Bank. It also prohibited technology transfer payments between subsidiaries and their parent companies and
between joint ventures and foreign partners who held more than a 50% stake in the
venture. The rationale was that the parent firms already earned a return on the technology, through profits, and therefore should not be allowed to deduct technology
licensing payments. The law maintained the 5% maximum royalty rate, and also
restricted deducting technology transfer payments for fiscal purposes to a maximum
period of 5 years.[30]

In 1970 the National Institute of Industrial Property (INPI) was created. Among
other responsibilities, it was to regulate technology transfer (taking over from the Central Bank). Technology transfer agreements were divided into five categories. Each
agreement must be registered with INPI as to terms and payments authorized, period
of validity, required Brazilian participation, and special provisions, depending on type
of contract. Royalties for *patent licenses* and *trademark licenses* may be paid only if
the licenses are registered in Brazil. Moreover, the intellectual property regime in Brazil does not offer significant patent protection in the areas of chemicals, pharmaceuticals, metal alloys and mixtures, and alloys in general. One of the principal rationales
of the Brazilian property rights system is to protect technologically less capable local
firms against potentially predatory behavior by foreign producers and to reduce the
cost of appropriating relevant foreign technology. However, a frail intellectual property rights regime, including weak trade secret protection, possibly deters foreign firms
from transferring or using locally their most advanced or up-to-date technology.

Industrial technology license agreements are less onerous since such licensing
does not depend on INPI's registering the patent or trademark.[31] However, INPI treats
such an agreement as a sale: after expiration of the contract, INPI regards the licensee
as the owner of the technology. In addition, the parties must satisfy INPI that the technology

- is not available domestically and that its transfer to a Brazilian licensee is in line with
  national development objectives;
- brings real advantages for the development of the industrial sector;
- improves product quality and allows for substitution of Brazilian products for
  imports; and
- allows the licensee to absorb and master the technology within the lifetime of the
  contract.

Registration of *technical and industrial cooperation agreements* depends on convincing INPI that the services are not available locally and that there will be short-term benefits to the sector. This might mean producing a quality product with export and/ or import substitution possibilities. For *technical service agreements,* INPI must be satisfied that the services are not available domestically. It also must approve the detailed schedule of payments for foreign technicians.[32]

Maximum approved royalty rates range from 2% for plastic and rubber articles to 5% for electrical equipment.[33] Those royalties are based on net sales, which can be considerably lower than total sales.[34] Royalties for trademarks have a maximum of 1%. In addition, royalty payments are taxed at a rate of 25%, and that tax is counted within the specified maximum royalty limits. The maximum duration is 5 years, with a possible extension for another 5 years, at the discretion of INPI. Also, as noted above, royalty payments are not permitted between subsidiaries and their parents or between joint venture firms and foreign partners holding more than a 50% stake in the venture.

Technology contracts prohibit restrictive clauses involving limits on exports, pricing guidelines, use of tied inputs, purchase of other technology, secrecy about the technology after expiration of the contract, and obligatory transfer to the seller of improvements made in the technology by the buyer. The seller, however, is obliged to pass on improvements made to the technology after it was sold and is liable for any legal action that originates because of defects in the technology or intellectual property right infringements, even by third parties. In addition, full disclosure of all technical data is required, and engineering drawings must be provided, as well as all information necessary to update the know-how. The latter requirement is of extreme concern to many technology suppliers who fear that technology information may be appropriated by third parties.

The impact of INPI's attempts to control technology imports has not been evaluated systematically but may be quite significant. Between 1972 and 1987 more than 23,500 contracts were submitted to INPI for approval. Of those, about 18,000, or roughly 75%, were approved. INPI's approval rate has followed a generally downward trend, the result of its stricter control, especially regarding technical services (Table 13.9).[35]

Table 13.9. INPI: Approvals of Technology Transfer Contracts, 1978–1987

Year	Contracts Presented for Approval	Contracts Approved	Percentage Approved
1978	1473	1451	98.5
1979	1456	1416	97.3
1980	1576	1332	84.5
1981	1426	1178	82.6
1982	1438	1135	78.9
1983	1296	969	74.8
1984	907	786	86.7
1985	1043	769	73.7
1986	1185	885	74.7
1987	1815	1213	65.8
Total	13615	11134	81.6

Source: Cardozo (1988), based on INPI data.

Fifty percent of all technology contracts approved between 1978 and 1987 were concentrated in four of the 70 economic sectors that INPI uses to classify contracts (mechanical, metallurgical, chemical, and mining). Although the shares of most of the leading sectors have been falling, electronics and electrical material are expanding rapidly, with the proportion of approved contracts increasing from 4% in 1978 to more than 15% in 1987. This partly reflects the increased importance of outright technology purchases by the electronics industry, since direct foreign investment has been severely restricted in a number of its segments.

Data on technology payments are available for 1979–1989 (Table 13.10), showing payments of US$2.4 billion during that period. Roughly 79% of the total was for specialized technical services even though their share fell markedly over the period. About 18% was for unpatented industrial technology (including 7.3% for unpatented industrial technology for made-to-order capital goods). The smallest share (just 3%) went for patent and trademark licenses. These values understate the actual inflows since payments by subsidiaries to their parent companies are not allowed. An almost continuous decline in the values recorded is notable and this fall is not explained by the economic recession alone.

It is not clear to what extent INPI has improved the bargaining position of domestic firms and helped them obtain technology more cheaply, however. There are various reasons to surmise that INPI's controls may have been deleterious to the national interest in two respects. First, the regulations discriminate against national firms because these firms must pass their contracts through a bureaucratic process for approval. In contrast, subsidiaries of foreign companies have direct access to their parent companies' technology and can transfer the technology even if they cannot deduct the cost for tax purposes. Second, for foreign technology suppliers, including investors, restrictive transfer controls as well as inadequacies in the direct foreign investment regime (e.g., not being able to capitalize technology contributions or to deduct technology fees) make it not worthwhile to license or even use their best technology in Brazil. This situation is aggravated by the lack of adequate protection from the intel-

Table 13.10. Payments for Technology Transfer Contracts 1979–1987 (in Millions of Current Dollars)

Year	Patents and Trademarks	Industrial Cooperation Agreements	Industrial Technology Licenses	Technical Services	Total
1979	9	6	11	287	313
1980	12	11	14	284	321
1981	12	18	12	234	276
1982	5	17	10	208	240
1983	12	10	14	182	218
1984	9	8	8	177	202
1985	5	21	41	108	175
1986	2	20	43	119	184
1987	3	40	27	123	193
1988	3	12	27	99	141
1989	3	15	39	112	169
Total	75	178	246	1,933	2,432

Source: Cardozo (1988), based on Annual Reports of the Central Bank.

lectual property regime. The net result is that Brazil may be receiving obsolete or outmoded technology.

Imports of Capital Goods

Access to the most productive capital goods is critical if an economy is to benefit from
embodied advances in technology. Brazil has relied much less than fast growing East
Asian economies on imported capital goods for acquiring foreign technology (Table
13.11). Moreover, the ratio of capital goods imports to gross domestic investment
(GDI) has decreased since 1980. This resulted from the policy of promoting the local
capital goods industry through trade restrictions on imports and special financial
incentives for local production. Excessive protection may be hampering the international competitiveness of local industry.

The restrictive capital goods import regime has had significant impact on modernization as well. A relatively large number of manufactures in many specialized
product areas (even more from the United States or Japan) has meant an overly diversified capital goods industry lacking the economies of scale or specialization necessary
to reduce costs, keep up with new technologies, and stay competitive. Excessive dependence on more expensive and often outmoded locally produced capital goods, especially in electronics and process control, has placed the downstream user industry at a
disadvantage with respect to Brazil's international competitors.

Foreign Investment

Brazil's foreign investment policy has reflected the government's objective of attracting capital to specific industrial segments and (after 1972) of obtaining export commitments from individual firms. Technology development has been of secondary
importance to import substitution and balance-of-payments considerations. Although
the inflow of direct foreign investment (DFI) has been considerable, Brazil may not
have been receiving the most advanced technology. The overall effect of restriction has
made foreign investment in Brazil, particularly investment with a high technology
content, relatively less attractive than in other locations.[36]

Table 13.11. Imports of Capital Goods[a] as Ratio of GDI

	1965	1970	1975	1980	1985	1986	1987
Hong Kong	1.949	3.76	2.962	2.224	4.073	3.826	3.848
South Korea	0.991	0.902	1.272	1.119	1.114	1.034	1.066
Malaysia	1.768	1.488	1.435	1.441	1.454	1.541	1.636
Singapore	5.878	3.357	3.592	4.42	3.489	3.801	4.160
Thailand	0.889	0.714	0.824	1.112	1.029	0.944	1.041
Brazil	0.251	0.327	0.409	0.455	0.376	0.299	0.259
Mexico	0.352	0.302	0.312	0.370	0.400	0.390	—
United States	0.181	0.270	0.442	0.575	0.559	0.574	0.591

[a]Capital goods are defined as the following SITC Revision 2 categories: 659, 711, 712, 714, 715, 716, 717, 718, 719 (minus
7194), 721, 722, 723, 7249, 726, 7295, 7296, 7297, 7299, 731, 7322, 7323, 7324, 7325, 7327, 7333, 734, 735, and 861. The
ratios in the table are greater than one for some of the Asian countries because many of the imported capital goods are reexported as part of new products.
Source: Own computations based on UN trade data and BESD system.

Profit remittances are limited to 12% of the original investment plus reinvested earnings.[37] In addition, the original foreign currency value of the investment is not corrected for inflation, which means that the original base for remittances decreases in real terms over time. Furthermore, parent companies may not receive royalty payments for patents and trademarks from their subsidiaries and may not capitalize their technology as equity contributions to the investments.[38]

For minority joint venture partners, there are also arbitrary and strict limits on maximum payments for technology transfer (as noted above). In addition, the foreign investor who brings technology to the joint venture has to pay a 25% tax on this part of his capital contribution to make it part of his remittance base.

Still, the foreign investment regime is quite open. In general, up to 100% foreign ownership has been allowed in most areas. Until recently, the only sectors closed to DFI were petroleum extraction and refining, certain segments of the informatics industry, communications media, and most domestic transport, although there were also some restrictions on mining, banking, insurance, and other financial activities. The new Constitution adopted in 1988 has taken a more nationalistic posture toward DFI. Its main restrictions were limiting foreign control in mining, mineral exploration, and production of electric power, and prohibiting foreign oil companies from engaging in oil exploration through risk contracts. However, the new Government that took power in March 1990 has announced a more open policy toward foreign investment, and a possible reduction in the scope of restrictions in the informatics sector.

Brazil has the largest stock of foreign capital of any developing country. Registered foreign investment was US$27.9 billion in 1987. Almost 75% of all foreign investment is in manufacturing, 20% in services, 3% in the extractive mineral industry, less than 1% in agriculture, and 2% in other activities. Within manufacturing, the subsectors accounting for the largest shares of foreign investment are automobiles (11%), basic chemicals (9%), mechanical (9%), and electrical and communications (8%). This particular concentration pattern resulted because most foreign investment was attracted under specific sectoral programs (e.g., for automobiles, shipbuilding, capital goods, and chemicals). Such programs provided fiscal and financial incentives (as well as protection in the local market) in exchange for performance requirements pertaining to investment volume, local content, and exports.[39] At the same time, foreign investment in key areas for industrial competitiveness has been limited or even totally excluded.

The most comprehensive attempt to block foreign investment and promote domestic firms' capabilities has been in "informatics," broadly defined to include computers and peripherals, professional and industrial electronics, and microelectronics. Brazil's informatics policies, set in mid-1976 and predetermined to last until late 1992, reserved the domestic market exclusively for national producers, fostering the establishment and growth of a sizable number of firms. These policies, managed until recently by a powerful Special Secretariat of Informatics, have been sufficiently focused to attract resources and create a new industrial segment in a relatively short period of time. However, they have not brought adequate levels of productive efficiency, while design efforts have resulted at most in incremental innovations within well-known and relatively open technologies. The industry has yet to become internationally competitive in most product lines, even though domestic prices have come down substantially for more mature goods. Particularly for products that have become high-volume commodities or that have undergone radical improvements, the price–performance differential between the international and domestic market has actually widened since the mid-1980s.[40]

Financial Incentives for Local Technology Development

Financial incentives have been the main instrument for encouraging the development of technological capabilities at the firm level. Since 1973, FINEP (Agency for Financing Studies and Projects) has used subsidized loans, risk-sharing instruments, and, to a lesser extent, equity participation to foster national firms' technological activities. In the period 1973–1989, FINEP contracted 1761 technology development support operations for approximately US$810 million. The focus has been on the development of import substitutes (as in chemicals and pharmaceuticals) and products that would allow national firms to compete with foreign-owned producers in the domestic market (as in capital goods, electronics, vehicles, and autoparts). There has been a growing emphasis on establishing R&D and quality control labs and developing and improving products, processes and tools.

Although there is not enough information to evaluate the impact of FINEP's programs, it is likely that most national firms with significant R&D activity have benefited from FINEP's assistance. Nonetheless, the effectiveness of its actions has been limited not only by relatively narrow lending criteria, but by internal bureaucratic obstacles to timely operation, and the difficulties small, technically based firms encounter in qualifying for its programs. Larger firms, on the other hand, increasingly find FINEP's financial capabilities too limited for their innovation finance requirements.[41]

In conclusion, the technology policy regime in Brazil has been characterized by objectives other than the acquisition of technological capabilities that would allow firms to become internationally competitive. Government interventions have been oriented instead toward enabling domestic firms to operate in new areas, design import substitutes with their own or acquired means, achieve a measure of technological "autonomy," and displace multinational firms from certain key industrial segments. As a result, the country has failed to attract best-practice technology via direct foreign investment or through arms-length transactions. A combination of weak domestic technological efforts and restrictive access to the most valuable foreign technology appears to have hampered the modernization efforts of Brazilian firms. As argued in the next section, substantial public sector involvement in technological activities has been a weak substitute for greater involvement by the productive sector and a more flexible technology policy regime.

INSTITUTIONAL NETWORK SUPPORTING TECHNOLOGY DEVELOPMENT

Background and Current Structure

Shortly after the inauguration of the new civilian government, in March 1985 a Ministry of Science and Technology (MCT) was created. Although initially MCT sought to take control of all existing institutions working in the area of S&T, including STI and EMBRAPA (the major government institution responsible for agricultural research), it ended up with direct responsibility over only three key agencies: CNPq, which still directly managed and oversaw a national network of research institutes, FINEP, and SEI. Subsequently it acquired control over the National Institute of Technology (INT) as well as several other specialized institutes.

With the creation of the MCT, clearer priorities were established. Policy was directed to the expansion of infrastructure in science and technology, principally related to human resource development. There was also an attempt to define strategic sectors for Brazil to keep up with international trends. The new policy emphasis reflected a greater awareness of the weaknesses still inherent in the S&T base of the country, especially in qualitative terms, and the view that a strategic focus on new technologies was necessary for a maturing economy seeking to close the gap with advanced nations.

Throughout 1985–1986 there were many broad-based meetings, conferences, and congresses on S&T, as many who had not had a chance to express their views saw their opportunity during this opening up of the system. There was much euphoria on the possible contribution of S&T to all aspects of economic and social development. There were also ambitious proposals to increase R&D expenditure to 2% of GDP by the 1990s. In addition there were proposals to include a section on science and technology in the new constitution being drafted.

The new National Development Plan placed special emphasis on S&T and devoted a chapter to the subject. It recognized that in the past, government support to technology suppliers was frequently based on academic criteria without considering the relevance of the technology to market needs. It also recognized that the vast network of publicly-supported R&D institutes suffered from excessive diversification and lack of sufficient integration with the needs of industry. Furthermore, in the area of regulation the plan recognized that numerous reforms were necessary in standardization, technical norms, and testing laboratories, to improve the performance of the productive sectors and reduce high rates of wastage.

The MCT hoped to promote the increase of total expenditures of R&D to nearly 1% of GDP in 1986 and to higher levels subsequently by encouraging the productive sector to invest more in R&D through an improved economic environment, increased financing for technology, and the introduction of fiscal incentives for R&D. However, due to the difficult budgetary situation and increasing macroeconomic instability, R&D expenditures remained flat, despite the fact that fiscal incentives for R&D were enacted as part of the new industrial policy program in 1988.

Since 1989 the Special Secretariat for Science and Technology has been the apex S&T institution in Brazil. In addition, 17 major federal implementing agencies for S&T policy receive at least 1% of the S&T budget. Combined they account for over 90% of total allocations for S&T (Table 13.12). Approximately 40% of the allocations finance research related activities (metrology, norms and standards, normative coordination, for example), and the remainder goes to postgraduate training and actual research.

Public R&D Institutes

A complex and differentiated government institutional network carries out public sector R&D activities in Brazil. In major areas, such as health and biological sciences, as

Table 13.12. Key S&T Agencies According to Budgetary Allocations[a]

Agency	Function	Final 1988 Budgetary Allocation	
		Amount[b]	Percent
CNPq—The National Council for S&T Development	T,R	291,639	17.01
EMBRAPA—Brazil Agricultural Research Corp.	T,R	200,542	11.69
Secretariat of Sec. of S&T[c]	N,R	183,903	10.72
CAPES—Coordinating Agency for Postgraduate Training	T,I	139,108	8.11
CNEN—National Council for Nuclear Energy	N,R,T	129,128	7.53
EMBRATER—Brazil Rural Extension Corp.	I	98,916	5.77
IFES—Federal University and Other Teaching Inst.	T,R	93,842	5.47
CSN—National Security Council	N	89,431	5.22
EMFA—Joint Chiefs of Staff	R	72,760	4.24
Secretariat of Min. of Mines and Energy[d]	N	65,617	3.83
INPE—Institute of Space Research	T,R	48,421	2.82
FIOCRUZ—Foundation Institute Oswaldo Cruz	T,R	33,137	1.93
Min. of Aeronautics	R	31,931	1.86
INMETRO—National Institute of Metrol., Stand.	I,N	27,178	1.58
Secretariat of Min. of Justice	—	25,199	1.47
CEDATE—Center for Tech. Supp. of Ed.[e]	—	21,083	1.23
CTI—Center for Informatics Technology	R	19,918	1.16
INPA—National Institute for Research of Amazon Reg.	R	18,981	1.11
Subtotal		1,590,644	92.75
Total S&T budget		1,714,851	100.0

[a]T, training; R, research; D, dissemination of information; I, institutional development; N, normative coordination.
[b]Amounts in 1987 dollars.
[c]Includes the FNDCT and the PADCT research funds.
[d]Eighty percent is allocated for equity investment in NUCLEBRAS.
[e]Ninety percent is allocated for classroom scientific equipment and instruments.
Source: CNPq, "Recursos do Tesouro da Uniao: Dotacao Inicial, Dotacao Final, e Despesa Realizada 1980–89," May 1989.

well as in experimental physics and chemistry, most resources are in the federal and State of São Paulo universities. Public enterprises' in-house R&D facilities cover energy generation and conservation, oil exploration, telecommunications, and aircraft development. Government institutions not attached directly either to federal or state universities, or to public sector enterprises, play an important role in agriculture, food technology, Amazon ecology, biotechnology, tropical disease research, physics and nuclear technology, aerospace, and computer sciences. In addition, development efforts in various areas of engineering and mining technology are undertaken by a few state-level institutions (the most important of which is IPT of São Paulo).

Government-undertaken industrial R&D has not been very effective due to the generally weak linkages with the productive sector. A survey of sources of technology in Brazilian industry notes that less than 2.5, 5.1, and 3.9% of product designs, tool designs, and manufacturing processes, respectively, has originated in research insti-tutes.[42]

Although industry ties are strong in some cases, the dispersion of resources through an excessive number of research projects and competing activities hampers efforts. An example of the dispersion of a research program in the public sector is the work program of CPqD, the research unit of Telebras, Brazil's public telephone holding company. In 1988 CPqD was the largest and most sophisticated applications laboratory in Latin America. It employed 400 professionals directly engaged in R&D work, in addition to sponsoring personnel from industry and universities. CPqD's budget of US$60 million was allocated to a very broad research agenda, approximately 80 R&D projects in seven priority areas: electronic switching, digital transmission, optical communications, data and text communications, satellite communications equipment, tools, and materials. Even adjusted for skilled labor cost differences, a budget of US$60 million is minute for the scope of CPqD's research agenda. Budgetary allocation would average less than US$8 million per program or US$1 million per project, whereas each program could in itself justify the whole budget. The absence of research focus and specialization has led to systematic delays in the CPqD research chronogram and, therefore, to delays in the market launching of its applications. These delays have had a high cost for the economy because in many cases, such as the digital exchange program, government policy prevented the use of existing, less costly, foreign technology while waiting for the local technology to be developed.[43]

In two areas, however, government R&D efforts have been quite effective: agrotechnology and aerospace. In agrotechnology, the government agency EMBRAPA (Empresa Brasileira de Pesquisa Agropecuaria) has coordinated and partly executed a complex and far-ranging national agricultural research program. This has resulted in, among other things, the incorporation of previously infertile land through a better understanding of soil biology and the successful introduction of new plant varieties.

In aerospace, Brazil (with China and India) probably has the most advanced research program among industrializing countries. CTA (Centro Tecnologico da Aeronautica) and INPE (Instituto Nacional de Pesquisas Espaciais) have been the core R&D institutes in this subsector. CTA, in particular, has generated and effectively transferred aircraft, rocket, fuel, and other aerospace-related technology to industry. In addition, it has had an important role in the development of gasohol-based engines.

Among industry-oriented institutes, IPT (Instituto de Pesquisas Tecnologicas) of the State of São Paulo is possibly the one that has forged the closest links with the productive sector. Other than IPT (and two more state-level R&D institutes—those serving Minas Gerais and Bahia), government-led, industry-directed efforts have been small and not very effective.

Public and Aggregate R&D Expenditures

Public sector R&D has been dominant not only in scope but in resources allocated. Although there are no firm estimates of total R&D expenditures in Brazil—private sector outlays are not known with certainty—most sources estimate that public sector expenditures account for between 70 to 90% of total R&D outlays. Based on actual public expenditures, a series of imputed private and total R&D expenditures can be constructed (Table 13.13).

Although in absolute terms R&D outlays in Brazil are not modest compared to other industrializing countries, they are small in comparison to developed economies (Table 13.14). Moreover, after a significant increase in the 1970s, R&D expenditures as a proportion of GNP remained basically flat throughout the 1980s, whereas they expanded substantially in the fast growing East Asian economies. As a result, absolute levels of R&D expenditures in South Korea, for example, are at least twice as large as

Table 13.13. R&D Expenditures in Brazil, 1981–1988 (in Constant 1987 Dollars)

Year	Public Expenditure[a]	GDP	PE/GDP	TE1/GDP[b]	TE2/GDP[c]
1981	966,133	253,785,250	0.38	0.54	0.42
1982	1,184,970	257,988,623	0.46	0.66	0.51
1983	938,207	247,500,345	0.38	0.54	0.42
1984	907,447	253,138,254	0.36	0.51	0.40
1985	1,242,271	282,347,174	0.44	0.63	0.49
1986	1,455,239	314,477,537	0.46	0.66	0.51
1987	1,485,365	323,573,075	0.46	0.66	0.51
1988	1,468,595	322,597,503	0.46	0.65	0.51

[a]For 1981–1987 these are actual expenditures; for 1988, it is the final budget allocation.
[b]TE1 is total imputed expenditures on the assumption that public expenditures make up 70% of R&D outlays in Brazil.
[c]TE2 is total imputed expenditures on the assumption that public expenditures make up 90% of R&D outlays in the country.
Source: CNPq, "Recursos do Tesouro da Uniao: Dotacao Inicial, Dotacao Final, e Despesa Realizada 1980–89," May 1989.

in Brazil, although the Brazilian economy is more than twice the size of the Korean economy.

Is Brazil devoting an insufficient amount of resources to R&D? It should be emphasized that even if R&D outlays are stagnant, it certainly does not imply that Brazil is spending too little on scientific and technological development. In the absence of knowledge about rates of return in R&D compared to other economic activities, not much can be said about the optimal level of R&D expenditures. On the one hand, a number of countries that are allocating larger amounts of resources to R&D are not necessarily reaping greater benefits. For example, between 1977 and 1985, India doubled its relative outlays to R&D without major gains in terms of technological capabilities in the productive sector. On the other hand, countries that have improved their competitive position have also been increasing their R&D efforts on a systematic basis. More important, most of these efforts have been undertaken by the productive sector.

In contrast, not only the level and intensity of Brazil's R&D expenditures have

Table 3.14. R&D Expenditures in Selected Countries (R&D Expenditures in Absolute Terms and as a Proportion of GNP)

Country	Absolute Expenditure[a]		R&D Intensity			
	Amount	Year	1970	1977	1982	Latest Year
Brazil	1448	1982	0.24	0.70	0.59	0.59 (1987)[b]
Argentina	1087	1981	n.a.	1.80	0.20	0.20 (1982)
Mexico	881	1984	0.20	0.30	0.20	0.60 (1984)
India	1482	1984	n.a.	0.50	0.76	1.0 (1985)
South Korea	1307	1983	0.39	0.60	0.90	1.8 (1986)
Taiwan	505	1985	n.a.	n.a.	0.90	1.06 (1985)
Japan	39117	1987	1.90	2.00	2.40	2.9 (1987)
United States	100823	1987	2.60	2.10	2.50	2.6 (1987)

[a]Expenditures in millions of 1982 dollars.
[b]Average between the low and high estimates of Table 13.13.
Source: UNESCO, *Statistical Yearbook 1988,* Paris, 1989.

been flat since the beginning of the decade, but more important, most R&D is both financed and undertaken by government (Table 13.15). At the beginning of the decade, government was responsible for 67% of R&D financing and industry for only 20%. Estimates for 1988 indicate that with an additional 10% transferred from government and other sources, industry's share of innovation financing may have reached 30%.

This pattern of government dominance of R&D expenditures is also apparent in other industrializing economies—such as Argentina, Mexico, and India—that have not been able to sustain their competitive position in world markets for more sophisticated goods. In South Korea and Japan, in contrast, industry both finances and carries out most R&D. In the United States, financing is shared equally by government (a good proportion of R&D being defense related) and industry, although industry ultimately undertakes most R&D.

Human Capital Formation

Brazil's education system is one of the main obstacles to the country's modernization and technological upgrading. Although major deficiencies characterize all components of the system, more fundamental weaknesses are observed in primary education and at the top end in science and engineering.

Primary and Secondary Schooling

Technical progress in industry is increasingly dependent on an educated labor force. Low levels of basic education and skills are not compatible with the complexity, precision, and consistency of modern industry. Yet in 1980, 73% of the Brazilian labor force either had no education or had not completed primary school, a figure among the highest for middle-income countries. In 1985 Brazil's total secondary enrollment represented only 35% of secondary school-age population, well below the average for middle income countries (Table 13.16).

Brazil's heavy investment in vocational and technical training has compensated to a limited extent for the weakness of the formal school system. Although the proportion of students enrolled in vocational training as a proportion of the working age population is less than in South Korea or Taiwan, it is comparable to that of Mexico

Table 13.15. R&D Funding and Expenditures in Selected Countries[a]

Country	Year	Source of Funding				Source of Expenditure		
		G	I	F	O	I	HE	GA
Brazil	1982	67	20	5	8	30	17	53
Argentina	1981	95	—	1	4	41	22	37
Mexico	1984	15	1	1	83	30	51	19
India	1984	87	13	—	—	26	—	74
South Korea	1986	19	81	—	—	67	11	22
Japan	1985	21	79	—	—	67	20	13
United States	1986	47	50	—	3	73	12	15

[a]G, government; I, industry; F, foreign; O, other; HE, higher education; GA, government agencies.
Source: Unesco, *Statistical Yearbook,* Paris 1988.

Table 13.16. Indicators of Investments in Human Capital in Selected NICs and Japan

	South Korea	Taiwan	Hong Kong	Singapore	Brazil	Mexico	India	Indonesia	Japan
Percent age group enrolled in									
Primary education									
(1965)	101	97	103	105	108	92	74	72	100
(1985)	96	100	105	115	104	115	92	118	102
Secondary education									
(1965)	35	38	29	45	16	17	27	12	82
(1985)	94	91	69	71	35	55	35	39	96
Tertiary education									
(1965)	6	7	5	10	2	4	5	1	13
(1985)	32	13	13	12	11	16	9	7	30
No. of tertiary students per 100,000 population									
(latest year)	3606	2080	1410	1406	1140	1508	776[a]	600	2006
No. of tertiary students in CSE[b] (1000)	585	207	36	22	535	563	1443	235	707
(Year)	(1987)	(1984)	(1984)	(1983)	(1983)	(1986)	(1980)	(1985)	(1986)
As % of population									
Total	1.39	1.06	0.67	0.89	0.40	0.70	0.21	0.14	0.58
Urban	2.02	1.36	0.72	0.89	0.58	1.02	0.97	0.53	0.77
No. of students in SME[c] (1000)	320.6	151.7	27.5	16.2	323.3	336.9	1269.9	137.3	486.9
As % of population									
Total	0.76	0.78	0.51	0.73	0.24	0.42	0.19	0.09	0.40
Urban	1.10	1.00	0.55	0.73	0.34	0.59	0.86	0.33	0.53
No. of students in engineering only (1000)	227.6	128.7	21.1	15.4	164.6	281.8	397.0	109.5	418.9
As % of population									
Total	0.54	0.68	0.41	0.61	0.13	0.35	0.06	0.07	0.34
Urban	0.78	0.85	0.42	0.61	0.17	0.50	0.27	0.27	0.45
No. of students enrolled in vocational training (1000)	814.5	404.6	31.7	9.4	1481.0	853.6	397.7	1061.3	1415.4
(Year)	(1986)	(1984)	(1984)	(1984)	(1985)	(1986)	(1981)	(1986)	(1986)
As % of population of working age	3.06	3.24	0.86	0.54	1.83	2.0	0.1	1.14	1.71

[a]1980.

[b]General science and engineering fields: natural science, mathematics and computer science, medicine, engineering, architecture, trade, craft, transport and communication, agriculture, forestry, fishery.

[c]Natural science, mathematics and computer science, engineering.

Source: Lall (1992). Original data from World Development Report, 1988; UNESCO, Statistical Yearbook 1988. Paris, 1989; and Government of Republic of China, Statistical Yearbook of Republic of China 1988; Taiwan. Government of Republic of China, Ministry of Education, Educational Statistics of Republic of China, 1984.

and considerably above other comparator countries (Table 13.16). Yet the trainability of students at vocational and technical schools increasingly depends on the quality of their basic school education. More generally, the technological content of industrial and other economic activities requires growing levels of formal education for the labor force, which the Brazilian education system has failed to provide.

Higher Education
Between 1960 and 1985, the total number of tertiary students went from 93,202 to 1,437,232, a rapid expansion. As a percentage of their age group, students enrolled in higher education comprised 11%, up from 2% two decades earlier (Table 13.16). Although that percentage does not compare poorly with other industrializing countries (with the exception of South Korea), certain features of the higher education system tend to undermine its effectiveness as a breeding ground for technical labor and innovation.

- First, the 3-fold expansion of undergraduate enrollment during the 1970s, combined with a decline in full-time faculty, has had an adverse effect on the quality of university education across the board. Many postgraduate courses have been redesigned to remedy the insufficiencies of undergraduate training. The low status and poor qualification of undergraduate teachers are the core of the problem. About 45,000 full-time teachers, hired initially on a provisional basis, without formal procedures or evaluation, are now tenured. Most lack academic training and have not gone beyond a B. A. degree. They serve some 450,000 students in free, public universities.[44] In addition, around 60,000 teachers, also not well qualified and many with a large teaching load in several institutions, serve 850,000 students in private schools.
- Second, the postgraduate system also faces severe quality problems. Although in 1970 there were 57 doctoral programs in Brazilian universities, in 1985 there were more than 300, with another 800 providing training at the M. A. level. Combined, they were graduating 5000 students at both levels each year.[45] Yet there is a wide quality variance among postgraduate programs, and according to CAPES' (Coordenação de Aperfeiçoamento do Ensino Superior) evaluations, only about one-fourth of new graduate programs are academically satisfactory. Most programs also face uncertain financial support from FINEP and CAPES, and very few have been able to diversify their funding by linking up with or supporting innovative efforts in the productive sector.
- Third, the proportion of students in science, mathematics, and engineering is relatively small compared to other industrializing countries, being considerably below fast growing East Asian economies and Mexico (Table 13.16). In engineering alone the disproportion is even greater: there are more than four times as many engineering students as a percentage of the population in South Korea, Hong Kong, Taiwan, and Singapore as there are in Brazil; and there are three times as many in Mexico (Table 13.17).

The combination of low-quality undergraduate teaching, few strong graduate programs, a relatively small pool of students in science, mathematics, and engineering, and underuse of existing educational capabilities outside formal institutions of higher learning has contributed to Brazil's lagging R&D manpower. Brazil has fewer scientists

Table 13.17. Human Resources Devoted to R&D According to Major Fields, 1986

Field	Total		Doctorates	
	No.	%	No.	%
Exact and earth sciences[a]	6,651	12.6	2,192	19.1
Biological sciences	5,117	9.7	1,900	16.5
Engineering	7,765	14.7	1,180	10.3
Health sciences	6,107	11.6	1,939	16.9
Agrarian sciences	7,607	14.4	1,340	11.7
Applied social sciences	4,543	8.6	842	7.3
Human sciences	4,993	9.4	1,516	13.2
Linguistics, letters and arts	1,471	2.8	583	5.1
No information	8,609	16.3	—	—
Total	52,863	100.0	11,492	100.0

[a]Includes physics, mathematics, and other "exact" disciplines.
Source: Martins and Queiroz (1987).

and engineers engaged in R&D in relation to population (256 per million) than Taiwan (1,426 per million), Singapore (960 per million), South Korea (804 per million), and Argentina (360 per million).

Moreover, the distribution of human resources allocated to R&D is concentrated in biological and health sciences, as well as applied social sciences, human sciences, and the arts/literature (Table 13.17). In two key fields, engineering and agrarian sciences, the proportion of researchers is relatively small. Their secondary position in the distribution of R&D researchers suggests that much R&D undertaken in Brazil is not closely related to productive activities.

The System at Work

Despite certain fundamental weaknesses in the institutional support network for technological advancement, there are many instances of successful cooperation with industry and other segments of the productive sector. In these cases strong and effective links have been forged, and producers have achieved international levels of competitiveness. We shall provide three examples to illustrate different ways in which this has occurred.

An impressive case of a top performing public enterprise with strong roots in the public research infrastructure is that of Embraer. In 1946 the Aeronautics Technology Institute (ITA) was established to train high-level human technical resources. Drawing heavily on ITA graduates, the Aeronautics Technology Center (CTA) was created in 1947.[46] Among other tasks, CTA was given the mission of designing an airplane suitable to Brazilian conditions. The Bandeirante turboprop had its first successful flight in 1968. The original team was then transferred from CTA to set up Embraer in 1969 and produce the Bandeirante on a commercial scale.[47] Five hundred Bandeirantes were produced and most sold internationally, where it found a niche in the commuter airplane market. Embraer followed the Bandeirante with several other models, again focused strongly on the international market.[48]

Embraer progressed from a heavily protected and subsidized public enterprise to a dynamic world-class competitor. Embraer has also been proficient at using public research institutions and universities as well as tapping finance from FINEP. Its strong focus on the export market has been crucial in offsetting development costs by permitting larger production scales, in bringing new ideas for further technical change, and in demanding exacting performance standards.

Metal Leve is a case that illustrates the trajectory of a very dynamic domestic private firm that has effectively used the public support infrastructure. Metal Leve started to operate in 1950 producing pistons for local subsidiaries of multinational companies manufacturing vehicles in Brazil (Ford, Volkswagen, GM, and Mercedes Benz). Its initial focus was on quality control, combined with well structured technology transfer programs, involving engineering of piston manufacturing processes. Metal Leve entered the international market in 1965 as a way to use up its excess capacity, and induced by fiscal and credit incentives. Export-output ratios rose to 8% in 1970, 17–20% in the 1980s, and 35% in 1988. The driving force for technical change during the early period was demanding foreign buyers. Efforts at quality improvement at Metal Leve were part of a managerial culture that continuously emphasized the importance of best practice techniques and methods. Effective absorption of imported technology was the result of prior and detailed studies of the processes that were to be transferred, intense training in-house and at the premises of the technology supplier, and systematic adaptation of the technology to local conditions.

In the late 1970s the firm began developing new products to compete in markets that required Metal Leve to supply designs.[49] In 1979 it set up its own research center with financial assistance from FINEP (on the order of US$2.2 million), spurred largely by the challenge posed by increased rivalry in export markets. By 1988 the staff of the R&D center had grown to 230, and Metal Leve spent 2.7% of sales on R&D. In addition, it contracted out research to local R&D centers and universities. In 1988 Metal Leve set up an Advanced Technology Center in Ann Arbor, Michigan, as an extension of its São Paulo R&D center, motivated by the need to be better informed about new developments and future plans of American buyers.[50] In September 1989 Metal Leve opened a manufacturing facility in South Carolina to produce articulated pistons for diesel engines (a Metal Leve innovation) to equip Caterpillar's new diesel engines (to be introduced in 1990) and also cater to demand from Volvo and Cummins.

The case of Metal Leve, like that of Embraer, illustrates the systematic, step-by-step technology efforts needed to become an internationally competitive producer. It also emphasizes the importance of export markets as a source not only of technical information (supplied by buyers or gleaned from competitors) but of continuous pressure to improve performance. Just as Embraer, Metal Leve also was quite successful in using Brazil's institutional system supporting innovation. It maintains close interaction with FINEP, as well as its collaborative ventures with universities and technical and research institutions. These arrangements suggest that a motivated management with long-term commitment to technological excellence and with a record of technological and commercial accomplishments is able to tap existing technology-oriented institutional, human, and financial resources effectively.

In agrotechnology, the Government agency EMBRAPA (Empresa Brasileira de Pesquisa Agropecuaria) has coordinated and partly executed a complex and far ranging "national agricultural research program," resulting, among other things, in the incorporation of previously infertile land through a better understanding of soil biology and the successful introduction of new varieties.

In 1987, agriculture accounted for 10% of Brazil's GDP, 25% of employment, and 43% of total exports. Prior to 1980 agriculture production growth was led by nontraditional exports (mainly soybeans and citrus), based almost entirely from new land expansion. Since the early part of the 1980s, the expansion of the agricultural frontier has come to a virtual halt (with the exception of areas in the north). To a large extent, it has been compensated by the introduction of new varieties, made possible by technological advances in agricultural research, which has led to significant increases in yields on traditional export crops (cotton, tobacco, and coffee) and many food crops (rice, maize, and wheat). In this and other agriculture-related innovations, the role of EMBRAPA has been critical.

EMBRAPA was created in 1972 as a public sector corporation attached to the Ministry of Agriculture, with a large degree of financial and administrative autonomy. It is the coordinating agency for the country's cooperative agricultural research system, which, besides EMBRAPA, comprises (1) state-level research companies and institutions, (2) universities, (3) the private sector, and (4) some 40 research institutions throughout the world with which EMBRAPA entertains technical cooperative arrangements.

EMBRAPA executes its own research program through a national network of research stations that comprises 6 regional centers, 21 national centers for commodity research, and 8 state-level research centers. The regional research centers concentrate and coordinate research on specific problems of the major agroecological regions in which they are located. At the commodity research centers, multidisciplinary teams work on priority programs related to agronomic problems and production systems for each specific commodity. State-level research stations (either managed by EMBRAPA or by state-owned companies) are responsible for taking the findings and technological components generated by the regional and national centers and incorporating these into adaptive research at the local level.

Finally, in support of all these research programs, EMBRAPA operates a number of special service centers: the Center for Genetic Resources and Biotechnology (Cenargen), the Service for Soil Surveys and Soil Conservation (SNLCS), the Basic Seeds Production Service (SPSB), the National Research Center for Agroindustry and Food Technology (CTAA), the National Center for Plant Protection and Environmental Research (CNPDA), the National Center for Irrigation and Drainage Research (CNPA), and the National Center for Soil Biology Research (CNPBS).

EMBRAPA's activities have been backed by strong and consistent Government commitment to agriculture research since the early 1970s, in contrast to the more fragmented and far less effective approach to industrial research. EMBRAPA's first year (1974) budget (in 1986 dollars) amounted to US$25 million. Funding increased steadily to about US$300.6 million by 1980 and an estimated US$324 million for 1989. Most other research institutions have not fared so well, having suffered frequent and unexpected budget cuts since the early 1980s due to a worsening fiscal crisis.

Although EMBRAPA has been successful in expanding agricultural production in less fertile areas and in introducing new seed varieties (for cotton, tobacco, coffee, rice, maize, and wheat), the diffusion of research results has been limited mostly to producers in better endowed regions. Many of the technologies generated by research need to be adapted and screened through on-farm tests before they can be disseminated to resource-poor, medium and small-scale producers, particularly in the less developed regions of the country. Formal mechanisms for coordination between research and extension, including consultation with the farming community, were initiated only in 1986. Still, research centers generally are endowed with only modest human and physical resources for technology transfer because technology diffusion has yet to be recognized as an explicit function of the research establishment.

CONCLUSIONS

This chapter's major contention is that a combination of limited technological involvement by domestic producers, regulatory and policy restrictions on both embodied and disembodied forms of technology imports, and weak institutional support to industrial firms has increased Brazilian firms' distance from the price–performance frontier. In addition, major gaps in the educational system, particularly low enrollment levels in secondary school and in science and engineering, compromise the supply of technical labor force and the acquisition of technological capabilities in the future.

As in most discussions of this kind, these propositions are subject to a number of caveats. First, the suggestion that relatively few firms are actively engaged in technology development omits the fact that not long ago, say in the early 1970s, far fewer than the present core of 350 R&D-active firms (with a contour of 1200 producers) were technologically active. In many cases, improved technological performance came as a result of competitive pressures from the international market. For national firms, particularly those in capital goods and electronics, support from government technology policies and institutions was critical.

This chapter suggests that much of the underlying motivation for the Brazilian Government's technology policies was not the improvement of the country's technical base but the more short-sighted consideration of saving or earning foreign exchange. A second caveat is now in order. Although that general statement is on the whole correct, the Government's technology policies also improved the bargaining position of local firms in negotiating arms-length technology transfer deals. In addition, they promoted entry of domestic firms in areas that normally would be precluded through patent protection or the exercise of overwhelming market power (pharmaceuticals and electronics), while stimulating the creation of a fairly sophisticated capital goods sector. Moreover, such policies effectively steered multinational firms that traditionally had been domestic market-oriented toward exporting, thereby forcing the technological upgrading of their domestic operations. Finally, the policies created for the first time a financing mechanism for the technological needs of Brazilian industrial and engineering consulting firms.

What is implicitly argued in this chapter, however, is that these government policies were carried too far and became outdated. Restrictive arms-length technology transfer policies, for example, assumed the presence of relatively unsophisticated domestic producers and the considerable eagerness of foreign suppliers to market their latest technological wares. Nearly two decades after these policies were first implemented, the assumptions are much less justifiable. Similarly, capacity creation in sophisticated industrial segments, such as capital goods and electronics, was regarded as double benefits for economic development: it allowed for import substitution in areas of heavy foreign exchange outflow while creating capabilities in strategic segments for the formation of skills and diffusion of knowledge. But across-the-board import substitution led to excessive diversification, fragmentation of efforts within firms, and substantial waste in government-supported technological pursuits.

A third and final caveat concerns the institutional support system for technical advance in industry. This chapter argues that despite a number of important exceptions (such as EMBRAPA, CTA, and IPT), the public R&D network is not very responsive to the productive needs of the economy. Moreover, overlapping and fragmentary efforts dissipate scarce resources. What was left unsaid, however, is that the faults of the institutional network are not unique to Brazil nor to industrializing countries, for that matter. A more demanding industrial sector, challenged by competitive markets and focused on fewer product areas, would be a far better user of existing institutional resources (as the experiences of Metal Leve and Embraer show) and an effective force for reform.

NOTES

1. See Furtado (1984).
2. See Pastore (1974).
3. See Pastore (1974) and S. Motoyama (1984).
4. See Fishlow (1980).
5. The enlarged demand for these services led to the expansion and transformation of the Laboratory of Material Resistance of the São Paulo Polytechnic into the Technological Research Institute (IPT) in 1934. IPT focused on testing key materials for the construction and mechanical industries, as well as providing support for the further development of civil and soil engineering for large industrial projects, including Volta Redonda, the first integrated flat steel plant, established in 1941. IPT remains the largest and one of the most respected industrial technology research institutes in Brazil. Another key industry-oriented research institute, the National Technology Institute (INT), was established in 1933, as an outgrowth of an experimental research station on combustibles and materials founded in 1921. The need for greater professional and technical skills and some research capability also led to the creation of the University of São Paulo (USP) in 1934. One Brazilian science historian has argued that the creation of USP was São Paulo's reaction to its defeat in the Constitutional Revolution of 1932. It sought its redemption by investing heavily in human resource development and betting on the increasing importance of science and development, a bet that seems to have paid off very well. See Motoyama (1984).
6. See Pastore (1974).
7. In this early period there was a strong emphasis on the development of human resources, especially in physics, because of the preoccupation with atomic energy. The focus on higher level technical human resources was institutionalized through the creation in 1951 of the Coordinating Agency for Advanced Training of High Level Personnel (CAPES). Its primary objective was to stimulate and finance the development of higher level technical resources in order to strengthen S&T capability, particularly in the universities and in R&D institutions. However, as suggested, compared to other middle-income developing countries, Brazil has underinvested in general education.
8. The Brazilian push for an independent development of atomic energy led by Admiral Alvaro Alberto conflicted with U. S. interests at the time, and he was forced to resign in 1955.

The atomic energy program was then redirected from an effort to gain greater autonomy over that important new technology to that of being a supplier of uranium and other strategic minerals. Furthermore, support for nuclear issues was transferred out of the CNPq to a new institution the National Nuclear Energy Commission (CNEN) established in 1956.

9. See Fishlow (1980).

10. FUNTEC was a special fund created within the National Bank of Economic Development (BNDE) to finance the training of specialized technical personnel for research and related activities in the universities. In 1964, BNDE also established the Fund for the Acquisition of Machinery and Industrial Equipment (FINAME), which was to play an important role in the development of the local capital goods industry. FINEP is the Agency for Financing Studies and Projects. It started out in 1965 as a fund in the Ministry of Planning and Coordination to finance feasibility studies and project development for investments in sectors and activities that were considered of priority for the country's economic and social development. In the administrative reforms that took place in 1967, the Government transformed FINEP into a public enterprise.

11. The plan also sought to prepare Brazil for more extensive use of nuclear energy (up to 10 million kW by 1990) and to continue working on other applications of nuclear energy such as isotopes in agriculture, medicine, and industry. It also included a massive effort for prospecting for nuclear minerals, and a large program for absorbing technology for uranium enrichment and for building nuclear reactors with local materials and components.

12. The STI was the promoter of the national alcohol program, which was supposed to supply 10.7 billion liters of alcohol by 1985 to substitute for 45% of the projected gasoline consumption for that year. This was the most ambitious program developed by the STI. The program involved not only the technological problems of blending and using various mixtures of gasoline and alcohol, but also adapting gasoline and diesel engines to run on pure alcohol, searching for different raw material sources of alcohol, increasing crop yields, and developing new processes to produce alcohol.

13. Market share is defined as X_i/X_{iw} where X_i is the country's exports of good i and X_{iw} is the world's exports of good i.

14. See Tavares de Araujo (1982, Table III).

15. The normalized market share index is defined as $(X_i/X)/(X_{iw}/X_w)$, where X_i is the country's exports of good i, X is total country exports, X_{iw} is the world exports of good i, and X_w is total world exports; hence, the share of a particular good in the country's exports is normalized by the share of world exports of that good in total world exports. The index is quite sensitive to the competitive position of individual subsectors in the national economy, and changes in the index are indicative of shifts with respect to the world prices.

16. The only major exception is "explosive pyrotechnical products," which continued to increase their normalized shares in the 1980s and showed in 1987 the highest "revealed" comparative advantage. This category is believed to contain many arms exports.

17. See Tavares de Araujo et al. (1989), Kume (1988). Kume's 1988 price comparisons were for 88 subsectors on the basis of a representative sample of 715 products (eight-digit BTN classification) of the IPEA–FUNCEX data base. International price comparisons tend to present well-known problems of choice of an appropriate exchange rate, and comparability of products differentiated by quality and performance. Yet such price data can be suggestive of broad trends in a country's competitive position in world markets.

18. See Confederação Nacional da Industria (1990).

19. In 1985 the top 254 exporters of manufactured goods were responsible for 70 to 80% of total manufactured exports. These producers comprise approximately 6% of all medium and large firms with published balance sheets and less than 3% of all establishments with over 100 employees. In addition, a number of smaller firms export through trading houses; these firms are concentrated in shoes, cast iron, steel, and autoparts. Overall, however, exports are undertaken by that narrow set of large producers in metal-mechanics, chemicals and petrochemicals, and traditional segments.

20. The number of firms filing income tax returns fell from 570,000 in 1977 to just 266,000 in 1985.

21. See Paulinyi (1990).

22. These are Petrobras (oil and petrochemicals), Telebras (telecommunications), Electrobras (electricity), Nuclebras (nuclear energy), Siderbras (steel), CVRD (minerals), Embraer (airplanes), and Cobra (informatics).

23. The limited participation of R&D personnel in the productive sector is even more accentuated in terms of researchers with doctoral degrees. The share for the productive sector is 0.46%, most in public enterprise R&D labs.

24. "R&D active" firms are defined as those that are known to have formal R&D laboratories or to undertake systematic R&D efforts. They are a subset of about one-third of all firms that declare R&D expenditure on their income tax returns.

25. See Braga and Matesco (1989). The study reports the answers to a detailed questionnaire on the technological activities of the Brazilian industry from a 1980/1981 sample of 4309 industrial firms operating 7156 plants.

26. Braga and Matesco (1989, pp. 12–14).

27. Braga and Matesco (1989) report that over 67% of respondents pointed out that copying of product lines from competitors is a common practice in their sector.

28. Substantial changes in the technology transfer and intellectual property rights regime are being considered, but have not been put into effect yet.

29. Law 4131.

30. Cardozo (1988).

31. For more information on the regulations covering the different types of agreements, see Rosenn (1988).

32. In 1983 INPI issued Normative Act 64 whose principal objective is to strengthen national technological capability. Under this Act, INPI's approval for a technology transfer agreement is conditioned on whether the receiving firm has an adequate program to assimilate the technology and carry out R&D to gain greater technological autonomy. The amount of the investment required depends on the financial situation of the Brazilian contractor and the amount to be paid for the imported technology.

33. However, it appears that since the "New Industrial Policy" was initiated in 1988, royalties as high as 10% are being permitted for some high-technology sectors such as software. See Rosenn (1988).

34. *Net sales* is calculated as total sales minus duties, taxes, imported inputs and components, commissions, transport, insurance, and other deductions.

35. Data from income declarations corroborate this downward trend in foreign technology contracts. The number of firms paying foreigners for royalties, and technical assistance has fallen from between 500 and 600 in the mid-1970s to just over 200 in the mid-1980s (see Paulinyi, 1990).

36. See Rosenn (1988).

37. Profit remittances above 12% of registered capital are subjected to a 40–60% supplemental income tax.

38. This causes tax problems for U. S. companies because Sections 367 and 382 of the U. S. Internal Revenue Code force companies to include imputed royalties on technology transfers in their U. S. income for tax purposes. See Rosenn (1988).

39. The main program was BEFIEX, established in 1972. This program, initially developed for the auto industry, gave firms incentives in the forms of reduction of imports duties and other fiscal exemptions as well as financial incentives in return for specific export commitments. The program was expanded to other sectors and also to national firms. In 1989 it was estimated that 50% of all Brazilian manufactured exports were covered under this program.

40. Take the example of printers. In the case of dot matrix, international–domestic price

differentials were in the range of 3:1 at the early stage of production in Brazil (and have remained so since), whereas for laser printers this lag has grown to 5:1.

41. Note in this respect that the value of contracted technology development operations in 1989 was less than US$18 million, little over one-tenth of what was contracted 2 years earlier in 1987.

42. Braga and Matesco (1989, Table 2.1).

43. CPqD, however, has been fairly successful in transferring many of the products it has developed to industrial firms for large-scale production. By the end of 1987, 75 different products developed singly by CPqD or in association with universities (which were in charge of carrying out most applied research) and industrial firms (generally focused on the later stages of development, such as prototyping) were being manufactured by 25 producers. See Frischtak (1989).

44. See Schwartzman (1988, pp. 99–119).

45. Schwartzman (1988, p. 104).

46. By 1988 ITA had trained more than 3000 engineers, 800 of which were in the aeronautics field.

47. The ITA/CTA graduate engineering, education/research nexus led to the spontaneous development of Brazil's first and largest industrial high technology park around San Jose dos Campos. Along with Embraer it has led to the establishment of many high-technology companies including Avibras (missiles), Orbita (missiles), Engesa (military equipment), Tecnasa (electronic communication equipment), Composite Tecnologica (composite materials), and Quantum (software).

48. As of February 1989 it had an accumulated production of 3983 aircraft.

49. Between 1970 and 1980, 31 new types of pistons and 59 types of sleeve bearings were introduced, including "heavy duty" pistons for large diesel engines and a special line for alcohol vehicles.

50. The reported cost of the new center was US$3 million, 90% of which was financed by FINEP. See *Gazeta Mercantil,* February 1, 1988.

REFERENCES

Baer, W., da Fonseca, M., and Guilhoto, J. (1987). "Structural Changes in Brazil's Industrial Economy: 1960-1980." *World Development* 15(2): 277–86.

Braga, H., and Matesco, V. (1989). "Desempenho Tecnólogico da Industrial Brasileira: uma Análise Exploratoria." *Textos Para Discussão Interna* No. 162, INPES/IPEA, February.

Cardozo, A. C. (1988). "A Implantação de Leis e Regulamentos Sobre Transferencia de Tecnologia: A Experiencia do Brasil." Mimeo.

CNPq. (1989). "Recursos do Tesouro da União: Dotacao Inicial, Dotacao Final, e Despesa Realizada 1980–89." May.

Confederacao Nacional da Industria. (1990). *Competitividade e Estrategia Industrial: a Visao de Lideres Industriais Brasileiros.* Rio. CNI.

Fishlow, A. (1980). "Brazilian Development in Long-Term Perspective." *American Economic Review* May, 102–8.

Frischtak, C. (1989). "Specialization, Technical Change and Competitiveness in the Brazilian Electronics Industry." *Industry Series Paper,* No.

15. The World Bank, Industry and Energy Department.

Furtado, C. (1984). *The Economic Growth of Brazil: A Survey from Colonial to Modern Times.* Westport, CT: Greenwood Press.

Government of Republic of China, Ministry of Education. (1984). *Educational Statistics of Republic of China.*

Government of Republic of China. (1988). *Statistical Yearbook of Republic of China 1988.* Taiwan.

Kume, H. (1988). "A Politica Tarifaria Brasileira no Periodo 1980–85: Avaliacão e Reforma." Mimeo.

Lall, S. (1992). "Explaining Industrial Success in Developing Countries." In S. Lall and V. N. Balasubramanyam (eds.), *Current Issues in Development Economics.* London: Macmillan (in press).

Martins, G., and Queiroz, R. (1987). "O Pertil do Pesquisador Brasileiro." *Revista Brasileira de Tecnologia* 18(6).

Motoyama, S. (1984). "Ciencia e Tecnologia e a Historia da Dependencia do Brasil." *Revista Brasileira de Tecnologia* 15(3).

Pastore, J. (1974). "Science and Technology in Brazilian Development." In W. Beranek, Jr. and G. Ranis (eds.), *Science, Technology, and Economic Development.* New York: Praeger.

Paulinyi, E. (1984). "Empresa Nacional—Panorama do Setor Empresarial em 1983." *Revista Brasileira de Tecnologia* 15(3).

Paulinyi, E. (1990). "Padroes de Capacitação e Atualização Tecnológica da Empresa Brasileira." *Informe Estatístico do CNPq.* 1(4).

Rosenn, K. (1988). "Regulation of Foreign Investment in Brazil." Mimeo.

Schwartzman, S. (1988). "Brazil: Opportunity and Crisis in Higher Education." *Higher Education* 17: 99–119.

Tavares de Araujo, J., Haguenauer, L., and

Machado, J. B. (1989). "Proteção, Competitividade e Desempenho Exportador da Economia Brasileira nos Anos 80." *Revista Brasileira de Comercio Exterior.* 26.

Tavares de Araujo, J. (1982). "Mudança Tecnólogica e Competitividade das Exportações Brasileiras de Manufaturados," IEI/FEA/UFRJ, *Texto para Discussão n. 8.* Table III

UNESCO. (1989). *Statistical Yearbook 1988,* Paris. U. N.

World Development Report. (1988, 1990).

14

National Systems of Innovation Supporting Technical Advance in Industry: The Case of Argentina

JORGE M. KATZ
NESTOR A. BERCOVICH

As a result of its successful integration into world markets for foodstuffs and agricultural raw materials Argentina was, at the beginning of the present century, a relatively rich nation with a fast growing economy. From 1895 to 1914 the number of acres under cultivation increased from 5 to 25 million. Wheat and maize exports multiplied by 3- and 4-fold, respectively, and the local population expanded from 3.9 to 7.8 million, due to heavy immigration from Europe. In 1914 one-third of the population had been born abroad, with nearly one million Italians and 800,000 Spaniards having taken up local residence; 90% of exports were primary products, most of which were directed toward western European countries (Diaz Alejandro, 1970; Rock, 1985).

Welfare indicators such as income and calories per capita clearly place Argentina among the richest nations in the world in those early years of the century.[1]

Contrary to the above picture, and in spite of a major process of industrialization, structural change, and social mobility, Argentina exhibits today a high level of macroeconomic instability, long-term decay in aggregate economic performance, and extreme forms of institutional fragility. Output per head is currently some 20% lower than two decades ago. The recent transition from a constitutional government to its freely elected civilian successor was the first to take place in many decades, pointing to the strong military presence in the country's political life, as well as to the weakness of the Argentine civilian institutions.

Thirty years of technological stagnation in its primary sector, a concentrated and oligopolistic industry that developed in an overprotected environment that relied basically on direct foreign investment as a source of technological dynamism, an entrepreneurial community that has increasingly involved itself in bureaucratic lobbying, opportunistic behavior, and rent-seeking activities rather than in technological and innovative efforts, a scientific and technological sector that has lacked in sense of purpose and direction as well as in incentives and accountability, and bureaucratic governments that have recurrently failed to incorporate the idea that a coherent network of institutions and policies supporting the process of technological change and modernization is needed if any given country is to adequately exploit its long-term opportunities constitute the main explanations of why the industrialization process has gradually lost strength and dynamism, and today faces major difficulties for its long-term consolidation.

Many of these difficulties relate to the weaknesses of Argentina's institutions and policies supporting technological change and innovation in industry and agriculture. In this chapter we shall examine the structure and performance of the country's National System of Innovation, its changes through time, and its relationship to the nation's long-term industrial and agricultural performance.

The first section of the chapter deals with the national system of innovation's support for technical change in industry. We begin by identifying various subperiods in the country's long-term industrialization process and examining the sources and nature of technological change and innovation as well as the functioning of the national system of innovation in each one of these. In the last of these periods—from the mid-1970s to the present—the country's industrial sector has been undergoing a major restructuring process, which has deeply affected the organization of work at the individual plant level as well as the functioning of markets and regulatory institutions. This process is also having a major impact on the national system of innovation supporting technological change and innovation in industry, the impact of which we will examine. The next section examines the network of agents, institutions, and policies influencing technological change and innovation in agriculture.

Having looked at agents and institutions related to innovation and technical change in agriculture and industry, we then proceed with the examination of R&D and knowledge-generating activities performed by public sector research agencies, universities, decentralized public enterprises, and the Armed Forces. We pay attention to the various ideologies, political and military lobbies, that in one way or another influenced the somewhat chaotic evolution of this major part of Argentina's national system of innovation.

The chapter concludes with an overall evaluation of the organization and performance of this system. It is quite clear that we cannot truly argue that the country has been able to develop a coherent and effective set of policies and institutions capable of inducing a successful process of generation, transfer, and diffusion of scientific and technological knowledge throughout the production structure. Nor can we say that Argentina has had anything close to a technological strategy reflecting its long-term development needs or its opportunities in the international marketplace.

Much could surely be achieved in this field if a major institutional build-up effort could be undertaken in the years to come. A less regulated macro policy environment, more respectful of the country's resource endowments and of its opportunities in world markets, a major reorganization of the educational system with the introduction of new mechanisms for the upgrading and recycling of the labor force and for the development of scientific and technological manpower; new ways of interaction and collaboration between manufacturing firms, universities, public R&D laboratories, and regulatory agencies; and better choice of priorities as far as public R&D and engineering efforts are concerned seem to all be different pieces of a complex puzzle to which Argentina will no doubt have to pay closer attention in the years to come, if it wants to regain the capacity for growth and the patterns of social equity that are currently being lost at a rapid pace.

In many of these fields we can identify powerful reasons for which decentralized market decisions might not necessarily be enough to ensure socially acceptable outcomes. Different types of externalities and public goods are involved, suggesting that new forms of intervention and institutional build-up efforts will probably have to be explored in the future even in spite of the fact that public intervention has had a clear record of failure as far as Argentina is concerned. How to work out an adequate balance between regulatory mechanisms and decentralized market decisions in the field of knowledge generation and diffusion or in relation to the training, upgrading, and recycling of human resources is of course a difficult question for which the country will have to work out imaginative new answers in the future.

THE NATIONAL SYSTEM OF INNOVATION SUPPORTING TECHNOLOGICAL CHANGE AND INNOVATION IN INDUSTRY

Argentina's industrial sector is today significantly different from what it was, say, two decades ago. The organization of production at the individual firm level, the structure of industry, and the behavior of markets have all been experiencing drastic changes during the course of the last decade. The national system of innovation supporting technical advance in industry has also been changing, as we shall see throughout the present section.

The Argentine industrialization process began in the early years of the present century. It acquired momentum in the 1930s and during World War II, when lack of foreign supplies induced local entrepreneurs into import substitution industrialization efforts.

Since the early 1960s, the massive arrival of foreign firms has significantly affected the rate and nature of the import substitution industrialization process, as well as technological change and innovation in industry. In the late 1970s the "foreign-led" expansionary phase came to a halt and since then a major industrial restructuring process—reflected in the contraction of metalworking industries and the concomitant expansion of raw material processing industries—has been taking place.

We shall now examine this industrialization process in some detail.

The Pre-1950s

The Argentine industrialization process of Argentina began with the establishment of food-processing industries linked to its primary production. Meatpacking houses, tanneries, flour mills, wineries and so on came into being and fared rather well before 1930.

A completely open economy and strict respect for Gold Standard principles, on the domestic side, along with a rapidly expanding foreign demand for foodstufs and raw materials allowed Argentine industries to prosper in world markets.

Capital goods for the locally established plants were at that point entirely imported. Their repair and maintenance, however, induced an early expansion of domestic technological capabilities in areas such as stamping, forging, and machining. Such technical skills were to become important some years later—in the 1940s—when the inconvertibility of the British pound, on the one hand, and the outbreak of World

War II, on the other, induced the military government in power into a "domestically oriented" import substitution industrialization strategy that was to have long lasting consequences on the country's social and economic performance.

Central to the new macroeconomic policy environment, we find two new policies that strongly affected the process of industrialization. We refer to the introduction of exchange control—which began to be applied late in 1931—and to import tariffs that soon followed. From 1930 onward, the economy became much more regulated and closed itself off to foreign trade, with imports and exports falling in their percentage of the GDP. In particular, tariff protection was to play a major role as a determinant of the structure and nature of the industrialization process that followed. The average firm size, market structure and behavior, and degree of vertical integration were all significantly affected by the new industrial policy that was adopted by the country.

In the late 1930s and 1940s, textiles and chemicals and later a whole range of electromechanical products began to be domestically produced under the incentives of a rapidly expanding internal market, tariff protection, and subsidized financing from public agencies, in particular from the Industrial Bank, which was created for such purposes in 1944. From 1945 onward, the nationalization of foreign trade and the expropriation of agricultural profits allowed the government to transfer resources from rural landlords to the rapidly growing urban–industrial sector that developed in those days under the incentives of an expanding real wage rate and of an industrial policy that promoted various so-called "industries of national interest." The role of Argentina's highly nationalistic military forces became central to the country's macroeconomic policy formulation mechanism during those years. A fortiori it also exerted a major impact on the way the national system of innovation behaved throughout the war period and during the 1950s.[2]

Whereas the pre-1930s industrialization process—involving mostly the local processing of primary raw materials—was carried out in modern and updated facilities and was highly competitive by international standards, the import substitution industrialization efforts of the 1940s and afterwards entailed the erection of a "second best" industrial sector exclusively catering to local demands. Foreign exchange shortages—originated in the stagnation of primary exports—introduced a major barrier to the expansion of manufacturing production.[3]

On the external front the situation was by no means better. The end of the war and the rapid technological reconstruction of DCs during the 1950s brought about an increasing technological gap between local manufacturing industries and their international counterparts.

Even before the military coup d'état of 1955 that ousted the Peronist government in power, the local administration had begun to revise its antagonistic attitude toward foreign capital and had accepted the idea that foreign investment and technology could become major "sources of economic growth." In April 1953 the Administration passed Argentina's first foreign investment law and started negotiations with a number of MNCs, trying to attract them to Argentina. It is important to note the weak bargaining position from where Argentina carried out these negotiations if we are to understand the extremely high level of protection—along with other advantages—that many of these firms managed to obtain from the local authorities in exchange for their promise of setting up domestic production facilities.

Be that as it may, the massive arrival of foreign firms in the late 1950s and early

1960s clearly signals the beginning of a somewhat different period in the country's industrialization history as well as in the functioning of the agencies and institutions supporting technical change and innovation. This period covers the years between 1960 and 1975, which we now examine.

1960-1975: The Establishment of the Automobile Industry and the Expansion of Metalworking Industries in General

The investment boom that took place between 1957 and 1961 clearly constitutes the starting point of a period of rapid expansion, both in manufacturing output and in the productivity of labor. Close to 200 foreign corporations established domestic production facilities during those years, bringing about a major change in the country's industrial culture.

The share of MNCs in manufacturing production grew quite significantly in those years until it reached about one-third of the total. Central to this overall episode is the establishment of the automobile industry that represented only 2.5% of the manufacturing GDP in 1951 and grew to 10.3% of the manufacturing GDP in 1965, exhibiting a growth rate of nearly 25% per year between 1958 and 1965.

The industrialization process we are describing had a number of highly idiosyncratic features in relation to both the size and nature of firms as well as in terms of market structure and performance. On the one hand, plant sizes were never bigger than 10% of comparable plants in European countries. On the other hand, and due to the low degree of standardization and normalization prevailing in local markets, as well as to the absence of reliable subcontractors, manufacturing plants started their local operation with a degree of vertical integration much higher than companies in Europe.

Given the small size of the domestic market—and the fact that very few of these firms originally expected to engage themselves in export activities—their output mix rapidly became wider than that of comparable plants elsewhere. Thus, the organization of work and the social division of labor did not develop as a copy of those prevailing in more mature societies. As a consequence of the above, many of the newly erected firms found themselves needing to gradually develop "in house" technological capabilities in areas such as product design, production engineering, industrial planning, and organization where "from the shelf" technology was not particularly well suited, given the highly idiosyncratic nature of the local production structure.

In other words, given the highly "localized" nature of their domestic operation, many of these newly created companies found themselves needing to establish "in house" engineering departments whose basic mission was to adapt foreign product designs and production processes to the local working and regulatory environment.[4] This process of industrial growth had a major impact on the functioning of the national system of innovation supporting technological change on industry, as we shall now show.

First, manufacturing output and labor productivity grew quite rapidly throughout the industrial structure. Between 1960 and 1974, Argentina's industrial output grew at about 8% per annum while employment and labor productivity grew at 2 and 6%, respectively.

Second, in spite of the domestic orientation of the industrialization process, manufacturing exports gradually began to expand in the late 1960s and early 1970s.

Third, foreign firms clearly acquired a leading role within the local manufacturing sector and had a major influence on the way the national system of innovation was to be developed. There are various reasons for this. On the one hand, these firms introduced quality control practices, tolerance limits, and subcontracting practices, which simply had not been available before within the local industrial environment. On the other hand, their new production facilities served as training grounds for local technicians and engineers. In spite of the obvious beneficial impact obtained by this process it should also be taken into account that it clearly restricted the spectrum of the technological "search" activities carried out by engineers and technologists, limiting them to "adaptive" technological efforts within the boundaries of the technology originally imported from abroad.

Three different studies document our previous points.

The first of these studies (Katz, 1974) constitutes an attempt to measure the flow of R&D and engineering expenditure carried out by domestic manufacturing firms throughout the 1960s, and their impact on individual firm productivity growth.

Taking the largest 200 industrial firms in Argentina, a survey was conducted that showed that some 20 million U. S. dollars per year were spent by the firms under examination in "adaptive" R&D and engineering activities as well as in production planning and organization. Many of these activities were nonroutine in the local context even though some of them would not have been covered by OECD or NSF standard definitions of R&D expenditure.

About half of the firms in the sample employed somewhere between 5 and 50 people in product design activities and/or in process engineering departments, whose function was "debugging" and adapting product designs and production processes brought from abroad to the local environment, under some form of licensing contract. Even in those cases in which no formal R&D departments could be identified—such as in the case of many medium-size family enterprises—knowledge creation activities were carried out by ad hoc groups or even by production personnel on a part-time basis. Pilot plant work and the construction of prototypes were quite frequently undertaken by the companies examined during our field work.

For each one of the companies in the sample, a total factor productivity growth rate was estimated covering the 1960s. Also output growth, employment, R&D, and engineering expenditure and royalties were measured for each firm over the same period and their relationship to labor productivity growth was examined using standard econometric techniques (Katz, 1974).

Our results show that labor productivity growth was "explained" both by a "scale" factor—measured by the expansion of output—and by a "technological" factor that in the present case was represented by the accumulated R&D and engineering expenditure carried out by each company throughout the 1960s. As mentioned before, this decade was, for many of these firms, one of rapid physical expansion in the domestic environment and of technological adaptation to its highly particular atmosphere.

Both "scale" and "technological learning" effects can be reasonably expected to underlie their observed performance. Concerning the impact the industrialization process had on the country's pattern of exports, two additional studies carried out a few years later (Ablin and Katz, 1985) provide evidence that industrial exports of an increasing degree of technological sophistication gradually expanded in the early 1970s. Manufacturing exports increased from some 100 million U S$ in 1959—less than 10% of total exports—to nearly 1500 million U S$ in 1974—close to 25% of a much higher figure of total exports. Among the newly exported products we find machine tools, agricultural equipment, electromechanical instruments, industrial boilers, and automobiles. Examining the experience of the largest 20 industrial exporters, we found that product design and process engineering efforts were by no means negligible as explanatory variables of these companies' gradual success in foreign markets.

On the other hand, we notice that during the 1970s the industrialization process resulted in not just manufacturing exports of an increasing degree of technological sophistication, but also an incipient export trade of pure technology—both under the form of licensing activities and through the delivery of complete manufacturing plants to enterprises of neighboring countries. Meatpacking houses, industrial dairies or bakeries, bottling and canning facilities, and machining plants appear on the list. Concomitant with such developments we also found evidence indicating that large domestic engineering firms engaged in the construction of hospitals, airports, pipelines, and so on to be delivered on a turnkey basis to other Latin American countries (Ablin et al., 1985).

Beyond doubt, export subsidies played a significant role in inducing such developments, but we cannot rule out the fact that technological "learning" and domestic engineering efforts gradually acquired significance as explanatory forces of the newly emerging trends.

Similar results were reported by other researchers looking at other NICs such as India (Lall, 1982), Brazil, Mexico, Hong Kong, and Taiwan (*World Development*, 1984), confirming the fact that technological "learning" from peripheral societies could be expected to have dynamic consequences that had not been previously examined in the development literature.

Direct foreign investment activities from local entrepreneurs also increased throughout those years (Katz and Kosacoff, 1983) suggesting that revenues could be captured in third markets through the export of goods and technology and also by means of "joint venture" agreements involving the direct investment of local entrepreneurs in neighboring societies.

The development process we have so far been describing reached a plateau in the mid-1970s.

Both domestic and external reasons account for the limitations encountered by local industries at that point. On the domestic side it is clear that many consumer durable markets became highly "saturated." Consider the case of automobiles. Whereas in the early 1950s Argentina had one automobile per 50 people, by 1975 the figure had fallen to around 6 people per vehicle. A similar case can be made for many other durables. The import substitution industrialization strategy became increasingly criticized for its overprotected nature as well as for its lack of a stronger export drive. Exports continued to be a small fraction of the total industrial output and the country's balance of payments fell into a recurrent 3 to 4 years cycle. A generalized perception developed concerning the fact that the import substitution industrialization process was leading to a dead end and that structural reforms were badly needed.

On the external side, the rapid diffusion of microprocessors and microelectronic technology quickly eroded the competitive advantage many local firms had managed to attain in Latin American markets for machine tools, electrical instruments, and capital goods in general. Local entrepreneurs were not able to follow the pace of the international technological frontier, which was introducing digital and numerical control devices and miniaturization, and rapidly lost external markets with their relatively less sophisticated electromechanical designs.

In addition to these economic circumstances, it should also be taken into consideration that the domestic institutional atmosphere became rather tense in the late 1960s and early 1970s with militant trade unions and student groups increasingly challenging the political status quo. The degree of social unrest increased considerably throughout the country in those years opening up major questions concerning the capabilities of the country's institutional fabric to survive under such pressure. Argentina was at that point entering into a turbulent period from which it has not as yet completely recovered. A major process of structural change began in the early 1970s with a civilian government in power and continued—in a more dramatic and repressive way—after the military coup d'état of March 1976. We turn now to the examination of this period.

1975 to the Present: Deregulation and Opening up of the Local Economy: From Mechanical Engineering to Raw Material Processing Industries

The perception that the economy was heading for a dead end and running into stronger balance of payment difficulties induced the Peronist government in office in the early 1970s to press import substitution industrialization efforts even further. With this purpose, it introduced a new set of fiscal incentives hoping to attract investment for industries such as petrochemical, aluminum, and pulp and paper, which were heavily dependent on foreign supplies. In the space of approximately one decade, a significant number of new, capital-intensive factories came into being with as much as 60–70% of the required capital investment coming from public sources under the form of tax concessions (Azpiazu, 1985). A small group of large domestic holdings benefited from such policy actions.

Shortly after, in early 1976, a new military takeover occurred, and in the context of a massive process of social repression, the authorities attempted to deregulate and open up the local economy to foreign competition. On the sociopolitical front the Armed Forces tried to curb worker activism through the physical intervention of trade unions and the imprisonment of labor leaders; on the economic front their disciplinary action came under the form of a drastic return to orthodox market principles. Among their initial economic policy actions we find (1) a major reduction in tariff protection: the average ad valorem rate was brought down from 95 to 55%, (2) a revaluation of the local currency of approximately 40% in real terms—intended as an instrument for inducing foreign competition in local markets and price restraints on the part of domestic entrepreneurs, and (3) the deregulation of the financial sector of the economy. On account of this measure the rate of interest—negative during previous decades—moved into positive levels.

These policies—together with the fiscal incentives for raw material processing industries approved in the early 1970s and not removed by the military authorities, probably because of the strong lobbying pressure exerted by large domestic corporate groups—had a major impact on the rate and nature of the industrialization process as well as on the behavior of the national system of innovation supporting technical advance in industry. Let us consider both these aspects. Concerning the process of industrialization we notice the following.

First, industrial production as a percentage of the GDP has fallen significantly during the course of the past 15 years. Industrial output has fallen from about one-third of the GDP in the mid-1970s to approximately 23% at present.

Second, the structure of industry has changed drastically in recent years. The production of metalworking products and capital goods in general has contracted, while resource-based industries producing steel, petrochemicals, aluminum, edible oil, and so on have expanded considerably. In the mid-1970s Argentina produced some 350,000 automobiles, 25,000 machine tools, and 60,000 tractors per annum. At present, it produces only 150,000, 6000, and 5000, respectively, in factories that have changed significantly as far as production organization, import content, subcontracting practices, and employment absorption, are concerned. Contrary to the above, production has increased from 865 to 1800 thousand tons worth of petrochemical products and from 2250 to 3670 thousand tons of steel products during the course of the same period. As far as edible oil is concerned, production rose from 630 thousand tons in 1975–1977 to nearly 2 million tons in 1984–1986.

Third, the share of MNCs in domestic manufacturing production has fallen from 32 to 25%. The local production facilities of major MNCs such as General Motors, Olivetti, and Citroen have been closed down in recent years.

Fourth, with takeovers, mergers, and exits, the degree of business concentration has increased quite dramatically in the automotive, steel, petrochemical, textile apparel and shoe production, and tobacco sectors.

Fifth, the consolidation of a small number of large domestic holdings can now be observed. These groups have expanded, taking advantage of the industrial promotion legislation of the early 1970s (Schvarzer, 1983). They have gradually diversified their activities from textiles to oil exploration and extraction and from automotive to atomic energy component production in a rapid process of horizontal and vertical expansion.

Sixth, together with the structural transformation, the pattern of industrial exports has experienced substantial changes. In the mid-1970s about one-third of the country's manufacturing exports—sold basically in the Latin American region—were electromechanical products such as vehicles, machine tools, and agricultural equipment. These products account for less than 10% of total industrial exports today. Instead, we now register large and growing exports of steel plate, edible oil, aluminum, and pulp and paper, all being industrial commodities where local firms behave as "price takers" in strongly competitive international markets. Companies frequently sell abroad at marginal cost, with domestic prices for the same products being significantly higher than their international quotations.

Seventh, the organization of work and labor relations at the individual firm level as well as the overall functioning of the labor market have also undergone major changes. On the one hand, the contraction of the metalworking sector has brought about a sharp reduction in Argentina's industrial labor force. The auto industry employs today some 70,000 workers, less than it did one decade ago, and a similar situation can be observed in the production of tractors, agricultural equipment, and capital goods in general. On the other hand, the production of industrial "commodities" in capital-intensive plants has scarcely required new workers. Moreover, the massive military repression among trade union members carried out between 1976 and 1979 significantly reduced worker activism and trade union bargaining strength within the society at large.

These aspects add up to a major "change of regime" in which the structure of industry, the organization of production at the individual firm level, the market structure, the degree of business concentration, the participation of foreign companies, the functioning of the labor market, trade union bargainig strength, and regulatory institutions all seem to be part of a global economic and institutional restructuring process of far-reaching dimensions. Firms, markets, and institutions all seem to be involved in this process. When compared with the old "mechanical engineering" period of the 1960s and early 1970s, it is clear that the import substitution efforts of the 1980s involve technologically more updated production facilities, a much higher degree of integration into world markets, and a different entrepreneurial constituency, insofar as large domestic corporate groups—and not foreign firms—now dominate the local industrial landscape.

A major question now emerges in relation to the impact of the previously described process on the country's national system of innovation (i.e., on agents, institutions, and policies supporting technical change and innovation in industry). A number of comments follow.

Consider first the impact that macroeconomic stabilization policies and the opening up of the domestic economy are having on the rate of new capital formation, entrepreneurial spirit, and locally performed R&D activities. Both the rate of savings and investment have fallen quite sharply relative to the 1960s and 1970s. A much higher degree of macroeconomic uncertainty and volatility, together with a completely open financial sector, account for the fact that capital flights from Argentina increased quite dramatically during the course of the 1980s. The reduced tendency to invest locally (Escude and Guerberoff, 1990) is reflected in the low level of imports of machinery and equipment that has prevailed throughout recent years (Katz and Kosacoff, 1989).

Direct foreign manufacturing investment has also fallen sharply throughout the 1980s reflecting the scarce interest and low expectations held by foreign firms concerning the future of the Argentine economy.

This behavioral pattern (i.e., the reduction in the rate of new capital formation and in the average propensity to invest on the part of the entreprenurial community) appears to be associated with an expansion of opportunistic and rent-seeking activities and with a general fall in spirit that permeates the production structure.

In addition to the above, yet another significant new structural element concerns the impact that the industrial restructuring process is having on the rate and nature of locally performed R&D and engineering efforts. Metalworking firms have reacted to the reduction in their level of activity by cutting down "in house" product design and production organization efforts. Raw material processing industries, on the other hand, have not yet significantly expanded their R&D commitments. Thus the fact that Argentina now produces about half the number of cars, machine tools, and tractors than it did 10 years ago and that capital-intensive factories producing industrial commodities have taken over their role as leaders within manufacturing production seems to have produced an absolute contraction in industrial R&D and engineering efforts.

The reasons for this are as follows. From an accounting point of view, activities such as product design engineering efforts, production planning and organization, plant layout balancing actions, and time and motion studies constitute an indirect cost of production. Therefore with the contraction of sales, many metalworking firms proceeded to reduce their engineering departments, particularly those concerned with product design activities.

On the other hand, the production of industrial commodities in new and technologically more updated facilities—many of which were purchased abroad on a turnkey basis—has so far required very little in the form of R&D and/or process engineering efforts on the part of local companies.

In addition to the previous explanation, we should also notice that the more turbulent and uncertain macroeconomic scenario of the last decade has probably militated against long-term technological and innovative commitments on the part of the local entrepreneurial community. Firms have turned more to the search for subsidies and special privileges than to investment and technological change. Moreover, the exchange rate overvaluation that existed during the period between 1979 and 1981 induced many firms to incorporate imported machinery and equipment with the expectation that the recession that was going on in the country at that time was to be a short one and that demand would soon return to normal levels. These expectations never materialized and idle production capacity was apparent throughout the industrial spectrum during the mid- and late 1980s.

So much for capital formation, entrepreneuric spirit, and domestic R&D activities. Furthermore, it is also evident that a new set of regulatory institutions is gradually gaining ground within the local environment and that its impact on the national system of innovation is going to be far from negligible. The deregulation of markets and the opening up of the economy to foreign competition, the privatization of public enterprises, and the capitalization of the country's external debt in exchange for domestic public utilities and industrial assets have now become central parts of the new—and implicit—industrial policy. It is still premature to evaluate the impact that this new regulatory regime is going to have on local industry, and particularly on the spirit and functioning of the national system of innovation supporting technical advance in industry, but there is no doubt that the impact will be a major one in the years to come. Recent investments in the petrochemical, steel, and automotive industries carried out with the purpose of establishing a strong export platform in Argentina suggest that large companies are gradually beginning to adapt themselves to the new regulatory environment and that a more open and competitive industrial structure, better integrated to world markets, might eventually emerge out of the ongoing structural transformation. It is still too early to determine whether the country is taking a good or a bad route in its industrialization process, but it is clear that the old route on the "mechanical engineering" front was running into a dead end and that fundamental changes in industrial policy were badly needed.

Having so far examined the functioning of the national system of innovation supporting technical advance in industry, we now proceed with the study of the way in which this system has worked in the case of the agricultural sector.

THE NATIONAL SYSTEM OF INNOVATION SUPPORTING TECHNOLOGICAL CHANGE IN AGRICULTURE

Argentina's agricultural sector presents us with one of the more intriguing puzzles in the country's long-term development history; Figure 14.1 presents the case.

After nearly four decades of rapid expansion—which brought the area under cultivation to nearly 20 million acres from 1938 to 1940, and the total grain output to 20 million tons—the sector entered into a long period of decay and stagnation that lasted nearly 30 years. In the early 1950s the area under cultivation had fallen to less than 15 million acres and total agricultural output was roughly equivalent to the 1919/1920 level. It was only in the late 1960s that the agricultural sector of Argentina returned to its 1939/1940 output levels, with 20 million acres under cultivation and production at about 23 million tons.

The process of expansion then proceeded quickly, with productivity per acre doubling between the late 1960s and the present. This improvement in productivity resulted initially from a more rapid rate of introduction of agricultural equipment and production organization technologies, and subsequently from the massive diffusion of maize hybrids, the use of new agrochemicals, and the introduction of new crops such as soybeans and sorghum. Public sector agencies (see the discussion of this topic in our next section) have played an important role with regard to the development of new product varieties, mainly in wheat and soybeans, and in the diffusion of production

Figure 14.1. Total production of grain for the country: 1911–1964.

organization technologies. On the other hand, private firms, in particular, local subsidiaries of large MNCs, are now playing an increasingly important role in the production and commercialization of agricultural machinery, agrochemicals, and hybrids.

How do we explain the poor performance of Argentine agriculture between the 1930s and 1960s? Which patterns of interaction prevailed among agents, institutions, and policies that locked Argentina into a vicious circle of agricultural stagnation and decay that lasted nearly 30 years? Which events unlocked this vicious circle in more recent times? We proceed with an analysis of these major questions.

Obviously there is not a single and universally valid view as to what happened to the rural sector of Argentina in the 1930s, when the agricultural frontier came to an end and the country had to face the limits of its natural resource endowments. The following considerations, however, should be taken into account:

First, in spite of the fact that prices for primary products suffered an important downfall during the 1930s and 1940s and world demand for grains, wool, and beef remained rather weak throughout those years, these should not be regarded as the principal explanations for what happened to the Argentine agricultural sector at that point in history. Rather, there were domestic reasons—a major increase in local consumption, a downfall in the rate of mechanization, a high degree of uncertainty concerning agricultural prices and profits, and political antagonism between the government in power and rural landlords that prevented a more entrepreneurial behavior on the part of the latter—that should be taken into consideration when trying to explain what actually happened to the sector during the war years and the 1950s.

The need to emphasize the "internal" explanation is obvious if we observe the dissimilar export performance of Argentina compared to that of other agricultural giants in the same designated period.

Wheat and maize exports can be used as examples of what happened on this front. In the prewar years Argentina's annual exports of wheat reached some 3.3 million tons and represented about 20% of total world exports. Canada with 4.8 million tons accounted for 28% of the total, Australia with 2.8 million tons absorbed 16%, and the United States with 1.3 million tons represented about 7%. From 1950 to 1954, with a much higher world demand for wheat, Argentine exports fell to 2.2 million tons, which constituted only 9% of total world exports, whereas Canada had doubled its exports, and the U. S. exports increased from 1.3 to 8.9 million tons (CEPAL, 1959).

Concerning maize, in the prewar period Argentina exported 6.3 million tons, absorbing as much as 64% of the world trade. From 1950 to 1954, exports fell to just over 1 million tons per annum whereas U. S. exports increased 3-fold from 800,000 to 2.6 million tons.

A similar situation can be found with regard to wool and beef exports where the Argentine share of the world trade fell from 12 to 9% in the first case and from 40 to 19% in the latter comparing the 1950/1954 period to the prewar years.

Summarizing: falling prices and a weak world demand for primary products obviously had a negative impact on Argentine exports in the late 1930s and 1940s, but the main explanation for its stagnation and decay is to be found in the fact that Argentina produced less grain and beef in those years than in the 1920s and simultaneously increased its domestic consumption of such goods, as a consequence of public policies aimed at benefiting urban working classes and import substitution industrialization efforts. As a result of this Argentina gradually lost its share of the world trade to the United States, Canada, Australia, and New Zealand.

Second, as far as domestic consumption is concerned, we should notice that whereas from 1925 to 1929 local consumption of agricultural products accounted for 48% of the total production, by 1950–1954 this proportion had expanded to 69%. During the war years wheat and maize were burned as substitutes for fuel, which could not be imported.

Third, although domestic consumption of wheat and maize expanded, the production fell in real terms. Labor shortages caused by heavy rural migration induced by the rapid expansion of industry led rural land owners into open-pasture cattle raising instead of agricultural production. On the other hand, the nationalization of foreign trade and the setting up of low agricultural prices for various consecutive years resulted in a climate of uncertainty and unrest among rural landlords. This antagonistic atmosphere created a barrier against mechanization and a more rapid diffusion of fertilizers.

Consider the following evidence (CEPAL, 1959). The United States employed less than 50 kg worth of fertilizers per acre in the prewar years and increased to around 170 kg per acre from 1950 to 1954. In contrast, Argentina employed less than 5 kg of fertilizers per acre from 1950 to 1954. Of course, relative prices were highly different among both countries, providing a good explanation for the observed differences in the use of fertilizers—consider that 100 kg worth of wheat was needed to purchase 11 kg of fertilizers in Argentina from 1950 to 1954 while the same amount of grain managed to obtain 44 kg of fertilizers in the United States. In addition to relative prices we should also notice the antagonistic atmosphere in which the rural sector operated in those days as a consequence of government policies.

A similar case can be made concerning the degree of mechanization. Between 1930/1934 and 1945/1949 the number of operating tractors decreased by about 40% in Argentina, whereas they multiplied 3-fold in the United States. Between 1940 and 1955 the United States increased its stock of tractors from 1.5 to 4.3 million. By 1955 the United States had 30 tractors per 1000 acres under cultivation, which was about 15 times more than Argentina, which at that point had approximately 2 tractors per 1000 acres under exploitation. Again, relative prices—as well as import difficulties during the war period—are good explanations for the observed differences in mechanization, although we should not disregard the political aspects and the antagonism between rural landlords and Peronist authorities that exacerbated risk-aversion attitudes on the part of the former.

Beginning in 1952, a number of major policy changes were implemented by the government, many of them directed at improving the position of the rural sector. A major currency devaluation and a drastic change in relative prices favoring primary production over industrial goods were particularly relevant in this respect. Slowly, the agricultural sector gave signs of reaction. The area under cultivation began to increase once again, reaching 18 million acres in 1956 and 1957.

Throughout the 1960s, the agricultural output grew by 30% whereas in the following 20 years the production of primary products multiplied 3-fold, and the productivity of labor increased nearly 4-fold, being at present at their all time historical peak.

Four different sources can be identified behind the observed trends (Obschatko, 1988). First, "disembodied" technical change—new agricultural practices—played an important role during the 1960s. The National Institute for Agricultural Technology (INTA)—created in 1956—was instrumental in the dissemination of new agricultural practices and patterns of production organization. Second, the expansion of the tractor industry, which took place during the 1960s, had a major impact on the degree of mechanization employed by the rural sector. The country's total stock of tractors expanded from around 77,000 in 1960 to 140,000 in 1970 and to 162,000 in 1980 (Huici, 1988). Four domestic subsidiaries of large multinational corporations entered the local market for tractors during the 1960s and various forms of tax concessions were used by the authorities to induce a rapid expansion in the degree of mechanization of the rural sector.

The third major source of technological change and productivity growth as far as agriculture is concerned, involved the diffusion of hybrids (in maize, sorghum, and sunflower), new varieties of wheat, and the introduction of soybean into production during the late 1970s.

Finally, the fourth and last set of innovative actions is related to the recent expansion in the use of agrochemicals, herbicides, and pesticides.

An important change in the institutional scenario underlying these processes should be noted at this point. Whereas in the 1950s and 1960s it is the public sector—mainly through the INTA—that carries out research activities in the field of new agricultural practices and hybrids, particularly in the case of maize, the most recent trend toward the more rapid diffusion of hybrids, new product varieties, herbicides, and pesticides seems to be increasingly in the hands of domestic subsidiaries of large multinational corporations. Whereas in the former period technological change had a more "disembodied" nature—involving agricultural practices and production organization technologies—in the latter it seems to have more of an "embodied" nature with hybrids and agrochemicals now being the major way of introduction. Yet another major technological innovation of recent years—this time of an institutional nature—relates to the diffusion of subcontracting practices as far as harvesting is concerned. New forms of market organization are now allowing medium size and small farmers to operate with capital-intensive equipment that the scale of their plots would not have allowed them to own.

Having examined the nature and behavior of the national system of innovation supporting technological change in industry and agriculture, we now turn to the study of other parts of this system, in particular to those related to public R&D efforts.

PUBLIC R&D EFFORTS IN ARGENTINA

The Aggregate Picture

Public R&D expenditure and knowledge generation efforts came close to 380 million U. S. dollars per annum in 1988. We arrive at this figure by adding up 330 million U. S. dollars accounted for under the relevant chapter of the National Budget plus some 50 million U. S. dollars spent by decentralized public enterprises (the National Petroleum Company—YPF—being the largest one in this group), not included in the previously mentioned Budget chapter.

Public R&D activities are highly concentrated. Eight agencies and institutions absorb nearly 90% of the total budget, as Table 14.1 indicates. Most of these agencies

Table 14.1. Major Public Agencies and Institutions Carrying or Financing R&D Activities in Argentina (Million U.S. Dollars), 1988

Agency or Institution	Total Expenditure
National Council for Science and Technology (CONICET)	135.4
Atomic Energy Commission (CNEA)	56.3
Institute for Agricultural Technology (INTA)	67.2
Institute for Industrial Technology (INTI)	14.2
National Petroleum Enterprise Yacimientos Petrolíferos Fiscales (YPF)	15.0
Armed Forces Instituto de Investigaciones Científicas y Técnicas de las Fuerzas Armadas (CITEFA)	12.2
Secretary of Science and Technology (SECYT)	8.2
Universities	30.0
Others	41.5
Estimated total public R&D expenditure	380.0

Sources: National Budget Law, complemented with direct information from YPF, CITEFA, and the University of Bs.As.

were created after World War II and at least some of them experienced a period of rapid expansion and institutional consolidation throughout the 1960s and early 1970s. Ideologies, academic as well as corporate, and military "lobbies" have played a major role as determinants of the budgetary allocation process as far as public R&D expenditure is concerned. We should therefore keep in mind the following aspects when dealing with the individual history of some of these agencies:

1. Argentina's traditionally strong military forces exerted major pressure in favor of developing domestic nuclear power capabilities and supporting the evolution of the Atomic Energy Commission, which thus received special treatment within the budgetary process for quite a long period of time.
2. INTA's late creation, in 1956, came about after a drastic rethinking of the role of agriculture in the country's long-term development process. As we have seen before, such rethinking came about after nearly three decades of neglect, which had dramatically negative consequences.
3. Almost as a matter of policy, Argentine universities have been kept as rather weak institutions, just marginally contributing to the national system of innovation. This was particularly so during authoritarian periods of military rule.
4. Research for the sake of new knowledge—rather than technologically oriented efforts—and little tendency to collaborate with the production sector of the economy appear as distinctive ideological features of the local academic community. This is particularly noticeable in the early history of CONICET.

Keeping in mind these ideological and political factors, let us now proceed with a brief presentation of the evolution of some of the agencies and institutions.

Brief Description of Some of the Main Public R&D Activities

The National Council for Science and Technology (CONICET)

CONICET was created in 1958 with the purpose of "promoting, coordinating and carrying out research both in applied and pure sciences." Whereas in 1971, CONICET had 490 research fellows and 13 affiliated institutes, by 1988 the figures had gone up to 198 affiliated institutes and 11 regional research centers with a total payroll of close to 7500 people. Such a dramatic institutional build-up took place in about one decade and in a somewhat chaotic and unplanned fashion, more as a consequence of a deliberate action by the military authorities to weaken the institutional position of the National Universities after the 1966 military coup d'état than as a result of serious long-term planning of public R&D activities. Needless to say, CONICET was by no means administratively prepared to handle this build-up and is still suffering from serious bureaucratic disorder.

In 1988 approximately 40% of CONICET's research personnel belonged to the medical and biological sciences, while the humanities absorbed 26% and the technological sciences 14% of the total payroll.

A few points stand out concerning CONICET's current situation. On the one hand, it is the largest and fastest growing R&D agency in Argentina. On the other hand, it exhibits a somewhat large interinstitute and interprogram variance in research quality and productivity and has not yet been able to introduce systematic quality control and peer evaluation actions.

A special comment should be made concerning technology transfers toward the production sector of the economy. A Technology Transfer Office was opened up by CONICET authorities in 1985 with the purpose of strengthening the technological linkages between its institutes and firms producing goods and services. Between 1985 and 1988, some 225 contracts were signed between both public and private firms. About half of these contracts involve R&D activities jointly performed and financed by both parts of the agreement, while another 40% of them correspond to services provided by CONICET personnel in areas such as quality control and metrology. Nearly one-half of the contracts relate to chemical and petrochemical firms, while a surprising 10% is accounted for by companies dealing in biotechnology. In most cases, medium size and small firms without their own R&D infrastructure are the ones engaged in these contracts. The average size of the agreements is rather small with just a few of them having funds of over 100 thousand U. S. dollars annually (Nivoli, 1990).

The Atomic Energy Commission (CNEA)

The Atomic Energy Commission was founded in 1951. It has a total labor force of nearly 6000 people, 1600 of whom perform R&D activities. Although during the war years the Argentine Military Forces entertained the idea of developing technological self-sufficiency in the atomic energy field, it was only in the mid-1960s that the country decided to build up nuclear power stations for electricity generation. The first such unit was put into operation in 1973 and the second one in 1983. Although both of these plants were purchased on a turnkey basis from international subcontractors, the degree of local participation and technological "unpackaging" increased considerably from the first to the second project (Tanis, 1986).

In May 1980, CNEA signed contracts with a German firm for a third nuclear power station. This time CNEA went much further into the basic engineering specification of the technology it wanted and took responsibility for the overall supervision of the project, thus indicating that the "learning" component had by no means been negligible in this particular field of activity.

Ever since its creation, CNEA has had an explicit policy aimed at upgrading both its technical personnel and its many subcontractors. A study carried out by Sabato et al. (1978) indicates that nearly 1000 scientists and technicians have been trained abroad in physics, chemistry, radiobiology, metallurgy, and material sciences. Also, and as part of its efforts in the development of human resources, various pilot plants and experimental research reactors were constructed during the late 1950s and 1960s, thus providing the infrastructure for further applied R&D efforts.

Besides developing "in house" technological capabilities, CNEA generated a significant flow of externalities by upgrading and developing an extensive number of subcontractors.

During recent years, CNEA signed various "joint venture" agreements with private firms. As in the case of subcontractors, CNEA's impact on the private nuclear industry has been far from negligible. It has also developed an engineering design capacity that is currently being offered both locally and in foreign markets through INVAP, an R&D and engineering firm presently employing more than 500 people and carrying out research both for CNEA and for private firms in fields such as electronic instruments, and biomedical equipment.

CNEA has recently suffered major reductions in its overall budget as well as the loss of scientific personnel. The fact that the country has, in recent years, discovered huge reserves of natural gas—it is now estimated that approximately 50 years of gas reserves are stored underground—casts strong doubts on the likelihood of the future expansion of Argentina's nuclear power sector.

The National Institute for Agricultural Technology (INTA)

This public R&D agency was created in 1956 with the purpose of strengthening agricultural research and extension activities. It is interesting to note that in a country where primary raw materials have always been a major source of economic growth, so little importance had been given before to R&D efforts related to the primary sector. Obviously, this is in sharp contrast to the early interest such activities received in similarly endowed countries such as Australia or Canada, where the upgrading of rural life, institutions, and production capabilities appeared as a major public commitment much before they did in Argentina (Fogarty, 1977).

INTA's budget is financed with a 1.5% ad valorem tax on agricultural and livestock exports. With a total personnel of close to 5000 people, INTA employs today some 1900 professionals and technicians, a figure that is about three times higher than its initial level in 1956/1957. Approximately 230 of these people pursued postgraduate studies at a Masters level while 54 completed Ph.D. training. Just over 100 students currently receive local training at a Masters level, while nearly 40 more are enrolled as Ph.D. candidates at various educational institutions around the world.

INTA runs a large number of regional experimental farms and extension agencies. Nearly 30 research programs have been organized and pursued by INTA's staff throughout the years. Obviously, not all of these programs have attained the same degree of success, but there is evidence that some of them have been highly successful in the generation and diffusion of genetic materials and in the design and diffusion of production organization technology. In particular Penna et al. (1983) have shown very high social returns for INTA's R&D efforts in relation to new wheat varieties derived from Mexican germoplasm. Similarly, successful results have been reported in yet another recent study (Katz and Bercovich, 1989) with regard to biotechnology. In spite of this, however, expert opinion suggests that in terms of molecular biology and genetics, INTA is presently lagging well behind the international technological frontier.

As previously explained Argentine universities do not constitute an important source of new technology. Basic research is normally performed for the "advancement of science." Only 30.0 million $US—5% of the total 640 million $US that make up the budget for the 26 National Universities—went to R&D activities in 1988. It is believed that just one of four university professors performs research efforts, and nearly one-third of those that do belong to the biomedical fields.

The University of Buenos Aires—the largest in the country with 110,000 students—has recently set up a Technology Transfer Office and signed some 20 contracts for the transfer of technical knowledge to the production sector. These contracts are of a somewhat modest size. Furthermore, this University has just completed building a company, UBATEC, jointly with private firms and the Municipality of Buenos Aires, with the objective of facilitating the transfer of technology to the productive sector.

University activities in general and R&D efforts in particular seem to be going through a period of decay and lack of financing that might prove difficult to overcome and damaging in the long run, from the point of view of the country's scientific capabilities.

Defense R&D Expenditure
Chapter 8 of the Budget Law indicates that defense R&D activities absorbed about 6% of the total public R&D expenditure in 1988.

Roughly 60% of these expenses were carried out by CITEFA (Instituto de Investigaciones Científicas y Técnicas de las Fuerzas Armadas), the largest research agency within the military sector. CITEFA employs close to 900 people, 200 of which are highly trained military engineers. The agency's annual budget is about 10 million U. S. dollars, 25% of which has been normally assigned to R&D projects.

Argentina has developed a certain degree of autonomy as far as the development and construction of weapons is concerned. Medium-range missiles, jet fighters, medium size tanks, and cannons are locally designed and constructed, largely in military factories.

Exports of military equipment and technology have taken place in the past both within Latin America and also to Middle Eastern countries such as Iraq and Iran, but Argentina has had a far less significant experience in this respect than Brazil, which has managed to develop a highly successful export sector in armaments, largely based on active R&D and engineering collaboration between state-owned enterprises and private firms. This kind of collaboration is not to be found in Argentina.

We conclude this overview of public R&D activities in Argentina as yet another part of the national system of innovation. In spite of the potential social value of public

R&D activities, many of the approximately 20,000 professionals now involved are grossly underutilized and could become important agents of modernization and technological change if only the country could find the institutional and economic mechanisms and the incentives for this to be so. We shall explore such matters in the last section of this chapter.

ARGENTINA'S NATIONAL SYSTEM OF INNOVATION: OVERVIEW AND POLICY IMPLICATIONS

A careful examination of Argentina's national system of innovation shows that the country is far from having an integrated and coherent network of agents, institutions, and policies dealing with questions of scientific and technological knowledge generation, diffusion, and utilization. Neither does it have a technological strategy that would reflect a successful exploitation of its opportunities in the international market place.

Consider first the situation of the Argentine manufacturing industry. Having relied on direct foreign investment and on external transfers of technology as a major source of technological dynamism and due to the fact that domestic production facilities are of a highly idiosyncratic nature as far as size, production organization, and degree of vertical integration are concerned it can scarcely be surprising to know that most R&D efforts performed by manufacturing firms have taken the form of "adaptive" engineering activities that, in many cases, would not fall under internationally accepted definitions of R&D activities. The lack of suitable technical know-how and engineering routines, differences in raw materials, and a highly particular legal and institutional environment frequently induced local subsidiaries of large MNCs to use domestic engineering and technological manpower with the purpose of recreating product design and/or process engineering technolgies that are simply not available "from the shelf." Locally owned companies have normally followed a similar pattern of behavior. Although "adaptive" R&D efforts can and have systematically been performed by firms, it is seldom the case that companies pass this stage and engage themselves in more complex state-of-the-art R&D activities, as we see is happening, for example, in the case of many Korean firms (Kim, 1990).

There might be various reasons for this phenomenon. On the one hand, the historically overprotected nature of the domestic industrialization process probably militated against a more dynamic outward-going attitude on the part of local entrepreneurs. Firms have never really felt the challenge of external competition domestically, nor have they been coached by policy makers to search for export markets. Tax concessions have not been handed out on a quid pro quo basis for R&D and export commitments as we see happening in many countries around the world.

Concomitant with the above, it is also true that macroeconomic instability has played a major role in this field, exacerbating risk-aversion attitudes and oportunistic behavior on the part of local entreprenurs. The search for subsidies and special privileges has normally been better rewarded than innovative behavior and investment in new production capacity. In actual fact investment in new capital equipment has dramatically been reduced during the course of the last decade and so have imports of machinery and equipment, R&D activities, and entrepreneurial spirit in general.

Yet as previously explained, the industrial sector of Argentina is presently undergoing a major transformation. The old overprotected industrial sector is gradually losing ground and a new breed of technologically more updated firms, involved in the production of intermediate industrial commodities and resource-based products, is taking its place. It is certainly much too early to make predictions as to the future success of these newcomers, as well as to their likely technological strategies in the years to come. A more stable macroeconomic environment, a higher degree of exposure to external competition, and a more active government policy on the technological front might well induce them into a stronger technological commitment in the years ahead.

So much for the industrial sector. As far as agriculture is concerned, we have pointed out that after many years of technological stagnation the sector is presently undergoing a period of rapid technological change associated with the diffusion of new product varieties and hybrids as well as with the massive utilization of herbicides, fertilizers, and new production organization techniques. Sunflower and soybean production have expanded massively in recent times. However, in spite of the fact that both the area under cultivation and yields per acre are currently at their all time historical peaks, we cannot fail to notice that the sector is still far from exploiting its real growth potential and available opportunities in the international market place. In this respect, the national system of innovation supporting technical change and innovation in agriculture is not performing an entirely successful task.

Let us now turn to public scientific and technological activities. Lack of priorities, of ex ante evaluating mechanisms, of ex post peer review missions, and of institutional coordination account for low research productivity, a scarce sense of purpose and direction, frustration, and a great deal of slack and inefficiency. Many of these shortcomings, however, can be found in other spheres of activity in contemporary Argentina and are by no means exclusive to public R&D agencies.

As explained before, much seems to be out of place in present day Argentina, with per capita income some 20% lower than a decade ago and a continuing uncertain situation as far as macroeconomic equilibrium is concerned.

It would be wrong to assume that the present state of affairs is exclusively due to lack of resources and that by providing more money to the public R&D system—without simultaneously acting on aspects of organization, coordination, and accountability—things could be improved significantly. No doubt research personnel is being grossly underpaid—the average monthly income of a professional graduate working in any of the previously mentioned agencies is presently somewhere in the order of 300 U. S. dollars per month, but overlapping programs, research groups that are just "empty boxes," and institutions that do not have the minimum critical scale in terms of experimental equipment or qualified personnel required to attain sensible results, suggest that a great deal has to be reorganized if the expansion of public R&D expenditure is to become socially worthwhile in the future. The Secretary of Science and Technology clearly has a long and complex agenda ahead of it, in terms of coordination, evaluation, and reorganization of R&D institutes and programs.

Part of such reorganization efforts could probably involve a new and different set of principles in relation to collaborative ventures and risk-sharing activities between public agencies and private firms producing goods or services. As we have seen before, both CONICET and the University of Buenos Aires are already exploring new mechanisms in this respect and it would be advisable to further proceed along these lines in the future.

Let us now turn to a few final comments concerning the national system of innovation as a whole, its priorities, and future possibilities.

Clearly, one of the major challenges Argentina faces today is how to regain the capacity for growth. After nearly two decades where output per head and the rate of new capital formation have been steadily declining it is quite clear that the question of how to return to a viable long-term growth path is a very major one.

Let us assume that the industrial restructuring process we have previously described will continue in the immediate future and that as a consequence of this, Argentina will eventually settle down to a new "industrial regime" in which the structure of industry, the organization of work, the social division of labor, and industrial relations will lose many of the idiosyncratic features associated with the "old" domestically oriented regime.[5] In such a scenario, manufacturing and agricultural exports will probably continue to grow.

Under such circumstances (i.e., large positive foreign trade balances) domestic fiscal and macroeconomic policy issues—obviously related to questions of fiscal equilibrium, social equity, and income distribution—are necessarily going to acquire increasing importance in the future. The transition from the old overprotected and domestically oriented regime to the new one—more deregulated and open up to market signals—is proving to be far from costless. Quite the contrary, high unemployment rates and a deteriorating pattern of social equity and income distribution seem to be undesirable consequences of the ongoing transformation. In a country where there is not yet an ex ante public debate of the national budget, where tax evasion is dramatically high, and where public authorities are not capable of managing a credible fiscal policy, there are obvious institutional shortcomings that need to be corrected if the country's growth potential is to be realized and if acceptable levels of social equity are to be maintained. The national system of innovation could significantly contribute to such goals in more than one direction. On the one hand, it could certainly collaborate in the modernization and upgrading of the nation's badly deteriorating social sectors—such as health or education—which are now lagging behind as a consequence of the drastic reduction in social public expenditure and investment (Dieguez et al., 1990). On the other hand, it could become an important source of new ideas and technology with which to undertake the country's transition to the new world of microelectronics—including flexible production automation and telecommunications—which is rapidly developing internationally and which Argentina will have to incorporate in the years ahead. In both of these spheres—as well as in many others—Argentina will probably have to face difficult decisions in the immediate future concerning redeployment of human resources, upgrading of its labor force, deciding how much foreign "from the shelf" technology it should use given its particular resource endowments and regulatory environment, and how much such technology is to be complemented by domestic R&D efforts to be adequately absorbed by the local society. As the previous examples suggest, there is a long list of issues related to the functioning of its national system of innovation to which Argentina will have to pay close attention in the future, if it is to successfully adapt itself to ongoing changes in the world's institutional, technological, and economic scenarios. In many of these fields, we can identify powerful reasons for which decentralized market decisions might not necessarily be enough to ensure socially acceptable outcomes. New forms of intervention will probably have to be explored in the future even in spite of the fact that government intervention has a clear history of failure as far as Argentina is concerned. How to work out an adequate balance between public regulation and decentralized market decisions in fields where there are obvious reasons for market failure constitutes, of course, a difficult problem for which the country will have to work out imaginative new answers if it is to regain the capacity for growth and to maintain acceptable levels of social equity.

NOTES

Both authors belong to Argentina's National Council for Scientific and Technological Research (CONICET). The former is Professor of Industrial Economics at the University of Buenos Aires and Consultant to the Economic Commission for Latin America (ECLA). The ideas hereby presented are their exclusive responsibility. The present chapter has been prepared as a contribution to the project "National Systems Supporting Technical Advance in Industry" and is based upon drafts presented by the authors at the seminars held in November 1989 in Maastricht, Holland, and in October 1990, at Stanford, California. The authors would like to acknowledge detailed comments from the participants at both such workshops.

1. It is usual among social scientists to compare the case of Argentina with that of Australia, which underwent a similar process of early integration into the world economy, but whose long-term performance has been significantly better than the one attained by Argentina. A wide variety of explanations of the observed differences have been put through in the literature. On the one hand, a richer natural endowment of gold and minerals allowed the Australian population to enjoy a higher income per capita than Argentina, even before the nineteenth century agricultural export boom had actually started (Diegues, 1969). On the other hand, various writers have argued (Fogarty, 1977) that the earlier exhaustion of the agricultural frontier induced the Australian government to press for a rapid and widespread diffusion of fertilizers and new varieties of wheat, this having a major and earlier impact on land productivity and agricultural profits.

In addition to the above we should notice that a different set of institutions, for example, highly different land leasing contracts, induced a much less careful land exploitation system in Argentina than in Australia as well as a longer lag in the adoption of new agricultural technologies. At a more general level, it is important to realize that in spite of its economic success, Argentina failed in those early years of the century to develop and consolidate civilian and political institutions of the sort Australia managed to establish together with its rapid economic expansion. Such weaker institutional fabric was to remain as a central feature of the Argentine society and still today recurrently appears as a major barrier to a more successful socioeconomic performance.

2. Political historians have shown that the Argentine Armed Forces have had a strong political and institutional presence in Argentina ever since the 1920's, or even earlier (Potash, 1980). It is, however, after the 1930 right-wing nationalistic coup d'etat headed by General Uriburu against the civilian government of President Yrigoyen that the political role of the Armed Forces and the nationalist ideas underlying military education became much more influential in relation to the country's long term development process. Notions of economic self-sufficiency, of a strong military production industry capable of designing and constructing different types of defense goods, etc, gain preeminence at that point (D. Rock, 1985). Such military presence has had a significant impact upon the national system of innovation thereafter, inducing patterns of institutional behavior with long lasting consequences for the country's development process. Consider, for example, that for many years the production of steel was regarded as an issue of 'national security' and that private entrepreneurs were not allowed to enter the market or to introduce new production technologies. 'Down stream' industries producing consumer durables and capital goods were negatively affected by such policies. Similar examples can be found in other areas of the production structure.

3. The structural model relating industrial growth, import requirements, foreign exchange shortages, devaluation, and income distribution effects—given the fact that Argentina's main exports are wage goods whose domestic prices immediately reflect changes in the value of the foreign currency—has been extensively discussed in the local and international professional literature since the early contribution by Diaz Alejandro (1970). See also Canitrot (1975).

4. The neoclassical methaphor of complete specification and perfect availability of "from-the-shelf" production functions just does not seem to be very useful if one is to make sense of the present case. Rather, evolutionary ideas based on notions of incomplete specification of production knowhow, imperfect information of domestic entrepreneurs, "adaptive" R&D efforts, "technological learning," bottlenecks, and disequilibrium seem to fit much better the set of issues we need to examine. In relation to such topics the reader could see Nelson and Winter (1982) and Dosi et al. (1988).

5. It is outside the scope of the present chapter to examine various potential difficulties that might in the future hamper the development of this new industrial regime. High structural unemployment, falling terms of trade in the field of industrial commodities, a continuously deteriorating pattern of income distribution, and a high level of social conflict could very well increase in the future, opening up major questions as to the likelihood of a steady consolidation of present trends.

REFERENCES

Azpiazu, D. (1985). *La promocion industrial en la Argentina 1973–1983.* Buenos Aires: CEPAL.

Ablin, E., and Katz, J. (1985). *De la Industria Incipiente a la Exportacion de Tecnologia. La experiencia Argentina en la venta internacional de plantas industriales y obras de Ingeneiria.* Cepal/Eudeba, Bs.As.

Ablin, E., Gatto, F., Katz, J., Kosacoff, B., and Soifer, D. (1985). *Internacionalización de empresas y tecnología de origen Argentino.* Buenos Aires: Cepal/Eudeba.

Bercovich, N., and Katz, J. (1988). "Innovación genética, esfuerzo público de I&D y la frontera tecnológica internacional. Nuevos híbridos en el INTA." *Desarrollo Economico,* Buenos Aires, July-September.

Canitrot, A. (1975). "La experiencia populista de redistribución de ingresos." *Desarrollo Economico,* Buenos Aires, October/December.

CEPAL (1959). Análisis y proyecciones del Desarrollo Económico. El desarrollo económico de la Argentina. Parte II. Naciones Unidas, Mexico.

Diaz Alejandro, C. (1970). *Essays in the Economic History of the Argentine Republic.* New Haven: Yale University Press.

Dieguez, H. (1969). "Argentina y Australia: algunos aspectos de su desarrollo económico comparado. *Desarrollo Económico.* Buenos Aires, January/March.

Dieguez, H., Llach, J., and Petrecolla, A. (1990). "El gasto Público social." Centro de Investigaciones Económicas, Instituto Torcuato DiTella, August, Buenos Aires.

Dosi, J., Freeman, C., Nelson, R., Silverberg, G., and Soete, L. (1988) *Technical Change and Economic Theory.* London: Pinter Publishers.

Escude, G., and Guerberoff, S. (1990). "Ajuste macroeconomico, deuda externa y ahorro en la Argentina." In *Ahorro y formación de capital.* CEPAL/ONUDI, Buenos Aires: Grupo Editor Lationamericano.

Fogarty, J. (1977). "Difusión de tecnología en areas de asentamiento reciente: el caso de Australia y de la Argentina." *Desarrollo Economico,* Buenos Aires, April/June.

Huici, N. (1988). *La industria de maquinaria agrícola en la Argentina.* Buenos Aires: CISEA.

Katz, J. (1973). *Patentes de invencion, Convenio de Paris y paises de menor grado de desarrollo relativo.* Mimeo, Instituto DiTella, Buenos Aires.

Katz, J. (1974). *Importacion de tecnología, aprendizaje e industrialización dependiente.* Mexico: Fondo de Cultura Económica.

Katz, J., & Kosacoff, B. (1983). "Multinationals from Argentina." In S. Lall (ed.), *The New Multinationals. The Spread of Third World Enterprises.* New York: Wiley.

Katz, J., and Kosacoff, B. (1989). *El proeeso de industrializacion en la Argentina: Evolucion, retroeeso y prospectiva.* Buenos Aires: CEAL/CEPAL.

Kim, L. (1990). Korea's National System for industrial innovation. *Mimeo,* presented at Stanford University, (Final version in this book.)

Lall, S. (1982). *Developing Countries as Exporters of Technology. A First Look at the Indian Experience.* London: Macmillan.

Nelson, R., and Winter, S. (1982). *An Evolutionary Theory of Economic Change.* Boston, MA: The Belknap Press of Harvard University Press.

Nivoli, A. (1989). "Balance de la experiencia de la Oficina de Transferencia de Tecnología." *Revista del Derecho Industrial,* Ediciones DEPALHA, Buenos Aires, January–April.

Obschatko, E. (1988). *Transformacion economica y*

tecnologica de la agricultura pampeana 1950–1984. Buenos Aires: Ediciones Culturales Argentinas.

Penna, J. (1983). *Difusion de las variedades de trigo con germoplasma mexicano y su impacto en la produccion nacional.* Buenos Aires: INTA.

Potash, R. (1969). *The Army and Politics in Argentina. 1928/1945 Yrigoyen to Peron.* Stanford: Stanford University Press, 1980.

Rock, D. (1985) *Argentina 1516–1987. From Spanish colonization to the Falklands war.* Berkeley, CA: University of California Press.

Sábato, J., Wortman, O., and Gargiulo, G. (1978). *Energia Atomica e Industria Nacional.* Washington, D. C.: OEA.

Schvarzer, J. (1983). "Cambios en el liderzgo industrial Argentino en el periodo de Martinez de Hoz." *Desarrollo Economico,* Buenos Aires, October/December.

Tanis, S. (1986). "Evaluación de la capacidad industrial Argentina y desarrollo de los proveedores para instalaciones nucleares." Paper submitted at the Seminar on Supporting Industrial Infrastructure Requirements and Development for Nuclear Power, organized by the International Atomic Energy Agency, Vienna, April.

World Development. (1984). Exports of Technology by Newly-Industrializing Countries. Case studies on Hong Kong, Taiwan, Korea, India, Egypt, Brazil, Mexico, Argentina, Vol. 12. Oxford: Pergamon.

15

The Innovation System of Israel: Description, Performance, and Outstanding Issues

MORRIS TEUBAL

The peculiarities of the Israeli innovation system stem to a large degree from the environment surrounding and the forces shaping Jewish immigration to Palestine during the first decade of the century. Specifically, the tradition of Jewish scholarship, the determination to create a modern state, and the Zionist ideology were driving forces that created functioning, institutionalized bases for modern scientific research, technological development, and the training of new generations of scientists. Both the Hebrew University and the Technion of Haifa were established almost a quarter of a century before the creation of the State in 1948. (The Weizmann Institute began operations in 1934.) So did the appearance of significant applied research in agriculture and in medicine, as well as the beginnings of industrial research.

The process of expansion and innovation in the science and technology system continued during the first decades after the creation of the State (the 1950s and 1960s),[1] a fact that explains some of its salient features: the high fraction of GNP devoted to R&D, the strength of the university system, and the dominant roles of both defense and government finance of R&D. This was also a period of significant economic growth by international standards.

The 1970s and 1980s represent a break from historical trends, both in terms of economic growth performance and in terms of innovation in the science and technology system. The first section of this chapter focuses primarily on economic performance and the second section on policies (primarily technological) and institutions of the 1970s and 1980s. The former section looks at the connection between structural change and economic growth. After briefly describing the 1950s and 1960s, it presents the "paradox" of the 1970s and 1980s: a continuation of deep structural change—facilitated by abundant skills and leading to the emergence and growth of high-tech industry—and the onset of economic decline and stagnation. Possible "crowding out" effects of activities in the defense sector during the eighties are considered. Finally, the second section describes the stagnation occurring in science and technology policy during the 1980s, one that parallels economic stagnation. Its maximum expression is absence of the new technological infrastructures, which, given the abundant stock of skills, could have propelled the economy back into reasonable growth. This institutional–organization–political (rather than market) failure takes place across the board: in relation to SMEs and conventional industry, in relation to defense and high-tech, and in connection with strategic science. In the final section I relate it to the inability to create new patterns of cooperation and networking within the economy, and with the incapacity of Israel's government in the 1980s to plan ahead and to crystallize a vision of its place in the world community.

GROWTH, STRUCTURAL CHANGE, AND SCIENCE/TECHNOLOGY BACKGROUND

In this section I present essential background and motivation for an in-depth analysis of technology policies and related institutions during the 1970s and 1980s—an important aspect, in our opinion, of Israel's declining economic performance.

Economic Development and Research Patterns during the 1950s and 1960s

Economic Structure
The Israeli economy—following the behavior of the Jewish economy during the Mandate period that preceded the establishment of the State in 1948—has a long tradition of rapid structural change actively promoted by government policy. Although the share of manufacturing (including mining) has not changed substantially since the 1920s—if anything, it has slightly declined during the period, standing at around 20% of GNP during 1986—there has been considerable change in the structure of manufacturing, particularly during World War II and after the establishment of the State. During the 1950s, a number of industrials sectors were targeted by the government: food processing, clothing and leather, and metals. These sectors, together with the agricultural sector, which also received preferential support, contributed to supply the needs of the almost 700,000 immigrants who came to the State during the 1948–1951 period, most of them Jewish refugees from Arab countries.[2] The industrial sectors supported were largely labor intensive, and the methods for support involved both import tariffs and quotas and investment grants and loans. During the 1960s, government targeting focused on another set of industrial branches, more capital intensive and possessing a larger export orientation. These sectors included textiles, chemicals, cement and mining, and, toward the end of the 1960s, high-tech industry. The methods involved both those mentioned above together with export subsidies and the beginnings of subsidization of R&D in industry. The general evaluation of such policies, which had only a minor explicit technology promotion component, was positive. Pack (1971), in his book on the Israeli economy, suggests that this was the case despite the fact that the growth path followed was not necessarily the efficient one from the benefit–cost analysis viewpoint. Thus, despite the inefficiencies of the government in executing what was largely an investment, population dispersal, and employment policy, the aggregate growth rate of the economy was one of the highest in the world, possibly second only to Japan during 1950–1970.[3] One can understand the contribution of government to this process, given market failures in the early stages of "modern" indus-

trial development: infant industries and technologies; scarcity of entrepreneurs; underdeveloped capital markets; the coordination requirements of industrial development, immigration absorption, and defense; and other factors. Moreover, the tasks confronting the young state were relatively clear at the time, and a set of quite remarkable individuals filled the ranks of government during what was, in fact, the "heroic" period of Israel's statehood.

Science and Technology

Scientific activities during the period of the Mandate (1918–1948) were mainly concerned with the study of characteristics of the land—climate, soil, water resources—plant and animal life, plagues and illnesses, geography, and geology. Basic research, conducted in accordance with the western tradition of academic freedom, and agricultural research achieved a high level relative to the standards of the period. There was practically no industrial research, except for some connected with the Dead Sea Works. After independence, Prime Minister D. Ben-Gurion himself headed the Research Council founded in 1949; its objective was to extend further the institutional structure of scientific work in Israel. The new government established a number of governmental research laboratories during the 1950s, for example, the Fibers Institute, the aim of which was to support the textile industry being developed to provide employment to the more than half a million Jewish refugees from Arab countries, and the National Physics Laboratory. It also established several new universities—Tel-Aviv, Bar Ilan, Negev—and founded other institutions such as the National Council for Research and Development (NCRD) in 1959 and the Israel Academy of Sciences in 1961.

By the mid-1960s, institutional arrangements for scientific work were well under way; additional efforts were made to reinforce existing institutions rather than to establish new ones. This period shows also the first attempts at a more systematic approach toward research and development. Thus among the objectives of the National Council for Research and Development we find planning governmental policy toward research and development and defining "national research needs" in various fields. The most significant event, however, was the nomination in 1966 of a committee for the organization and administration of government research—the Kachalsky committee. The committee's main recommendation was that bureaus of chief scientists be created in ministries such as the Ministry of Commerce and Industry to coordinate their activities in research and technology and to stimulate applied research. This is an essential background to the growth of civilian R&D expenditure in industry during the 1970s.

Agricultural Research

Research in agriculture played an important role during the Mandate period and during the two first decades of the State of Israel.[4] Scientific knowledge was perceived as instrumental for a shift from the traditional dry-farming methods (involving both separate animal and plant husbandry and manual work) to a mixed crop pattern that would be combined with the raising of cattle and with irrigation. Organized agricultural research began in the 1920s with the establishment of the Jewish Agricultural Research Stations (A.R.S., now the Volcani Institute), founded on the pattern of American agricultural and mechanical colleges. The knowledge required in the early period fell into two categories: knowledge concerning the natural characteristics of land and knowledge that could be directly applied. A significant part of the activities of the A.R.S. consisted of research into the botany, zoology, and geology of the territory. This "generic research" was both of scientific interest and directly relevant for the local agricultural community—it provided basic information needed for the selection of areas of settlement; and without surveying the conditions of the soils, climate, plants, and animals the possibility of applying the results of new experiments done in the country or elsewhere would have been extremely limited. In spite of the freedom of agricultural research workers from bureaucratic controls and political pressures, there emerged close informal contacts between them and the agriculturalists with the result that the contribution of agricultural research to productivity growth in agriculture was, and is still, substantial (e.g., for ideological reasons scientists originally also did extension work and provided essential services to agriculturalists such as seed testing and artificial insemination). During the 1930s, the relationships between the two groups began to take a more institutionalized form with the emergence of "branch committees" (field crops, citrus, cattle, etc.) where both researchers, users, and administrators were represented.

In the 1940s and 1950s, with the creation of the Faculty of Agriculture at the Hebrew University, agricultural research—even at the Vulcani Institute, where scientific publications increasingly became the basis for promotion—became increasingly academized. Moreover a functional separation of research from services/extension has gradually emerged. The contribution of agricultural research, however, to agricultural productivity seems to have continued throughout the 1980s, although few systematic studies have attempted to make such an assessment.

The Rise of High-Tech Industry and Declining Growth Performance During the 1970s and 1980s

The relationship between rapid structural change and fast aggregate and per capita income growth was reversed in some sense after 1973–1974. This was precisely the period of emergence and development of high-tech industry in what is widely regarded as a successful result of industrial and technological policy. The most salient feature of the past 20 years is the rise in the relative importance of this group of skill- and R&D-intensive industries. Table 15.1 shows an industry categorization based on skill intensity at a three-digit industrial branch level. Skill intensity is defined as the proportion of scientists and engineers in the labor force (see Halperin et al., 1988; Teubal, 1989). This seems to be the most crucial variable in defining degree of sophistication, at least in Israel where R&D data exclude defense R&D. The three clearly defined categories of industry are Category "H" (high-tech), which includes electrooptics and fine machinery (SIC numbers 280, 281), aircraft and ships (262, 263), and electronics and communications equipment (254, 253); Category "OS" (other sophisticated), which includes various categories of metal products, heavy and specialty chemicals, and electrical goods; and Category "C" (conventional), which includes all the rest, such as food and textiles, pulp and paper, and wood and furniture. The skill intensities for the three categories were 16, 6, and 2%, respectively, in 1984. These three categories largely correspond to the categories proposed by Pavitt (1984)—science-based, production-intensive, and traditional—with some differences that are largely specific to Israel (e.g., the pharmaceutical industry is not yet as high-tech in Israel as it is in most advanced countries).

Table 15.1. Israel: Industry Categories and Skill Intensity, 1984[a]

Subsector/Category	SIC	Skill Intensity (1984)	%
Category "H"			
	(280,281)	Electrooptics and fine machinery	12
	(262,3)	Aircraft and ships	16
	(254,3)	Electronics and communications equipment	18.5
		1984	16.0
		1987	(18.5)
Category "OS"			
Basic metals	(220,1)	Iron and steel castings	4.1
	(223)	Pipes	6.4
Metal products	(233,4)	Heating and cooking equipment	4.8
Machinery	240,1,3	For agriculture, industry, and construction, pumps and compressors	7.0
	242	Used in services and in households	4.9
Electrical	250	Electric motors	6.4
machinery	251,2,3	Batteries, household consumer durables, illuminating equipment	4.3
Mining	100,3,4,8	Mining of salts and minerals	7.2
Chemicals	200	Basic chemicals	8.6
	201	Pharmaceuticals	5.7
	202,3,4,8	Soaps and detergents, paints and other chemical products	5.6
	205	Disinfectants and insecticides (and herbicides)	8.4
		Average Category "S" (1984)	6.0
Category "C"			
All other 3-digit subsectors		(Food, textiles, wood products, leather and shoes, etc.)	
		Average Category "C" (1984)	2.0

[a]Share of qualified scientists and engineers in total sector/category employment.

Table 15.2 describes structural change within the Israeli industrial sector between 1968 and 1983, in terms of percentage shifts in shares of industrial outputs and inputs among the various categories mentioned above. The increase in the share of both industrial product and industrial exports in favor of Category "H" (and largely against Category "C") is truly dramatic: from 6 and 5%, respectively, in 1968 to 24 and 28% in 1983. The shift in the share of inputs is also quite dramatic: a more than doubling of the percentage share of skills, physical capital, and labor allocated to Category "H"

Table 15.2. Structural Change in Israeli Industry,[a] 1968–1983

	Share of Product			Share of Export			Share of Skills			Share of Capital			Share of Labor		
	"H"	"OS"	"C"	"H"	"S"	"C"	"H"	"S"	"C"	"H"	"S"	"C"	"H"	"S"	"C"
1968	6	20	74	5	42	53	~30		~70	4	30	66	6	15	79
1983	24	20	56	28	32	40	~70		~30	11	32	57	17	14	69
Change in share	+18	0	−18	+23	−10	−13	+40		−40	+7	+2	−9	+11	−1	−10

[a]Excluding diamonds (all figures in percentages).

Sources: Halperin et al. (1988) and Teubal (1989).

Table 15.3. Growth Performance of Israeli Industry and Business Sector (Average Annual Percentage Change)

	1968–1972	1973–1979	1980–1984
Industry			
Product	15.1	4.9	2.5
TFPG[a]	7.0	1.4	0.0
		1961–1972	1973–1981
Business sector performance			
Gross domestic product		9.7	3.4
GDP[b] per hour of work		5.8	2.4
TFPG		4.2	0.6

[a]TFPG, total factor productivity growth.
[b]GDP, gross domestic product.
Sources: Industry: Bregman (1987); business: Metzer (1986).

between those two dates. In particular, note that the share of scientists and engineers employed in high-tech increased from 30 to 70% of the total pool employed in industry.

The process of structural change occurring in industry was profound and far reaching. Prima facie and following Kuznetz (1971) and the structuralist perspective more generally, this should have prevented a sustained decline or stagnation of aggregate manufacturing growth and of manufacturing total factor productivity growth (TFPG).[5] These have been declining sharply during the 1970s and early 1980s as can be seen in Table 15.3 with industrial TFPG declining to zero during 1980–1984 (Bregman, 1987).[6] The same trend can be seen when looking at the business sector (which involves much more than industry)—see the lower part of the table. Similar tendencies can be shown when observing the economy as a whole (see Syrquin, 1986).

Growth of Skills and Quantitative Science and Research Indicators

The high growth of skills is a central factor explaining the rise of high-tech industry since the Six-Day War. Tables 15.4–15.6 show the growth of skills, principally in Israeli industry, since the 1960s. In Table 15.4, which is based on data from the Ministry of Industry and Trade (MI&T), we see that scientists and engineers in manufacturing rose from 3400 in 1968 to almost 20,000 in 1987 (an annual rate of growth of

Table 15.4. Israel: Employment, Skills, and Skill Intensity in Manufacturing (Aggregate)

Year	Total Employment	Total Skills	Skill Intensity (%)
1968	227,000	3,400	1.3
1971	272,000	4,184	1.5
1975	292,000	6,749	2.4
1978	308,000	8,860	2.9
1981	313,500	12,158	4.0
1984	331,000	17,450	5.3
1987	341,150	19,735	5.8

Source: Ministry of Industry and Trade.

Table 15.5. Skilled Labor in Israel

	1961	1972	1983
Scientists and engineers			
Industry	1,470	3,560	10,180
Total	6,870	15,985	33,070
Percent industry	21.4	22.3	30.8
Technicians			
Industry		9,225	15,315
Total		30,295	45,990
Percent industry		30.5	32.6

Sources: Central Bureau of Statistics, Census 1961, 1972, 1983; and additional publications on the Labor Force (No. 13). A comparison of these figures to those from the Ministry of Industry and Trade data shows them to be consistently smaller. We believe that this reflects a more compact definition of both industry and engineers in the census, as well as a possible bias in the reporting of firms in the Ministry of Industry and Trade data base.

9.2%). The table also shows a very significant increase in the skill intensity of manufacturing industry during the period—from 1.3 to 5.8%. Table 15.5 also provides data on skills in the manufacturing industry, not only our narrow definition including scientists and engineers but also numbers of technicians (including practical engineers). In addition, there exists information on the share of total skills employed in industry (e.g., the share of Israel's scientists and engineers employed in industry increased from 21.4% in 1961 to 30.8% in 1983). Note that the increase in the share of technicians and practical engineers employed in industry increased relatively little between 1972 and 1983 (it stands at around 1/3). Finally, Table 15.6 provides an international perspective of the growth in skilled manpower in Israel; it shows what was already becoming clear, namely, that the growth of scientists and engineers in Israeli industry has been phenomenal since 1967, probably one of the highest recorded (due provision should be given to the fact that the base of skills in industry during 1967 was very low, even less than one-half on a per-capita basis compared with the United States). It has certainly outstripped the growth of skills for the country as a whole. This fact is related to the growth of high-tech industry since 1967, to the university system, and to immigration. If we accept the "structuralist perspective" viewpoint that skills are the critical factor in economic growth, then the potential growth of the manufacturing sector could have been enormous during the period in question. Why hasn't it materialized? One aspect relates to the role of defense in industry, and, in particular, in high-tech industry. Before considering this, let us present some additional quantitative indica-

Table 15.6. Scientists and Engineers in Industry—OECD and Israel

	United States	United Kingdom	West Germany	France	Japan	Israel
1967	495,500	49,900	61,000	42,800	117,600	3,400
1980	573,900	80,700	111,000	68,000	272,000	12,150
						(1981)
Percent increase	16	62	82	59	132	257

Source: Halperin (1986).

tors of science and research in Israel, part of which are related to the growth of skills (see Table 15.7).

Israel possesses one of the highest ratios of total R&D to GNP—an estimate of over 3% in the mid-1980s, compared to ratios approaching this number for three of the major powers—the United States, Germany, and Japan (this ratio was also one of the highest of the world during the mid-1970s); probably the highest ratio of defense-related R&D to total R&D in the world. Our estimate is probably 2/3, from which it follows that the non-defense-to-GNP ratio for Israel is most certainly surpassed by those of Japan, West Germany, and other countries. Another feature is the extremely high share of total and civilian R&D that is paid for by government. In the mid-1970s, the proportion of civilian R&D financed by government was 62%, a number attained only by Norway at the time (the figures for the other countries in the seventies range from 27% for Japan to 47% for Belgium). Presumably, Israel preserves a very high ranking in this respect even today. Some figures on skill intensity of the population and skills involved in R&D (with skills defined as numbers of scientists and engineers) are also known from other sources: during the mid-1970s, Israel possessed one of the highest ratios of skills to total population—40 per 10,000—compared with the highest ratio of 42 reached by the United States at the time. For the mid-1980s, we have some figures (Table 15.7C) showing the numbers of recipients of academic degrees in the

Table 15.7. Israel: Some Basic Science and Technology-Related Indicators

A. Aggregate R&D Ratios[a]

Year	Total R&D $\times$ 100 GNP		Defense R&D $\times$ 100 Total R&D		Government Financing of Civilian R&D (%)	
	1974–1976	1987	1970s	1981	1970s	1984
1974–1976, 1987	2.2	>3.0	40	65	62	79[7]

B. The Distribution of Civilian R&D (percent)

Year	University	Industry	Government
1974–1975	60.0	22.0	18.0
1978	45.0	43.0	12.0
1982–1983	47.0	37.0	16.0
various sources			

C. Recipients of Academic Degrees in the Natural Sciences and Engineering per 10,000 Participants in the Labor Force

	First Degree		Advanced Degree	
Year	Natural Sciences[8]	Engineering	Natural Sciences	Engineering
1986–1987	9.5	8.1	4.2	2.0

[a]Ministry of Science and Development (1988).

Sources: UNESCO, *Statistical Yearbook 1987,* Paris, 1988; and for Israel: Israel Central Bureau of Statistics, *Recipients of Degrees from Universities 1986/87,* Jerusalem, 1988; Council for Higher Education—Planning and Grants Committee, *Higher Education in Israel—Statistical Abstract 1986/87,* Jerusalem, 1988.

natural sciences and engineering per 10,000 participants in the labor force; both for advanced and for first degrees, Israel ranks very high in a sample of advanced countries (only surpassed by Japan or the United States, depending on the specialty and on the degree).

A second important aspect is the distribution of civilian R&D among broadly defined performing sectors—industry, universities, and government. The situation in the mid-1970s is striking—almost 60% of all civilian R&D was being performed at universities, while the figures for all of the other countries ranged between 8% (United Kingdom) and 33% (Norway). Correspondingly, the share being performed in industry was very low (22%) compared to the next in rank—51% for Norway. This clearly points out to a structural disequilibrium in Israel at the time—strong universities and a weak industrial base. This imbalance has since then partially corrected itself, for example, the share of industry in total civilian R&D rose to 43% already in 1978 (see Table 15.7B). It probably is more than this now, although the share of R&D performed by universities is probably still relatively high by international standards.

The growth of skills and the general strength of science and technology in Israel suggest a *paradox* in Israeli growth: rapid structural change (fueled by these factors) but declining growth performance. I will address it in two stages, first in terms of macroeconomic factors and the role of defense and then in terms of inefficient policies and institutions (particularly during the 1980s).

Explaining the Israeli Paradox: Macroeconomic Factors and Defense R&D

The most important factor mentioned by neoclassical economists in explaining declining overall performance is the extremely high and accelerating rates of inflation experienced during 1982–1983 and 1985–1986—the yearly rate reached a level of about 400% in 1983–1984. Such levels and acceleration of inflation are usually associated with violent changes in relative prices, increased uncertainty that affects investment decisions, increased time and effort devoted to financial management relative to productivity growth and efficiency improvements, and so on. For an attempt at a quantitative estimate of the effects see Bregman (1987). A related factor is government investment policy, which led to extremely high levels of capital subsidization during periods of rapid and increasing inflation: during most of the period after the Yom Kippur War of 1973 either none or only part of the interest paid on government loans was indexed. The resulting *excessive* investment led to substantial capacity underutilization and to choice of highly capital-intensive techniques of production in industry. The effects of these policies are analyzed in Metzer (1986), Bregman (1986), and Mayshar (1986). They are the result of an industrial policy that, if not misconceived, was certainly not adapted to the macroeconomic disorder of the late 1970s and 1980s.

Effects of the Military Sector
The Six-Day War led to a perception that a large measure of autonomy or autarchy in the major pieces of military hardware was required, both for military and political reasons. It was also thought, in line with prevailing thinking in the United States at the time, that the indirect effects and spinoffs of military industries to the national economy would be significant (e.g., in the area of industrial exports). Thus the perception was that the military industries to be developed were strategic also from the economic

Table 15.8. The Military Industrial Sector[a] in Israel, 1984

Sector	Number
1. Employees	65,000
2. Engineers and scientists	11,000–12,000
3. Technicians	14,000
In millions of US$	
4. Sales	2,250
5. R&D	750
6. Export	850

[a]Military industrial sector includes IAI (Israel Aircraft Industries); Rafael (the Ministry of Defense's armaments development authority—A.D.A.); IMI (Israel Military Industries); internal activity in the IDF, in the fields of R&D, upgrading, and production (not including maintenance); national laboratories for nuclear research; and firms and factories that deal in military R&D and production and have not been included in the previous list (Tadiran, Elta, Elbit, El-Op, Soltam, Urdan, Elisra, and some smaller firms).

Source: Halperin (1986).

point of view. Table 15.8 provides a quantitative definition of the military–industrial sector of Israel while Table 15.9 sets some skill-related aspects of the sector in an industry-wide perspective. This at least suggests the possibility of strong competition between military and civilian uses of skills.

A central point to be highlighted is that high defense expenditures that resulted both from the security problem facing the country and from the above perspective concerning the strategic importance of military industries and military R&D have caused both inflationary problems and the absorption of a significant fraction of the growth of skills.[9] The latter effect has dampened the growth of civilian high-tech during the early eighties through a "crowding out" phenomenon similar to that mentioned in connection with the science/technology system of countries such as the United

Table 15.9. Military Industry and Civilian Industry: Competition for Critical Resources

Skills	Military–Industrial System (1984) (a)	Industry (b)	a/b (%)
Scientists and engineers	11,000	17,450[a]	63
Technicians	14,000	15,315[b]	91
Skill Intensity	1978	1984	1987
Industry Category "S"[c]			
Civilian	3.1	8.6	9.1
Military	5.6	9.3	11.0
Industry Category "H"[c]			
Civilian	6.3	12.6	14.5
Military	9.0	17.6	19.4

[a]Data from Ministry of Commerce and Industry (1984).

[b]Data from Central Bureau of Statistics (1983).

[c]"H" includes the two-digit sectors 25 and 26 rather than (254,3): (262,3); (280,81) which compose "H." It thus includes electrical machinery (250-3) but excludes electrooptics and precision machinery. The share of "H" in total skills for 1987 is approximately 60%.

Kingdom and France (Ergas, 1986). I will attempt to delineate the basis for such an argument by looking at the data of both the military industries and civilian high-tech during the 1970–1985 period.

The 1970s were a period of fast growth of domestic sales of the military industries—which include both hardware and R&D procurement to the Ministry of Defence (MOD)—and of military exports. Although domestic sales experienced an acceleration during the first half of the 1970s followed by a reduction in the rate of growth (and even absolute decline in some years), the growth in military exports was rapid and sustained throughout the 1980s. A significantly divergent behavior of the two occurred during the first half of the 1980s: whereas domestic sales of military industries increased sharply, military exports experienced a sharp decline with the subsequent recovery enabling the level achieved in 1980 to be attained only in 1985. One of the main reasons for this divergence in behavior was the beginning of large military R&D projects during the period such as that of the ill-fated Lavi fighter plane. This implied sharp increases in domestic procurement that, together with the slump in military export markets, explains the declining export performance of the military-industrial sector.[10] During the 1970s both the level of civilian high-tech exports and their rate of growth were lower compared to that of military exports. However, civilian high-tech exports continued to grow throughout the 1980s, despite the crisis in the sector during 1985–1986, and briefly exceeded military high-tech exports during 1983–1985. This is one indication of the increasing maturity of the civilian high-tech industry and the increasing contribution to the national economy.

The relative "success" of the infant high-tech sector to achieve maturity in the 1980s was compromised by, among other factors, the sharp expansion of military R&D during this decade.

This is for a number of reasons. First, average wages in the military high-tech sector invariably exceeded those of civilian high tech[11]; second, and more important, military high-tech wage raises pace those occurring in civilian high-tech industry. Thus the sharp increases in salaries of scientists and engineers employed in civilian high-tech during the early 1980s were significantly influenced by increased salaries paid then in the military high-tech sector (and despite declining military exports). These raises partly explain the problems facing civilian high-tech during the period since at that time many firms were planning and executing significant investments directed to penetrate or expand their share in export markets. The sharp increases in the cost of employing skilled labor blocked a more vigorous expansion of civilian high-tech exports during the period and contributed to the crisis of the mid-1980s.[12]

The second, and no less important, reasons for declining economic performance (especially during the 1980s) that we focus on relates to technological policies and institutions. To these we now turn.

TECHNOLOGICAL POLICIES AND INSTITUTIONS

The stage is set for a more explicit discussion both of technology policy and of the Israeli innovation system. During the late 1960s, Israel pioneered the establishment of a mechanism for *direct* state subsidy of industrial R&D, one that focused on the activity performed *within* an industry that was almost wholly composed of small firms. In the 1980s, however, a fundamental weakness of the Israeli innovation system has been revealed, in particular a striking failure to establish the new technological infrastructures required by the technological revolution. This will be analyzed in the next section, where we will also consider national failure in creating new patterns of cooperation and new institutions and networks, both for policy formulation and for implementation.

Direct Support of Civilian R&D in Industry[13]

The Israeli system for the promotion of civilian technology is centered at the Office of the Chief Scientist, Ministry of Industry and Trade (MI&T). The system was established in the late 1960s as part of a shift in focus in national R&D policy toward applied research and development. Most applied R&D at the time was centered in the agricultural and defense areas, and the objective was to extend this activity to other areas as well. For this purpose a number of Chief Scientist offices were established, the most important of which was centered at the MI&T.

The objectives of the promotion system were (1) promotion of exports of high-tech products, more specifically, exports resulting from local R&D efforts; and (2) more broadly, promotion of structural change, in the direction of high-tech, R&D-intensive industries. The specific goals were promotion of R&D performed directly by industrial firms rather than by research institutes; and, related to this, stimulating the development of innovation capabilities and high-tech entrepreneurship.[14] The target population for the newly established promotion scheme (around 1967–1968) consisted, first, of small- and medium-sized enterprises (SMEs) including those that did not yet exist—the so-called new start ups (NSUs)—rather than large industrial firms, few of which were in existence at the time.

Instruments of Policy and Locus of Support

Implementation involved the allocation of grants supporting the R&D performed directly by industrial firms. The locus of support was not government laboratories (in fact, the relative allocation of subsidies for R&D to these laboratories declined in the aftermath of the new scheme), nor was there an attempt at that time to support a venture capital segment of financial institutions. The approach was quite revolutionary at the time, since the prevailing philosophy for supporting technological development in industry was first, to support R&D performed at government laboratories, and second, to stimulate the transfer of the technology so developed to industrial firms (for example, the case of India, and even today, the emphasis given in Taiwan).[15]

Concerning the policy instrument used—grants—it seems to me that at the time few countries, if any, used this method. The United States and Canada, which supported R&D, favored the use of tax concessions rather than grants. Grants are more adapted to a small firm environment, especially to those that are not currently profitable.

The formulators of the policy rightly understood that the critical bottleneck to innovation was R&D: the result was support of only this stage in the innovation process. Preexisting schemes would supposedly provide incentives for other steps such as physical investments and export marketing. Experience has shown that this was probably not the right design, at least in the longer run. There is a feeling today that probably too much R&D may have been done, which means that an unduly small propor-

488   LOWER INCOME COUNTRIES

tion was effectively applied. Part of the problem was the enormous investments associated with the post-R&D stages, particularly export market penetration investments. These would normally exceed investments in R&D, and Israeli financial institutions seldom extended loans for these nonconventional purposes. In the last few years, the definition of R&D has been broadened to take care of at least part of the problem (it now includes what is called Beta-Site prototype testing). There is still, however, no integrated mechanism to support the innovation process as a whole. This is probably one of the major weaknesses of Israeli direct support of industrial R&D.

Extent of Support and Policy Approach
The 50% rate of subsidization of R&D was considered a reasonable division of effort and risk between government and the firm. This basic rate is even today the standard one used in most projects.

Support was and continues to be universal (i.e., any R&D project satisfying some minimal criteria of honesty, technical feasibility, and lately a checklist of marketing factors could be supported). It did not matter to which industrial sector or technology the project belonged. Moreover, the 50% rate applies to all projects—provided they were aiming at exports—and this assures at least formal neutrality in the R&D promotion scheme.[16]

Quantitative Trends and the Effects of Policy
A statistical overview is found in Table 15.10. More specifically, Table 15.11 presents information on civilian R&D expenditures in Israeli industry between 1966 and 1985. The nominal amount in 1966 was a mere $4.6 million, and this rose to $335 million in 1985. The real rate of growth of R&D between 1969 and 1984 was 18% per annum—a substantial growth rate. After 1986, industrial R&D declined considerably for a number of reasons, including a reduction in government support (which accompanied a switch back to R&D grants to large firms after the failure of the tax concession promotion systems introduced in the early 1980s). Parallel to the significant increase in R&D, Table 15.11 also shows the significant increase in the ratio of civilian R&D

Table 15.10. Growth of Industrial R&D[a] in Israel[19]

	1969–1970	1985–1986	Change (%)
Current expenditures on R&D (million constant 1984–1985 US$)	26	347	1230
Current expenditure on R&D as a percentage of total sales of industry (%)	0.45	2.2	390
Scientists and engineers[b] engaged in R&D			
Absolute numbers	890	4300	380
Share in total industrial employment (%)	0.45	1.4	220
Practical engineers and technicians			
Absolute numbers	671	3260[c]	
Share in total industrial employment (%)	0.34	1.72[c]	
Establishments conducting R&D	210	370[c]	

[a]Civilian industrial firms only.
[b]Not in full-time equivalents.
[c]For 1984/1985.
Source: Israel Central Bureau of Statistics, *Survey of Research and Development in Industry, 1985/86,* Jerusalem, 1988.

Table 15.11. Israel: Civilian R&D in Industry, 1966–1985[a]

Year	R&D[b] (Millions of Nominal US$)	Total Industry (%)	R&D/Sales "S"[c] (%)	"C" (%)
1970	14.7	0.45	1.45	0.08
1973	22.8			
1974	30.5	0.54	1.59	0.09
1976	64.0			
1977	99.0			
1979		1.14	3.21	0.18
1984	292.0	1.91	5.29	0.22
1985	335.0			
1986	460.0			

[a]Real annual rates of growth 1969–1984 = 18%. Real reduction during 1985–1987 period = 36%.

[b]R&D Industry Surveys, CBS.

[c]Two categories of industry are used; the "S" category includes electronics and electrical machinery, transportation equipment, miscellaneous manufacturing, machinery, chemicals and oil, and metal products. The "C" category includes all others.

to industry sales—from 0.45% in 1970 to 1.91% in 1984. A simple industry breakdown into the sophisticated group (which roughly covers our "H" and "S" categories) and the conventional group of industries essentially highlights the tremendous difference in R&D intensity between these sectors—a dual economy-type situation, possibly with the intensity increasing much faster in the first group than in the second. Table 15.10 also shows the parallel development of technological manpower employed in civilian, industrial R&D. Using our broad definition of skilled manpower (i.e., scientists, engineers, practical engineers, and technicians) the numbers employed in R&D increased from 1557 in 1969 to around 7000 in 1984. The number of establishments involved in civilian R&D has not, however, increased so substantially—from 210 in 1969 to 370 in 1984–1985. This reflects both birth and death of firms and an increase in the average size of the R&D-performing establishment. Finally, Table 15.12 shows both the growth in R&D support from the government and in R&D-related exports—"outputs" of government support of R&D. Despite data and identification problems, there is a strong presumption that R&D-intensive exports have increased very fast—at least during the first 15 years—thus contributing both to the high rate of growth of industrial exports and to the change in the structure of exports previously mentioned.

Evaluation of System
The Israeli promotion system of civilian technology in industry is generally considered to have been successful in promoting R&D expenditures in industry, in promoting the employment of qualified manpower in industry (including absorption of immigrant scientists and engineers) and in industrial R&D, and in promoting industrial exports. More importantly, it was certainly one of the two or three important factors helping to explain the profound structural transformation occurring since 1967 in the direction of high-tech and, more generally, of R&D-intensive industry. Its success during the first decade or two derives from (1) it being a grant system, particularly adapted to SMEs under conditions of imperfect capital markets, and (2) the universality of sup-

Table 15.12. Growth in Governmental Support of Research and Development in Industry and in Related Exports

Year	(Nominal) R&D Grants to Industry from Ministry of Commerce and Industry[20]	Exports Resulting from Grants for R&D (Current US$ in Millions)[21]	High Technology Industrial Exports (Category H) (Millions of 1983 US$)[22]
1968	1.5	3.7	44
1970	3.0	8.0	54
1972	3.7	20.8	89
1974	9.0	233.4	144
1975	10.0	289.9	176
1976	20.0	283.6	265
1977	25.2	416.3	373
1978	27.0	550.0	438
1979	32.0	750.0	574
1980	—	—	643
1981	—	1000.0	816
1982	60.0	1400.0	811
1984–1985			922
1986			1299

port and its neutrality, which fits well with the "innovation capabilities" perspective. The system, however, has problems derived from (1) supporting R&D rather than the whole innovation process (which results in "excessive"—even duplicate—R&D and low-rate of application of R&D results), (2) the lack of evolution of the policies, particularly the need of reducing universality (e.g., focusing on SMEs and/or high-risk R&D only) without loss of neutrality, and (3) insufficient incentives to cooperative R&D.[17] We should also mention that direct support of R&D in industry is the main direction of Israel's direct policy support of technological promotion in industry. There is no policy for explicitly promoting technology adoption and diffusion by business firms such as that increasingly applied in Europe.[18]

Technological Infrastructure and Related Institutions[23]

We separately consider SMEs and conventional industry, defense and high-tech industry, and industry–university relationships.

SMEs and Conventional Industry
Problems of Industrial Research Institutes. Most of them belong to the Industrial Research Authority (IRA), which depends on the Ministry of Industry and Trade (MI&T).[24] These include Israel Fibers Institute, Israel Institute of Metals, National Physics Lab, Israel Ceramics and Silicate Institute, Institute of Plastics, and the Rubber Research Association. Most of these institutes were founded during the 1950s and 1960s. They cater to the needs of traditional industry with "services" or consultancy probably comprising a large fraction of their activity. Turnover has been declining since the 1970s relative both to conventional industry turnover and to R&D expenditures (see Table 15.13) (Toren, 1989).

The general impression is that these institutions are not effective in catering to the

Table 15.13. Share of the Budgets of Government Laboratories (G.L.)[27] in Total Civilian Industrial R&D (CR&D) and in CR&D Support by Government

	1976	1980	1985	1989[28]
Budgets of G.L. ($\times$100)				
CR&D support (%)	16.0	7.4	4.2	2.2
Total CR&D (%)	4.5	1.6	0.5	—
CR&D of non-R&D-intensive sectors (%)	37.8	9.6	7.2	—

Source: Adapted from Table 7 in Beni Toren (1989): "R&D in non-R&D intensive industrial sectors and in Government Labs," Industrial Policy Development Group (IPDG), The Jerusalem Institute, September.

needs of the small and medium-sized enterprises (SMEs) comprising a significant part of conventional industry. On the one hand, we hear that the labs undertake too little long-term research[25]; on the other hand, that they perform too little R&D commissioned by industry (e.g., in relation to the largest lab, The Fibers Institute). This apparent paradox can be solved once we recognize that the problem is not insufficient longer term research per se, but rather insufficient research of the kind that is relevant to the longer term needs of industry and that would enable the gradual build-up of capabilities for the associated industrial sectors—more specifically, development of an engineering and technological support network for SMEs and more generally for industrial categories "C" and "S." In the plastics industry, for example, the skills and capabilities required, and rarely supplied, include an understanding of raw materials and of the relationships between their characteristics and those of the final product, control of the production process, material compounding capabilities, and design.[26]

Defense and High-Tech Industry
I will focus here on some structural aspects of the high-tech-oriented innovation system, particularly that which is military oriented. The emphasis will be development during the past 10–15 years affecting infrastructure development (mainly technological capabilities) and patterns of firm cooperation within the military–industrial complex of Israel. These aspects provide a partial explanation for the "skills crowding out" argument previously mentioned, but also have independent effects on economic performance.

Defense R&D of the late 1970s and early 1980s involved a number of projects of significantly larger size and complexity compared to the past. Some of these involved linking and integrating a number of scientific and technological areas such as communications, computers, optronics, software, and propulsion systems. Moreover the ambition of developing a local version of each major piece of military hardware led also to some attempts at developing a new "platform" (e.g., such as that for the now-defunct Lavi fighter plane) and not only the electronics and avionics attached to existing platforms. The increased complexity and cost of these new military systems would naturally have dictated new patterns of cooperation and division of labor at least within the military–industrial complex—both in relation to infrastructures *and* in relation to specific projects. There is clear evidence, however, that this was not the case, at least for a wide array of technologies and projects. Rather than cooperate, defense-related firms attempted to add new capabilities to those they historically possessed.[29]

The results involved (1) considerable duplication of effort in establishing new technological infrastructures (e.g., optoelectronics), (2) failed and/or delayed projects, as a result of less than critical size of effort, (3) inadequate exploitation of export potential due to excessive competition—a striking example being the mutual price undercutting in the sale of "drones,"[30] and (4) insufficient "market creation" in connection with the assembly for export of complex projects and systems, the success of which depends critically on creating a network of (long-term relationships connecting) supplier firms.[31] Since the above-mentioned failures occurred within the defense-related industrial sector—a sector with heavy government involvement and even ownership of firms—they are of a "governmental–institutional–organizational" nature rather than traditional failures in the working of market forces. They provide, in my opinion, a central characterization of the military-oriented innovation system of Israel (one part of the overall national industrial innovation system), one that was shaped by the policies of the Ministry of Defense (MOD). The main causes seem to be (1) MOD's desire to promote competition among suppliers in order to reduce the cost of procuring military equipment, (2) absence of a clear policy assigning new technological infrastructures and capabilities to specific firms, and (3) the special treatment received by the Armaments Development Authority (ADA, or Rafael).[32,33] Thus policy focused on advancing competition rather than in achieving an appropriate competition–cooperation configuration. It also distinguished only imperfectly between specific innovations and technological infrastructure.

University–Industry Linkages
Israeli universities, which developed very early an awareness of the importance of linking with industry, pioneered during the 1960s the establishment of research authorities and science parks. These fostered the commercialization of research results and the establishment of new high-technology firms headed by entrepreneurs spun-off from the ranks of university staff. Both should be considered at least moderately successful.[34] One aspect of this success is captured by Herskovic's (1988) data on university patenting (see Table 15.14). The relative "success" of Israeli universities in becoming more industry oriented in the past 10 years does not hide the fact that there exists a "structural imbalance" between the university system and industry (or application of university research more generally). One possible indication of this is the share of uni-

Table 15.14.[39] A Comparison of University Patenting Activity in the United States, Canada, and Israel in 1984

	United States Universities	Canadian Universities	Israeli Universities
Domestic patents granted	520	21	34
Domestic patents granted to universities as a percentage of total domestic patents granted (%)	1.4	1.0	14.7
Domestic patents granted per million US$ expenditure on R&D in universities in 1981 (%)	0.08	0.02	0.18

Source: S. Herskovic, University Patenting Activity—the Case of Israel, Ministry of Science and Development, Jerusalem, 1988. This paper was presented at a workshop, Science Indicators: Their Use in Science Policy and Their Role in Science Studies, Leiden University, Leiden, Netherlands, November 14–15, 1988.

versities in national R&D compared to that of other countries. Table 15.2 showed that despite the significant decline in the past 10–15 years (and the corresponding rise of R&D performed in industry) this share is still very high by international standards— 47% in 1982/1983.

The broad-based scientific infrastructure, however, may be a significant facilitating factor in the continued movement to ever-increasing industrial sophistication, although the contribution need not flow from university research directly. Materializing such potential requires new interfaces between the traditional areas of basic research at universities and applied research in industry, such as those which emerged in a number of OECD countries during the 1980s.[35] It has been increasingly recognized that the effective transfer to industry of basic research performed at universities requires, prior to specific attempts at application, additional (1) "translation" into engineering terms and (2) bundling with complementary capabilities. All of this may also imply some need for priorities in science[36]: thus, the importance of generic research and the emergence of what has been termed strategic science.[37]

The Israeli system for financing universities is totally neutral vis-à-vis strategic areas of research. Moreover, there is very little awareness of the need to experiment with the emerging trends in this type of research. This derives from a number of factors. First, there is no effective separation between the financing of student education and training on the one hand, and the financing of research, on the other.[38] Second, the system is viewed by academicians as effectively blocking outside political interference into the university system and therefore as a bulwark of academic freedom. Third, there is no forum of experts or of leaders of academia where strategic issues concerning the future of the university system are discussed. PGC not only does not attempt to establish research priorities or to identify strategic areas of science in cooperation with users in industry, defense, and so on, but it also does not make a serious attempt at rationalizing the allocation of resources within the university system, promoting cooperation among parties, or constructing future growth scenarios under alternative assumptions. Fourth, the crisis of the universities is perceived as a basic research crisis rather than as reflecting, among other things, an insufficiently developed interfacing with other segments of society, (e.g., industry) (see Israel Academy of Science, 1988).

We conclude that the Israeli university system, despite its successes, has failed to adapt to the changing needs dictated both by the dynamic external environment (new trends in cooperation and in industry–university relationships) and by internal developments (economic stagnation and massive immigration). This failure to adapt parallels the failure mentioned in relation to the defense and civilian industrial sectors— a general inability to develop new forms of cooperation and infrastructure both within the sector and with outside organizations and institutions.

SUMMARY AND CONCLUSIONS

Gaps in the Israeli Innovation System

The industrial innovation system of Israel has failed to develop in the 1980s a number of institutions, mechanisms, and infrastructures that increasingly have been found useful in other countries—both large and small, advanced and newly industrialized. These include the following:

1. *Branch-specific organizations* to house new technological capabilities for conventional industry—including management reorientation of existing institutions (from simple shift to demand pull to "strategic" capability development) and to promote technology diffusion.
2. University-related *Centers of Excellence* in multisector functional areas of science and technology such as biotechnology, microelectronics, optoelectronics, and new materials. *Existence of these centers would have eliminated fragmentation and duplication of effort in that part of overall national effort that should essentially remain curiosity oriented.* They also could play a role in generating new technological infrastructures.
3. A *Technological Council* to assist in the identification of desired technological infrastructure, to coordinate the establishment of the various infrastructures (e.g., CIM for a particular sector with a nationwide, multisector CIM program), to develop criteria for evaluating the economic and other contribution of cooperative infrastructure-type R&D programs, and to represent a national locus of capabilities in the technological infrastructure policy area.
4. *A system for the support of small and medium-sized enterprises (SME),* both on technological and business matters—such as the DTI (Department of Trade and Industry) schemes in the United Kingdom, the Technological Service Network in Denmark, and the ITRI network of institutions of Taiwan.
5. *Secretariats and temporary joint labs in high-tech areas,* such as those involved in the Esprit program of the EEC and the microelectronics and optoelectronics programs of Japan.
6. *Vision exercises and policies,* at the branch, sectorial (e.g., high-tech industry), and national levels. These are essential ingredients for effective development of new technological capabilities.

In most cases the above institutions are critical nodes in important networks linking firms and other agents. Their absence implies insufficient networking in science and technology and between them and industry.

Anomalies and Distortions in Technological Effort

There is no obvious underinvestment in R&D relative to the international norm if we look at the aggregate R&D/GNP ratios (maybe the opposite), although the situation is less clear when we consider civilian R&D or civilian R&D performed in industry. The major problem, however, relates to the *structure of R&D in industry: too little generic R&D* or cooperative infrastructure type R&D,[40] and *probably excessive project R&D* (due to duplication and relative to actual incorporation of R&D results into innovations). A second important problem is *insufficient engineering (non-R&D) effort,* especially of the cooperative type required for the development of capabilities in conventional industry. This is related to the issue of diffusion, a central aspect of technology and technology policy of countries such as Italy (see Malerba, 1992), Germany, and Switzerland (see Ergas, 1986), and other countries.

    It is pretty clear that Israel is not a case of a diffusion-oriented innovation system, and for several reasons. **First,** there is very little explicit policy that promotes diffusion—not in connection with the technologies developed within the military industries or in connection with the adoption and diffusion of civilian (specifically, imported) technology[41]; and **second,** there is little actual diffusion, from the military to civilian industries and from abroad to small- and medium-sized firms within conventional industries. In addition, insufficient diffusion of technologies has characterized the situation *within* the defense industries as evidenced by excessive project and technological infrastructure duplication. Having said this we should add that *the mechanism for promoting civilian R&D within industrial firms should, to some extent, be regarded as a mechanism of diffusion*—in the sense of adapting and applying foreign technology (e.g., new electronic components) to numerous industrial applications. This mechanism, however, favors R&D-intensive firm rather than firms in conventional industries. In addition, it is a direct-support rather than an infrastructure-support method of diffusion. On both counts, this diffusion system is imperfect and incomplete.

A Network Interpretation of Transition Problems

The design and implementation of the new institutions, mechanisms, and infrastructures required for the 1980s necessitate the development of new sorts of relationships among the major players involved: government, industry, and universities. More concretely, what is required is a shift from an atomistic, noncollaborative pattern that also emphasizes control, power, and secrecy to a spontaneously interactive and collaborative pattern—one that recognizes the pervasiveness of potential positive game situations opened up by the technological revolution. Israel has also been extremely short of what may be termed network-entrepreneurs,[42] whose main function is to *create* the new networks of agents (firms, universities, individuals, etc.) required to generate these new collaborative patterns.[43]

In fact, I would like to postulate that the fundamental problem has been the non-creation of these new networks. The cause of this failure is not, first, market failure (as could be the case in relation to component producers–assembler networks or with innovator–user networks), since we are concerned with public/private mechanisms and with institutions associated with technological infrastructure rather than with specific innovations. Rather, the failure is institutional–organizational–governmental. Since network *creation* may have to overcome significant indivisibilities,[44] and since success in this effort may require a PBX-entrepreneur to perform the necessary coordination, we may fairly safely state that a root cause of the malaise probably lies in a political system that has not nurtured such (public sector) entrepreneurs.

Government Objectives, the Bureaucracy, and Politicians

The Israeli government has lost its capacity for long-term strategic decision making especially on economic matters. This probably is a result of the evolution of politics and the political system during the past 10–15 years, symbolized by the transition from traditional dominance by the center-left Labour Party to a two-party system effectively dominated by the center-right Likud. Such a long-term strategic capability did exist in the past, and served the needs of the country very well in its first two decades of existence. The loss of such capability is in part *conceptual,* not only a problem of implementation (e.g., lack of awareness of the nature and importance of technological infrastructure). Moreover, economic growth does not figure centrally or explicitly in the list of objectives of the Israeli government. The main nonpolitical objectives beyond social welfare (including housing) are employment, price stability, and others of a short-term macroeconomic nature. Moreover, the government's (and most of academia's) thinking concerning economic growth is neoclassical rather than structuralist (and evolutionary) with lip service adherence to the virtues of the free market implicitly precluding long-term, strategic thinking.[45] Finally, Israeli governments essentially act to what amounts to the political economy of maintaining the existing system rather than as a developmental state.[46] This relates to the other side of the government—its significant powers and extensive interference at the microeconomic level, one that generates an enormous amount of (neoclassical) inefficiencies. The sources of political power derive, apparently, from this political and distributional micromanagement rather than from leadership and courage in promoting change.[47]

Professor Y. Dror (1989) asserts that the main problems affecting Israel's capacity to govern (including long-term decision-making) relate to (1) the nature and capabilities of the bureaucracy, (2) excessive political interference in decision making (vis-à-vis the bureaucracy), and (3) incapable ministers who cannot restrain some excesses of the bureaucracy.[48] These are very important points, which bear directly on Israel's capacity to adopt long-term policies for the cooperative development of new capabilities.

First, it is clear that Israel has not yet developed a self-conscious, well-educated civil service, and especially one whose education has been strengthened to the extent of understanding the importance of, and mutual relationships between, technology and society in this day and age, and moreover, one where its long-term interests as a group (or subgroup) can predominate over partisan, short-term benefits. We should mention in this connection the lack of awareness and misperceptions concerning generic R&D and infrastructure, in all ministries including Treasury and (even more strikingly) the MI&T. Second, it is clear that coalition politics has frequently led to the nomination of ministers lacking sufficient capabilities and that short-term political considerations figure prominently in their agenda. The lack of implementation of the 1984 R&D Laws calling for the creation of a Technology Council within the MI&T may be ascribed both to this factor and (possibly) to partisan opposition from other bureaucrats within the Ministry (whose relative power on the subject matter of the Council would presumably diminish). Third, "uneducated ministers" mean that the political leadership is ineffective in controlling partisan bureaucratic interests. Y. Dror mentions the lack of control of MOD over Israel defense forces (concerning *professional* matters only).[49]

The weaknesses mentioned above block both the emergence and the activity of potential network entrepreneurs wishing to coordinate various parts of the bureaucracy in relation to initiatives in the area of generic R&D–technological infrastructure. Interministerial coordination is a serious problem in Israel, and it is known that interministerial committees have frequently not led to the application of the policies agreed on. The Treasury, despite its potential coordinating function, is a weak force in this respect.[50]

Final Thoughts

The transition to cooperative technology infrastructure development programs may require a greater measure of political leadership than that seen in the past. This includes a number of components: taking a longer, more strategic view of the economy and technology; a more capable political leadership and especially, one more open to the need for change and to new approaches to experiment with; and a will to coordinate the various parts of a fragmented bureaucracy. Within this context, public sector network entrepreneurs may conceptualize and coordinate specific programs. However, even then, initial obstacles are great, due to the generalized absence of trust prevailing in society as a whole.[51]

The result of Israel's case is that abundant skills are not sufficient for steady economic growth, since failures of an institutional, organizational, and governmental character may create strong obstacles in the way of successfully adapting to changes in the external environment. In Israel, these failures are not only static neoclassical distortions but failures of a dynamic, strategic nature starting, in my opinion, from lack of a clear vision of Israel's future in the world community. More specifically, the brilliant successes of Israel's entrepreneurs (market forces) to a very large extent have been achieved *despite* the existence of a vast array of government policies and semipublic mechanisms and institutions, at least in the last decade and a half.

The above is intimately related, in my opinion, to Israel's nonadaptive reaction to the Palestinian question and to the Palestinian uprising of the past 4 years. The mechanisms are subtle, but as with a lot of those insinuated in this chapter, they do not seem to be less real. First, the day-to-day dealing with the uprising puts a great deal of pressure on the government's "management time," and this enhances the already existent short-term bias of government policy, one inimical to infrastructure and new network creation. Second, absence of a dialogue with the Palestinians exacerbates the noncooperative, noninteractive traits developed in the past, which also block the transition to the new approach to policy. And finally, the associated international friction, especially with Europe, makes the whole area of international networking more difficult. This is serious for a small country searching for its place in an increasingly connected world. It directly relates to technological infrastructure once one realizes that an enormous share of capability and knowledge inputs must come from abroad— from the "external network." Therefore, its potential impact on the central message of this chapter concerning Israel's inability to adapt is very serious indeed.

NOTES

Previous drafts of this chapter have benefited from Richard Nelson's comments and suggestions.

1. See Ministry of Science and Development, *Scientific Research in Israel* (1989, Ch. 16). For a useful discussion of the attitude towards science of the prestate Zionist leadership, see Katz and Ben David (1975, pp. 152–54).

2. The share of agriculture in GNP rose somewhat during the 1950s, probably in response to government incentives.

3. See Syrquin (1986).

4. The main points in what follows were taken from Katz and Ben David (1975).

5. For the structuralist perspective on economic growth and development see Justman and Teubal (1987, 1989, 1991b).

6. A reduction in economic growth and in productivity growth has also characterized other industrialized countries since the energy crisis; however, there are numerous indicators that show that Israel's decline has been sharper and more persistent than that of many other countries. See Bruno (1989) for the brief resuscitation after 1988, followed by subsequent stagnation.

7. Total expenditure in R&D.

8. Includes mathematics and computer science.

9. The share of defense expenditure in GNP (*plus* import surplus) has grown from 7–9% during 1958–1966 to almost 18–21% during 1968–1980 (Berglas, 1986). This share probably did not decline, at least during the first half of the 1980s.

10. The Lavi plane's contribution to national security was also probably negative, the project having been discontinued in 1987 after a long political debate and after immense investments in critical resources.

11. There are indications that this is not fully explainable by higher average skills, but rather it has a lot to do with the management environment associated with a large public-sector organization operating on a cost-plus basis.

12. Thus, large military R&D programs of the early 1980s may have *delayed the take-off* of civilian high tech.

13. See also Teubal (1983).

14. Development of **innovation** capabilities at the early stage of high-tech development is of crucial importance, much more than at a more mature stage of the sector. It implies the desirability of supporting the R&D activity of large numbers of firms with a significant probability of failing—the reason being the very significant learning process taking place so that while direct private profitability might be negative, total social profitability might be positive. Thus, promotion of R&D is a target in itself at the early stage of high-tech industry. The usual "market failure" arguments for supporting R&D apply even more to the generation of capabilities. Externalities are rampant, due to the significant flow of knowledge and experience going from firms that go broke to newly established and other firms. Capability creation is a social or collective phenomenon, rather than a process occurring exclusively within the realm of the single firm, so the public good and indivisibility/critical mass argument are applicable here. Finally, the need to finance costly learning—an activity not existing previously, at least in the high-tech context— almost inevitably leads to capital market problems, since the required financial institutions or mechanisms have not yet had the opportunity to develop.

15. The relative lack of emphasis on government laboratories can be explained by a number of factors: first, there were numerous opportunities for small projects whose R&D could be carried out by small firms (e.g., attaching a minicomputer and even more so later on, a microprocessor, to a measuring or medical instrument); second, the high quality of the engineers and scientists involved, which also relates to the high quality of the institutions of higher learning; third, related to the first reason, the fact that the promotion scheme did not deal with the "strategic level" of technology promotion—one normally involving the development of technological infrastructures that are inevitably "lumpy"—but rather, with the current support level dealing with specific, commercially oriented products or process development. At the strategic level, many more indivisibilities will be present, so cooperative R&D with the participation of government labs is essential (this was the case to some extent within the military sector).

16. This means that the system did not formally discriminate among projects belonging to different sectors, branches, or technologies. The fact that the share of electronics in total industrial R&D and in total MI&T support for industrial R&D has increased is not an indication of an explicit preference given to this sector vis-à-vis others. It is rather the result of a process of natural selection of products, entrepreneurs, and firms that took place as a result of the neutral

policy environment (see Teubal, 1983). This process expresses the main advantage of neutrality in support.

17. Despite the world trend toward cooperation in R&D, Israel has lagged in this respect. Although lately some incentive to undertake cooperative industrial R&D projects has been introduced, the main thrust of the Office of the Chief Scientist is overwhelmingly in the direction of supporting individual projects in individual firms. However, a new scheme, BIRD—Israel–U. S. Bi-national Industrial Research and Development Foundation—has been instrumental in promoting international cooperation in innovation, including strategic partnering between small Israeli firms and larger foreign ones.

18. Israel's Law for the Encouragement of Capital Investment, in fact, has traditionally favored the "hardware" over the "software" component of capital investment. It thereby implicitly discriminates against the diffusion of new information technologies in industry, such as computer-integrated manufacturing (CIM), which possess a significant software component (see Justman and Teubal, 1988). Discussions are underway for formulating a more rational diffusion of technology policy.

19. From Ministry of Science and Development (1989).

20. Current US$ in millions. Central Bureau of Statistics, Industrial R&D Surveys, various years. Grants for 1989 approximate US$ 100 million.

21. Internal information, Office of the Chief Scientist, MI&T.

22. Data Bank of the Industrial Development Policy Group (IDPG), Jerusalem Institute. For a definition of category "H" see Table 15.1.

23. Some of the issues dealt with here were considered in Justman and Teubal (1990) and in Brodet et al. (1990)—Summary and Conclusions.

24. The exceptions include some non-high-tech institutes belonging to the Technion such as the Building Materials Institute and the Food Industry R&D Center.

25. See the report of the Yiftach Committee (1984), which also proposes a better balance between longer term R&D (which they identify as "infrastructure R&D") and shorter term problem-solving, consulting, and performance of R&D commissioned by industry; and also the earmarking of a certain proportion of the overall budget for the purpose of purchasing equipment.

26. See Yinnon and Meron (1990).

27. Government Laboratories include The Institute for Applied Research, The Fibers Institute, The Metals Institute, The Ceramics Institute, The Institute of Rubber Research, The Plastics Institute, and the Physics Laboratory.

28. Approved budgets.

29. An ideal example: a firm traditionally involved in communications would attempt to add a radar capability in order to compete in the supply of certain new military systems with the firm possessing a long-standing radar capability. The latter in turn would attempt to add a communications capability in order to be able to compete in the next generation of such systems. Critical mass problems indicate that the national economy would, in principle, have benefited from a joint venture in system development and production and from a division of labor in relation to capabilities.

30. The competing firms were Israel's largest electronics firm—Tadiran—and Israel's largest company—Israel Aircraft Industries (IAI). At some stage, the Ministry of Defense (MOD) forced the firms into a joint venture that was subsequently dissolved. A "drone" is an unmanned light reconnaissance plane developed in Israel in the early 1980s.

31. The unexploited potential in the export of military systems and turnkey projects has been emphasized by close observers of the military–industrial scene such as U. Galil and B. Peled. There also exists significant unexploited potential in relation to the supply of civilian systems and turnkey projects (e.g., in the areas of education, health, and agriculture).

32. MOD policies of the late 1970s and early 1980s that aimed at enhancing competition among alternative suppliers were probably justified during the 1970s when systems were rela-

tively small and simple. However, they were inappropriate for a small country such as Israel during the 1980s when the supply of enhanced system complexity necessitated the prior establishment of a spectrum of indivisible new R&D and production capabilities.

33. Absence of an explicitly civilian technological infrastructure and insufficient cooperation and networking among firms (at least until 1988; see Teubal et al., 1989) also characterize civilian high-tech industry. No government ministry has assumed a role in generating technological infrastructures for civilian industry, nor has there been any consideration of civilian industry's needs (and no consultation regarding such needs) when designing technological infrastructures for the military.

34. Spinoffs from the Weizmann Institute, for example, include a number of highly innovative biotechnology firms.

35. See Mowery and Rosenberg (1992) and OECD (1984).

36. See Martin and Irvine (1984, 1989). A well-documented example is biotechnology research in the United Kingdom organized and directed by the Biotechnology Directorate of the Science and Engineering Research Council (SERC) (Senker, 1989). Additional examples are the Alvey and Esprit programs on information technology for the United Kingdom and the EEC, respectively.

37. The nature and significance of generic research were first analyzed by Nelson et al. (1967). Further analyses of their importance for growth and innovation can be found in Nelson (1983, 1984). Effective application of strategic science for capability development requires industry relevance, multidisciplinarity, integration with engineering capabilities, excellence, and the creation of tailor-made institutions and mechanisms (e.g., the Engineering Research Centers in the United States. See Chemical Engineering (1989)).

38. The Planning and Grants Committee (PGC) of the Council of Higher Education performs in Israel most of the role performed in the United Kingdom both by the University Grants Committee (UGC) and the Science and Engineering Research Council (SERC).

39. Ministry of Science and Development (1988).

40. This problem has been mentioned also for the United States. See Nelson (1983, 1984) and Nelson and Winston (1982).

41. Both Malerba (1992) and Ergas (1986) have emphasized the role in diffusion policies played by collective institutions and even spontaneous cooperative effort. We have seen that these have been particularly absent in Israel.

42. See Imai and Baba (1989) and Teubal et al. (1990).

43. For a survey of the various modes of interaction and collaboration of OECD countries in information technologies, see Arnold and Guy (1987, pp. 67–68). Networks—involving patterns of long-term relationships and spontaneous interaction among many agents—are particularly required in the new collaborative forms of *systemic* technological development (see Imai and Baba, 1989). They are required in order to ensure orderly patterns of division of labor and cooperation among firms, to exploit new (unhidden) opportunities arising from spontaneous interaction, and, more generally, as an organizational framework assuring technological system evolution. In the cooperative development of new technological infrastructure, they are also essential in order to establish priorities and for formulating a joint, efficient, and mutually acceptable R&D agenda.

44. Network creation (or new network creation) may be difficult for a number of reasons: first, the fixed costs of establishing new channels and new codes of communication among agents, a fact that may cause existing relationships to persist despite the need for fundamental change [see Lundvall's (1989) "stubborn" user-producer relationships and his "incomplete" networks case, as applied to the Danish agroindustrial complex); second, critical mass problems that may hinder network take-off and lead to stagnation within a low-level-equilibrium trap [Teubal et al.'s (1990) case of inventor–user networks]. I suggest that this also partly explains problems

facing the creation of the new cooperative, *public/private,* technological infrastructure networks in Israel.

45. The ideology and interests of Israel's political establishment are to some extent inimical to systematic screening of world trends, to the building of alternative economic, political, and social scenarios based on Israel's strengths, and to open public discussion of alternative policy trajectories.

46. For the notion of "developmental state," see Johnson (1982).

47. Prevailing economic thinking is thus right in assessing the enormous costs of government intervention in the economy. It is wrong, however (even when abstracting from political economy considerations), to judge that simply reducing government's role is sufficient for the renewal of economic growth. They may be right in periods of "normal" growth but are definitely wrong at the *nodes* of structural change (see Justman and Teubal, 1990).

48. See Dror (1990). This summarizes a book that also reflects, among other things, the author's participation in, and in the conclusions of, the Kubarsky Committee (calling for the professionalization of Israel's public service).

49. I emphasized lack of control of MOD ministers and bureaucrats over the military–industrial complex.

50. A possible coordination failure involving both the Ministry of Science and Technology and the PGC concerns the application of the policies agreed on concerning biotechnology.

51. The short-term perspective within segments of the business sector was nurtured by years of macroeconomic instability and by some negative effects of the (generally successful) Stabilization Program of 1986 (e.g., long periods of extremely high real interest rates). Moreover the 1980s also witnessed the partial destruction of the "trust fund" of society (e.g., the demise of a large number of cooperative arrangements involving mutual insurance between members such as those within the moshav and kibbutz movements).

REFERENCES

Arnold, E., and Guy, K. (1987). *Information Technology and Emerging Growth Areas.* SPRU, August.

Berglas, E. (1986). "Defence and the Economy." In Y. Ben-Porath (ed.), *The Israeli Economy—Maturing through Crisis,* Ch. 8. Cambridge: Harvard University Press.

Bregman, A. (1986). *Industry and Industrialization Policy in Israel.* Bank of Israel, Research Department (in Hebrew).

Bregman, A. (1987). "Technological Progress, Structural Changes and Productivity in Manufacturing: The Case of Israel." *Journal of Development Economics* 25.

Brodet, D., Justman, M., and Teubal, M. (1990). *An Industrial and Technological Policy for Israel.* Jerusalem, Israel: The Jerusalem Institute for Israel Studies (Hebrew).

Bruno, M. (1989). "Economic Recuperation in Historical Perspective." Typescript, May.

Chemical Engineering (1989). "Engineering Research Centers: The Jury Is Still Out." May.

Dror, Y. (1989). *A Grand Strategy For Israel.* Jerusalem's Academon, The Hebrew University students printing and publishing house.

Ergas, H. (1986). "Does Technology Policy Matter?" Center for European Policy Studies.

Halperin, A. (1986). "The Military Buildup and Economic Growth in Israel." Paper presented at the Falk Institute Conference on Economic Issues and Policy in Israel, June.

Halperin, A., Berman, E., and Teubal, M. (1988). "The Trade-Off Between Economic Growth and Military Industries." Draft.

Herskovic, S. (1988). "University Patenting Activity—The Case of Israel." Paper presented at workshop on *Science Indicators: Their Use in Science Policy and Their Role in Science Studies.* Leiden, Netherlands: University of Leiden.

Imai, K., and Baba, Y. (1989). "Systemic Innovation and Cross-Border Networks." Paper presented at the International Seminar on the *Contributions of Science and Technology to Economic Growth,* at the OECD, Paris, June.

Israel Academy of Sciences. (1988). *The Basic Research Fund, 13th Annual Report, 1988–89.*

Johnson, C. (1982). *Miti and the Japanese Miracle: The Growth of Industrial Policy 1925–1975.* Stanford: Stanford University Press.

Justman, M., and Teubal, M. (1987) "A Framework For an Explicit Industrial and Technological Policy for Israel and Some Specific Policies." In C. Freeman and B. Lundvall (eds.) *Small Countries*

Facing The Technological Revolution. London: Frances Pinter.

Justman, M., and Teubal, M. (1989). "The Structuralist Perspective on Economic Growth and Development: Conceptual Foundations and Policy Implications." Reprinted in Evenson, R., and Ranis, G. (1990). The Role of Science and Technology in Development. Boulder, CO: Westview Press.

Justman, M., and Teubal, M. (1991). "A Structuralist Perspective on the Role of Technology in Economic Growth and Development." Typescript. World Development, 19(9) 1167–1183.

Justman, M. and Teubal, M. (1990). "A Framework for an Industrial and Technological Policy for Israel." In D. Brodet, M. Justman, and M. Teubal (eds.), An Industrial and Technological Policy for Israel, Ch. 3. Jerusalem, Israel: The Jerusalem Institute for Israel Studies (Hebrew). 79–96.

Katz, S., and Ben-David, J. (1975). "Scientific Research and Agricultural Innovation in Israel." Minerva 13(2), 151–182.

Kuznetz, S. (1971). Economic Growth of Nations. Cambridge, MA: Belknap Press of Harvard University Press.

Lundvall, B. A. (1989). "Innovation, the Organized Market and the Productivity Slow-Down," typescript.

Malerba, F. (1990). "Italy: The National System of Innovation." This volume.

Martin, B., and Irvine, J. (1989) Research Foresight—Priority Setting in Science, Netherlands Ministry of Education and Science.

Martin, B., and J. Irvine (1984). Foresight in Science—Picking the Winners. London: Pinter Publishers.

Mayshar, J. (1986). "Investment Patterns." In Y. Ben-Porath (ed.), The Israeli Economy—Maturing through Crisis. Cambridge: Harvard University Press.

Metzer, J. (1986). "The Slowdown of Economic Growth: A Passive Phase or the End of the Big Spurt." In Y. Ben-Porath (ed.), The Israeli Economy—Maturing through Crisis. Cambridge: Harvard University Press.

Ministry of Science and Development. (1989). Scientific Research in Israel, 8th ed. N. Greenwald and S. Herskovic.

Mowery, D. C., and Rosenberg, N. (1992). "The U. S. National Innovation System." This volume.

National Agency for Technology. (1983). A Technological Development Program. Denmark: Ministry of Industry.

National Council for Research and Development. (1988). Policy for the Promotion of Biotechnology R&D in Israel. Report of the National Committee for Biotechnology (Katzir Report).

Nelson, R. (1983). "Government Support of Technical Progress: Lessons from History." Journal of Policy Analysis and Managements 2(4): 499–514.

Nelson, R. (1984). High Technology Policy: A Five-Nation Coparison. Washington D. C.: American Enterprise Institute of Public Policy Research.

Nelson, R., and Winston, S. (1982). An Evolutionary Theory of Economic Change. Cambridge, MA: Harvard University Press.

Nelson, R., Peck, M., and Kalachek, E. (1967). Technology, Economic Growth and Public Policy. Washington, D. C.: Brookings Institution.

OECD. (1984). Industry and University: New Forms of Cooperation and Communication. Paris: OECD.

OECD. (1988). Reviews of National Science and Technology Policy—Denmark. Paris: OECD.

Pack, H. (1971). Structural Change and Economic Policy in Israel. New Haven, CT: Yale University Press.

Senker, J. (1989). Evaluating the Funding of Strategic Science—Some Lessons from the British Experience. SPRU, typescript, September.

Syrquin, M. (1986). "Economic Growth and Structural Change: An International Perspective." Reprinted in Y. Ben-Porath, (ed.), The Israeli Economy—Maturing through Crisis. Cambridge, MA: Harvard University Press.

Teubal, M. (1982). "The R&D Performance Through Time of an Electronics Firm." Reprinted in M. Teubal (ed.), Innovation Performance, Learning, and Government Policy. Madison, WI: University of Wisconsin Press, 1987.

Teubal, M. (1983). "Neutrality in Science Policy: The Development of Sophisticated Industrial Technology in Israel." Minerva. Reprinted in M. Teubal (ed.), Innovation Performance, Learning, and Government Policy. Madison, WI: University of Wisconsin Press, 1987.

Teubal, M. (1987). Innovation Performance, Learning, and Government Policy. Madison, WI: University of Wisconsin Press.

Teubal, M. (1989). "Israel's High Tech Industry, Where To?" Published in 1988. Proceedings of the Israel Economists' Association, December.

Teubal, M., Yinnon, T., and Zuscovitch, E. in press. "Networks and Market Creation." Research Policy, 20:381–92.

Toren, B. (1989). "R&D in Non-R&D Intensive Sectors and in Government Labs," IDPG, Jerusalem Institute, Israel

Yiftach Committee Report (1984). R&D, Technology, and Science-Based Industry in Israel. Report of the Committee for the Evaluation of Government Research Organization and Management, Ministry of Science and Development.

Yinnon, T., and Meron, M. (1990). Industrial Capability in the Israeli Plastics Industry. Draft (Hebrew).

PART IV

NATIONAL INNOVATION SYSTEMS

16

A Retrospective

RICHARD R. NELSON

It is customary for a concluding chapter to summarize the findings presented in the text. However, here such an objective is impossible. The 15 country studies that make up the heart of this book cover an enormous amount of material. No other project has come remotely close to treating the range of countries considered here. Many of the individual studies stand as major contributions in their own right to the understanding of the innovation systems of particular countries going far beyond anything written on that subject before. To try to summarize would be absurd.

However, it is possible to try to assess the extent to which the project has had success in achieving the goals that were foremost in the minds of the researchers. This concluding chapter offers such a retrospective on the project.

The principal motivations and objectives of this study were laid out in some detail in Chapter 1. Therefore they need only brief recapitulation here. The first objective was, simply, to describe, to compare, and to try to understand the similarities and differences across countries in their innovation systems. We noted that until this project, studies of national innovation systems almost always focused on one country, in recent years commonly Japan, in earlier ones the United States, with comparisons with other countries left mostly implicit. Thus, prior to this one, there existed no systematic comparative study covering a sizable range of countries, which probed explicitly for what were the common elements, and what were the apparently significant differences, and what were the factors that seemed to lie behind these. Such a study seemed highly worthwhile in itself.

Yet these earlier studies had spawned considerable argument about what made an innovative system effective, in the sense that it contributed positively to national economic performance. As we noted in Chapter 1, the originators of this project were bothered by the tendency of various analysts to argue, on the basis of very little evidence or analysis, that this feature, or that one, was a major factor behind country performance differences, a tendency checked neither by strong conceptual understanding of what is and what is likely not a causal factor, nor by the requirement that the proposed causal connections be consistent with a wide range of country observations. We hoped that significantly expanding the comparison group would constrain such practice, and that the proposed causal arguments that survived the stronger empirical constraints might be worthy of serious analytic consideration. This was the second major objective of this project.

To a considerable extent, the arguments about the role of innovation in national economic performance explicit or implicit in the normative studies characterized above were drawing or rationalizing attention to a small set of industries and technologies marked by high R&D intensity—specifically semiconductors, computers and telecommunications, aerospace, and modern biotechnology—and calling for or justifying significant government support for national firms engaged in these areas. Although the arguments struck the project organizers as analytically loose, and empirically unsubstantiated, national governments were heeding them. Thus, trade in "high-technology" products, the behavior of companies in these industries, and in particular national policies in support of these industries had become major issues of contention among nations. At the same time, companies in these industries were becoming increasingly transnational. A third objective of this project was to throw some light on this complex of issues.

From another point of view the project as a whole can be considered a test of a set of intellectual commitments that guided the work. In particular, the basic notion of a "national innovation system" that oriented the project is a complex and somewhat problematic one. Our concept of innovation was broad and not necessarily tied to leadership in a technology but rather to effective competitive performance in a dynamic context. The participants in the project felt that the key questions demanded that the studies go beyond narrow examination of research and development, patenting, and the like, and had the faith that our wider exploration could be kept analytically compact. But this was an open question.

Also, using either the broad or the narrower concept of innovation, the participants in the project were well aware that innovation systems are not neatly divided by national borders. The transnational aspects of technological advance, and of the key actors involved, has grown increasingly prominent in recent years. Nonetheless, our belief was that nations continue to be meaningful units of observation. Another objective of this study was to explore in what ways this was the case, while at the same time considering how internationalization has affected how one ought to think about national systems.

COUNTRY DIFFERENCES AND WHAT LIES BEHIND THEM

To compare means to identify similarities as well as differences. Certainly the broad view of technical innovation that we laid out in Chapter 1 and that guided this study implies certain commonalities. That view applies to economies in which profit-oriented firms are the principal providers of goods and services, and where central planning and control are weak. These conditions hold in all of the countries in our set, although in some a certain portion of industry is nationalized, and in some governments do try to mold the shape of industrial development in at least a few economic sectors. In all of the countries in our set, the bulk of education, including university education, is conducted in public institutions. In all, the government is presumed to have major responsibility for the funding of basic research, although there are major differences across countries regarding how much of that they do, and where basic research is mostly carried out, and in the kinds of applied research and development the governments finance. From one point of view, what is most striking about the country comparisons is the amount of basic similarity. Had the old Soviet Union been included in the set, or China, or Nigeria, the matter would have been different. But, as it is, the differences across our set of countries must be understood as differences of individuals of the same species.

Within our group of countries, it would appear that to a considerable extent the differences in the innovation systems reflect differences in economic and political circumstances and priorities. First, size and the degree of affluence matter a lot. Countries with large affluent populations can provide a protected market for a wide range of manufacturing industries and may engage in other activities that "small" countries cannot pursue, at least with any chance of success, and their innovation systems will reflect this. Low-income countries tend to differ from high-income ones in the kinds of economic activities in which they can have comparative advantage, and in internal demand patterns, and these differences profoundly shape the nature of technical innovation that is relevant.

The 3-fold division of our countries into large high-income industrial nations, small high-income countries, and low-income countries thus turned out to be a useful first cut analytic separation. By and large the economies in the first group had a significantly larger fraction of their economies in R&D-intensive industry, such as aerospace, electronics, and chemical products, which require large sales to be economic, than economies in the second group. There are some anomalies, at the surface at least. Thus Sweden in the second group and Israel and Korea in the third have higher R&D to GNP ratios than several of the countries in the first group. Some of the mystery disappears when Israel's ambitious military R&D is recognized, and Sweden's and Korea's strong presence in several R&D-intensive industries that live largely through export. Both of the latter two countries also have strong defense programs and this also undoubtedly affected their R&D intensities. There are certain interesting similarities of countries in different groups—Japan and Korea for example. However, by and large there were strong intragroup similarities and strong intergroup differences. Thus the United States and Japan look much less different than advertised, once one brings Australia and Israel into the comparison set. And much of the United States–Japan difference can be seen to reside in differences in their resource bases and defense policies.

Whether a country had rich natural resources or ample farming land clearly is another important variable influencing the shape of its innovation system. It turns out that all our "small" high-income countries also were well endowed in this respect. Among the large high-income countries the United States was by far the best endowed here. Countries that possess resources and good farm land face a different set of opportunities and constraints than countries without these assets.

Countries that lack them must import resources and farm products, which forces their economies toward export-oriented manufacturing, and an innovation system that supports this. One sees this strikingly in the cases of Germany, Japan, and Korea. On the other hand, countries with a rich resource base can support relatively high living standards with these and the affiliated industries providing exports to pay for imported manufactured goods. The countries that have been able to do this—Denmark, Canada, and Australia stand out in our set—have developed significant publicly supported R&D programs to back these industries. So also has the United States. Although effective agriculture and resource exploitation does require R&D, compared with "high-tech" industry the R&D intensity here is low.

The discussion above suggests that to some extent at least, a nation's innovation system is shaped by factors such as size and resource endowments that affect comparative advantage at a basic level. But it also is true that a nation's innovation system tends to reflect conscious decisions to develop and sustain economic strength in certain areas, that is, it builds and shapes comparative advantage.

Some of the project members were surprised to find that in many of our countries national security concerns had been important in shaping innovation systems.

First, among high-income countries defense R&D accounts for the majority of the differences among the countries in government funding on industrial R&D, and the presences of large military programs thus explains why government industrial R&D spending in the United States, and the United Kingdom, and France is so much greater than in Japan and Germany. Second, the industries from which the military procures tend to be R&D intensive, whether the firms are selling to the military or to civilians. The study of Japan shows clearly that the present industrial structure was largely put in place during an era when national security concerns were strong. This structure, now oriented to civilian products, is one of the reasons for Japan's high R&D intensity. It is possible that to some extent, this argument also holds for Germany.

Interestingly, every one of the low-income countries in our study has been influenced by national security concerns, or a military government, or both. Thus much of high-tech industry in Israel is largely oriented toward the military. The broad economic policies, industrial structures, and innovation systems of Korea and Taiwan were molded in part by their need to have a capable military establishment. The pockets of "high tech" atop the basically backward Brazilian and Argentine economies clearly reflect the ambitions of their military elites.

As noted, all of the countries in our set are, basically, ones in which firms are mostly expected to fend for themselves in markets that are, to a considerable extent, competitive. However, all are marked by significant pockets of government overview, funding, and protection. In our countries with big military procurement programs, the defense industries are the largest such pocket. However, in many of our countries government support and protection extend into space, electric power, and telecommunications, and other areas of civilian "high tech." Although these extensions are most significant in the big high-income countries, Canada has large public programs in electric power and telecommunications, and so does Sweden.

There clearly are significant differences across the nations regarding beliefs about the kind of role government should play in shaping industrial development. The role of military concerns clearly is a powerful variable influencing this. But a relatively active government also is associated with "late" development, along the lines put forth by Alexander Gerschenkron (1962). Aside from the arena of national security and related areas, Britain and the United States are marked by restrained government. On the other hand all of our low-income late-developing countries have quite active governments. However, there certainly are exceptions to this rule. France's Etatism goes way back in history, and although Italy is a late developer, except during the Fascist era her government has been weak.

The above discussion suggests that one ought to see considerable continuity in a nation's innovation system, at least to the extent that the basic national objectives and conditions have a continuity. Although this proposition clearly has only limited bearing on the countries in our set that were formed or gained independence only in recent years—Israel, Taiwan, and Korea—even here one can see a certain consistency within these nation's short histories. All of these countries have experienced dramatic improvements in living standards from the 1950s, and their industrial structure has changed markedly. Their innovation systems have changed as well, but as our authors tell the story, in all of these countries today's institutional structures supporting innovation clearly show their origins in those of 30 years ago.

For countries with longer histories, the institutional continuity is striking, at least to the study authors. Thus one can see many of the same things in 1990 in France, Germany, and Japan that were there in 1890, and this despite the enormous advances in living standards and shifts in industrial structure all have experienced, and the total defeat of the latter two nations in World War II and the stripping away of their military. Britain in 1990 continues many the institutional characteristics of Britain in 1890, although they seemed to work better then than now.

Indeed, it seems that of the countries with long histories the one that has changed most institutionally is the United States. The governmental roles in funding university research, and defense R&D, that came into place only after World War II, had little precedent prior to the war, and profoundly changed the nature of the innovation system.

WHAT IS REQUIRED FOR EFFECTIVE INNOVATIVE PERFORMANCE?

We have defined innovation broadly so that the term basically stands for what is required of firms if they are to stay competitive in industries where technological advance is important. Such industries span a large share of manufacturing, many service sectors such as air transport, telecommunications, and medical care, and important areas of agriculture and mining. Staying competitive means different things in different national contexts. For firms located in high-wage countries, being competitive may require having a significantly more attractive product or a better production process than firms in low-wage countries. For the latter, being competitive may not require being at the forefront. Indeed much of innovation in low-income countries involves the learning of foreign technology, its diffusion, and perhaps its adaption to local circumstances of demand or production. But in either kind of country, if technological advance in the industry is significant, staying competitive requires continuing innovation.

We, the group that has produced the country studies, think we can discern several basic features that are common to effective innovative performance, and that are lacking or attenuated in countries where innovation arguably has been weak. First, the firms in the industry were highly competent in what mattered to be competitive in their lines of business. Generally this involved competence in product design and production, but usually also effective overall management, ability to assess consumer needs, links into upstream and downstream markets, and so on. In most cases significant investments lay behind these firm capabilities. All this enabled firms to master the relevant technologies and other practices needed to compete and to stay up with or lead with new developments.

This observation does contain a hint of tautology, but is better regarded as confirmation of a point stressed in Chapter 1, that the bulk of the effort in innovation needs to be done by the firms themselves. Although they may draw on outside developments, significant internal effort and skill are needed to complement and implement these. One cannot read the studies of Japan, Germany, Italy, Korea, and Taiwan, all arguably countries in which firms have displayed strong performance in certain industries, without being impressed by the authors' description of the firms. On the other hand, one is impressed the other way by the authors' commentary on the weaknesses of firms in certain industries in Britain, France, Australia, Argentina, and Israel.

Being strong did not necessarily mean that firms were large. Economists long have understood that although in some industries a firm has to be large to be a capable innovator, in other industries this is not the case. Many of the strong Italian, Taiwanese, and Danish firms are relatively small. Nor does it mean that the firms spend heavily on formal R&D. In some fields such as electronics generally it did, at least for firms in our first two groups of countries; however in Korea and Taiwan electronics firms often were doing well with technical efforts mostly oriented toward "reverse engineering." The Italian textile industry is strong on fashion and design, but little of that work is accounted as R&D. In Chapter 1 we noted that scholars of technological innovation now understand that there are significant interindustry differences in the extent to which resources allocated to innovation, in the broad sense in which we are using the term, get counted as R&D. Nor does it imply that the firms were not benefiting from publicly funded R&D programs, or favored procurement status. However, as our authors describe it, the bulk of the inputs and direction for innovative activity were coming from the firms themselves.

Although our concept of strong firm entails ability to compete, in all of our cases becoming strong involved actually being exposed to strong competition and being forced to compete. As Michael Porter (1990) noted, in a number of cases the firms faced strong rivals in their own country. Thus the Japanese auto and electronics companies compete strongly with each other, and American pharmaceutical companies and Italian clothing producers compete. However, it is not clear that this generalization holds for small countries, where there may be only one or a few national firms as Ericson in Sweden and Northern Telecom in Canada. For these firms most of their competition is with foreign rivals.

Porter (1990) and Bengt-Åke Lundvall (1988) proposed that firms in industries where a country is strong tend to have strong interactive linkages with their upstream suppliers, who also are national firms. Our studies show many cases in which this proposition is verified. The supplier networks of Japanese automobile firms, and the upstream–downstream connections in Danish agricultural product processing, are good examples. The cooperation of Italian textile producers with each other and with their equipment suppliers is another. However, there are a number of examples in which the proposition does not seem to hold. Pharmaceutical companies, strong in Germany and the United States, do not seem generally to have any particularly strong supplier connections, international or national. In aircraft production, the producers of components and subcomponents increasingly are located in countries other than that of the system designer and assembler.

A similar observation is obtained regarding the proposed importance of a demanding set of home market customers. In many cases this holds. But in small countries or for industries that from their start have been export oriented, the main customer discipline may come from foreign customers.

Although "strong firms" are the key, that only pushes the question back a stage. Under what conditions do strong firms arise? As the discussion above suggests, to some extent the answer is "spontaneously." However, our studies do indicate strongly that aspects of the national background in which firms operate matter greatly.

One important feature distinguishing countries that were sustaining competitive and innovative firms was education and training systems that provide these firms with a flow of people with the requisite knowledge and skills. For industries in which university-trained engineers and scientists were needed, this does not simply mean that the universities provide training in these fields, but also that they consciously train their students with an eye to industry needs. The contrast here between the United States and Germany on the one hand, and Britain and France on the other, is quite sharp, at least according to the authors of our studies. Indeed these studies suggest strongly that a principal reasons why the former two countries surged ahead of the latter two, around the turn of the century, in the science-based industries emerging then is that the university systems of the former were much more responsive to the training needs of industry.

Although strength in "high tech" depends on the availability of university-trained people, industry more generally requires a supply of literate, numerically competent people in a wide range of functions outside of R&D, who are trained to industry demands either by the firms themselves (as in Japan) or in external training systems linked to firms (as in several German and Swedish industries). Countries differed in the extent to which their public education and training systems combined with private training to provide this supply, and the differences mattered. Thus among high-income countries Germany, Japan, and Sweden came through much stronger in this respect than Britain and Australia. Among developing countries the contrast is equally sharp between Korea and Taiwan on the one hand, and Brazil on the other.

The examples of Korea and Taiwan, and the other Asian "tigers," can be read as remarkably successful cases of education led growth. As the authors indicate, the ability of firms in these countries to move quickly from the relatively simple products they produced in the 1950s and 1960s to the much more complex and technologically sophisticated products they produced successfully in the 1980s was made possible by the availability of a young domestic workforce that had received the schooling necessary for the new jobs. On the other hand, the cases of Argentina and Israel suggest that the availability of an educated workforce is not enough by itself. The economic incentives facing firms must be such as to compel them to mind the market and to take advantage of the presence of a skilled work force to compete effectively with their rivals.

Another factor that seems to differentiate countries in which firms were effectively innovative from those in which they were not, is the package of fiscal, monetary, and trade policies. Where these combined to make exporting attractive for firms, firms have been drawn to innovate and compete. Where they have made exporting difficult or unattractive, firms have hunkered down in their home markets, and when in trouble called for protection. As I shall indicate later, in some cases at the same time firms were competing abroad, they were working within a rather protected home market, so the argument is not a simple one for "free trade." Rather, it is that export incentives matter significantly because for most countries if firms do not compete on world markets they do not compete strongly. Until recently the United States possibly was an exception to this rule. The U. S. market was large enough to support considerable competition among domestic firms, which kept them on their toes and innovative. No other country could afford the luxury of not forcing their firms to compete on world markets. Now the United States cannot either.

Of course much of the current interest in national systems of innovation reflects a belief that the innovative prowess of national firms is determined to a considerable extent by government policies. Above I have identified two features of the national environment in which firms live that seem to affect their ability and incentives to innovate profoundly, and which are central responsibilities of government in all of the countries in our sample: the education of the work force and the macroeconomic climate. But what of government policies and programs more directly targeted at technological advance? This is where much of the contemporary interest is focused. How effective have these kinds of policies been?

In assessing this question in the light of the 15 country systems studied in this project, one strong impression is the wide range of policies targeted at technological advance. Thus in recent years government policies toward industrial mergers and requisitions, interfirm agreements and joint ventures, and allowable industry-wide activities often have been strongly influenced by beliefs about the effects of such policies on innovative performance. Many countries (and the E. C.) now are encouraging firms to cooperate in R&D of various sorts. Similarly, in recent years a number of governments have worked to restructure or augment financial institutions with the goal of fostering industrial innovation; thus several have tried to establish their analogue to the "venture capital" market that exists in the United States. As suggested, these policies are a very diverse lot and differ from country to country. Our case studies do provide scattered evidence on them, but, simply because they are so diverse, I cannot see any strong generalizations that can be drawn.

Of course our country study authors were primed to look at government programs directly supporting R&D, and here I think the evidence collected is more systematic. It seems useful to distinguish between government programs that largely provide funds for university research or for research in government or other laboratories not tied to particular business firms, and government programs that directly support R&D done in firms. I consider each in turn.

Scholars of innovation now understood that in many sectors, publicly supported research at universities and in public laboratories is an important part of the sectoral innovation system. A substantial share of the funding of such institutions goes into fields directly connected with technological or industrial needs, such as agronomy, pathology, computer science, materials science, and chemical and electrical engineering.

Do our country studies support the proposition that strong research at universities or public laboratories aids a country's firms in innovation, defining that term broadly as we have? Not surprisingly, the answer seems to differ from field to field, and to be sensitive to the mechanisms in place to mold and facilitate interactions with industry. All the countries that are strong and innovative in fine chemicals and pharmaceuticals have strong university research in chemistry and the biomedical sciences. A strong agriculture, and a strong farm product processing industry, is associated in all of our cases with significant research going on relevant to these fields in national universities, or other types of public research institutions dedicated to these industries. In contrast Argentine agriculture is surprisingly weak, despite favorable natural endowments. The authors of the chapter on Argentina lay the blame on Argentina's failure to develop an adequate agricultural research system.

Where countries have strong electronics firms, for the most part there is some strong research in university departments of electrical engineering, and this would appear to include Japan. Government laboratories have been important sources of new designs later taken over by firms in Taiwan. On the other hand, university research does not seem of much importance to technical advance in automobiles and aerospace.

Where universities or public laboratories do seem to be helping national firms, one tends to see either direct interactions between particular firms and particular faculty members or research projects, as through consulting arrangements, or mechanisms that tie university or public laboratory programs to groups of firms. Thus in the United States agricultural experimentation stations do research of relevance to farmers, and seed producers, and have close interactions with them. Various German universities have programs designed to help machinery producers. Taiwan's electronics industry is closely linked to government laboratories. In all of these cases, the relationships between the university or government labs and the industry are not appropriately described as the universities or public laboratories simply doing research of relevance to the industry in question. The connections were much broader and closer than that, involving information dissemination and problem solving. They were co-partners in a technological community. Although not important in all industries, a strong case can be made that such technology and industry-oriented public programs have made a big difference in many fields.

These programs do not cost a great deal, and are far less politically visible than government programs that directly support industrial R&D. Countries differ significantly in the extent to which the government directly funds industrial R&D. And although most of these programs tend to be concentrated on a narrow range of "high-tech" industries, programs of this sort vary significantly and have been put in place for different reasons.

I noted above that in most of our countries, military R&D accounts for the largest portion of government funding of industrial R&D. Analysts have been divided as to whether military R&D and procurement has been a help, or a hinderance, to the commercial competitiveness of national industry. Of the major industrial nations, the United States spends by far the largest share of industrial R&D on military projects. A strong case can be made that in the 1960s this helped the American electronics and aircraft industries to dominate commercial markets, but that since the late 1960s there has been little "spillover." Britain has the second largest defense R&D budget among our set of nations, but most of the companies receiving R&D contracts have shown little capability to crack the nonmilitary markets. The same can be said for most of the French companies. Although until recently civilian commercial spillover seldom has been a central objective of military R&D, except in the sense that it was recognized that selling on civilian markets could reduce the public costs of sustaining a strong military procurement base, it is interesting to try to understand where military R&D did lend civilian market strength and where it did not.

Analysis of the U. S. experience suggests that civilian strength is lent when military R&D programs are opening up a broad new generic technology, as contrasted with focusing virtually exclusively on procuring particular new pieces of fancy hardware wanted by the military. Increasingly, the U. S. military effort has shifted from the former to the latter. A much smaller share of military R&D now goes into research and exploratory development than during the 1960s, and a larger share now goes into highly specialized systems development. And the efforts of the other countries in our set that have invested significantly in military R&D—Britain, France, and Israel—have from the beginning focused largely on the latter.

Space programs and nuclear power programs have much in common with military R&D and procurement. They tend to involve the same kind of government agency leadership in determining what is done. They also tend to be concentrated on large-scale systems developments. Spillover outside the field has been quite limited.

Government programs in support of company R&D in telecommunications, other civilian electronics, and aircraft may overlap the technical fields supported by military and space programs, and in some cases the support may go to the same companies. These programs also tend to involve the same blend of industrial R&D support and protection from foreign competition. However, there are several important differences. One is that compared with military R&D, the public funds almost invariably are much smaller. Indeed programs such as Eureka, Esprit, Jessi, Fifth Generation, and Sematech are small relative to industry funding in the targeted areas. Second, the firms themselves largely determine the way the public monies are spent, and the projects are subject to far less detailed public management and overview than are defense projects. Third, these programs are targeted to firms and products in civilian markets, and although their home base may be protected through import restriction or preferential procurement, the hope is that the firms ultimately will be able to stand on their own.

Thus although they involve a commitment to high R&D spending, these programs have much in common with other "infant industry" protection programs, many of which have grown up for reasons with no connections to national security or a belief in the importance of "high tech," but simply because of the desire of a government to present or create a "national" industry. Infant industry protection, subsidy, and government guidance are policies that have been around for a very long time. They mark French policy since Colbert. During the nineteenth century and through World War II the United States was protectionist. The Japanese and Korean steel and auto industries, which were highly protected up until the 1980s, are more contemporary examples.

Do the infants ever grow up? Some do and some do not. The Japanese auto and electronics companies and the Korean *chaebol*-based enterprises are well-known examples of presently strong firms that grew up in a protected market, but it also should be recognized that the American computer and semiconductor industries grew up with their market shielded from foreign competition and with their R&D funded to a considerable extent by the Department of Defense. After a period of such shelter and support, these firms came to dominate the world's commercial markets. Airbus may or may not be another successful example. On the other hand, the country studies in this project give many examples of protected and subsidized industries that have never got to the stage at which the firms can compete on their own. France's electronics industry is a striking example, but so also are the import-substituting industries of Argentina and Brazil.

What lies behind the differences? If I were to make a bet it is that the differences reside in two things. First, the education and training systems that in some cases did and in others did not provide the protected firms with the strong skills they needed to make it on their own. Second, at least in today's world, the extent to which economic conditions, including government policies, provide strong incentives for the firms to quickly start trying to compete on world markets, as contrasted with hunkering down in their protected enclave.

The picture of government policies supporting industrial innovation that I have been presenting highlights the diversity of such policies and programs, and their generally fragmented nature—some supporting research and other activities aimed to help industry in universities or public labs, others connected with defense or space or nuclear power, and still others aimed directly at supporting or protecting certain industries or industry groups. This is what I conclude from the country studies of this project. These studies play down the existence of active coherent industrial policies more broadly. The interpretation they present of the policies of nations widely believed to have them is closer to that of modern day infant industry protection with some R&D subsidy than to a well-structured and thought through general policy.

Some readers will dispute this conclusion, arguing that the failure of the studies in this project of countries well known to have active coherent industrial policies to highlight them and their successes reflects a serious misjudgment of the authors. And it is fair to say that it is not yet clear whether programs such as Esprit and Jessi will in fact be successful in enabling European companies to become competitive in semiconductors. The authors of those studies respond by arguing that in fact government policies in their countries are highly decentralized, and by pointing, with the case of Airbus an exception, to the very small fraction of industry R&D accounted for by government programs.

The skeptics rejoin that although the policies did not involve massive public monies, they had a lot of leverage on private decisions and investments. The authors respond that government leverage has been exaggerated and that where strong policies have been executed, they as often lead to failure as to success. This clearly is the position taken by our Japanese authors on MITI. Without a better understanding of technological innovation than we now have, there is no way of resolving this debate in a way that will persuade all people.

THE DISPUTE OVER "HIGH-TECH" POLICIES

Above I stressed that the bulk of government R&D support, particularly support of industrial R&D, goes into "high tech," a portion of it through programs expressly designed to lend their firms a commercial edge. Where these latter programs exist, they tend to be complemented by various forms of protection and, sometimes, export subsidy. They are motivated and justified by the argument that if an economy does not have considerable strength in "high tech" it will be disadvantaged relative to countries that do.

But does this seem to be the case? The logic of the case and the evidence supporting it is not strong.

For a firm or industry to be competitive in a high-wage country certainly requires that it make effective use of skills, and technological and managerial sophistication, that are not readily available in low-wage countries. The "high-tech," high-R&D intensity industries are of this sort, but there are many others as well. The definition of "high" tech used by statistical agencies is directly tied to R&D intensity. However, we have stressed that an industry can be characterized by considerable innovation and not have a high R&D intensity. If firms are relatively small, or if there is significant design work aimed at particular customers or market niches, although considerable innovation may be going on, the firms may not report much R&D.

Further, although national programs have tended to focus on areas such as semiconductors, computers, and new materials, where technical advance clearly is dramatic, much of the economic value created by these advances occurs downstream, in the industries and activities that incorporate these new products into their own processes and products—automobiles, industrial machinery, financial services, shipping. To do this effectively often involves significant innovation and creative innovation here may generate major competitive advantage, but not much in the way of large-scale formal R&D may be involved. On the other hand, it can be argued that active government policies often can be more effective when aimed to help an industry take advantage of new upstream technologies than when oriented toward subsidizing major breakthroughs. A large portion of the clearly effective public programs discussed in the various country studies of this project were or are focused on bringing an industry up to world practice (this certainly characterizes many of the successful Japanese programs) or to spread knowledge about new developments (American agriculture and several of the government programs in Germany and Denmark and Sweden).

Of course, the lure of "high tech" to countries that know they must be highly innovative if they are to compete with lower wage countries is not based solely on statistical illusion. The discussion above acknowledges the special place of innovation in semiconductors, computers, new materials, and the like in the contemporary pattern of industrial innovation more broadly. Advances in these fields provide the building blocks, the key opportunities, for technical innovation in a wide range of downstream industries, from high-speed trains to cellular telephones to commercial banking. Many observers noting this have proposed that a nation that wants its firms to be strong over the coming years in the downstream industries had better not let foreign firms control the key upstream technologies. This argument is prevalent in some newly developing countries, such as Brazil, Korea, and Taiwan, as well as today's high-income ones.

Another argument seems to square the circle. It is that a nation needs to have strength in the downstream industries to provide a market for the key component industries. Thus, nations are supporting firms working on high definition T. V., and telecommunications, partly on the argument that without a home market a nation's semiconductor and computer firms will be disadvantaged. Similarly, public support of aerospace is justified partly on alleged stimulation to upstream technology.

The authors of our country studies clearly have different, and perhaps mixed, minds about this matter. There is a certain plaintiveness expressed in the studies of the major European countries that, although doing well in some other areas, national firms are not doing well in these critical "high-tech" fields. The authors of the studies of Australia and Canada, on the other hand, seem to regard electronics envy as silly and expensive fadism.

Although our country studies cannot resolve the issues, they can at least bring attention to three matters that ought to give pause to the zealots. In the first place, there does not seem to be strong empirical support for the proposition that national economies are broadly advantaged if their firms are especially strong in high tech and disadvantaged if they are not. Thus the United States continues to be strong (and a major net exporter) in a wide range of "high-technology" R&D-intensive industries, but its economic growth has been lagging badly for nearly 20 years. Italy has very limited capacity in these industries, but its overall productivity and income levels have been growing briskly for many years. One can argue that France has had broad economic success more despite her efforts to nurture and subsidize her high-technology industries than because of them. Japan is strong in DRAMS, but also in automobile production, which accounts for much more employment and export value, and her efficiency in producing cars seems to have little to do with "high tech." And Canada, Australia, Denmark, and the United States all continue to be strongly competitive in industries based on agriculture or natural resources.

Also, as we have noted, the record of national policies expressly aimed to help high-tech industries through support of industrial R&D is very uneven. Indeed, the strongest positive examples occurred long ago, when the U. S. government provided broad support for advances in electronics and aircraft, and the American edge here has not proved to be durable. The European success with Airbus may or may not be a recent positive example. Other successful cases are largely "infant industry" cases (e.g., Japanese electronics during the 1960s and 1970s, and Korea during the early 1980s) where, as the companies became strong, the active and protective role of government diminished.

And of crucial importance, firms and projects in the aircraft and electronics industries are rapidly becoming transnational. Partly this is because of a need to share very high up-front R&D costs, which can be met by joining with other firms. Traditional intranational rivalries tend to make firms look for foreign partners. And this tendency, of course, is increased to the extent that governments try to keep the products of foreign firms out of domestic markets and to channel subsidy to national firms. Unless the home market is very rich and the subsidies very high, firms have strong incentives to somehow form links with other firms so that they have a chance at other markets.

Today, there probably is no other matter that so forces one to step back, and consider the contemporary meaning of a "national innovation system." To what extent are there really "innovation systems," and to the extent that there are, in what ways are they defined by nation states?

WHAT REMAINS NATIONAL ABOUT INNOVATION SYSTEMS?

There obviously are a number of difficulties with the concept of a "national innovation system." In the first place, unless one defines innovation very narrowly and cuts the institutional fabric to that narrow definition, and we did neither, it is inevitable that analysis of innovation in a country sometimes would get drawn into discussion of labor markets, financial systems, monetary fiscal and trade policies, and so on. One cannot draw a line neatly around those aspects of a nation's institutional structure that are concerned predominantly with innovation in a narrow sense excluding everything else, and still tell a coherent story about innovation in a broad sense. Nonetheless, most of our authors were able to tell a pretty coherent story about innovation in their country focusing largely on institutions and mechanisms that fit the narrow definition, with discussion of country institutions more broadly serving largely as a frame.

Second, the term suggests much more uniformity and connectedness within a nation than is the case. Thus, one can discuss Canadian agriculture pretty independently of Canadian telecommunications. R&D and innovation in the American pharmaceutical industry and R&D of aircraft by American companies have little in common. And yet, one cannot read the studies of Japan, Germany, France, Korea, Argentina, and Israel, to name just a few, without coming away with the strong feeling that nationhood matters and has a persuasive influence. In all these cases, a distinctive national character pervades the firms, the educational system, the law, the politics, and the government, all of which have been shaped by a shared historical experience and culture.

I believe that most of us would square these somewhat divergent observations as follows. In the spirit of the discussion above, if one focuses narrowly on what we have defined as "innovation systems" these tend to be sectorally specific. But if one broadens the focus the factors that make for commonality within a country come strongly into view, and these largely define the factors that make for commonality across sectors within a country.

And from the start of this project we recognized that borders around nations are porous, and increasingly so. Indeed, one of the questions that motivated this study was whether the concept of *national* innovation systems made sense anymore. I suspect that many of us come out on this as follows.

It is safe to say that there will be increasing internationalization of these aspects of technology that are reasonably well understood scientifically. Efforts on the part of nations, and firms, to keep new understandings won in research and development privy increasingly will be futile. Among firms with the requisite scientific and technical people, the competitive edge will depend on the details of design, production process, firm strategy and organization, upstream–downstream connections, and so on. Today, this is quite clearly the case in fields such as semiconductors, aircraft, computers, and automobiles. In these fields, there are no broad technological secrets possessed by individual countries or particular firms. On the other hand, strong firms have a good deal of firm specific know-how and capability.

It is also safe to say that differences across firms stamped into them by national policies, histories, and cultures will diminish in importance. Partly that will be because the world is becoming much more unified culturally, for better or for worse. Partly it will be because firm managers and scholars of management increasingly are paying attention to how firms in other countries are organized and managed. And cross-country interfirm connections are likely to grow in importance. Firms in industries where there are large up front R&D design and production engineering costs increasingly are forging alliances with firms in other countries, to share some of the costs, and to get over government-made market barriers. The establishment of branch plants in protected countries or regions is another mechanism. Thus, increasingly, the attempts of national governments to define and support a national industry will be frustrated because of internationalization.

What will remain of "national systems"? The firms that reside in the country will remain, but people and governments will have to get used to dealing with plants whose headquarters are abroad. The countries of Europe have been struggling with this matter for some time, and many of the Latin American countries, too. The United States is now having to try to deal with this, and Japan and Korea are beginning to. As yet, no large country seems to have made its peace with the problem, however. Although in most countries, resident firms will be largely national, the presence of "foreign" firms in important industries is something that nations will have to learn to cope with better.

We noted earlier the striking continuity of a nation's basic institutions bearing on industrial innovation. A good example is national education systems, which sometimes seem never to change in their basics. Although top level scientists and engineers may be highly mobile, and some high level students will continue to take training abroad, below the Ph.D. level, by and large, countries will be stuck with their nationals who are trained at home.

The nations system of university research and public laboratories will continue to be, largely, national, particularly the programs that are specifically keyed to advancing technology or otherwise facilitating technical progress in industry, and with built in mechanisms for interacting with industry. These programs will have to work with foreign branch firms as well as domestic ones in certain fields. But the notion that universities and public laboratories basically provide "public goods" and that therefore there are no advantages to firms that have close formal links simply does not fit the facts in many industries.

The nation's other public infrastructure, and laws, its financial institutions, its fiscal monetary and trade policies, and its general economic ambiance still will be a major influence on economic activity, including innovating, and these are very durable. For large high-income countries at least, the majority of private investment will continue to be domestic, and constrained by domestic savings. And nations will continue to have their own distinctive views of the appropriate relationships between government and business.

And these will strongly influence a nation's policies bearing explicitly on science and technology. From the evidence in this study, these must be understood as an agglomeration of policies directed toward different national objectives, each with a somewhat special domain in terms of the fields and the institutions most affected, rather than as a coherent package.

All can hope that there will be a significant diminution of defense programs, but military R&D will probably continue to account for most government industrial R&D spending in the United States, France, Britain, and Israel. It is likely, however, that there will be little commercial "spillover."

Outside of defense and space, a nation's programs of R&D support will in all likelihood continue to reflect both the needs of industry and broad attitudes toward what government should be doing and how. Although there will be exceptions, particularly when a defense connection is argued, the United States will continue to resist programs that directly fund industrial R&D, but will use the universities as the base for a variety of programs including some directly targeted at certain technologies and industries. European countries are likely to make much more use of programs that directly support civil industrial R&D, either in individual firms, or in industry wide research organizations. And in Japan, France, and various other countries, government agencies and high-tech firms will continue to be quite close.

THE DIVERSITY OF NATIONAL SYSTEMS: DO WE NEED SOME STANDARDS REGARDING WHAT IS FAIR?

At present nations seem to be conscious as never before of their "innovation systems" and how they differ from those of their peers. This consciousness of differences is leading in two very different directions.

On the one hand, it is leading to attempts on the part of nations to adopt aspects of other systems that they see as lending them strength. However, the experimentation is far from systematic, and it is highly influenced by perceptions that may have little contact with reality. Thus the United States and the European countries (and the E. C.) have been loosening laws that restrict interfirm R&D cooperation, and establishing programs to encourage and subsidize it in some areas. If the chapter on Japan has got it right, this may be somewhat ironic in view of the argument that the role in Japan's rapid postwar growth of cooperative R&D among firms in the same line of business probably has been exaggerated, and in any case is diminishing.

The LDCs are looking, with good reason, to Korea and Taiwan for models. But aside from their strong support of education, high levels of investment in plant and equipment, and their pressure on firms to go for exports, these two countries have quite different innovation systems. In one, Taiwan, government research laboratories have been an important source of industrial technology; in the other, Korea, apparently they have not, at least until recently. Korea has encouraged the growth of large industrial conglomerates, and resisted foreign ownership; Taiwan has not especially encouraged the growth of large firms and has admitted foreign firms selectively. But both have been successful in building innovative competitive manufacturing industry based on foreign created technologies and other low income countries are trying to learn from their experience.

Although today attempts at emulation are at a peak, they are nothing new. The study of Japan shows how earlier in the century the Japanese tried to pick and choose from European and American experience, and came out with something quite different. The Americans earlier tried to adopt the German university system, and actually built a very different one.

At the same time, perceptions of differences are leading nations to declare certain aspects of their rival's systems as illegitimate. Prominent Americans have expressed the opinion that MITI support and guidance of key Japanese industries, together with the special connections between Japanese firms and their customers and their sources of finance, amount to an unfair system, involving subsidy and dumping as well as protection. Similar complaints have been lodged against Eureka and Airbus. The Europeans complain about Japan, and about U. S. programs such as the SDI, claiming that such large-scale government R&D support, although aimed at a military target, is sure to build commercial advantages, and that that requires response on their part. The Japanese make similar complaints, but particularly about the import barriers being imposed by other countries. Some have gone so far as to argue that presently there is a war between competing national innovation systems that can be resolved only if there are new accepted standards regarding what is fair and what is not (see, e.g., Ostry, 1990). Otherwise, nations will have to adopt the norm of managed trade in high-technology products.

These two aspects of the current concern about differences in national innovation systems—attempts at emulation and expressions of hostility—are opposite sides of the same coin. They reflect a combination of beliefs that a nations performance in "high tech" is vital to its broader economic performance and security, real uncertainty regarding just how to achieve high performance, and lack of agreed on criteria for judging what are legitimate and illegitimate government policies.

In my view, which may not be shared by all of my colleagues, the current argument seems somewhat hysterical. There is no more reason to get upset over inter-country differences in the government's role in industrial innovation than there is to complain about many other areas where the government's role in economic activity differs across nations. For one thing, governments' anguish that their economies are fated to be surely disadvantaged if they do not have a "high-tech" industry of their own probably is unwarranted. For another, beliefs that strength in high-tech is due largely to promotional government policies seem grossly exaggerated.

At the same time, the studies in this project show that the institutional structures supporting technical innovation are complex and variegated. Technology and science interact in complex ways. Both private for profit and public institutions play roles in virtually all arenas of technological advance and the efficient division of labor is not obvious. Arguments that private enterprise does industrial innovation and that public institutions have little useful role in it are simple minded.

In this area it is not totally clear what one should call subsidy or protection, as contrasted with legitimate public spending or coordination or regulation.

Economists tend to draw the line in terms of whether government spending or regulation or guidance can be justified by market failure arguments. If so, although public action may give advantage to a particular national industry, such support can be argued to increase economic efficiency. If not, it is considered naked subsidy or protection, and is not to be condoned. Thus, although international trade theorists have long known that a nation could enhance the well-being of its own citizens vis-à-vis those in other countries by selected naked subsidy or protection, the argument was that under the theory then in vogue, for nations taken as a group, this was a negative sum game.

But the problem with this line of argument is that "market failure" is ubiquitous in the activities associated with industrial innovation, and thus subsidy or protection or guidance could be efficiency enhancing; hence the game of active industrial policy need not be negative sum. What has come to be called "the new trade theory" recognizes some of this, nervously. If there are large "up front" R&D costs, or significant learning through doing or using, or major externalities in certain activities such as research and training, the simple arguments that free trade is "Pareto Optimal" (in the parlance of economists) falls apart.

Of course "market failure" is greater in certain activities than in others. Also, government competence and incentives are more likely to lead to productive programs in certain arenas than in others. Further, it is apparent that competitive protection and subsidy among nations can get beyond any level conceivably justified on grounds of "efficiency." It is in the interest of all nations to reign in such tendencies.

However, it seems unlikely that simple rules—for example, that government support of R&D on public sector needs and for "basic" research is efficient and fair and direct support of industrial R&D aimed to develop products for a civilian market is both inefficient and unfair—will carry the discussion very far. This argument certainly can be used to attack Airbus. But Europeans rejoin that government help was needed to overcome the huge headstart American companies had won in large part as a spillover from military R&D, and can be justified economically both on infant industry grounds, and as a policy to avoid the development of a one company world monopoly. And what of government support for telecommunications R&D where telecommunications is a government service? Americans are prone to argue that telecommunications should be privatized, but there surely is limited agreement on that. And what to one eye is blockage to competition in public procurement to another is a valuable close relationship between customer and supplier.

Nor are there clean lines separating "basic" from applied research. No one seems to object to government support for research on the causes of cancer (although a breakthrough here may give the firms with close contact with the research a major advantage in coming up with a proprietary product). But what about research to advance agricultural productivity? To deal improve crops growing in a particular national soil and climate? Research on superconductivity, or on surface phenomena in semiconductors, conducted in universities? Conducted in an industry-cooperative research organization? In a particular firm?

The argument about whether government funding of certain kinds of R&D is appropriate and efficient or unfair subsidy of course gets intertwined with arguments about protection, and about constraints in direct foreign investments. Here countries clearly disagree regarding what they regard as appropriate. The disagreements can be discussed, and agreements negotiated. However, it does not seem to me that the question of whether a protected industry is "high-tech" changes the nature of the discussion, or the stakes, that much.

All this is no argument against trying to establish some norms and rules regarding government policies bearing on industrial innovation, and in certain areas aiming for uniform or at least comparable policies. However, it is an argument against one nation or another getting self-righteous that its ways are efficient, fair, and quite justified, and the policies of other nations are not. And it is an argument against the belief that agreeing on ground rules will be simple, if only the advice of economists is heeded.

And finally, it is an argument against trying to impose too much uniformity. Countries differ in their traditions, ideologies, and beliefs about appropriate roles for government, and they will guard the differences they think matter. A central reason why this project was undertaken was, by expanding the set of countries considered, and by trying to enable comparisons where these seemed most interesting, to try to determine what features of national systems seemed systematically to enhance innovation performance, and what features seemed useless or worse. My colleagues and I like to believe that we have learned a good deal. But there still is a lot of room for informed differences of opinion. Given that there is, it is not appropriate for our group or another to argue for its preferred uniformity. We still can learn from observing diversity closely. Although (as this project testifies) it is not easy to differentiate signal from noise, potentially we all can learn from each other about what seems to be effective and what is not.

REFERENCES

Dosi, G., Freeman, C., Nelson, R., Silverberg, G., and Soete, L. (1988). *Technical Change and Economic Theory.* London: Pinter Publishers.

Gerschenkron, A. (1962). *Economic Development in Historical Perspectives.* Cambridge: Harvard University Press.

Lundvall, B. A. (1988). "Innovation as an Interactive Process: From User-Producer Interaction to the National System of Innovation." In G. Dosi, C. Freeman, R. Nelson, G. Silverberg, and L. Soete (eds.), *Technical Change and Economic Theory.* London: Pinter Publishers.

Ostry, S. (1990). *Governments and Corporations in a Shrinking World.* New York: Council on Foreign Relations Press.

Porter, M. (1990). *The Competitive Advantage of Nations.* New York: The Free Press.

Index

ABB, 284
Academia Sinica (Taiwan), 402
Académie Royale des Sciences (France), 194
Acer group, 399, 404
Act on the Mining and Manufacturing Industry
    Technology Research Association, 87
Adams Act (1906), 37
Advanced Micron Devices, 377
AECL, 306
AEG, 129, 143
Aerodynamics, 7
Aeronautical engineering, 7
Aeronautics industry, Canada, 318
Aronautics technology
    Brazil, 437, 442
    U.S., 35
Aerospace industry, Great Britain, 167
Aérospatiale, 218
Aerospace technology, Brazil, 418, 437
Agrarian reform, France, 196
Agricultural cooperatives, Denmark, 270, 276
Agricultural extension agencies/activities
    Argentina, 468–69
    U.S., 37, 52
Agricultural industry
    Argentina, 462–65, 471
    Denmark's agroindustrial complex, 269–70,
        284, 288
    Great Britain, 161
Agricultural research
    Argentina, 465, 468–69
    Brazil, 416
    Israel, 478–79
    U.S., 36–38, 51–52
Agricultural research stations/farms, 12
    Argentina, 468
    Brazil, 416
    Canada, 319
    Israel, 478–79
    U.S., 37

Agrotechnology, Brazil, 437, 443–44
Airbus, 59, 145, 201
Aircraft design
    cumulative, incremental, 8–9
    scientific development and, 7
Aircraft industry
    France, 201
    Germany, 145
    Korea, 379
    technical advance in, 13, 14
Alberta Oil Sands Technology Research Agency
        (AOSTRA), 311, 317
Alcatel NV, 220
Alfa Laval, 271
Aluminum-smelting industry, Japan, 89
Alvey Project, 173, 184
"American system of manufactures," 31
Antitrust legislation, U.S., 29, 32, 34
    start-up firms and, 49
    technological development and, 62–63
ANVAR, 205, 211
Applied Research Fund (Italy), 253
Apprenticeships
    Germany, 121
    Great Britain, 180
Argentina, 451–73
    agricultural industry, 462–65, 471
        farm mechanization, 464–65
    arms exports, 469
    automobile industry, 455, 457, 459
    deregulation and economic liberalization,
        458–61
    economic characteristics, international
        comparisons, 355–56
    foreign direct investment, 457, 460
    foreign trade, 463, 464
    history and present innovation status, 451–52
    industrialization process, 453–61
        multinationals and, 454–58, 459, 463, 465
        restructuring, 458–60

Argentina *(continued)*
  labor market, 459
    productivity in, 456
  manufacturing industries, 455–57, 470–71
  R & D activities, 460–61
    agricultural research, 465
    defense R & D, 469–70
    government-supported, 465–70, 471
    industrial research, 456, 470–71
    university research, 469
  technology transfer, 467
Arianspace, 201, 204
Arms industry/exports
  Argentina and Brazil, 469
  France, 215–16
  Israel, 486, 487–90
ASEA, 271
ASEA-ATOM, 281
ASICs, Taiwan, 398
Assistance Program for Strategic Industries
    (APSI) (Taiwan), 395
Association of German Engineers, 131
Association of the Beet Sugar Industry
    (Germany), 126
Atomic Energy Commission (CNEA)
    (Argentina), 467–68
ATT, 32
Australia, 263, 324–49
  Civil Offsets Program, 341
  "colonial socialism" in, 324
  economic characteristics, 324–25
  education system, 342–45
    higher education, 342–44
  employment population changes (1983–90),
    348
  foreign debt, effects of, 334–35, 345–48
  foreign trade, 329–30, 332, 333, 334
  government assistance to industries, 335–36
    150% R & D allowance, 336
  government technology procurement, 340–42
  immigration policy since 1945, 332
  international economic and R & D
    comparisons, 264
  manufacturing industries, 329–35
  multinationals in, 339
  on-the-job training, 345
  Partnerships for Development, 341–42
  R & D expenditures, 325–31
    government, 327–29, 331
    private sector, 329–31
  research centers, 345
  rural R & D, 327–29
  tariff protection, 335
Auto Pact (1965) (Canada), 301, 308
Automobile industry
  Argentina, 455, 457, 459
  Australia, 336, 337

Canada, 301, 307–08
Germany, 129, 131
Great Britain, 168–70
Japan, 97–101
Korea, 365
Avro Arrow inteceptor program (Canada),
  303

Bandeirante turboprop, 442
Banks and banking
  France, 196
  role in British industry, 181–82
BASF, 138
Basic research. *See also* Scientific research
  applied research *vs.,* value in innovation
    systems, 522
  British expenditures, 172–73
  Canada, 305
  Israel, 478
  Japan, 110–11
  Korea, 370, 371–72
  U.S., 42
Basic Research Promotion Law (Korea), 372
Bayer, 126, 138, 139
BCE, 305–06
Beecham, 167
Beet-sugar industry, Germany, 125–26
Belgium, German technological development
    and, 116–17
Bell Canada, 313, 315, 318
Bell Northern Research, 318
Benetton, 241
Bercovich, Nestor A., "National Systems of
    Innovation Supporting Technical
    Advance in Industry: The Case of
    Argentina," 451–73
Berlin Technical Institute, 120
Berlin University, 118
Biotechnology
  Denmark, 288
  U.S.
    postwar development, 49
    start-up firms and, 57
    university/industry research cooperation,
      54
Boeing, 14, 379
"Brain-drain," in Taiwan, 393–94
Brazil, 414–46
  aeronautics research, 442
  capital goods importation, 432
  economic characteristics, 414–15
    international comparisons, 355–56
  education system, 439–42
    higher education, 441–42
  foreign direct investment, 432–34
  history of industrialization, 416–30
  industrial research, 419, 425–28, 442–45

"informatics" industries, 433–34
international competitiveness, 420–23
local technology development incentives
 (FINEP programs), 434
manufacturing industries, 421–28
military R & D, 418
Ministry of Science and Technology (MCT),
 434–35
multinationals in, 427
national agricultural research program, 443–
 44
National Development Plans, 418
piston-manufacturing industry, 443
R & D expenditures, 437–39
science & technology research development,
 417–20
 institutions, 417, 434–37
 technology policies, 428–34
 technology transfer, 429–32
Breguet, 200
"Bridging" institutions, 180
British Aerospace, 167
British Petroleum (BP), 161
Bull Machine Company, 204
Business schools, Germany, 121

CAD systems, diffusion in Sweden and
 Denmark, 284–85
CAE industries, 318
Canada, 263, 299–321
 aeronautics industry, 318
 automobile industry, 301
 chemicals industry, 317
 economic characteristics, 300–04
 education system, 301
 higher education, 301
 electric power complex, 316
 energy industry, 310
 forestry industry, 313, 316–17
 high-technology entrepreneurship (Ottawa),
 314–15
 hydroelectric development, 313
 information technology industry, 318–19
 innovation failures, 303
 innovation linkages, 299–300, 309–19
 user-supplier relationships, 312–14
 international economic and R & D
 comparisons, 264
 international linkages, 300
 logging-equipment industry, 312
 manufacturing industries, 300–01, 309
 metallurgy complex, 316
 natural resources industries, 300
 petroleum industry, 311, 317
 pulp and paper industry
 machinery, 312
 wood innovation cluster, 316

R & D activities, 302–03
 agricultural experimental stations, 319
 government funding, 304–05, 311
 industrial research, 303, 305–08, 310–11
 military R & D, 311
 provincial research councils, 304–05
 university research, 305
 relationship with U.S. economy, 301, 307–09
 research organizations, 309–11
 Electrical Association, 310
 Gas Research Institute, 310
 Steel Industry Research Association, 310
 steel industry, 310–11
 technology diffusion, 308–09
 telecommunications industry, 318, 320
 U.S. patents, 303, 306–07, 317
Canadair, 318
CANDU nuclear reactor, 303, 306
Capital-goods industry, France, 224
Cement industry, Denmark, 277
CGE-Alcatel, 219
CGE/Alsthom, 216, 217
Chaebols, 362–63, 366–68, 375–80
Chemical engineering, 7
Chemicals industry
 Australia, 336, 337
 Canada, 317
 Germany, 126, 131
 Great Britain, 167
 Korea, 365–66
 scientific development and, 6
 technical advance in, 14
 U.S., 33
Chemistry, polymer, development of, 7
Chesnais, Francois, "The French National
 System of Innovation," 192–226
Chung-Shan Science Colleague, 406
CITEFA, 469
CNES, 218–19
CNET, 219
CNRS, 192, 202–03, 210
COGEMA, 217
Combustion engine, 129
Commissariat à l'Energie (CEA), 202, 216–18
Committee for German Industry Norms (DIN),
 131
Committee for Space Research (France), 203
Commodities industries. See also Foodstuffs/
 food-processing industries; Petroleum
 and oil industries
 technical advance in, 14–15
Commonwealth Scientific and Industrial
 Research Organization (CSIRO)
 (Australia), 327–28, 331
Communication-equipment industry. See also
 Telecommunications industry
 Japan, 95–97

Computer industry
  Brazil, 433
  Canada, 318–19
  Great Britain, 168
  Korea, 379
  postwar U.S. development, 49
Computer Numerical Control (CNC)
  machinery, diffusion in Sweden and
  Denmark, 284–85
Computer technology/software development
  France, 204
  Korean *chaebol* activities, 375–77
  Taiwan, 400–01
Computing Devices of Canada, 315
Concorde, 201
Construction industry, Denmark, 277
Cooperative research. *See* Research
  collaboration
Cooperative Research Centre Scheme
  (Australia), 345
Corporatism
  Denmark, 275
  Great Britain, 182
  Sweden, 273
Council of Scientific and Industrial Research
  (CSIR) (Australia), 328
Counterpoint Computers, 404
CPqD, 436–37
Craftsmenship, Great Britain, 179–80
Cream separator, development of, 269
CRITTs, 211

Daeduck Science Town, 380–81
Daewoo, 375, 376, 377, 378, 379
Dahlman, Carl J., "National Systems
  Supporting Technical Advance in
  Industry: The Brazilian Experience,"
  414–46
Daihatsu, 98, 100
Daimler-Benz, 138, 145
Dairy industry, Denmark, 269–70, 276–77
Data-processing development. *See also*
  Computer industry
  France, 204
"Datsun," 98, 100
Defence Industry Productivity Program
  (Canada), 311
Defense electronics
  Great Britain, 167
Defense industry, France, 215–16
Defense Production Act (U.S.), 46
Defense R & D. *See* Military R & D
DeHavilland, 318
Denmark, 265–92
  agroindustrial complex, 269–70, 284, 288
  development blocks, 276–77

economic concentration and multinational
  capital, 266–67
employment rates, 273, 283
food/drink/tobacco industries, 279
foreign trade, 270
industrialization, 269–70
international economic and R & D
  comparisons, 264
labor market, 273
lack of innovation coordination, 290–91
macroeconomic performance, 282–83
manufacturing industries, 279
process of technical change, 275
production system, 275
small firms in, 289
socio-political aspects, 272–75
structural problems in the economy, 288–89
Sweden and, comparisons, 265–69
technological contributions, 283–84
Technology Development Programme, 280
technology diffusion, 285–87
technology policy, 280–82
U.S. patents, 266, 283
Design, in process of technical advance, 8
Deutsche Forschungsgeneinschaft, 132, 133,
  141
Development blocks
  definition, 275–76
  Sweden and Denmark, 275–78
Digital Equipment Corporation (DEC)
  in Canada, 318
  in Great Britain, 164
Direct foreign investment (DFI). *See* Foreign
  investment
Direction Générale des Télécommunications
  (DGT), 219
Directorate for Military Research and Testing
  (DRME) (France), 204
Délégation Générale à l'Armament (DGA)
  (France), 214, 215–16
DMR, 318
DRAM technology
  Korea, 377
  Taiwan, 398–400
Du Pont, 32, 50, 62
Dwoty and Smiths Industries, 167
DYNA, 404

Eastman Kodak, 32, 50
Ecole Normale Supérieure, 198
Ecole Polytechique, 198, 213
Edison effect, 8
Edquist, Charles, "Comparing the Danish and
  Swedish Systems of Innovation," 265–92
Education systems. *See also* Engineering
  education/training
  Australia, 342–45

Brazil, 439–42
Canada, 301
  competitive innovation systems and, 511
France, 197–99
Germany, 147
  19th cent., 117–23
  current status, 139–41
Great Britain, 178–80
international comparisons, 140, 440
Japan, 78–80
Korea, 358–59
Taiwan, 385, 392–94
U.S., 48
Electric power complex, in Canada, 316
Electric Research Institution (Japan), 83
Electrical-equipment industries
  Australia, 336, 337
  Japan, 93–95
  scientific development and, 6
Electronic Research and Service Organization
    (ERSO), 397
Electronics industry. See also Microelectronics
    industry
  Brazil, 433
  Denmark, 277, 288
  Great Britain, 168, 174, 175–76
  Italy, 256–57
  Korea, 365, 374, 378
  Scotland, 187
  Taiwan, 397–400
Electronics switching system (ESS),
    development in Korea, 374, 378
Electronuclear industry, France, 216–18
Electrotechnical industry, Germany, 127–28,
    131
Embraer, 442
EMBRAPA, 437, 443–44
Emergency Association of German Science,
    131–32
Employment, long-term, in Japan, 106, 107
Encyclopedia, 194, 198
ENEA, 254
Energy industries
  Canadian research institutes, 310
  Great Britain, 161
  Japan, 88–89
Engineering design, technical advance and, 8
Engineering education/training
  France, 197–98, 211, 213–14
  Germany, 119–21, 123
  Great Britain, 178–79
  Japan, 79–80
  Taiwan, 393
  U.S., 36
Engineering industries
  Denmark, 277, 284–86
  Sweden, 271, 277–78, 284, 289–90

"Enterprise," concept in Great Britain, 184–85
Entrepreneurship
  Canada, 314–15
  Great Britain, 185
  Japan, 98, 101–02
  Israel, 495
Equipment-manufacturing industry, Italy, 237–
    39. See also Electrical-equipment
    industry
Ericsson, 271
ESPRIT, 254
EUCLID, 186
European Community
  British research cooperation and, 174
  defense R & D program (EUCLID), 186
  German exports and, 136
  innovation, Germany, and, 147
  Single European Act, 188
European Space Agency, 201, 204, 255
European system of innovation, 16
Export/import performance
  Argentina, 455, 456–57, 459, 463, 464, 469
  Australia, 329, 332, 333, 334
  Brazil, 422–24, 425, 426–27
  British (1978–88), 164–65
  Denmark, 270
  France, 222, 224–26
  Germany, 115, 128, 129–30, 133–37
  large, high-income countries, 25
  promotion in Korea, 363
  Sweden, 271–72, 278
Exxon, Canadian innovation system and, 318

Fair Trade Act (Korea), 367
Farm mechanization, Argentina, 464–65
Farman, 200
Federal Ministry for Research and Technology
    (Germany), 142, 143, 146
Federally funded research and development
    centers (FFRDCs), 42, 47
FIAT, 249
Fibers Institute (Italy), 478, 490
Filter technology, Denmark, 283
FINAME, 419
FINEP, 419, 435
Firms. See Industrial research; Large firms;
    Multinationals; Small firms; Small- and
    medium-sized firms (SMEs)
Flexible manufacturing systems (FMS),
    diffusion in Sweden and Denmark, 284–
    85
Foodstuffs/food-processing industries
  Argentina, 453
  Denmark, 276–77, 279, 288
  Great Britain, 161, 168
Ford Company
  British auto industry and, 168

Ford Company *(continued)*
  German factory, 131
  Japanese auto industry and, 97, 99
Fordism, U.S., 31
Foreign investment/foreign direct investment
    (FDI)
  Argentina, 457, 460
  Brazil, 417, 432
  Great Britain, 168–70, 174–75
  Japan, 86, 102
  Korea, 360–62
  Sweden and Denmark, 266–67
  Taiwan, 388–91, 405–06
Foreign licensing (FL), Korea, 360, 365
Foreign trade. *See also* Export/import
    performance
  Argentina, 454, 463, 464
  Australia, 329–30, 332, 333, 334
  competitive innovation systems and, 511–12
  Denmark, 270
  France, 222, 224–26
  Germany (1913), 128, 129–30, 133–37
  Great Britain, 164–65, 168–70
  Sweden, 271–72
  technological competitiveness and, 60–61
Forestry industry
  Canada, 313, 316–17
Framatome, 216, 217
France, 192–226
  aeronautics industry, 199–200
  automobile industry, 199–200
  data-processing industry, 204
  defense industry, 215–16
  financial system development, 196
  foreign trade performance, 222, 224–26
  government's role in technological
      development, 192–93
  "Grandes Ecoles," 197, 198, 211, 213–14
  high-technology sector, 214–20
  higher education, 197–98
  industrialization & economic development,
      195–96, 200–01
  large firms (nationalized enterprises) in, 193
  military-industrial complex development, 204
  R & D structure, 205–11
    government funding, 206–08
    industrial research, 208–09
    military R & D, 203–04, 215–16
    research laboratories, 13, 205
    science & technology institution building,
        201–03
    scientific research, 194–95
    university research, 198–99, 210–11
  revealed technological advantage (RTA), 221
  space industry, 218–19
  state/industry alliance, 212–13
  technology information dissemination, 211

  telecommunications industry, 219–20
  U.S. patents, 221–22, 223
  vital statistics, 25–27
France Telecom, 219, 220
"Free market," in Great Britain, 182, 183
Frischtak, Claudio R., "National Systems
    Supporting Technical Advance in
    Industry: The Brazilian Experience,"
    414–46
Fuji Electric, 94
FUNTEC, 419
Furukawa Mine, 94

Gakushin, 84
GEC, 163, 167
Gee, San, "National Systems Supporting
    Technical Advance in Industry: The Case
    of Taiwan," 384–412
General Electric, 32, 50
  Japanese electrical equipment industry and,
      94–95
General Motors (GM)
  British auto industry and, 168
  Japanese auto industry and, 97, 99
Germany, 115–47
  Airbus program, 145
  beet-sugar industry, 125–26
  education system, 139–41
    university system, 117–20, 140–41, 147
    vocational training, 139–40
  engineering profession in, 179
  European Community and, 136
  Federal Ministry for Research and
      Technology, 142, 143, 146
  foreign trade, 128, 129–30
    export performance, 115, 133–37
  future of innovation system, 146
  government funding of research, 137, 138,
      141, 142–45
  government laboratories in, 13
  history of industrialization, 116–33
  industrial research
    19th century, 125–29
    20th century, 124, 131–33, 138–39
  Japanese industry and trade, effects, 137
  military R & D, 132
  research organizations, 123–24, 131–32
  science parks, 145
  technology policy, 142–45
  U.S. patents (1975–85), 137, 139
  university research in, 12
  vital statistics, 25–27
G.I. Bill (U.S.), 48
Glass & rubber industries, U.S., 33, 34
Glaxo, 167
Globalization (concept), 63
  Japan and, 110

Goto, Akira, "The Japanese System of Innovation: Past, Present, and Future," 76–111
Gottingen University, 117
Government funding/support. *See also* Military funding
    Argentine R & D, 465–70, 471
    Australian R & D, 327–29, 331, 335–40, 345
    Brazilian R & D, 434–39
    British R & D, 172–74, 182–87
    Canadian R & D, 304, 311
    Danish R & D, 280
    French R & D, 206–08, 212–13
    Germany
        higher education and science, 124–25
        R & D, 117, 137, 138, 141, 142–45
        specialized research organizations, 123–24
        universities (19th cent.), 119
    Israeli industrial research, 487–90
    Italy
        R & D, 244
        small-firm networks, 241–42
    Japan
        auto industry, 100–101
        electrical & communication equipment industries, 96
        industrial plants in Meiji, 80
        industrial research, 87–89
    Korea
        education system, 358
        R & D, 370–74
    R & D, fairness questions, 522–23
    Swedish R & D, 279
    Taiwanese industrial R & D, 391–92, 394–400, 402–03
    U.S. R & D, 30
        agricultural research, 37, 51–52
        during World War II, 39–40
        postwar, 40–48
        prior to 1945, 34–36
        university research, 47–48
Government policies, for technology development
    Australian high-technology, 345–48
    effects of, 512–15
    Italy, 251–55
    Japan's industrial development, 103
    U.S., 58–61
Government research laboratories, 12–13
    Germany, 144
Government's role, in national innovation systems, 508, 512–13
GTP, 168
"Grandes Ecoles," 197, 199, 211, 213–14
    Ecole Polytechnique, 198, 213
    technical experts, 192
Grands corps, 213, 214, 218

Grants for Industrial Research and Development Scheme (GIRD) (Australia), 336
Great Britain, 158–89
    Advisory Committee on Science and Technology (ACOST), 184
    agricultural sector, 161
    coordination problems, 180–82
    craftsmen and apprenticeships in, 179–80
    economic decline, 158–60
    economic performance (1980s), 160
    economic structure, 160–65
    education system, 178–80
        higher education, 178–79
    electronics industry, 174, 175–76
    engineering profession in, 179
    "enterprise" concept in, 184–85, 186
    European Community and, 188
    foodstuffs industry, 161
    foreign investment (multinationals), 164, 166, 168–70, 174–75, 176, 188
    foreign trade, 164–65, 168–169
    "free market" in, 182, 183
    German technological development and, 116–17
    high-technology industries, 165–66
    innovation system weaknesses, 176–82
    "Levene" reforms, 177
    manufacturing industries, 163, 165–70
    petroleum industry, 161
    political structure, 182
    R & D activities
        government funding, 172–74, 183–87
        industrial research, 170–72, 174–75
        military R & D, 172–73, 177–78
        university research, 12
    R & D expenditures (1970s; 1980s), 172–76
    regional development agencies, 186
    revealed technological advantage (RTA) (1978–86; 1988), 168–69, 176
    science parks, 186–87
    service industries, 162–64
    U.S. patents, 175
    vital statistics, 25–27
Gregory, Robert G., "The Australian Innovation System," 324–39
Gross national expenditures and production
    Denmark and Sweden, 282–83
    Japan (1875–1940), 82
Gruppo Finanziario Tessile (GFT), 241

Hakunetsusha, 93, 94
Halle University, 117
Hatch Act (1887), 37
Heavy industries
    Brazil, 417–18
    Japan, 84

Heavy oil extraction, Canada, 311, 317
Hebrew University, 479
High-definition television (HDTV), U.S.
   initiatives, 59
High-technology sector/industries
   Australia, 345–48
   France, 214–20
   Great Britain, 165–66
   Israel, 479–82, 491–92
   Japan, 89
   Korea, 375–79
   national innovation systems and, 515–17, 521
   U.S. development, 49
High-temperature superconductivity (HTS), 58
Higher education. See also University research
   Australia, 342–43
   Brazil, 441–42
   Canada, 301
   France, 197–99
   Germany, 147
      19th century, 117–19, 124–25
      business schools, 121
      current system, 140–41
   Great Britain, 178–79
   Japan, 79
   Taiwan, 392, 393
   U.S., 35–36, 48
Hino, 100
Hitachi, 94, 95
Hoechst, 138, 139
Honda, 100
Hou, Chi-ming, "National Systems Supporting
   Technical Advance in Industry: The Case
   of Taiwan," 384–412
Hsinchu Science-based Industrial Park, 405
Human resources development. See Education
   systems
Hydro-Quebec, 313
Hydroelectric development, Canada, 313
Hyundai, 375, 376, 377, 378

IBM, 14
   Canada, 306, 318
   Great Britain, 164
   PC clones, Korea and, 379
   Taiwan, 400–01
IC chip technology, Taiwan, 397–400
ICI, 167
ID Focus, 375
IG Farben, 131
IHI, 98
Immigration policies, Australia, 332
Imperial Institute of Physics and Technology
   (Germany), 123–24
Imperial Oil, 312, 318
Incubators, 314

Industrial Base Technology Development
   Projects (IBTDP) (Korea), 372–74
Industrial Parks, Taiwan, 405
Industrial policies. See also Government
   policies; Technology policies
   Japan, 102–03
Industrial research, 10–11
   Argentina, 456, 470–71
   Australia, 329–31, 336–40
   Brazil, 419, 425–28, 442–45
   British productivity and, 170–72
   Canada, 303, 305–08, 310–11
   expenditures, international comparisons, 175
   France, 208–09
   Germany, 124, 125–29, 138–39, 144
   government support and, 13
   Great Britain, foreign investment in, 174–75
   Israel, 484
   Italy, 231–32, 247–50
   Japan, 84–85, 87–89, 105–09
   Korea, 364, 370–71, 372–74, 375–80
   Sweden and Denmark, 278–79
   Taiwan, 394–96
   U.S., 30
      antitrust policy and, 34
      before 1945, 31–39
      post-World War II, 39–52
      decline in 1970s, 50–51
      1980s, 53–56
Industrial Research Institution (Japan), 83
Industrial research laboratories, 10–11
   Germany, 144
   Japan, 84–85
   U.S., 33–34, 50
Industrial Upgrading Statute (IUS) (Taiwan),
   395
Infant-industry protection
   Japan, 99–100
   national innovation systems and, 514–15
INFN, 254
Information technology industry
   Australia, 341–42
   Canada, 318
   Taiwan, 396–400
"Innovation," definition, 4
"Innovation clustering," 316
Innovation systems. See National innovation
   systems; and names of individual
   countries, e.g. Korea, United States, etc.
INPE, 437
Institute for Chemical Science and Technology
   (Canada), 317
Institute for Research into Data-Processing and
   Automation (IRIA) (France), 204
Institute for the Information Industry (III)
   (Taiwan), 396, 400–01

Institute of Physical and Chemical Research
    (Riken) (Japan), 83–84
Integrated Systems Development Corp (ISDC),
    401
Intel, 377
Intellectual property rights
  Brazil, 429
  Taiwan, 406
  U.S.
    agricultural research, 51
    protection initiatives, 59
    trade policies and, 60–61
International competitiveness
  Brazil, 420–23
  national innovative performance and, 509
International research cooperation
  Great Britain, 174–75
  Italy, 251, 254–55
  U.S., 55, 56
International Data-Processing Company (CII),
    204
International Integrated System Inc. (IIS), 401
Internationalization, 17–18
  Germany and, 147
  Italy, 234, 251
  national innovation systems and, 518–19
  Sweden and, 291–92
IPT, 437
Iron and steel industries
  Canadian R & D, 310–11
  development in Japan, 90–92
  France, 196
  Germany, origins, 127
  Sweden, 271
Israel, 476–97
  Academy of Sciences, 478
  defense R & D, 483, 484–86, 491–92
  early scientific activities, 478–79
  economic characteristics, international
      comparisons, 355–56
  economic development (1950s; 1960s), 477–
      79
  entrepreneurship in, 495
  high-tech industries, 479–82, 491–92
  industrial research, 484, 487–90
  innovation system gaps, 493–94
  manufacturing industries, 481–82
  Ministry of Industry & Trade, 487, 490
  research networking, 495
  scientific & engineering personnel, 479–80,
      481–82, 483, 489
  small- and medium-sized enterprises (SMEs),
      490–91
  technology diffusion, 494–95
  total factor productivity, 481
  U.S. patents, 492–93

university research, 484, 492–93
university-industrial linkages, 492–93
ISS, 254
Isuzu, 98, 99, 100
Italy, 230–57
  electronics industry, 256–57
  high-technology sector, 250, 251
  industrialization, 231–34
  inter-institution research cooperation, 254
  North-South industrial differences, 232–33
  public enterprises, 233–34
  public policy and technological development,
      251–55
  public research network, 246–47
  R & D activities, 231–34
    European research programs, 254–55
    government-funded research, 241–42, 244
    industrial research, 247–50
    large-firm R & D, 230, 231, 232–33, 235,
        243–55
    small-firm networks, 230–31, 232, 234–
        43
    university research, 245–46
  R & D expenditures, 243–44, 245
  Sabatini Law, 241–42
  science parks, 242
  technological information dissemination,
      236, 242–43
  technology diffusion, 255–56
  textile industry, 235, 236, 241
  U.S. patents, 237–38, 244, 245
  virtuous and vicious innovative cycles, 255–
      57
  vital statistics, 25–27

Japan, 76–111
  automobile industry, 97–101
  basic research in, 110–11
  education system
    early schools, 78–79
    higher education, 79
    public education, 78–80
  electrical & communication equipment
      industries, 93–97
  energy-saving R & D, 88–89
  External Trade Organization (JETRO), 103
  foreign investment in Great Britain, 188
  globalization of research and, 110
  industrial policy, 102–03
  industrial research
    current status, 105–09
    government support, 87–89
    managers and, 106–07
    new technology introduction, 108
    since 1960s, 87–89

Japan *(continued)*
  industrialization history
    Tokugawa Era and before (to 1868), 77–79,
      90
    Meiji Era (1868–1911), 79–81
    1914–1945, 83–85
    postwar era, 1945–1970s, 85–87
    since 1960s, 87–89
  iron and steel industries, 90–92
  national model of innovation, 17
  National Railways, 103
  national research institutions, 83–85
  patents, 104–05
    in U.S., 104–05, 137
  R & D expenditures (1989), 103–04
  total factor productivity (1960s–80s), 105
  Unequal Treaties, 80–81
  university research, 110–11
  vital statistics, 25–27
JESSI project, 147
Jitsuyo Jidosha, 98

Kachalsky committee, 478
Kaiser-Wilhelm-Society, 124, 133, 141
  government funding, 132
  research institutes, 131
Kaishinsha, 97, 98
Kamaishi plant, 90–91
Karakuri masters, 78
Katz, Jorge M., "National Systems on
    Innovation Supporting Technical
    Advance in Industry: The Case of
    Argentina," 451–73
Kawasaki, 91, 92
  Japanese auto industry and, 98
Keck, Otto, "The National System for
    Technical Innovation in Germany,"
    115–47
Kim, Linsu, "National System of Industrial
    Innovation: Dymnamics of Capability
    building in Korea," 357–82
Korea, 357–82
  aircraft industry, 379
  automobile industry, 365
  chaebols, 362–63, 366–68, 375–80
  chemicals industry, 365–66
  economic characteristics, 357
    international comparisons, 355–56
  economic liberalization progarm, 367–69
  effects of civil war (1945–53), 358
  electronics industry, 365
    electronics switching system (ESS), 374,
      378
  export promotion, 363–64
  foreign technology transfer, 360–62
  high-technology transfer, 375–79
    high-tech "valleys," 380–81

  human resources development, 358–60
    education system, 358–59
  Institute of Science and Technology (KIST),
    364
  interorganizational research cooperation, 374
  labor movement, 369
  multinationals in, 376
  national defense and heavy-machinery
    industries, 362, 380
  promotion of big business, 362–63
  R & D activities, 369–75
    government support, 370–74
    industrial research, 364, 370–71, 372–74,
      375–80
    university research, 371, 374
  small- and medium-sized firms promotion,
    368
  "strategic" industry development, 362–63,
    369
  technological capability, large firm *vs.* small
    firm behavior, 364–67
  technology development policies, 367–69
  tradition of overseas training and observation,
    359–60
  U.S. military presence and, 361–62
  working habits, 360
Korean Air, 379
Korsil, 377

Labor market, Sweden and Denmark, 273, 274
Labor productivity, Taiwan, 385
Labor relations
  Japan, 107, 108, 109–10
  Korea, 369
Large firms
  France, 193
  Italy, 230, 231, 232–33, 235, 243–55
  Korea, 364–67
Laser industry, FIAT and, 255–56
LM-Tel, 281
Logging-equipment industry, Canada, 312
Louis Pasteur University, 210
Lucas Aerospace, 167
Lucky-Goldstar, 375, 376, 377, 378
Luis de Queiroz Agricultural College, 416

Machine-construction industry, Germany, 127,
    129
MacMillan Blodel, 312
Malerba, Franco, "The National System of
    Innovation: Italy," 230–57
Management
  Australia, 335–36
  British, industrial innovation and, 181
  France, 213–14
  role in Japanese firms, 106–07
Manhattan Project, 39

Manufacturing industries
  Argentina, 454–58, 470
  Australia, 324, 325, 329–35
  Brazil, 421–28
  Canada, 300–01, 309
  Denmark, 270, 279
  France, 194
  Germany, 128, 129–30, 136, 137
  Great Britain, 163, 165–72
  Israel, 481–82
  Italy, 232, 234–43
  Japan, 86
  R & D in, international comparisons, 329–30
  U.S., 31–32, 33–34
Marks & Spencer, 181
Mass production, in U.S., 31
Massachusetts Institute of Technology (MIT),
    40
  Industrial Liaison Program, 54
Matra, 218
Max-Planck- Society, 133, 141
Mazda, 98
McFetridge, Donald G., "The Canadian System
    of Industrial Innovation," 299–321
Meikosha, 95
Merck Company, 126
Mergers
  Taiwan, 403–05
  U.S. (1895–1904), 32
Metal Leve, 443
Metal-processing industry
  Germany, origins, 127
  Sweden, 271
Metallurgy complex, in Canada, 316, 317
Metalworking industry, Argentina, 460, 461
Michelin, 200
Microelectronics industry
  Brazil, 433
  U.S., 49, 57, 59
Micron Technologies, 377
Microsystems International, 303, 315
Microtex, 404
Midi-Robots, 205
Military funding
  Japanese auto industry, 97–99
  U.S. commercial technologies, 58–59
Military R & D
  Argentina, 469–70
  Brazil, 418
  Canada, 311
  effects on national innovation systems, 508,
      513–14
  France, 203–04, 215–16
  Germany, 132, 142
  Great Britain, 172–73, 177–78
  Israel, 483, 484–86, 491–92
  Korea, 380

  Sweden and Denmark, 281
  Taiwan, 406
  U.S., 30, 37, 42–43, 46–47, 49–50, 514
Military/civilian technology spillovers, U.S., 43,
    46–47, 49–50, 57, 58–59
Mining industries
  Germany, origins, 127
  Sweden, 271
Ministerial Delegation for Armaments (DMA)
    (France), 204
Ministry for Scientific and Technological
    Research (MRST) (Italy), National
    Research Programs (NRPs), 252–53
Minitel videotex, 219
Miroglio, 241
Mitac, 404–05
MITI (Japan)
    information collection and diffusion, 103
    Japanese auto industry and, 98, 100
    support of Japanese RAs and, 88
Mitsubishi, 84, 91, 94, 98
Mitsui, 98, 99
Modern Electrosystems, 375
Moonlight Project (Japan), 89
Morrill Act (1862), 37
Motor-vehicle industry. *See* Automobile
    industry
Mouse System Company, 404
Mowery, David C., "The U.S. National
    Innovation System," 29–64
Multinationals
  Argentina, 454–58, 459, 463, 465
  Australia, 339
  Brazil, 427
  Great Britain, 164, 166, 168–70, 174–75,
    176
  Korea, 360, 361, 376
  Sweden, 267, 281, 291, 292

National Advisory Committee on Aeronautics
    (NACA) (U.S.), 35
National Aeronautics and Space Administration
    (NASA), 35
National Center for Manufacturing Sciences
    (NCMS) (U.S.), 58–59
National Centre for Scientific Research (CNRS)
    (France), 192, 202–03, 210
National Centre for Space Studies (CNES)
    (France), 203
National Centre for the Study of
    Telecommunications (CNET) (France),
    202
National Cooperative Research Act (1984), 59–
    60
National Council for Metrology, Normalization
    and Quality Control (CONMETRO)
    (Brazil), 419

National Council for Research and
    Development (NCRD) (Israel), 478
National Council for Science and Technology
    (CONICET) (Argentina), 467
National development plans, Brazil, 418
National Economic Development Council
    (Great Britain), 183
National Fund for Scientific and Technological
    Development (FNDCT) (Brazil), 419
National innovation systems. *See also* names of
    individual countries, e.g. Korea, United
    States, etc.
  advantages of large countries *vs.* small
      countries, 302–04
  concept of, 15–17
  defense R & D and, 508, 513–14
  definitions & characteristics, 4–5, 267–69
  education systems and, 511
  "emulation" and "fairness" concepts, 520–23
  government technology policies and, 512–13
  government's role, 508, 512–13
  high-tech industrial development and, 515–
      17, 521
  infant-industry protection and, 514–15
  international competitiveness and, 509
  internationalization and, 518–19
  "market failure" arguments and, 521
  "mission-oriented," 220
  "national systems" concept, 15–17
  national continuity and, 509
  natural and agricultural resources,
      significance of, 507
  structural change in highly-industrialized
      countries, 63
  technological globalization and, 63
  university research and, 512–13
National Institute for Agricultural Technology
    (INTA) (Argentina), 465, 466, 468–69
National Institute of Agricultural Research
    (INRA) (France), 202
National Institute of Health (INH) (France), 202
National Institute of Industrial Property (INPI)
    (Brazil), 419, 429–32
National Office of Aeronautical Studies and
    Research (ONERA) (France), 202, 205
National Plan for Science and Technology
    (Taiwan), 409–10
National R & D Projects (NRP) (Korea), 372,
    373
National Research Council (CNPq) (Brazil),
    417, 435
National Research Council (CNR) (Italy), 246
  Finalized Programs, 252
National Research Council (NRC) (Canada), 304
  Industrial Research Assistance Program
      (IRAP), 311

National research institutions/laboratories
  Japan, 83–85
  Germany, 144–45
National Science Council (Taiwan), 392, 402
National Science Foundation (U.S.),
    interdisciplinary engineering research
    centers, 53
"National system," definition, 5
National System of Scientific and Technological
    Development (SNDCT) (Brazil), 419
National technology programs, Sweden and
    Denmark, 279–80
Nationalization, industrial, in France, 193, 213
Natural-resources industries
  Canada, 300, 307
Nelson, Richard R.
  "A Retrospective," 505–23
  "Technical Innovation and National
      Systems," 3–21
Neotech Development Corp. (NDC), 400–01
New process/product technology
  diffusion in Denmark and Sweden, 284–87
  introduction, in Japanese firm, 108
Nippon Electric Co. (NEC), 95–96
Nippon Kokan, 84, 91
Nippon Steel, 91–92
Nissan Motors, 98, 99, 100
NKK (Japan), 84, 91
Nordic countries. *See* Denmark; Sweden
Northern Securities decision (1904), 32
Northern Telecom, 306, 307, 313, 315, 318, 320
Notgemeinschaft, 131–32
Novatel, 318
Nuclear industry
  Argentina, 467–68
  France, 202, 216–18
Nuclear power development
  German government funding, 143, 145
  national innovation systems and, 514
  Swedish, 281

Odargiri, Hiroyuki, "The Japanese System of
    Innovation: Past, Present, and Future,"
    76–111
Office of Overseas Scientific and Technical
    Research (ORSTOM) (France), 202
Oki, 95
Olivetti, 251
Omnibus Trade and Competitiveness Act
    (1988), 60
Ontario Hydro, 320
Opel, 131
Ouro Preto School of Mines (Brazil), 417
Oxygen converter gas recovery system, 92
Oxygen furnace method, steelmaking, 92

Panhard, 200
Paris Radium Institute, 199
Partnerships for Development, Australia, 341–42
Patents. *See also* Intellectual property rights; Patents, U.S.
  international comparisons, 104–05
  Taiwan, 409
Patents, U.S.
  Canada, 306–07, 317
  France, 221–22, 223
  Germany, 130, 137, 139
  Great Britain (1981–86), 175
  Israel, 492–93
  Italy, 237–38, 244, 245
  Japan (1855–1902), 81, 137, 139
  large *vs.* small countries, 303
Petroleum and oil industries
  Australia, 36, 337
  Canada, 311, 317
  Great Britain, 161
  U.S., 33, 34
Peugeot, 200
Pharmaceuticals industry. *See also* Chemicals industry
  Germany, 126, 127
  Great Britain, 167
Physics, rise of research in U.S., 36
Pilot plant, 7, 8
Plan Calcul (France), 204
Plant Patent Act (1930), 51
Plant Variety Protection Act (PVPA) (1970), 51
Plessey, 163
Polymer chemistry, 7
Polytechnical schools, Germany, 120, 121
Prato (Italy), Sprint project, 242–43
Pratt (U.K.), 99, 318
Productivity rates
  Great Britain (1980s), 170–72
  Israel, 481
  Taiwan, 385
  total factor productivity (TFP), international comparison, 105
Prototypes, 8
Pulp and paper industry
  Canada, 310, 312, 316
  Sweden, 271
Pulp and Paper Research Institute of Canada, 310

Raw materials processing industries, Argentina, 460, 461
RCA, 50
Regional development agencies, 186
Renault, 200

Research & development activities. *See also* Industrial research; Military R & D; University research
  Argentina, 460–61, 465–70
  Canada, 302–03
  France, 201–03, 205–11
  Italy, 231–34, 243–55
  Korea, 369–75
  large, high-income countries, 27
  Sweden and Denmark, 278–79
Research & development expenditures
  Australia, 325–31
  Brazil, 425, 426, 437–39
  Germany, 138, 139, 142–45
  Great Britain, 172–76
  international comparisons, 438
  Italy, 232
  Japan, 103–04
  Korea, 369–70
  Taiwan, 407–08
Research associations/consortia
  Canada, 310–11
  Japan, 87–88
  Microelectronics and Computer Technology Corporation (U.S.), 59
Research centers
  Australia, 345
  Brazil EMBRAPA, 444
  Italy, 242
  Korea, 371, 380–81
  U.S., interdisciplinary engineering, 53
Research collaboration/cooperation
  Canada, 310–11
  Germany, 144
  Great Britain, 174–75
  Israel, 495
  Italy, 249, 251
  Japan, 87–88
  Korea, 374
  Sweden, 281
  U.S., 53–54, 55, 56, 59–60
Research councils
  Canada, 304–05
  Israel, 478
Research institutes
  Brazil, 435–37
  Canada, 310
  France, 202, 203
  Germany, 131, 145
  Israel, 490–91
  Korea, 371, 372
  Taiwan, 406
Research institutions/organizations. *See also* names of specific types of organizations, e.g. Research associations/consortia, Research laboratories, etc.

Research institutions/organizations *(continued)*
  France, 202–04
  Germany, 123–24
  Italy, 252–54
  Japan, 83–85
  Taiwan, 392
Research laboratories
  France, 198, 199, 205, 210, 211
  Germany, 126, 144–45
  government, 12–13, 513
  industrial, 10–11
  Israel, 478
  Japan, 83, 84, 110
  Korea, 370–71
  U.S., 33–34, 50
Research personnel. *See* Scientists and engineers
Revealed technological advantage (RTA)
  France, 221
  Great Britain, 168–69, 176
Reverse engineering, 11
  Korea, 365, 366, 369, 378–79
Riken, 83–85
Robotics
  development in Korea, 378–79
  diffusion in Sweden and Denmark, 284–85
  FIAT and, 255–56
Rolls-Royce, 167
Rosenberg, Nathan, "The U.S. National
  Innovation System," 29–64

Sabatini Law, 241–42
Saint-Gobain, 195
Samsung, 375, 377, 378, 379
  research organizations, 376
Sao Paulo Polytechnic, 417
Scandanavian countries. *See* Denmark; Sweden
Schneider-Empain group, 217
Science Council (Japan), 84
Science parks
  Germany, 145
  Great Britain, 186–87
  Israel, 492
  Italy, 242
Scientific research, 402. *See also* University
  research
  British expenditures, 172–73
  Canada, 305
  France, 194–95, 198–99
  Germany, 117–24, 131–32
  Israel, 478
  Italy, 245–46
  Japan, 110–11
  Taiwan, 392
  technological advance and, 6
  U.S., 35–36, 42

Scientist and engineers
  Australia, 344–45
  Brazil, 425–26, 442
  France, 197, 199
  Great Britain, 178–79
  in industry, international comparisons, 482
  Israel, 479–80, 481–82, 483, 489
  Japan, 104
  large, high-income countries, 26
  Taiwan, 408–09
Scotland, electronics industries in, 187
Sematech consortium, 47, 58–59
Semiconductor Chip Protection Act (1984), 57
Semiconductors
  Korean *chaebol* activities, 375–77
  U.S., 43, 57
Seoul Science Park, 380
Service industries, Great Britain, 162–64
Shell, 161
Shibaura Engineering Works, 94
Shibaura Seisakusho, 84
Shipbuilding industry, Denmark, 277
Siemens, 94, 127–28, 138, 139, 143, 163, 168
Single European Act, 188
Single European Market, 174
SKF, 271
Skilled labor. *See* Scientists and engineers
Small and Medium Enterprise Formation Act
  (1986), 368
Small- and medium-sized enterprises (SMEs)
  Israel, 490–91
  Korea, 368
  Taiwan, 384, 388, 390–91, 396–400, 403–05,
    411
Small firms
  Denmark, 289
  Great Britain, 167
  Italy, 230–31, 231, 234–43, 250
  Korea, 364–67, 368
  U.S., 29, 48–49, 56–57
South Korea. *See* Korea
Space technology programs
  France, 201, 203, 204, 218–19
  Germany, 145
  national innovation systems and, 514
Sprint project, 242–43
Start-up firms, U.S., 29, 48–49, 56–57
Statute for Encouragement of Investment (SEI)
  (Taiwan), 394
Steel industry. *See* Iron and steel industries
Stifterverband, 132
Stoneville, 404
Sumitomo Metal, 91, 92
Sunshine Project (Japan), 89
Suzuki, 100

Sweden, 263, 265–92
  Board for Technical Changes, 290
  Board for Technical Development (STU),
      279
  Denmark and, comparisons, 265–69
  employment rates, 273, 283
  engineering industry, 290
  exports, 271–72
  industrialization, 271–72, 273–74
  international economic and R & D
      comparisons, 264
  labor market, 273–74
  macroeconomic performance, 282–83
  multinationals in, 266–67, 281, 291, 292
  national technology programs, 279–80
  natural resources, importance to economy,
      289
  product innovations, 271–72
  production system, 273–74
    development blocks, 275, 277–78
    R & D activities, 278–79
      nuclear power research program, 281
  socio-political aspects, 272–75
  structural problems in economy, 288–89
  technological contributions, 283–84
  technology diffusion, 284–87
  technology policy, 279–82
  U.S. patents, 266, 283
Synthetic dyestuffs industry, Germany, 126,
    130
System X (Great Britain), 176
"System(s)," concepts, 4–5

Taiwan, 384–412
  "brain-drain" problem, 393–94
  computer software development, 400–01
  economic characteristics, international
      comparisons, 355–56
  education system, 385, 392–94
    engineering education, 393
    higher education, 392, 393
  foreign direct investment, 388–91, 405–06
  government's role in industrial technology
      development, 391–92
    assistance programs, 394–95
  industrial base in 1950s, 386
  industrial research, 394–96
  intellectual property rights protection, 406
  Japanese occupation, 386
  labor productivity, 385
  national defense industries, 406
  National Plan for S & T, 409–10
  patents, 409
  publicly-owned enterprises in, 387

  R & D expenditures, 407–08
  research organizations
    government-sponsored, 396–400
    research institutes, 406
  scientific research, 392, 402
  scientist and engineers, numbers of, 408–09
  small- and medium-sized enterprises (SMEs)
      in, 384, 387–88, 411
    overseas mergers and, 403–05
    technology development and, 388–91, 396–
        400
  sources of economic growth, 385–86
  technology transfer among firms, 389
Tanaka Seisakusho, 93
Tariff protection
  Argentina, 454
  Australia, 335
TDX-1/TDX-10, 374, 378
Technical advance/change
  concept of "national systems," 15–17
  cumulative, incremental, 8–9
  Danish production system and, 275
  government support, 12–13
  interindustry differences, 13–15
  process of, 5, 267–68
  R & D facilities and, 5–6
    industrial research laboratories, 10–11
  rise of science and, 6–9
  start-up firms and, 48–49, 56–57
  Swedish trade unions and, 273–74
  transnational aspects, 17–18
  university research and, 11–12
Technical education/training. See also
      Engineering education/training
  Brazil, 439–40
  Germany, 120, 121, 139–40
  Great Britain, 179–80
  Taiwan, 393
Technical innovation. See National innovation
      systems; Technical advance/change
Technische Hochschulen, 120, 123
"Technological community," concept, 15
Technological Innovation Fund (Italy), 253
Technology, indigenous
  Great Britain, 167–68
  Japan, 77–78, 81, 87–88, 101
Technology Development Promotion Act
    (1977) (Korea), 375
Technology Development Reserve Fund
    (Korea), 374
Technology diffusion
  Canada, 308–09
  France, 211
  international comparisons, 256
  Israel, 494–95

Technology diffusion *(continued)*
　Italy, 236, 242–43, 255–56
　Sweden and Denmark, 284–87
Technology policies
　Brazil, 428–34
　effects on innovation, 512–13
　Germany, 142–45
　Israel, 487–88
　Italy, 251–55
　Korea, 367–69
　Sweden and Denmark, 279–82
Technology transfer
　Argentina, 467
　Brazil, 429
　Canada, 305, 308–09
　France, 211
　Germany, 116–17
　Italy, 242–43
　Japan, 81, 85–87, 92, 96, 100, 101
　Korea, 360–62, 364–67, 368
　Taiwan, 389–91
"Technonationalism," 3
Tekijuku, 78
Telecommunications industry
　Canada, 313, 315, 318, 320
　France, 219–20
　Great Britain, 168
　Korea, 374, 378
Terakoya, 78
Teubal, Morris, "The Innovation System of
　Israel: Description, Performance, and
　Outstanding Issues," 476–97
Texas Instruments, 377
Textile industry
　Italy, 235, 236, 241
"Thatcherism," 159
Thermodynamics, 7
Thomson-CSF, 218
Tokyo Denki, 84
Tokyo Electric Power Company, 93, 94
Tokyo Gas Electric, 98
Tokyo Ishikawajima Zosensho, 98
Tokyo Shibaura Electric, 94
Toshiba, 84, 93, 94
Total factor productivity (TFP)
　international comparison (1960s–80s), 105
　Israel, 481
Toyota, 98, 99, 100
Trade associations, Canadian R & D and,
　310
Transistor, development, 9
Transnational aspects, of technical advance, 17–
　18
Transportation equipment industry, U.S., 34
TSMC, 398–99

UBATEC, 469
Unequal Treaties, 80–81
Union of German Engineers, 120
Unions
　Denmark, 273
　Germany, 133
　Japan, 108
　Korea, 369
　Sweden, 273–74, 291–92
United Kingdom. *See* Great Britain
United States, 29–64
　agricultural research, 36–38, 51–52
　American model of innovation, 16
　antitrust statutes, 29, 32, 34, 49, 59–60, 62–
　　63
　education system, 48
　　engineering training, 36
　　higher education, 35–36, 48
　government R & D funding, 34–36
　industrial research
　　before 1945, 31–39
　　post-World War II, 39–52
　　decline in 1970s, 50–51
　　1980s, 53–56
　　strength of, 30
　intellectual property rights protection
　　initiatives, 59
　Korean *chaebol* activities in, 375, 377
　living standards, 52
　military R & D, 30, 42–43, 46–47, 514
　military funding of commercial technologies,
　　58–59
　national R & D investment, 29, 30
　Northern Securities decision (1904), 32
　patents, 104
　public policies for technology development,
　　58–61
　relationship with Canadian economy, 301,
　　307–09
　research collaboration initiatives, 59–60
　start-up firms in, 29, 48–49, 56–57
　university/industry research cooperation, 53–
　　54
　university research system, 12, 35–36, 40, 47–
　　48
　vital statistics, 25–27
U.S. Defense Advanced Research Projects
　Agency (DARPA), 59
U.S. Department of Health and Human
　Services, basic research budget, 42
U.S./Japan Agreement on Scientific
　Cooperation, 60
U.S. Office of Scientific Research and
　Development (OSRD), 39
U.S. patents. *See* Patents, U.S.

U.S. Pentagon, R & D development initiatives, 58
University of Buenos Aires, 469
University research
    Argentina, 469
    Canada, 305
    France, 198–99, 210–11
    Germany, 117–20, 140–41
    industrial innovation and, 512–13
    Israel, 478, 484, 492–93
    Italy, 245–46
    Japan, 110–11
    Korea, 371
    Taiwan, 402
    technical advance and, 7, 11–12
    U.S., 12, 35–36, 40, 42, 47–48
Uruguay Round, 60

Vitelic, 399
Vocational/technical training
    Brazil, 439–40
    Germany, 120, 121, 139–40
    Taiwan, 393
Vulcani Institute, 478–79

Volksschule, 121
Volkswagen, 138
Volvo Uddevalla factory, 274

Walker, William, "National Innovation Systems: Britain," 158–89
Welding Institute, 183
West Germany. *See* Germany
Western Electric, 40
    Japanese communications equipment industry and, 95
Westinghouse, 94
Wood and paper industry. *See* Pulp and paper industry
Work organization
    Danish and Swedish innovations, 284
    Fordist/Taylorist, 31–32
    Worker rotation, in Japan, 107
    WYSE Technology, 404–05

Yawata Steel Works, 90, 91–92, 101

Zaibatsus, 98, 101